THE BIRDWATCHER and DIARY

Designed and published by
Hilary Cromack

Edited by
David Cromack

Dedicated to
Leslie and Doris Cromack with love and in admiration of their fortitude in the face of serious illness.

in association with

Published in 2001 by:
Buckingham Press
55 Thorpe Park Road, Peterborough
Cambridgeshire PE3 6LJ
United Kingdom

01733 561739
e-mail: buck.press@btinternet.com

ISBN 0 9533840 3 9
ISSN 0144-364 X

Cover: *Eiders* - detail from an oil painting by Martin Ridley.
Visit the artist's website: www.martinridley.com
A Creative Process Revealed: View how sketches, preparatory drawings and a gallery of more than 200 wildlife paintings evolve from initial field encounters. E-postcards to send and artwork slideshow screensavers.
Martin exhibits at: The British Birdwatching Fair; Nature in Art, Gloucestershire; Tryon Gallery, London; Nigel Stacey-Marks Gallery, Perth; Wildfowl & Wetlands Trust, Slimbridge; RSPB, Vane Farm.

Printed and bound in Great Britain by:
Biddles Ltd Book Manufacturers, Guildford, Surrey.

CONTENTS

CONTENTS

CONTENTS

Key contributors in this Edition

GORDON HAMLETT, a freelance writer, is a regular contributor to *Bird Watching* magazine, both as a reviewer of books and computer software and also as sub-editor of the UK Bird Sightings section. Gordon is not only an active committeeman of both the Greater Peterborough Ornithological Group and Peterborough Bird Club, but an incorrigable Net surfer. Who better to nominate the most useful 150 websites for birders?

CHRIS MEAD, since retiring as head of the British Trust for Ornithology's ringing section has devoted much time to researching garden birds, and continues to spearhead the Trust's dealings with the media. A prolific writer, Chris was greatly praised for his latest book, *The State of the Nation's Birds*, which charted the decline in many familar species. In this edition of *The Yearbook*, Chris reviews the most interesting ornithological discoveries of the past 12 months.

MARTIN RIDLEY scored the highest ever marks for wildlife illustration when he graduated from Carmarthenhire College of Technology and Art in 1988. A regular exhibitor at Society of Wildlife Artists shows and art galleries in Glos, London and Perthshire, he has had more than 100 images used for greetings cards, books and calendars etc. You can see examples of his work on his website www.martinridley.com

PREFACE

DURING THE COURSE of creating the 2002 Edition, the analogy with childbirth has never been far from my mind. A long gestation period with disturbed sleep patterns was then followed by the strenuous, and sometimes painful 'labour' of checking and re-checking thousands of facts and then designing and proofing pages for 'delivery' to the printers. Like any parent, I'm immensely proud of my new 'baby', and I hope it grows up to be as useful a member of the birdwatching society as its 21 siblings.....

At those moments of greatest stress, it was heartening to have the support of so many people. I am greatly indebted to Chris Hamlett, Cherry Hadley and Kim Richardson for their willingness to 'pitch in' at short notice, and to artists Dan and Rosie Powell for responding so promptly for drawings to illustrate our main editorial feature.

It was also a great comfort to have the enduring support of John Pemberton, the founder of *The Yearbook* who devoted many hours to making databases available to me and to cheerfully answering the hundreds of questions I fired in his direction. Likewise, Derek Toomer at the BTO has been unfailingly helpful, while new *British Birds* Editor Roger Riddington and his managing council deserve thanks for allowing us to use artwork from their annual Illustrator of the Year competition to enhance this year's book.

It has been a pleasure to work with sponsors Swarovski UK, whose financial support has allowed us to introduce the new features in this Edition. To the scores of artists, photographers, lecturers and company representatives who have been so warm in their comments about *The Yearbook* and the new Trade Directory I say a heartfelt 'thank-you'. It does make the hard work seem worth it.

Regular readers will be instantly aware that change is the order of the day within this Edition. We have changed the book size to A5, and hope you find that the extra page width makes it easier to write in the Diary and Checklist sections. We also felt that the Quick Reference section did not live up to its name buried in the centre of the book, so we have relocated it at the back.

As long-time users of *The Yearbook* we found that we often needed to cross-refer from the Reserves Section to the County Directory and to make that task easier we have moved them to adjacent positions. The Reserves Section can be instantly identified by the yellow page edging.

Within the County Directory, the most significant changes we have made is to adopt the recording areas used by the Scottish Ornithologists Club part of the UK. We are grateful for the advice they have given us on this matter, and also for the continued support of hundreds of information providers.

We trust that all regular users of *The Yearbook* will find our changes are genuine improvements, and recommend it to their friends. We look forward to hearing that listed artists, photographers, lecturers and retailers are receiving more enquiries as a result of being in this Edition. Our goal is to see *The Yearbook* develop in a collaborative way for the mutual benefit of all people within birdwatching. We have many more ideas for the future, but, naturally, their introduction will depend on the success of this Edition.

Hilary A Cromack
Publisher
August 26, 2001

A message from our sponsor

Mr John Brinkley,
Sales and Marketing Director of Swarovski Optik

NO OTHER NATION can compare to Britain when it comes to an interest in wild birds. The number of active birdwatchers is remarkably high compared to the overall population and more than one million souls care enough about the future of birds to give their whole-hearted financial support to the Royal Society for the Protection of Birds. Hundreds of thousands also support local wildlife trusts and more specialist organisations such as the British Trust for Ornithology and the Wildfowl and Wetlands Trust.

This commitment to the hobby means that British birdwatchers demand the very highest standards - both in the field of optics and publishing. For a company such as Swarovski, which is totally dedicated to the quest of producing the very best binoculars and telescopes, it is a pleasure to be associated with *The Birdwatcher's Yearbook*, which has become a prized institution during its 22-year history.

It is pleasing to note that our sponsorship support has been invested in expanding and improving *The Yearbook*. Within the pages of the 2002 Edition you will find an amazing amount of information and many new features.

This year sees the introduction of a Trade Directory designed to aid communication between artists, photographers, lecturers, bird tour companies, optical dealers and many other companies and the customers they are serving. I feel confident many of you will appreciate the improved Reserves Section as you travel about the UK looking at wild birds. Swarovski is delighted to be associated with this publishing venture to help you get the most from your hobby.

THE YEARBOOK AND ITS READERS

by David Cromack

INHERITING the role of Editor of a treasured institution such as *The Birdwatcher's Yearbook* is an awesome challenge. Though 14 years at the helm of *Bird Watching* magazine has given me the technical skills for the task, it is the thought of emulating the rigorous standards set by founding Editor John Pemberton which gives pause for thought. Over a 21-year period John and his wife Joyce moulded *The Yearbook* into an indispensable and trusted Bible of the ornithological world. As they say, how do you follow that?

Step one for me and my wife Hilary (who as Publisher, Financial Controller, Designer and General office Hercules must take credit for doing 95% of the work to produce the 2002 Edition) was to conduct some research among the most loyal purchasers of *The Yearbook*. We are grateful that so many responded to our questionnaire and for the wealth of goodwill that came with so many of the returned forms.

One of the few preconceptions we harboured was the feeling that few purchasers would actually use the Diary section. How wrong we were. No fewer than 42% told us they use this part of the *The Yearbook,* so instead of removing it we have given it more space and a better layout to make it even more useful. The jury is split on a proposal to separate the Logbook, Diary and Notebook elements from the rest of *The Yearbook*, with 47% being opposed.

Regular readers will have already noticed our decision to revert to using a painting as part of our cover design, a tradition that lapsed in 1990. Though we are great admirers of our first chosen artist Martin Ridley it is our intention to invite different painters and print-makers to contribute each year so that each edition becomes a collector's item. The other most noticeable change is the introduction of colour to make it easy to locate the Reserves Section, and we are grateful to Swarovski for the sponsorship that makes this possible.

Here's a breakdown of the most important findings revealed by the research questionnaire:

• A total of 94% thought *The Yearbook* was 'very good value' or 'good value'.

• The County Directory was the most useful of the existing contents, closely followed by Bird Reserves, National Organisations and Tide Tables.

• When asked what new features should be included, the top item was more information

A first-winter Yellow-rumped Warbler was recorded by Andrew Stevenson for one of his entries in the 2001 *British Birds* Bird Illustrator of the Year competition.

about bird reserves including maps, and you will see from our new colour section we have responded to that request.

• No fewer than 33% of the respondents go birdwatching on a daily basis, while a further 38% manage at least one weekly outing to see birds and 22% go between three to five times a month. It's clear why reserve information is in demand with that level of activity.

• We have also followed up a strong signal that information about birding websites should be included. No fewer than 51% of respondents have access to the Internet at home and a further 33% at work. We will be interested to get feedback from readers about the websites nominated by Gordon Hamlett, and would encourage you to send us your own recommendations for new sites for the 2003 Edition.

• Respondents were equally enthusiastic for information about sites for butterflies and dragonflies, dealing with sick and injured birds, a directory of speakers, artists, photographers and those companies serving the needs of active birdwatchers. Lack of time has not allowed us to move forward on the first items, but we hope you find the Trade Directory a valuable addition.

• Not surprisingly, there was enthusiasm for a Calendar of Birding Events to be included. Duly done. If you are planning conferences or other activities for 2003, please let us know as soon as details are confirmed.

• It was reassuring to learn that 63% bought *The Yearbook* every year, and gratifying to discover that 11% had been persuaded by our advertising campaign in *Bird Watching* to try it for the first time. As a 'cottage industry' we do not have massive marketing budgets, so we are grateful for the word-of-mouth recommendations and bird club mailshots that help make the business financially viable.

Producing the 2002 Edition from scratch has been a monumental task, particularly as I have not yet given up my 'day job', and a number of proposed initiatives will have to wait until next year. Hilary and I are keen to open a dialogue with as many of our current and future readers as possible, so if you have ideas for subsequent Editions please feel free to let us have them.

NEW ARTISTIC PARTNERSHIP

Yearbook joins forces with *British Birds*

GRACING this edition of *The Yearbook* is a selection of black and white drawings entered for the 2001 *British Birds* Illustrator of the Year contest. The quality of the competition is so high that none of these works won prizes, but we are delighted to ensure they are seen by a wider public.

The competition to find the Bird Illustrator of the Year has been run by *British Birds* since 1979, and the list of past winners contains a large proportion of Britain's top bird artists. Amateur and professional artists alike can enter, and must submit four line-drawings (of precise, specified dimensions) to be eligible for the main award. The subjects should be birds recorded in the Western Palearctic.

Two additional awards and one further category are included in the competition. The Richard Richardson award, for the best work submitted by an artist under 22 years of age, was established in 1979, in honour of Richard Richardson, the renowned Norfolk ornithologist and artist, while the PJC Award, for a single work of merit, was established in 1987 by David Cook, in memory of his wife Pauline. Finally, entrants may also submit a colour painting, suitable for use on the cover of *British Birds*. Sponsorship of the event by T. & A. D. Poyser, Academic Press and Christopher Helm ensures that winners of the various categories are suitably rewarded for their efforts.

All the winning entries are displayed at the Society of Wildlife Artists annual exhibition, and at the British Birdwatching Fair, where a presentation ceremony for the winners take place.

For further details of the award, contact Roger Riddington, *British Birds*, Chapel Cottage, Dunrossness, Shetland ZE2 9JH. e-mail: editor@britishbirds.co.uk

Well known artist David Cook, who drew these two drake Smew, also sponsors a prize in the *British Birds* competition each year.

FEATURES

Though Tree Sparrows are monogamous, a new study shows up to a fifth of chicks result from extra-pair copulation. See page 21 for full details.

SCIENTIFIC DISCOVERIES IN 2001

(A REVIEW OF THE YEAR'S LITERATURE)

Renowned ornithologist Chris Mead provides a resume of some results from the scientific literature relevant to Britain's birds and their conservation, published over the last year. Most come from surveys run by the British Trust for Ornithology or research undertaken by its staff or the staff of the RSPB. All illustrations by Dan and Rosie Powell.

Duck! It's a speeding bird

HOW FAST birds fly has been a bone of contention for many years. Hugely unrealistic estimates – up to 300mph for a stooping Peregrine – were rife in Victorian times. More recently, estimates have come from birds being tracked against cars, but even these estimates are subject to all sorts of difficulties – particularly the role of wind assistance.

A report in *Ibis*, the scientific journal of the British Ornithologists' Union breaks new ground as the measurements are all taken by radar tracking, allowing for both wind speed and direction. Swiss ornithologists Bruno Bruderer and Andreas Bolt measured 139 different species using their specially modified radar – that will accurately track species as small as a Chaffinch.

They tried to measure the normal flying speed of birds, and discovered in general that bigger birds flew faster, and those with smaller wings were faster than those with larger.

Of all the species measured, Mallard produces the highest average flying speed.

SCIENTIFIC DISCOVERIES IN 2001

The highest mean speed came from Mallard at 21.4 metres per second (m/s) equivalent to about 48 mph This was almost matched by another duck, the Goosander.

The fastest records for bigger birds – over half a pound in weight – in flapping flights were:

Species	Max speed	Average speed
Mallard	56mph	48mph
Woodpigeon	53mph	38mph
Goosander	48mph	–
Raven	45mph	32mph
Kestrel	44mph	28mph

Big birds, like buzzards, vultures and eagles, gliding from one thermal to another, reached high speeds. However they were effectively going downhill as they were losing height to gain speed.

Griffon Vulture	55mph	37mph
Honey Buzzard	54mph	31mph
Golden Eagle	50mph	33mph
Common Buzzard	49mph	32mph
White Stork	45mph	31mph

Small birds, weighing only an ounce or two, can fly almost as fast and are very closely matched. Three of them spend most of their life in the air:

Swift	44mph	37mph
Tree Pipit	44mph	27mph
Swallow	43mph	25mph
House Martin	42mph	25mph
Chaffinch	42mph	29mph

These realistic figures for birds on migration are very important. The range of speeds recorded show that the birds can fly faster, and slower, if they have to – especially if they can lose height by diving. The very fastest speeds come from hunting birds. Goshawk at 30 m/s (67mph) is probably matched by the Sparrowhawk as well, but the top bird seems to still be the Peregrine at 51 m/s – more than 110mph after a 1,000 foot dive!

These speeds are very interesting when related to the bird carnage on our roads caused by speeding cars. Speeds now regularly attained on roads, in excess of 60 mph, are much faster than any bird would normally expect danger to approach. They are thus taken by surprise. Some studies show that there is a huge increase in bird casualties where traffic travels at 55mph compared to 40mph and this may be the reason.

Size is important after all

A STORY covered enthusiastically by *The Sun* was a real puzzle for many birdwatchers. It emerged that a close relative of the Ruddy Duck, the Argentinean Lake Duck, has a penis measuring a full 20cm (nearly eight inches). Drakes apparently impress the females by showing them the size of their penis and this may lead them to choose particular males. So size does matter, and overt 'willie waving' may be very important for these rather special ducks.

This anatomical preference may be an explanation for the preference shown by some female White-headed Ducks for the smaller drake Ruddy Ducks: a relatively bigger penis on the smaller drake might be very impressive and desirable – leading to the White-headed Duck choosing the wrong mate. This would, at last, explain their apparently unnatural preference in Spain, one of the last strongholds for the endangered White-headed population.

This concern reinforces the scientists' view that the Ruddy Duck cull in Britain should be continued to prevent the species migrating to Spain and Turkey and contaminating the White-headed gene pool.

Latest trends show mixed results

The single most important annual results in the UK are those generated by the Breeding Bird Survey (BBS) which reported more than 217 species of birds from 2,378 different 1km squares in 1999.

There are now five-year changes from the survey for 100 widespread species recorded from a good number of squares. The year-on-year changes are very interesting but long-term trends are more important. More than half of the hundred show statistically significant changes – 30 of these are increases and 25 declines.

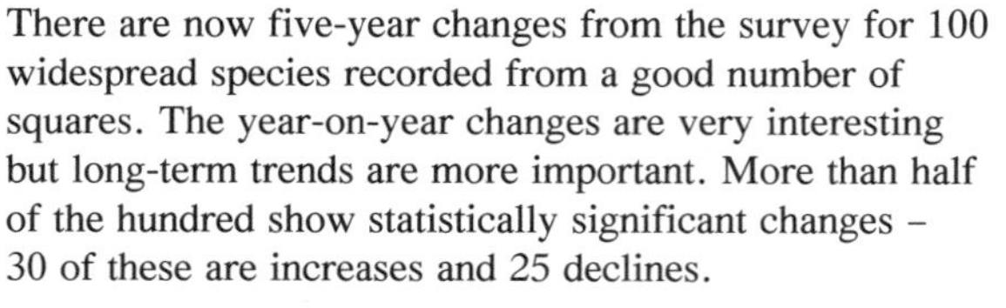

How the survey works

Volunteers are allocated 1km squares, close to them but chosen at random, which they survey every year by walking a designated

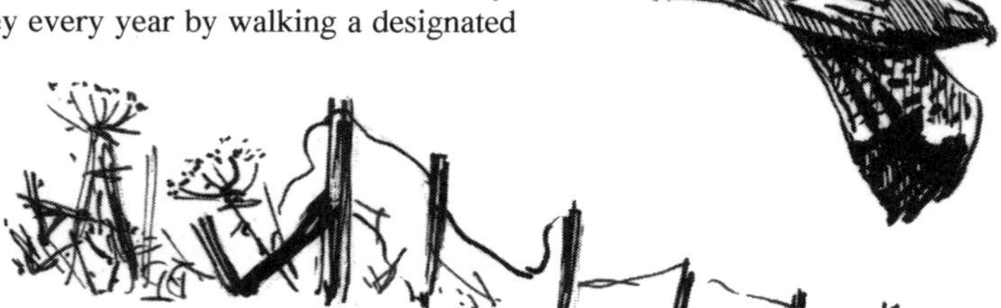

There would be no shortage of BBS volunteers if all patches could boast a pair of Montagu's Harriers!

route once in the first part of the breeding season and once in the second. Every bird seen and heard is recorded along with the habitats present.

I couldn't visit my three allocated squares this year because of Foot and Mouth restrictions, but in previous years there have been real highlights. One had the first record of a Montagu's Harrier for the survey and another has had 50 Skylark records on one visit. However, the other is very ordinary. By combining records from all over the country we obtain a very good picture for the ordinary species of the countryside. The survey is not very good for colonial and nocturnal species and very bad for colonial seabirds (especially nocturnal ones!).

Downward trends
These trends feed into the Red and Amber lists of Bird of Conservation Concern (BoCC) The former is basically for birds, which have gone down by 50% over 25 years, and the later by 25%.

Species	List	5-year change
Shelduck	Amber	-40%
Kestrel	Amber	-30%
Grey Partridge	Red	-43%
Oystercatcher	Amber	-18%
Lapwing	Amber	-20%
Curlew	Amber	-12%
Redshank	Amber	-36%
Lesser BB Gull	Amber	+46%
Turtle Dove	Red	-18%
Green Woodpecker	Amber	+14%
Skylark	Red	-16%
Swallow	Amber	+10%
Dunnock	Amber	+7%
Redstart	Amber	+37%
Stonechat	Amber	+80%
Blackbird	Amber	+12%
Willow Tit	Amber	-42%
Linnet	Red	-14%
Bullfinch	Red	-28%
Corn Bunting	Red	-26%

Britain's Bullfinch population has declined dramatically in the past five years

Regional changes
The latest survey reports detailed investigations into regional changes for the first time. The country was divided into the nine Regional Development Areas within England as well as for Scotland, Wales and Northern Ireland. Though these do not have significant changes for all that many species very interesting comparisons can be made. There are several species for which all the significant changes are in the same direction but others where some are up and some are down.

SCIENTIFIC DISCOVERIES IN 2001

For the BBS, summaries are given with S, W and I indicating Scotland, Wales and Northern Ireland respectively and the English regions represented by SW (South West), SE (South East), L (London), E (East), EM (East Midlands), WM (West Midlands), NW (North West) YH (Yorkshire and Humberside) and NE (North East).

These regions are mentioned if the changes are significant and the largest declines are to the left and highest increases to the right. The 18 species listed are the ones with five or more significant changes from 1994-1999:

Species	Declines	Increases
Mallard	W	NW, SE, SW, S
Pheasant	W, S, EM,	SW, YH, WM, NW
Cuckoo	SW, YH, WA, SE, E,	
Swift	SW, SE,	EM, WM, YH, W, E
Skylark	WM, NE, NW, EM, E, SE, SW, S	
Wren		WM, W, EM. NE, YH, NW, I, S
Robin		S, E, WM, YH, NW, NE
Blackbird	L	SW, W, WM, YH, NW, I, NE
Blackcap		SW, E, YH, SE, EM, W, WM, NW
Willow Warbler	SE, E, SW,	NW, S, I
Goldcrest		W, SE, E, SW, S, I
Great Tit		W, NW, S, I, S
Rook	NW, WM, SE	SW, E, I
Crow		E, NW, EM, SE, L, I
Starling	W, SE, WM, L	EM
House Sparrow	L, I, SE, E	W
Chaffinch	W, SW	NW, E, I
Greenfinch		SW, E, WM, NW, EM

Quite a few of these findings are all good news – all the separate regions reporting significant changes show increases for Wren, Robin, Blackcap, Goldcrest, Great Tit, Carrion Crow and Greenfinch.

Mallard and Blackbird only had a single negative area, and as there have been real worries about the Blackbird (it is currently on the Amber list of Birds of Conservation Concern) this is very good news.

Cuckoo breeding success is falling in many parts of the UK.

Unfortunately there were two species where all the significant changes were decreases – Cuckoo and Skylark – and there were two others where there was only one positive of the five results – Starling and House Sparrow. Skylark (Red) and Starling (Amber) are already on the BoCC list and there has been much concern about the recent plunge of House Sparrow numbers. Many have been worried, in recent years, by the fate of the Cuckoo.

The five other species, with conflicting results, are very interesting. Pheasant (-3, +4) may be doing better in areas where shooting is more important. Swift (-2, +5) seem to be doing much less well in the south of England and Willow Warbler (-3, +3) is definitely doing worse in the south and east and better in the west and north. Rook (-3, +3) numbers might be improving in areas where outside pigs are kept and they can exploit the food available. Finally Chaffinch (-2, +3) changes are very confusing, with losses in Wales and the south-west but increases in Ireland and the north-west as well as the east.

Concern about Swallows

Two species with only four significant changes were Swallow and House Martin. While both increased in Wales, Swallows also increased in the south-west and north-east, but declined in eastern England. House Martins were up in Scotland and the north-west but declined in the south-east. This fits in well with the concerns expressed to me by correspondents for several years.

One new problem for the Swallows might be the insistence that birds should be excluded from buildings where the milking of cows takes place. Clearly there might be problems where milk is processed but Swallows nesting in the milking parlour can surely not be a problem. A paper by Anders Pape Møller on more than 30 years of study at farms in Denmark recorded a 47% decline in dairy farms that gave up milking. Where they continued the population of Swallows remained stable.

* The Breeding Bird Survey is run by the British Trust for Ornithology, the Joint Nature Conservation Committee and the Royal Society for the Protection of Birds.

Singing with wet feet!

AFTER THE BTO's national Nightingale survey in 1999, it was realised that the British population was still in decline, with birds retreating from their former haunts in the north and west. However, the BTO launched several extra investigations in 2000, one of which highlighted a real hot spot for the species around the Fenlands of East Anglia.

In partnership with Anglian Water a 60km x 60km area, including most of the Fens, was re-surveyed in 2000 and no fewer than 382 singing Nightingales were found. They were almost all on peatland alluvial soils, particularly down the eastern side from Downham Market (Norfolk) to just outside Newmarket (Suffolk). Chris Day, an undergraduate from the University of East Anglia spent a sticky time surveying 100 of the territories with Nightingales and 100 carefully matched sites without. This seems to show that the Nightingales like wetter sites where the patches of scrub are completely enclosed and bare inside.

The archives of various long-term BTO surveys were examined by Gavin Siriwrdena to try to find out the mechanisms of the decline. Nest Record Cards seem to show that Nightingale nests have not varied much in their productivity over the last 35 years, though they begin breeding earlier, in line with many other species, as a result of global warming.

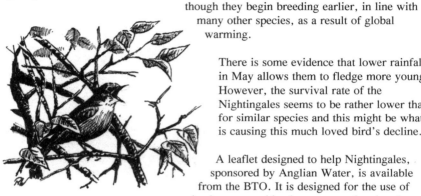

Scientists are still trying to discover why Nightingales prefer wetter sites.

There is some evidence that lower rainfall in May allows them to fledge more young. However, the survival rate of the Nightingales seems to be rather lower than for similar species and this might be what is causing this much loved bird's decline.

A leaflet designed to help Nightingales, sponsored by Anglian Water, is available from the BTO. It is designed for the use of landowners and land managers who already have, or think they might be able to attract, the species nesting on their holdings.

Nest records show how birds decline

EIGHT SPECIES having problems maintaining breeding success have been flagged up by analysis of the BTO's Nest Records Scheme. Alerts have been issued to the government Joint Nature Conservation Committee for these. The eight species with current alert status include two new species and six with existing alerts.

Current alerts, with the number of years notified, are as follows:

Reed Bunting (9 years): Egg stage nest failure rate more than trebled.
Linnet (9 years): Nest failure rate up from 39% to 53% over whole cycle.
Yellow Wagtail (New): Brood size falling over the last 30 years.
Moorhen (8 years): Increasing egg-stage failure (from 31% to 40%).
Lapwing (5 years): Increasing egg-stage failure (from 40% to 49%).
Ringed Plover (4 years): Increasing egg-failure rates (from 56% to 70%).
Willow Warbler (2 years): Chick-stage failure rates up by a half (18% to 27%)
Red-throated Diver (New): Egg-stage failure up from 13% to 40% since 1980.

Other declining species may show better breeding statistics as the species' density declines and there is less competition. This may be happening for Ring Ouzel, Stonechat, Whinchat and Wheatear.

In addition there are several species – Chaffinch, Woodlark, Robin, Redstart, Nuthatch and three common species of tit (Great, Blue and Long-tailed) – whose populations are increasing because the birds are breeding better.

Further analysis, extending the period over which the data were considered, have enabled the alerts on five species to be lifted. Three of these were newly notified last year (Yellowhammer, Sedge Warbler and Dunnock), one for three years (Meadow Pipit) and the final one (Greenfinch) had been on the list for five years.

Countryside picture looks grim

A NEW REPORT on *Breeding Birds in the Wider Countryside* – in full on the web (www.bto.org) - at the beginning of 2001 covers the changes shown in commoner birds as measured by the Common Birds Census and Waterways Bird Survey mainly over the 25 years (1973-1998).

No fewer than 22 species showed a decline of 50% or more, and a further ten had more than 25% losses. These figures are worse than those released in 1996, with the Little Grebe a new species for the list (at -51%) and Yellow Wagtail (–81%), Marsh Tit (-52%), Starling (–61%) and Linnet (–55%) now on the fastest declining list.

The two worst declines are reported for Lesser Redpoll and Tree Sparrow – both down by an appalling 94% in the 25 years.

The BTO authors (Humphrey Crick, John Marchant, David Noble and Stephen Baillie) point out that the most worrying aspect of this analysis is that eight species have declined in the CBC plots by more than 25% just in the last five years. Indeed some are becoming so rare that it is difficult to keep track of them!

Falling numbers mean Little Grebe is now a species in need of active conservation help.

They are as follows

Species	Change over 25 years	5 years
Grey Partridge	-83%	-29%
Lesser Spotted Woodpecker	-73%	-42%
Tree Pipit *	-77%	-31%
Yellow Wagtail	-81%	-41%
Willow Tit	-75%	-25%
Starling	-61%	-27%
Tree Sparrow	-94%	-30%
Lesser Redpoll.	-94%	-44%

* Not representative of most of Britain's Tree Pipits

These results are vital for conservation planning and several of the species have Biodiversity Action plans devoted to them and others are in urgent need of them. For the Grey Partridge the aim is to halt the decline by 2005. For Tree Sparrow, Bullfinch (down 56%) and Corn Bunting (down 86%) the aim is to achieve a 50% increase in the Breeding Bird Survey index between 1996 and 2008. At the moment one might characterise these targets as ambitious but all sorts of actions are being undertaken to help them.

Shelduck displaced by rising water in Cardiff Bay moved only short distances.

Barrage has impact on waders and wildfowl

THE ERECTION of a barrage across the end of Cardiff Bay, completed in November 1999 as part of the Cardiff Docks regeneration scheme, marked the end of the tidal mudflats as a habitat for the birds that had used them for centuries. Niall Burton of the BTO reported on a study started several years before to find out what would happen. The birds involved included many species but the main ones were Shelduck (average population 307 the winter before the barrage was operative) and three waders: Dunlin (786), Curlew (161) and Redshank (344). These birds lived on the 200ha (500 acres) of the Bay composed of mudflat and the surrounding salt marsh – an average of about eight birds per hectare just for these four species.

In the first winter after completion the bay was flushed once a week but, from

September 2000, it has been a permanent lake. Less than 100 (1999/2000) and about 200 (2000/2001) birds of these four species remained on site. The Curlew and Shelduck seemed to have settled locally but Dunlin populations in western Britain were falling through the period and it was not possible to say, definitively, where the displaced birds had gone.

The main part of the study was aimed at Redshanks, which are very site faithful, and ringing, colour marking and radio-tagging techniques were used to try to find out what was happening. The majority of the birds stayed within ten kilometres of Cardiff Bay though a few were about 20 kilometres NE of the bay on the Welsh side of the Severn and three were found across the estuary. This indicates that the resources were not totally occupied on the local areas but there are ongoing studies to determine if the displaced birds are at greater risk than others which had not been forced to relocate.

The study has relevance to all sorts of other areas where habitat for waders and wildfowl may be destroyed. And, because the Redshank only winter in South Wales, the findings are also really important for the areas where they breed. The colour-marked birds have been found in Norfolk, Lancashire, Northumberland, the Outer Hebrides (five) and even in Iceland (five).

And finally.........

BRITAIN'S most rapidly dwindling farmland bird should be encouraged to have more sex, according to a Swiss ornithologist. The Tree Sparrow population is down by 95% from 1970 to 1998, according to the British Trust for Ornithology's Common Bird Census, but a new study reveals that most sexually active pairs laid more eggs and had more fledglings. They also spent less time incubating before the eggs hatched.
A paper in the journal *Avian Biology* by a Swiss ornithologist, Philipp Heeb reports on detailed studies of breeding Tree Sparrows in the grounds of Lausanne University.

These birds clearly show that the pair bond is very important for the quality of the breeding attempt. The fact that our birds are not doing so well is not a consequence of the breeding birds losing out on nooky! However if they are able to do better, because we get the habitat right for them, they will respond by having bigger clutches, producing more young and, yes, having more sex!

Small birds like Tree Sparrows are monogamous and so it is very important that the male and female get on well together and cooperate efficiently in tending their young. DNA fingerprinting shows that about 19% of the chicks result from extra-pair copulations (that is matings by the female not to her 'husband'). Frequent matings, with her partner, might make such activities less likely and reinforce the urge of the male to do his best to rear the eggs in their nest. Some human studies suggest that the expected man does not father about 10% of children born to couples in long-term relationships. So it may be that Tree Sparrow society is not too different from our own!

THE TOP 150 BIRDING INTERNET WEBSITES

by Gordon Hamlett

THE INTERNET has changed markedly since I started to use it about three years ago. There is much less American bias now, but of the thousands of bird-related pages to choose from, only a small fraction are of any great interest or relevance to most British birdwatchers.

I am a great believer in using the Net to gather information and I don't like gimmicks, animations, flashing bits and bobs that take ages to load but add little to the experience. Over-designed pages irritate and some of my comments reflect this. Give me content over design any day.

In terms of birdwatching, the Net is really good for providing information on places, with lists of birds to see, reserves to visit and trip reports aplenty. It is less good on images, songs, and reference material on the birds themselves: not many people have the confidence to create a cyber fieldguide; and those who have, or at least their publishers, haven't found a way to make money out of it yet.

One of the problems with the Net is that it is like a vast, constantly changing sand dune system. All the recommended links from one site to another worked at the time of writing, but that is not to say that they will work when you come to read them. If a link no longer works, then I apologise but it is something that happens.

Star site for 2002
Being forced to choose the Best Bird Website for 2002 is an invidious task, when you consider the huge range of sites, but, under pressure from the Editor, I declare the winner is... Surfbirds (www.surfbirds.com)

You can tell that this site is still evolving as it seems to look totally different every time you visit, but slowly but surely, they are getting their act together, even if there are still a lot of menu options on the home page that don't appear on subsequent pages.
What makes this site a winner is that it is written by birders for birders. Consequently, the material is both interesting and relevant. This is very important. Contrast this to the RSPB site below where it gives the impression of being for the benefit of staff rather than the casual browser.

Content on Surfbirds is rich and varied: breaking news stories, major identification articles, trip reports, latest rarity photographs (including birds seen the day before so it is bang up to date), artists' sketch books, photo essays, book and product reviews (still a bit weak here) and interviews as well as more trivial items such as the ability to send bird greeting cards by e-mail and take part in on-line quizzes.

Even if you don't visit the site regularly, you can sign up for a weekly e-mail which tells you what new features, stories and photos have just been added. If something appeals, click on the relevant link; if not, wait until next week.

The mix of the articles is just right too. It is not a site just for twitchers. There is lots of interesting material here if you are an artist, conservationist, photographer or just simply someone who enjoys birds. And that is just how it should be.

Best newsgroup award

All the subscribers to the newsgroup uk.rec.birdwatching were invited to vote for their favourite website as designed by a fellow contributor and sponsored by *The Birdwatchers' Yearbook.*

The clear winner with more than 60% of the votes polled was Richard Smith's Dee Estuary site (www.deeestuary.freeserve.co.uk/). This is a real labour of love, featuring site guides, monthly newsletter, tide times, suggested walks, all the latest sightings and plenty of other relevant information.

It just goes to show what one person can achieve and is a worthy winner. Congratulations.

...and the worst of the lot!

Nominating the worst website was a lot easier, because just as I was finishing this article, the RSPB launched its newly designed website http://www.rspb.org.uk

It is awful, a triumph of ill-conceived design over content. I am sure that all the information is still there, there are several thousand pages after all, but you just can't find it easily. To illustrate this, let's assume that you want references for Bitterns, Loch Garten and your local members' group. To start the search you must select from the following unhelpful topic headings:

- Current affairs
- Closer to you
- Helping the RSPB
- Wildlife and Conservation
- Community Centre
- Shopping and Services
- Special Features or Resources

A search for Bittern led me to a web-cam with a relevancy rating of 57% and was not what I wanted. Searching for Loch Garten returned no details on how to find the reserve. Looking for local groups through their search engine was equally futile. The search facility on the website is particularly poor.

I did eventually find a database entry for Bitterns. Hands up if you guessed you had to start off through the Special Features box. To find out about Loch Garten, I started off at Wildlife and Conservation (why?) then had to filter through – Reserves – Visiting our reserves – Scotland – and then click on Loch Garten before finding what I wanted. Even then, there is no map – you have to link to another web page (Multimap). Nor was there any mention of the Capercaillie watch there, the information I was specifically seeking. As for local groups, I'm still looking.

Did the site designers ever consider that the needs of the casual browser? It is not unreasonable to think that a non-birder would want to discover something about birds and reserves and think RSPB. This is a prime example of everything a website shouldn't be.

As it is intended that this feature is repeated in future *Yearbooks*, please alert me to any links that no longer work, or if you want to recommend a marvellous new website you believe should be added, feel free to e-mail me on gordon.hamlett@btinternet.com

To help you navigate around this survey I have divided the websites into the following categories:

Biology/science
Bird books
Birds and the law
Conservation
Discussion groups
Foreign birding
Garden birds
History/mythology
Images/sound
Latest sightings
Links
Magazines
Miscellaneous
Non-birding
Optics
Other organisations
Rare birds and listing
Reference
Ringing
Software
Species accounts and ID
Trip reports
Weather
Webcams
Where to watch in Britain

BIOLOGY AND SCIENCE

www.birdingonthe.net
This wonderfully named site contains a list of all the birds in the world, arranged according either to Sibley & Monroe or Clements. You can either browse online or download for your own use. There are plenty of other links too, plus a few recent news snippets (American).

http://birdsource.cornell.edu/
Animated maps of raptor migration and details of recent counts are typical of the information on this site. A massive source of data on North American avian facts and figures, complete with odd snippets and trivia updated each month.

http://www.bto.org/birdtrends/index.htm
We are constantly told that populations of common birds such as House Sparrows and Starlings are crashing, but what's the evidence? Well, there's plenty here from the various surveys conducted by the British Trust for Ornithology.

http://www.english-nature.org.uk/redkite/default.asp
I wanted an overview of the whole Red Kite re-introduction project with facts and figures from the various release schemes and so on. Instead, there is a bit about the East Midlands birds but I couldn't find anything else. Less than friendly for casual browsers, and in view of the interest in this species, I hope the site will be upgraded soon.

http://www.nmnh.si.edu/BIRDNET/index.html
An umbrella organisation covering ten different North American groups, this site is aimed at serious ornithologists with details of various studies and job

offers. Useful sections include a checklist of American birds and lots of copyright-free images though the ones I looked at were very old, not very good and all in black and white.

http://www.mbr-pwrc.usgs.gov/bbs/bbs.html
Wow! An unbelievable source of data on breeding birds, including distribution maps and trends in the USA. This is the sort of thing that you hope one day will be available for other countries as well. A link also gives you identification notes and photos of all American species.

http://www.ospreys.org.uk/AWOP/Home.htm
This site is almost what the Internet was designed for! Dealing with the Osprey re-introduction programme at Rutland Water, the most exciting part is following the journeys of migrating birds as they are tracked by satellites.

http://www.uct.ac.za/depts/stats/adu/seabirds/
BirdLife International is increasingly concerned about the conflict between fishing boats and seabird conservation, with albatrosses, in particular, falling foul of a technique known as long-lining. Here are the grim facts.

http://virtual.clemson.edu/groups/birdrad/index.htm
Ever since it was discovered in the Second World War, radar operators have noticed strange shadows appearing on their screens, caused by migrating birds. This site looks at all the latest research details.

BIRD BOOKS

http://www.hbw.com/
Here you can follow the progress of forthcoming volumes and check out sample plates from the *Handbook of the Birds of the World*, one of the most ambitious publishing projects ever. The six volumes released so far are simply stunning.

http://www.oup.co.uk/academic/science/ornithology/
Birds of the Western Palearctic (BWP) is the standard reference book on its subject. Find out all about it – in book and CD-ROM format – as well as details on various other ornithological titles.

http://groups.yahoo.com/group/bwpusers
http://www.oup.co.uk/ep/prodsupp/sci/combwp/
If you use the CD version of *BWP*, you might encounter a few glitches when running it. These sites contain the archives of a newsgroup discussing those problems as well as OUP's suggested fixes.

http://www.bookbrain.co.uk/
If you want to find the best offers on new bird books this site searches lots of online bookstores for you and finds the cheapest price.

http://www.abebooks.com/
For out-of-print books, take a look at this excellent site.

http://www.nhbs.com/
http://www.wildlifebooks.com/
These two sites specialise in natural history books and offer a huge range of titles. The first is Natural History Book Service, while the latter is also known as Subbuteo Books.

http://www.xs4all.nl/~sbpoley/fgfaq.htm
Want to know what other people think about various fieldguides for Britain and Europe? Here are a series of comments culled from the archives of the newsgroup uk.rec.birdwatching.

http://www.harcourt-international.com/imprints/poyser.htm
Bird books published by Poyser are renowned for their quality. Many of the early titles are extremely sought-after (and consequently expensive to buy). It is a real pity that this site doesn't do the imprint justice. Now part of a larger parent company, there is no obvious enthusiasm here.

BIRDS AND THE LAW

http://www.indaal.demon.co.uk/rbbp.html
Who do you tell if you discover a rare breeding bird? The aptly named Rare Birds Breeding Panel will advise you and treat your records in total confidence. There is also a list of protected species.

http://www.defra.gov.uk/wildlife-countryside/index.htm
In the post-election shake-up in government departments, all the official websites were in the process of name changing from DETR to DEFRA (Department for Environment Food and Rural Affairs). Lots of links but, not surprisingly, very 'official' looking.

http://www.natureNet.Net/law/index.html
This wonderful Web page will answer all your queries about wildlife law, including links to Scottish and Northern Irish laws. I was expecting just the Wildlife and Countryside Act 1981 but there is so much more. Definitely worth bookmarking.

http://www.ramsar.org/index.html
The Convention on Wetlands, signed in Ramsar, Iran, in 1971 is involved with 'the conservation and wise use of wetlands by national action and international cooperation as a means to achieving sustainable development throughout the world.' Find out all the latest developments here.

CONSERVATION

http://www.wing-wbsj.or.jp/birdlife/
Around a tenth of the birds in the world are threatened in some way. BirdLife International breaks the stories on the latest natural and man-made disasters. A depressing but vitally important read.

http://www.habitat.org.uk/news1.htm
For a good selection of British conservation stories, culled from a variety of sources, this site does an excellent job. You can search by date, region (England, Scotland etc.) and theme (birds, flowers etc.) Nothing too technical and well designed.

DISCUSSION GROUPS

Mailing lists

These are a wonderful source of information and debate on a range of topics from the finer points of identification to what's going on in your local area. Once you have joined a list, any e-mail you send is forwarded to every other member on the list who can then reply in turn.

Net etiquette demands that if you can answer a question, you should do so – you might want to ask one yourself one day.

In Britain, local coverage is patchy. Groups that are particularly active include Berkshire, Cambridgeshire, Cornwall, Hampshire, Kent, Oxfordshire and NE Scotland. Surprisingly, there is practically no traffic for London, East Anglia, Yorkshire and the Northwest, so sign up and get writing to see if you can change things. The benefits can be immense – on my local group, the number of records submitted is far greater than if we just used pen and paper. News of locally rare birds gets disseminated much quicker, too.

http://dir.groups.yahoo.com/dir/Recreation_Sports/Outdoors/Birding
Many mailing lists and groups are run by Yahoo, and the site above has a list of more than 350 groups. Some are local, such as Peterbirder dealing with birds around the Peterborough area, while others are more global e.g. African birds. More abstract groupings include teenage bird chat. Something for everyone.

http://www.fatbirder.com/links/signpost_and_discussion/mailing_lists.html
Another excellent source is the page on Fatbirder which also includes lots of non-Yahoo groups.

http://www.osme.org/ebn/lists.html
This site has lots of links to foreign groups

http://www.Netlink.co.uk/users/ag/ebn/
UK-BirdNet (UKBN) is one of the longest running mailing lists and many of the contributors, mostly top birders, have been arguing with each other for many years. Discussions tend to be quite serious and recent topics have included crossbill taxonomy, Crested Tit distribution and colour-ringed gulls as well as various personality threads revolving round which twitcher has seen which bird.
To subscribe: Send an e-mail to ukbirdNet-request@dcs.bbk.ac.uk or fill in the form on the website.

Newsgroups

Imagine newsgroups as giant notice boards. You post your message and everyone else can see it and reply at will. They are not always for the fainthearted, as people tend to speak first and think afterwards. However, they are a good source of information and a good way of getting your questions answered, though do look at the Frequently Asked Questions(FAQ) first (see below).

If you do subscribe to a newsgroup (technical term, no money involved) your best bet is to lurk for a week or so and see what sort of messages get posted before jumping in yourself.

To subscribe to a newsgroup, you first need to set up your system to access them. Your Internet Service Provider (ISP) should handle this for you (search for newsgroups in the help section if you don't know what to do). You will then have to download a list of all the newsgroups currently available – about 30-35,000 on every subject imaginable at the time of writing depending on your ISP. You can then subscribe to as many of these as you want and read and send messages to your heart's content.

There are currently three UK newsgroups dealing directly with birds plus others interested in other aspects of wildlife.

uk.rec.birdwatching (ukrb)
Typical traffic is largely beginners and improvers though the likes of Chris Mead and Malcolm Ogilvie often answer your questions and very helpful and knowledgeable they are, too.

Some of the threads, especially on matters of conservation – the Ruddy Duck cull is a prime example – can lead to some pretty robust debates, though timid newcomers should be aware that this is one of the milder news groups by a long way.

Sadly, a few idiots think it is great fun to spoil things by resorting to considerable personal abuse. The only way to deal with these posters is to put them into your kill file so you don't get to see their messages. Don't be put off. There is a lot of good debate here, too.

scot.birds
As its name suggests this site deals with matters Scottish but gets very little traffic, most people using ukrb instead.

rec.birds
This site contains mostly North American traffic. For some reason, they hardly seem to debate things at all, certainly not the full and frank discussions sometimes seen on ukrb.

http://www.xs4all.nl/~sbpoley/ukrbfaq.htm
All the FAQ (frequently-asked questions) for uk.rec.birdwatching can be found here. These include such diverse topics as how to get rid of cats, seeing Red Kites over the M40, mosquito repellents, dealing with birds that have flown into your room and what is a Caspian Gull.

FOREIGN BIRDING

http://www.camacdonald.com/birding/birding.htm
There is not enough scope in this article to cover every foreign country but this site does it all for you! Simply click on the country you are interested in and you get a whole range of Websites covering nature reserves, endemic birds, places to stay and trip reports. Your number one site when researching your next birding holiday.

http://www.bsc-eoc.org/links/links1.html
This is another site with a massive number of links. Simply click on the world map, narrowing it down from continent, to country etc to find a host of useful sites.

http://worldtwitch.virtualave.Net/
WorldTwitch concentrates on some of the more remote areas of the world. It is also strong on conservation matters and has a good section on appropriate books.

http://americanbirding.org/
The American Birding Association is where you will find the most active North American birders. They also produce some superb magazines. When you join, you get a nationwide list of members who may be able to help you plan your next visit there.

http://www.neotropicalbirdclub.org/index.html
The Neotropical Bird Club deals with all matters South and Central American. Their Website is aimed at recruiting new members, so there isn't much general information available online.

http://www.orientalbirdclub.org/
The Oriental Bird Club is much better. Despite a very simple design, there are plenty of mini articles and stories to get you interested in the club's activities. There is also an e-mail group to join.

http://www.osme.org/
If the Middle East is your thing, then OSME's site is an excellent starting point with lots of news stories, latest sightings, and, especially welcome, lots of trip reports.

http://www.africanbirdclub.org/
The African Bird Club has a fairly simple Web page with only a few articles to browse. There is quite a bit of detail about applying for grants if you are interested in research projects.

http://www.ausbird.com/
For everything that you want to know about birding Down Under, this site has probably got it, with information, articles and links to just about every aspect of Australian birding.

http://www.fco.gov.uk/travel/
If you are planning a trip abroad, especially to somewhere remote, then check the latest travel advice from the Foreign Office.

http://www.free-living.com/
If you are thinking of booking a specialised bird holiday, this site has links to all the major tour companies, plus the latest travel news that may affect birders.

http://www.virtualbirder.com/vbirder/index.html
Can't afford a foreign trip this year? Take a virtual tour instead. Visit various hotspots, identify the birds, rack up the points, beat the Americans! New tours appear periodically – among others I've been to Churchill, Florida Everglades and tried some New England wader (sorry, shorebird) identification. A great way to waste an afternoon.

http://www.camacdonald.com/birding/eufranceCALAIS2.htm
A day's birding doesn't have to be in this country. How about a day trip on the ferry across to France? John Cantelo's article looks at some of the best places to watch, easily accessible from Calais, together with some of the key species.

GARDEN BIRDS

http://www.wildlifeforever.Net/
Hints and tips for setting up a wildlife garden, as seen through the eyes of a Devon gardener. A nicely designed home Web page.

http://www.bto.org/gbw/gbwhome.htm
Anyone with a back yard, no matter how small, can take part in the BTO's garden bird scheme, which helps monitor populations across the country.

http://www.abcissa.force9.co.uk/birds/
Just because you are house bound, doesn't mean that you can't enjoy your birding. This delightful and award-winning Website details the bird life in a Cheshire garden, including a section on Meadow Pipit

migration as well as the usual birds. Nearly 70,000 visitors can't be wrong.

HISTORY AND MYTHOLOGY

http://www.daily-tangents.com/Aves/Archaeop/
If you are interested in how birds evolved, then this site tells you everything that is known about Archaeopteryx, one of the first fossils with feathers. Articles, animations, theories and counter-theories, all fossilized life is here.

http://www.kami.demon.co.uk/gesithas/birdlore/fugellar.html
Just to show that even the most obscure research can be fascinating, this site looks at birds in Anglo-Saxon England, the evidence for them and the origin of their names. Delightfully illustrated with contemporary images.

http://www.advanceNet.Net/~jscole/wren.htm
Across most Celtic countries, the Wren is known as the King of the Birds and great misfortune befell anyone who harmed it, except on St Stephen's Day when it was ritually hunted and given a ceremonial burial. Explore more myths here.

http://www.geocities.com/carmelbird/birds/
Nearly 100 species have become extinct in the last 300 years. This site, which is still being completed, has illustrations and text on all of them, a depressing comment on man's effect on the environment.

IMAGES AND SOUND

http://www.wildsounds.co.uk/
If you are looking for CDs of bird song, or CD-ROMs, then WildSounds have an impressive selection of titles for sale. They can also help you if you fancy having a go at making your own recordings.

http://www.bl.uk/collections/sound-archive/wild.html
The British Library National Sound Archive boasts more than 130,000 recordings. If you need to research something obscure, this is a good starting place though it is aimed fairly and squarely at the academic end of the market.

http://www-stat.wharton.upenn.edu/~siler/masi/eurosongs3.html
For a free site where you can download short snippets of bird song and examine the appropriate songagram, take a look at this excellent site.

http://www.instnat.be/Soorten/Broedvogels/atlas/Engels/distribution.htm
Bird photographs and pictures can be found at a variety of sites. For European species, try this first-rate Belgian site that also has an ongoing sound quiz to test your skills.

http://www.rspb-images.com
For top quality photographic images, you will find it hard to beat the RSPB's collection. After registering, you can browse the catalogue and download the image for your own personal use. If you want a print or slide, these can be ordered with a sliding scale of fees, increasing markedly if you want to use them for commercial purposes. You will need Flash to access this site though I would have preferred less gimmicks and faster loading.

http://www.martinridley.com/
If you like the front cover of this book, take a look at the artist Martin Ridley's home page which shows a selection of his work including various sketches and work in progress.

http://www.birdsireland.com/pages/birdart.html
Here is a selection of bird paintings by artist Michael O'Clery on the Birds Ireland website. It also contains plenty of other information on birding in the Emerald Isle.

http://freespace.virgin.Net/swla.Web/
The pages of the Society of Wildlife Artists have details of members, what the society is looking for and how to apply for bursaries. Such a pity then that it can't include a representative sample of art.

http://www.birdillustrators.com
This is more like it. Despite an awful front page, there are some amazing treasures inside with artwork from many of today's top bird artists, including Ian Lewington, Hilary Burn and Alan Harris. I particularly liked the sketchbooks. You can buy online though prices aren't too cheap - £200 was the lowest price I found.

http://www.camacdonald.com/birding/birdindex.html
There are photos of an excellent range of species on this page though the pictures themselves are of variable quality. Search according to the bird's specific name (a la Sibley and Monroe) or you can follow a link if you are looking for something on a broader scale such as 'eagles'. New pictures are being added all the time

LATEST SIGHTINGS

http://dialspace.dial.pipex.com/town/close/xdu72/
Whether you want the latest rare bird sightings

e-mailed to you or sent as a text message to your mobile phone, Focalpoint offer a range of services starting at £7.50 per year. If you don't want the e-mails, there is a free Web page accessible from this site that has brief details of all the latest news.

http://www.jjstroud.freeserve.co.uk/latest.htm
Birdlinks has a few latest sightings on its pages, together with a selection of weather forecasts, news stories links and books.

http://www.birdguides.com/birdnews/about.asp
Most birders I know use the pages from BirdGuides. You can register for a free Web page of the latest sightings, but you only get full details of the last bit of news to be phoned in. The full service delivers complete details of everything, and again you can have e-mails delivered to you. A nice touch is that you click on links to get more information on a particular bird or maps showing exactly where it was seen.

LINKS

http://www.fatbirder.com
Why do all the hard work of searching for yourself when someone has already done it for you? Fatbirder contains many thousands of links to birding sites and mailing lists across the world and is especially good for finding local British information.

http://directory.google.com/Top/Recreation/Birdwatching/
Google is my favourite search engine and this page will do a lot of the initial searching for you with categories for birds based on a scientific basis and also looking at birdwatching as a recreation.

http://birding.al-info.com/
Another birding search engine, though not one that I have personally used.

http://www.bsc-eoc.org/links/
There are supposed to be more than 6,000 links to other birdwatching sites listed on these pages, arranged by geographical area. That should keep you quiet for a bit.

http://www.best.com/~petrel/AngusBirdingWebSites.html
Lots of links to pelagic birding, gull sites and all things marine, plus other birding links. It was last updated back in 2000 though so not all the links might work.

MAGAZINES

http://www.surfbirds.com/
Here you'll find the latest news from both sides of the Atlantic including plenty of stunning rarity photographs. There are lots of interesting articles such as a detailed discussion of the 2000 Honey Buzzard invasion, complete with animated map and plenty of trip reports, too. The quirky site navigation is improving a lot.

http://www.birding.com/
Though it is American in its bias, you will constantly discover new sections to explore. Whether you want information on using and choosing optics or help with identifying birds, it is probably in here somewhere.

http://www.birdsofbritain.co.uk/
Updated monthly, there are a few news stories, a major article, a guide to more than 100 species taken from the Eastern Daily Press and lots of suggestions as to places to watch birds. More than 170 pages.

http://www.bbc.co.uk/nature/birds/
Part of the BBC's huge Website, there are links to news stories, Web cameras, building nest boxes, weather and, of course, radio and television programmes. You can also send an e-card to a friend.

MISCELLANEOUS

http://www.bird-stamps.org/
http://www.birdtheme.org/
Themed stamp collecting is something of a recent phenomenon and it comes as no surprise to find that 'birds' are the most collected subject. These two sites between them should tell you everything you ever wanted to know about ornithophilately, including pictures of every bird stamp issued (and there are thousands). It is interesting to note that the British Post Office mistakenly depicted a very non-British Cape Gannet rather than a Northern Gannet on one recent issue!

http://www.babelbird.de/start_e.html
If your favourite search engine turns up a useful site written in a foreign language, head for this site as it will search through a Web page for you and translate all the bird names into the language of your choice. Currently translates to and from English, scientific, French, German and Spanish.

http://birdingpal.com/
There is nothing to beat a bit of local knowledge. Birding Pals aims to put you in touch with fellow birders around the world who are prepared to help you plan your next trip or even take you out. Of course you should offer your help in return.

http://birdtop50.com/
http://www.supertop100.com/bird/
Want to know which sites are visited most often? Take a look at the Top 50 and Top 100 rated according to numbers of visitors to a particular site. Some very strange results are caused by having to register your site first, something that not everyone does.

http://www.pbs.org/lifeofbirds/index.html
Find out more about the making of Sir David Attenborough's stunning television series *The Life of Birds*. There are sections on bird evolution, songs, bird intelligence etc. Strangely, this link comes from the American PBS pages – I couldn't find very much on the BBC website at all.

http://www.bbc.co.uk/education/birding/
Another television programme that captured the public's imagination was *Birding with Bill Oddie*. This site has all the background information on locations used, species seen and transcripts of the live question and answer session.

http://www.thayerbirding.com/birdjokes.htm
All work and no play makes Jack a bad birder to paraphrase a well known saying. When the boss isn't looking try reading a few of these birding jokes. Some are truly awful, the rest a lot worse.

NON-BIRDING

http://www.cathate.co.uk/
You've spent a fortune on bird food and feeders and what happens? Next door's moggie helps itself to one of your Blackbirds. Whether you want tips on keeping cats out of your garden or you want to know exactly what the law allows you do, this humorous site is for you.

http://www.geocities.com/SiliconValley/Horizon/1195/wxtide32.html
The time of high tide is crucial to birders. Get it wrong and you won't see a bird all day. This is a free programme you can download that helps you plot tide times at 9,000 locations round the world. As with all tide information, the further ahead you look, the less accurate it becomes.

OPTICS

http://betterviewdesired.com/
Independent optics reviews are in short supply. This site tells you everything you need to know about a whole range of binoculars and telescopes for birders. Be prepared for some surprising conclusions though.

http://www.digiscoping.co.uk/
Digiscoping is term that might be new to a lot of you but basically involves taking pictures through your telescope using either a digital still camera or video camera. This site takes you through some of the basics and there are some great pictures on view too.

http://www.md.ucl.ac.be/peca/test/a.html
Another good digiscoping site with plenty of technical advice and tips and tricks. Of course, there are some mind-blowing pictures – just take a look at the American Avocet. If that doesn't make you want to go out and try for yourself, nothing will.

http://www.optics4birding.com/
If you want to know what fellow birders think about various makes and models of binocular, scopes and tripods, then take a look here. There is also a huge section of frequently-asked questions which cover most of the things you ever wanted to know about optics.

OTHER ORGANISATIONS

http://www.arocha.org/
A Rocha is an international Christian organisation concerned with all conservation matters. Their website has plenty of information on the group itself, various projects and opportunities for volunteering.

http://www.disabledbirdersassociation.org.uk/DBAindex.htm
Birding in a wheelchair is no fun. But there are still plenty of places you can go and the website of the Disabled Birders Association is compiling a list. They also organise various birding holidays including Scotland and Kenya.

http://dspace.dial.pipex.com/gay.birders/index.shtml
If you are a gay or lesbian birder, then take a look at the pages of the Gay Birders Club where you can read extracts from their quarterly newsletter, use the message board or see what trips are planned.

RARE BIRDS AND LISTING

http://www.uk400clubonline.co.uk/
If you are into twitching and listing, you might be interested in joining Lee Evans' UK400 Club. There is a subscription charge of £12 per annum to access his information.

http://www.Webbsteve.freeserve.co.uk/
Steve Webb, Lee Evans' arch rival has also set up a Web page which includes various checklists you can download, though the chosen colour schemes mean that you probably won't want to linger.

http://birdlist.org/
This ambitious project aims to provide bird lists (not including vagrants) for every country in the world though at the time of writing, it still has a few teething problems. The British list starts off well enough though there haven't been too many Black-and-yellow Silky-flycatchers recently!

http://www.bou.org.uk/recgen.html
For an up-to-date British list and any recent taxonomic splits and lumps, visit the Website of the British Ornithologists' Union.

http://Web.oNetel.Net.uk/~wcswift/index.html
If the whole idea of twitching appals you the Society

for the withholding information from Twitchers (SWIFT) which operates out of the West Country has images of rare birds that were not advertised to the hordes. They also explain why they feel the need to take this action.

http://www.birdNet.ltd.uk/
http://www.rarebirdalert.co.uk/
If you have to have up-to-the-minute news, you are going to need a pager. There are currently two main companies in Britain offering their services to birders. The first site needs better navigation but gives details of recent pager messages so you can see what you will be getting for your money. The second address consists of little more than a phone number and e-mail address though with the promise of more to come!

http://www.gadwall.com/birding/rules.html
It's always the same. You go looking for a bird only to be greeted with "It was here ten minutes ago." But there are plenty of other reasons why the bird won't show. Here are a list of excuses and apologias for use in the pub afterwards. Very silly. And heartfelt.

REFERENCE

http://www.birdcare.com/birdon/
An excellent source of material including a comprehensive dictionary of birding terms, the complete text of Chris Mead's *State of the Nation's Birds*, hints and tips for feeding and attracting birds to your garden.

http://www.sca.org.au/lochac/scribes/hrld_6.html
This site is unlikely to be of use unless you are about to be ennobled with the title of Sir Twitcher of Titchwell, but heraldry terms do come up in crossword clues on occasions and you wouldn't want to get a bird question wrong would you?

http://bible.christiansunite.com/Torreys_Topical_Textbook/ttt056.shtml
There are all sorts of references to birds in the Bible, though scholars still argue about the species referred to in the ancient Hebrew scripts. This site lists every reference and links take you to the passage in question.

RINGING

http://www.bto.org/ringing/ringinfo/ring-found.htm
What do you do if you find a bird with a ring on its leg? Fill in the details on the form on this page and send it off to the BTO. You should get an answer in about five weeks. There is also information on how to become a ringer as well as plenty of other information.

http://www.birdsinthe.Net/
This site details everything to do with ringing birds around the world and covers observatories, equipment suppliers, ongoing studies and mailing lists.

SOFTWARE

http://www.birdsoftware.co.uk/
http://www.wildlife.co.uk/
http://www.avisys.Net/index.htm
http://www.thayerbirding.com/prod.htm

If you want to use your computer to record all your bird sightings, you can either design your own spreadsheet or database or buy an off-the-shelf package such as those listed above. The first two packages are British in origin, the other two American, which means that you might have to spend extra time setting up in a British format. The Websites all describe the sorts of things you can do with recording software, including a whole host of reporting options. Thayer also produces other North American CD-ROMS.

http://www.birdguides.com/html/estore/CDROMS.ASP
For CD-ROMS covering Britain and Europe, the best ones by far are the BAFTA-winning titles from BirdGuides.

http://members.aol.com/sbsp/
As a way of advertising their database, Santa Barbara Software Products will send you a free checklist for any country in the world.

SPECIES ACCOUNTS AND ID

http://montereybay.com/creagrus/index.html
There are, depending on what system you use to count them, about 202 different bird families. At the time of writing, Don Roberson has written well researched essays on about half of them, together with a few trip reports, sundry other essays, lots of photos etc.

http://www.goldeneagle.ie/
After the success of reintroducing White–tailed Eagles to Scotland and Red Kites to England and Scotland, an attempt is now being made to bring back Golden Eagles to Ireland. Read all about the project here.

http://www.ospreywatch.co.uk/
England's first acknowledged pair of totally wild Ospreys for over 150 years bred in the Lake District in 2001. Find out all about them on this site.

http://owlpages.com/
Birds of ill omen or something far more lovable? Mankind has always had a huge fascination with owls and this site will tell you everything you ever wanted to know, ranging from biology through mythology to owl antiques.

http://www.owls.org/
Despite its name, the site of the World Owl Trust has a decidedly British feel to it. Though primarily a conservation charity, there is plenty of information on various species of owl as well as designs for building your own nesting box.

http://www.best.com/~petrel/index.html
If sitting staring out to sea all day is your favourite birding activity, you will love this site, which is devoted to seabirds. There are annotated checklists with links to photos of all the species as well as all the best pelagic sites round the world.

http://ourworld.compuserve.com/homepages/peter_and_barbara_barham/Pengies.htm
Everything you wanted to know about penguins boasts the introduction to this site and with more than 150 pages of text and 200 photos, who am I to argue? Covers everything from evolution to penguin boxer shorts.

http://www.gigrin.co.uk
With Red Kites being successfully introduced into England and Scotland, more people are getting the chance to see this exciting raptor. But if you want to see them really closely, you want to go to one of the feeding stations such as Gigrin Farm in Wales. All the details are here as well as lots of news about this once common bird.

http://www.martinreid.com/gullinx.htm
Gull-watchers are the most fanatical birders in the known universe. The rest of us just can't see what the fuss is about. Phenomenally detailed discussions of all sorts of species/subspecies/different ages etc. Hundreds of photos, even more links. It makes you wonder if these people ever get out into the field.

http://www.sandmartintrust.org.uk/
There are groups and individuals interested in just about any group of birds you can imagine. Here we go even further, down to species level. The Sand Martin Trust is collating data on these harbingers of spring and welcomes input and queries from you.

http://users.ox.ac.uk/~wolf0977/projectparakeet.html
More frequent than Jumbo Jets round Heathrow, Ring-necked Parakeets are slowly colonising the south-east. A doctoral thesis into these and other parrots in Britain sounds pretty dull but I found it all fascinating. Updated maps show the latest sightings and you can send in your own records, too. Plenty of information and pictures add to the interest.

http://www.peregrinefund.org/notes_condor.html
These pages – very well designed – deal with the problems faced by the Californian Condor, brought back from the verge of extinction by a captive breeding programme.

http://www.home.istar.ca/~amon/bluetits_index_.htm
Blue Tits in Cyberspace screams the title page though there is information about other tit species too. Very much a one person design with some hideously garish backdrops and cheesy buttons. The enthusiasm bubbles through though.

http://www.bsc-eoc.org/lpbo/swans/swans.html
Another satellite tracking site, this time looking at Tundra Swans, the North American version of our Bewick's Swans in the area of Long Point, one of Canada's main migration hotspots. Plenty of other pages look at other birds in the area.

http://www.rspb.org.uk/wild_info/view_wi.asp?fld_faq_id=171
Capercaillie and Black Grouse are two of the most sought-after species in the Scottish Highlands. Unfortunately, behaviour by some birders is putting undue pressure on these birds. As a result of that, a voluntary code of conduct has been drawn up. If you want to be able to continue to watch these stunning birds, then please read it here.

http://www.bsc-eoc.org/links/links2.html
If you can't find anything to interest you above, then this site has links to all sorts of individual species and bird families around the world.

TRIP REPORTS

Want to know what you are likely to see in Tibet in spring, or Namibia in autumn? There are thousands of trip reports on the Net, but they are not always easy to find. The sites below have large numbers of reports available ranging from a few paragraphs to more than 50 pages in length. Most have links to other trip report sites. If you do look at lots of reports, take the trouble to write up your own trip and post it for the benefit of others.

http://www.crosswinds.Net/~birdtrips/TripReports.html
A good selection of sites on offer, but it is no longer taking new reports.

http://www.birdtours.co.uk/
Growing every month, so check it out regularly.

http://www3.ns.sympatico.ca/ns/maybank/Trips.htm
This site covers both North and South America.

http://www.azstarNet.com/~lisab/triplist.html
Another large collection of North American reports.

http://www.ukbishosting.co.uk/fbris/about.htm
Once upon a time Steve Whitehouse and his Foreign

TOP 150 BIRDING INTERNET SITES

Birdwatching Reports and Information Service (FBRIS) had the printed trip report market to himself. Then the Internet came along offering information for free. However, if you can't find what you want elsewhere, have a look Steve's site.

WEATHER

Want to know what the weather is going to be doing when you are out searching for migrants? The following sites all have UK weather information.

http://www.met-office.gov.uk/weather/europe/uk/ukforecast.html
Information direct from the Met Office so it must be good, but there are no wind details given – useless for seawatching and migration information!

http://www.onlineweather.com/
This site includes wind speeds and directions but the maps aren't the best.

http://www.bbc.co.uk/weather/ukweather/wind.shtml
Trust Auntie to get it right. Nice clear maps, lots of arrows showing wind strength and direction.

WEBCAMS

By their very nature, Web cameras are something of a hit or miss affair. If the camera is pointing at a nest site, you will only see pictures in the breeding season, assuming of course that the birds are obliging enough to use the right nest in the first place. Then of course, you have to allow for time differences, or different seasons when looking at cameras elsewhere in the world and so on.

http://www.fatbirder.com/links/images_and_sound/Webcams.html
For a good list of currently operating cameras, take a look at this site.

http://www.quetzalcam.com/tour/qcam/
The chance to see live action of Quetzals makes this one of the international sites worth looking for.

http://www.storchennest.de/livecam.en.html
This German site records White Storks, but you do get English translations.

http://www.rspb.org.uk/features/
Roam around some RSPB reserves, perhaps watching Ospreys at Loch Garten, Hen Harriers at Forsinard and so on. There is usually a selection of highlights if nothing much is happening.

http://www.owlcam.com/
Enjoy pictures of Barred Owls here.

If you subscribe to the newsgroup uk.rec.birdwatching (see Discussion groups) there are usually fellow subscribers with cameras inside tit boxes during the breeding season.

WHERE TO WATCH IN BRITAIN

http://www.fatbirder.com/links_geo/europe/uk.html
If you want details of the reserves in any county in Britain and Ireland, then by far the most comprehensive list of sites is on the Fatbirder pages. Select your county and you get details and links to all the appropriate reserve and club pages, as well as a list of top birding sites, places to stay and books to read. Excellent.

There are far too many sites to list individually but the ones below show some of the different approaches to 'where to watch guides' including country, county, area straddling several counties, local birding and individual sites.

http://www.deeestuary.freeserve.co.uk/
Covering both the English and Welsh sides of the Dee, this site has maps and site details for plenty of places to watch as well as tide tables, counts, recent sightings and newsletters. A very well constructed site.

http://www.surfbirds.com/kernowbirds/kernowsite.html
This is a fairly basic site to Cornish locations, though there are links to Streetmap so you can get a detailed map of the area in question.

http://www.peterboroughbirdclub.org.uk/
My local club so guaranteed a plug! There are 20 locations on line at present, nearly all local rather than national sites, the sort of place a non-local birder would never get to hear about. This is just the sort of things that local clubs should be doing.

http://members.aol.com/SNetbirds/index.htm
Snettisham is celebrated with a couple of maps, a few photos, tide tables and so on this private one person website. Though the site is still being constructed and seems slow to load, you end up with a much better feel for the place than from the official RSPB site.

http://www.andrewsi.freeserve.co.uk/lothian-sites.htm
Lothian: A highly detailed account of an entire county. At the moment, there is just one overall map of the county with screeds of text but individual site maps are promised.

http://www.wildlifeWeb.co.uk/
Scotland: As well as having all the latest bird sightings from Grampian, there is also a clickable map for the various regions of Scotland giving details of the best places to go (some areas of the website are still under construction).

http://users.ox.ac.uk/~mert0096/publictransport.html
If you don't have a car, this site has some suggestions for reserves which can reached by public transport. Design is basic in the extreme but there are links to maps and railway timetables.

http://www.sk58.freeserve.co.uk/
Fans of local patch birding should have a look at this site concentrating on a 10x10km square in South Yorkshire. The pages are simple to use and well designed, though I would prefer to go straight into the site rather than a title page that just says 'click here to enter'.

http://cos.users3.50megs.com/finder.html
Rather than looking at one site and telling you what to see there, Bird Finder targets a few speciality species in Wales such as Black Grouse and suggests places to find them. Naturally, there are no breeding sites for birds such as Goshawk given.

http://www.seabird.co.uk/
The Scottish Seabird Centre overlooks Bass Rock. Considering how hi-tech the whole thing is, I was somewhat disappointed with the website. There is a good article on the birds of Bass Rock but by and large, birds feature very little. Where is the

Derbyshire artist Richard Whittlestone produced this highly detailed pen and ink drawing of a Meadow Pipit (*Anthus pratensis*) brooding a newly-hatched Cuckoo. Her own eggs lie abandoned outside the nest.

BREAKTHROUGH IN HEARING BIRD SOUND

SOUNDS NATURAL HEARING SUPPORT SYSTEM

by Dennis Furnell

SOME YEARS ago my hearing was permanently damaged following a car accident and, as a consequence, I found certain aspects of nature closed to me. I simply could not hear birds with a low frequency song - birds like the Cuckoo.... And other quiet natural sounds were also hard to hear. It's dispiriting not to be able to listen to the Bittern booming or the churr and chortle of a reedbed full of nesting warblers.

Fortunately, because of my job as a natural history radio and television broadcaster and wildlife sound recordist, I'm familiar with sound recording equipment, the niceties of amplification and the intricacies of microphones and I set about looking for ways in which to improve my ability to hear in the field. I came across a portable sound amplifier, but it was cumbersome, especially as I was already carrying binoculars, camera, tripod, recorder etc...

The more I researched, the more I realised just how many people share a similar hearing loss. About 12% of the population (nearly 8.5 million people) are hearing impaired - ranging from a slight or moderate hearing loss to profound loss where sign language and lip reading, as well as electronic aids, are necessary.

I began to think about how I might help other deaf or disabled countryside enthusiasts to overcome some of the disadvantages of their disability. It brought me into close contact with other hard-of-hearing birdwatchers and with organisations such as the Royal National Institute for the Deaf and The Fieldfare Trust (which gives advice about access to the countryside for people with various types of disabilities - not only hard of hearing). I found too that conservation organisations like the Royal Society for the Protection of Birds (RSPB), the Wildfowl and Wetlands Trust (WWT) and the Wildlife Trust Partnerships were only too happy to become involved and help wherever possible.

Eventually I discovered a company that markets mechanical and electronic aids for people with hearing disability and, with their help, was able to design a system of electronic hearing support for use in bird observatories. The system feeds a signal to a loop and amplified headphone sockets. This loop allows users with a 'T' position switch on their hearing-aid to receive a clear signal from the microphone, avoiding the ambient noise and speech from within the hide itself.

SOUNDS NATURAL HEARING

I've already mentioned that millions of people do not enjoy good hearing. Some of them for one reason or another do not (or will not) wear an aid. For these people, I reasoned, that a simple system incorporating amplified headphones and a volume control would provide an enhanced level of sound from within the hide and add to their enjoyment of wildlife.

It's all very well having an idea, recognising a need and designing a system, but in the end it all comes down to money. By it's very nature this type of equipment is expensive and has to be installed by experts if it is to work properly. Fortunately I had worked with BT on a number of conservation and education projects and was encouraged to present this project to them as part of their 'BT Hear for All Campaign'.

Within two years the project was up and running. Called Sounds Natural Hearing Support Systems there are now five installations up and down the country:

- the RSPB reserves at Strumpshaw Fen in Norfolk and Leighton Moss in Lancashire,
- the Wildfowl & Wetlands Trust Reserves at Welney on the Ouse Washes in Cambridgeshire and Slimbridge in Gloucestershire,
- the Anglian Water/LRTNC Birdwatching Centre at Rutland Water.

But it's not enough to equip these major wildlife sites with highly sophisticated electronics to help hearing-impaired birdwatchers if they don't know about it... And being deaf often makes it harder to come by information about special facilities.

This is where the World Wide Web comes into its own. To complement the facilities in the wildlife observatories a multi-layered web-site was built to provide information for people at home. Birdsong has been added for atmosphere and a commentary for people with visual impairment. There's a 'Kid's Page' too. The web address is www.soundsnatural-hss.com and the site runs to some 20 or more pages - and gets thousands of 'hits' per month.

BOOKS THAT HAVE BEEN SENT IN FOR REVIEW

Alaska – The Traveller's Wildlife Guide by Denis Paulson and Les Beletsky. Published by Academic Press 2001. ISBN 0125469608, price £19.95.

Bill Oddie's Birds of Britain and Ireland. Illustrated by David Daly, Stephen Message and Clive Byers. Softback editon, published by New Holland 2001. ISBN 1853684880, price £12.99.

The Wetland Bird Survey 1998-1999. Published by BTO, WWT, RSPB and JNCC 2000. Available from WeBS Secretariat, WWT Slimbridge, Glos GL2 7BT. ISBN 0900806303, price £30.

Report of the UK Raptor Working Group, chaired by DETR and JNCC. Available from Scottish Natural Heritage Publications, Battleby, Redgorton, Perth PH1 3EW. ISNB 1853970786, price £9.99.

Migration and International Conservation of Waders, edited by H.Hötker et al 2000. Available from International Wader Study Group, c/o National Centre for Ornithology, Nunnery Place, Thetford, Norfolk IP24 2PU. Price £35.

A Study into the Raptor Predation of Domestic Pigeons by Colin Shawyer, Roger Clarke and Nicholas Dixon. Published by DETR 2000.

The influence of Moorland Management on Grouse and their Predators edited by Adam Smith, Stephen Redpath and Steven Campbell. Published by DETR 2000.

EVENTS DIARY 2002

JANUARY

26th 'Migration from the Isles of Scilly to Slapton'.
A one-day conference for BTO members and ringers.
Derriford Hall, Plymouth, Devon.
Contact Roger Swinfen Tel: 01752 704184 e-mail:
roger@swinfen5.freeserve.co.uk or John Woodland Tel: 01647 252494
jwoodland@btodv.fsnet.co.uk

FEBRUARY

14th – 21st National Nest Box Week
Contact BTO.
2nd – 3rd The Great West Bird Fair.
WWT, Slimbridge, Glos.
Contact WWT.

MARCH

2nd 'Birds, Weather and Climate'
Meeting organised by Royal Meteorological Society.
London Zoo 10:30am - 4pm.
Contact Ken Milne, Met Office, +44 (0) 1344 856 070
9th North-East Ringers' Conference.
University of Durham. (Hosted by The Natural History Society of Northumbria Ringing Group).
Contact: Ian Johnston,
0191 2370709 e-mail:
dij@oldhartley.freeserve.co.uk
18th – 19th Association of Applied Biologists conference.
'Birds and Agriculture'.
Heriot-Watt University, Edinburgh.
Contact Dr Nick Carter, BTO.
22nd – April 7th National Exhibition of Wildlife Art.
Road Range Gallery, Liverpool.
Contact NEWA, e-mail:
newa@mtuffrey.freeserve.co.uk
www.newa.cwc.net
23rd – 25th British Ornithologists Union Annual Conference
'Global change and coastal birds'.
University of Hull.
Contact BOU.

APRIL

5th – 7th RSPB member's weekend in York.
Contact Christine McDowell at the RSPB.

MAY

19th A Forum for Bird Clubs, organised by West Midlands Bird Club.
Venue Leamarston Hotel, Nr Kingsbury Water Park.
Contact Club.
18th - 19th SE Bird Fair
WWT, Arundel.
01903 883355.

JUNE

15th National Moth Night 2002.
Various locations.
For further details visit the websites: www.atroposuk.co.uk and www.insectline.co.uk
9th Bedfordshire Bird Club's 10th Anniversary Conference.
Forest Centre, Marston Vale Millennium Country Park.
Contact Club.
29th - 30th Wildlife Photo and Bird Fair.
Brandon Marsh
www.birder.co.uk

JULY

4th – 7th British Ornithologists Union Conference – 'Derby Days'.
University of Liverpool.
Contact BOU.

AUGUST

26th Oriental Bird Club's Norfolk meeting.
Blakeney Village Hall, Norfolk.
Contact Club.
11th – 17th The 23rd International Ornithological Congress.
Beijing, China
Contact BOU.
16th - 18th The British Birdwatching Fair
Rutland Water
www.birdfair.org.uk

SEPTEMBER

7th – 8th The Scottish Wildlife and Countryside Fair.
Vane Farm,
Contact the RSPB Scotland.
25th - 6th October SWLA annual exhibition.
Mall Galleries, London.
Contact SWLA.

OCTOBER

5th RSPB AGM.
Queen Elizabeth II Conference Centre, London,
Contact Christine McDowell at RSPB.
6th - 7th World Birdwatch.
Various venues,
Contact RSPB.
7th 10am – 4pm Part of 'World Birdwatch', (SE Herts RSPB Group).
Hourly bird walks. Fishers Green car park, N of Waltham Abbey.
Contact Club.
Norfolk Bird Fair
(to be confirmed).
Titchwell, Norfolk.
01485 210779.

NOVEMBER

Scottish Ringers Conference,
(date and venue to be confirmed).
Contact BTO.
NW Bird Fair (date to be confirmed).
WWT, Martin Mere
01704 895181.

DECEMBER

1st Oriental Bird Club AGM.
London Zoo meeting rooms
Contact Club.
6th – 8th The BTO's Members' Weekend.
Hayes Conference Centre, Swanwick, Derbyshire.
Contact Nick Carter, BTO.

Full contact details for the clubs and organisations listed here can be found under their entries in the County, National and International directories.

JANUARY 2002

1 Tuesday *New Year's Day*	2 Wednesday *Bank Holiday - Scotland*
3 Thursday	4 Friday
5 Saturday	6 Sunday
7 Monday	8 Tuesday
9 Wednesday	10 Thursday
11 Friday	12 Saturday
13 Sunday	14 Monday
15 Tuesday	16 Wednesday

JANUARY 2002

17 Thursday	18 Friday
19 Saturday	20 Sunday
21 Monday	22 Tuesday
23 Wednesday	24 Thursday
25 Friday	26 Saturday
27 Sunday	28 Monday
29 Tuesday	30 Wednesday
31 Thursday	Notes

FEBRUARY 2002

1 Friday	2 Saturday
3 Sunday	4 Monday
5 Tuesday	6 Wednesday
7 Thursday	8 Friday
9 Saturday	10 Sunday
11 Monday	12 Tuesday
13 Wednesday	14 Thursday
15 Friday	16 Saturday

FEBRUARY 2002

17 Sunday	18 Monday
19 Tuesday	20 Wednesday
21 Thursday	22 Friday
23 Saturday	24 Sunday
25 Monday	26 Tuesday
27 Wednesday	28 Thursday

Notes

MARCH 2002

1 Friday	2 Saturday
3 Sunday	4 Monday
5 Tuesday	6 Wednesday
7 Thursday	8 Friday
9 Saturday	10 Sunday
11 Monday	12 Tuesday
13 Wednesday	14 Thursday
15 Friday	16 Saturday

MARCH 2002

17 Sunday *St Patrick's Day - Northern Ireland*	18 Monday *Bank Holiday - Northern Ireland*
19 Tuesday	20 Wednesday
21 Thursday	22 Friday
23 Saturday	24 Sunday
25 Monday	26 Tuesday
27 Wednesday	28 Thursday
29 Friday *Good Friday*	30 Saturday
31 Sunday *Easter Sunday*	Notes

APRIL 2002

1 Monday *Easter Monday*	2 Tuesday
3 Wednesday	4 Thursday
5 Friday	6 Saturday
7 Sunday	8 Monday
9 Tuesday	10 Wednesday
11 Thursday	12 Friday
13 Saturday	14 Sunday
15 Monday	16 Tuesday

APRIL 2002

17 Wednesday	18 Thursday
19 Friday	20 Saturday
21 Sunday	22 Monday
23 Tuesday	24 Wednesday
25 Thursday	26 Friday
27 Saturday	28 Sunday
29 Monday	30 Tuesday

Notes

MAY 2002

1 Wednesday	2 Thursday
3 Friday	4 Saturday
5 Sunday	6 Monday *May Day*
7 Tuesday	8 Wednesday
9 Thursday	10 Friday
11 Saturday	12 Sunday
13 Monday	14 Tuesday
15 Wednesday	16 Thursday

MAY 2002

17 Friday	18 Saturday
19 Sunday	20 Monday
21 Tuesday	22 Wednesday
23 Thursday	24 Friday
25 Saturday	26 Sunday
27 Monday *Spring Bank Holiday*	28 Tuesday
29 Wednesday	30 Thursday
31 Friday	Notes

JUNE 2002

1 Saturday	2 Sunday
3 Monday	4 Tuesday
5 Wednesday	6 Thursday
7 Friday	8 Saturday
9 Sunday	10 Monday
11 Tuesday	12 Wednesday
13 Thursday	14 Friday
15 Saturday	16 Sunday

JUNE 2002

17 Monday	18 Tuesday
19 Wednesday	20 Thursday
21 Friday	22 Saturday
23 Sunday	24 Monday
25 Tuesday	26 Wednesday
27 Thursday	28 Friday
29 Saturday	30 Sunday

Notes

JULY 2002

1 Monday	2 Tuesday
3 Wednesday	4 Thursday
5 Friday	6 Saturday
7 Sunday	8 Monday
9 Tuesday	10 Wednesday
11 Thursday	12 Friday *Battle of the Boyne - Northern Ireland*
13 Saturday	14 Sunday
15 Monday	16 Tuesday

JULY 2002

17 Wednesday	18 Thursday
19 Friday	20 Saturday
21 Sunday	22 Monday
23 Tuesday	24 Wednesday
25 Thursday	26 Friday
27 Saturday	28 Sunday
29 Monday	30 Tuesday
31 Wednesday	Notes

AUGUST 2002

1 Thursday	2 Friday
3 Saturday	4 Sunday
5 Monday *Summer Bank Holiday - Scotland*	6 Tuesday
7 Wednesday	8 Thursday
9 Friday	10 Saturday
11 Sunday	12 Monday
13 Tuesday	14 Wednesday
15 Thursday	16 Friday

AUGUST 2002

17 Saturday	18 Sunday
19 Monday	20 Tuesday
21 Wednesday	22 Thursday
23 Friday	24 Saturday
25 Sunday	26 Monday *Summer Bank Holiday - England and Northern Ireland*
27 Tuesday	28 Wednesday
29 Thursday	30 Friday
31 Saturday	Notes

SEPTEMBER 2002

1 Sunday	2 Monday
3 Tuesday	4 Wednesday
5 Thursday	6 Friday
7 Saturday	8 Sunday
9 Monday	10 Tuesday
11 Wednesday	12 Thursday
13 Friday	14 Saturday
15 Sunday	16 Monday

SEPTEMBER 2002

17 Tuesday	18 Wednesday
19 Thursday	20 Friday
21 Saturday	22 Sunday
23 Monday	24 Tuesday
25 Wednesday	26 Thursday
27 Friday	28 Saturday
29 Sunday	30 Monday

Notes

OCTOBER 2002

1 Tuesday	2 Wednesday
3 Thursday	4 Friday
5 Saturday	6 Sunday
7 Monday	8 Tuesday
9 Wednesday	10 Thursday
11 Friday	12 Saturday
13 Sunday	14 Monday
15 Tuesday	16 Wednesday

OCTOBER 2002

17 Thursday	18 Friday
19 Saturday	20 Sunday
21 Monday	22 Tuesday
23 Wednesday	24 Thursday
25 Friday	26 Saturday
27 Sunday	28 Monday
29 Tuesday	30 Wednesday
31 Thursday	Notes

NOVEMBER 2002

1 Friday	2 Saturday
3 Sunday	4 Monday
5 Tuesday	6 Wednesday
7 Thursday	8 Friday
9 Saturday	10 Sunday
11 Monday	12 Tuesday
13 Wednesday	14 Thursday
15 Friday	16 Saturday

NOVEMBER 2002

17 Sunday	18 Monday
19 Tuesday	20 Wednesday
21 Thursday	22 Friday
23 Saturday	24 Sunday
25 Monday	26 Tuesday
27 Wednesday	28 Thursday
29 Friday	30 Saturday

Notes

DECEMBER 2002

1 Sunday	2 Monday
3 Tuesday	4 Wednesday
5 Thursday	6 Friday
7 Saturday	8 Sunday
9 Monday	10 Tuesday
11 Wednesday	12 Thursday
13 Friday	14 Saturday
15 Sunday	16 Monday

DECEMBER 2002

17 Tuesday	18 Wednesday
19 Thursday	20 Friday
21 Saturday	22 Sunday
23 Monday	24 Tuesday
25 Wednesday *Christmas Day*	26 Thursday *Boxing Day*
27 Friday	28 Saturday
29 Sunday	30 Monday
31 Tuesday	Notes

YEAR PLANNER 2003

January	February
March	April
May	June
July	August
September	October
November	December

LOG CHARTS

A pair of Long-eared Owls (*Asio otus*) drawn by Peter Beeson of Suffolk.

SPECIES, CATEGORIES, CODES AND GUIDE TO USE

Species list

The charts include all species on the British List and is based on the 1992 BOU Checklist of Birds of Britain and Ireland and the various BOURC reports published after that date. These include changes to the List, with the exception of the extinct Great *Auk Pinguinus impennis.* They are augmented by birds which breed or occur regularly in Europe - almost 600 species altogether.

Vagrants which are not on the British List, but which may have occurred in other parts of the British Isles, are not included. Readers who wish to record such species may use the extra rows provided on the last page. In this connection it should be noted that separate lists exist for Northern Ireland (kept by the Northern Ireland Birdwatchers' Association) and the Isle of Man (kept by the Manx Ornithological Society), and that Irish records are assessed by the Irish Rare Birds Committee.

Species are arranged in Voous order; their names are those most widely used in the current field guides (with some proposed changes shown in parentheses); each is followed by its scientific name, printed in italics.

Species categories

The following categories are those assigned by the British Ornithologists' Union.

A Species which have been recorded in an apparently natural state at least once since January 1, 1950.

B Species which would otherwise be in Category A but have not been recorded since December 31, 1949.

C Species that, although originally introduced by man, either deliberately or accidentally, have established breeding populations derived from introduced stock that maintain themselves without necessary recourse to further introduction. (This category has been subdivided to differentiate between various groups of naturalised species, but these subdivisions are outside the purpose of the log charts).

D Species that would otherwise appear in Categories A or B except that there is reasonable doubt that they have ever occurred in a natural state. (Species in this category are included in the log charts, though they do not qualify for inclusion in the British List, which comprises species in Categories A, B and C only. One of the objects of Category D is to note records of species which are not yet full additions, so that they are not overlooked if acceptable records subsequently occur. Bird report editors are encouraged to include records of species in Category D as appendices to their systematic lists).

E Species that have been recorded as introductions, transportees or escapees from captivity, and whose populations (if any) are thought not to be self-sustaining. They do not form part of the British List and are not included in the log charts.

EU Species not on the British List, or in Category D, but which either breed or occur regularly elsewhere in Europe.

LOG CHARTS

Life list

Ticks made in the 'Life List' column suffice for keeping a running personal total of species. However, added benefit can be obtained by replacing ticks with a note of the year of first occurrence. To take an example: one's first-ever Marsh Sandpiper, seen on April 14, 2002, would be logged with '01' in the Life List and '14' in the April column (as well as a tick in the 2002 column). As Life List entries are carried forward annually, in years to come it would be a simple matter to relocate this record.

First and last dates of migrants

Arrivals of migrants can be recorded by inserting dates instead of ticks in the relevant month columns. For example, a Common Sandpiper on March 11 would be recorded by inserting '11' against Common Sandpiper in the March column. The same applies to departures, though dates of last sightings can only be entered at the end of the year after checking one's field notebook.

Unheaded columns

The three unheaded columns at the right hand end of each chart are for special (personal) use. This may be, for example, a, second holiday, a particular county or a 'local patch'. Another use could be to indicate species on, for example, the Northern Ireland List or the Isle of Man List.

BTO species codes

British Trust for Ornithology two-letter species codes are shown in brackets in the fourth column from the right. They exist for many species, races and hybrids recorded in recent surveys. Readers should refer to the BTO if more codes are needed. In addition to those given in the charts, the following are available for some well-marked races or forms - Whistling Swan (WZ), European White-fronted Goose (EW), Greenland White-fronted Goose (NW), dark-bellied Brent Goose (DB), pale-bellied Brent Goose (PB), Black Brant (BB), Green-winged Teal (TA), Yellow-legged Gull (YG), Kumlien's Gull (KG), Feral Pigeon (FP), White Wagtail (WB), Black-bellied Dipper (DJ), Hooded Crow (HC), intermediate crow (HB).

Rarities

Rarities are indicated by a capital letter 'R' immediately preceding the 'Euring No.' column.

EURING species numbers

EURING species numbers are given in the last column. As they are taken from the full Holarctic bird list there are many apparent gaps. It is important that these are not filled arbitrarily by observers wishing to record species not listed in the charts, as this would compromise the integrity of the scheme. Similarly, the addition of a further digit to indicate sub-species is to be avoided, since EURING has already assigned numbers for this purpose. The numbering follows the Voous order of species.

Rare breeding birds

Species monitored by the Rare Breeding Birds Panel (see National Directory) comprise all those on Schedule 1 of the Wildlife and Countryside Act 1981 (see Quick Reference) together with all escaped or introduced species breeding in small numbers. The following annotations in the charts (third column from the right) reflect the RBBP's categories:

- (b)[A] Rare species. All breeding details requested.
- (b)[B] Less scarce species. Totals requested from counties with more than 10 pairs or localities; elsewhere all details requested.
- (b)[C] Less scarce species (specifically Barn Owl, Kingfisher, Crossbill). County summaries requested.
- (b)[D] Escaped or introduced species. Treated as less scarce species.

	DIVERS, GREBES, ALBATROSS, FULMAR, PETRELS, SHEARWATERS.		Life list	2002 list	24 hr	Garden	Holiday	Jan	Feb	Mar	Apr	May	Jun	Jul	Aug	Sep	Oct	Nov	Dec							EU No
A	**Red-throated Diver**	*Gavia stellata*																					(RH)	(b)B		0002
A	**Black-throated Diver**	*G. arctica*																					(BV)	(b)A		0003
A	**Great Northern Diver**	*G. immer*																					(ND)			0004
A	**White-(Yellow)billed Diver**	*G. adamsii*																					(IW)		R	0005
A	**Pied-billed Grebe**	*Podilymbus podiceps*																					(PJ)		R	0006
A	**Little Grebe**	*Tachybaptus ruficollis*																					(LG)			0007
A	**Great Crested Grebe**	*Podiceps cristatus*																					(GG)			0009
A	**Red-necked Grebe**	*P. grisegena*																					(RX)	(b)A		0010
A	**Slavonian Grebe**	*P. auritus*																					(SZ)	(b)A		0011
A	**Black-necked Grebe**	*P. nigricollis*																					(BN)	(b)A		0012
A	**Black-browed Albatross**	*Diomedea melanophris*																					(AA)		R	0014
A	**Fulmar**	*Fulmarus glacialis*																					(F)			0020
A	**'Soft-plumaged Petrel'**	*Pterodroma mollis?* *																							R	0026
B	**Capped Petrel**	*P. hasitata*																							R	0029
B	**Bulwer's Petrel**	*Bulweria bulwerii*																							R	0034
A	**Cory's Shearwater**	*Calonectris diomedea*																					(CQ)			0036
A	**Great Shearwater**	*Puffinus gravis*																					(GQ)			0040
A	**Sooty Shearwater**	*P. griseus*																					(OT)			0043
A	**Manx Shearwater**	*P. puffinus*																					(MX)			0046
A	**Mediterranean Shearwater**	*P. yelkouan*																								0046
A	**Little Shearwater**	*P. assimilis*																							R	0048
A	**Wilson's Petrel**	*Oceanites oceanicus*																							R	0050
B	**White-faced Petrel**	*Pelagodroma marina*																							R	0051
A	**Storm Petrel**	*Hydrobates pelagicus*																					(TM)			0052
	Sub-total																									

*alternative sub-species

	PETRELS, cont. GANNET, CORMORANTS, PELICANS, BITTERNS, HERONS, STORKS		Life list	2002 list	24 hr	Garden	Holiday	Jan	Feb	Mar	Apr	May	Jun	Jul	Aug	Sep	Oct	Nov	Dec							EU No
A	**Leach's Petrel**	*Oceanodroma leucorhoa*																					(TL)	(b)B		0055
A	**Swinhoe's Petrel**	*0. Monorhis*																							R	0056
B	**Madeiran Petrel**	*0. castro*																							R	0058
A	**Gannet**	*Morus bassanus*																					(GX)			0071
A	**Cormorant**	*Phalacrocorax carbo*																					(CA)			0072
A	**Double-crested Cormorant**	*P. auritus*																							R	0078
A	**Shag**	*P. aristotelis*																					(SA)			0080
EU	**Pygmy Cormorant**	*P. pygmeus*																								0082
D	**Great White Pelican**	*Pelecanus onocrotalus*																					(YP)		R	0088
EU	**Dalmatian Pelican**	*P. crispus*																								0089
A	**Magnificent Frigatebird**	*Fregata magnificens*																							R	0093
A	**Bittern**	*Botaurus stellaris*																					(BI)	(b)A		0095
A	**American Bittern**	*B. lentiginosus*																					(AM)		R	0096
A	**Little Bittern**	*Ixobrychus minutus*																					(LL)		R	0098
A	**Night Heron**	*Nycticorax nycticorax*																					(NT)	(b)AD	R	0104
A	**Green Heron**	*Butorides virescens*																					(HR)		R	0107
A	**Squacco Heron**	*Ardeola ralloides*																					(QH)		R	0108
A	**Cattle Egret**	*Bubulcus ibis*																					(EC)		R	0111
A	**Little Egret**	*Egretta garzetta*																					(ET)	(b)A		0119
A	**Great White Egret**	*Ardea alba*																					(HW)		R	0121
A	**Grey Heron**	*A. cinerea*																					(H)			0122
A	**Purple Heron**	*A. purpurea*																					(UR)			0124
A	**Black Stork**	*Ciconia nigra*																					(OS)		R	0131
A	**White Stork**	*C ciconia*																					(OR)			0134
	Sub-total																									

IBIS, SPOONBILL, FLAMINGO, SWANS, GEESE, DUCKS			Life list	2002 list	24 hr	Garden	Holiday	Jan	Feb	Mar	Apr	May	Jun	Jul	Aug	Sep	Oct	Nov	Dec							EU No
A	**Glossy Ibis**	*Plegadis falcinellus*																					(IB)			0136
A	**Spoonbill**	*Platalea leucorodia*																					(NB)	(b)A		0144
D	**Greater Flamingo**	*Phoenicopterus ruber*																					(FL)		R	0147
AC	**Mute Swan**	*Cygnus olor*																					(MS)			0152
A	**Bewick's (Tundra) Swan**	*C columbianus*																					(BS)			0153
A	**Whooper Swan**	*C cygnus*																					(WS)	(b)AD		0154
A	**Bean Goose**	*Anser fabalis*																					(BE)	(b)D		0157
A	**Pink-footed Goose**	*A. brachyrhynchus*																					(PG)	(b)AD		0158
A	**White-fronted Goose**	*A. albifrons*																					(WG)	(b)D		0159
A	**Lesser White-fr Goose**	*A. erythropus*																					(LC)	(b)B	R	0160
AC	**Greylag Goose**	*A. amser*																					(GJ)			0161
A	**Snow Goose**	*A. caerulescens*																					(SJ)	(b)D		0163
AC	**Canada Goose**	*Branta canadensis*																					(CG)			0166
A	**Barnacle Goose**	*B. leucopsis*																					(BY)	(b)D		0167
A	**Brent Goose**	*B. bernicla*																					(BG)	(b)D		0168
A	**Red-breasted Goose**	*B. ruficollis*																					(EB)	(b)B	R	0169
C	**Egyptian Goose**	*Alopochen aegyptiacus*																					(EG)	(b)D		0170
B	**Ruddy Shelduck**	*Tadorna ferruginea*																					(UD)	(b)D		0171
A	**Shelduck**	*T. tadorna*																					(SU)			0173
C	**Mandarin Duck**	*A. galericulata*																					(MN)			0178
A	**Wigeon**	*Anas Penelope*																					(WN)	(b)B		0179
A	**American Wigeon**	*A. americana*																					(AW)		R	0180
D	**Falcated Duck**	*A. falcata*																					(FT)		R	0181
AC	**Gadwall**	*A. strepera*																					(GA)	(b)B		0182
	Sub-total																									

	DUCKS continued		Life list	2002 list	24 hr	Garden	Holiday	Jan	Feb	Mar	Apr	May	Jun	Jul	Aug	Sep	Oct	Nov	Dec				EU No
D	**Baikal Teal**	*A. formosa*																		(IK)		R	0183
A	**Eurasian Teal**	*A. crecca*																		(T)			0184
A	**Green-winged Teal**	*Anas carolinensis*																					
AC	**Mallard**	*A. platyrhynchos*																		(MA)			0186
A	**American Black Duck**	*A. rubripes*																		(BD)		R	0187
A	**Pintail**	*A. acute*																		(PT)	(b)A		0189
A	**Garganey**	*A. querquedula*																		(GY)	(b)A		0191
A	**Blue-winged Teal**	*A. discors*																		(TB)	(b)B	R	0192
A	**Shoveler**	*A. clypeata*																		(SV)			0194
D	**Marbled Duck**	*Marmaronetta angustirostris*																				R	0195
A	**Red-crested Pochard**	*Netta rufina*																		(RQ)	(b)D		0196
A	**Canvasback**	*Aythya valisineria*																				R	0197
A	**Pochard**	*A. ferina*																		(PO)	(b)B		0198
A	**Redhead**	*A. americana*																		(AZ)		R	0199
A	**Ring-necked Duck**	*A. collaris*																		(NG)			0200
A	**Ferruginous Duck**	*A. nyroca*																		(ED)			0202
A	**Tufted Duck**	*A. fuligula*																		(TU)			0203
A	**Scaup**	*A. marila*																		(SP)	(b)A		0204
A	**Lesser Scaup**	*A. affinis*																		(AY)		R	0205
A	**Eider**	*Somateria mollissima*																		(E)			0206
A	**King Eider**	*S. spectabilis*																		(KE)		R	0207
A	**Steller's Eider**	*Polysticta stelleri*																		(ES)		R	0209
A	**Harlequin**	*Histrionicus histrionicus*																		(HQ)		R	0211
A	**Long-tailed Duck**	*Clangula hyemalis*																		(LN)	(b)A		0212
	Sub-total																						

	DUCKS continued and RAPTORS		Life list	2002 list	24 hr	Garden	Holiday	Jan	Feb	Mar	Apr	May	Jun	Jul	Aug	Sep	Oct	Nov	Dec							EU No
A	**Common Scoter**	*Melanitta nigra*																					(CX)	(b)A		0213
A	**Surf Scoter**	*M. perspicillata*																					(FS)			0214
A	**Velvet Scoter**	*M. fusca*																					(VS)			0215
A	**Bufflehead**	*Bucephala albeola*																					(VH)		R	0216
A	**Barrow's Goldeneye**	*B. islandica*																							R	0217
A	**Goldeneye**	*B. clangula*																					(GN)	(b)AD		0218
A	**Smew**	*Mergellus albellus*																					(SY)			0220
A	**Red-breasted Merganser**	*Mergus serrator*																					(RM)			0221
A	**Goosander**	*M. merganser*																					(GD)			0223
C	**Ruddy Duck**	*Oxyura jamaicensis*																					(BY)			0225
EU	**White-headed Duck**	*0. Leucocephala*																					(WQ)			0226
A	**Honey Buzzard**	*Pernis apivorus*																					(HZ)	(b)A		0231
EU	**Black-winged Kite**	*Elanus caeruleus*																								0235
A	**Black Kite**	*Milvus migrans*																					(KB)		R	0238
AC	**Red Kite**	*M. milvus*																					(KT)	(b)A		0239
A	**White-tailed Eagle**	*Haliaeetus albicilla*																					(WE)	(b)A		0243
D	**Bald Eagle**	*H. leucocephalus*																							R	0244
EU	**Lammergeier**	*Gypaetus barbatus*																								0246
BD	**Egyptian Vulture**	*Neophron percnopterus*																							R	0247
D	**Black (Monk) Vulture**	*Aegypius monachus*																							R	0255
A	**Short-toed Eagle**	*Circaetus gallicus*																								0256
A	**Marsh Harrier**	*Circus aeruginosus*																					(MR)	(b)A		0260
A	**Hen Harrier**	*C. cyaneus*																					(HH)	(b)B		0261
A	**Pallid Harrier**	*C macrourus*																							R	0262
	Sub-total																									

	RAPTORS continued		Life list	2002 list	24 hr	Garden	Holiday	Jan	Feb	Mar	Apr	May	Jun	Jul	Aug	Sep	Oct	Nov	Dec							EU No
A	**Montagu's Harrier**	*C. pygargus*																					(MO)	(b)A		0263
AC	**Goshawk**	*Accipiter gentilis*																					(GI)	(b)B		0267
A	**Sparrowhawk**	*A. nisus*																					(SH)			0269
EU	**Levant Sparrowhawk**	*A. brevipes*																								0273
A	**Buzzard**	*Buteo buteo*																					(BZ)			0287
EU	**Long-legged Buzzard**	*B. rufinus*																								0288
A	**Rough-legged Buzzard**	*B. lagopus*																					(RF)			0290
EU	**Lesser Spotted Eagle**	*Aquila pomarina*																								0292
B	**Greater Spotted Eagle**	*A. clanga*																							R	0293
EU	**Imperial Eagle**	*A. heliaca*																								0295
A	**Golden Eagle**	*A. chrysaetos*																					(EA)	(b)B		0296
EU	**Booted Eagle**	*Hieraaetus pennatus*																								0298
EU	**Bonelli's Eagle**	*H. fasciatus*																								0299
A	**Osprey**	*Pandion haliaetus*																					(OP)	(b)A		0301
A	**Lesser Kestrel**	*Falco naumanni*																							R	0303
A	**Kestrel**	*F. tinnunculus*																					(K)			0304
A	**American Kestrel**	*F. sparrrius*																							R	0305
A	**Red-footed Falcon**	*F. vespertinus*																					(FV)		R	0307
A	**Merlin**	*F. columbarius*																					(ML)	(b)B		0309
A	**Hobby**	*F. subbuteo*																					(HY)	(b)B		0310
A	**Eleonora's Falcon**	*F. eleonorae*																							R	0311
EU	**Lanner**	*F. biarmicus*																					(FB)			0314
D	**Saker**	*F. cherrug*																					(JF)		R	0316
A	**Gyrfalcon**	*F. rusticolus*																					(YF)		R	0318
	Sub-total																									

	RAPTORS contd, GAMEBIRDS, RAILS, CRAKES, GALLINULES		Life list	2002 list	24 hr	Garden	Holiday	Jan	Feb	Mar	Apr	May	Jun	Jul	Aug	Sep	Oct	Nov	Dec							EU No
A	**Peregrine**	*F. peregrinus*																					(PE)	(b)B		0320
EU	**Hazel Grouse**	*Bonasa bonasia*																								0326
A	**Red (Willow) Grouse**	*Lagopus lagopus*																					(RG)			0329
A	**Ptarmigan**	*L. mutus*																					(PM)			0330
A	**Black Grouse**	*Tetrao tetrix*																					(BK)			0332
BC	**Capercaillie**	*T. urogallus*																					(CP)			0335
EU	**Rock Partridge**	*Alectoris graeca*																								0357
C	**Red-legged Partridge**	*A. rufa*																					(RL)			0358
EU	**Barbary Partridge**	*A. barbara*																								0359
AC	**Grey Partridge**	*Perdix perdix*																					(P)			0367
A	**Quail**	*Coturnix coturnix*																					(Q)	(b)B		0370
C	**Pheasant**	*Phasianus colchicus*																					(PH)			0394
C	**Golden Pheasant**	*Chrysolophus pictus*																					(GF)	(b)D		0396
C	**Lady Amherst's Pheasant**	*C. amherstiae*																					(LM)	(b)D		0397
EU	**Andalusian Hemipode**	*Turnix sylvatica*																								0400
A	**Water Rail**	*Rallus aquaticus*																					(WA)			0407
A	**Spotted Crake**	*Porzana porzana*																					(AK)	(b)A		0408
A	**Sora**	*P. carolina*																							R	0409
A	**Little Crake**	*P. parva*																					(JC)		R	0410
A	**Baillon's Crake**	*P. pusilla*																					(VC)		R	0411
A	**Corncrake**	*Crex crex*																					(CE)	(b)A		0421
A	**Moorhen**	*Gallinula chloropus*																					(MH)			0424
B	**Allen's Gallinule**	*Porphyrula alleni*																							R	0425
A	**American Purple Gallinule**	*P. martinica*																							R	0426
	Sub-total																									

	GALLINULES contd, COOTS, CRANES, BUSTARDS, WADERS		Life list	2002 list	24 hr	Garden	Holiday	Jan	Feb	Mar	Apr	May	Jun	Jul	Aug	Sep	Oct	Nov	Dec							EU No
EU	**Purple (Swamp-hen) Gallinule**	*Porphyrio porphyrio*																								0427
A	**Coot**	*Fulica atra*																					(CO)			0429
A	**American Coot**	*F. americana*																							R	0430
EL	**Crested Coot**	*F. cristata*																								0431
A	**Crane**	*Grus grus*																					(AN)	(b)A		0433
A	**Sandhill Crane**	*G. canadensis*																							R	0436
A	**Little Bustard**	*Tetrax tetrax*																							R	0442
A	**Houbara Bustard**	*Chlamydotis undulata*																							R	0444
A	**Great Bustard**	*Otis tarda*																					(US)		R	0446
A	**Oystercatcher**	*Haematopus ostralegus*																					(OC)			0450
A	**Black-winged Stilt**	*Himantopus himantopus*																					(IT)		R	0455
A	**Avocet**	*Recurvirostra avosetta*																					(AV)	(b)A		0456
A	**Stone Curlew**	*Burhinus oedicnemus*																					(TN)	(b)A		0459
A	**Cream-coloured Courser**	*Cursorius cursor*																							R	0464
A	**Collared Pratincole**	*Glareola pratincola*																							R	0465
A	**Oriental Pratincole**	*G. maldivarum*																					(GM)		R	0466
A	**Black-winged Pratincole**	*G. nordmanni*																					(KW)		R	0467
A	**Little Ringed Plover**	*Charadrius dubius*																					(LP)	(b)B		0469
A	**Ringed Plover**	*C. hiaticula*																					(RP)			0470
A	**Semipalmated Plover**	*C. semipalmatus*																					(TV)		R	0471
A	**Killdeer**	*C vociferus*																					(KL)		R	0474
A	**Kentish Plover**	*C. alexandrinus*																					(KP)			0477
A	**Lesser Sand Plover**	*C. mongolus*																							R	0478
FA	**Greater Sand Plover**	*C. leschenaultii*																					(DP)		R	0479
	Sub-total																									

	WADERS continued		Life list	2002 list	24 hr	Garden	Holiday	Jan	Feb	Mar	Apr	May	Jun	Jul	Aug	Sep	Oct	Nov	Dec							EU No
A	**Caspian Plover**	*C. asiaticus*																							R	0480
A	**Dotterel**	*C. morinellus*																					(DO)	(b)B		0482
A	**American Golden Plover**	*Pluvialis dominica*																					(ID)		R	0484
A	**Pacific Golden Plover**	*P. fulva*																					(IF)		R	0484
A	**Golden Plover**	*P. apricaria*																					(GP)			0485
A	**Grey Plover**	*P. squatarola*																					(GV)			0486
EU	**Spur-winged Plover**	*Hoplopterus spinosus*																					(UW)			0487
A	**Sociable Lapwing**	*Vanellus gregarius*																					(IP)		R	0491
A	**White-tailed Lapwing**	*V. leucurus*																							R	0492
A	**Lapwing**	*V. vanellus*																					(L)			0493
A	**Great Knot**	*Calidris tenuirostris*																					(KO)		R	0495
A	**Knot**	*C. canutus*																					(KN)			0496
A	**Sanderling**	*C alba*																					(SS)			0497
A	**Semipalmated Sandpiper**	*C pusilla*																					(PZ)		R	0498
A	**Western Sandpiper**	*C mauri*																					(ER)		R	0499
A	**Red-necked Stint**	*C. ruficollis*																							R	0500
A	**Little Stint**	*C minuta*																					(LX)			0501
A	**Temminck's Stint**	*C temminckii*																					(TK)	(b)A		0502
A	**Long-toed Stint**	*C. subminuta*																							R	0503
A	**Least Sandpiper**	*C. minutilla*																					(EP)		R	0504
A	**White-rumped Sandpiper**	*C. fuscicollis*																					(WU)		R	0505
A	**Baird's Sandpiper**	*C bairdii*																					(BP)		R	0506
A	**Pectoral Sandpiper**	*C. metanotos*																					(PP)			0507
A	**Sharp-tailed Sandpiper**	*C. acuminata*																					(VV)		R	0508
	Sub-total																									

WADERS continued			Life list	2002 list	24 hr	Garden	Holiday	Jan	Feb	Mar	Apr	May	Jun	Jul	Aug	Sep	Oct	Nov	Dec							EU No
A	**Curlew Sandpiper**	*C. ferruginea*																					(CV)			0509
A	**Purple Sandpiper**	*C. maritima*																					(PS)	(b)A		0510
A	**Dunlin**	*C. alpina*																					(DN)			0512
A	**Broad-billed Sandpiper**	*Limicola falcinellus*																					(OA)		R	0514
A	**Stilt Sandpiper**	*Micropalama himantopus*																					(MI)		R	0515
A	**Buff-breasted Sandpiper**	*Tryngites subruficollis*																					(BQ)			0516
A	**Ruff**	*Philomachus pugnax*																					(RU)	(b)A		0517
A	**Jack Snipe**	*Lymnocryptes minimum*																					(JS)			0518
A	**Snipe**	*Gallinago gallinago*																					(SN)			0519
A	**Great Snipe**	*G. media*																					(DS)		R	0520
A	**Short-billed Dowitcher**	*Limnodromus griseus*																								
A	**Long-billed Dowitcher**	*Limnodromus scolopaceus*																					(LD)		R	0527
A	**Woodcock**	*Scolopax rusticola*																					(WK)			0529
A	**Black-tailed Godwit**	*Limosa limosa*																					(BW)	(b)A		0532
A	**Hudsonian Godwit**	*L. haemastica*																					(HU)		R	0533
A	**Bar-tailed Godwit**	*L. lapponica*																					(BA)			0534
A	**Little Whimbrel (Curlew)**	*Numenius minutus*																							R	0536
B	**Eskimo Curlew**	*N. borealis*																							R	0537
A	**Whimbrel**	*N. phaeopus*																					(WM)	(b)A		0538
A	**Curlew**	*N. arquata*																					(CU)			0541
A	**Upland Sandpiper**	*Bartramia longicauda*																					(UP)		R	0544
A	**Spotted Redshank**	*Tringa erythropus*																					(DR)			0545
A	**Redshank**	*T. totanus*																					(RK)			0546
A	**Marsh Sandpiper**	*T. stagnatilis*																					(MD)		R	0547
	Sub-total																									

	WADERS contd, WADERS, GULLS		Life list	2002 list	24 hr	Garden	Holiday	Jan	Feb	Mar	Apr	May	Jun	Jul	Aug	Sep	Oct	Nov	Dec							EU No
A	**Greenshank**	*T. nebularia*																					(GK)	(b)B		0548
A	**Greater Yellowlegs**	*T. metanoleuca*																					(LZ)		R	0550
A	**Lesser Yellowlegs**	*T. flavipes*																					(LY)		R	0551
A	**Solitary Sandpiper**	*T. solitaria*																					(I)		R	0552
A	**Green Sandpiper**	*T. ochropus*																					(GE)			0553
A	**Wood Sandpiper**	*T. glareola*																					(OD)	(b)A		0554
A	**Terek Sandpiper**	*Xenus cinereus*																					(TR)		R	0555
A	**Common Sandpiper**	*Actitis hypoleucos*																					(CS)			0556
A	**Spotted Sandpiper**	*A. macularia*																					(PQ)		R	0557
A	**Grey-tailed Tattler**	*Heteroscelus brevipes*																					(YT)		R	0558
A	**Turnstone**	*Arenaria interpres*																					(TT)			0561
A	**Wilson's Phalarope**	*Phalaropus tricolor*																					(WF)		R	0563
A	**Red-necked Phalarope**	*P. lobatus*																					(NK)	(b)A		0564
A	**Grey Phalarope**	*P. fulicarius*																					(PL)			0565
A	**Pomarine Skua**	*Stercorarius pomarinus*																					(PK)			0566
A	**Arctic Skua**	*S. parasiticus*																					(AC)			0567
A	**Long-tailed Skua**	*S. longicaudus*																					(OG)			0568
A	**Great Skua**	*Catharacta skua*																					(NX)			0569
B	**Great Black-headed (Pallas's) Gull**	*Larus ichthyaetus*																							R	0573
A	**Mediterranean Gull**	*L. melanocephalus*																					(MU)	(b)A		0575
A	**Laughing Gull**	*L. atricilla*																					(LF)		R	0576
A	**Franklin's Gull**	*L. pipixcan*																					(FG)		R	0577
A	**Little Gull**	*L. minutus*																					(LU)			0578
A	**Sabine's Gull**	*L. sabini*																					(AB)			0579
	Sub-total																									

GULLS continued, TERNS

			Life list	2002 list	24 hr	Garden	Holiday	Jan	Feb	Mar	Apr	May	Jun	Jul	Aug	Sep	Oct	Nov	Dec				EU No
A	**Bonaparte's Gull**	*L. Philadelphia*																		(ON)		R	0581
A	**Black-headed Gull**	*L. ridibundus*																		(BH)			0582
A	**Slender-billed Gull**	*L. genei*																		(EI)			0585
FU	**Audouin's Gull**	*L. audouinii*																					0588
A	**Ring-billed Gull**	*L. delawarensis*																		(IN)			0589
A	**Common (Mew) Gull**	*L. canus*																		(CM)			0590
A	**Lesser Black-backed Gull**	*L. fuscus*																		(LB)			0591
A	**Herring Gull**	*L. argentatus*																		(HG)			0592
A	**Iceland Gull**	*L. glaucoides*																		(IG)			0598
A	**Glaucous Gull**	*L. hyperboreus*																		(GZ)			0599
A	**Great Black-backed Gull**	*L. marinus*																		(GB)			0600
A	**Ross's Gull**	*Rhodostethia rosea*																		(QG)		R	0601
A	**Kittiwake**	*Rissa tridactyla*																		(KI)			0602
A	**Ivory Gull**	*Pagophila eburnea*																		(IV)		R	0604
A	**Gull-billed Tern**	*Sterna nilotica*																		(TG)		R	0605
A	**Caspian Tern**	*S. caspia*																		(CJ)		R	0606
A	**Royal Tern**	*S. maxima*																		(QT)		R	0607
A	**Lesser Crested Tern**	*S. bengalensis*																		(TF)	(b)A	R	0609
A	**Sandwich Tern**	*S. sandvicensis*																		(TE)			0611
A	**Roseate Tern**	*S. dougallii*																		(RS)	(b)A		0614
A	**Common Tern**	*S. hirundo*																		(CN)			0615
A	**Arctic Tern**	*S. paradisaea*																		(AE)			0616
A	**Aleutian Tern**	*S. aleutica*																				R	0617
A	**Forster's Tern**	*S. forsteri*																		(FO)		R	0618
	Sub-total																						

	TERNS contd, AUKS, SANDGROUSE, DOVES/PIGEONS, PARAKEET, CUCKOOS		Life list	2002 list	24 hr	Garden	Holiday	Jan	Feb	Mar	Apr	May	Jun	Jul	Aug	Sep	Oct	Nov	Dec						EU No
A	**Bridled Tern**	*S. anaethetus*																						R	0622
A	**Sooty Tern**	*S. fuscata*																						R	0623
A	**Little Tern**	*S. albifrons*																				(AF)	(b)B		0624
A	**Whiskered Tern**	*Chlidonias hybridus*																				(WD)		R	0626
A	**Black Tern**	*C niger*																				(BJ)			0627
A	**White-winged Black Tern**	*C leucopterus*																				(WJ)		R	0628
A	**Guillemot**	*Uria aalge*																				(GU)			0634
A	**Brünnich's Guillemot**	*U. lomvia*																				(TZ)		R	0635
A	**Razorbill**	*Alca torda*																				(RA)			0636
A	**Black Guillemot**	*Cepphus grylle*																				(TY)			0638
A	**Ancient Murrelet**	*Synthliboramphus antiquus*																						R	0645
A	**Little Auk**	*Alle alle*																				(LK)			0647
A	**Puffin**	*Fratercula arctica*																				(PU)			0654
EU	**Black-bellied Sandgrouse**	*Pterocles orientalis*																							0661
EU	**Pin-tailed Sandgrouse**	*P. alchata*																							0662
A	**Pallas's Sandgrouse**	*Syrrhaptes paradoxus*																						R	0663
AC	**Rock Dove**	*Columba livia*																				(DV)			0665
A	**Stock Dove**	*C oenas*																				(SD)			0668
A	**Woodpigeon**	*C palumbus*																				(WP)			0670
A	**Collared Dove**	*Streplopelia decaocto*																				(CD)			0684
A	**Turtle Dove**	*S. turtur*																				(TD)			0687
A	**Rufous (Oriental) Turtle Dov**	*S. orientalis*																						R	0689
A	**Mourning Dove**	*Zenaida macroura*																						R	0695
C	**Rose-ringed Parakeet**	*Psittacula krameri*																				(RI)	(b)D		0712
	Sub-total																								

	CUCKOOS, OWLS, NIGHTJARS, SWIFTS		Life list	2002 list	24 hr	Garden	Holiday	Jan	Feb	Mar	Apr	May	Jun	Jul	Aug	Sep	Oct	Nov	Dec							EU No
A	**Great Spotted Cuckoo**	*Clamator glandarius*																					(UK)		R	0716
A	**Cuckoo**	*Cuculus canorus*																					(CK)			0724
A	**Black-billed Cuckoo**	*Coccyzus erythrophthalmus*																							R	0727
A	**Yellow-billed Cuckoo**	*C. americanus*																							R	0728
A	**Barn Owl**	*Tyto alba*																					(BO)	(b)C		0735
A	**Scops Owl**	*Otus scops*																							R	0739
EU	**Eagle Owl**	*Bubo bubo*																					(EO)	(b)D		0744
A	**Snowy Owl**	*Nyctea scandiaca*																					(SO)	(b)A	R	0749
A	**Hawk Owl**	*Surnia ulula*																							R	0750
EU	**Pygmy Owl**	*Glaucidium passerinum*																								0751
C	**Little Owl**	*Athene noctua*																					(LO)			0757
A	**Tawny Owl**	*Strix aluco*																					(TO)			0761
EU	**Ural Owl**	*S. uralensis*																								0765
EU	**Great Grey Owl**	*S. nebulosa*																								0766
A	**Long-eared Owl**	*Asio otus*																					(LE)			0767
A	**Short-eared Owl**	*A. flammeus*																					(SE)			0768
A	**Tengmalm's Owl**	*Aegolius funereus*																							R	0770
A	**Nightjar**	*Caprimuigus europaeus*																					(NJ)			0778
B	**Red-necked Nightjar**	*C. ruficollis*																							R	0779
A	**Egyptian Nightjar**	*C. aegyptius*																							R	0781
A	**Common Nighthawk**	*Chordeiles minor*																							R	0786
A	**Chimney Swift**	*Chaetura pelagica*																							R	0790
A	**White-throated Needletail**	*Hirundapus caudacutus*																					(NI)		R	0792
A	**Pallid Swift**	*A. pallidus*																							R	0796
	Sub-total																									

SWIFTS etc, KINGFISHERS, BEE-EATERS, ROLLER, HOOPOE, WOODPECKERS, PHOEBE, LARKS			Life list	2002 list	24 hr	Garden	Holiday	Jan	Feb	Mar	Apr	May	Jun	Jul	Aug	Sep	Oct	Nov	Dec							EU No
A	**Swift**	*Apus apus*																					(SI)			0795
A	**Pacific Swift**	*A. pacificus*																							R	0797
A	**Alpine Swift**	*A. melba*																					(AI)		R	0798
EL	**White-rumped Swift**	*A. caffer*																								0799
A	**Little Swift**	*A. affinis*																							R	0800
A	**Kingfisher**	*Alcedo atthis*																					(KF)	(b)C		0831
A	**Belted Kingfisher**	*Ceryle alcyon*																							R	0834
A	**Blue-checked Bee-eater**	*Merops superciliosus*																							R	0839
A	**Bee-eater**	*M. apiaster*																					(MZ)			0840
A	**Roller**	*Coracias garrulus*																							R	0841
A	**Hoopoe**	*Upupa epops*																					(HP)			0846
A	**Wryneck**	*Jynx torquilla*																					(WY)	(b)A		0848
EU	**Grey-headed Woodpecker**	*Picus canus*																								0855
A	**Green Woodpecker**	*P. viridis*																					(G)			0856
EU	**Black Woodpecker**	*Dryocopus martius*																								0863
A	**Yellow-bellied Sapsucker**	*Sphyrapicus varius*																							R	0872
A	**Great Spotted Woodpecker**	*Dendrocopos major*																					(GS)			0876
EU	**Syrian Woodpecker**	*D. syriacus*																								0878
EU	**Middle Spotted Woodpecker**	*D. medius*																								0883
EU	**White-backed Woodpecker**	*D. leucotos*																								0884
A	**Lesser Spotted Woodpecker**	*D. minor*																					(LS)			0887
EU	**Three-toed Woodpecker**	*Picoides tridactylus*																								0898
A	**Eastern Phoebe**	*Sayornis phoebe*																							R	0909
EU	**Dupont's Lark**	*Chersophilus duponti*																								0959
	Sub-total																									

	LARKS contd, MARTINS, SWALLOWS, PIPITS		Life list	2002 list	24 hr	Garden	Holiday	Jan	Feb	Mar	Apr	May	Jun	Jul	Aug	Sep	Oct	Nov	Dec							EU No
A	**Calandra Lark**	*Melanocorypha calandra*																							R	0961
A	**Bimaculated Lark**	*M. bimaculata*																							R	0962
A	**White-winged Lark**	*M. leucoptera*																							R	0965
A	**Short-toed Lark**	*Calandrelia brachydactyla*																					(VL)			0968
A	**Lesser Short-toed Lark**	*C rufescens*																							R	0970
A	**Crested Lark**	*Galerida cristata*																							R	0972
EU	**Thekla Lark**	*G. theklae*																								0973
A	**Woodlark**	*Lullula arborea*																					(WL)	(b)B		0974
A	**Skylark**	*Alauda arvensis*																					(S)			0976
A	**Shore (Horned) Lark**	*Eremophila alpestris*																					(SX)			0978
A	**Sand Martin**	*Riparia riparia*																					(SM)			0981
A	**Tree Swallow**	*Tachycineta bicolor*																							R	0983
A	**Crag Martin**	*Ptyonoprogne rupestris*																							R	0991
A	**Swallow**	*Hirundo rustica*																					(SL)			0992
A	**Red-rumped Swallow**	*M. daurica*																					(VR)		R	0995
A	**Cliff Swallow**	*H. pyrrhonota*																							R	0998
A	**House Martin**	*Delichon urbica*																					(HM)			1001
A	**Richard's Pipit**	*Anthus novaeseelandiae*																					(PR)			1002
A	**Blyth's Pipit**	*A. godlewskii*																							R	1004
A	**Tawny Pipit**	*A. campestris*																					(TI)			1005
A	**Olive-backed Pipit**	*A. hodgsoni*																					(OV)		R	1008
A	**Tree Pipit**	*A. trivialis*																					(TP)			1009
A	**Pechora Pipit**	*A. gustavi*																							R	1010
A	**Meadow Pipit**	*A. pratensis*																					(MP)			1011
	Sub-total																									

	PIPITS contd, WAGTAILS, WAXWINGS, DIPPER, WREN, ACCENTORS, ROBINS		Life list	2002 list	24 hr	Garden	Holiday	Jan	Feb	Mar	Apr	May	Jun	Jul	Aug	Sep	Oct	Nov	Dec						EU No
A	**Red-throated Pipit**	*A. cervinus*																				(VP)		R	1012
A	**Rock Pipit**	*A. petrosus*																				(RC)			1014
A	**Water Pipit**	*A. spinoletta*																				(WI)			1014
A	**Buff-bellied Pipit**	*A. rubescens*																						R	1014
A	**Yellow Wagtail**	*Motacilla flava*																				(YW)			1017
A	**Citrine Wagtail**	*M. citreola*																						R	1018
A	**Grey Wagtail**	*M. cinerea*																				(GL)			1019
A	**Pied (White) Wagtail**	*M. alba*																				(PW)			1020
A	**Cedar Waxing**	*Bombycilla cedrorum*																						R	1046
A	**(Bohemian) Waxwing**	*B. garrulus*																				(WX)			1048
A	**Dipper**	*Cinclus cinclus*																				(DI)			1050
A	**Wren**	*Troglodytes troglodytes*																				(WR)			1066
A	**Northern Mockingbird**	*Mimus polyglottos*																						R	1067
A	**Brown Thrasher**	*Toxostoma rufum*																						R	1069
A	**Dunnock**	*Prunella modularis*																				(D)			1084
A	**Alpine Accentor**	*P. collaris*																						R	1094
A	**Rufous-tailed Scrub Robin**	*Cercotrichas galactotes*																						R	1095
A	**Robin**	*Erithacus rubecula*																				(R)			1099
A	**Thrush Nightingale**	*Luscinia luscinia*																				(FN)		R	1103
A	**Nightingale**	*L. megarhynchos*																				(N)			1104
A	**Siberian Rubythroat**	*L. calliope*																						R	1105
A	**Bluethroat**	*L. svecica*																				(BU)			1106
A	**Red-flanked Bluetail**	*Tarsiger cyanurus*																						R	1113
A	**White-throated Robin**	*Irania gutturalis*																						R	1117
	Sub-total																								

	REDSTARTS, CHATS, WHEATEARS, THRUSHES		Life list	2002 list	24 hr	Garden	Holiday	Jan	Feb	Mar	Apr	May	Jun	Jul	Aug	Sep	Oct	Nov	Dec							EU No
A	**Black Redstart**	*Phoenicurus ochruros*																					(BX)	(b)A		1121
A	**Redstart**	*P. phoenicurus*																					(RT)			1122
A	**Moussier's Redstart**	*P. moussieri*																							R	1127
A	**Whinchat**	*Saxicola rubetra*																					(WC)			1137
A	**Stonechat**	*S. torquata*																					(SC)			1139
A	**Isabelline Wheatear**	*Oenanthe isabellina*																							R	1144
A	**Wheatear**	*0. Oenanthe*																					(W)			1146
A	**Pied Wheatear**	*0. Pleschanka*																					(PI)		R	1147
A	**Black-eared Wheatear**	*0. Hispanica*																							R	1148
A	**Desert Wheatear**	*0. Deserti*																							R	1149
A	**White-crowned(tailed) Black Wheatear**	*0. Leucopyga*																								1157
EU	**Black Wheatear**	*0. Leucura*																							R	1158
A	**Rock Thrush**	*Monticola saxatilis*																					(OH)		R	1162
A	**Blue Rock Thrush**	*M. solitarius*																							R	1166
A	**White's Thrush**	*Zoothera dauma*																							R	1170
A	**Siberian Thrush**	*Z. sibirica*																							R	1171
A	**Varied Thrush**	*Z. naevia*																					(VT)		R	1172
A	**Wood Thrush**	*Hylocichla mustelina*																							R	1175
A	**Hermit Thrush**	*Catharus guttatus*																							R	1176
A	**Swainson's Thrush**	*C ustulatus*																							R	1177
A	**Grey-cheeked Thrush**	*C minimus*																							R	1178
A	**Veery**	*C fuscescens*																							R	1179
A	**Ring Ouzel**	*Turdus torquatus*																					(RZ)			1186
A	**Blackbird**	*T. merula*																					(B)			1187
	Sub-total																									

	THRUSHES continued, WARBLERS		Life list	2002 list	24 hr	Garden	Holiday	Jan	Feb	Mar	Apr	May	Jun	Jul	Aug	Sep	Oct	Nov	Dec						EU No
IA	**Eyebrowed Thrush**	*T. obscurus*																						R	1195
A	**Dusky Thrush**	*T. naumanni*																						R	1196
A	**Dark-throated Thrush**	*T ruficollis*																				(XC)		R	1197
A	**Fieldfare**	*T. pilaris*																				(FF)	(b)A		1198
A	**Song Thrush**	*T. philomelos*																				(ST)			1200
A	**Redwing**	*T. iliacus*																				(RE)	(b)A		1201
A	**Mistle Thrush**	*T. viscivorus*																				(M)			1202
A	**American Robin**	*T. migratorius*																				(AR)		R	1203
A	**Cetti's Warbler**	*Cettia cetti*																				(CW)	(b)A		1220
A	**Zitting Cisticola (Fan-tailed Warbler)**	*Cisticola juncidis*																						R	1226
A	**Pallas's Grasshopper Warbler**	*Locustella certhiola*																						R	1233
A	**Lanceolated Warbler**	*L. lanceolata*																						R	1235
A	**Grasshopper Warbler**	*L. naevia*																				(GH)			1236
A	**River Warbler**	*L. fluviatilis*																				(VW)		R	1237
A	**Savi's Warbler**	*L. luscinioides*																				(VI)	(b)A	R	1238
A	**Moustached Warbler**	*Acrocephalus melanopogon*																						R	1241
A	**Aquatic Warbler**	*A. paludicola*																				(AQ)			1242
A	**Sedge Warbler**	*A. schoenobaenus*																				(SW)			1243
A	**Paddyfield Warbler**	*A. agricola*																				(PY)		R	1247
A	**Blyth's Reed Warbler**	*A. dumetorum*																						R	1248
A	**Marsh Warbler**	*A. palustris*																				(MW)	(b)A		1250
A	**Reed Warbler**	*A. scirpaceus*																				(RW)			1251
A	**Great Reed Warbler**	*A. arundinaceus*																				(QW)		R	1253
A	**Thick-billed Warbler**	*A. aedon*																						R	1254
	Sub-total																								

WARBLERS continued

			Life list	2002 list	24 hr	Garden	Holiday	Jan	Feb	Mar	Apr	May	Jun	Jul	Aug	Sep	Oct	Nov	Dec				EU No
A	**Olivaceous Warbler**	*Hippolais pallida*																				R	1255
A	**Booted Warbler**	*H.caligata*																					1256
EU	**Olive-tree Warbler**	*H. olivetorum*																					1258
A	**Icterine Warbler**	*H. icterina*																		(IC)			1259
A	**Melodious Warbler**	*H. polyglotta*																		(ME)			1260
A	**Marmora's Warbler**	*Sylvia sarda*																		(MM)			1261
A	**Dartford Warbler**	*S. undata*																		(DW)	(b)B		1262
A	**Spectacled Warbler**	*S. conspicillata*																					1264
A	**Subalpine Warbler**	*S. cantillans*																					1265
A	**Sardinian Warbler**	*S. melanocephala*																					1267
EU	**Cyprus Warbler**	*S. melanothorax*																					1268
A	**Rüppell's Warbler**	*S. rueppelli*																					1269
A	**Desert Warbler**	*S. nana*																					1270
A	**Orphean Warbler**	*S. hortensis*																					1272
A	**Barred Warbler**	*S. nisoria*																		(RR)			1273
A	**Lesser Whitethroat**	*S. curruca*																		(LW)			1274
A	**Whitethroat**	*S. communis*																		(WH)			1275
A	**Garden Warbler**	*S. borin*																		(GW)			1276
A	**Blackcap**	*S. atricapilla*																		(BC)			1277
A	**Greenish Warbler**	*P. trochiloides*																		(NP)			1293
A	**Arctic Warbler**	*P. borealis*																		(AP)			1295
A	**Pallas's Warbler**	*P. proregulus*																		(PA)			1298
A	**Yellow-browed Warbler**	*P. inornatus*																		(YB)			1300
A	**Hume's Leaf Warbler**	*P. humei*																					1300
	Sub-total																						

	WARBLERS continued, 'CRESTS', FLYCATCHERS, TITS		Life list	2002 list	24 hr	Garden	Holiday	Jan	Feb	Mar	Apr	May	Jun	Jul	Aug	Sep	Oct	Nov	Dec				EU No
A	**Radde's Warbler**	*P. schwarzi*																					1301
A	**Dusky Warbler,**	*P. fuscatus*																		(UY)		R	1303
A	**Western Bonelli's Warbler**	*P. bonelli*																		(IW)		R	1307
A	**Eastern Bonelli's Warbler**	*P. orientalis*																				R	1307
A	**Wood Warbler**	*P. sibilatrix*																		(WO)			1308
A	**Common Chiffchaff**	*P. collybita*																		(CC)			1311
A	**Iberian Chiffchaff**	*P. brehmii*																				R	1311
A	**Willow Warbler**	*P. trochilus*																		(WW)			1312
A	**Goldcrest**	*Regulus regulus*																		(GC)			1314
A	**Firecrest**	*R. ignicapillus*																		(FC)	(b)A		1315
D	**Asian Brown Flycatcher**	*Muscicapa dauurica*																					1335
A	**Spotted Flycatcher**	*M. striata (SF)*																					1335
A	**Red-breasted Flycatcher**	*Ficedula parva*																		(FY)			1343
D	**Mugimaki Flycatcher**	*F. mugimaki*																				R	1344
EU	**Semi-collared Flycatcher**	*F. semitorquata*																					1347
A	**Collared Flycatcher**	*F. albicollis*																				R	1348
A	**Pied Flycatcher**	*F. hypoleuca*																		(PF)			1349
A	**Bearded Tit**	*Panurus biarmicus*																		(BR)	(b)B		1364
A	**Long-tailed Tit**	*Aegithalos caudatus*																		(LT)			1437
A	**Marsh Tit**	*Parus palustris*																		(MT)			1440
EU	**Sombre Tit**	*P. lugubris*																					1441
A	**Willow Tit**	*P. montanus*																		(WT)			1442
EU	**Siberian Tit**	*P. cinctus*																					1448
A	**Crested Tit**	*P. cristatus*																		(CI)	(b)B		1454
	Sub-total																						

TITS contd, NUTHATCHES, TREECREEPERS, ORIOLE, SHRIKES, CROWS			Life list	2002 list	24 hr	Garden	Holiday	Jan	Feb	Mar	Apr	May	Jun	Jul	Aug	Sep	Oct	Nov	Dec				EU No
A	**Coal Tit**	*P. ater*																		(CT)			1461
A	**Blue Tit**	*P. caeruleus*																		(BT)			1462
A	**Great Tit**	*P. major*																		(GT)			1464
EU	**Krüper's Nuthatch**	*Sitta krueperi*																					1469
EU	**Corsican Nuthatch**	*Sitta whiteheadi*																					1470
A	**Red-breasted Nuthatch**	*S. canadensis*																				R	1472
A	**Nuthatch**	*S. europaea*																		(NH)			1479
EU	**Rock Nuthatch**	*S. neumayer*																					1481
A	**Wallcreeper**	*Tichodroma muraria*																				R	1482
A	**Treecreeper**	*Certhia familiaris*																		(TC)			1486
A	**Short-toed Treecreeper**	*C. brachydactyla*																		(TH)		R	1487
A	**Penduline Tit**	*Remiz pendulinus*																		(DT)		R	1490
A	**Golden Oriole**	*Oriolus oriolus*																		(OL)	(b)A		1508
A	**Brown Shrike**	*Lanius cristatus*																				R	1513
A	**Isabelline Shrike**	*L. isabellinus*																		(IL)		R	1514
A	**Red-backed Shrike**	*L. collurio*																		(ED)	(b)A		1515
A	**Lesser Grey Shrike**	*L. minor*																				R	1519
A	**Great Grey Shrike**	*L. exubitor*																		(SR)			1520
A	**Southern Grey Shrike**	*L. meridionalis*																				R	1520
A	**Woodchat Shrike**	*L. senator*																		(OO)			1523
EU	**Masked Shrike**	*L. nubicus*																					1524
A	**Jay**	*Garrulus glandarius*																		(J)			1539
EU	**Siberian Jay**	*Perisoreus infaustus*																					1543
EU	**Azure-winged Magpie**	*Cyanopica cyana*																					1547
	Sub-total																						

	CROWS continued, STARLINGS, SPARROWS, FINCHES		Life list	2002 list	24 hr	Garden	Holiday	Jan	Feb	Mar	Apr	May	Jun	Jul	Aug	Sep	Oct	Nov	Dec							EU No
A	**Magpie**	*Pica pica*																					(MG)			1549
A	**Nutcracker**	*Nucifraga caryocatactes*																					(NC)		R	1557
EU	**Alpine Chough**	*Pyrrhocorax graculus*																								1558
A	**Chough**	*P. pyrrhocorax*																					(CF)	(b)B		1559
A	**Jackdaw**	*Corrus monedula*																					(JD)			1560
A	**Rook**	*C frugilegus*																					(RO)			1563
A	**Carrion (Hooded) Crow**	*C. corone*																					(C)			1567
A	**Raven**	*C. corax*																					(RN)			1572
D	**Daurian Starling**	*Sturnus sturninus*																							R	1579
A	**Starling**	*S. vulgaris*																					(SG)			1582
EU	**Spotless Starling**	*S. unicolor*																								1583
A	**Rose-coloured (Rosy) Sta**	*S. roseus*																					(OE)		R	1594
A	**House Sparrow**	*Passer domesticus*																					(HS)			1591
A	**Spanish Sparrow**	*P. hispaniolensis*																							R	1592
A	**Tree Sparrow**	*P. montanus*																					(TS)			1598
A	**Rock Sparrow**	*Petronia petronia*																							R	1604
D	**Snow Finch**	*Montifringilla nivalis*																							R	1611
A	**Yellow-throated Vireo**	*Vireo flavifrons*																							R	1628
A	**Philadelphia Vireo**	*V. philadelphicus*																							R	1631
A	**Red-eyed Vireo**	*V. olivaceus*																					(EV)		R	1633
A	**Chaffinch**	*Fringilla coelebs*																					(CH)			1636
A	**Brambling**	*F. montifringilla*																					(BL)	(b)A		1638
A	**Serin**	*Serinus serinus*																					(NS)	(b)A		1640
A	**Greenfinch**	*Carduelis chloris*																					(GR)			1649
	Sub-total																									

	FINCHES continued, NORTH AMERICAN WARBLERS		Life list	2002 list	24 hr	Garden	Holiday	Jan	Feb	Mar	Apr	May	Jun	Jul	Aug	Sep	Oct	Nov	Dec							EU No
A	**Goldfinch**	*C carduelis*																					(GO)			1653
A	**Siskin**	*C. spinus*																					(SK)			1654
A	**Linnet**	*C. cannabina*																					(LI)			1660
A	**Twite**	*C. flavirostris*																					(TW)			1662
	Lesser Redpoll	*C. cabaret*																								
A	**Mealy Redpoll**	*C. flammea*																					(LR)			1663
A	**Arctic Redpoll**	*C. hornemanni*																					(AL)		R	1664
A	**Two-barred Crossbill**	*Loxia leucoptera*																					(PD)		R	1665
A	**Crossbill**	*L. cutvirostra*																					(CR)	(b)C		1666
A	**Scottish Crossbill**	*L. scotica*																					(CY)	(b)B		1667
A	**Parrot Crossbill**	*L. pytyopsittacus*																					(PC)	(b)A	R	1668
A	**Trumpeter Finch**	*Bucanetes githagineus*																							R	1676
A	**Common Rosefinch**	*Carpodacus erythrinus*																					(SQ)	(b)A		1679
A	**Pine Grosbeak**	*Pinicola enucleator*																							R	1699
A	**Bullfinch**	*Pyrrhula pyrrhula*																					(BF)			1710
A	**Hawfinch**	*Coccothraustes coccothraustes*																					(HF)			1717
A	**Evening Grosbeak**	*Hesperiphona vespertin*																							R	1718
A	**Black-and-white Warbler**	*Mniotilta varia*																							R	1720
A	**Golden-winged Warbler**	*Vermivora chrysoptera*																							R	1722
A	**Tennessee Warbler**	*V. peregrina*																							R	1724
A	**Northern Parula**	*Parula americana*																							R	1732
A	**Yellow Warbler**	*Dendroica petechia*																							R	1733
A	**Chestnut-sided Warbler**	*D. pensylvanica*																							R	1734
A	**Blackburnian Warbler**	*D. fusca*																							R	1747
	Sub-total																									

	NORTH AMERICAN WARBLERS continued, NEW WORLD SPARROWS, BUNTINGS		Life list	2002 list	24 hr	Garden	Holiday	Jan	Feb	Mar	Apr	May	Jun	Jul	Aug	Sep	Oct	Nov	Dec							EU No
A	**Cape May Warbler**	*D. tigrina*																							R	1749
A	**Magnolia Warbler**	*D. magnolia*																							R	1750
A	**Yellow-rumped Warbler**	*D. coronata*																							R	1751
D	**Palm Warbler**	*D. palmarum*																							R	1752
A	**Blackpoll Warbler**	*D. striata*																							R	1753
A	**Bay-breasted Warbler**	*D. castanea*																							R	1754
A	**American Redstart**	*Setophaga ruticilla*																					(AD)		R	1755
A	**Ovenbird**	*Seiurus aurocapillus*																							R	1756
A	**Northern Waterthrush**	*S. noveboracensis*																							R	1757
A	**Yellowthroat**	*Geothlypis trichas*																							R	1762
A	**Hooded Warbler**	*Wilsonia citrina*																							R	1771
A	**Wilson's Warbler**	*W. pusilla*																							R	1772
A	**Summer Tanager**	*Piranga rubra*																							R	1786
A	**Scarlet Tanager**	*P. olivacea*																							R	1788
A	**Eastern Towhee**	*Pipilo erythrophthalmus*																							R	1798
A	**Lark Sparrow**	*Chondestes grammacus*																							R	1824
A	**Savannah Sparrow**	*Passerculus sandwichensis*																							R	1826
A	**Song Sparrow**	*Melospiza melodia*																							R	1835
A	**White-crowned Sparrow**	*Zonotrichia leucophrys*																							R	1839
A	**White-throated Sparrow**	*Z. albicollis*																							R	1840
A	**Dark-eyed Junco**	*Junco hyemalis*																					(JU)		R	1842
A	**Lapland Bunting**	*Calcarius lapponicus*																					(LA)			1847
A	**Snow Bunting**	*Plectrophenax nivalis*																					(SB)	(b)A		1850
A	**Black-faced Bunting**	*Emberiza spodocephala*																							R	1953
	Sub-total																									

	BUNTINGS continued, NORTH AMERICAN GROSBEAKS etc.		Life list	2002 list	24 hr	Garden	Holiday	Jan	Feb	Mar	Apr	May	Jun	Jul	Aug	Sep	Oct	Nov	Dec				EU No
A	**Pine Bunting**	*E. leucocephalos*																		(EL)		R	1856
A	**Yellowhammer**	*E. citrinella*																		(Y)			1857
A	**Cirl Bunting**	*E. cirlus*																		(CL)	(b)A		1958
A	**Rock Bunting**	*E. cia*																				R	1860
EU	**Cinereous Bunting**	*E. cineracea*																					1865
A	**Ortolan Bunting**	*E. hortulana*																		(OB)			1866
A	**Cretzschmar's Bunting**	*E. caesia*																				R	1868
A	**Yellow-browed Bunting**	*E. chrysophrys*																				R	1871
A	**Rustic Bunting**	*E. rustica*																				R	1873
A	**Little Bunting**	*E. pusilla*																		(LJ)			1874
D	**Chestnut Bunting**	*E. rutila*																				R	1875
A	**Yellow-breasted Bunting**	*E. aureola*																				R	1876
A	**Reed Bunting**	*E. schoeniclus*																		(RB)			1877
A	**Pallas's Bunting**	*E. pallasi*																				R	1878
D	**Red-headed Bunting**	*E. bruniceps*																					1880
A	**Black-headed Bunting**	*E. melanocephala*																				R	1881
A	**Corn Bunting**	*Miliaria calandra*																		(CB)			1882
A	**Rose-breasted Grosbeak**	*Pheucticus ludovicianus*																				R	1887
D	**Blue Grosbeak**	*Guiraca caerulea*																				R	1891
A	**Indigo Bunting**	*Passerina cyanea*																				R	1892
A	**Bobolink**	*Dolichonyx oryzivorus*																				R	1897
A	**Brown-headed Cowbird**	*Molothrus ater*																				R	1899
A	**Baltimore Oriole**	*Icterus galbula*																				R	1918
	Sub-total																						

PREVIOUSLY UNLISTED SPECIES	Life list	2002 list	24 hr	Garden	Holiday	Jan	Feb	Mar	Apr	May	Jun	Jul	Aug	Sep	Oct	Nov	Dec						EU №
Sub-total																							

DIRECTORY OF ART, PHOTOGRAPHY AND LECTURERS

A preening drake Smew recorded by author/artist David Cook of Norfolk.

DIRECTORY OF WILDLIFE ART GALLERIES

NATURE IN ART MUSEUM AND ART GALLERY

Key exhibitions for 2002: World's first museum dedicated to art inspired by nature. Picasso to David Shepherd, Flemish Masters to contemporary crafts. Permanent collection plus regular special exhibitions and 70 artists in residence each year. Look on our website.
Opening times: Tues-Sun (10am-5pm) and Bank holidays. Closed Dec 24-26.
Address: Wallsworth Hall, A38, Twigworth, Gloucester, GL2 9PA; 01452 731422; (Fax)01452 730937.
e-mail: ninart@globalnet.co.uk
www.nature-in-art.org.uk

OLD BREWERY STUDIOS

Key exhibitions for 2002: On-going and changing display of work by John Paige and Jane Leycester Paige. Greeting cards and train friezes.
Opening times: Variable, best to telephone first.
Address; The Manor House, Kings Cliffe, Peterborough, PE8 6XB; 01780 470247; (Fax)01780 470334.
www.oldbrewerystudios.co.uk

SLADMORE SCULPTURE GALLERY

Key exhibitions for 2002: A constantly changing exhibition of England's very best, bird and animal sculptors including: Geoffrey Dashwood, Mark Coreth and Philip Blacker.
Opening times: Mon-Fri (10am-6pm).
Address; 32 Bruton Place, Mayfair, London, WJ1 6NW; 020 7499 0365; (Fax)020 7409 1381.
www.sladmore.com

DIRECTORY OF WILDLIFE ARTISTS

ALLEN, Richard

Watercolour paintings and illustrations of birds, wildlife and flowers, recently published work in *Sunbirds* (Helm). Also black and white scraperboard illustrations for a variety of publications.
Address: 34 Parkwood Avenue, Wivenhoe, Essex, CO7 9AN; 01206 826753.
e-mail: richardallen@romanriver.freeserve.co.uk
www.birdillustrators.com

BARRETT, Priscilla

Watercolour, pastel and mixed media studies of all wild mammals, (domesticated also!). Line drawings of behaviour a speciality. Commissions accepted. Published many books: HarperCollins, Academic etc.
Address: Jack of Clubs, Lode, Cambridge, CB5 9HE; 01223 812229; (Fax)01223 330869.
e-mail: gh105@cus.cam.ac.uk

BINNS, David SWLA

Watercolours of British wildlife. Published work includes book illustrations, jigsaw designs for RSPB, RSNC, designs for Country Artists Ltd, Medici Society and in house designs and limited edition prints for the Brent Gallery, run with wife Molly at 60a Keighley Rd, Cowling, BD22 0BH. Award winning member of the SWLA. Commissions usually accepted.
Exhibitions for 2002: NEWA (Liverpool), SWLA (London), Brent Gallery (Cowling), Milnethorpe (Silverdale).
Address: Homestead, 9 Boundary Avenue, Sutton-in-Craven, Nr Keighley, Yorkshire, BD20 8BL; (Tel/Fax)01535 632774.

BURTON, Philip

Acrylics on canvas; current enthusiasm seabirds. Many book illustrations e.g. in recent *Raptors of the World*. Founder member of SWLA.
Exhibitions in 2002: Some at SWLA, London, annually.
Address: High Kelton, Doctors Commons Road, Berkhamsted, Herts, HP4 3DW; 01442 865020.
e-mail: pjkburton@aol.com

BUSBY, John SWLA

Illustrator of natural history books and articles, especially bird and animal behaviour. Lifelong field experience. Over 30 books illustrated, including nine Poyser titles. Also oil and w/c landscapes. See website for

---

Key: SWLA = Annual exhibition of Society of Wildlife Artists. BBF = British Birdwatching Fair.

examples of latest work.
Address: Easter Haining, Ormiston Hall, Tranent, E.Lothian, EH35 5NJ; (Fax)01875 341011. e-mail: jj.busby@lineone.net www.johnbusby-artist.com

BYERS, Clive

Paints in gouache and watercolour crayon. Birds in natural settings a speciality. Many available as greetings cards, some as prints. Original illustrations for various fieldguides and other bird books also available.
Address: 167 Unthank Rd, Norwich, NR2 2PG. 01603 615231. e-mail: clive@unthank167.freeserve.co.uk www.birdillustrators.com

CHESHIRE, David

Wildlife wood carvings in relief and specializing in miniature three dimensional subjects. Using wood from sustainable sources, subjects are carved utilizing its natural beauty. Commissions accepted.
Exhibitions in 2002: Willoughby Memorial Gallery, Corby Glen, Lincs, Sept 18 - Oct 16
Address: Chater Cottage, Station Road, Little Bytham, Nr Grantham, Lincs, NG33 4QY; 01780 410678. e-mail: david.cheshire@talk21.com

CHESTER, Mark

Mark has painted tigers in India, big game in Africa and raptors in America. Over 200 of his paintings have been reproduced as prints, calendars, collectors' plates and stamps.
Exhibitions for 2002: Mark exhibits at many shows each year. Contact him for details of all events.
Address: Greenlands Farm, Denham, Suffolk, IP21 5DN; 01379 668077. www.markchester.co.uk

COOK, David

Original paintings, drawings, paper cuts and paper sculptures of wildlife, especially waterfowl. Workshops for *Bird Watching* magazine. Publications include HarperCollins art book, three videos, RSPB and WWT greetings cards.
Exhibitions in 2002: SWLA, London. RSMA October.
Address: Holly House, 3 Lynn Road, South Runcton, King's Lynn, Norfolk, PE33 0EW; 01553 811980.

CROMACK, Peter

Specialising in wildfowl and gamebirds, mainly in oils. Twice a BASC prize winner. Exhibits at game fairs. commissions accepted.
Address: Flat 6, Wychnor Hall, Burton-on-Trent, Staffs, DE13 8BU. 01283 791054.

DAVIS, John SWLA

Watercolours, oils and acrylics of birds, mammals, general wildlife and landscapes. Published illustrations in various books and magazines. Commissions accepted for framed and unframed originals.
Exhibitions in 2002: Frank.T.Sabin Gallery, London W1; SWLA, London
Address: 6 Redmoor, Birdham, Chichester, West Sussex, PO20 7HS; 01243 512351.

FORKNER, Andrew

Detailed pencil drawings and studies of birds and mammals. Commissions accepted for framed or unframed originals. Limited edition prints.
Exhibitions in 2002: The Gallery, Bampton, Oxon Feb 3-

Glasgow artist Steve McQueen submitted this study of Coots and a Pied Wagtail for the 2001 *British Birds* competition

17. The BBF. The Wetland Centre, Barnes, London, Dec.
Address: 149 Manor Road, Witney, Oxon, OX28 3UF; 01993 776322.
e-mail: andrew@forkner.freeserve.co.uk

GILLMOR, Robert

Original watercolours, linocut prints and line drawings, mainly of British birds. Illustrator of many books.
Exhibitions in 2002: Work available at Wildlife Art Gallery, Suffolk; Bircham Gallery, Holt, Norfolk. SWLA Sept.
Address: North Light, Hilltop, Cley-next-the-Sea, Holt, Norfolk, NR25 7SE; 01263 740729.

HAMPTON, Michael SWLA

Watercolours of birds and mammals. John Aspinall, the late zoo owner, commissioned many paintings of his animals. Via the Federation of British Artists, he painted Arabian mammals for the Sultan of Oman in 2000. Michael's work has appeared on many magazine covers and calendars.
Exhibitions in 2002: SWLA, London. WWT, Arundel, Spring 2002.
Address: 13 Sandy Way, Shirley, Croydon, Surrey, CR0 8QT.
www.croydonartsociety.org.uk

JONES, Chris

International Young Artist of the Year 1998. Highly realistic oils and acrylics of British and exotic wildlife. *Bird Watching* magazine's current artist for bird identification series. Commissions accepted.
Exhibitions in 2002: Nature in Art, Gloucester June 11-16, Crossing Gate Gallery, Kingsley, Hampshire, all year.
Address: 47 Church Lane, North Bradley, Trowbridge, Wilts, BA14 0TE; (Tel/Fax) 01225 769717.
e-mail: chrisjones@eco-art.freeserve.co.uk

Essex artist Simon Patient was well placed to sketch a Canvasback among Tufted Ducks at Abberton Reservoir.

KOSTER, David

Original prints - etchings, woodcuts, linocuts, lithographs - of birds, fish, flowers, insects etc. Watercolours, oils. Commissions accepted. Published work includes wood engravings for *Down to Earth* by John Collis, ink drawings for *Fellow Mortals*, anthology of animal poetry.
Exhibitions in 2002: Nevill Gallery, Canterbury; SWLA London, as founder member.
Address: 5 East Cliff Gardens, Folkestone, Kent, CT19 6AR; 01303 240544.

LANGMAN, Mike

Bird identification illustrations, published illustrations for four fieldguides and numerous magazines. Interpretive and interactive displays produced for RSPB and National Trust. Limited edition prints and original paintings available.
Address: 38 Brantwood Drive, Paignton, Devon, TQ4 5HZ; (Tel/Fax)01803 528008.
e-mail: mikelangman38@aol.com
www.birdillustrators.com

LATIMER, Jonathan

Original acrylics of birds and other subjects. Commissions undertaken. Limited edition prints. Published interpretation material commissioned by National Geographic and Royal Botanic Gardens.
Address: 92 Swinley Road,

Wigan, Lancs, WN1 2DL; 01942 230502. e-mail: jlatimer2510@aol.com www. jonathanlatimer-wildart.co.uk

LEAHY, Ernest

Original watercolours and drawings of Western Palearctic birds, wildlife and country scenes. Illustrations for many publications including Poysers. Wide range of framed and unframed originals available. Commissions accepted and enquiries welcome.
Exhibitions for 2002: BBWF 2002, Redbourn Exhibition, Nov 29 - Dec 1, contact for details.
Address: 32 Ben Austins, Redbourne, Herts, AL3 7DR; 01582 793 144. e-mail: ernest.leahy@ntlworld.com

NEILL, William

Watercolours of landscape and wildlife of the Outer Hebrides. Illustrated Scottish Wildlife Trust *Discovery Book of Western Isles*. Commissions accepted. Six limited edition reproductions, catalogue available.
Exhibitions in 2002: SWLA, London. Studio Gallery Askernish Apr - Sept.
Address: Rannachan, Askernish, South Uist, Western Isles, HS8 5SY; 01878 700237. e-mail: Bill@askernish.fsnet.co.uk

NURNEY, Dave

Original gouache illustrations of birds plates from *Woodpeckers, Nightjars, Pica Pocket Guide*. Individual A5 size birds from Eco-Guides to Brazil, Malaysia, Thailand. Commissions undertaken, client roughs provided.
Address: 43 Abington Grove, Elm, Wisbech, Cambs, PE14 0BL; (Tel/fax)01945 860786.

PAIGE, John SWLA, & PAIGE, Jane Leycester FSBA

Wildlife and wild flowers in their natural surroundings. Watercolour, oil, acrylic, collage, mono-screen and lino prints.
Address: The Manor House, Kings Cliffe, Peterborough, PE8 6XB; 01780 470247; (Fax)01780 470334. www.oldbrewerystudios.co.uk

PARSONS, Joy SWLA, FRSA

Watercolours of birds, field mice, penguins, landscape, flowers (some pastels). Latest book *Holiday Painting and Wildlife Tales.* Work appears in *Leisure Painter* periodically. Work available from studio.
Exhibitions in 2002: Own studio gallery, Christchurch. SWLA, London.
Address: 3 Willow Place, Bridge Street, Christchurch, Dorset, BH23 1ED; 01202 482613.

PARTINGTON, Peter

Beloved medium is watercolour followed by oils and etching. Happiest in the field with sketchbook. Travels widely. Many one man shows, work widely collected. Commissions welcome. Books; *Learn to Draw* series, *Wildlife*, *Birds*, and *Farm Animals* (all HarperCollins).
Exhibitions in 2002: Slimbridge WWT Feb; The BBF (Aug) SWLA, London, Sept.
Address: The Hall, Kettlebaston, Suffolk, IP7 7QA; 01449 741538; (Fax)01449 744286. e-mail: peter.partington@kettlebaston.co.uk www. peter-partington.fsnet.co.uk

PEARSON. Bruce

Working in oils, watercolour and mixed media, paintings are completed either directly in the field or re-evaluated and reworked in the studio to express the natural rhythm, elemental energy and sheer excitement of 'being there'.
Exhibitions in 2002: Brian Sinfield Gallery, Burford, June 22 - July 6, 'Recent Work'.
Address: The Old Plough, Caxton Road, Great Gransden, Sandy, Beds, SG19 3BE; 01767 677558; (Fax)01767 677964. e-mail: b&p@openstudio.demon.co.uk

PHILLIPS, Antonia

Original watercolours and acrylics, specialising in birds and marine landscape, capturing atmosphere and movement within the natural world. Commissions accepted for framed/unframed works.
Exhibitions in 2002: Galleri Smidar og Skart, Reykjavik, Iceland, May/June; Wildfowl and Wetlands Trust, Arundel, October.
Address: 116 Sandbanks Road, Poole, Dorset, BH14 8DA. e-mail: antonia@artist100.fsnet.co.uk

POOLE, Greg

Best known as printmaker making stylised images of nature. Examples of work can be seen and bought on website- www.gregpoole.co.uk
Exhibitions for 2002: Artists for Nature Foundation Pyrenees exhibition, Barcelona, and related book.
SWLA, London.
Address: Eagle Tap, Eagle

Lane, Kings Cliffe, Nr Peterborough, PE8 6XD; 01780 470095.
e-mail: greg.poole@virgin.net

REANEY, John SWLA

Original watercolours of mainly British wildlife in a land or seascape, often at dusk. Illustrated *Birds of Sussex* 1996. Commissions accepted.
Exhibitions of 2002: SWLA, London. RSPB, Pulborough, Brooks Reserve, August.
Address: 1 Buxton Road, Brighton, East Sussex, BN1 5DE; 01273 551993.

RIDLEY, Martin

Artist specialising in British wildlife. Original oils and watercolours of birds and animals in their natural habitat. Prints, cards and commissions. RSPB 2002 calendar, this book cover. Extensive website.
Exhibitions for 2002: WWT, Slimbridge July 28 - Aug 28.
Address: Beinn a'Ghlo, Dalguise, Dunkeld, Scotland, PH8 0JU; 01350 727388;
e-mail: art@martinridley.com
www.martinridley.com

SCOTT, Dafila

Original oil paintings of wildlife and landcape. Has illustrated articles and books and has exhibited paintings widely in UK.
Exhibitions in 2002: SWLA, London.
Address: White Roses, The Hythe, Reach, Cambridgeshire, CB5 0JQ; 01638 742344.
e-mail:
dafila@dafila.freeserve.co.uk

SMITH, James P

Original colour and black-and-whites of British, European and Middle Eastern birds. Finished 'Runner-up' in *British Birds* 'Bird Illustrator of the Year' 1992. Commissions accepted, originals for sale.
Address: 157 Standon Rd, Sheffield, South Yorkshire, S9 1PH; (Tel/Fax)0114 2491378.
e-mail: jameslotan@yahoo.com
www.birdingisrael.com

STOCK, Andrew SWLA, ARE

Watercolour, oil and mixed-media paintings of wildlife and landscape. Also etchings. Member of SWLA since 1983 (currently Hon Sec), and RE since 2001. Exhibits SWLA, Tryon Gallery, Royal Academy and locally.
Exhibitions in 2002: SWLA, London, Solo show: Mall Galleries, November.
Address: The Old Schoolhouse, Ryme Intrinseca, Sherborne, Dorset, DT9 6JX; (Tel/Fax)01935 873620.
e-mail:
Andrewstock1@compuserve.com

SYKES, Thelma SWLA

Printmaker, linocuts, woodcuts, mainly birds. Published illustrations in *New Breeding Bird Atlas, European Atlas, Birdwatcher's Yearbooks*, 1986-1996, BTO publications. Founder member Nature in Art, where exhibited and artist in residence. Exhibits with Printmakers' Council and Society of Wood Engravers. Exhibited Festival of Printmaking, Chong Qing, China, 2000.
Exhibitions of 2002: SWLA, London. Solo exhibition, WWT Slimbridge, Nov 21 2001 - Jan 8 2003.
Address: Blue Neb Studios, 18 Newcroft, Saughall, Chester, CH1 6EL; 01244 880209.

WALLACE, D.Ian.M.

Gouache paintings, pencil and ink drawings; "paints birds like birdwatchers see them", supplies roughs free for commissions. Many published illustrations in own/other books.
Exhibitions in 2002:
SWLA London.
Address: Mount Pleasant Farm, Main Road, Anslow, Burton-on-Trent, Staffs, DE13 9QE; 01283 812364.

WARREN, Michael

Original watercolour paintings of birds, all based on field observations. Books, calendars, cards and commissions.
Exhibitions for 2002: WWT, The Wetland Centre, Barnes, London, Aug 31 - Oct 28; The BBF, Aug. SWLA, London.
Address: The Laurels, The Green, Winthorpe, Nottinghamshire, NG24 2NR; 01636 673554; (Fax)01636 611569. e-mail:
mike.warren.birdart@
care4free.net

WATSON, Donald SWLA

Artist and author. Many exhibitions 1948-2001. Gouache, watercolour, some oils, (UK and abroad), scraperboard and pen drawings. Author and illustrator of *The Hen Harrier* (Poyser) 1979, *A Bird Artist in Scotland* (Witherby 1988), *Birds of Moor and Mountain* (Academic Press 1972), *One Pair of Eyes* (Arlequin 1994). Contributor to many other books.
Agent: Wildlife Art Gallery, Suffolk.
Address: Barone, 54 High Street, Dalry, Castle Douglas, Kircudbrightshire, DG7 3UW; 01644 430246.

A Wood Sandpiper on the Cork Estuary was recorded by Dublin's Barry Ryan and entered for the 2001 *British Birds* competition.

WILCZUR, Jan

Original gouache/watercolours of birds and landscapes. Published illustrations for *Handbook of Birds of the World*, *Concise Birds of the Western Palearctic* and other fieldguides. Commissions accepted.
Address: 30 Dover House Rd, London, SW15 5AV; 0208 878 8925. www.birdillustrators.com

WILLIAMSON-BELL, James, SWLA, HC (Paris)

Any wildlife subject, in watercolour and acrylics. Also limited edition original prints. Chinese watercolours and woodblock prints a speciality. Illustrated details available. Commisions welcome.
Exhibitions in 2002: SWLA, London.
Address: 2 Pauline Gardens, Newcastle-upon-Tyne, NE15 7TD; (Tel/Fax)0191 274 6594. e-mail: autumnleaves@supanet.com

WOOLF, Colin

Original watercolour paintings. The landscape atmosphere and the character of his subject are his hallmark, with a technique that imparts a softness to his subjects. Owls, birds of prey and ducks are specialities. Wide range of limited editions and greetings cards, special commissions also accepted.
Exhibitions in 2002: Annual solo exhibitions in N Wales (Dec-Easter), BBF 2002 and galleries and shows country wide.
Address: Tremallt, Penmachno, Betws y Coed, Conwy, LL24 0YL; (Tel/ fax) + 44 (0) 1690 760 308. e-mail: colin@wildart.co.uk www.wildart.co.uk

WOODCOCK, Martin

Original watercolours and oils of birds. Illustrations published in many reference works and field guides, including the Birds of Africa. Commissions accepted.
Exhibitions of 2002: SWLA, London.
Address: Furlongs, Long Lane, Wiveton, Norfolk, NR25 7DD; (Tel/Fax)01263 741124 e-mail: woodcock@dircon.co.uk

WOODHEAD, Darren MA(RCA), SWLA

Original watercolours and woodcuts of birds, butterflies, mammals and other wildlife subjects, as well as landscapes and cloudscapes. All subjects painted direct in the field. Commissions undertaken.
Exhibitions for 2002: SWLA, London.
Address: 44F(2F3), Millhill, Musselburgh, East Lothian, EH21 7RN; 0131 665 6802. e-mail: darren.woodhead@virgin.net

WOOTTON, Tim

Watercolours and oils of birds and rural subjects. Widely published in magazines and periodicals etc. Works professionally in environmental interpretation and design. Accepts the occasional commission. Shorlisted for 'Young European Bird Artist' 1991.
Exhibitions in 2002: Mail for details.
Address: 8 Walker Road, Tankersley, Barnsley, South Yorks, S75 3DB 01226 740142. e-mail: natterjack@barnsley.ac.uk

DIRECTORY OF PHOTOGRAPHERS

BENVIE, Niall
Wildlife and landscape photographer and writer.
Subjects: Specialising in Scotland, Norway and Latvia. Special interest in human/ nature relations.
Formats: 35mm, 24x65mm panoramas, digitally enhanced images from hi-res scans for publication on CD.
Address: 24 Park Road, Brechin, Angus, DD9 7AP; 01356 626128.
e-mail: niall@niallbenvie.com

BORG, Les
Photographer, course leader.
Subjects: Mostly British wildlife, with some from Florida and elsewhere.
Formats: Mounted, unmounted or framed, inkjet prints or Ilfochromes if required.
Address: 17 Harwood Close, Tewin, Welwyn, Herts, AL6 0LF; 01438 717841, (Fax)01438 840459.
e-mail: les@les-borg-photography.co.uk
www.les-borg-photography.co.uk

BROADBENT, David
Professional photographer.
Subjects: UK birds and wild places.
Formats: 35mm, 6x7, CD-ROMs, scans.
Address: 12 Thomas Street, Glossop, Derbyshire, SK13 8QN; 01457 862997, (W)07889 47266. e-mail: info@davidbroadbent.com
www.davidbroadbent.com

BROOKS, Richard
Wildlife photographer, writer, lecturer.
Subjects: Owls (Barn especially), raptors, Kingfisher and a variety of European birds (Lesvos especially) and landscapes.
Formats: Mounted and unmounted computer prints (6x4 - A3+ size), framed pictures, surplus slides for sale.
Address: 24 Croxton Hamlet, Fulmodeston, Fakenham, Norfolk, NR21 0NP; 01328 878632. e-mail: email@richard-brooks.co.uk
www.richard-brooks.co.uk

CAMPBELL, Laurie
Professional nature photographer.
Subjects: Land-use, flora, fauna, landscapes of northern UK, particularly Scottish Highlands.
Formats: 120,000 35mm transparencies available for publication or to hang as digital or conventional prints.
Address: Hestia, Paxton, nr Berwick-upon-Tweed, Scotland, TD15 1TE; 01289 386736; (fax)01289 386746.
e-mail: laurie@lauriecampbell.com
www.lauriecampbell.com

CHAPMAN, David
Natural history photographer, writer, speaker and workshop leader.
Subjects: British natural history (esp.birds) and farm animal images.
Formats: 35mm slides, mounted &/or framed photos, photo cards.
Address: 41 Bosence Road, Townshend, Cornwall, TR27 6AL ; (Tel/fax) 01736 850 287. e-mail: David@Ruralimages.freeserve.co.uk
www.Ruralimages.freeserve.co.uk

CHITTENDEN, Robin
Photographer, Birdline East Anglia partner, writer and wildlife enthusiast.
Subjects: Wildlife in UK, Europe, Middle East, Africa, India, Americas, plus abstract nature, landscapes, habitat and environmental subjects.
Formats: 35mm transparencies, high quality prints, framed photographs, digital CD-ROM.
Address: PO Box 740, Norwich, NR2 3SH; +44 (0) 1603 633326.
e-mail: chittenden.robin@virgin.net
www.harlequinpictures.co.uk

CONWAY, Wendy
Award-winning wildlife photographer.
Subjects: Birds, mammals, landscapes : UK, USA, Lesvos and Africa.
Formats: 35mm and medium format. Prints matted and unmatted.
Address: 4 Meriden Close, Winyates Green, Redditch, B98 0QN; 01527 457793.
e-mail: wendy@terry-wall.com

COOK, Garry
Photographer, birder.
Subjects: UK rarities, many published in monthly bird magazines.
Formats: Unmounted prints.
Address: Herons Flight, New Road, Blakeney, Nr Holt, Norfolk, NR25 7PA; 01263 741614.

DICKSON, Wendy
Tour leader, photographer, writer.
Subjects: Birds and landscapes

of Shetland, Northumberland/ Farnes, Iceland, Arctic Siberia (incl Spectacled Eider), Spitsbergen, Senegal, Falklands, NZ.
Formats: Mostly 35mm transparencies, some prints.
Address: Flat 4, Muckle Flugga Shore Station, Burrafirth, Haroldswick, Unst, Shetland , ZE2 9EQ ; 01957 711 275. e-mail: wendy.dickson@ukgateway.net

GARBUTT, Nick

Author, photographer, artist, tour leader.
Subjects: Madagascar (Ground rollers, Vangas, Couas, Mesites etc), East/Southern Africa, Indian subcontinent.
Formats: Mounted 35mm and 70mm transparencies, cibachrome prints to order.
Address: c/o 30 School Road, Wales, Sheffield, S26 5QJ; 01909 770954.
e-mail: nick@nickgarbutt.com
www.nickgarbutt.com

GOMERSALL, Chris

Photographer, author of *Photographing Wild Birds*.
Subjects: Birds, wildlife and habitats, principally British Isles and Europe, also Florida, Seychelles, Morocco.
Formats: 35mm transparency library, loans available to bona-fide picture researchers & publishers, BAPLA terms and conditions. Digital supply (CD, e-mail) facility.
Address: 14 Judith Gardens, Potton, Bedfordshire, SG19 2RJ; 01767 260769.
e-mail: chris@ c-gomersall.demon.co.uk
www.chrisgomersall.co.uk

GREEN, Iain

Wildlife photographer, writer.
Subjects: Birds and wildlife of India, UK and Africa.
Formats: Mounted, unmounted and framed prints, including limited editions.
Address: 28 Woodside Road, Tonbridge, Kent, TN9 2PD; 01732 771570.
e-mail: iain@iaingreen.co.uk
www.iaingreen.co.uk

HORNE, Robert

Wildlife photographer.
Subjects: Specialising in British wildlife, reserves and landscapes.
Formats: Mounted and unmounted prints and framed photographs.
Address: 5 Dalton Close, Broadfield, Crawley, West Sussex, RH11 9JR.
e-mail: robert.horne@virgin.net

KNIGHTS, Chris

Farming, wildlife photography and filming.
Subjects: British wildlife, North America, Eastern Europe, East Africa, Siberia, Lesbos and Canada.
Fomats: 35mm mounted and digital prints, framed pictures and slides, copies to CD ROM.
Address: Crow Hall Farm, Gooderstone, King's Lynn, Norfolk, PE33 9DA; 01366 328646. e-mail: chris.knights@talk21.com

LANGSBURY, Gordon FRPS

Professional lecturer, wildlife photographer, author and tour leader.
Subjects: Birds and mammals from UK, Europe, Scandinavia, N America, Gambia, Kenya, Tanzania, Morocco and Falklands.
Formats: 35mm transparencies for publication, lectures and prints.
Address: Sanderlings, 80 Shepherds Close, Hurley, Maidenhead, Berkshire, SL6 5LZ; (Tel/fax)01628 824252.
e-mail: gordon_langsbury@onetel.net.uk

MOCKLER, Mike

Safari guide, tour leader, writer and photographer.
Subjects: Birds and wildlife of Britain, Europe, Central America, India and several African countries.
Formats: 35mm transparencies.
Address: Gulliver's Cottage, Chapel Rise, Avon Castle, Ringwood, Hampshire, BH24 2BL; 01425 478103. e-mail: mikemockler@lineone.net

OFFORD, Keith

Photographer, writer, tour leader, conservationist.
Subjects: Raptors, UK wildlife and scenery, birds and other wildlife of USA, Africa, Spain, Australia, India.
Formats: Conventional prints, greetings cards, framed pictures.
Address: Yew Tree Farmhouse, Craignant, Selattyn, Nr Oswestry, Shropshire, SY10 7NP; 01691 718740.
e-mail: keith-offord@virgin.net
www.keithofford.co.uk

DAVID PIKE

Photographer, presenter and writer.
Subjects: Wildlife, including birds from Japan, N America and Africa.
Formats: 35mm mounted. Conventional prints and digital.
Address: Uffington Manor, Main Road, Uffington, Lincs, PE9 4SN; 01780 751944;(W)01780 767711;

(Fax)01780 489218.
e-mail:
david.pike@dpikephotos.com
www.dpikephotos.com

READ, Mike

Photographer (wildlife and landscapes), tour leader, writer.
Subjects: Birds, mammals, plants, landscapes, and some insects. UK, France, USA, Ecuador (including Galapagos).
Formats: 35mm.
Address: Claremont, Redwood Close, Ringwood, Hampshire, BH24 1PR; 01425 475008, (Fax)01425 473160.
e-mail: mike@mikeread.co.uk
www.mikeread.co.uk

SMITH, Gary

Natural history photographer supplying agencies, runs library of own work.
Subjects: North Norfolk a speciality including birds and animals, other general wildlife subjects and rural scenes.
Formats: 35mm transparencies and CD-ROM available for publication.
Address: 19 The Elms, Hindringham, Fakenham, Norfolk, NR21 0PP; 01328 878 718. e-mail:
gksmithf4@callnetuk.com

SWASH, Andy

Photographer, author, tour leader.
Subjects: Birds, habitats/ landscapes and general wildlife from all continents; photographic library currently 1,400 bird species.
Formats: Slides for publication and duplicates for lectures. High resolution scans on CD-ROM. Conventional and digital prints, unmounted, mounted or framed.
Address: Stretton Lodge, 9 Birch Grove, West Hill, Ottery St Mary, Devon, EX11 1XP; (H&fax)01404 815383, (W)01392 822901. e-mail:
andy_swash@wildguides.co.uk
www.wildguides.co.uk

TATE, Alan

Birder, twitcher, photographer.
Subjects: UK rarities, 450+ W.Palearctic species, birds from all continents especially seabirds, waders, gulls. Some habitat shots.
Formats: Prints, copy slides, CD-ROM.
Address: 55 Woodlands Way, Mildenhall, Suffolk, IP28 7JA. 01638 717 699.
e-mail: alantate.birdphotos@ btinternet.com

TIPLING, David

Wildlife and landscape photographer, photographic tour leader, author.
Subjects: Worldwide wildlife and landscapes. Specialist areas include; UK, Antarctic, Finland and Arctic Norway, N India, Amazon, Alaska and China.
Formats: 35mm to 6 x 17 panoramas available as transparencies for commercial use only. Mounted prints available for sale, plus greetings cards.
Address: 99 Noah's Ark, Kemsing, Sevenoaks, Kent, TN15 6PD; 01732 763486.
e-mail:
windrushphotos@hotmail.com

WALL, Terry ARPS EFIAP PSA4

Wildlife photographer.
Subjects: Birds, mammals, landscapes from UK, USA, Lesvos, Africa and Galapagos..
Formats: 35mm/medium. Prints matted/unmatted. 35mm scanning service and restoration and retouching service. Quality printing service.
Address: 4 Meriden Close, Winyates Green, Redditch, B98 0QN; 01527 452145. e-mail:
wildimages@terry-wall.com
www.terry-wall.com

WARD, Chris

Photographer.
Subjects: Birds and landscapes, plus some other wildlife. UK (mostly commoner species, some rarities), W.Palearctic, S.Africa, Florida, California, Venezuela, Argentina, Australia.
Formats: Prints and framed pictures, slide copies for lectures.
Address: 276 Bideford Green, Linslade, Leighton Buzzard, Beds, LU7 7TU; 01525 375528.

WILKES, Mike FRPS

Professional prize winning wildlife photographer, tour leader.
Subjects: African, European and British birds.
Address: 43 Feckenham Road, Headless Cross, Redditch, Worcestershire, B97 5AS; 01527 550686.
e-mail: wilkes@photoshot.com

WILLIAMS, Nick

Photographer, lecturer, author, tour leader.
Subjects: W.Palearctic including Cape Verde Islands and Falkland Islands.
Formats: Duplicate slides, some originals, prints also available.
Address: Owl Cottage, Station Road, Rippingale, Lincs, PE10 0TA; (Tel/Fax)01778 440500.
e-mail:
magick2@hotmail.co.uk
www.wildlifebreaks.co.uk

WILMSHURST, Roger
Wildlife photographer, particularly birds.
Subjects: All aspects of wildlife, particularly British and European birds, butterflies, plants, mammals etc.
Formats: 35mm, 6x6, 6x7, 645.
Address: Sandhill Farmhouse, Sandhill Lane, Washington, Pulborough, West Sussex, RH20 4TD; 01903 892210, (fax)01903 893376.

DIRECTORY OF LECTURERS

For convenience, we have divided the lecturers into regional areas but please check the entries as most entrants are prepared to travel across the country.

SOUTH EAST ENGLAND

BEVAN, David
Photographer, Conservation officer, writer.
Subjects: Nature conservation, natural history of the garden, butterflies, wild flowers. SAE for full details.
Fees: £70+petrol. **Limits:** 50 miles without o.n. acc. 150 mls otherwise. **Times:** Evenings, days possible.
Address: 3 Queens Road, Bounds Green, London, N11 2QJ; (H)020 8889 6375, (W)020 8348 6005, Fax 020 8342 8754. e-mail: conserving.bevan@virgin.net

BRIGGS, Kevin
Freelance ecologist.
Subjects: General wildlife in NW and S England; specialist topics - raptors, Oystercatcher, Ringed Plover, Goosander, Yellow Wagtail, Ring Ouzel.
Fees: £50 + petrol. **Limits:** None. **Times:** Any.
Address: 2 Osborne Road, Farnborough, Hampshire, GU14 6PT; 01252 519881.

BUCKINGHAM, John
Lecturer, photographer, tour leader.
Subjects: 60+ titles covering birds, wildlife and habitats in UK, Europe, Africa, Australia, India and the Americas.
Fees: £55 + expenses. **Limits:** Any reasonable distance.
Times: Any.
Address: 3 Cardinal Close, Tonbridge, Kent, TN9 2EN; Tel/fax 01732 354970.

CANIS, Robert
Professional photographer, tour leader.
Subjects: Illustrated talks (including British and Finnish wildlife).
Fees: £30 + petrol. **Limits:** None, add fee for distance over 100 mls one way.
Times: Jan - Apr.
Address: 26 Park Avenue, Sittingbourne, Kent, ME10 1QY; 01795 477017. e-mail: rm.canis@btinternet.com

CLEAVE, Andrew MBE
Head of environmental education centre, author, tour leader.
Subjects: 30 talks (including Galapagos, Arctic, Mediterranean and Indian birds, dormice, woodlands). List available.
Fees: £50+ petrol. **Limits:** 60 mls without o.n accom.
Times: Evenings, not school holidays.
Address: 31 Petersfield Close, Chineham, Basingstoke, Hampshire, RG24 8WP; (H)01256 320050, (W)01256 882094, (Fax)01256 880174. e-mail: andrew.cleave@care4free.net

COOMBER, Richard
Tour leader, photographer, writer.
Subjects: Alaska, Australia, Botswana, Namibia, Seychelles, Falklands, S America, USA, seabirds.
Fees: £60+petrol. **Limits:** 50 mls without o.n. accom. 150 mls otherwise. **Times:** Afternoons or evenings.
Address: 1 Haglane Copse, Lymington, Hampshire, SO41 8DT; 01590 674471. e-mail rcoomber@compuserve.com

DUGGAN, Glenn
Ex-commander Royal Navy, tour leader, researcher.
Subjects: 10 talks including, birds of paradise and bower birds, history of bird art

(caveman to present day), famous Victorian bird artists (John Gould, the Birdman and John James Audubon.
Fees: £50+ expenses. **Limits:** none with o.n accom.
Times: Any.
Address: 25 Hampton Grove, Fareham, Hampshire, PO15 5NL; 01329 845976, (M)07771 605320. e-mail: lennduggan@ cardinal-ours.com www.cardinal-tours.com

EYRE, John
Chairman Hampshire Ornithological Society.
Subjects: World birding, From home in Hampshire to Europe, Africa, Australia and the Americas.
Fees: £50+travel. **Limits:** Any considered. **Times:** Any.
Address: 3 Dunmow Hill, Fleet, Hampshire, GU51 3AN; 01252 677850, (Fax)01252 677851. e-mail: johneyre@compuserve.com

GALLOP, Brian
Speaker, photographer, tour leader.
Subjects: 25+ talks covering UK, Africa, India, Galapagos and Europe - All natural history subjects.
Fees: £40+ 20p per ml.
Limits: None - o.n acc. if over 100 mls. **Times:** Any.
Address: 13 Orchard Drive, Tonbridge, Kent, TN10 4LT; 01732 361892.

GREEN, Iain
Wildlife photographer, writer.
Subjects: Birds and wildlife of India (including Keoladeo, Ghana), also tigers and other subjects.
Fees: To be arranged. **Limits:** To be arranged. **Times:** To be arranged.
Address: 28 Woodside Road, Tonbridge, Kent, TN9 2PD; 01732 771570.
e-mail: iain@iaingreen.co.uk
www.iaingreen.co.uk

HOLCOMBE, Brenda
Wildlife lecturer, photographer, travelled worldwide.
Subjects: 20+ talks (worldwide coverage, birds, mammals, plants, insects, scenery). List available.
Fees: £50+travel, neg. for smaller groups. **Limits:** SE England, further considered with o.n. accom. **Times:** Any.
Address: 2 Vicarage Way, Hurst Green, Etchingham, East Sussex, TN19 7QQ; 01580 860628.

KNYSTAUTAS, Algirdas
Ornithologist, photographer, writer, tour leader.
Subjects: Birds and natural history of USSR, Baltic States, S America, Indonesia (6 talks).
Fees: £1 per person. £70 minimum + £20 travelling.
Limits: None - in UK, o.n accom. needed.
Times: Oct and Nov.
Address: 7 Holders Hill Gardens, London, NW4 1NP; 020 8203 4317.
e-mail: ibisbill@talk21.com

LANGSBURY, Gordon FRPS
Professional wildlife photographer, lecturer, author and tour leader.
Subjects: 20 talks - Africa, Europe, USA, Falklands and UK. Full list provided.
Fees: £75 + travel. **Limits:** None. **Times:** Any.
Address: Sanderlings, 80 Shepherds Close, Hurley, Maidenhead, Berkshire, SL6 5LZ; (Tel/fax)01628 824252.
e-mail:
gordon_langsbury@onetel.net.uk

LOSEBY, Tim
Photographer, tour leader, birdwatcher for 45 years.
Subjects: 10 talks (Fair Isle, Nepal, Hong Kong, Sri Lanka, various on India, Russia, Central Asia, garden birds). Detailed list available.
Fees: £65+ petrol.
Limits: None. **Times:** Any.
Address: 34 Meteor Road, West Malling, Kent, ME19 4TH; 01732 870283.
e-mail:
timloseby@btinternet.com

McCARTHY, George
Professional wildlife and nature photographer.
Subjects: Various including birds of New Mexico, Florida and Lesvos. Full list available by post or on website.
Fees: £50+ 25p per ml.
Limits: No limits (check website).
Times: Any during Sept - Dec.
Address: 12 Searles View, Horsham, West Sussex, RH12 4FG; 01403 257917, (Fax)01403 267503.
www.georgemccarthy.com

MOCKLER, Mike
Safari guide, tour leader, writer and photographer.
Subjects: Birds and other wildlife of: Botswana, Kenya, Tanzania, Spain, Finland and Norway, Costa Rica, India.
Fees: negotiable. **Limits:** None. **Times:** evenings.
Address: Gulliver's Cottage, Chapel Rise, Avon Castle, Ringwood, Hampshire, BH24 2BL; 01425 478103. e-mail: mikemockler@lineone.net

MOIR, Geoffrey DFC, FRGS, FRPSL
Ret. Schoolmaster, lecturer, writer, philatelist, lived in Falkland Islands.

Subjects: Falklands wildlife, South Georgia wildlife, all fully illustrated.
Fees: £20. **Limits:** none.
Times: Any.
Address: 37 Kingscote Road, Croydon, Surrey, CR0 7DP; Tel/fax 020 8654 9463.

MORRIS, Pat

University lecturer, author, broadcaster.
Subjects: Hedgehogs, dormice, edible dormice, saving Kestrels and killing shrews (conservation projects in Mauritius).
Fees: £50.
Limits: 80 mls from Ascot.
Times: Evenings, not weekends.
Address: West Mains, London Road, Ascot, Berkshire, SL5 7DG; 01344 621001.
e-mail: P.Morris@rhul.ac.uk

NOBBS, Brian

Amateur birdwatcher and photographer.
Subjects: Wildlife of the Wild West, Israel, Mediterranean, Florida, wildlife gardening.
Fees: £30 + 25p per ml.
Limits: Kent, Surrey, Sussex.
Times: Evenings.
Address: The Grebes, 36 Main Road, Sundridge, Sevenoaks, Kent, TN14 6EP; 01959 563530. e-mail: Brian.Nobbs@talk21.com

READ, Mike

Photographer, tour leader, writer.
Subjects: 12 talks featuring British and foreign subjects (list available on receipt of sae).
Fees: £70 + travel.
Limits: 175 mls. **Times:** Any.
Address: Claremont, Redwood Close, Ringwood, Hampshire, BH24 1PR; 01425 475008, (Fax)01425 473160.
e-mail: mike@mikeread.co.uk
www.mikeread.co.uk

RUMLEY-DAWSON, Ian

Photographer, course leader.
Subjects: 96 talks using twin dissolving projectors. Birds, mammals, insects, plants, habitats, ethology. Arctic, Antartic, Falklands, N and S America, N.Z, Seychelles. albatrosses, penguins, Snowy Owls, polar bears etc.
Fees: £50+expenses. **Limits:** None. **Times:** Any.
Address: Oakhurst, Whatlington Road, Battle, East Sussex, TN33 0JN; 01424 772673.

TAYLOR, Don

Tour leader, author, photographer, chairman Kent OS editorial and records committee.
Subjects: Various illustrated talks on birding in Kent, Europe, the Americas, Africa and Nepal.
Fees: £50 + petrol. **Limits:** South-east without own accom, elsewhere otherwise.
Times: Any.
Address: 1 Rose Cottages, Old Loose Hill, Loose, Maidstone, Kent, ME15 0BN; 01622 745641. e-mail: don.taylor@care4free.net

TIPLING, David

Wildlife photographer, author, tour leader.
Subjects: Bird Journeys (Emperor Penguins etc), Adventures with a Camera (life of a wildlife photographer).
Fees: £80 + expenses. **Limits:** None. **Times:** Any in Nov-Feb preferred.
Address: 99 Noah's Ark, Kemsing, Sevenoaks, Kent, TN15 6PD; 01732 763486.
e-mail:
dt.windrush@care4free.net

TODD, Ralph

Tour leader.
Subjects: 6 talks incl. Galapagos Wildlife, Antarctica, Pyrenees, Iceland, Osprey wardening at Loch Garten, Wintering in Africa.
Fees: £55 + expenses. **Limits:** None, neg over 120 mls.
Times: Any - also short notice.
Address: 9 Horsham Road, Bexleyheath, Kent, DA6 7HU; (Tel/fax)01322 528335.
e-mail: rbtodd@globalnet.co.uk
www.users.globalnet.co.uk/~rbtodd/todd.htm

WRIGHT, Barry

Biomedical scientist, widely travelled abroad.
Subjects: Various South American countries and West Indies. 'A Year Abroad!', 'Journey across South America' - all talks based on birding trips.
Fees: £50 + petrol. **Limits:** 60 mls without o.n accom.
Times: Evenings.
Address: 18 Chestnut Grove, Wilmington, Kent, DA2 7PG; (H)01322 527345, (W)01322 428100 (4895). e-mail: barry@birding98.fsnet.co.uk

SOUTH WEST ENGLAND

CHAPMAN, David

Natural history photographer, writer, speaker and workshop leader.
Subjects: British natural history, birds, photography, small-holding wildlife.
Fees: £30 + travel. **Limits:** Negotiable. **Times:** Negotiable.

Address: 41 Bosence Road, Townshend, Cornwall, TR27 6AL; (Tel/fax) 01736 850 287. e-mail: David@ Ruralimages.freeserve.co.uk www.Ruralimages.freeserve.co.uk

GALE, John

Bird illustrator, artist.
Subjects: One talk - Bird Illustrating in East Africa (based on new field guide).
Fees: £50 + petrol. **Limits:** Approx 150 mls.
Times: Evenings.
Address: 6 Underdown, Kennford, Exeter, Devon, EX6 7YB; 01392 832026. www.galleryofbirds.com

GREEN, Dr George

Author and tour leader.
Subjects: Nine talks (including Dorset birds, African wildlife safari, birds of Gambia, Florida, N.Africa and Middle East.
Fees: £50+ petrol. **Limits:** 100 mls. **Times:** Evenings.
Address: 20 Paget Close, Wimbourne, Dorset, BH21 2SW; (H)01202 886885, (W)01258 843414.

KERSHAW, Richard

Global birdwatcher, music teacher and composer.
Subjects: Birds in Music.
Fees: £50+ petrol. **Limits:** 50 mls without o.n. accom. 150 mls otherwise.
Times: Evenings.
Address: 1 Priestlands House, Priestlands, Sherborne, Dorset, DT9 4HN; 01935 814525.

ROBINSON, Peter

Former Scilly resident and RSPB staff consultant.
Subjects: Various talks on sea and landbirds of Scilly and life in an island environment; Song Thrushes, Storm Petrels and Kittiwakes.
Fees: £45 + Petrol. **Limits:** None (by arrangement).
Times: Any.
Address: 19 Pine Park Road, Honiton, Devon, EX14 2HR; 01404 549873. e-mail: pjrobinson2@compuserve.com

SWASH, Andy

Photographer, author, tour leader.
Subjects: Ten talks (birds and general wildlife: Antarctica, Brazil, Argentina, Galapagos, Africa, Australia, China, USA, Costa Rica, Venezuela).
Fees: £75+ petrol. **Limits:** None. **Times:** Evenings.
Address: Stretton Lodge, 9 Birch Grove, West Hill, Ottery St Mary, Devon, EX11 1XP; (H&fax)01404 815383, (W)01392 822901. e-mail: andy_swash@wildguides.co.uk www.wildguides.co.uk

TULLY, John

Amateur bird surveyor.
Subjects: Eight talks (including Peregrines,feral pigeons, woodland birds, garden nesting, bird surveying).
Fees: £45+ travel. **Limits:** None. **Times:** Sept - March.
Address: 6 Falcondale Walk, Bristol, BS9 3JG; 0117 9500992.
e-mail: johntully4@aol.com

EAST ENGLAND

APPLETON, Tim

Reserve Manager, Rutland Water.
Subjects: Rutland Water, British Birdwatching Fair, Return of Ospreys to England, Trips and birds of Spain, Australia, Papua New Guinea, various African countries, Argentina and more.
Fees: Negotiable. **Limits:** Preferably within 2hrs of Rutland. **Times:** Winter preferred but can be flexible.
Address: Fishponds Cottage, Stamford Rd, Oakham, Rutland, LE15 8AB. 01572 724101; (W)01572 770651; (Fax)01572 755931.

BORG, Les

Photographer, course leader.
Subjects: Florida (mostly birds), nature photography, Cetaceans of the Azores, Parts I, II and III.
Fees: Negotiable. **Limits:** 150 mls without o.n accom.
Times: Any.
Address: 17 Harwood Close, Tewin, Welwyn, Herts, AL6 0LF; 01438 717841.
e-mail: les@ les-borg-photography.co.uk www. les-borg-photography.co.uk

BROADBENT, David

Professional photographer.
Subjects: UK birds and wild places. In praise of natural places.
Fees: £70+ travel. **Limits:** 50mls without o.n accom. Anywhere otherwise.
Times: Any.
Address: 12 Thomas Street, Glossop, Derbyshire, SK13 8QN; 01457 862997, (W)07889 47266. e-mail: info@davidbroadbent.com www.davidbroadbent.com

BROOKS, Richard

Wildlife photographer, writer, lecturer.
Subjects: 12 talks (including Lesvos, N.Greece, Israel, Canaries, E.Anglia, Scotland, Wales, Oman).

Fees: £65+ petrol. **Limits:** None if accom. provided.
Times: Any.
Address: 24 Croxton Hamlet, Fulmodeston, Fakenham, Norfolk, NR21 0NP; 01328 878632. e-mail: email@richard-brooks.co.uk www.richard-brooks.co.uk

BROOKS, David

Took early retirement to concentrate on wildlife interests.
Subjects: Various talks on wildlife, principally birds, in UK and overseas.
Fees: £50+ petrol. **Limits:** 50 mls without o.n. accom. 100 mls otherwise. **Times:** Any.
Address: 2 Malthouse Court, Green Lane, Thornham, Norfolk, PE36 6NW; 01485 512548. e-mail: david.g.brooks@tesco.net

CLARKE, Roger

Author of books on harriers, Phd in raptor feeding ecology.
Subjects: Harriers (overview and feeding ecology), other raptors if pressed.
Fees: £50 + petrol. **Limits:** Negotiable. **Times:** Flexible.
Address: New Hythe House, Reach, Cambridge, CB5 0JQ; 01638 742447.

COOK, Tony MBE

35 years employed by WWT. Travelled in Europe, Africa and N. America.
Subjects: 22 talks from Birds of the Wash, garden birds to travelogues of Kenya, E and W North America, Europe (Med to North Cape).
Fees: £35 + 15p per ml.
Limits: 100 mls. **Times:** Any.
Address: 43 Church Street, Market Deeping, Peterborough, PE6 8AN; 01778 342559.

CROMACK, David

Editor of *Bird Watching* magazine, bird tour leader.
Subjects: 1) 'Evolution of a Bird Magazine' and 2) 'Birds of Arizona and California'.
Fees: 1) No fee - expenses only, 2) £50+ expenses.
Limits: 150 mls.
Times: Jan/Feb.
Address: c/o *Bird Watching* Magazine, Bretton Court, Peterborough, PE3 8DZ. e-mail: david.cromack@emap.com

ELCOME, David

Wildlife lecturer, course leader, formerly head of education RSPB.
Subjects: Bird behaviour, adaptations; British butterflies, wild orchids; wildlife conservation in India; Gilbert White.
Fees: £80 + expenses. **Limits:** None if expenses paid.
Times: Any.
Address: 2 Charnocks Close, Gamlingay, Sandy, Bedfordshire, SG19 3JX; 01767 650489. e-mail: david.elcome@btinternet.com

FURNELL, Dennis

Natural history writer, radio and television broadcaster, artist and wildlife sound recordist.
Subjects: British and European wildlife and landscape, Thailand and West Africa. Wildlife sound recording, wildlife and disability access issues.
Fees: £100.
Limits: 30 miles, further with o.n. accom. **Times:** Afternoons or evenings according to commitments.
Address: 19 Manscroft Road, Gadebridge, Hemel Hempstead, Hertfordshire, HP1 3HU; 01442 242915, (Fax)01442 264852. e-mail; dennis.furnell@btinternet.com www.natureman.co.uk

GARNER, David

Wildlife photographer.
Subjects: 15 live talks and audio-visual shows on all aspects of wildlife in UK and some parts of Europe - list available.
Fees: £35 + 15p per ml.
Limits: None. **Times:** Any.
Address: 73 Needingworth Road, St Ives, Cambridgeshire, PE27 5JY; (H)01480 463194; (W)01480 463194.

GIBSON, Chris

Conservation professional, tour leader, photographer, writer, broadcaster.
Subjects: Includes the wildlife, lepidoptera and botany of Essex, East Anglia and the Mediterranean.
Fees: £50+ expenses in Essex and Suffolk, £100 + expenses elsewhere. **Limits:** None.
Times: Evenings.
Address: 1 Dove House Cottage, Oakley Road, Dovercourt, Essex, CO12 5DR; 01255 502960. e-mail: gibson@dovehc.freeserve.co.uk

GLADWIN, Alan B

Wildlife photographer, lecturer, tour leader, environmental consultant.
Subjects: Ten talks (inc. Birds in the Peak District, birding in Scotland, Southern Spain, Florida, British birds of prey, British owls, coastal birds, Australian wildlife, nature photography).
Fees: £50 + petrol. **Limits:** 1hr travelling without o.n accom. **Times:** Evenings.
Address: Hillside, 2 Castle

Mount Way, Bakewell, Derbyshire, DE45 1BQ; 01629 812215. e-mail: alanbgladwin@rdplus.net

GOMERSALL, Chris
Professional photographer, writer.
Subjects: 1) 'Taking Flight' (experiences as RSPB staff photographer), 2) 'Photographing Wild Birds' (illustrating Chris's new book).
Fees: £75 + 25p per mile.
Limits: None. **Times:** Oct-Mar evenings preferred.
Address: 14 Judith Gardens, Potton, Bedfordshire, SG19 2RJ; 01767 260769.
e-mail: chris@c-gomersall.demon.co.uk
www.chrisgomersall.co.uk

HAMMOND, Nicholas
Writer, wildlife trust director.
Subjects: Nine talks (including Modern Wildlife Painting, In Search of Tigers, Wildlife artists in Extremadura, Wildlife Trusts, Island Wildlife, Carl Linnaeus).
Fees: £70+ petrol. **Limits:** 50 mls without o.n. accom.
Times: Evenings/weekends.
Address: 30 Ivel Road, Sandy, Bedfordshire, SG19 1BA; (H)01767 680504, (W)01223 712406, (Fax)01767 683967.
e-mail: nhammond@mcmail.com

HASSELL, David
Ex-YOC leader, ex-RSPB assistant group leader.
Subjects: Five talks (including Seabirds, Shetland Birds, British Birds, USA Birds).
Fees: £40 + petrol. **Limits:** 100 mls. **Times:** Evenings.
Address: 15 Grafton Road, Enfield, Middlesex, EN2 7EY; (H)020 8367 0308, (W)020 7587 4500. e-mail: david@hassell99.freeserve.co.uk
www.davidhassell.co.uk

JOHNSTONE, Leslie
Photographer.
Subjects: Several (St Kilda, Hebrides and Shetland and offbeat view of bird photography).
Fees: £45 or 45p per ml (whichever greater). **Limits:** 70 mls without o.n. accom, 200 mls otherwise. **Times:** Any.
Address: 3 Muirfield Way, Woodhall-Spa, Lincs, LN10 6WB; 01526 354696.

KNIGHTS, Chris
Farming and conservation, photographer.
Subjects: British wildlife, North America, Eastern Europe, East Africa, Siberia, Lesvos, Canada.
Fee: £60+ petrol. **Limits:** 60 mls without o.n. accom.
Times: Evenings only.
Address: Crow Hall Farm, Gooderstone, King's Lynn, Norfolk, PE33 9DA;01366 328646. e-mail: chris.knights@talk21.com

MASON, Barrie
Wildlife photographer, RSPB group leader.
Subjects: The Brilliant Kingfisher, Grassholm and Skokholm, Wildlife of Scotland, trips by lorry in Peru and Africa.
Fees: £30 + petrol. **Limits:** 100 mls. **Times:** Evening.
Address: 6 Landseer Walk, Bedford, MK41 7LZ; (H)01234 262280.

PIKE, David
Photographer, presenter and writer
Subjects: Winter Birds of Japan.
Address: Uffington Manor, Main Road, Uffington, Lincs, PE9 4SN; 01780 751944;(W)01780 767711; (Fax)01780 489218. e-mail: david.pike@dpikephotos.com
www.dpikephotos.com

SCOTT, Ann and Bob
Ex-RSPB staff, tour leaders, writers, lecturers, tutors, trainers.
Subjects: 16+ talks (including nature reserves, RSPB, tours, gardening, Europe, Africa, S America, after dinner talks etc).
Fees: £60+travel over 50 mls.
Limits: None (by arrangement). **Times:** Any.
Address: 8 Woodlands, St Neots, Cambridgeshire, PE19 1UE; 01480 214904. e-mail: abscott@tinyworld.co.uk

TREVIS, Barry
Nature reserve warden, bird-ringer, widely travelled birdwatcher.
Subjects: Birding in Peru, Birds of Churchill, Manitoba, Tanzania - birds, parks and Kilimanjaro, Birding 'Down-under', Lemford Springs Nature Reserve.
Fees: £75. **Limits:** Up to 20mls, travel costs otherwise.
Times: Any.
Address: 11 Lemsford Village, Welwyn Garden City, Hertfordshire, AL8 7TN; (H)01707 335517.
e-mail: trevis@unisonfree.net

WARD, Chris
Photographer.
Subjects: 16 talks UK and worldwide (W.Palearctic, Americas, Africa, Australia) - primarily birds, some other wildlife.
Fees: £30 + petrol. **Limits:** 100 mls. **Times:** Evenings, afternoons poss.
Address: 276 Bideford Green,

Leighton Buzzard, Bedfordshire, LU7 7TU; 01525 375528.

WILLIAMS, Nick
Photographer, lecturer, author, tour leader.
Subjects: Several audio visual shows (including Spain, Camargue, Turkey, Canaries and Cape Verde Islands, Falklands).
Fee: £80-£99 depending on group size and distance.
Limits: None. **Times:** Any.
Address: Owl Cottage, Station Road, Rippingale, Lincs, PE10 0TA; (Tel/Fax)01778 440500. e-mail: magick2@hotmail.co.uk www.wildlifebreaks.co.uk

WREN, Graham ARPS
Wildlife photographer, lecturer, tour guide.
Subjects: 17 talks, birds - UK and Scandinavia, the environment - recent habitat changes and effect on bird populations, wildlife - Ohio and Kenya.
Fees: £50-70 + petrol.
Limits: None. **Times:** Any.
Address: The Kiln House, Great Doward, Whitchurch, Ross-on-Wye, Herefordshire, HR9 6DU; 01600 890488, (Fax)01600 890294.

WYATT, John
Tour leader, photographer, writer, co-author of *Teach Yourself Bird Sounds* cassette series.
Subjects: Over 25 talks (including birds and other wildlife of Africa, Central America, Europe and of specific habitats within these areas, bird identification by sight and sound).
Fees: £55 + travel. **Limits:** None. **Times:** Any.
Address: Little Okeford, Christchurch Road, Tring, Hertfordshire, HP23 4EF; 01442 823356. e-mail: wyatt@waxwing.u-net.com

WEST MIDLANDS

BOND, Terry
Bank director, photographer, group field leader.
Subjects: Eight talks (including Scilly Isles, Southern Europe, USA - shorebirds and inland birds, Birdwatching Identification - a new approach.
Fees: By arrangement (usually only expenses). **Limits:** Most of UK. **Times:** Evenings.
Address: 3 Lapwing Crescent, Chippenham, Wiltshire, SN14 6YF; (H)01249 462674, (W)020 7382 5476, (Fax)01249 446082. e-mail:(W) terry.bond@barclays.co.uk (H) terrybond@barclays.net

BROWN, David
Lecturer, photographer, lepidopterist.
Subjects: Butterflies, moths, survival techniques to avoid bird predation, habitats, ecology, migration, techniques for recording moths.
Fees: £50+petrol. **Limits:** None, needs o.n. accom. over 150 mls. **Times:** Any.
Address: Jacksons Lawn, Charlecote, Warwick, CV35 9EW; 01789 840295.

BROWN, Charles ARPS
Bird photographer, tour leader.
Subjects: 12 talks which cover worldwide areas and various bird-related subjects (list avail).
Fees: Expenses by arrangement. **Limits:** 160 ml round trip preferred. **Times:** Winter evenings.
Address: Riverside, Victoria Street, Yoxall, Burton on Trent, DE13 8NG; 01543 472280, (Fax)01543 473659.

CONWAY, Wendy
Award-winning wildlife photographer.
Subjects: Several talks, birds, mammals, landscapes from UK, USA, Lesvos.
Fees: £45 + petrol. **Limits:** over 50mls please contact.
Times: Any.
Address: 4 Meriden Close, Winyates Green, Redditch, B98 0QN; 01527 457793.
e-mail: wendy@terry-wall.com

CROUCHER, Roy
Wildlife tour leader, local authority ecologist.
Subjects: 4 talks (Northern France, Montenegro, Wildfowl, Bird song).
Fees: £50+ petrol. **Limits:** Mainland Britain. **Times:** Any.
Address: Uplands Lodge, Manor Road, Smethwick, West Midlands, B67 6SA; 0121 558 7658. e-mail: roy_croucher@lineone.net

GARBUTT, Nick
Author, photographer, artist, tour leader.
Subjects: Madagascar, (mammals, birds, reptiles, frogs), India, East and Southern Africa.
Fees: £150 + expenses.
Limits: None. **Times:** Any.
Address: c/o 30 School Road, Wales, Sheffield, S26 5QJ; 01909 770954.
e-mail: nick@nickgarbutt.com
www.nickgarbutt.com

LANE, Mike
Wildlife photographer.
Subjects: Seven talks from the UK and worldwide, mostly on birds.

Fees: Varies. **Limits:** None. **Times:** Flexible. **Address:** 37 Berkeley Road, Shirley, Solihull, West Midlands, B90 2HS; 0121 744 7988, e-mail: mikelane@nature-photograph.co.uk www.nature-photography.co.uk

MORRIS, Rosemary and YATES, Basil

Wildlife enthusiasts, photographers.
Subjects: Talks on birds and wildlife, including England, Lesvos, Ecuador and Galapagos, Kenya, Tanzania, around the world.
Fees: £30 + petrol. **Limits:** Negotiable. **Times:** Any.
Address: Wrens Nest, Droitwich Road, New End, Astwood Bank, Redditch, Worcestershire, B96 6NE; 01527 893581.

OFFORD, Keith

Photographer, writer, tour leader, conservationist.
Subjects: 14 talks covering raptors, uplands, gardens, migration, woodland wildlife, Australia, Southern USA, Tanzania, Gambia, Spain, SW.Africa.
Fees: £80+ petrol. **Limits:** none. **Times:** Sept - April.
Address: Yew Tree Farmhouse, Craignant, Selattyn, Nr Oswestry, Shropshire, SY10 7NP; 01691 718740.
e-mail: keith-offord@virgin.net www.keithofford.co.uk

SHERWIN, Andrew

Interests in natural history and photography.
Subjects: Ten talks including Kenya, Gambia, Israel, California, Canada, India, Lesvos, Pyrenees.
Fees: £40. **Limits:** 50 mls. **Times:** Evenings only.
Address: 26 Rockingham Close, Ashgate, Chesterfield, Derbyshire, S40 1JE; 01246 221070. e-mail: andrew.sherwin@btinternet.com

SIMPSON, Geoff

Tour leader, professional photographer, writer.
Subjects: 1) 'A Nature Photographer's Diary', 2) 'Wild Britain', 3) 'The Flora and Fauna of the Peak District'.
Fees: £100+petrol. **Limits:** 50 mls, neg otherwise. **Times:** Any.
Address: Camberwell, 1 Buxton Road, New Mills, High Peak, Derbyshire, SK22 3JS; 01633 743089, (Fax)01663 744843. e-mail: info@geoffsimpson.co.uk www.geoffsimpson.co.uk

WALL, Terry ARPS EFIAP PSA4

Wildlife photographer.
Subjects: Several (birds, mammals, landscapes - USA, UK, Lesvos, Galapagos).
Fees: £50 + petrol. **Limits:** Over 50 mls please contact.
Times: Any.
Address: 4 Meriden Close, Winyates Green, Redditch, B98 0QN; 01527 457793.
e-mail: wildimages@terry-wall.com: www.terry-wall.com

WALLACE, D.Ian.M.

Field ornithologist, writer, artist.
Subjects: Early birdwatching (1930s-1960s), patchwork, the Rosefinch enigma, adventurous collectors (19th/20th Century).
Fees: Negotiable + travel.
Limits: None, overnight accom. over 150 mls. **Times:** Any.
Address: Mount Pleasant Farm, Main Road, Anslow, Burton on Trent, Staffordshire, DE13 9QE; 01283 812364.

WILKES, Mike FRPS

Professional wildlife photographer, tour leader.
Subjects: 13 talks - natural history - Africa, America, South America, Europe, Gt Britain.
Fees: According to distance on request. **Limits:** None.
Times: Any.
Address: 43 Feckenham Road, Headless Cross, Redditch, Worcestershire, B97 5AS; 01527 550686.
e-mail: wilkes@photoshot.com

NORTH EAST ENGLAND

BELL, Graham

Cruise lecturer worldwide, photographer, author.
Subjects: Arctic, Antarctic, America, Siberia, Australia, Canada, Iceland, Seychelles, UK - identification, behaviour, seabirds, bird imitations etc.
Fees: £35 + travel. **Limits:** None. **Times:** Any.
Address: Ros View, The Bungalow, South Yearle, Wooler, Northumberland, NE71 6RB; (H&fax)01668 281310.
e-mail: seabirds@talk21.com

DOHERTY, Paul

Videomaker/photographer.
Subjects: Five talks (Birds of Prey, Waders, Wetlands, Israel and California).
Fees: £60 + petrol. **Limits:** 100 mls. **Times:** Any.
Address: 28 Carousel Walk, Sherburn in Elmet, N.Yorks,

LS25 6LP. (Tel/fax)01977 684666. e-mail: paul@ birdimages.swinternet.co.uk

LAWSON, Tom
Retired hospital doctor, tour leader, photographer.
Subjects: Travel talks on Israel, Oman, Kazakhstan, Antarctica, Namibia, Venezuela and N. America. Bird illustration, bird literature.
Fees: Donation to bird charity + petrol. **Limits:** 100 mls without o.n. accom. **Times:** Any.
Address: Burton Garth, Main Street, Knapton, York, YO26 6QG; 01904 795489, (Fax)01904 339493.

MATHER, John Robert
Ornithologist, writer, tour guide, lecturer.
Subjects: Birds and wildlife of: Kenya, Tanzania, Uganda, Costa Rica, India, Nepal. 'Bird on the Bench'.
Fees: £65+ 20p per ml.
Limits: 100 mls. **Times:** Eve.
Address: Eagle Lodge, 44 Aspin Lane, Knaresborough, North Yorkshire, HG5 8EP; 01423 862775.

PARKER, Susan and Allan ARPS
Professional photographers, (ASPphoto - Images of Nature), lecturers and tutors.
Subjects: Talks on birds and natural history, natural history photography - countries include UK, USA (Texas, Florida), Spain, Greece, Cyprus.
Fees: On application. **Limits:** Up to 120 mls without o.n accom. **Times:** Any.
Address: Ashtree House, 51 Kiveton Lane, Todwick, Sheffield, S Yorkshire, S26 1HJ; 01909 770238. e-mail: aspaspphoto@clara.co.uk

RICHMAN, Peter William
Lecturing since 1989.
Subjects: Ten AV travelogs - USA, India, Africa - includes birds, mammals, scenery.
Fees: £35 + petrol. **Limits:** 50 ml radius of York. **Times:** Evenings.
Address: 4 Cherry Tree Avenue, New Earswick, York, YO32 4AR; 01904 760269. e-mail: peter@ birding-audio-visual.co.uk www. birding-audio-visual.co.uk

TRINDER, Geoff
Photographer, reserve manager.
Subjects: Ten talks (including Falklands, Galapagos, Lincolnshire wildlife, North America various).
Fees: £50 + 25p per ml.
Limits: 120 mls. **Times:** Day or evenings.
Address: The Croft, Carrhouse Road, Belton, Doncaster, South Yorkshire, DN9 1PG; 01427 872051. e-mail: geoff@trinderg.freserve.co.uk

NORTH WEST ENGLAND

CARRIER, Michael
Lifelong interest in natural history.
Subjects: 1) 'Birds in Cumbria', 2) 'The Solway and its Birds' and 3)'The Isle of May'.
Fees: £20. **Limits:** None but rail connection essential.
Times: Sept-March, afternoons or evenings.
Address: Lismore Cottage, 1 Front Street, Armathwaite, Carlisle, Cumbria, CA4 9PB; 01697 472218.

McKAVETT, Mike
Photographer.
Subjects: Five talks, Birds and Wildlife of India, North and Western Kenya and the Gambia, Bird Migration in North America.
Fees: £30 + expenses. **Limits:** None. **Times:** Any.
Address: 34 Rectory Road, Churchtown, Southport, PR9 7PU; 01704 231358.

MELLOR GREENHALGH, Pauline
Photographer,countryside ranger, writer.
Subjects: Hebridean wildlife - birds, flora, insects, fauna.
Fees: £50 + petrol. **Limits:** 100 mls from Leigh. **Times:** Evenings.
Address: 78 Firs Lane, Leigh, Lancashire, WN7 4SB; (H)01942 606576, (W)01695 625338.

OWEN, Charles
Ornithologist, photographer, countryside warden.
Subjects: Ten talks (including UK birds, butterflies, dragonflies, plants and conservation issues.
Fees: £45 + expenses. **Limits:** 50 - 60 mls but negotiable.
Times: Evenings.
Address: 21 Pembroke Road, Hindley Green, Wigan, Lancs, WN7 4TG; 01942 256163.

PICKFORD, Terry
Co-ordinator NW Raptor Protection Group, advisory member to the government's raptor forum committee.
Subjects: 1) Raptor conservation/persecution NW England;
2) Home Life of the Golden Eagle in Scotland;
3) Wildlife of the Czech Republic.
Fees: £70 + 15p per ml.
Limits: None. **Times:** Any.
Address: 114 Pilling Lane,

Preesall, Lancs,FY6 0HG; 01253 810620, (M)07977 890116. e-mail: conservation@raptor.uk.com

POWER, John FRPS
Bird photographer.
Subjects: British birds - three talks (slides) plus photographic workshop (equipment/prints).
Fees: To be agreed. **Limits:** To be discussed. **Times:** Evenings (days poss).
Address: 15 Brynmor Road, Mossley Hill, Liverpool, L18 4RW; 0151 724 5004, (W)0151 729 0094,(Fax)0151 724 3667.

WALES

DENNING, Paul
Wildlife photographer.
Subjects: 15 talks, (birds, mammals, butterflies etc, western and eastern Europe, north and central America, Canaries).
Fees: £30 + petrol. **Limits:** 80 mls. **Times:** Eve, weekends.
Address: 17 Maes Maelwg, Beddau, Pontypridd, CF38 2LD; (H)01443 202607; (W)02920 673243.
e-mail: pgdenning.naturepics @virgin.net

HOLT, Brayton
Photographer, writer, county recorder, BTO rep.
Subjects: 20 talks (world wide - all continents plus UK).
Fees: £25 + 25p per ml.
Limits: 100 mls without o.n. accom. 150 mls otherwise.
Times: Evenings.
Address: Scops Cottage, Pentre Beirdd, Welshpool, Powys, SY21 9DL; 01938 500266.

LAWTON ROBERTS, John
Writer, photographer, field ornithologist.
Subjects: Upland wildlife; remote/ unfamiliar destinations; emphasis on interesting behaviour/ ecology.
Fees: £65 + petrol. **Limits:** 70 mls without o.n. accom, 130 mls otherwise (inc London).
Times: Any.
Address: Belmont, Berwyn, Llangollen, Denbighshire, LL20 8AL; (Tel/Fax)01978 860343. e-mail: jlawtonroberts@onetel.net.uk

LINN, Hugh ARPS
Experienced lecturer, photographer.
Subjects: Various: location-based (UK and Europe) plus subject-based (eg. photography understanding birds, etc).
Fees: £40+ petrol. **Limits:** 75 mls without o.n. accom. 150 mls otherwise.
Times: Flexible.
Address: 4 Stonewalls, Rosemary Lane, Burton, Rossett, Wrexham, LL12 0LG; 01244 571942.

ROGERS, Paul
Tour leader, lecturer.
Subjects: 15+ talks on USA, Africa, Antarctica, Ecology etc. Tunnicliffe's Anglesey.
Fees: £35 + petrol. **Limits:** 3-4 hrs travelled, (150-200 mls).
Times: Not weekends.
Address: Shorelands, Malltraeth, Bodorgan, Anglesey, LL62 5AT; 01407 840396.

SCOTLAND

BENVIE, Niall
Wildlife and landscape photographer and writer.
Subjects: Photo techniques based on his books *The Art of Nature Photography* and *Creative Landscape Photographer*; Latvia, Norway, Scotland, issues.
Fees: £200 + exp within Scotland, £350 + exp. rest of UK. **Limits:** UK wide. **Times:** Nov, Dec, Jan.
Address: 24 Park Road, Brechin, Angus, DD9 7AP; 01356 626128.
e-mail: niall@niallbenvie.com

DICKSON, Wendy
Freelance naturalist.
Subjects: Wildlife of Northumberland coast, Shetland wildlife, some NZ birds.
Fees: £20. **Limits:** Since I live in Shetland I am willing to negotiate expenses/etc. **Times:** usually south in Dec, other times by arrangement.
Address: Flat 4, Muckle Flugga Shore Station, Burrafirth, Haroldswick, Unst, Shetland, ZE2 9EQ; 01957 711275. e-mail: wendy.dickson@ukgateway.net

DENNIS, Roy
Ornithologist, ecologist, lecturer, writer.
Subjects: More than ten talks (Ospreys, eagles, raptors, re-introductions of birds and large mammals, ecosystem restoration, conservation strategies, Scotland and worldwide).
Fee: Negotiable.
Limits: Any. **Times:** Any.
Address: Inchdryne, Nethybridge, Inverness-shire, Scotland, PH25 3EF; 01479 831384; (W)14779 831714; (Fax)01479 831686.
e-mail: roydennis@aol.com

TRADE DIRECTORY

Craig Chapman used scraperboard to create this study of a nesting Spoonbill (*Platalea leucorodia*).

BIRD GARDEN SUPPLIERS

CJ WILDBIRD FOODS LTD

Company ethos: High quality products, no-quibble guarantee, friendly, professional service.
Key product lines: Complete range of RSPB Birdcare feeders, food and accessories, alongside a collection of other wildlife related products.
Other services: Mail order company, online ordering, 24hr delivery service. Free handbook.
Opening times: Mon-Fri (9am-5pm).
Contact: The Rea, Upton Magna, Shrewsbury, Shropshire, SY4 4UR; 0800 731 2820; Fax; 01743 709504. e-mail: enquiries@birdfood.co.uk www.birdfood.co.uk

ERNEST CHARLES

Company ethos: Member of Birdcare Standards Assoc. ISO 9002 registered. Offering quality bird foods/wildlife products through a friendly mail-order service.
Key product lines: Bird foods, feeders, nest boxes and other wildlife products.
Other services: Own label work for other companies considered and trade enquiries.
Opening times: Mon to Fri (8am-5pm).
Contact: Stuart Christopher, Ernest Charles, Crediton, Devon, 01363 84842; (Fax)01363 84147. e-mail: stuart@ernest-charles.com www.ernest-charles.com

GARDEN BIRD SUPPLIES LTD

Company ethos: The very best for your garden birds, direct to your door. Fast and friendly service. RSPB Corporate Partner. BTO Business Ally. BSA founder member.
Key product lines: Huge range of high-quality wild bird foods, feeders, tables, nest boxes, birdbaths, poles, baffles, books, videos, CDs and more.
Other services: Exclusively mail order.
Opening times: Mon to Fri (8;30-5pm).
Contact: By phone or e-mail for free *Garden Bird Feeding Guide* and catalogue, Garden Bird Supplies, Wem, Shrewsbury, Shropshire, SY4 5BF; 01939 232233; (Fax)01939 233155. e-mail: info@gardenbird.com www.gardenbird.com

JACOBI JAYNE & CO.

Company ethos: To supply products of proven conservation worth and highest quality. To offer expertise and special prices to wildlife groups, schools and colleges.
Key product lines: Birdfeeders, birdfoods, nest boxes & accessories. UK distributor of Schwegler woodcrete nest boxes, Droll Yankees feeders and Jacobi Jayne wildlife foods.
Other services: *Wild Bird News* mail-order catalogue.
Opening times: 24hrs (use websites or answering service when office is closed).
Contact: Graham Evans/Sally Haynes, Jacobi Jayne & Co, Wealden Forest Park, Canterbury, Kent, CT6 7LQ; 0800 072 0130; (Fax)01227 719235. e-mail: enquiries@jacobijayne.com www.jacobijayne.com www.birdon.com www.wildbirdnews.com

JAMIE WOOD PRODUCTS

Company ethos: Quality hand-made products at competitive prices as supplied to the RSPB, universities, film units, householders. Thirty years experience.
Key products: Hides, photographic electronics, nest boxes, feeders, bird tables, patio stands.
Other services: Mail order, delivery ex-stock, within seven days.
Opening times: Mon to Fri (8:30am-4:30pm),
Contact: Pam or Brian, Jamie Wood Products, Dept BYD, 1 Green Street, Old Town, Eastbourne, Sussex, BN21 1QN; Tel/Fax; 01323 727291. e-mail: Jamiewood@birdtables.com www.birdtables.com

www.thebirdtable.co.uk

Company ethos: A family business that supplies an extensive range of quality products combined with superb service. Supporters of The Essex Wildlife Trust.
Key product lines: Bird tables, bird feeders, nest boxes, bird baths and a variety of mixes and feeds for wild birds and other wildlife.
Other services: Courier service, 48 hour delivery.
Contact: Browse our website for our extensive range of products, advice, drawings and photographs; 01268 413109; (Fax)01268 419258. e-mail: enquiries@thebirdtable.co.uk www.thebirdtable.co.uk

BOOK PUBLISHERS

ARLEQUIN PRESS

Imprints; Arlequin Press — birdwatching site guides, monographs, limited edition natural history art books.
New for 2002: *A Birdwatching Guide to Bermuda* by Andrew Dobson. *A Birdwatching Guide to Brittany* by Stephanie Coghlan.
Address: 26 Broomfield Road, Chelmsford, Essex, CM1 1SW; 01245 267771; (Fax)01245 280606. e-mail: info@arlequinpress.co.uk www.arlequinpress.co.uk

BRITISH ORNITHOLOGISTS' UNION

Single imprint specialising in the highly acclaimed Checklists Series providing detailed avifaunas for poorly known countries, regions and islands around the world.
Expected during 2002: *The Birds of Hispaniola; The Birds of Principé, Sáo Tome and Annobon; The Birds of Morocco.*
Address: The Natural History Museum, Tring, Herts, HP23 6AP; 01 442 890 080; (Fax)020 7942 6150. e-mail: sales@bou.org.uk www.bou.org.uk

BUCKINGHAM PRESS

Imprints: Single imprint company - publishers of *The Birdwatcher's Yearbook* since 1980 and *The Who's Who in Ornithology* (1997).
New for 2002: *Best Bird Sites in Norfolk;* (Neil Glen), *Best Bird Sites in the Highlands of Scotland* (Gordon Hamlett).
Address: 55 Thorpe Park Rd, Peterborough, PE3 6LJ, 01733 561739; e-mail: buck.press@btinternet.com

CHRISTOPHER HELM PUBLISHERS

Imprints: An imprint of A & C Black (Publishers) Ltd, incorporating Pica Press (acquired Oct 2000),
New for 2002: *Raptors of the World* (Helm), *Birds of Western Africa* (Helm).
Address: 37 Soho Square, London, W1D 3QZ; 020 7758 0200; (Fax)020 7758 0222. e-mail: ornithology@acblack.com

HARCOURT PUBLISHERS LTD

Imprints; T and AD Poyser — mainly dealing with British/ European birds.
AP Natural World — all areas of natural history and ecology.
Academic Press — science for the professional or devoted enthusiast.
Poyser Natural History — cover natural history issues and wildlife.
New for 2002: *The Lost Land of the Dodo* (AP Natural World); *The Migration Atlas* (Poyser).
Address: Harcourt Place, 32 Jamestown Road, London, NW1 7BY; 020 7424 4200; (Fax)020 7482 2293. e-mail: wildlife@harcourt.com www. harcourt-international.com

HARPERCOLLINS PUBLISHERS

Imprints: Collins Natural History — publisher of fieldguides to the natural world.
Collins New Naturalist Series - the encyclopaedic reference for British natural history.
HarperCollins, publisher of illustrated books.
New for 2002: *Collins Birds by Colour* by Norman Arlott (CNH); *The Broads* by Brian Moss (CNNS); *Vanishing Flowers* by Bob Gibbons and David Woodfall (HC).
Address: 77-85 Fulham Palace Rd, Hammersmith, London, W6 8JB; 020 8307 4225; (Fax)020 8307 3037. e-mail: katie.piper@harpercollins.co.uk www.fireandwater.com

NEW HOLLAND PUBLISHERS (UK) LTD

Imprints; New Holland, illustrated bird books, general wildlife and personality-led natural history.
New for 2002: Bill Oddie's *Introduction to Birdwatching;* Wildlife Trusts' *Handbook of Garden Wildlife; Nick Baker's Bug Book; Field Guide to the Birds of Thailand.*
Address: Garfield House, 86-88 Edgware Road, London, W2 2EA; 020 7724 7773; (Fax)020 7258 1293. e-mail: postmaster@nhpub.co.uk www.newhollandpublishers.com

OCTOPUS PUBLISHING

Imprints; Mitchell Beazley, Hamlyn, Bounty-Brimax, Phillips.
New for 2002: *The Complete Guide to Birdwatching in Britain and Europe.*
Address: 2-4 Herons Quay, London, E14 4JB; 020 7531 8480; (Fax)020 7531 8534. www.mitchell-beazley.co.uk

PRION LTD

Imprints: Birdwatchers' Guides — a series of guides providing the travelling birdwatcher with information he or she needs to make the

most of a birdwatching holiday or tour. Soft-back, with maps. Titles include: Nepal, Morocco, Canary Islands, Gambia, Turkey, India, Portugal & Madeira.
New for 2002: *A Birdwatchers' Guide to New Zealand.*
Address: Kings Head Cottage, Cley-next-the-Sea, Norfolk, NR25 7RX.

WILD*Guides* LTD

Imprints; WILD*Guides* — natural history fieldguides.
OCEAN*Guides* — identification guides to marine wildlife.
Your Countryside Guides — regional heritage guides for walkers.
WILD eARTh — illustrated celebrations of wildlife and natural places.
New for 2002: *Butterflies of the British Isles* (WG); *Whales & Dolphins of the North American Pacific* (OG); *The Thames Valley* (YCG).
Address: Parr House, 63 Hatch Lane, Old Basing, Hants, RG24 7EB; 01256 478309; (Fax)01256 818039.
e-mail: info@wildguides.co.uk
www.wildguides.co.uk

BOOK SELLERS

ATROPOS/ATROPOS BOOKSHOP

Company ethos: All the latest information published in a lively and entertaining style. Books supplied quickly at competitive prices.
Key subjects: Journals suited to birdwatchers interested in butterflies, moths and dragonflies. Field guides and key books supplied.
Address: Mark Tunmore, 36 Tinker Lane, Meltham, Holmfirth, West Yorkshire, HD9 4EX; 01326 290287.
e-mail:
atropos@atroposed.freeserve.co.uk
www.atroposuk.co.uk

BOOKS FOR BIRDERS/ BIRDING WORLD SALES

Company ethos: Friendly and informative staff, providing a fast delivery service.
Key subjects: Ornithology, (fieldguides, site guides and monographs).
Other services: *Birding World* magazine. Mail-order.
Opening times: Mon-Fri (9am-5pm), answerphone outside office hours.
Address; Stonerunner, Coast Road, Cley, Norfolk, NR25 7RZ; 01263 741139. e-mail: sales@birdingworld.co.uk

CALLUNA BOOKS

Company ethos: Providing a wide selection of second-hand titles at competitive prices.
Key subjects: Natural history, including birds, flora, invertebrates, general topics, New Naturalists, Poysers, reports.
Opening times: Mail order. Viewing by appointment only.
Address; c/o Syldata, Arne, Wareham, Dorset, BH20 5BJ; 01929 552560 (evenings); (Fax)01929 550969. e-mail: neil&yuki@onaga54.freeserve.co.uk

NHBS MAIL ORDER BOOKSTORE

Company ethos: A unique natural history, conservation and environmental bookstore.
Key subjects: Natural history, conservation, environmental science, zoology, habitats and ecosystems, botany, marine biology.
Other services: NHBS.com offers a searchable and browsable web catalogue with more than 75,000 titles.
Opening times: Mon-Fri (9am-5pm).
Address; 2-3 Wills Road, Totnes, Devon, TQ9 5XN; 01803 865913; (Fax)01803 865280. www.nhbs.com
e-mail: nhbs@nhbs.co.uk

PORTLAND OBSERVATORY BOOK SHOP

Company ethos: To meet the needs of amateur and professional naturalists.
Key subjects: Ornithology, general natural history, topography, art and local history. New and secondhand.
Other services: Mail order, discount on new books, increased discount for observatory members.
Opening times: Wed, Thur and weekends; (10am to 5pm). Other times on request.
Address; Bird Observatory, Old Lower Light, Portland Bill, Dorset, DT5 2JT; 01305 820553.
e-mail: obs@btinternet.com
www.
portlandbirdobs.btinternet.co.uk

SECOND NATURE

Company ethos: Buying and selling out-of-print/secondhand/ antiquarian books on natural history, topography and travel.
Key subjects: Birds, mammals and travel with a natural history interest. Very large specialist stock.
Other services; Occasional catalogues issued. Often exhibiting at bird/natural history fairs.
Opening times: Mail order only.
Address; Knapton Book Barn, Back Lane, Knapton, York, YO26 6QJ; (Tel/fax) 01904 339493.

SUBBUTEO BOOKS

Company ethos: Specialist knowledge on all aspects of natural history, friendly service.
Key subjects: Wildlife, natural history and travel books.
Other services: Source any natural history book from around the world. Online ordering, free catalogue.
Opening times: Mon-Fri (9am-5pm).
Address: The Rea, Upton Magna, Shrewsbury, Shropshire, SY4 4UR; 0870 010 9700; (Fax)0870 010 9699.
e-mail:info@wildlifebooks.com
www.wildlifebooks.com

CLOTHING SUPPLIERS

BOULTERS OF BANWELL LTD

Company ethos: Friendly advice by well-trained local staff, with competitive prices to match.
Key product lines: A full range of outdoor clothing including Lowe Alpine, Crag Hoppers, Columbia, Regatta, Berghaus. Boots from Brasher, Scarpa and Hi-tec.
Other services: A full range of equestrian clothing and equipment, mowers, quads, trailers, pressure washers.
Opening times; Mon-Fri (8am-6pm), Sat (8am-5pm), Sun (10am-3pm).
Address: Phillip Cook, Banwell, Weston-super-Mare, Somerset, BS29 6HT; 01934 822137; (Fax)(01934 823301.
e-mail: mail@boulters.co.uk
www.boulters.co.uk

COUNTRY INNOVATION

Company ethos: Friendly advice by well-trained staff.
Key product lines: Full range of outdoor wear: Jackets, fleeces, trousers, walking boots, poles, lightweight clothing, hats, gloves, bags and pouches. Ladies fit available.
Other services: Mail order, special order service.
Opening times; Mon-Fri (9am-5pm).
Address: The Bridge, Langford Road, Lower Langford, North Somerset , BS40 5HU; 01934 863863; (Fax)01934 863016.
e-mail:
sales@countryinnovation.com

EQUIPMENT SUPPLIERS

BIRDGUIDES LTD

Company ethos: Top quality products and services especially using new technologies such as CD-ROM, DVD, websites, plus one-stop on-line shop for books, bird food etc.
Key product lines: CD-ROM, DVD, video guides to British, European and American birds. Rare bird news services via e-mail and website.
New for 2002: Electronic field guide for hand-held PCs, new online news/information services.
Address: Dave Gosney, Jack House, Ewden, SheffieldS36 4ZA; 0114 2831002; (Fax)0114 2831003.
e-mail: sales@birdguides.com
www.birdguides.com

EagleEye OpticZooms

Company ethos: Innovative design, quality manufacturing, custom products and expert advice on all aspects of digital photography.
Key product lines: Telephoto lenses for digital cameras/ camcorders, digiscoping adapters and products, custom digital camera accessories.
New for 2002: Digiscoping adapters and products (cam-mount and image locating sight), plus Digiscoping advice service.
Opening times: Mon-Sat (9am-6pm).
Address: Carlo Bonacci, 61 Yorkland Avenue, Welling, Kent, DA16 2LE; Tel/(Fax)020 8298 0352.
e-mail: sales@eagleeyeuk.com
www.eagleeyeuk.com

MONDELL

Company ethos: Supplying products not readily available through retail outlets, that meet our customer requirements. We are always keen to hear of individual needs.
Key product lines: Products to ease carrying of binoculars, and telescope and tripod combinations.
New for 2002: Constantly trying to improve and develop new lines.
Opening times: Any reasonable time. Mainly mail order.
Address: Chris Montgomery, 4 Pound Lane, Woodbury, Exeter, EX5 1JE; (Tel/fax)01395 232192.

PAUL M HILL NATURAL HISTORY SERVICES

Company ethos: Friendly service and competitive.
Key product lines: Moth trap components.
New for 2002: Details of new products listed on our website www.papilio.co.uk
Opening times: Mon-Fri (9am-5pm), answerphone at other times.
Address: Paul M Hill, 1 Clive Cottage, London Rd, Allostock, Knutsford,

Cheshire, WA16 9LT; (Tel/fax)01565 722938. e-mail: paul@papilio.co.uk www.papilio.co.uk

THE PENNA PRESS

Company ethos: Selling high quality products featuring colourful wildlife illustrations by Robert Gillmor.
Key product lines: Appointment calendar 2002, Christmas and greeting cards, stationery, giftwrap (all featuring birds).
New for 2002: Free wildlife catalogue of Penna goods.
Opening times: Weekdays, normal office hours.
Address: 132 Beechwood Avenue, St Albans, Herts, AL1 4YD; 01727 860281; (Fax)01727 846167. e-mail: gillmor@pennapress.co.uk

WILDLIFE WATCHING SUPPLIES

Company ethos: To bring together a comprehensive range of materials, clothing and equipment to make it easier and more comfortable for you to blend in with the environment. Quick and friendly service.
Key product lines: Hides, camouflage, bean bags, lens and camera covers, clothing etc.
New for 2002: Wider range of hides and equipment. Free CD of website available.
Opening times: Mon to Fri (9am-5pm), Mail order. Visitors by appointment.
Address: Town Living Farmhouse, Puddington, Tiverton, Devon, EX16 8LW; 01884 860692(24hr); (Fax)01884 860994. e-mail: enquiries@wildlifewatchingsupplies.co.uk www.wildlifewatchingsupplies.co.uk

WILDSOUNDS

Company ethos: Donates a significant proportion of profits to bird conservation, committed to sound environmental practices, official bookseller to African Bird Club and Oriental Bird Club.
Key product lines: Mail order, post-free books and mult-media guides i.e. the award winning *Bird Songs & Calls of Britain and Europe* on four CDs. Field recording equipment.
New for 2002: Practical field recording kits. 2002 catalogue.
Address: Cross Street, Salthouse, Norfolk, NR25 7XH. Tel/fax; +44(UK) (0)1263 741100. e-mail: duncan@wildsounds.com www.wildsounds.com

HOLIDAY COMPANIES

AVIAN ADVENTURES

Company ethos: Quality tours, escorted by friendly, expert leaders at a relaxed pace. ATOL 3376.
Types of tours: Birdwatching, birds and wildlife photography and wildlife safaris. Suitable for both first-time and more experienced travellers.
Destinations: 70 tours to Europe, Africa, Asia & Australasia, North & South America.
New for 2002: Estonia, Ecuador, Hawaii, Guyana, Oregon, New Zealand.
Brochure from: 49 Sandy Road, Norton, Stourbridge, DY8 3AJ; 01384 372013; (Fax)01384 441340. e-mail: aviantours@argonet.co.uk www.avianadventures.co.uk

BIRDFINDERS

Company ethos: Good-value birding tours to see all specialities/endemics of a country/area, using top UK and local guides.
Types of tours: Birdwatching for all abilities.
Destinations: 34 tours in Europe, Africa, Asia, Australasia, North and South America and Antarctica.
New for 2002: Nepal, Egypt, Russia, Australia, Thailand, Sri Lanka, Arizona (winter) and New England.
Brochure from: Vaughan Ashby, 18 Midleaze, Sherborne, Dorset, DT9 6DY.(Tel/fax)01935 817001 e-mail: BirdFinders@compuserve.com www.BirdFinders.co.uk

BIRD HOLIDAYS

Company ethos: Relaxed pace, professional leaders, small groups, exciting itineraries.
Types of tours: Birdwatching for all levels, beginners to advanced.
Destinations: Worldwide (40 tours, 5 continents).
New for 2002: Mexico, Kerala, Midway Atoll, Venezuela, Tuscany, Arizona, Brazil, Andalusia.
Brochure from: 10 Ivegate, Yeadon, Leeds, LS19 7RE; (Tel/fax)0113 3910 510. e-mail: pjw.birdholidays@care4free.net

BIRDSEEKERS

Company ethos: Value-for-money birdwatching tours, with an enviable success at finding the most sought-after species.
Types of tours: High standard birdwatching tours with an emphasis on seeing the birds and other wildlife as well!
Destinations: Britain, Europe and worldwide.

New for 2002: Galapagos, Nepal, Australia, Cuba, S.Africa, Kenya.
Brochure from: 19 Crabtree Close, Marshmills, Plymouth, Devon, PL3 6EL; 01752 220947; (Fax)01752 220947. e-mail: Bird@birdseekers.freeserve.co.uk www.birdseekers.co.uk

BIRDQUEST

Company ethos: Superb leaders and small groups are behind our worldwide reputation. ATOL no 2937.
Types of tours: Birdwatching tours, wildlife tours (including Antarctica), bird and wildlife photography.
Destinations: More than 140 different tours worldwide (more than 80 offered annually).
New for 2002: Yunnan, Eastern Bolivia, Polynesia.
Brochure from: Two Jays, Kemple End, Stonyhurst, Clitheroe, Lancashire, BB7 9QY; 01254 826317; (Fax)01254 826780. e-mail: birders@birdquest.co.uk www.birdquest.co.uk

BIRDWATCHING BREAKS

Company ethos: Professional guides and local experts in the countries we visit, a winning combination.
Types of tours: Birdwatching holidays.
Destinations: 50 tours in North, Central and South America, Europe, Asia and Africa.
New for 2002: Ghana, Korea, Corsica, Dominican Republic/Puerto Rico, China (Sichuan), Uganda, Sweden (Olano), India (W.Ghats+ Andaman Islands), Malaysia.
Brochure from: 26 School Lane, Herne, Kent, CT6 7AL; 01227 740799; (Fax)01227 363946. e-mail: m.finn@birdwatchingbreaks.com www.birdwatchingbreaks.com

CAMBRIAN BIRD HOLIDAYS

Company ethos: Friendly and personal attention, we don't twitch – our aim is to enjoy good views of those birds and other wildlife that we find.
Types of tours: Birdwatching and general natural history. Some themed holidays: Birds and Flowers, Birds and Butterflies, Birds and Geology, Birding for Beginners etc.
Destinations: West Wales and Southern Ireland.
New for 2002: A continuation of our recent and evolving programme.
Brochure from: Rhydlewis, Llandysul, Ceredigian, SA44 5SP; 01239 851758. www.cambihols.co.uk

CARPATHIAN WILDLIFE SOCIETY

Company ethos: A non-profit organisation bringing together people with an interest in conserving large mammals and birds.
Types of tours: Wildlife tours contributing to research. Tracking of wolves, bears and lynx. Birdwatching and working holidays.
Destinations: Slovakia. Five national parks, seven primeval forests and one wetland reserve.
New for 2002: New holidays to all the above sites.
Brochure from: Information currently only available on our website; 01692 598135; (Fax)01692 598141. e-mail: cws@szm.com www.cws.szm.com

CELTIC BIRD TOURS

Company ethos: Relaxed, bird-filled holidays suitable for all levels of birdwatching ability.
Types of tours: General birdwatching, birding for beginners, some general wildlife holidays, pelagics.
Destinations: Wales, UK, Europe, Middle East, Africa and Indian sub-continent.
New for 2002: Poland, Lesvos, Sri Lanka and The Gambia.
Brochure from: 84 Coity Road, Bridgend, CF31 1LT; 01656 645709; (mobile) 07971 983227. e-mail: birds@celtictours.org.uk

CLASSIC JOURNEYS

Company ethos: Professional and friendly company, providing well organised and enjoyable birdwatching holidays.
Types of tours: General birdwatching and wildlife holidays on the Indian sub-continent.
Destinations: Nepal, India, Bhutan.
New for 2002: Sri Lanka.
Brochure from: 33 High Street, Tibshelf, Alfreton, Derbyshire, DE55 5NX; 01773 873497; (Fax)01773 590243. e-mail: birds@classicjourneys.co.uk www.classicjourneys.co.uk

GREAT GLEN WILDLIFE

Company ethos: Quality wildlife watching experience at a relaxed pace.
Types of tours: General wildlife watching, (mainly birds and mammals, also butterflies and wild flowers). Small groups (eight participants), high standard of accommodation.
Destinations: Full range of

Scottish Highland and Island destinations, also Belarus, France, Sweden, Spain, Greece, Norway.
New for 2002: Greece - Macedonia; Spain - Picos de Europa.
Brochure from: Sherren, Harray, Orkney, KW17 2JU; (Tel/fax)01856 761604. e-mail: davidkent@onetel.net.uk

GULLIVERS NATURAL HISTORY HOLIDAYS

Company ethos: We are the 'small company that takes care of you', we aim to fulfil your holiday dreams. ATOL 4256.
Types of tours: Relaxed, friendly, fun holidays. Birdwatching, botany, wildlife, general natural history. Singles welcome. No-hassle quotes and arrangements for your club/ society trips.
Destinations: Worldwide.
New for 2002: South Africa, Colorado and Wyoming.
Brochure from: Bob Gulliver, Oak Farm (H), Stoke Hammond, Milton Keynes, MK17 9DB; 01525 270100; (Fax)01525 270777.

HEATHERLEA

Company ethos: Exciting holidays to see all the birds of Scotland. Experienced guides and comfortable award-winning hotel for great customer service.
Types of tours: Birdwatching and other wildlife watching tours in the beautiful Scottish Highlands.
Destinations: Scottish Highlands, plus Outer Hebrides, Orkney, Shetlands and more.
New for 2002: A full range throughout the year.
Brochure from: Mountview Hotel, Nethybridge, Inverness-shire, PH25 3EB; 01479 821248; (Fax)01479 821515. e-mail: hleabirds@aol.com www.heatherlea.co.uk

HONEYGUIDE WILDLIFE HOLIDAYS

Company ethos: Relaxed natural history holidays with wildlife close to home. Quality accommodation, expert leaders, beginners welcome.
Types of tours: Birds, flowers and butterflies, with a varied mix depending on the location.
Destinations: Europe, including Extremadura, Pyrenees, Crete, Menorca, Camargue, Slovakia and Danube Delta.
New for 2002: The Dordogne.
Brochure from: 36 Thunder Lane, Thorpe St Andrew, Norwich, Norfolk, NR7 0PX; (Tel/fax)01603 300552 (Evenings).
e-mail: honeyguide@tesco.net www.honeyguide.co.uk

HOSKING TOURS LTD

Company ethos: The best in wildlife photographic holidays.
Types of tours: Wildlife photography for all levels of experience.
Destinations: Africa, America, Europe.
New for 2002: Madagascar, Cyprus.
Brochure from: Pages Green House, Wetherinsett, Stowmarket, Suffolk, IP14 5QA; 01728 861113; (Fax)01728 860222. www.hosking-tours.co.uk

IBIS EXCURSIONS

Company ethos: Providing you with the 'holiday of a lifetime'. Specialists in Scandinavia/ Finland - particularly owls.
Types of tours: Longer bird tours, weekend bird breaks, photography, walking and customised holidays.
Destinations: 28 tours - Arizona, Bharatpur, Cape May, Estonia, Falklands, Finland (7), Namibia, Nepal, Norway, South Georgia, Spain (5), Spitsbergen, Sweden (5) - plus customised anywhere.
New for 2002: Antarctic, Namibia.
Brochure from: Ganloseparken 46, 3660 Stenlose, Denmark.(UK no)01327 831225, (DK no)0045 48195940; (Fax)0045 48195945. e-mail: jeffprice@ibis-excursions.dk www.ibis-excursions.dk

ISLAND HOLIDAYS

Company ethos: Relaxed pace holidays with conservation and responsibility to the environment paramount.
Types of tours: Relaxed birding and natural history tours. We like to enjoy all aspects of the islands we visit, not just the birds.
Destinations: More than 20 island destinations in the UK and worldwide.
New for 2002: Iceland/Faroes/ Shetland (a 17-day tour).
Brochure from: Drummond Street, Comrie, Perthshire, PH6 2DS; 01764 670107; (Fax)01764 670958. e-mail: enquiries@islandholidays.net www.islandholidays.net

KUONI TRAVEL

Company ethos: Our buying power brings you value for money as well as a professional dedication to quality and service.
Types of tours: Itineraries for birdwatchers using the expert knowledge of local guides.
Destinations: Sri Lanka, Egyptian Nile cruise, Costa Rica, Finland, South Africa,

Cuba and Caribbean cruise, Madeira, Dubai, Ecuador and Galapagos, Kenya, USA, India.
New for 2002: Trinidad and Tobago and the Seychelles.
Brochure from: Specialist Products Dept, Kuoni House, Dorking, Surrey, RH5 4AZ; 01306 744 477;(Fax)01306 744155. e-mail: specialist.products@kuoni.co.uk www.kuoni.co.uk

LIMOSA HOLIDAYS

Company ethos: The finest birdwatching tours - expertly led, fun, friendly and full of birds.
Types of tours: Wide range of general birding and wildlife tours, plus 'First Steps' holidays tailored to your 'first steps' abroad.
Destinations: Limosa 2002 Brochure and 'First Steps' programme feature more than 80 holidays worldwide.
New for 2002: 18 destinations, including Portugal, Switzer-land, China, Thailand, Chile, Venezuela & USA.
Brochure from: Suffield House, Northrepps, Norfolk NR27 0LZ. 01263 578143; (Fax)01263 579251. E-mail: limosaholidays@compuserve.com

NATURETREK

Company ethos: Friendly, gentle-paced, birdwatching holidays with broad-brush approach. Sympathetic to other wildlife interests, history and local culture. ATOL 2962.
Types of tours: Escorted birdwatching, botanical and natural history holidays worldwide.
Destinations: Worldwide - see brochure.
New for 2002: Egypt, Iran, Queensland, Bulgaria, Siberia, Papua New Guinea, etc.
Brochure from: Cheriton Mill, Cheriton, Alresford, Hampshire, SO24 0NG; 01962 733051; (Fax)01962 736426. e-mail: info@naturetrek.co.uk www.naturetrek.co.uk

NORTH WEST BIRDS

Company ethos: Friendly, relaxed and unhurried but targetted to scarce local birds.
Types of tours: Very small groups (up to four) based on large family home in South Lakes with good home cooking. Short breaks with birding in local area. Butterflies in season.
Destinations: Local to Northwest England. Lancashire, Morecambe Bay and Lake District.
Brochure from: Mike Robinson, Barn Close, Beetham, Cumbria, LA7 7AL; (Tel/fax)015395 63191. e-mail: mike@nwbirds.co.uk www.nwbirds.co.uk

ORNITHOLIDAYS AND CRUISES FOR NATURE

Company ethos: Full-time tour leaders and a company with more than 35 years experience. ABTA member. ATOL 0743.
Types of tours: Birdwatching and natural history tours as well as cruises to Antarctica.
Destinations: 80 tours to all seven continents.
New for 2002: Azores, Egypt, Estonia.
Brochure from: 29 Straight Mile, Romsey, Hampshire, SO51 9BB; 01794 519445; (Fax)01794 523544. e-mail: ornitholidays@compuserve.com www.ornitholidays.co.uk

SPEYSIDE WILDLIFE

Company ethos: Expert leaders, personal attention and a sense of fun - it's your holiday. ATOL 4259.
Types of tours: Experts in Scotland and leaders worldwide - birdwatching, mammals and whale watching.
Destinations: Speyside and the Scottish Islands, Scandinavia, the Arctic, Europe, Middle East, N America.
New for 2002: Spitsbergen, Poland, Bears in Finland, Oman, S.Africa.
Brochure from: 9 Upper Mall, Grampian Road, Aviemore, Inverness-shire, PH22 1RH; (Tel/fax)01479 812498. e-mail: enquiries@speysidewildlife.co.uk www.speysidewildlife.co.uk

SUNBIRD

Company ethos: Enjoyable birdwatching tours led by full-time professional leaders. ATOL no 3003
Types of tours: Birdwatching, Birds & Music, Birds & History, Birds & Butterflies, Sunbirder events.
Destinations: Worldwide.
New for 2002: Oman, South Korea, South Africa total eclipse tour.
Brochure from: PO Box 76, Sandy, Bedfordshire, SG19 1DF; 01767 682969; (Fax)01767 692481. e-mail: sunbird@sunbird.demon.co.uk www.sunbird.demon.co.uk

THE BIRD ID COMPANY

Company ethos: Expert leaders with skills in bird identification, fieldcraft and teaching all aspects of birding.
Types of tours: Daily tour specialists, weekend breaks. Five day migration tours. Rare bird tours. Maximum six participants.
Destinations: Norfolk, France, Greece, Fair Isle.
New for 2002: Specialist days on warblers and raptors.

Brochure from: 37 Westgate, Warham Road, Binham, Norfolk, NR21 0DQ; 01328 830617; (Fax)01328 830020. www.birdtour.co.uk

THE TRAVELLING NATURALIST

Company ethos: Friendly, easy-going, expertly-led birdwatching and wildlife tours.
Types of tours: Tours include birds and history, birds and bears, whale-watching, birds and flowers.
Destinations: Worldwide, with Latin America and Spain our specialities.
New for 2002: Azores, Corsica, Guyana, Hawaii, Mongolia, Syria & Lebanon, Tanzania, Vancouver & Rockies.
Brochure from: PO Box 3141, Dorchester, Dorset, DT1 2XD; 01305 267994; (Fax)01305 265506.

WORLDWIDE JOURNEYS

Company ethos: Shared enjoyment of the natural world.
Types of tours: Relaxed wildlife and birdwatching holidays with friendly groups and Britain's most experienced leaders.
Destinations: 26 locations in Africa, Australasia, North and South America, India, Indian Ocean and Europe.
New for 2002: Australia, Bhutan, Arizona, Texas, Portugal, Romania, Pyrenees, Crete, Islay, Isle of Man.
Brochure from: Worldwide Journeys and Expeditions, 27 Vanston Place, London, SW6 1AZ; 020 7386 4676; (Fax)020 7381 0836. e-mail: wwj@wjournex.demon.co.uk

WILDLIFE WORLDWIDE

Company ethos: Specialist wildlife consultants ensure the finest wildlife holidays.
Types of tours: Tailor-made wildlife holidays and small group departures, accommodating individuals, couples and specialist groups. Polar and South Sea expedition voyages.
Destinations: Worldwide.
New for 2002: New lodges and itineraries.
Brochure from: Chameleon House, 162 Selsdon Rd, South Croydon, Surrey, CR2 6PJ; 020 8667 9158; (Fax)020 8667 1960. e-mail: sales@wildlifeworldwide.com www.wildlifeworldwide.com

WILDWINGS

Company ethos: Superb value holidays led by expert guides.
Types of tours: Birdwatching holidays, whale and dolphin watching holidays, wildlife cruises, ecovolunteers.
Destinations: Europe, Arctic, Asia, The Americas, Antarctica, Africa, Trinidad and Tobago.
Brochure from: 577-579 Fishponds Road, Fishponds, Bristol, BS16 3AF; 0117 9658333; (Fax)0117 9375681. e-mail: wildinfo@wildwings.co.uk

OPTICAL MANUFACTURERS & IMPORTERS

CARL ZEISS LTD

Company ethos: World renowned, high quality performance and innovative optical products.
Product lines: Product ranges of stabilised, Victory, Dialyt, compacts and binoculars and Diascope telescopes.
Address: PO Box 78, Woodfield Road, Welwyn Garden City, Hertfordshire, AL7 1LU; 01707 871350; (Fax)01707 871287. e-mail: binos@zeiss.co.uk www.zeiss.co.uk

CT DISTRIBUTION

Company ethos: Distributor of Manfrotto tripods and accessories for the wildlife and birding specialist. National dealer network.
Product lines: Manfrotto tripods, heads and accessories. Available as separates or kits, suitable for video, scope and camera use.
Address: PO Box 3128, Tilbrook, Milton Keynes, MK7 8JB; 01908 646444; (Fax)01908 646434.
e-mail: sales@ctdistribution

INTROPHOTO

Company ethos: Experienced importer of photo and optical products.
Product lines: Summit (binoculars), Velbon (tripods), Kenko (range of telescopes).
Address: Unit 1, Priors Way, Maidenhead,Berkshire, SL6 2HR; 01628 674411; (Fax)01628 771055. e-mail: jane@introphoto.co.uk www.introphoto.co.uk

LEICA CAMERA LTD

Company ethos: Professional advice from Leica factory-trained staff.
Product lines: Trinovid binoculars, eight full size and six compacts. Televid spotting scopes, four models available with a choice of four eyepieces and a photo-adaptor to attach a camera. Minox binoculars, nine

models full size and compacts, two Minox monoculars, plus four new spotting scopes and three eyepieces.
Address: Davy Avenue, Knowlhill, Milton Keynes, MK5 8LB; 01908 666663;(Fax)01908 671316.
e-mail: info@leica-camera.co.uk
www.leica-camera.com

SOVIET BAZAAR LTD

Company ethos: Affordable introduction to birdwatching. Fast, efficient, friendly service with replacement or refund policy.
Product lines: Siore optics, variable powered spotting scopes. These are lightweight, compact and very affordable with competitive optical performance
Address: Clachan Beag, Castlebay, Isle of Barra, Western Isles, HS9 5XD; 01871 810832;(Fax)01871 810911.
e-mail: halstudio@aol.com
www.sovietbazaar.co.uk

MARCHWOOD

Company ethos: Quality European optics offering outstanding value for money.
Product lines: Kahles binoculars from Austria, Meopta telescopes from the Czech Republic and Eschenbach Optik binoculars from Germany.
Address: Unit 308 Cannock Ent Centre, Walkers Rise, Hednesford, Staffs WS12 5QU; 01543 424255.

OPTICRON

Company ethos: To provide the highest quality, value-for-money optics for today's birdwatcher.
Product lines: Official importers of Opticron and Optolyth binoculars and telescopes, plus mounting systems and accessories.
Address: PO Box 370, Luton LU4 8YR; 01582 726 522; (Fax)01582 273559.
e-mail: info@opticron.co.uk

SWAROVSKI OPTIK

Company ethos: Constantly improving on what is good in terms of products, and committed to conservation world-wide.
Product lines: ATS 65 spotting scope, the latest addition to a market-leading range of telescopes and binoculars. Swarovski tripods also available.
Address: Perrywood Business Park, Salfords, Surrey RH1 5JQ. 01737 856812; (Fax)01737 856885. e-mail: christine.percy@swarovski.com

VICKERS SPORTS OPTICS

Company ethos: Importers of world renowned products from American companies Bausch & Lomb and Bushnell.
Product lines: High performance Bausch & Lomb binoculars (including compacts) and telescopes. The extensive Bushnell list includes market-leading Natureview range and Glasses-On models for spectacle wearers. New models expected in 2002.
Address: Vickers Sports Optics, Unit 9, 35 Revenge Road, Lords Wood, Kent ME5 8DW; 01634 201284; (Fax)01634 201286.
e-mail: info@jjvickers.co.uk
www.jjvickers.co.uk

OPTICAL DEALERS

South East England

In focus

Company ethos: The binocular and telescope specialists, offering customers informed advice at birdwatching venues throughout the country. Main sponsor, British Birdwatching Fair.
Viewing facilities: Available at all shops (contact your local outlet), or at field events (10am-4pm) at bird reserves (see *Bird Watching* magazine or website www.at-infocus.co.uk for calendar).
Optical stock: Most leading makes of binoculars and telescopes, plus own-brand Delta range of binoculars and tripods.
Non-optical stock: Wide range of tripods, clamps and other accessories. Repair service available.
Opening times: Vary - please contact local shop or website before travelling.
ST ALBANS: Bowmans Farm, London Colney, St Albans, Herts AL2 1BB; 01727 827799; (Fax)01727 827766.
SOUTH WEST LONDON: WWT The Wetland Centre, Queen Elizabeth's Walk, Barnes, London SW13 9WT: 020 8409 4433.

KAY OPTICAL

Company ethos: Unrivalled expertise, experience and service since 1962.
Viewing facilities: At Morden. Also field-days every weekend at reserves in South.
Optical stock: All leading makes of binoculars and

telescopes stocked. Also giant binoculars and astronomical.
Non-optical stock: Tripods, clamps etc.
Opening times: Mon-Sat (9am-5pm) closed (1-2pm).
Address: 89(B) London Road, Morden, Surrey, SM4 5HP; 020 8648 8822; (Fax)020 8687 2021.
e-mail: info@kayoptical.co.uk www.kayoptical.co.uk and www.bigbinoculars.co.uk

LONDON CAMERA EXCHANGE

Company ethos: To supply good quality optical equipment at a competitive price, helped by knowlegeable staff.
Viewing facilities: In shop and at local shows. Contact local branch.
Optical stock: All leading makes of binoculars and scopes.
Non-optical stock: All main brands of photo, digital and video equipment.
Opening times: Mon-Sat (9am-5.30pm).
FAREHAM: 135 West Street, Fareham, Hampshire, PO16 0DU; 01329 236441; (Fax)01329 823294; e-mail: fareham@lcegroup.co.uk
GUILDFORD: 8/9 Tunsgate, Guildford, Surrey, GU1 2DH; 01483 504040; (Fax)01483 538216; e-mail: guildford@lcegroup.co.uk
PORTSMOUTH: 40 Kingswell Path, Cascados, Portsmouth, PO1 4RR; 023 9283 9933; (Fax)023 9283 9955; e-mail: portsmouth@lcegroup.co.uk
READING: 7 Station Road, Reading, Berkshire, RG1 1LG; 0118 959 2149; (Fax)0118 959 2197; e-mail: reading@lcegroup.co.uk
SOUTHAMPTON: 10 High Street, Southampton, Hampshire, SO14 2DH; 023 8022 1597; (Fax)023 8023 3838; e-mail: southampton@lcegroup.co.uk
STRAND, LONDON: 98 The Strand, London, WC2R 0AG; 020 7379 0200; (Fax)020 7379 6991;
e-mail: strand@lcegroup.co.uk
WINCHESTER: 15 The Square, Winchester, Hants, SO23 9ES; 01962 866203; (Fax)01962 840978; e-mail: winchester@lcegroup.co.uk

South West England

ACE CAMERAS

Company ethos: To be the best - service, price and stock.
Viewing facilities: Bird of prey at 100 yds, Leica test card to check quality.
Optical stock: All the top brands, including Questar.
Non-optical stock: All the best tripods and an array of optical related accessories.
Opening times: Mon-Sat (8:45am-6pm).
Address: 16 Green Street, Bath, BA1 2JZ; 01225 466364; (fax)01225 469761. e-mail: aceoptics@balzjz.freeserve.co.uk

LONDON CAMERA EXCHANGE

(See entry in South East England).
BATH: 13 Cheap Street, Bath, Avon, BA1 1NB; 01225 462234; (Fax)01225 480334.
e-mail: bath@lcegroup,co.uk
BOURNEMOUTH: 95 Old Christchurch Road, Bournemouth, Dorset, BH1 1EP; 01202 556549; (Fax)01202 293288; e-mail: bournemouth@lcegroup.co.uk
BRISTOL: 53 The Horsefair, Bristol, BS1 3JP; 0117 927 6185; (Fax)0117 925 8716; e-mail: bristol.horsefair@lcegroup.co.uk
EXETER: 174 Fore Street, Exeter, Devon, EX4 3AX;01392 279024/438167; (Fax)01392 426988.
e-mail: exeter@lcegroup.co.uk
PAIGNTON: 71 Hyde Road, Paignton, Devon, TQ4 5BP;01803 553077; (Fax)01803 664081. e-mail: paignton@lcegroup.co.uk
PLYMOUTH: 10 Frankfort Gate, Plymouth, Devon, PL1 1QD; 01752 668894; (Fax) 01752 604248. e-mail: plymouth@lcegroup.co.uk
TAUNTON: 6 North Street, Taunton, Somerset, TA1 1LH; 01823 259955; (Fax)01823 338001. e-mail: taunton@lcegroup.co.uk

Eastern England

A.R.HAWKINS (NORTHAMPTON)

Company ethos: We appreciate you may need advice with your purchase. All staff are birders and fully conversant with optics.
Viewing facilities: Good viewing facilities.
Optical stock: All the top names, Leica, Zeiss, Minox, Opticron, Kowa, plus a full binocular-repair service.
Opening times: Mon-Sat (9am-5.30pm).
Address: 9 Marefair , Northampton, NN1 1SR; 01604 639674.

In focus

(see entry in South East England).
NORFOLK: Main Street, Titchwell, Nr Kings Lynn, Norfolk PE31 8BB; 01485 210101.
RUTLAND: Anglian Water Birdwatching Centre, Egleton

Reserve, Rutland Water, Rutland LE15 8BT; 01572 770656.

LONDON CAMERA EXCHANGE

(See entry in South East England).
LINCOLN; 6 Silver Street, Lincoln, LN2 1DY; 01522 514131; (Fax)01522 537480; e-mail: lincoln@lcegroup.co.uk
NOTTINGHAM: 7 Pelham Street, Nottingham, NG1 2EH; 0115 941 7486; (Fax)0115 952 0547; e-mail: nottingham@lcegroup.co.uk

WAREHOUSE EXPRESS

Company ethos: Mail order and website.
Viewing facilities: By appointment only.
Optical stock: All major brands including Leica, Swarvoski, Opticron, Kowa, Zeiss, Nikon, Bushnell, Slik, Canon, Minolta etc.
Non-optical stock: All related accessories including hides, tripods and window mounts etc.
Opening times: Mon-Fri (9am-5.30pm).
Address: PO Box 659, Norwich, Norfolk, NR2 1UJ; 01603 626222; (Fax)01603 626446.
www.warehouseexpress.com

West Midlands

BIRDNET OPTICS LTD

Company ethos: To provide the birdwatcher with the best value for money on optics, books. Plus rare bird information on pagers and mobile phones.
Viewing facilities: Clear views to distant hills for long-range comparison and wide variety of textures and edges for clarity and resolution comparison.
Optical stock: Most leading binocular and telescope ranges. If we do not have it we will endeavour to get it for you.
Non-optical stock: Books, videos, CDs, audio tapes, tripods, hide clamps, accessories and clothing.
Opening times: Mon-Sat (9:30am-5:30pm). Sundays by appointment only.
Address: 5 London Road, Buxton, Derbyshire, SK17 9PA;01298 71844; (Fax)01298 73052.
e-mail: paulflint@birdnet.co.uk
www.birdnet.co.uk

FOCUS OPTICS

Company ethos: Friendly, expert service. Top quality instruments. No 'grey imports'.
Viewing facilities: Our own pool and nature reserve with feeding stations.
Optical stock: Full range of leading makes of binoculars and telescopes.
Non-optical stock: Waterproof clothing, fleeces, walking boots and shoes, bird food and feeders. Books, videos, walking poles.
Opening times: Mon-Sat (9am-5pm). Some bank-holidays.
Address: Church Lane, Corley, Coventry, CV7 8BA; 01676 540501/542476; (Fax) 01676 540930.
e-mail: focopt1@aol.com
www.focusoptics.co.uk

FORESIGHT OPTICAL

Company ethos: Personal service is our pleasure. Quality optical products - no 'grey imports'.
Viewing facilities: Showroom with viewing facilities.
Optical stock: Most popular brands stocked. New, secondhand and ex-demonstration stock for sale. Part exchange undertaken. Mail order available, credit cards accepted and credit facilities.
Non-optical stock: Night vision equipment, magnifiers, microscopes, tripods and accessories.
Opening times: Mon-Fri (8:30am-5:30pm).
Address: 13 New Road, Banbury, Oxon, OX16 9PN; 01295 264365.

In focus

(See entry in South East England).
GLOUCS: WWT Slimbridge, Gloucestershire GL2 7BT; 01453 890978.

LONDON CAMERA EXCHANGE

(See entry in South East England).
CHELTENHAM: 10-12 The Promenade, Cheltenham, Gloucestershire, GL50 1LR; 01242 519851; (Fax)01242 576771; e-mail: cheltenham@lcegroup.co.uk
CHESTERFIELD: 1A South Street, Chesterfield, Derbyshire, S40 1QZ; 01246 211891; (Fax)01246 211563; e-mail: chesterfield@lcegroup.co.uk
DERBY: 17 Sadler Gate, Derby, Derbyshire, DE1 3NH; 01332 348644; (Fax)01332 369136;
e-mail: derby@lcegroup.co.uk
GLOUCESTER: 12 Southgate Street, Gloucester, GL1 2DH; 01452 304513; (Fax)01452 387309; e-mail: gloucester@lcegroup.co.uk
LEAMINGTON: Clarendon Avenue, Leamington, Warwickshire, CV32 5PP; 01926 886166; (Fax)01926 887611; e-mail: leamington@lcegroup.co.uk
SALISBURY: 6 Queen Street,

Salisbury, Wiltshire, SP1 1EY; 01722 335436; (Fax)01722 411670; e-mail: salisbury@lcegroup.co.uk
WORCESTER: 8 Pump Street, Worcester, WR1 2QT; 01905 22314; (Fax)01905 724585; e-mail: worcester@lcegroup.co.uk

Northern England

FOCALPOINT

Company ethos: Friendly advice by well-trained staff, competitive prices, no 'grey imports'.
Viewing facilities: Fantastic open countryside for superb viewing from the shop, plenty of wildlife. Parking for up to 20 cars.
Optical stock: All leading brands of binoculars and telescopes from stock, plus many pre-owned binoculars and telescopes available.
Non-optical stock: Bird books, outdoor clothing, boots, tripods plus full range of Skua products etc. available from stock.
Opening times: Mon-Sat (9:30am-5pm).
Address: Marbury House Farm, Bentleys Farm Lane, Higher Whitley, Warrington, Cheshire, WA4 4QW; 01925 730399; (Fax)01925 730368. e-mail: focalpoint@dial.pipex.com www.fpoint.co.uk

In focus

(see entry in South East England).
LANCASHIRE: WWT Martin Mere, Burscough, Ormskirk, Lancs L40 0TA; 01704 897020.
WEST YORKSHIRE: Westleigh House Office Est, Wakefield Road, Denby Dale, West Yorks HD8 8QJ; 01484 864729.

LONDON CAMERA EXCHANGE

(See entry in South East England).
CHESTER: 9 Bridge Street Row, CH1 1NW;01244 326531
MANCHESTER: 37 Parker Street, Picadilly, M1 4AJ; 0161 236 5819.

PENNINE BINOCULAR AND TELESCOPE CENTRE

Company ethos: Experienced staff are on hand to help you select the optics which are right for you.
Viewing facilities: First floor vantage point.
Optical stock: Leading brands of binoculars and telescopes: Leica, Swarovski, Opticron, Kowa, Zeiss, Optolyth, Kahles.
Non-optical stock: Tripods, clamps, photographic equipment.
Opening times: Mon, Wed, Thur, Fri, (9am-5.30 pm), Sat (9am-5pm).
Address: Binocular House, 74 Drake Street, Rochdale, Lancs, OL16 1PQ; 01706 524965, (Fax)01706 646567. www.penninephoto.f9.co.uk

Scotland

DEAYTON PHOTOGRAPHICS LTD

Company ethos: Expert advice and friendly service. Serving Paisley's photographers since 1965.
Viewing facilities: Uninterrupted view outside shop door for ½ mile or more.
Optical stock: Wide range of binoculars and telescopes. Pentax, Helios, Opticron, Bushnell, etc.
Non-optical stock: Full range of SLR, compact and digital cameras and accessories from all leading manufacturers. 1-hour 35mm and APS developing and printing.
Opening times: Mon-Fri (9am-5:30pm), Sat (9am-5pm).
Address: 24 Lawn Street, Paisley, Renfrewshire, PA1 1HF; 0141 889 6229; (Fax)0141 887 7695. www.deayton.co.uk

BIRD RESERVES AND OBSERVATORIES

Rooks react as a Grey Heron flies over the Mount Ephraim rookery – recorded by Mark James of Kent.

Bedfordshire

Key to sites:
1. Harrold Odell Country Park
2 Martson Vale Millenium Country Park
3. Priory Marina Country Park

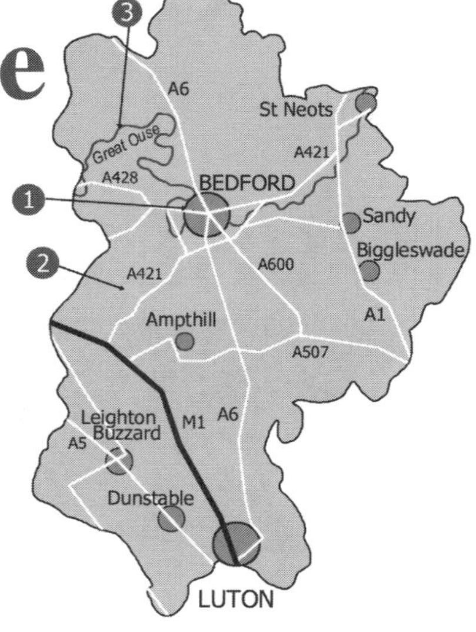

HARROLD ODELL COUNTRY PARK

Location: SP 960 570. 10 miles NW of Bedford off the Harrold to Carlton road.
Access: Open at all times.
Facilities: Visitor centre. Restaurant and cafe open Wed-Sun (10am-4.30pm). Hide.
Public transport: None.
Habitat: Lakes (one with island), lagoons, osier beds, meadows adjacent River Great Ouse, woodland.
Key birds: *Summer*: Breeding Reed and Sedge Warblers, Lesser Whitethroat. Passage waders, Common and Black Terns, late summer Hobby. *Winter*: Wildfowl, Water Rail.
Contact: Bill Thwaites,
Country Park, Carlton Road, Harrold, Bedford, MK43 7DS. 01234 720016.

MARSTON VALE MILLENNIUM COUNTRY PARK

Marston Vale Trust (Regd Charity No 1069229).
Location: SW of Bedford off A421 at Marston Moretaine. Only five mins from J13 of M1.
Access: Park and forest centre open seven days. Summer 10am-6pm, winter 10am-4pm. No dogs in reserve, reserve path unsurfaced.
Facilities: Cafe bar, gift shop, art gallery, exhibition. Free parking.
Public transport: Marston Vale Line - trains direct from Millbrook and Stewartby station.
Habitat: Lake - 284 acres/freshwater marsh (man made), reedbed, hawthorn scrub and grassland.
Key birds: *Winter:* Iceland and Glaucous Gulls (regular), gull roost, wildfowl, Great Crested Grebe. Spring: Passage waders and terns (Black Tern, Arctic Tern, Garganey. *Summer:* Nine species of breeding warblers, Hobby, Turtle Dove, Nightingale. *Autumn:* Passage waders and terns. Rarities: White-winged Black Tern, Laughing Gull, divers, Manx Shearwater, Bittern.
Contact:
Forest Centre, Station Road, Marston Moretaine, Beds, MK43 0PR. 01234 767037.
e-mail: info@marstonvale.org
www.marstonvale.org

PRIORY MARINA COUNTRY PARK

Bedford Borough Council.
Location: TL 071 495. 1.5 miles from Bedford town centre. Signposted A428 and A421.
Access: Open at all times.
Facilities: Toilets, visitor centre, hides, nature trail. Provision for disabled visitors.
Public transport: Stagecoach bus service 103 passes Barkers Lane (main) entrance.
Habitat: Lakes, reedbeds, scrub/plantations, meadows adjoining River Great Ouse.
Key birds: *Winter*: Wildfowl, Water Rail, bunting roosts. *Summer*: Breeding warblers, terns. *Passage*: Waders, terns, raptors, hirundines, Swift.
Contact: Errol Newman,
Wardens Office, Visitor Centre, Priory CP, Barkers Lane, Bedford, MK41 9SH. 01234 211182.

Berkshire

Key to sites:

1. Dinton Pastures Country Park
2. Lavell's Lake
3. Moor Green Lakes

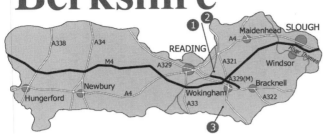

DINTON PASTURES COUNTRY PARK

Wokingham District Council.
Location: SU 784 718. E of Reading, off B3030 between Hurst and Winnersh.
Access: Open all year, dawn to dusk.
Facilities: Hides, information centre, car park, café, toilets. Suitable for wheelchairs.
Public transport: Information not available.
Habitat: Mature gravel pits and banks of River Loddon.
Key birds: Kingfisher, Water Rail, Little Ringed Plover, Common Tern, Nightingale. *Winter*: Wildfowl (inc. Goldeneye, Wigeon, Teal, Gadwall).
Contact: Dave Webster, Ranger,
Dinton Pastures Country Park, Davis Street, Hurst, Berks. 0118 934 2016.

LAVELL'S LAKE

Wokingham District Council.
Location: SU 781 729. Via Sandford Lane off B3030 between Hurst and Winnersh, E of Reading.
Access: Dawn to dusk. No permit required.
Facilities: Hides.
Public transport: Information not available.
Habitat: Gravel pits, two wader scapes, rough grassland, marshy area, between River Loddon and Emm Brook.
Key birds: Sparrowhawk. *Summer*: Garganey, Common Tern, Redshank, Lapwing, Hobby. Passage waders. *Winter*: Green Sandpiper, ducks (inc. Smew), Bittern.
Contact: Dave Webster, Ranger,
Dinton Pastures Country Park, Davis Street, Hurst, Berks. 0118 934 2016.

MOOR GREEN LAKES

Blackwater Valley Countryside Service.
Location: SU 805 628. Main access and parking off Lower Sandhurst Road, Finchampstead. Alternatively, Rambler's car park, Mill Lane, Sandhurst (SU 820 619).
Access: Car parks open dawn-dusk. Two bird hides open to members of the Moor Green Lakes Group (contact us for details). Dogs on leads. Site can be used by people in wheelchairs though surface not particularly suitable.
Facilities: Two bird hides, footpaths around site, Blackwater Valley Long-distance Path passes through site.
Public transport: Nearest bus stop, Finchampstead (approx 1.5 miles from main entrance). Local bus companies - Stagecoach Hants & Surrey, tel 01256 464501, First Beeline & Londonlink, tel 01344 424938.
Habitat: Thirty-six hectares (90 acres) in total. Three lakes with gravel islands, beaches and scrapes. River Blackwater, grassland, surrounded by willow, ash, hazel and thorn hedgerows.
Key birds: *Spring/summer*: Redshank, Little Ringed Plover, Sand Martin, Willow Warbler, and of particular interest, a flock of Goosander. Also Whitethroat, Sedge Warbler, Common Sandpiper, Common Tern, Dunlin and Black Terns. Lapwings breed on site and several sightings of Red Kite. *Winter*: Ruddy Duck, Wigeon, Teal, Gadwall.
Contact:
Blackwater Valley Countryside Service, Ash Lock Cottage, Government Road, Aldershot, Hants, GU11 2PS. 01276 686615.
e-mail: enquiries@blackwatervalleyservice.com
www.blackwatervalleyservice.com http://members.aol.com/berksbirds/moorgreen.htm

Buckinghamshire

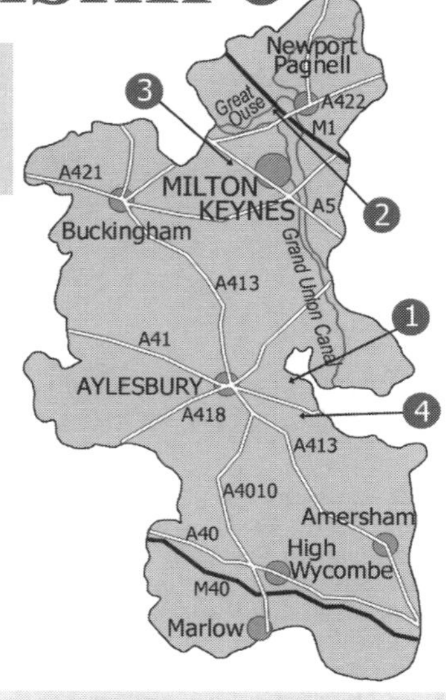

Key to sites:
1. College Lake Wildlife Centre
2. Hanson Environmental Study Centre
3. Stony Stratford Wildlife Conservation Area
4. Weston Turville

COLLEGE LAKE WILDLIFE CENTRE

Berks, Bucks & Oxon Wildlife Trust with Castle Cement (Pitstone) Ltd.
Location: SP 935 139. On B488 Tring/Ivinghoe road at Bulbourne.
Access: Open daily 10am-5pm. Permits available on site or from Trust HQ.
Facilities: Hides, nature trails, visitor centre, toilets.
Public transport: None.
Habitat: Marsh area, lake, islands, shingle.
Key birds: *Spring/summer*: Breeding Lapwing, Redshank, Little Ringed Plover. Hobby. Passage waders inc. Green Sandpiper.
Contact: Graham Atkins,
College Lake Wildlife Centre, Upper Icknield Way, Bulbourne, Tring, Herts, HP23 5QG. H: 01296 662890.

HANSON ENVIRONMENTAL STUDY CENTRE

Milton Keynes Council.
Location: SP 842 429. Two miles N of central Milton Keynes. Entrance almost opposite Proud Perch public house on Wolverton to Newport Pagnell road.
Access: Open daily dawn-dusk. Day or annual permit from warden – no access without permission. No dogs. Please ring in advance.
Facilities: Three hides (two lakeside, one woodland) for keyholders.
Public transport: None.
Habitat: Lake (with islands), lagoons, meadows, woodland, ponds.
Key birds: *Spring/summer*: Breeding warblers, wildfowl and waders, terns, hirundines, heronry, Hobby, Barn Owl. *Winter*: Wildfowl, Cormorant, Water Rail, Long-eared Owl (occasional), Siskin.
Contact: Andrew Stevenson,
Hanson Environmental Study Centre, Wolverton Road, Great Linford, Milton Keynes, Bucks, MK14 5AH. 01908 604810.

STONY STRATFORD WILDLIFE CONSERVATION AREA

Berks, Bucks & Oxon Wildlife Trust.
Location: SP 786 411. Off Stony Stratford loop road (A5).
Access: Open daily.
Facilities: Public footpath. Public hide.
Public transport: None.
Habitat: Wet riverside meadow, lakes, islands.
Key birds: *Summer*: Breeding Redshank. Passage waders. *Winter*: Wildfowl.
Contact: Trust HQ, 01865 775476.

WESTON TURVILLE

Berks, Bucks & Oxon Wildlife Trust.
Location: SP 859 095. From Wendover take A413 north; turn right after one mile opp Marquis of Granby pub; park in lay-by after 600 yards and reserve is on right.
Access: Public access on perimeter path.
Facilities: Hide.
Public transport: None.
Habitat: Reservoir, large reed fen.
Key birds: Water Rail. *Summer*; Breeding wablers. *Winter*: Wildfowl and gulls.
Contact: Trust HQ, 01865 775 476.

Cambridgeshire

Key to sites:
1. Brampton Wood
2. Fowlmere
3. Grafham Water
4. Hayley Wood
5. Nene Washes
6. Ouse Washes
7. Paxton Pits
8. Wicken Fen

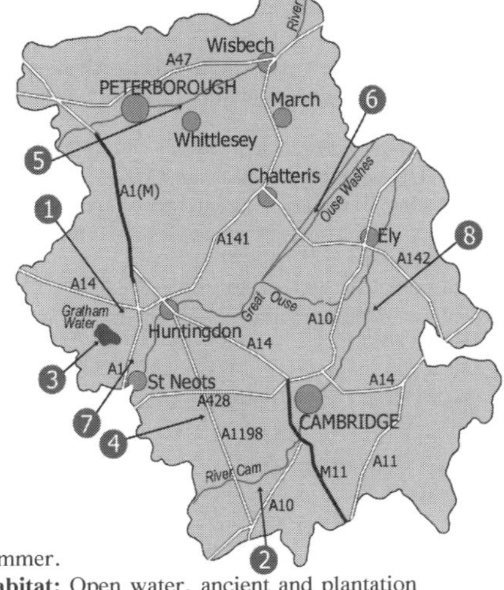

BRAMPTON WOOD

Beds, Cambs & Northants Wildlife Trust.
Location: TL 185 698. Two miles E of Grafham village on N side of road to Brampton. From A14 take main road S from Ellington.
Access: Open daily.
Facilities: Car park, interpretative shelter.
Habitat: SSSI. Primarily ash and field maple with hazel coppice.
Key birds: *Summer*: Breeding Grasshopper Warbler, Nightingale, Spotted Flycatcher, Woodcock; all three woodpeckers. *Winter*: thrushes. **Contact:** Trust HQ, 01233 712412.

FOWLMERE

RSPB (East Anglia Office).
Location: TL 407 461. Turn off A10 Cambridge to Royston road by Shepreth and follow sign.
Access: Access at all times along marked trail.
Facilities: None.
Habitat: Reedbeds, meres, woodland, scrub.
Key birds: *Summer*: Nine breeding warblers. Corn Bunting roost. *All Year:* Water Rail, Kingfisher. *Winter*: Snipe, raptors.
Contact: Doug Radford, RSPB, Manor Farm, High Street, Fowlmere, Royston, Herts, SG8 7SH. Tel/fax 01763 208978.

GRAFHAM WATER

Wildlife Trust for Beds, Cambs & Northants.
Location: TL 143 671. Follow signs for Grafham Water from A1 at Buckden or A14 at Ellington. Nature reserve entrance is from Mander car park, W of Perry village.
Access: Open all year. Permits required for settlement lagoons only. Dogs barred in wildlife garden only, on leads elsewhere.
Facilities: Six bird hides in nature reserve. Two in wildlife garden accessible to wheelchairs. Cycle track accessible to wheelchairs. Visitor centre with restaurant, shop and toilets. Disabled parking. Wildlife cabin open weekends in summer.
Habitat: Open water, ancient and plantation woodland, grassland.
Key birds: *Winter*: Wildfowl, gulls. *Spring/ summer*: Breeding Nightingale, Reed, Willow and Sedge Warblers, Common and Black Terns. *Autumn*: Passage waders.
Contact: Jo Calvert, Grafham Water Nature Reserve, c/o The Lodge, West Perry, Huntingdon, Cambs, PE28 0BX. 01480 811075. e-mail: grafham@cix.co.uk
www.wildlifetrust.org.uk/bcnp

HAYLEY WOOD

Beds, Cambs & Northants Wildlife Trust.
Location: TL 292 529. Between Cambridge and Sandy. Take B1046 W out of Longstowe for one and a half miles and park opposite water tower. Walk up old track to wood.
Access: Open at all times.
Facilities: Interpretative centre.
Habitat: Ancient semi-natural woodland. Active coppice cycle and derelict coppice.
Key birds: Woodland species inc. Nightingale, Blackcap, Garden Warbler, Nuthatch, Treecreeper, Marsh Tit, Woodcock, woodpeckers.

NENE WASHES

RSPB (East Anglia Office).
Location: TL 290 995. Six miles E of Peterborough, off B1040 to Thorney, one mile N

of Whittlesey.
Access: Open at all times on droves and south barrier bank. Group visits by arrangement. No access to fields.
Public transport: Bus and trains to Whittlesey.
Habitat: Wet grassland with ditches. Frequently flooded.
Key birds: *Spring/early summer*: Breeding waders, including Black-tailed Godwit, duck, including Garganey, Marsh Harrier and Hobby. *Winter*: Waterfowl including Bewick's Swan and Pintail, Barn Owl, Hen Harrier.
Contact: Charlie Kitchin, RSPB Nene Washes, 21a East Delph, Whittlesey, Cambs, PE7 1RH. 01733 205140.

OUSE WASHES

RSPB (East Anglia Office).
Location: TL 471 861. Between Chatteris and March on A141, take B1093 to Manea and follow signs. Reserve office and visitor centre located off Welches Dam.
Access: Access at all times from visitor centre (open every day except Christmas Day and Boxing Day). Welches Dam to public hides approached by marked paths behind boundary bank. No charge. Dogs to be kept on leads at all times. Disabled access to Welches Dam hide, 350 yards from car park.
Facilities: Car park and toilets. Visitor centre. Ten hides overlooking the reserve: nearest 350 yards from visitor centre (with disabled access) and furthest one mile from visitor centre. Boardwalk over pond – good for dragonflies.
Public transport: No public transport to reserve. Train station at Manea – three miles away.
Habitat: Lowland wet grassland – seasonally flooded. Open pool systems in front of some hides, particularly Stockdale's hide.
Key birds: *Summer:* Around 70 species breed including Black-tailed Godwit, Lapwing, Redshank, Snipe, Shoveler, Gadwall, Garganey and Spotted Crake. Also Hobby and Marsh Harrier. *Autumn*: Passage waders including Wood and Green Sandpipers, Spotted Redshank, Greenshank, Little Stint, plus terns and Marsh and Hen Harrier. *Winter:* Large numbers of Bewick's and Whooper Swans, Wigeon, Teal, Shoveler, Pintail, Pochard.
Contact: Cliff Carson, (Site Manager), Ouse Washes Reserve, Welches Dam, Manea, March, Cambs, PE15 0NF. 01354 680212
e-mail: cliff.carson@rspb.org.uk

PAXTON PITS

Huntingdonshire District Council.
Location: TL 197 629. Access from A1 at Little Paxton, two miles N of St Neots.
Access: No charge. Open 24 hours. Visitor centre manned at weekends. Dogs allowed under control. Heron trail suitable for wheelchairs during summer.
Facilities: One toilet in visitor centre (open weekends), two bird hides (always open), marked nature trails.
Public transport: Stagecoach X46. Runs between Huntingdon-Bedford. Tel 0870 608 2608.
Habitat: Grassland, scrub, lakes.
Key birds: *Spring/summer*: Nightingale, Kingfisher, Common Tern, Sparrowhawk, Hobby, Grasshopper, Sedge and Reed Warblers, Lesser Whitethroat. *Winter*: Smew, Goldeneye, Goosander, Gadwall, Pochard.
Contact: Ron Elloway, Ranger, The Visitor Centre, High Street, Little Paxton, St Neots, Cambs, PE19 6ET. 01480 406795.
e-mail: tony@howfreeserve.co.uk
www.paxton-pits.org.uk

WICKEN FEN

The National Trust.
Location: TL 563 705. Lies 17 miles NE of Cambridge and ten miles S of Ely. From A10 drive E along A1123.
Access: Daily (9am-5pm). Permit required from visitor centre. National Trust members free. Disabled access along approx 0.75 miles boardwalk. Dogs must be on leads.
Facilities: Toilets in car park. Visitor centre with hot/cold drinks, sandwiches at weekends, three nature trails, seven hides.
Public transport: Nearest rail link either Cambridge or Ely. Buses only on Thu and Sun (very restricted service).
Habitat: Open Fen – cut hay fields, sedge beds, grazing marsh – partially flooded wet grassland, reedbed, scrub, woodland.
Key birds: *Spring*: Passage waders and passerines. *Summer*: Marsh Harrier, Long-eared Owl, breeding waders and warblers. *Winter*: Wigeon, Hen Harrier, Merlin.
Contact: Martin Lester, Lode Lane, Wicken, Cambs, CB7 5XP. 01353 720274.
e-mail: awnmdl@smtp.ntrust.org.uk
www.wicken.org.uk

Cheshire

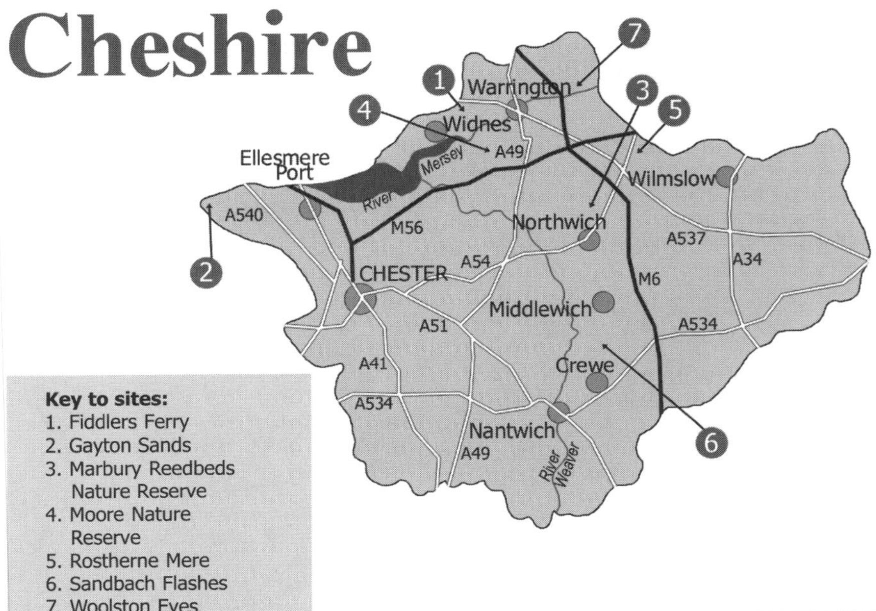

FIDDLERS FERRY

Edison Mission Energy.
Location: SJ 552 853. Off A562 between Warrington and Widnes.
Access: Parking at main gate of power station. Summer (8am-8pm); winter (8am-5pm). For free permit; apply in advance with sae to Manager, Fiddlers Ferry Power Station, Warrington WA5 2UT.
Facilities: Hide, nature trail.
Public transport: None.
Habitat: Lagoons, tidal and non-tidal marshes with phragmites and great reedmace, meadow grassland with small wooded areas.
Key birds: *Summer*: Breeding Oystercatcher, Ringed and Little Ringed Plovers.
Winter: Glaucous, Iceland and Yellow-legged Gulls, Short-eared Owl, Peregrine. Jack Snipe. Recent rarities inc. Black-necked Grebe, Little Egret, Goshawk, Little Crake, Red-necked Phalarope, Pectoral Sandpiper, Hoopoe, Greenish Warbler.
Contact: Keith Massey, 4 Hall Terrace, Great Sankey, Warrington, WA5 3EZ. 01925 721382.

GAYTON SANDS

RSPB (North West England Office).
Location: SJ 275 785. On W side of Wirral, S of Birkenhead. View high tide activity from the Old Baths car park near the Boathouse public house, Parkgate.
Access: Open at all times. Viewing from public footpaths and car parks overlooking saltmarsh. Please do not walk on the saltmarsh, the tides are dangerous.
Facilities: Car park, picnic area, group bookings, guided walks, special events, wheelchair access. Toilets at Parkgate village opposite the Square.
Public transport: Bus – Parkgate every hour. Rail – Neston, two miles.
Habitat: Estuary – saltmarsh, pools, mud and sandflats.
Key birds: *Spring/summer/autumn*: Greenshank, Spotted Redshank, Curlew Sandpiper. *Winter*: Shelduck, Teal, Wigeon, Pintail, Oystercatcher, Black-tailed Godwit, Curlew, Redshank, Merlin, Peregrine, Water Rail, Short-eared Owl.
Contact: Colin E Wells,
Burton Point Farm, Station Road, Burton, Nr Neston, Cheshire, CH64 5SB. 0151 3367681

MARBURY REEDBEDS NATURE RESERVE

Cheshire Wildlife Trust.
Location: SJ 651 768. North of Northwich.
Access: By permit only. The reedbed is viewable from a screen hide at Marbury Country Park which is open at all times.
Facilities: Toilets, hide and nature trails within Marbury Country Park.
Public transport: None.
Habitat: Reedbed and woodland.
Key birds: Waterfowl, Reed and Willow Warbler.
Contact: Cheshire Wildlife Trust, Grebe House, Reaseheath, Nantwich, Cheshire, CS5 6DG. 01270 610180.
e-mail: jhulse@cheshirewt.cix.co.uk
www.wildlifetrust.org.uk/cheshire

MOORE NATURE RESERVE

Waste Recycling Group.
Location: SJ 577 854. Located SW of Warrington. Take A56 towards Chester. At Higher Walton follow signs for Moore village into Moore Lane. Cross swing bridge and park beyond crossroads.
Access: Open all year. Not suitable for disabled.
Facilities: Hides, nature trails.
Public transport: None.
Habitat: Wetland, woodland, grasslands.
Key birds: *Spring/summer*: Breeding wildfowl and waders (including Little Ringer Plover). *Winter*: Wigeon, Gadwall, Goldeneye and waders (including Snipe, Jack Snipe and Green Sandpiper). Excellent for gulls (including Glaucous, Iceland and Mediterranean).
Contact: Miss Estelle Linney, c/o Arpley Landfill Site, Forest Way, Sankey Bridge, Warrington, WA4 6YZ. 01925 444 689.
e-mail: Estelle.Linney@wrg.co.uk

ROSTHERNE MERE

English Nature.
Location: SJ 744 843. Lies N of Knutsford and S of M56 (junction 8).
Access: View from Rostherne churchyard and lanes; no public access, except to A W Boyd Observatory (permits from D A Clarke, 1 Hart Avenue, Sale M33 2JY, tel 0161 973 7122).
Facilities: None.
Public transport: None.
Habitat: Deep lake, woodland, willow bed, pasture.
Key birds: *Winter*: Good range of duck (inc Ruddy Duck and Pintail), gull roost (inc. occasional Iceland and Glaucous). Passage Black Tern.
Contact: Tim Coleshaw, Site Manager, Parks Development Officer, English Nature, Attingham Park, Shrewsbury, SY4 4TW. 01743 709611; fax 01743 709303; e-mail tim.coleshaw@english-nature.org.uk.

SANDBACH FLASHES

Management Committee.
Location: SJ 720 590. Leave M6 at junction 17 for Sandbach.
Access: Elton Hall Flash from new road at SJ 716 595; Foden's Flash from road at SJ 730 614; Watch Lane Flash from car park at SJ 728 608.
Facilities: None.
Public transport: None.
Habitat: Fresh and brackish water, reedbed, carr woodland, inland saltmarsh.
Key birds: Passage waders; nesting and wintering wildfowl; many rarities occur.
Contact: Patrick Whalley, 3 Barracks Lane, Ravensmoor, Nantwich, Cheshire, CW5 8PR. 01270 624420.

WOOLSTON EYES

Woolston Eyes Conservation Group.
Location: SJ 654 888. E of Warrington between the River Mersey and Manchester Ship Canal. Off Manchester Road down Ferry Lane or from Latchford to end of Thelwall Lane.
Access: Open all year. Permits required from Chairman, £5 each (see address below).
Facilities: No toilets or visitor centre. Good hides and elevated hides.
Public transport: Buses along A57 nearest stop to Ferry Lane.
Habitat: Wetland, marsh, scrubland, wildflower meadow areas.
Key birds: Breeding Black-necked Grebe, warblers, all raptors (except Golden Eagle), many duck breeding (most species).
Contact: B R Ankers, Chairman, 9 Lynton Gardens, Appleton, Cheshire, WA4 5ED. 01925 267355. http://home.clara.net/franklinley

Cornwall

BRENEY COMMON

Cornwall Wildlife Trust.
Location: SX 054 610. Three miles S of Bodmin. Take minor road off A390 one mile W of Lostwithiel to Lowertown.
Access: Open at all times but please keep to paths. Disabled access.
Facilities: Wilderness trail.
Public transport: None.
Habitat: Wetland, heath and scrub.
Key birds: Willow Tit, Nightjar, Tree Pipit, Sparrowhawk, Lesser Whitethroat, Curlew.
Contact: Eric Higgs,
Crift Farm, Lanlivery, Bodmin, PL30 5DE. 01208 872702.

BUDE MARSHES

North Cornwall District Council.
Location: SS 208 057. By public footpath beside Bude Canal.
Access: Keep to paths. Public hide.
Facilities: None.
Public transport: None.
Habitat: Reedbed, grassland and pools.
Key birds: *Summer*: Breeding Reed, Sedge and Cetti's Warblers. *Winter*: Wildfowl (inc. Shoveler, Teal, Goosander), Snipe and occasional Bittern. *Late summer/autumn*: Little Egret.
Contact: R Braund,
36 Killerton Road, Bude, Cornwall, EX23 8EN. 01288 353906.

DRIFT RESERVOIR

South West Lakes Trust/Cornwall BWPS.
Location: Three miles W of Penzance on A30 (signposted).
Access: No restrictions (not suitable for disabled).
Facilities: Walk round S side of reserve to the unlocked hide.
Public transport: None.
Habitat: Reservoir, fresh water with muddy margins.
Key birds: *Autumn*: Gulls, ducks, waders plus regular rarities.
Contact: Graham Hobin,
Lower Drift Farmhouse, Buryas Bridge, Drift, Penzance. 01736 362206

HAYLE ESTUARY

RSBP (South West England Office).
Location: SW 550 370. In town of Hayle. Follow signs to Hayle from A30.
Access: Open at all times. No permits required. No admission charges. Dogs on leads please.
Facilities: Eric Grace Memorial Hide at Ryan's Field has disabled parking and viewing. Nearest disabled toilets at Wyevale Garden centre, Lelant, 600 yards W just off the roundabout. No visitor centre but information board at hide.
Public transport: Buses and trains at Hayle.
Habitat: Intertidal mudflats, saltmarsh, lagoon and islands, sandy beaches and sand dunes.
Key birds: *Winter*: Wildfowl, gulls, Kingfisher, Ring-billed Gull, Great Northern Diver. *Spring/summer*: Migrant waders, breeding Shelduck. *Autumn*: Rare waders, often from N America! Terns, gulls.
Contact: Dave Flumm,
RSBP, The Manor Office, Marazion, Cornwall, TR17 0EF. Tel/fax; 01736 711862.

LOVENY RESERVE - COLLIFORD RESERVOIR

Cornwall Birdwatching & Preservation Society.
Location: SX183744. By foot from SW Water Deweymeads car park, A30 E of Bodmin.
Access: Open at all times; access restricted to SW edge of reserve.
Facilities: None.
Public transport: Not known.
Habitat: Wetlands, moorland.
Key birds: Wildfowl (inc. Shoveler, Wigeon, Smew); passage waders can inc. N American species.
Contact: David Conway,
Tregenna, Cooksland, Bodmin, Cornwall, PL31 2AR. 01208 77686.

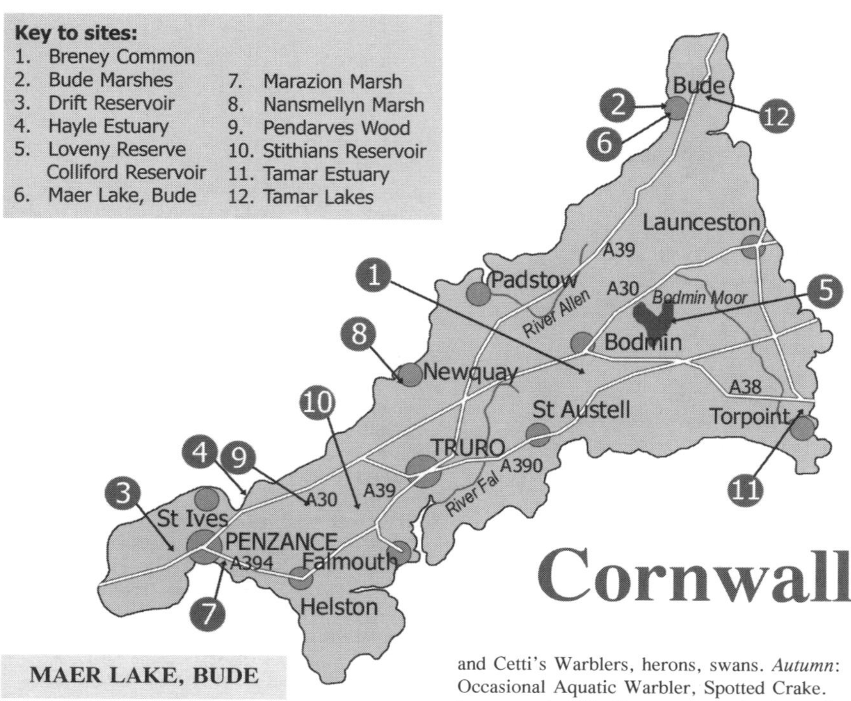

MAER LAKE, BUDE

Cornwall Birdwatching & Preservation Society.
Location: SS 208 075. View from private road next to Maer Lodge Hotel, heading N.
Access: Keep to road.
Facilities: None.
Public transport: Not known.
Habitat: Wetland meadows.
Key birds: Wildfowl and waders (inc. rarities eg. Temminck's Stint, Wilson's Phalarope).

MARAZION MARSH

RSBP (South West England Office).
Location: SW 510 315. Reserve is one mile E of Penzance, 500 yards W of Marazion. Entrance off seafront road near Marazion.
Access: Open at all times. No permits required. No admission charges. Dogs on leads please.
Facilities: One hide. No or visitor centre. Nearest toilets in Marazion and seafront car park.
Public transport: Bus from Penzance.
Habitat: Wet reedbed, willow carr.
Key birds: *Winter*: Wildfowl, Snipe, occasional Bittern. *Spring/summer*: Breeding Reed, Sedge and Cetti's Warblers, herons, swans. *Autumn*: Occasional Aquatic Warbler, Spotted Crake. Large roost of Swallows and martins in reedbeds, migrant warblers and waders.
Contact: Dave Flumm, RSBP, The Manor Office, Marazion, Cornwall, TR17 0EF. Tel/fax; 01736 711862.

NANSMELLYN MARSH

Cornwall Wildlife Trust.
Location: SW 762 541. Access from Perranzabuloe Sports Club car park, off the road to Goonhavern, just E of Perranporth.
Access: Open at all times with access suitable for disabled. Dogs on leads.
Facilities: Bird hide and circular path/boardwalk.
Public transport: None.
Habitat: Four and a half hectares of reedbed with willow carr.
Key birds: Cetti's Warbler, Grasshopper Warbler, Willow Warbler, Sedge Warbler, Snipe, Water Rail, Reed Bunting.
Contact: Stuart Hutchings, 5 Acres, Allet, Cornwall, TR4 9DJ. 01827 273939.
e-mail stuart@cornwt.demon.co.uk
www.wildlifetrust.org.uk/cornwall

PENDARVES WOOD

Cornwall Wildlife Trust.
Location: SW 640 376. From the B3303, two miles S of Camborne. Entrance on left.
Access: Open at all times. No dogs.
Facilities: Bird hide.
Public transport: None.
Habitat: Mixed woodland, glades and ornamental lake.
Key birds: Little Grebe, Spotted Flycatcher, Long-tailed Tit. Wintering duck. Woodland species.
Contact: Malcolm Perry, 7 Relistian Park, Reawla, Gwinear, Hayle, TR27 5HF. 01736 850612.

STITHIANS RESERVOIR

Cornwall Birdwatching & Preservation Society.
Location: SS 715 365. From B3297 S of Redruth.
Access: Good viewing from causeway. Key to hides from Debbie Melarickas, 20 Midway Drive, Truro TR1 1NQ. 01872 241558.
Facilities: None.
Public transport: None.
Habitat: Open water, marshland.
Key birds: Wildfowl and waders (inc. rarities, eg. Pectoral and Semipalmated Sandpipers, Lesser Yellowlegs).

TAMAR ESTUARY

Cornwall Wildlife Trust.
Location: SX 434 631. (Northern Boundary). SX 421 604 (Southern Boundary). From Plymouth head W on A38. Access parking at Cargreen and Landulph from minor roads off A388.
Access: Open at all times.
Facilities: Information boards at Cargreen and Landulph.
Public transport: None.
Habitat: Tidal mudflat with some saltmarsh. 404 hectares.
Key birds: *Winter*: Avocet, Snipe, Black-tailed Godwit, Redshank, Dunlin, Curlew, Whimbrel, Spotted Redshank, Green Sandpiper, Golden Plover, Kingfisher.
Contact: Stuart Hutchings, 5 Acres, Allet, Cornwall, TR4 9DJ. 01827 273939.
e-mail: stuart@cornwt.demon.co.uk
www.wildlifetrust.org.uk/cornwall

TAMAR LAKES

Tamar Lakes Country Park.
Location: SS 295 115. Leave A39 at Kilkhampton. Take minor road E to Thardon, car park off minor road running between upper and lower lakes.
Access: Open all year.
Facilities: Hide open all year round. New birdwatching centre on lower Tamar. Cafe, toilets (Apr-Sep).
Public transport: None.
Habitat: Two large bodies of water.
Key birds: Migrant waders (inc. North American vagrants). *Spring*: Black Tern. *Winter*: Wildfowl (inc. Goldeneye, Wigeon, Pochard).
Contact: Ranger,
Tamar Lakes Water Park, Kilkhampton, N Cornwall, 01288 321262.

Cumbria

CAMPFIELD MARSH

RSPB (North of England Office).
Location: NY 207 620. On S shore of Solway estuary, W of Bowness-on-Solway. Follow signs from B5307 from Carlisle.
Access: Open at all times, no charge. Views of high-tide roosts from roadside lay-bys (suitable for disabled).
Facilities: Viewing screens overlooking wetland areas, along nature trail (1.5 miles). No toilets or visitor centre.
Public transport: Nearest railway station – Carlisle (13 miles). Infrequent bus service to reserve.
Habitat: Saltmarsh/intertidal areas, open water, peat bog, wet grassland.
Key birds: *Winter*: Waders and wildfowl include

Cumbria

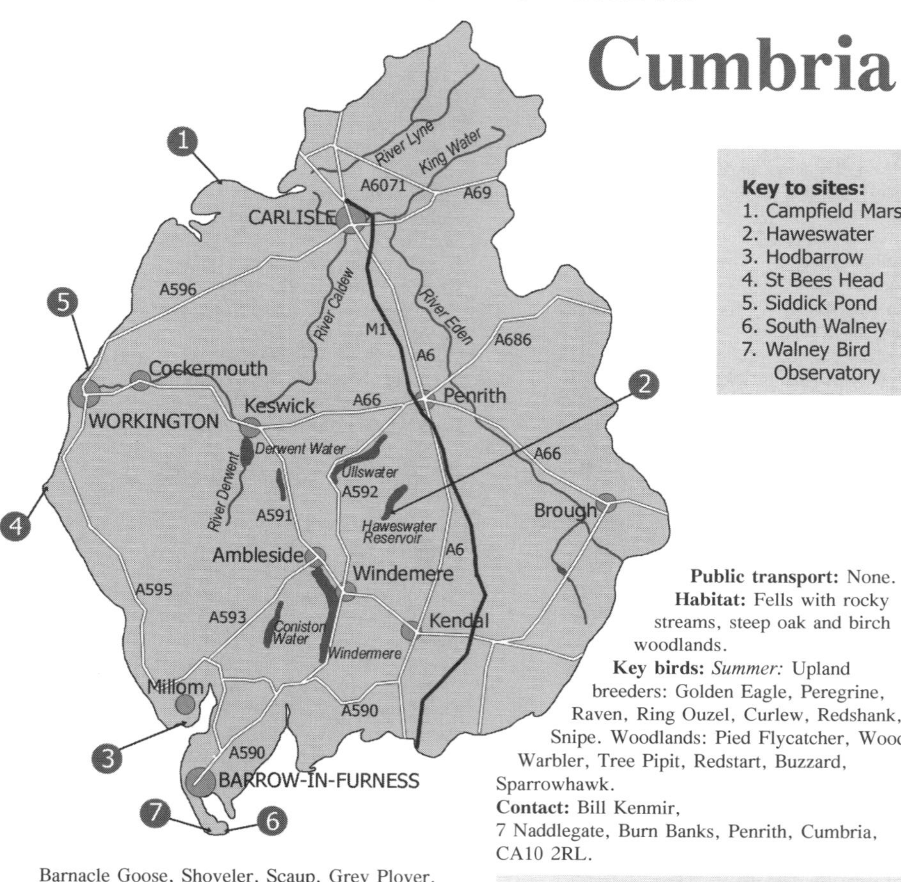

Key to sites:
1. Campfield Marsh
2. Haweswater
3. Hodbarrow
4. St Bees Head
5. Siddick Pond
6. South Walney
7. Walney Bird Observatory

Barnacle Goose, Shoveler, Scaup, Grey Plover. *Spring/summer*: Breeding Lapwing, Redshank, Snipe, Tree Sparrow and warblers. *Autumn*: Passage waders.
Contact: Norman Holton,
North Plain Farm, Bowness-on-Solway, Wigton, Cumbria, CA7 5AG.
e-mail: norman/holton@rspb.org.uk
www.rspb.org.uk

HAWESWATER

RSPB (North of England Office).
Location: NY 470 108. Off A6 at Shap, follow signs to Bampton and turn L in village; car park at S end of reservoir.
Access: Access at all times.
Facilities: Viewpoint in Summer.
Public transport: None.
Habitat: Fells with rocky streams, steep oak and birch woodlands.
Key birds: *Summer:* Upland breeders: Golden Eagle, Peregrine, Raven, Ring Ouzel, Curlew, Redshank, Snipe. Woodlands: Pied Flycatcher, Wood Warbler, Tree Pipit, Redstart, Buzzard, Sparrowhawk.
Contact: Bill Kenmir,
7 Naddlegate, Burn Banks, Penrith, Cumbria, CA10 2RL.

HODBARROW

RSPB (North of England Office).
Location: SD 174 791. Lying beside Duddon Estuary on the outskirts of Millom. Follow signs via Mainsgate Road.
Access: Open at all times, no charge.
Facilities: One hide overlooking island. Public toilets in Millom (two miles). Nature trail around the lagoon.
Public transport: Nearest railway station is in Millom (two miles).
Habitat: Brackish coastal lagoon bordered by limestone scrub and grassland.
Key birds: *Winter*: Waders and wildfowl includes Redshank, Dunlin, Goldeneye, Red-breasted Merganser. *Spring/summer*: Breeding gulls and

terns, Eider, grebes, Lapwing. *Autumn*: Passage waders.
Contact: Norman Holton, (Site Manager), North Plain Farm, Bowness-on-Solway, Wigton, Cumbria, CA7 5AG.
e-mail: norman/holton@rspb.org.uk
www.rspb.org.uk

ST BEES HEAD

RSPB (North of England Office).
Location: NX 962 118. S of Whitehaven via the B5345 road to St Bees village.
Access: Open at all times, no charge. Access via coast to coast footpath. The walk to the viewpoints is long and steep in parts.
Facilities: Three viewpoints overlooking seabird colony. Public toilets in St Bee's beach car park at entrance to reserve.
Public transport: Nearest railway station in St Bees (0.5 mile).
Habitat: Three miles of sandstone cliffs up to 300 ft high.
Key birds: *Summer*: Largest seabird colony on W coast of England: Guillemot, Razorbill, Puffin, Kittiwake, Fulmar and England's only breeding Black Guillemots.
Contact: Norman Holton, (Site Manager), North Plain Farm, Bowness-on-Solway, Wigton, Cumbria, CA7 5AG.
e-mail: norman/holton@rspb.org.uk
www.rspb.org.uk

SIDDICK POND

Allerdale Borough Council/EN/Cumbria WT.
Location: NY 001 305. One mile N of Workington, adjacent to A596.
Access: Access to hide by arrangement with Iggesund Paperboard (Workington) Ltd on site.
Facilities: None.
Public transport: None.
Habitat: Shallow pond with reedbeds.
Key birds: *Winter*: Wildfowl (inc. Goldeneye, Shoveler, Whooper Swan). *Spring/summer*: 35 nesting species. Occasional visitors inc. Black-necked Grebe, Black-tailed Godwit, Black Tern, Ruff, Osprey.
Contact: Patrick Joyce, Parks Development Officer, Allerdale BC, Allerdale House, Workington, Cumbria, CA14 3YJ.
01900 326324; fax 01900 326346.

SOUTH WALNEY

Cumbria Wildlife Trust.
Location: SD 215 620. Six miles S of Barrow-in-Furness.
Access: Open Tue-Sun (10am-5pm) plus Bank Holidays. No dogs except assistance dogs. Small charge for day permits but Cumbria Wildlife Trust members free.
Facilities: Toilets, nature trails, six hides (one of which is wheelchair accessible), cottage available to rent.
Public transport: None.
Habitat: Shingle, lagoon, sand dune, saltmarsh.
Key birds: *Spring/autumn*: Passage migrants. *Summer*: Breeding Eider, Herring and Lesser Black-backed Gulls, Shelduck. *Winter*: Teal, Wigeon, Redshank, Oystercatcher, Knot, Dunlin, Twite.
Contact: Mick Venters, No 1 Coastguard Cottages, South Walney Nature Reserve, Walney Island, Barrow-in-Furness, Cumbria, LA14 3YQ.
e-mail: cumbriawt@cix.co.uk
www.wildlifetrusts.org.uk/cumbria

WALNEY BIRD OBSERVATORY

Location: S tip of Walney Island, Barrow-in-Furness.
Access: Open daily.
Facilities: Monitoring and ringing of breeding and migrant birds. Cottage accommodation plus facilities for qualified ringers. For bookings write to Walney Bird Observatory, South End, Walney Island, Barrow-in-Furness, Cumbria LA14 3YQ.
Public transport: None.
Habitat: Mud flats, sandy beaches and dunes, pools.
Key birds: Uncommon and rare species on spring and autumn migration.
Contact: As above,

Derbyshire

DRAKELOW WILDFOWL RESERVE

Powergen PLC.
Location: SK 22 72 07. Drakelow Power Station, one mile NE of Walton-on-Trent.
Access: Permit by post from Drakelow Power Station, Burton-on-Trent. Open daily 9:30am-dusk (closed to 11am for wildfowl count on Sun). Closed Jun. No dogs. Unsuitable in parts for disabled. Parties by arrangement, limit ten.
Facilities: Seven hides, no other facilities
Habitat: Disused flooded gravel pits with wooded islands and reedbeds.
Key birds: *Summer*: Breeding Reed and Sedge Warblers. Water Rail, Hobby. *Winter*: Wildfowl (Goldeneye, Gadwall, Smew), Merlin. Regular sightings of Peregrine in Station area. Recent rarities include Little Egret, Cetti's Warbler and Golden Oriole. Excellent for dragonflies and butterflies.
Contact: Tom Cockburn, Ranger,1 Dickens Drive, Swadlincote, Derbys, DE11 0DX. 01283 217146.

OGSTON RESERVOIR

Severn Trent Water Plc.
Location: From Matlock, take A615 E to B6014. From Chesterfield take A61 S of Clay Cross onto B6014.
Access: View from roads, car parks or hides
Facilities: Four hides (three for Ogston BC members, one public), toilets. Information pack.
Public transport: None.
Habitat: Open water, pasture, mixed woodland.
Key birds: All three woodpeckers, Little and Tawny Owls, Kingfisher, Grey Wagtail, warblers. Passage raptors (inc. Osprey), terns and waders. *Winter*: Gull roost, wildfowl, tit and finch flocks.
Contact: Ogston Bird Club, c/o 2 Sycamore Avenue, Glapwell, Chesterfield, S44 5LH.

Devon

AYLESBEARE COMMON

RSPB (South West England Office).
Location: SY 058 897. Eight miles E of Exeter, off A3052, signposted Hawkerland.
Access: Open at all times.
Facilities: Long and short nature trails, disabled access via metalled track to private farm.
Public transport: Bus service - Exeter to Sidmouth (No 52).
Habitat: Lowland heathland, woodland, ponds.
Key birds: *Resident:* Dartford Warbler, Stonechat. *Summer*: Nightjar, Hobby, pipits. *Winter*: Occasional Hen Harrier, Great Grey Shrike.
Contact: Toby Taylor,Hawkerland Brake Barn, Exmouth Road, Aylesbeare, Nr Exeter, Devon, EX5 2JS. 01395 233655.

BOWLING GREEN MARSH

RSPB (South West England Office).
Location: SX 972 876. On the E side of River Exe, four miles SE of Exeter, 0.5 miles SE of Topsham.
Access: Open at all times. Please park at the public car parks in Topsham, not in the lane by the reserve.
Facilities: One hide suitable for wheelchair access. Viewing platform overlooking estuary reached by steps from track. No toilets. No visitor centre.
Public transport: Exeter to Exmouth railway has regular (every 30 mins) service to Topsham station (half a mile from reserve). Stagecoach Devon - T bus has frequent service (every 10-20 mins) from Exeter to Topsham.

Devon

Key to sites:
1. Aylesbeare Common
2. Bowling Green Marsh
3. Chapel Wood
4. Dart Valley
5. Dawlish Warren NNR
6. Exminster Marshes
7. Old Sludge Beds
8. Otter Estuary
9. Prawle Point
10. Rackenford & Knowstone Moors
11. South Milton Ley
12. Yarner Wood

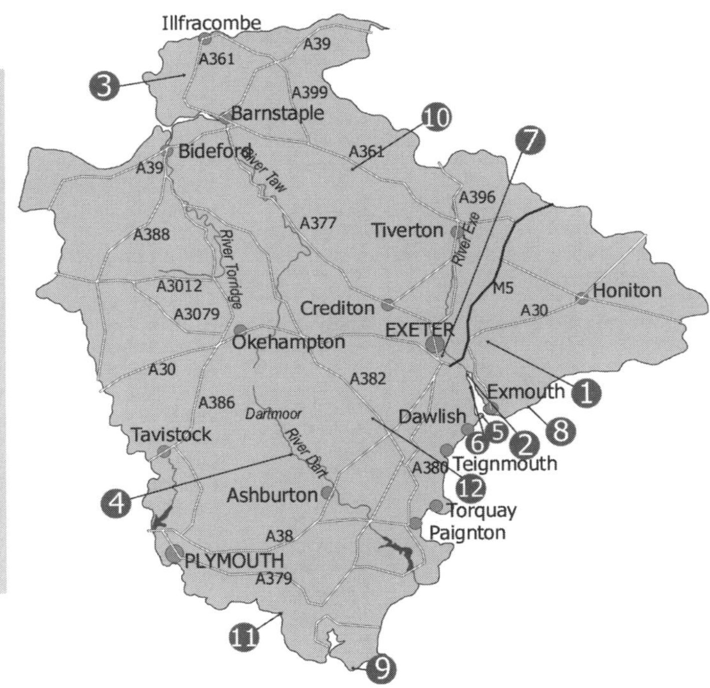

Habitat: Coastal grassland, open water/marsh, hedgerows.
Key birds: *Winter:* Wigeon, Shoveler, Teal, Black-tailed Godwit, Curlew, Golden Plover. *Spring:* Shelduck, *passage waders* – Whimbrel, passage Garganey and Yellow Wagtail. *Summer:* Gull/tern roosts, high tide wader roosts contain many passage birds. *Autumn:* Wildfowl, Peregrine, wader roosts.
Contact: RSPB, Unit 3, Lions Rest Estate, Station Road, Exminster, Exeter, EX6 8DZ. 01392 824614. www.rspb.org.uk

CHAPEL WOOD

RSPB (South West England Office).
Location: SS 483 413. Off minor road to Georgeham, W of A361 two miles N of Braunton.
Access: Permit required (send sae).
Facilities: None.
Public transport: None.
Habitat: Mixed woodland.
Key birds: Sparrowhawk, Buzzard, Raven, all three woodpeckers, Grey Wagtail, Dipper, warblers, Pied Flycatcher.
Contact: Alan Worth,
65 Chanters Hill, Barnstaple, North Devon, EX32 8DE.

DART VALLEY

Devon Wildlife Trust.
Location: SX 680 727. On Dartmoor nine miles NW from Ashburton. From A38 'Peartree Cross' near Ashburton, follow signs towards Princetown. Access from National Park car parks at New Bridge (S) or Dartmeet (N).
Access: Designated 'access land' but terrain is rough with few paths. It is possible to walk the length of the river (eight miles). A level, well-made track runs for a mile from Newbridge to give easy access to some interesting areas.
Facilities: Dartmoor National Park toilets in car parks at New Bridge and Dartmeet.

Public transport: Enquiry line 01392 382800. Summer service only from Newton Abbot/Totnes to Dartmeet.
Habitat: Upland moor, wooded valley and river.
Key birds: *All Year*: Raven, Buzzard. *Spring/ summer*: Wood Warbler, Pied Flycatcher, Redstart in woodland, Stonechat and Whinchat on moorland, Dipper, Grey Wagtail, Goosander on river.
Contact: Devon Wildlife Trust, Shirehampton House, 35-37 St David's Hill, Exeter, EX4 4DA. 01392 279244. e-mail: devonwt@cix.co.uk www.devonwildlifetrust.org

DAWLISH WARREN NNR

Teignbridge District Council.
Location: SX 983 788. At Dawlish Warren on S side of Exe estuary mouth. Turn off A379 at sign to Warren Golf Club, between Cockwood and Dawlish. Turn into car park adjacent to Lea Cliff Holiday Park. Pass under tunnel and turn left away from amusements. Park at far end of car park and pass through two pedestrian gates.
Access: Open public access but avoid mudflats. Also avoid beach beyond groyne nine around high tide due to roosting birds. Parking charges apply. Dogs to be kept under close control.
Facilities: Visitor centre (tel 01626 863980) open most weekends all year (10.30am-1pm and 2pm-5pm). Summer also open most weekdays as before, can be closed if warden on site. Toilets at entrance tunnel and in resort area only. Hide open at all times - best around high tide.
Public transport: Train station at site, also regular bus service operated by Stagecoach.
Habitat: High tide roost site for wildfowl and waders of Exe estuary on mudflats and shore. Dunes, dune grassland, woodland, scrub, ponds.
Key birds: *Winter:* Waders and wildfowl - large numbers. Also good for divers and Slavonian Grebe off shore. *Summer:* Particularly good for terns. Excellent variety of birds all year, especially on migration.
Contact: Keri Walsh/Andrew Buckley/Philip Chambers,
Countryside Management Section, Teignbridge District Council, Forde House, Brunel Road, Newton Abbot, Devon, TQ12 4XX. Visitor centre: 01626 863980. Teignbridge District Council: 01626 361101 (Ext 5754)

EXMINSTER MARSHES

RSPB (South West England Office).
Location: SX 954 872. Five miles S of Exeter on W bank of River Exe. Marshes lie between Exminster and the estuary.
Access: Open at all times.
Facilities: No toilets or visitor centre. Information in RSPB car park and marked footpaths across reserve.
Public transport: Stagecoach Devon (01392 427711). Exeter to Newton Abbot/Torquay buses - stops are 400 yds from car park.
Habitat: Grazing marsh with freshwater ditches and pools, reed and scrub-covered canal banks.
Key birds: *Winter*: Brent Goose, Wigeon, Water Rail, Short-eared Owl. *Spring*: Lapwing, Redshank and wildfowl breed, Cetti's Warbler on canal banks. *Summer*: Gull roosts, passage waders. *Autumn*: Peregrine, winter wildfowl.
Contact: RSPB,
Unit 3, Lions Rest Estate, Station Road, Exminster, Exeter, Devon, EX6 8DZ. 01392 824614. www.rspb.org.uk

OLD SLUDGE BEDS

Devon Wildlife Trust.
Location: SX 952 888. Located on S edge of Exeter. Park at University boathouse car park at entrance to SWW sewage treatment works off A379 towards Dawlish. Walk along canal past sewage works to reach reserve.
Access: Open at all times. Please keep dogs on short lead and keep to paths.
Facilities: Path with boardwalks runs through reserve. There are steps and ramps to negotiate.
Public transport: Stagecoach, tel 01392 427711. Buses run from Exeter city centre to Countess Wear roundabout, services 57, K and T.
Habitat: Freshwater reedbed, open water and willow carr.
Key birds: *Summer*: Reed and Sedge Warblers. *All year*: Cetti's Warbler and Water Rail.
Contact:
Devon Wildlife Trust, (see Dart Valley).

OTTER ESTUARY

Devon Wildlife Trust.
Location: SY 076 822. Lies on E edge of Budleigh Salterton. Park at Lime Kiln car park at eastern end of seafront.
Access: Open at all times. Access is along public footpaths (which run both sides of estuary) only. Path on western side is suitable for wheelchairs.
Facilities: Viewing platforms on western side; a hide (maintained by DBWPS) is on eastern side.
Public transport: Stagecoach, tel 01392 427711. Service 57 runs from Exeter Bus Station to Budleigh Salterton approx every 20 minutes.
Habitat: Estuary, saltmarsh and reedbed.
Key birds: Wintering and passage waders and wildfowl - Curlew, Redshank, Lapwing, Snipe, Wigeon, Teal, Little Egret, Water Rail and Kingfisher.
Contact: Devon Wildlife Trust (see Dart Valley).

PRAWLE POINT

Devon Birdwatching & Preservation Society.
Location: SE of Salcombe. Two acres by NT car park & two plots in Pigs Nose Valley.
Access: Strictly DBW&PS members only.
Facilities: None.
Public transport: None.
Habitat: Coastal migration watch point.
Key birds: Over 230 species recorded in area. Noted for seabird movements. Good list of raptors. Breeding Cirl Bunting. American vagrants inc. Red-eyed Vireo, Black-and-white Warbler, Blackpoll Warbler. Also Pallas's and Yellow-browed Warblers.
Contact: See contact in County Directory,

RACKENFORD AND KNOWSTONE MOOR

Devon Wildlife Trust.
Location: SS 858 211. Approx nine miles W of Tiverton along A361 (North Devon link road) to Barnstaple. Turn off at Moortown Cross junction to access reserve.
Access: Open at all times. Please keep dogs on short lead at all times. Terrain is rough and can be boggy, wellingtons essential! Please do not disturb grazing livestock.
Facilities: None.
Public transport: None.
Habitat: Culm grassland (wet grassland, heath, bog and scrub).
Key birds: *Summer*: Curlew, Willow Tit, Whinchat, Reed Bunting, Grasshopper Warbler. Occasional Hen Harrier in winter.
Contact: Devon Wildlife Trust,(see Dart Valley).

SOUTH MILTON LEY

Devon Birdwatching & Preservation Society.
Location: South coast near Thurlestone. W of Kingsbridge.
Access: Strictly DBW&PS members only, but can be overlooked from public footpath.
Facilities: None.
Public transport: None.
Habitat: Second largest freshwater reedbed in Devon.
Key birds: *Summer*: Breeding Reed and Sedge Warblers, and usually Cetti's Warbler. *Spring/ autumn:* Good for observing passages: Aquatic Warbler most years. Cirl Bunting close by.
Contact: See contact in County Directory,

YARNER WOOD

English Nature.
Location: SX 778 787. Part of East Dartmoor Woods and Heaths NNR. Two miles out of Bovey Tracey on the road to Becky Falls and Manaton.
Access: Open from 8.30am-7pm or dusk if earlier. Dogs must be on leads.
Facilities: Information/interpretation display and self-guided trails available. Hide.
Public transport: Nearest bus stops are in Bovey Tracey. Buses from here to Exeter/ Plymouth (every two hours off-peak, one hour peak) and Newton Abbot (hourly).
Habitat: Upland Western oakwood and lowland heathland.
Key birds: *All year*: Raven, Buzzard, Sparrowhawk, Lesser Spotted, Great Spotted and Green Woodpeckers. *Spring/summer*: Pied Flycatcher, Wood Warbler, Redstart, Tree Pipit, Linnet, Stonechat. *Autumn/winter*: Good range of birds with feeding at hide - Siskin, Redpoll.
Contact: Site Manager, English Nature, Yarner Wood, Bovey Tracey, Devon, TW13 9LJ. 01626 832330.
www.english-nature.org.uk

Dorset

Key to sites:
1. Arne
2. Brownsea Island
3. Durlston Country Park
4. Garston Wood
5. Holt Heath
6. Lodmoor
7. Portland Bird Observatory
8. Radipole Lake
9. Sopley Common
10. Stanpit Marsh
11. Studland & Godlingston Heaths

ARNE

RSPB (South West England Office).
Location: SY 973 882. Four miles SE of Wareham, turn off A351 at Stoborough.
Access: Shipstal Point and hide open all year, with access from car park. Coaches and escorted parties by prior arrangement.
Facilities: Toilets in car park. Bird hide at Shipstal. Various footpaths. Reception hut (open end-May-early Sept).
Public transport: None.
Habitat: Lowland heath, woodland reedbed and saltmarsh leading to extensive mudflats of Poole Harbour.
Key birds: *All year*: Dartford Warbler, Little Egret, Stonechat. *Winter*: Hen Harrier, Red-breasted Merganser, Black-tailed Godwit. *Summer*: Nightjar, warblers. *Passage*: Spotted Redshank, Whimbrel, Greenshank, Osprey.
Contact: Neil Gartshore, (Senior Warden), Syldata, Arne, Wareham, Dorset, BH20 5BJ. 01929 553360.
e-mail: neil.gartshore@rspb.org.uk
www.rspb.org.uk

BROWNSEA ISLAND

Dorset Wildlife Trust.
Location: SZ 026 883. Half hour boat ride from Poole Quay. Ten minutes from Sandbanks Quay (next to Studland chain-ferry).
Access: Apr, May, Jun, Sept. Access by self-guided nature trail. Costs £2 adults, £1 children. Jul, Aug access by afternoon guided tour (2.45pm daily, duration 105 minutes). Costs £2 adults, £1 children.
Facilities: Toilets, information centre, five hides, nature trail.
Public transport: Poole Rail/bus station for access to Poole Quay and boats.
Habitat: Saline lagoon, reedbed, lakes, coniferous and mixed woodland.
Key birds: *Spring*: Avocet, Black-tailed Godwit, waders, gulls and wildfowl. *Summer*: Common

and Sandwich Terns, Yellow-legged Gull, Little Egret, Little Grebe, Golden Pheasant. *Autumn*: Curlew Sandpiper, Little Stint.
Contact: Chris Thain,
The Villa, Brownsea Island, Poole, Dorset, BH13 7EE. 01202 709445.
e-mail: dorsetwtisland@cix.co.uk
www.wildlifetrust.org.uk/dorset

DURLSTON COUNTRY PARK

Dorset County Council.
Location: SZ 032 774. One mile S of Swanage (signposted).
Access: Visitor centre in car park open weekends during winter and daily in other seasons (phone for times).
Facilities: Guided walks.
Public transport: None.
Habitat: Grassland, hedges, cliff.
Key birds: Cliff-nesting seabird colonies; good variety of scrub and woodland breeding species; spring and autumn migrants; seawatching esp. Apr/May & Aug/Nov.
Contact: Hamish Murray,
Durlston Country Park, Swanage, Dorset, BH19 2JL. 01929 424443.

GARSTON WOOD

RSPB (South West England Office).
Location: SU 004 194. Small car park on Sixpenny Handley to Bowerchalke minor road, off B3081 midway between Salisbury and Blandford Forum.
Access: Open at all times. Keep to paths.
Facilities: None.
Public transport: None.
Habitat: Remnant of Cranborne Chase mixed woodland.
Key birds: *Summer*: Breeding Great Spotted Woodpecker, Turtle Dove, Garden Warbler, Blackcap, Spotted Flycatcher, Nuthatch, Treecreeper, Bullfinch. Sparrowhawk and Buzzard frequent.
Contact: Warden: Jack Edwards c/o Arne, above.

HOLT HEATH

English Nature (Dorset Team).
Location: SU 047 036 (Whitesheet car park). Located W of Ringwood and four miles NE of Wimborne Minster. From A31, two miles E of Wimborne, take minor road N to Broomhill and Holt. After two miles, turn right at Broomhill crossroads. From there, 1.5 miles to Whitesheet car park.
Access: Open access on foot. Dogs to be kept under close control.
Facilities: None.
Public transport: Buses to Colehill about three miles away - Wilts & Dorset.
Habitat: Heathland, woodland.
Key birds: *Spring/summer*: Dartford Warbler, Stonechat, Nightjar, Tree Pipit. *Winter*: Hen Harrier, Merlin.
Contact: Ian Nicol, (Site Manager),
English Nature, Slepe Farm, Arne, Wareham, Dorset, BH20 5BN. 01202 841026.
e-mail: ian.nicol@english-nature.org.uk

LODMOOR

RSPB (South West England Office).
Location: SY 686 807. Adjacent Lodmoor Country Park, in Weymouth, off A353 to Wareham.
Access: Open all times.
Facilities: One viewing shelter, network of paths.
Public transport: Local bus service.
Habitat: Marsh, shallow pools, reeds and scrub, remnant saltmarsh.
Key birds: *Spring/summer*: Breeding Common Tern, warblers (including Reed, Sedge, Grasshopper and Cetti's), Bearded Tit. *Winter*: Wildfowl and waders. Passage waders and other migrants.
Contact: Keith Ballard,
RSPB Visitor Centre, Swannery Car Park, Weymouth, DT4 7TZ. 01305 778313.
www.rspb.org.uk

PORTLAND BIRD OBSERVATORY

Portland Bird Observatory (independent registered charity).
Location: SY 681 690. Six miles S of Weymouth beside the road to Portland Bill.
Access: Open at all times. Parking only for members of Portland Bird Observatory. Self-catering accommodation for up to 20. Take own towels, sheets, sleeping bags.
Facilities: Displays and information, toilets, natural history bookshop, equipped kitchen,

laboratory.
Public transport: Bus service from Weymouth (First Dorset Transit Route 1).
Habitat: Scrub and ponds.
Key birds: *Spring/autumn*: Migrants including many rarities. *Summer*: Breeding auks, Fulmar, Kittiwake.
Contact: Martin Cade,
Old Lower Light, Portland Bill, Dorset, DT5 2JT.
e-mail: obs@btinternet.com
www.portlandbirdobs.btinternet.co.uk

RADIPOLE LAKE

RSPB (South West England Office).
Location: SY 677 796. In Weymouth. Enter from Swannery car park on footpaths.
Access: Visitor centre and nature trail open every day (9am-5pm). Hide open (8.30am-4.30pm). Permit available from visitor centre required by non-RSPB members.
Facilities: Network of paths, one hide, one viewing shelter.
Public transport: Close to train station which serves London and Bristol.
Habitat: Lake, reedbeds.
Key birds: *Winter*: Wildfowl. *Summer*: Breeding reedbed warblers (including Cetti's), Bearded Tit, passage waders and other migrants. Garganey regular in Spring. Good for rarer gulls.
Contact: Keith Ballard, (see Lodmoor).

SOPLEY COMMON

Dorset Wildlife Trust.
Location: SZ 132 975. Four miles NW of Christchurch near Hurn village.
Access: Open at all times. Permits required for surveying and group visits. Dogs allowed under close control. Limited access for disabled.
Facilities: None.
Public transport: None.
Habitat: Lowland heath (dry and wet) and deciduous woodland.
Key birds: *Summer*: Breeding Dartford Warbler, Nightjar, Woodlark, Stonechat. Also Hobby. *Winter*: Snipe.
Contact: Rob Brunt,
Dorset Wildlife Trust, Brooklands Farm, Forston, Dorchester, Dorset, DT2 7AA. 01305 264620.
e-mail: rbrunt@dorsetwt.cix.co.uk
www.wildlifetrust.org.uk/dorset

STANPIT MARSH

Stanpit Marsh Advisory Panel, Planning & Environmental Service, Christchurch Borough Council.
Location: SZ 167 924. Alongside mouth of River Avon in Christchurch.
Access: Public open space.
Facilities: Information centre.
Public transport: Wilts & Dorset bus no 123 (tel 01202 673555). Bournemouth Yellow Buses no 20 (tel 01202 522661).
Habitat: Salt, fresh, brackish marsh, sand dune and scrub.
Key birds: Estuarine: Waders, winter wildfowl, migrants. Reedbed: Bearded Tit, Cetti's Warbler. Scrub: Sedge Warbler, Reed Warbler. River/streams/bankside: Kingfisher. Feeding and roosting site.
Contact: Peter Holloway,
Christchurch Countryside Service, Steamer Point Woodland, Highcliffe, Christchurch, Dorset, BH23 4XX. 01425 272479.
e-mail: countrysideservice@christchurch.gov.uk

STUDLAND & GODLINGSTON HEATHS

English Nature (Dorset Team).
Location: SZ 030 846. From Ferry Road N of Studland village, on the Isle of Purbeck, N of Swanage.
Access: Open all year.
Facilities: Hides, nature trails.
Public transport: None.
Habitat: Woodland, heath, dunes, inter-tidal mudflats, saltings, freshwater lake, reedbeds, carr.
Key birds: Water Rail, Reed and Dartford Warblers, Nightjar, Stonechat. *Winter*: Wildfowl. Studland Bay, outside the reserve, has winter Black-necked and Slavonian Grebes, Scoter, Eider.
Contact:
English Nature, Slepe Farm, Arne, Wareham, Dorset, BH19 3AX. 01929 450259.

Durham

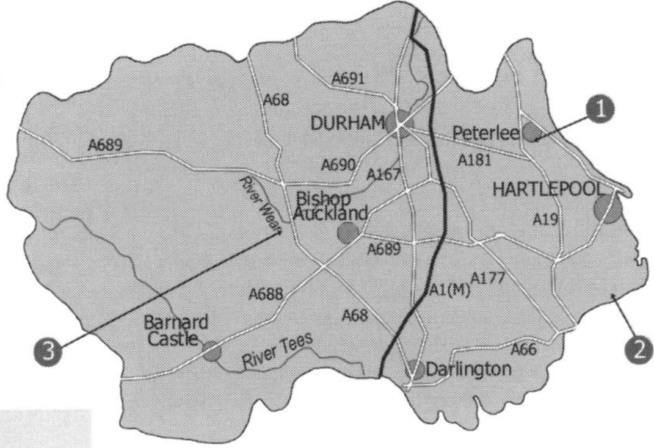

Key to sites:

1. Castle Eden Dene
2. Teesmouth
3. Witton-Le-Wear (Low Barns)

CASTLE EDEN DENE

English Nature (Northumbria Team).
Location: NZ 435 397. Adjacent to Peterlee, signposted from A19 and Peterlee town centre.
Access: Open from 8am-8pm or sunset if earlier. Car park. Dogs under tight control please.
Facilities: Car parking at Oakerside Dene Lodge. 12 miles of footpath, two waymarked trails.
Public transport: Bus service to Peterlee town centre.
Habitat: Yew/oak/sycamore woodland, paramaritime, limestone grassland.
Key birds: More than 170 recorded, 50 regular breeding species, typical woodland species.
Contact: Rob Lamboll,
Oakerside Dene Lodge, Stanhope Chase, Peterlee, Co Durham, SR8 1NJ. 0191 586 0004.

TEESMOUTH

English Nature (Northumbria).
Location: Two components, centred on NZ 535 276 and NZ 530 260, three and five miles S of Hartlepool, E of A178. Access to northern component from car park at NZ 534 282, 0.5 miles E of A178. Access to southern compartment from A178 bridge over Greatham Creek at NZ 510 254.
Access: Open at all times. In northern component, no restrictions over most of dunes and North Gare Sands (avoid golf course, dogs must be kept under close control). In southern component, disabled access path to public hides at NZ 516 255 and NZ 516 252 (no other access).
Facilities: Nearest toilets at Seaton Carew, one mile to the N. Disabled access path and hides (see above), interpretive panels and leaflet. Teesmouth Field Centre (Tel: 01429 264912).
Public transport: Hourly bus service operates Mon-Sat between Middlesbrough and Hartlepool, along A178 (service X9, Stagecoach Hartlepool, Tel: 01429 267082).
Habitat: Grazing marsh, sand dune, intertidal flats.
Key birds: Passage and winter wildfowl and waders. Passage terns and skuas in late summer. Scarce passerine migrants and rarities. *Winter*: Merlin, Peregrine, Snow Bunting, Twite, divers, grebes.
Contact: Mike Leakey,
English Nature, c/o British Energy, Tees Road, Hartlepool, TS25 2BZ. 01429 853325.
e-mail: michael.leakey@english-nature.org.uk
www.english-nature.org.uk

WITTON-LE-WEAR (Low Barns)

Durham Wildlife Trust.
Location: NZ 160 315. Off unclassified road between Witton-le-Wear (signposted on A68) and High Grange.
Access: Open all year.
Facilities: Three hides two with disabled access), observation tower above visitor centre (manned), nature trail.
Public transport: None.
Habitat: Former gravel workings, lake, ponds, riverbank.
Key birds: *All Year*: Greylag Geese, Kingfisher. *Summer*: Goosander, Grey Wagtail, Redpoll have bred. *Winter*: Wildfowl (inc. Goldeneye, Shoveler).
Contact: Visitor Centre Manager,
Low Barns Nature Reserve, Witton-le-Wear, Bishop Auckland, Co Durham, DL14 0AG.

Essex

ABBERTON RESERVOIR

Essex Wildlife Trust.
Location: TL 963 185. Six miles SW of Colchester on B1026. Follow signs from Layer-de-la-Haye.
Access: Open Tue-Sun (9am-5pm) except Christmas Day and Boxing Day.
Facilities: Visitor centre, toilets, nature trail, five hides (disabled access). Also good viewing where roads cross reservoir.
Public transport: Phone Trust for advice.
Habitat: Nine acres on edge of 1200a reservoir.
Key birds: Nationally important for Mallard, Teal, Wigeon, Shoveler, Gadwall, Pochard, Tufted Duck, Goldeneye (most important inland site in Britain). Smew regular. Passage waders, terns, birds of prey. Tree-nesting Cormorants (largest colony in Britain); raft-nesting Common Tern. *Summer*: Yellow Wagtail, warblers, Nightingale, Corn Bunting; *Autumn*: Red-crested Pochard, Bearded Tit, Water Rail; *Winter*: large numbers of waders.
Contact: Annette Adams, Essex Wildlife Trust, Abberton Reservoir Visitor Centre, Layer-de-la-Haye, Colchester, CO2 0EU. 01206 738172.

BRADWELL BIRD OBSERVATORY

Location: 100 yards S of St Peter's Chapel, Bradwell-on-Sea. Mouth of Blackwater estuary, between Maldon and Foulness.
Access: Open all year.
Facilities: Accommodation for eight in hut; two rooms each with four bunks; blankets, cutlery, etc. supplied.
Public transport: None.
Habitat: Mudflats, saltmarsh.
Key birds: *Winter*: Wildfowl (inc. Brent Geese, Red-throated Diver, Red-breasted Merganser), large numbers of waders; small numbers of Twite, Snow Bunting and occasional Shore Lark on beaches, also Hen Harrier, Merlin and Peregrine. Good passage of migrants usual in spring and autumn. *Summer*: Small breeding population of terns and other estuarine species.
Contact: Graham Smith, 48 The Meads, Ingatestone, Essex, CM4 0AE. 01277 354034.

COLNE POINT

Essex Wildlife Trust.
Location: TM 108 125. W of Clacton, via B1027 to St Osyth then Lee Wick Lane. Car park just inside reserve on seaward side of sea wall (liable to flood at very high tides).
Access: Day permit for non-Trust members.
Facilities: None.
Public transport: Phone Trust for advice.
Habitat: Mudflats, shingle pools.
Key birds: On major migration route for finches and chats. *Spring/autumn*: Birds of prey. *Summer*: Breeding Little Tern, Ringed Plover, Oystercatcher, Redshank. *Winter*: Divers, grebes, ducks, and feeding ground for Brent Geese.
Contact: C Cuthbert, Conservation Officer, Trust HQ, 01206 729678.

Key to sites:
1. Abberton Reservoir
2. Bradwell Bird Observatory
3. Colne Point
4. Fingringhoe Wick
5. Hanningfield Reservoir
6. Leigh
7. Old Hall Marshes
8. Stour Estuary
9. Tollesbury Wick Nature Reserve

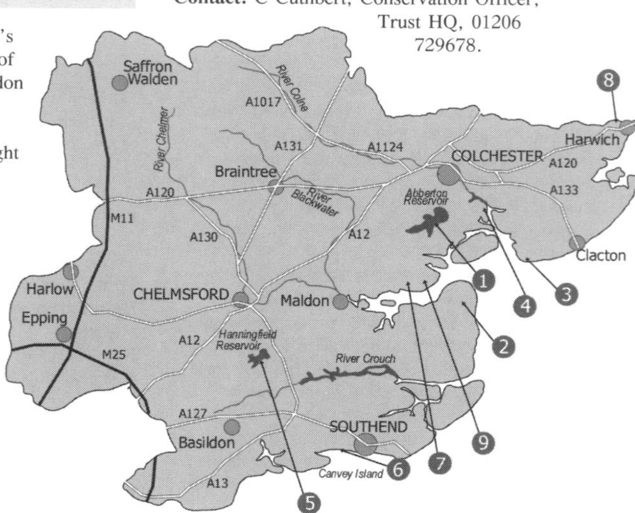

FINGRINGHOE WICK

Essex Wildlife Trust.
Location: TM 046 197. Colchester five miles. The reserve is signposted from B1025 to Mersea Island, S of Colchester.
Access: Open six days per week (not Mon or Christmas or Boxing Day). No permits needed. Donations invited. Centre/reserve open (9am-5pm). Dogs must be on a lead.
Facilities: Visitor centre – toilets, shop, light refreshments, car park, displays. Reserve – seven bird hides, two nature trails, plus one for disabled visitors.
Public transport: The reserve is best reached by car, or group coach.
Habitat: Old gravel pit, large lake, many ponds, sallow/birch thickets, young scrub, reedbeds, saltmarsh, gorse heathland.
Key birds: *Autumn/winter*: Brent Goose, waders, Hen Harrier, Little Egret. *Spring*: 40 male Nightingales. Good variety of warblers in scrub, thickets, reedbeds and Turtle Doves, Green/Great Spotted Woodpeckers. *Winter*: Little Grebe, Mute Swan, Teal, Wigeon, Shoveler, Gadwall on lake.
Contact: Laurie Forsyth, Wick Farm, South Green Road, Fingringhoe, Colchester, Essex, CO5 7DN. e-mail: admin@essexwt.org.uk
www.essexwt.org.uk

HANNINGFIELD RESERVOIR

Essex Wildlife Trust.
Location: TQ 725 972. Three miles N of Wickford. Exit off A130 at Rettendon onto South Hanningfield Road. Follow this for two miles until reaching the T-junction with Hawkswood Road. Turn right and the entrance to the Visitor Centre and reserve is one mile on the right.
Access: Open Tue-Sun (9am-5pm) plus Bank Holiday Mon. Disabled parking, toilets, and adapted birdwatching hide. No dogs. No cycling.
Facilities: Visitor centre, gift shop, optics, refreshments, toilets, four bird hides, nature trails, picnic area, coach parking, education room.
Public transport: Take Chelmsford to Wichford bus (no 14) to Downham village and walk half mile down Crowsheath Lane.
Habitat: One hundred acre mixed woodland with grassy glades and rides, adjoining the 870 acre Hanningfield Reservoir, designated an SSSI due to its high numbers of wildfowl.
Key birds: *Spring*: Good numbers and mix of woodland warblers. *Summer*: Vast numbers of Swifts, Swallows and martins feeding over the water. Hobby and Osprey. *Winter*: Good numbers and mix of waterfowl. Large gull roost.
Contact: Clare Cadman, Hanningfield Reservoir Visitor Centre, Hawkswood Road, Downham, Billericay, CM11 1WT. 01268 711001.
e-mail: Claire@essexwt.org.uk
www.essexwt.org.uk

LEIGH

Essex Wildlife Trust.
Location: TQ 824 852. Two Tree Island, approached from Leigh on Sea, W of Southend.
Access: Important to keep to marked footpaths.
Facilities: Hide, nature trail.
Public transport: Phone Trust for advice.
Habitat: Intertidal mudflats, saltmarshes.
Key birds: *Autumn*: Dark-bellied Brent Geese.
Contact: Trust HQ, 01206 729 678.

OLD HALL MARSHES

RSPB (East Anglia Office).
Location: TL 97 51 25. Approx eight miles S of Colchester. From A12 take B1023, via Tiptree, to Tolleshunt D'Arcy. Then take Chapel Road (back road to Tollesbury), after one mile turn left into Old Hall Lane. Continue up Old Hall Lane, over speed ramp and through iron gates to cattle grid, then follow signs to car park.
Access: By permit only in advance from Warden, write to address below. Open 9:00am-9pm or dusk, closed Tue.
Facilities: Two trails – one of three miles and one of 6.5 miles. Two viewing screens overlooking saline lagoon area at E end of reserve. No visitor centre or toilets.
Public transport: None.
Habitat: Coastal grazing marsh, reedbed, saline lagoon, saltmarsh and mudflat
Key birds: *Summer*: Breeding Avocet, Redshank, Lapwing, Pochard, Shoveler, Gadwall, Garganey, Barn Owl. *Winter*: Brent Goose, Wigeon, Teal, Shoveler, Goldeneye, Red-breasted Merganser, all the expected waders, Hen Harrier, Merlin, Short-eared Owl

and Twite. *Passage*: All expected waders (particularly Spotted Redshank, Green Sandpiper and Whimbrel), Yellow Wagtail, Whinchat and Wheatear.
Contact: Chris Tyas,
1 Old Hall Lane, Tolleshunt D'Arcy, Maldon, Essex, CM9 8TP. 01621 869015.
e-mail: chris.tyas@rspb.org.uk

STOUR ESTUARY

RSBP (East Anglia Office).
Location: TM 191 310. Car park - by B1352 Harwich-Manningtree Road, five miles W of Harwich, 0.5 miles E of Wrabness.
Access: No charges - donation appreciated. Open at all times, except Christmas Day. Only suitable for disabled in the driest conditions, access not possible to hides.
Facilities: Three hides. No visitor centre/toilets. Cycle racks in car park, height barrier to restrict overnight parking.
Public transport: Harwich/Colchester via Wrabness. Bus service passes entrance. Wrabness railway station 0.5 mile W of the reserve.
Habitat: Extensive areas of mudflats and saltmarsh with adjacent woodland and scrub.
Key birds: *Winter*: Wading birds and wildfowl, Dunlin, Grey Plover, Knot, Black-tailed Godwit, Pintail, Brent Goose. *Summer*: Nightingale, migratory warblers and all three woodpeckers.
Contact: Russell Leavett, 24 Orchard Close, Great Oakley, Harwich, Essex, CO12 5AX. 01255 886043.
e-mail: russell.leavett@RSBP.org.uk
www.RSBP.org.uk

TOLLESBURY WICK

Essex Wildlife Trust.
Location: GR 970 104. On Black Water Estuary eight miles E of Maldon. From A12 at Kelvedon, follow B1023 to Tollesbury via Tiptree. Then follow Woodrolfe Road S towards the marina. Use car park at Woodrolfe Green.
Access: Open all times along public footpath on top of sea wall.
Facilities: Public toilets at Woodrolfe Green car park.
Public transport: Bus services run to Tollesbury from Maldon, Colchester and Witham.
Habitat: Estuary with fringing saltmarsh and mudflats with some shingle. Extensive freshwater grazing marsh, brackish borrowdyke and small reedbeds.
Key birds: *Winter*: Wildfowl and waders, Short-eared Owl, Hen Harrier. *Summer*: Breeding Avocet, Redshank, Lapwing, occasional Little Tern, Reed and Sedge Warblers, Reed, Corn Bunting, Barn Owl. *Passage*: Whimbrel, Spotted Redshank.
Contact: Jonathan Smith,
Tollesbury, Maldon, Essex, CM9 8RJ. 01621 868628. e-mail: jonathans@essexwt.org.uk

---

Gloucestershire

ASHLEWORTH HAM & MEEREND THICKET

Gloucestershire Wildlife Trust.
Location: SO830265. Leave Gloucester N on A417; R at Hartpury and follow minor road through Ashleworth towards Hasfield.
Access: Access prohibited at all times but birds may be viewed from hide in Meerend Thicket.
Facilities: None.
Public transport: None.
Habitat: Low-lying grassland flood plain.
Key birds: *Winter*: Wildfowl (inc. 4000 Wigeon, 1500 Teal, Pintail, Goldeneye, Bewick's Swan); passage waders; Peregrine, Hobby.
Contact: Trust HQ, 01452 383333.

COKE'S PIT

Gloucestershire Wildlife Trust.
Location: SU 027 953. S of Cirencester, just E of Somerford Keynes, between the village and Spratgates Lane.
Access: Open at all times.
Facilities: Hide.
Public transport: None.
Habitat: Flooded gravel workings.
Key birds: *Winter*: Wildfowl (inc. Smew,

Gloucestershire

Key to sites:
1. Ashleworth Ham & Meerend Thicket
2. Coke's Pit
3. Coombe Hill Canal
4. Highnam Woods
5. Nagshead
6. Slimbridge
7. Whelford Pools
8. Woorgreens Lake And Marsh

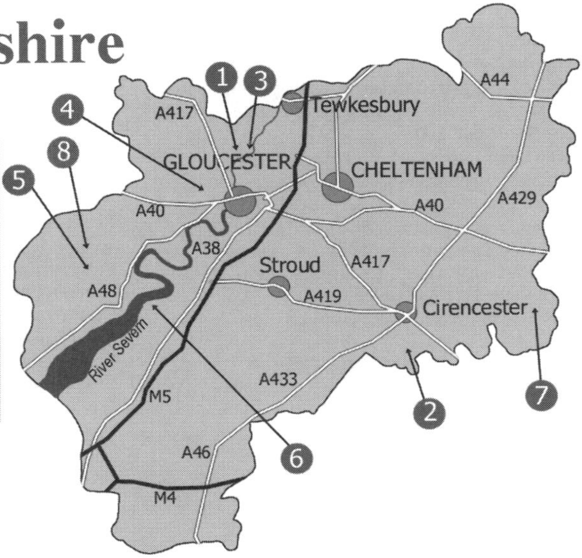

Goldeneye). Red-crested Pochard.
Contact: Trust HQ, 01452 383333.

COOMBE HILL CANAL

Gloucestershire Wildlife Trust.
Location: SO 887 272. NNE of Gloucester. W of A38 between Apperley and The Leigh.
Access: Open at all times.
Facilities: None.
Public transport: None.
Habitat: Disused canal and adjacent flood meadows.
Key birds: *Winter*: Wildfowl (large numbers of Wigeon and Teal; also Bewick's Swan, Pintail, Gadwall, Goldeneye). Good range of migrant warblers.
Contact: Trust HQ, 01452 383333.

HIGHNAM WOODS

RSPB (Central England Office).
Location: SO 778 190. Signed on A40 three miles W of Gloucester.
Access: Open at all times, no permit required. Disabled access to a hide 120 yards from car park. The nature trails can be very muddy. Dogs allowed on leads.
Facilities: One nature trail (approx 1.5 miles), one birdwatching hide with winter bird-feeding programme.
Public transport: Contact Glos. County Council public transport information line. Tel: 01452 425543.
Habitat: Ancient woodland in the Severn Vale with areas of coppice and scrub.
Key birds: *Spring/summer:* The reserve has Gloucestershire's main concentration of Nightingales - about 20 pairs. Resident birds include all three woodpeckers, Buzzard and Sparrowhawk. Ravens are frequently seen.
Contact: Ivan Proctor,
The Puffins, Parkend, Lydney, Glos, GL15 4JA. 01594 562852. www.rspb.org.uk
e-mail: ivan.proctor@rspb.org.uk

NAGSHEAD

RSPB (Central England Office).
Location: SO 097 085. In Forest of Dean, N of Lydney. Signed immediately W of Parkend village on the road to Coleford.
Access: Open at all times, no permit required. The reserve is hilly and there are some stiles to negotiate on the nature trails. Dogs must be kept under close control.
Facilities: There are two nature trails (one mile and 2.25 miles). Information centre open at weekends mid-Apr to end Aug.
Public transport: Contact Glos. County Council

public transport information line, 01452 425543.
Habitat: Much of the reserve is 200-year-old oak plantations, grazed in some areas by sheep. The rest of the reserve is a mixture of open areas and conifer/mixed woodland.
Key birds: *Spring*: Pied Flycatcher, Wood Warbler, Redstart, warblers. *Summer*: Siskin, Crossbill in some years. *All year*: Buzzard, Raven, all three woodpeckers.
Contact: Ivan Proctor,
The Puffins, Parkend, Lydney, Glos, GL15 4JA. 01594 562852. www.rspb.org.uk
e-mail: ivan.proctor@rspb.org.uk

SLIMBRIDGE

The Wildfowl & Wetlands Trust.
Location: SO 723 048. Signposted from M5 (exit 13 or 14).
Access: Open daily except Christmas Day, (9am-5.30pm, 5pm in winter).
Facilities: Hides, observatory, observation tower, Hanson Discovery Centre, wildlife art gallery, exhibition, tropical house, facilities for disabled, worldwide collection of wildfowl species.
Public transport: None.
Habitat: Reedbed, saltmarsh, freshwater pools, mudflats.
Key birds: Kingfisher, waders, raptors. *Winter*; Wildfowl esp. Bewick's Swans, White-fronted Geese, Wigeon, Teal.
Contact: Neil Woodward, Centre Manager, The Wildfowl & Wetlands Trust, Slimbridge, Gloucester, GL2 7BT. 01453 890333.

WHELFORD POOL

Gloucestershire Wildlife Trust.
Location: SU 174 995. SE of Fairford. Leave Fairford E on A417, turn towards Whelford and reserve is on left (just before Whelford sign).
Access: Open at all times.
Facilities: Two hides, one with wheelchair access.
Public transport: None.
Habitat: Flooded gravel pits in eastern section of Cotswold Water Park.
Key birds: On main passage flight route (Yellow Wagtail, Black Tern, Osprey, waders). *Summer:* Breeding Common Tern, Hobby. *Winter*: Wildfowl.
Contact: Trust HQ, 01452 383333.

WOORGREENS LAKE AND MARSH

Gloucestershire Wildlife Trust.
Location: SO 630 127. Forest of Dean, W of Cinderford, N of B4226 Cannop road.
Access: Open at all times.
Facilities: None.
Public transport: None.
Habitat: Marsh, lake, heath on reclaimed opencast coalmine.
Key birds: Stonechat, Tree Pipit, Nightjar; birds of prey (inc, Buzzard, Goshawk, occasional Hobby). Passage waders (inc. Greenshank, Spotted Redshank, Green Sandpiper).
Contact: Trust HQ, 01452 383333.

Hampshire

FARLINGTON MARSHES

Hampshire Wildlife Trust.
Location: SU 685 045. E side of Portsmouth. Entrance of roundabout at junc A2030 (Eastern Road) and A27, or from Harts Farm Way, Broadmarsh, Havant (S side of A27).
Access: Open at all times, no charge or permits, but donations welcome. Dogs on leads only. Not presently suitable for disabled. Groups please book to avoid clash of dates.
Facilities: Information at entrance and in shelter area of building. No toilets.
Habitat: Coastal grazing marsh with pools and reedbed within reserve. Views over intertidal mudflats/saltmarshes of Langstone Harbour.
Key birds: *Autumn to spring*: Waders and wildfowl. *Winter*: Brent Goose, Wigeon, Pintail etc and waders (Dunlin, Grey Plover etc). On migration wide range of waders including rarities. Reedbeds with Bearded Tit, Water Rail etc, scrub areas attract small migrants (Redstart, Wryneck, warblers etc).
Contact: Bob Chapman, c/o Hampshire Wildlife Trust, Woodside House, Woodside Road, Eastleigh, Hants, SO50 4ET. 013 9221 4683. www.hwt.org.uk

Hampshire

Key to sites:
1. Farlington Marshes
2. Hook-With-Warsash LNR
3. Langstone Harbour
4. Lower Test
5. Lymington Reedbeds
6. Lymington-Keyhaven NNR
7. Martin Down
8. North Solent
9. Pilsey Island
10. Titchfield Haven NNR

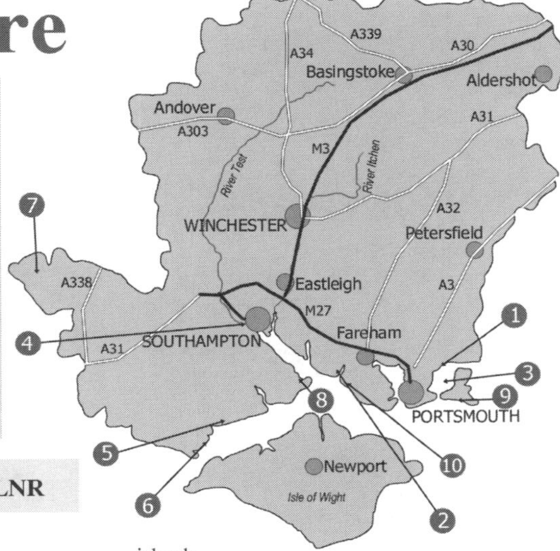

HOOK-WITH-WARSASH LNR

Hampshire County Council.
Location: SU 490 050. W of Fareham. Car parks by foreshore at Warsash. Reserve includes Hook Lake.
Access: Open all year.
Facilities: Public footpaths.
Public transport: Call for advice.
Habitat: Shingle beach, saltings, marsh, reedbed, scrape.
Key birds: *Winter*: Brent Geese on Hamble estuary. Waders. Stonechat, Cetti's Warbler.
Contact: Barry Duffin, Haven House Visitor Centre, Cliff Road, Hill Head, Fareham, Hants, PO14 3JT. 01329 662145; fax 01329 667113.

LANGSTONE HARBOUR

RSPB (South East England Office).
Location: SU 695 035. Harbour lies E of Portsmouth, a mile from Havant, SE of A27/A3(M) junction. Car park off Hayling Island road by Esso garage. View from footpath along N shore off junction of A27/A2030, Farlington Marshes (qv).
Access: Restricted access. good views from Farlington Marshes LNR and from footpaths of Broadmarsh. Winter boat trips may be booked at the close by Portsmouth Outdoor Centre.
Facilities: None.
Public transport: Mainline trains all stop at Havant.
Habitat: Intertidal mud, saltmarsh, shingle islands.
Key birds: *Summer*: Breeding Little, Sandwich and Common Terns, Black-headed and Mediterranean Gulls, waders. *Autumn/winter*: Waders (inc. Black-tailed and Bar-tailed Godwits, Oystercatcher, Ringed and Grey Plover, Dunlin). Wildfowl (inc. Shelduck, Shoveler, Goldeneye, Merganser and c7,000 dark-bellied Brent Geese), Black-necked Grebe, Short-eared Owl, Peregrine.
Contact: Chris Cockburn (Warden), 20 Childe Square, Stamshaw, Portsmouth, PO2 8PL. 023 9265 0675.
e-mail: chris.cockburn@rspb.org.uk

LOWER TEST

Hampshire Wildlife Trust.
Location: SU 364 150. M271 S to Redbridge, three miles from Southampton city centre.
Access: Open at all times, no dogs except guide dogs.
Facilities: Three hides, one suitable for disabled (access by arrangement with the warden).
Public transport: Totton train station and bus stops within easy walking distance.
Habitat: Saltmarsh, brackish grassland, wet meadows, reedbed, scrapes and meres.
Key birds: *Spring/summer*: Breeding Cetti's Warbler, Bearded Tit, Lesser Spotted Woodpecker. *Passage/winter*: Waders including Green and Common Sandpipers, wintering wildfowl, Water Pipit, Jack Snipe, Peregrine.

Contact: Jess Pain,
Hampshire Wildlife Trust, Woodside House, Woodside Road, Eastleigh, Hants, SO50 4ET. 023 8066 7919.
e-mail: jessp@hwt.org.uk
www.hwt.org.uk

LYMINGTON REEDBED

Hampshire Wildlife Trust.
Location: SZ 325 963. E of Lymington town centre, on E side of river, stretching up to A3054 road to Beaulieu.
Access: Good views from adjacent roads to S and E of reserve; otherwise access only on public paths
Facilities: None.
Public transport: Five minutes walk from train station.
Habitat: One of largest reedbeds on S coast, fringed by alder and willow woodland.
Key birds: One of highest concentrations of Water Rail in the country; resident but most evident in winter. *Summer:* Breeding Cetti's Warbler. Otters use site regularly.
Contact: Michael Boxall, 01590 622708.

LYMINGTON-KEYHAVEN

Hampshire County Council.
Location: SZ 315 920. S of Lymington along seawall footpath; car parks at Bath Road, Lymington and at Keyhaven Harbour.
Access: Open all year
Facilities: None.
Public transport: None.
Habitat: Coastal marshland and lagoons.
Key birds: *Spring*: Passage waders (inc. Knot, Sanderling, Bar-tailed and Black-tailed Godwits, Whimbrel, Spotted Redshank), Pomarine and Great Skuas. Breeding Oystercatcher, Ringed Plover, and Sandwich, Common and Little Terns. *Autumn*: Passage raptors, waders and passerines. *Winter*: Wildfowl (inc. Brent Geese, Wigeon, Pintail, Red-breasted Merganser), waders (inc. Golden Plover), Little Egret, gulls.

MARTIN DOWN

English Nature (Wiltshire Team).
Location: SY 05 19. Nine miles SW of\Salisbury, car park on A354.
Access: Open access, organised groups should book in advance.
Facilities: Two car parks, interpretative boards and leaflets.
Public transport: One bus Salisbury/Blandford.
Habitat: Chalk downland.
Key birds: *Spring/summer*: Grey Partridge, warblers, Nightingale, Stone Curlew. *Winter*: Merlin, Hen Harrier.
Contact: David Burton, Parsonage Down NNR, Cherry Lodge, Shrewton, Nr Salisbury, Wilts, 01980 620485.
e-mail: david.burton@english-nature.org.uk

NORTH SOLENT

English Nature (Hampshire and Isle of Wight Team).
Location: 1. Beaulieu Estate. SZ 420 975. Fifteen miles Southampton – minor roads from Beaulieu.
2. Cadland Estate. SU 460 015. Minor roads from Hythe/Fawley.
Access: 1. Permits available from Beaulieu Estate (tel 01590 614621). No dogs, designated parts only. No public right of way at Needs Ore. Public footpath along Beaulieu River (Beaulieu-Bucklers Hard).
2. Public rights of way only.
Facilities: 1. Hides (one with disabled access).
2. None.
Public transport: 1. None.
2. Southampton to Blackfield/Fawley bus.
Habitat: 1. Coastal – saltmarsh/estuary, grazing marsh, reedbed.
2. Heathland, river valleys.
Key birds: 1. Coastal-seabirds/waders all year and woodland species.
2. Heathland/woodland species.
Contact: Bob Lord, Sites Manager,
English Nature, 1 Southampton Road, Lyndhurst, SO43 7BU. 023802 86428.
e-mail: bob.lord@english-nature.org.uk
www.english-nature.org.uk

PILSEY ISLAND

RSPB (South East England Office).
Location: SU 770 006. Approach via coastal footpath around Thorney Island, E of Portsmouth.
Access: No access on to island but good views from surrounding areas at low tide.
Facilities: None.

Public transport: None.
Habitat: Saltmarsh and shingle.
Key birds: Major wader roost at high tide. *Winter*: Waterfowl.
Contact: Langstone Harbour (page 122),

TITCHFIELD HAVEN NNR

Hampshire County Council.
Location: SU 535 025. From A27 W of Fareham; public footpath follows derelict canal along W of reserve and road skirts S edge.
Access: Open Wed-Sun all year, plus Bank Hols.
Facilities: Centre has information desk, toilets, tea room and shop. Guided tours (book in advance). Hides.
Public transport: None.
Habitat: Reedbeds, freshwater scrapes, wet grazing meadows.
Key birds: *Spring/summer*: Bearded Tit, waders (inc. Black-tailed Godwit, Ruff), wildfowl, Common Tern, breeding Cetti's Warbler, Water Rail. *Winter*: Bittern.
Contact: Barry Duffin,
Haven House Visitor Centre, Cliff Road, Hill Head, Fareham, Hants, PO14 3JT. 01329 662145; fax 01329 667113.

Hertfordshire

LEMSFORD SPRINGS

Herts & Middlesex Wildlife Trust.
Location: TL 223 123. Lies 1.5 miles W of Welwyn Garden City town centre, off roundabout leading to Lemsford village on B197, W of A1(M).
Access: Access, via key, by arrangement with warden. Open at all times, unless work parties or group visits in progress. Keep to paths. No dogs. Not ideal for disabled due to steps up to hides.
Facilities: Two hides, chemical toilet, marked paths.
Public transport: Bus service to Valley Road, WGC No 366 (Sovereign Bus & Coach Co Ltd, tel 01438 726688). Nearest railway station Welwyn Garden City.
Habitat: Former water-cress beds, open shallow lagoons. Stretch of the River Lea, marsh, hedgerows.
Key birds: *Spring/summer*: Breeding warblers, Grey Wagtail, Kestrel. *Autumn/winter*: Green Sandpiper, Water Rail, Snipe, Siskin, occasional Jack Snipe. *All Year*: Kingfisher, Grey Heron, Sparrowhawk.
Contact: Barry Trevis,
11 Lemsford Village, Welwyn Garden City, Herts, AL8 7TN. 01707 335517.
e-mail: hertswt@cix.co.uk
www.wildlifetrust.org.uk/herts

RYE MEADS (RSPB)

RSPB (Central England Office).
Location: TL 387 099. E of Hoddesdon, near Rye House railway station.
Access: Open every day 10am-5pm (or dusk if earlier).
Facilities: Hides.
Public transport: None.
Habitat: Marsh, willow scrub, pools, scrapes, lake and reedbed.
Key birds: *Summer*: Breeding Tufted Duck, Gadwall, Common Tern, Kestrel, Kingfisher, nine species of warblers. *Winter*: Bittern, Shoveler, Water Rail, Teal, Snipe, Jack Snipe, Redpoll and Siskin.
Contact: Mike Pollard,
RSPB Rye Meads Nature Reserve, Rye Meads Sewage Treatment Works, Stanstead Abbotts, Herts, SG12 8JY. 01279 793720; fax 01279 793721.

RYE MEADS

Herts & Middlesex Wildlife Trust.
Location: TQ 044 931. Rickmansworth, off A412 into Springwell Lane (TQ 043 932) L after bridge, or via Bury Lake Aquadrome (parking).
Access: Open every day 10am-5pm or dusk if earlier.
Facilities: Hides,

Hertfordshire

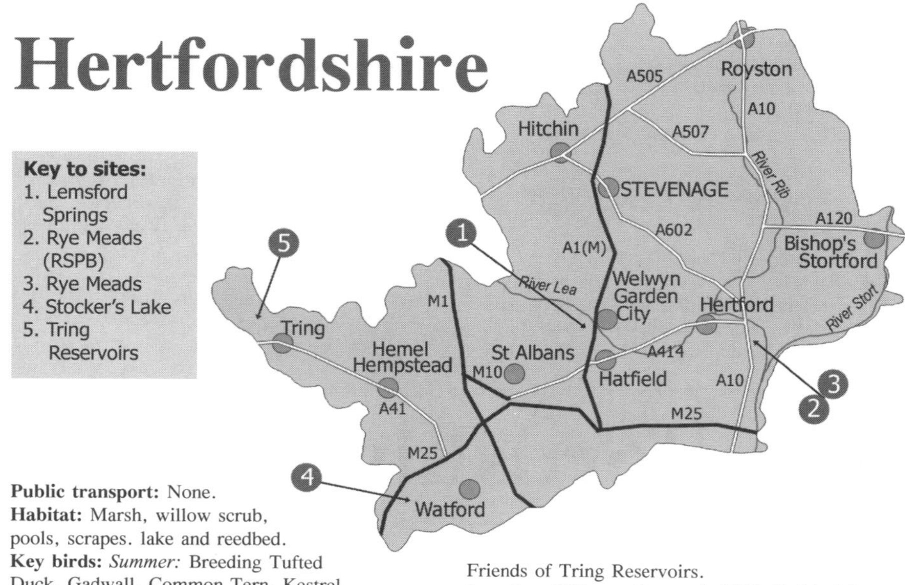

Public transport: None.
Habitat: Marsh, willow scrub, pools, scrapes. lake and reedbed.
Key birds: *Summer:* Breeding Tufted Duck, Gadwall, Common Tern, Kestrel, Kingfisher, nine species of warblers. *Winter:* Bittern, Shoveler, Water Rail, Teal, Snipe, Jack Snipe, Redpoll and Siskin.
Contact: Mike Pollard, RSPB Rye Meads Nature Reserve, Ry Meads Sewage Treatment Works, Stanstead Abbotts, Herts, SG12 8JY, 01279 793720, fax: 01279 793721.

STOCKER'S LAKE

Herts & Middlesex Wildlife Trust.
Location: TQ 044 931. Rickmansworth, off A412 into Springwell Lane (TQ043932) L after bridge, or via Bury Lake Aquadrome (parking).
Access: Open all year.
Facilities: None.
Public transport: None.
Habitat: Mature flooded gravel pit with islands.
Key birds: 50 species breed; over 200 recorded. Heronry. *Summer*: Breeding Pochard, Gadwall, Common Tern. Large numbers of migrants. *Winter*: Duck (inc. Goldeneye and nationally significant numbers of Shoveler).
Contact: Trust HQ, 01727 858901.

TRING RESERVOIRS

Wilstone Reservoir - Herts & Middlesex Wildlife Trust; other reservoirs - British Waterways and Friends of Tring Reservoirs.
Location: Wilstone Reservoir SP90 51 34. Other reservoirs SP 92 01 35. WTW Lagoon SP 92 31 34 adjacent to Marsworth Reservoir. From B489 which leaves A41 at Aston Clinton 1.5 miles due N of Tring.
Access: Reservoirs - open at all times. WTW Lagoon: open at all times by permit from FOTR.
Facilities: Café and public house adjacent to Startops Reserve. Car park Also disabled trail from here. Hides with disabled access at Startops/ Marsworth Reserve & WTW Lagoon.Other hides.
Public transport: Buses are available to and from Aylesbury & Tring including a weekend service, tel. 0870 6082608. Tring Station is 2½ miles away via canal towpath.
Habitat: Four reservoirs with surrounding woodland, scrub and meadows. Two of the reservoirs with extensive reedbeds. WTW Lagoon with islands, surrounding hedgerows and scrub.
Key birds: *Spring/summer*: Breeding warblers, regular Hobby, occasional Black Tern, Marsh Harrier, Osprey. *Autumn*: Passage waders and wildfowl. *Winter*: Gull roost, large wildfowl flocks, bunting roosts, occasional Bittern.
Contact: Herts & Middsx Wildlife Trust: 01727 858901.
FOTR: see Peter Hearn in Bucks BTO entry, British Waterways, Watery Lane, Marsworth, Tring HP23 4LZ. 01442 825938.
www.tringreservoirs.btinternet.co.uk

Kent

BLEAN WOODS (RSPB)

RSPB (South East England Office).
Location: TR 126 592. From Rough Common (off A290, one and a half miles NW of Canterbury).
Access: Open 8am-9pm.
Facilities: Public footpaths and four waymarked trails.
Public transport: None.
Habitat: Woodland (mainly oak and sweet chestnut), relics of heath.
Key birds: Nightingale, Nightjar, Hawfinch, three species of woodpecker.
Contact: Michael Walter,
11 Garden Close, Rough Common, Canterbury, Kent, CT2 9BP. 01227 462491.

BLEAN WOODS

English Nature (Kent Team).
Location: TR 120 609. NW of Canterbury on A290. Road opposite Chapel Lane at Blean.
Access: Keep to paths.
Facilities: None.
Public transport: None.
Habitat: Mixed coppice with standard sessile oak, glades, rides.
Key birds: *Summer:* Some 70 breeding species, inc. Woodcock, all three woodpeckers, Tree Pipit, Redstart, Nightingale, Wood Warbler, Hawfinch.
Contact: David Maylam,
Colharbour Farm, Wye, Ashford, Kent, TN25 5DB. 01233 812525.

BOUGH BEECH RESERVOIR

Kent Wildlife Trust.
Location: TQ49 64 89. Bough Beech is situated 3.5 miles S of Ide Hill, signposted off B2042, SW of Sevenoaks.
Access: Confined to holders of permits granted for recording and study purposes only on application to the warden. The whole of the reserve may be viewed from the public road just S of Winkhurst Green (49 64 94). Park on roadside (one side only).
Facilities: Toilets and visitor centre open between Apr-Oct, Wed, Sat, Sun & Bank Holiday Mon (11am-4.30pm).
Public transport: Rail service to Penshurst Station (two miles south).
Habitat: Reservoir.
Key birds: Approx 60 species of birds breed in and around the reserve annually, with Mallard, Tufted Duck, Canada Goose, Coot and Great Crested Grebe notable among the waterfowl. Little Ringed Plover nest most years.
Autumn: Especially good for numbers of waders like Green and Common Sandpipers and Greenshank. Many rarities have been recorded. Ospreys recorded most years. *Winter:* Wildfowl numbers are much higher than summer including Goldeneye and Goosander.
Contact: Dave Hutton, Kent Wildlife Trust, Tyland Barn, Sandling, Maidstone, Kent, ME14 3BD. 01622 662012.
e-mail: kentwildlife@cix.co.uk
www.kentwildlife.co.uk

BURHAM MARSHES

Kent Wildlife Trust.
Location: TQ 71 46 15. On E bank of the River Medway to the W of Burham Village. 4.5 miles from J3 (M2) S or J6 (M20) N.
Access: Visitors must adhere to the public footpath which runs along the riverbank. This may be reached most conveniently from the track leading W from Burham Court TQ 717 620.
Facilities: None.
Public transport: Bus - Arriva Bus No 155 (Maidstone to Chatham) passes through Burham Village.
Habitat: Wetland, large reed beds on River Medway.
Key birds: Bearded Tit, Water Rail. *Winter:* The river attracts duck and waders.
Contact: Dave Hutton, Kent Wildlife Trust, Tyland Barn, Sandling, Maidstone, Kent, ME14 3BD. 01622 662012. www.kentwildlife.co.uk
e-mail: kentwildlife@cix.co.uk

DUNGENESS

RSPB (South East England Office).
Location: TR 063 196. SE of Lydd.
Access: Open daily 9am-9pm or sunset when earlier. Visitor centre open (10am-5pm, 4pm Nov-Feb). Parties over 20 by prior arrangement.

Key to sites:

1. Blean Woods (RSPB)
2. Blean Woods
3. Bough Beech Reservoir
4. Burham Marshes
5. Dungeness (RSPB)
6. Dungeness Bird Observatory
7. Elmley Marshes
8. Hamstreet Woods
9. Nor Marsh
10. Northward Hill
11. Sandwich And Pegwell Bay
12. Sandwich Bay Bird Observatory
13. Sevenoaks Wildfowl Reserve
14. Stodmarsh
15. Oare Marshes LNR
16. Swale
17. Tudeley Woods
18. Wye

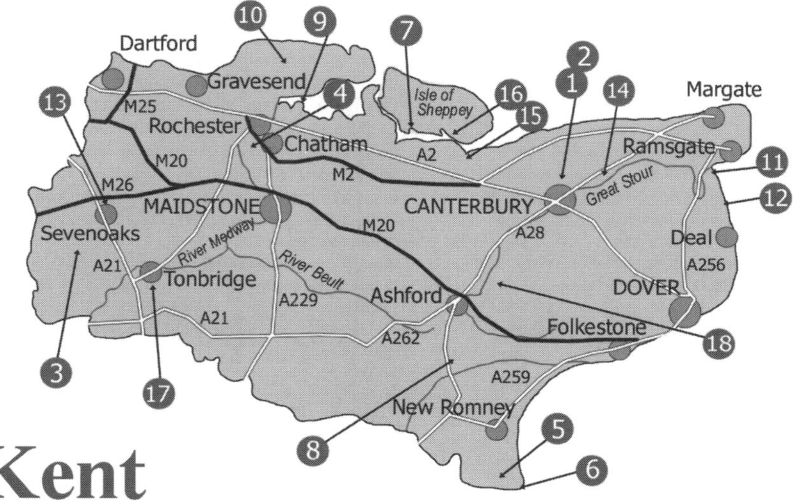

Facilities: Visitor centre, toilets (including disabled access), five hides, nature trail, wheelchair access to visitor centre and four hides.
Public transport: Service 12 from Lydd or Folkestone stops at reserve entrance on request - one mile walk to visitor centre.
Habitat: Shingle, flooded gravel pits, sallow scrub, reedbed, wet grassland.
Key birds: Resident Corn Bunting. *Winter*: Wildfowl (including Wigeon, Goldeneye, Goosander, Smew), divers and grebes. Migrant waders, landfall for passerines. *Summer*: Breeding Lapwing, Redshank, wildfowl, terns and gulls.
Contact: Christine Hawkins/Simon Busuttil, Boulderwall Farm, Dungeness Road, Lydd, Romney Marsh, Kent, TN29 9PN. 01797 320588/fax 01797 321962.
e-mail: dungeness@rspb.org.uk
www.rspb.org.uk

DUNGENESS BIRD OBSERVATORY

Dungeness Bird Observatory Trust.
Location: TR 085 173. Three miles SE of Lydd. Turn south off Dungeness Road at TR 087 185 and continue to end of road.
Access: Observatory open throughout the year.
Facilities: Accommodation available. Bring own sleeping bag/sheets and toiletries. Shared facilities including fully-equipped kitchen.
Public transport: Bus service between Rye and Folkestone, numbers 11, 12, 711, 712. Alight at the Pilot Inn, Lydd-on-Sea. Tel 01227 472082.
Habitat: Shingle promontory with scrub and gravel pits. RSPB reserve nearby.
Key birds: Breeding birds include Wheatear and Black Redstart and seabirds on RSPB Reserve. Important migration site.
Contact: David Walker, Dungeness Bird Observatory, 11 RNSSS, Dungeness, Kent, TN29 9NA. 01797 321309.
e-mail dungeness.obs@tinyonline.co.uk

ELMLEY MARSHES

RSPB (South East England Office).
Location: TQ 93 86 80. Isle of Sheppey, signposted from A249, one mile beyond Kingsferry Bridge. Reserve car park is two miles from the main road.
Access: Open every day except Tue, Christmas and Boxing days. 9am-9pm or dusk if earlier. No charge to RSPB members. Dogs are not allowed on the reserve. Less able may drive closer to the hides with Warden's permission.
Facilities: Five hides, no provision at present for disabled visitors but one hide with disabled access is planned. No visitor centre. Toilets located in car park 1.25 miles from hides.
Public transport: Swale Halt, a request stop is nearest railway station on Sittingbourne to Sheerness line. From there it is a three mile walk.
Habitat: Coastal grazing marsh, ditches and pools alongside the Swale Estuary with extensive intertidal mudflats and saltmarsh
Key birds: *Spring/summer*: Breeding waders - Redshank, Lapwing, Avocet, Yellow Wagtail, passage waders, Hobby. *Autumn*: Passage waders. *Winter*: Spectacular numbers of wildfowl especially Wigeon and White-fronted Goose. Waders. Hunting raptors - Peregrine, Merlin, Hen Harrier and Short-eared Owl.
Contact: Bob Gomes,
Elmley RSPB Reserve, Kingshill Farm, Elmley, Sheerness, Kent, ME12 3RW. 01795 665969.

HAMSTREET WOODS

English Nature (Kent Team).
Location: TR 003 337. Follow A2070 S from Ashford to hamstreet. Go E on B2067, car park first L at green.
Access: Keep to paths.
Public transport: None.
Habitat: Damp oak woodland, coppice/standards.
Key birds: Over 90 species recorded. Woodcock, Great and Lesser Spotted Woodpeckers, Nightingale, Redstart, warblers, Hawfinch; Hoopoe regular summer visitor.
Contact: English Nature (see Blean Woods).

NOR MARSH

RSPB (South East England Office).
Location: TQ 810 700. One mile NE of Gillingham in the Medway Estuary.
Access: No access, it is an island. It is viewable from Riverside Country Park (B2004) at the Horrid Hill Peninsula, giving overviews of the Medway Estuary saltmarsh and mudflats.
Public transport: Buses can be caught to Riverside Country Park. Phone Medway Council for the bus numbers, 01634 727777.
Habitat: Saltmarsh and mudflats.
Key birds: *Spring/summer*: Breeding Redshank, Oystercatcher, Shelduck and Black-headed Gull. *Winter*: Dunlin (2-3,000), Knot, Curlew, Redshank, Oystercatcher, Turnstone, Brent Goose, Teal, Wigeon, Shelduck.
Contact: Michael Ellison, Bromhey Farm, Eastborough, Cooling, Rochester, Kent, ME3 8DS. 01634 222480.

NORTHWARD HILL

RSPB (South East England Office).
Location: TQ 780 765. Adjacent to village of High Halstow, off A228, approx six miles N of Rochester.
Access: Open all year, free access, trails in public area of wood joining Saxon Shoreway to give access adjacent to grazing marsh. Sanctuary area accessible by permit only - write to warden. Dogs allowed in public area on leads. Trails often steep and not suitable for wheelchair users.
Facilities: Three nature trails in the wood and one joining with long distance footpath. Toilets at village hall, small car park adjacent to wood.
Public transport: Buses to village of High Halstow. Contact Arriva buses for times.
Habitat: Ancient and scrub woodland (approx. 130 acres), grazing marsh (approx.350 acres).
Key birds: *Spring/summer*: Wood holds UK's largest heronry (155 pairs in 2001), breeding Nightingale, Turtle Dove, scrub warblers and woodpeckers. Marshes - breeding Lapwing, Redshank, Avocet (most years), Marsh Harrier, Shoveler, Pochard. *Winter*: Wigeon, Teal Shoveler. Passage waders (ie Black-tailed Godwit). Long-eared Owl roost.
Contact: Michael Ellison, Bromhey Farm, Eastborough, Cooling, Rochester, Kent, ME3 8DS. 01634 222480

SANDWICH & PEGWELL BAY

Kent Wildlife Trust.
Location: TR 342 635. Main car park is off A256 Sandwich - Ramsgate road at Pegwell Bay.
Access: Open 8.30am-8pm or dusk if earlier.
Facilities: Toilets, hide, car parking and trails
Public transport: Bus stop within 500 yards

(Stagecoach). Sustrans National Bike Route passes along the edge of the reserve.
Habitat: Saltmarsh, mudflats, sand dunes and coastal scrub.
Key birds: Good range of wetland birds throughout the year.
Contact: Pete Forrest, Kent Wildlife Trust, Tyland Barn, Sandling, Maidstone, Kent, ME14 3BD. 01622 662012. www.kentwildlife.co.uk e-mail: kentwildlife@cix.co.uk

SANDWICH BAY BIRD OBSERVATORY

Sandwich Bay Bird Observatory Trust.
Location: TR 355 575. 2.5 miles from Sandwich, five miles from Deal, 15 miles from Canterbury. A256 to Sandwich from Dover or Ramsgate. Follow signs to Sandwich Station and then Sandwich Bay.
Access: Open daily. Disabled access.
Facilities: New Field Study Centre. Visitor centre, toilets, refreshments, hostel-type accomm.
Public transport: Sandwich train station two miles from Observatory. No public transport, but within walking distance.
Habitat: Coastal, dune land, farmland, marsh, small scrape.
Key birds: *Spring/autumn passage*: Good variety of migrants and waders, specially Corn Bunting. Annual Golden Oriole. *Winter*: Golden Plover.
Contact: Gaynor Cross, Sandwich Bay Bird Observatory, Guildford Road, Sandwich Bay, Sandwich, Kent, CT13 9PF. 01304 617341. e-mail: sbbot@talk21.com

SEVENOAKS WILDFOWL RESERVE

Jeffery Harrison Memorial Trust.
Location: TQ 519 568. From A25 immediately N of Sevenoaks.
Access: Wed, Sat, Sun 10am-5pm (or dusk if earlier).
Facilities: Visitor centre, nature trail, hides.
Habitat: Flooded gravel pits.
Key birds: Wintering wildfowl; woodland birds.
Contact: John Tyler, Tadorna, Bradbourne Vale Road, Sevenoaks, Kent, TN13 3DH. 01732 456407.

STODMARSH

English Nature (Kent Team).
Location: TR 222 618. Lies alongside River Stone and A28, five miles NE of Canterbury.
Access: Open at all times.
Facilities: Fully accessible toilets are available at the Stodmarsh entrance car park and also at the picnic area adjoining the Grove Ferry entrance.
Public transport: There is a regular bus service from Canterbury to Margate/Ramsgate. Alight at Upstreet for Grove Ferry. Hourly on Sun.
Habitat: Open water, reedbeds, wet meadows, dry meadows, woodland.
Key birds: *Spring/summer*: Breeding Bearded Tit, Cetti's Warbler, Garganey, Reed, Sedge and Willow Warblers, Nightingale. Migrant Black Tern, Hobby, Osprey, Little Egret. *Winter*: Wildfowl. Hen Harrier, Bittern.
Contact: David Feast, English Nature, (see Blean Woods).

OARE MARSHES LNR

Kent Wildlife Trust.
Location: TR 01 36 48 (car park). Two miles N of Faversham. From A2 follow signs to Oare and Harty Ferry.
Access: Open at all times. Access along marked paths only. Dogs under strict control to avoid disturbance to birds and livestock.
Facilities: Information centre, open weekends, Bank Holidays. Two hides.
Public transport: Bus to Oare Village one mile from reserve. Train station in Faversham (two miles)
Habitat: Grazing marsh, mudflats/estuary.
Key birds: *All year*: Waders and wildfowl. *Winter*: Hen Harrier, Merlin, Peregrine; divers, grebes and sea ducks on Swale. *Spring/summer*: Avocet, Garganey, Green and Wood Sandpipers, Little Stint, Black-tailed Godwit etc. Black Tern.
Contact: Tony Swandale, Kent Wildlife Trust, Tyland Barn, Sandling, Maidstone, Kent, ME14 3BD. 01622 662012. www.kentwildlife.co.uk e-mail: kentwildlife@cix.co.uk

SWALE

English Nature (Kent Team).
Location: TR 052 682. From Leysdown-on-Sea (Isle of Sheppey) along sea front to Muswell Manor; rough track for one mile to car park. Permissive track to Shellness Point, may be closed.
Access: Keep to pathways.
Facilities: Hides, one tower hide overlooking flood areas.

Public transport: None.
Habitat: Coastal saltmarsh, freshwater grazing marsh, shell/shingle beach.
Key birds: *Autumn*: Large seabird movements viewed from Shellness inc. Gannet, skuas, divers, grebes. *Winter*: Large numbers of wildfowl and waders (roosts of Oystercatcher, Black-tailed Godwit, Knot, Dunlin, Grey Plover), Hen Harrier, Short-eared Owl. *Summer*: Breeding birds inc. Gadwall, Teal, Pochard, Avocet, Snipe, Lapwing, Redshank, Yellow Wagtail.
Contact: English Nature,
Coldharbour Farm, Wye, Ashford, Kent, TN25 5DB. 01233 812525.

TUDELEY WOODS

RSPB (South East England Office).
Location: TQ 618 434. Beside A21, one mile S of Tonbridge. Take minor road to Capel on left immediately before Fairthorne Garage. Car park 0.25 miles on left.
Access: Open every day except Christmas Day. No dogs. No disabled facilities.
Facilities: Leaflet, two nature trails.
Public transport: None.
Habitat: Semi-natural ancient woodland, lowland heathland (restored), pasture.
Key birds: *Spring/summer*: Willow Warbler, Garden Warbler, Blackcap, Turtle Dove, Spotted Flycatcher, Nightingale, Tree Pipit, Wood Lark, Nightjar, Hobby, Whitethroat. *All year*: Marsh Tit, Willow Tit, Nuthatch, three woodpecker species, Yellowhammer, Treecreeper.
Contact: Martin Allison,
12 The Grove, Crowborough, East Sussex, TN6 1NY. 01273 775333 (South East Regional Office). www.rspb.org.uk
e-mail: martin/allison@rspb.org.uk

WYE

English Nature (Kent Team).
Location: TR 079 454. From Wye up hill towards Hastingleigh, car park at roadside.
Access: Open daily except Christmas Day. No dogs. Keep to paths.
Facilities: Three nature trails.
Public transport: None.
Habitat: Downland, scrub, woodlands, grazing meadows.
Key birds: *Summer*: Breeding Sparrowhawk, Tawny Owl, Nightingale, Spotted Flycatcher, Lesser Whitethroat, Hawfinch.
Contact: David Maylam,
Coldharbour Farm, Wye, Ashford, Kent, TN25 5DB. 01233 812525.

Lancashire

HEYSHAM NATURE RESERVE

Lancashire Wildlife Trust.
Location: SD 404 596. A683 to Heyshamport. Turn left at traffic lights by Duke of Rothersay pub, then first right after 300m.
Access: Gate to car park usually open 9.30am-6pm (sometimes longer in summer and shorter in winter). Pedestrian access at all times.
Dogs on lead. Disabled access tel 859101 and ask for security.
Facilities: One hide overlooking power station outfalls. No manned visitor centre, or toilet access, but always worth checking if anyone is in reserve office next to main car park.
Public transport: Train services connect with nearby Isle of Man and Belfast ferries.
Plenty of buses from various Heysham sites within walking distance to Lancaster (ask for nearest stop to the harbour).
Habitat: Varied: wetland, acid grassland, alkaline grassland, foreshore.
Key birds: Good passage of seabirds in spring, especially Arctic Tern late April/early May. *Summer*: Breeding Lesser Whitethroat and Reed Warbler. Other warblers can be heard singing at the same time on the reserve. *Autumn*: Leach's Petrel in gales. *Passage*: Regular rarities. Latest was a Tawny Pipit that turned up on May 16, 2001.
Contact: Pete Marsh,
17 Albion Street, Lancaster, LA1 1DY. 01524 66775.
e-mail: pete@pbmarsh.prestel.co.uk
www.libweb.lancs.ac.uk/ldbws.htm (covers N Lancs)

Key to sites:
1. Heysham Nature Reserve & Bird Observatory
2. Leighton Moss
3. Martin Mere
4. Marton Mere
5. Mere Sands Wood
6. Morecambe Bay
7. Ribble Estuary
8. Upper Coldwell Reservoir
9. Wigan Flashes

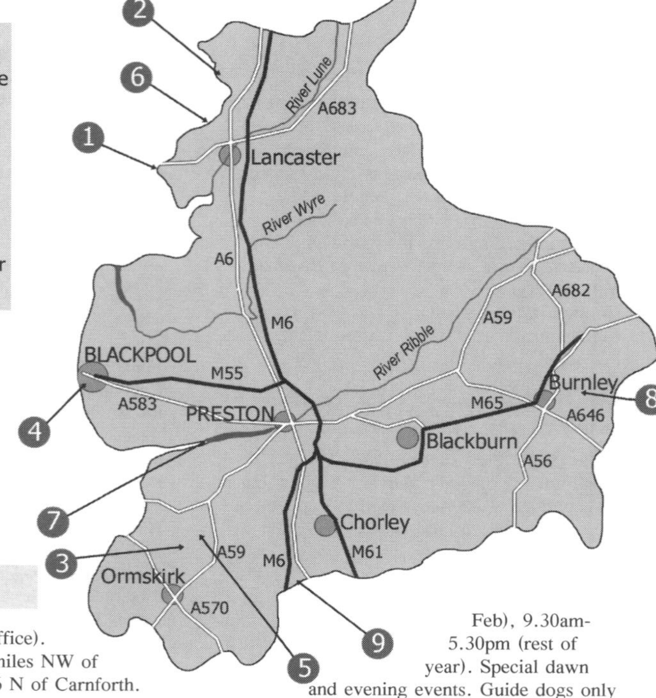

LEIGHTON MOSS

RSBP (North West England Office).
Location: SD 478 750. Four miles NW of Carnforth. Signposted from A6 N of Carnforth.
Access: Reserve open daily 9am-dusk. Visitor centre open daily 10am-5pm (except Christmas Day). No dogs. No charge to RSBP members.
Facilities: Visitor centre, shop, tea-room and toilets. Nature trails and five hides (four have wheelchair access).
Public transport: Silverdale Train Station 150 metres from reserve. Tel: 08457 484950.
Habitat: Reedbed, shallow meres and surrounding woodland.
Key birds: *All year*: Bittern, Bearded Tit, Water Rail, Pochard and Shoveler. *Summer*: Marsh Harrier, Reed and Sedge Warblers.
Contact: Robin Horne, Leighton Moss RSBP Nature Reserve, Myers Farm, Silverdale, Carnforth, Lancashire, LA 0SW. 01524 701601. www.RSBP.org.uk

MARTIN MERE

The Wildfowl & Wetlands Trust.
Location: SD 428 145. Six miles N of Ormskirk via Burscough Bridge (A59), 20 miles from Liverpool and Preston.
Access: Opening times: 9.30am-4.30pm (Nov-Feb), 9.30am-5.30pm (rest of year). Special dawn and evening events. Guide dogs only allowed. Admission charge. No charge for members. Fully accessible to disabled.
Facilities: Visitor centre with toilets, gift shop, restaurant, education centre, play area, nature reserve and nature trails, hides, waterfowl collection and sustainable garden. Provision for disabled visitors.
Public transport: Bus service to WWT Martin Mere from Ormskirk. Train to Burscough Bridge or New Lane Stations (both 1.5 miles from reserve).
Habitat: Open water, wet grassland, moss, copses, reedbed, parkland.
Key birds: *Winter*: Whooper and Bewick's Swans, Pink-footed Goose, various duck, Ruff, Black-tailed Godwit, Peregrine, Hen Harrier, Tree Sparrow. *Spring*: Ruff, Shelduck, Little Ringed and Ringed Plover, Lapwing, Redshank. *Summer*: Marsh Harrier, Garganey, hirundines, Tree Sparrow. *Autumn*: Pink-footed Goose, waders on passage.
Contact: Patrick Wisniewski, WWT Martin Mere, Fish Lane, Burscough, Lancs, L40 0TA. 01704 895181. www.martinmere.co.uk
e-mail: christine@martinmere.co.uk

MARTON MERE

Blackpool Borough Council.
Location: SD 345 352. Signposted from Blackpool Zoo car park (free) and De Veres Hotel car park.
Access: Open at all times. Dogs on lead.
Facilities: Hides.
Public transport: None.
Habitat: Open water surrounded by patchwork of grassland, scrub and reedbed.
Key birds: *Summer*: Breeding warblers. Migrant waders (inc. Little Ringed Plover, Jack Snipe), Black Tern. *Winter*: Good range of duck, also Bittern annual. Regular Mediterranean and Little Gulls.
Contact: David McGrath, Community & Tourism Services, c/o Blackpool Zoo, East Park Drive, Blackpool, FY3 8PP,

MERE SANDS WOOD

Wildlife Trust for Lancashire, Manchester and North Merseyside.
Location: SD 44 71 57. Four miles inland of Southport, 0.5 miles off A59 Preston – Liverpool road, in Rufford along B5246 (Holmeswood Rd).
Access: Visitor centre open 9am-5pm daily except Christmas Day. Car park open until 8pm in summer. 750m of wheelchair-accessible path, leading to two hides and viewpoint.
Facilities: Visitor centre with toilets (disabled), seven hides, two trails, exhibition room, latest sightings board. Feeding stations
Public transport: Bus: Southport-Chorley 347 stops in Rufford, ½ mile walk. Train: Preston-Ormskirk train stops at Rufford station, one mile walk.
Habitat: Freshwater lakes, mixed woodland, sandy grassland/heath. 105h.
Key birds: *Winter*: Nationally important for Teal and Gadwall, good range of waterfowl, Kingfisher. Feeding stations attract Tree Sparrow, Bullfinch, Reed Bunting. Woodland: Treecreeper. *Summer*: Little Ringed Plover, Kingfisher, Lesser Spotted Woodpecker. *Passage*: Most years, Osprey, Crossbill, Green Sandpiper, Greenshank, Wood Warbler, Turtle Dove.
Contact: Dominic Rigby, Warden, Mere Sands Wood Nature Reserve, Holmeswood Road, Rufford, Ormskirk, Lancs, L40 1TG. 01704 821809. e-mail: lancswtmsw@cix.co.uk www.wildlifetrust.org/lancashire

MORECAMBE BAY

RSBP (North West England Office).
Location: SD 468 667. Two miles N of Morecambe at Hest Bank.
Access: Open at all times. Do not venture onto saltmarsh or intertidal area, there are dangerous channels and quicksands.
Facilities: Viewpoint at car park.
Public transport: No 5 bus runs between Carnforth and Morecambe. Tel: 0870 608 2608.
Habitat: Saltmarsh, estuary.
Key birds: *Winter*: Wildfowl (Pintail, Shelduck, Wigeon) and waders – important high tide roost for Oystercatcher, Curlew, Redshank, Dunlin, Bar-tailed Godwit.
Contact: Robin Horner, Leighton Moss & Morecambe Bay RSBP Reserves, Myers Farm, Silverdale, Carnforth, Lancashire, LA5 0SW. 01524 701601. www.rspb.org.uk

RIBBLE ESTUARY

English Nature (North West Team).
Location: SD 380 240.
Access: Open at all times.
Facilities: No formal visiting facilities.
Public transport: None.
Habitat: Saltmarsh, mudflats.
Key birds: High water wader roosts (of Knot, Dunlin, Black-tailed Godwit, Oystercatcher and Grey Plover) are best viewed from Southport, Marshside, Lytham and St Annes. Pink-footed Geese and wintering swans are present in large numbers from Oct-Feb on Banks Marsh and along River Douglas respectively. The large flocks of Wigeon, for which the site is renowned, can be seen on high tides from Marshside but feed on saltmarsh areas at night. Good numbers of raptors also present in winter.
Contact: Kevin Wilson. (Warden), Pier House, Wallgate, Wigan, WN3 4AL. 01942 820342; fax 01942 820364.
e-mail north.west@english-nature.org.uk.

UPPER COLDWELL

Lancashire Wildlife Trust.
Location: SD 905 360. Three miles SE of Nelson. Enter from junction 13 of M65, then take minor road towards Hebden Bridge.
Access: Public footpath along N perimeter wall. Access to reserve area by permit.
Facilities: None.

Public transport: None.
Habitat: Upland reservoir, coniferous woodland, moorland.
Key birds: Breeding Tufted Duck, Little Ringed Plover, Whinchat; moors have Twite, Short-eared Owl, Golden Plover.
Contact: Trust HQ, 01772 324129..

WIGAN FLASHES

Lancashire Wildlife Trust/Wigan Council/RSPB.
Location: SD 580 035. One mile from J25 of M6.
Access: Free access, open at all times. Areas suitable for disabled but some motor cycle barriers with gates. Paths being upgraded.
Facilities: None.
Public transport: 610 bus (Hawkley Hall Circular).
Habitat: Wetland with reedbed.
Key birds: Black Tern on migration. *Summer*: Nationally important for Reed Warbler and breeding Common Tern. Willow Tit, Grasshopper Warbler, Kingfisher. *Winter*: Wildfowl especially diving duck and Gadwall. Bittern (especially winter).
Contact: Mark Champion, 225 Poolstock Lane, Wigan, Lancs, WN3 5JE. 01942 236337. e-mail: mark@championx.freeserve.co.uk

Leicestershire and Rutland

EYEBROOK RESERVOIR

Corby & District Water Co.
Location: SP 853 964. Reservoir built 1940. S of Uppingham, from unclassified road W of A6003 at Stoke Dry.
Access: Access to 150 acres private grounds granted to members of Leics and Rutland Ornithological Society, and Rutland Nat Hist Soc. Organised groups with written permission (from Corby Water Co, PO Box 101, Weldon Road, Corby NN17 5UA).
Facilities: SSSI since 1955. Good viewing from public roads. Trout fishery season Apr-Oct.
Public transport: None.
Habitat: Open water, plantations and pasture.
Key birds: *Summer*: Good populations of breeding birds, sightings of Ospreys. Passage waders and Black Tern. *Winter*: Wildfowl (inc. Goldeneye, Goosander, Bewick's Swan) and waders.

RUTLAND WATER

Leics and Rutland Wildlife Trust.
Location: SK 866 676. Large reservoir with two reserve areas.
1. Egleton Reserve: from Egleton village off A6003 S of Oakham, home of the British Birdwatching Fair each August.
2. Lyndon Reserve: south shore E of Manton village off A6003 S of Oakham.
Access: 1. Open daily 9am-5pm. 2. Open winter (Sat, Sun 10am-4pm), summer daily except Mon (10am-4pm). Day permits available for both reserves.
Facilities: 1: Anglian Water Birdwatching Centre, now enlarged. Toilets and disabled access to 10 hides, electric buggies, conference facilities. 2: Interpretive centre.
Public transport: None.
Habitat: Reservoir, lagoons, scrapes, woods, meadows, plantations.
Key birds: *Spring/autumn*: Outstanding wader passage. Also harriers, owls, passerine flocks, terns (Black, Arctic, breeding Common, occasional Little and Sandwich). *Winter*: Wildfowl (inc Goldeneye, Goosander, rare grebes, all divers), Ruff flock. *Summer:* First Osprey breeding success in 2001 following translocation of Scottish birds.
Contact: Tim Appleton, Fishponds Cottage, Stamford Road, Oakham, Rutland, LE15 8AB. 01572 770651; fax 01572 755931; e-mail awbc@rutlandwater.u-net.com www.rutlandwater.u-net.com.

Lincolnshire

DONNA NOOK-SALTFLEETBY

Lincolnshire Wildlife Trust.
Location: TF 422 998. Near North Somercotes, off A1031 coast road, S of Grimsby.
Access: Open all year. Dogs on leads. Some disabled access.
Facilities: No toilets or visitor centre. Interpretation boards and paths.
Public transport: None.
Habitat: Dunes, slacks and intertidal areas, seashore, mudflats, sandflats.
Key birds: *Summer*: Little Tern, Ringed Plover, Oystercatcher. *Winter*: Brent Goose, Shelduck, Twite, Lapland Bunting, Shore Lark, Linnet.
Contact:
c/o Lincolnshire Wildlife Trust, Banarallum House, Manor House Street, Horncastle, Lincs, LN9 5HT. 01507 526667.
e-mail: lincstrust@cix.co.uk
www.lincstrust.co.uk

FAR INGS

Lincolnshire Wildlife Trust.
Location: TA 011 229 and TA 023 230. Off Far Ings Lane, W of Barton-on-Humber, the last turn off before the Humber Bridge.
Access: Open all year. No dogs. Some disabled access.
Facilities: Toilets, visitor centre open some weekends and weekdays - not all week. Hides and paths.
Public transport: None.
Habitat: Chain of flooded clay pits and reedbeds.
Key birds: *Summer*: Marsh Harrier, Bittern, Bearded Tit, Water Rail. *Winter*: Wildfowl (Mallard, Teal Gadwall, Pochard, Tufted and Ruddy Ducks).
Contact: Lional Grooby, Far Ings Visitor Centre, Far Ings Road, Barton on Humber, DN18 5RG. 01652 634507. www.lincstrust.co.uk
e-mail: farings@lincstrust.co.uk

FRAMPTON MARSH

RSPB (East Anglia Office).
Location: TR 36 43 85. Four miles SE of Boston. From A16 follow signs to Frampton then Frampton Marsh.
Access: Open at all times. Free.
Facilities: Footpaths, bench, two car parks. Free information leaflets available (please contact the office), guided walks programme.
Public transport: None.
Habitat: Saltmarsh.
Key birds: *Summer*: Breeding Redshank, passage waders (inc Greenshank, Ruff and Black-tailed Godwit) and Hobby. *Winter*: Hen Harrier, Short-eared Owl, Merlin, dark-bellied Brent Goose, Twite, Golden Plover.
Contact: John Badley,
RSPB Lincolnshire Wash Office, 61 Horseshoe Line, Kirton, Kirton, Boston, Lincs, PE20 1LW. 01205 724678. www.rspb.org.uk
e-mail: john.badley@rspb.org.uk

FREISTON SHORE

RSPB (East Anglia Office).
Location: TF 39 74 24. Four miles E of Boston. From A52 at Haltoft End follow signs to Freiston Shore.
Access: Open at all times, free.
Facilities: Footpaths, two car parks, information leaflets available free - please contact the office guided walks programme.
Public transport: None.
Habitat: Saltmarsh, saline lagoon, mudflats.
Key birds: *Summer*: Breeding Redshank, Corn Bunting and Tree Sparrow. *Winter*: Lapland Bunting, Twite, dark-bellied Brent Goose, wildfowl, waders, birds of prey including Short-eared Owl and Hen Harrier. *Passage*: Waders, including Curlew Sandpiper and Little Stint.
Contact: John Badley,
RSPB Lincolnshire Wash Office, 61 Horseshoe Line, Kirton, Boston, Lincs, PE20 1LW. 01205 724678. www.rspb.org.uk
e-mail: john.badley@rspb.org.uk

GIBRALTAR POINT NNR & BIRD OBSERVATORY

Lincolnshire Wildlife Trust.
Location: TF 556 580. Three miles S of Skegness on the N edge of The Wash. Signposted from Skegness town centre.
Access: Reserve is open dawn-dusk. Seasonal

Lincolnshire

Key to sites:
1. Donna Nook-Saltfleetby
2. Far Ings
3. Frampton Marsh
4. Freiston Shore
5. Gibraltar Point NNR & Bird Observatory
6. Saltfleetby Theddlethorpe Dunes
7. Snipe Dales Nature Reserve
8. Tetney Marshes
9. Whisby Nature Park

charges for car parking. Free admission to reserve, visitor centre and toilets.
Some access restrictions to sensitive sites at S end, open access to N. Dogs on leads at all times - no dogs on beach during summer. Visitor centre and toilets suitable for wheelchairs, also network of surfaced foot paths. Bird observatory and two hides suitable for wheelchairs. Day visit groups must be booked in advance. Contact Doreen Lilley, bookings secretary for residential or day visits.
Facilities: Site also location of Wash Study Centre and Bird Observatory. Field centre is an ideal base for birdwatching/natural history groups in spring, summer and autumn. Visitor centre and gift shop open daily (May-Oct) and weekends for remainder of the year. Toilets open daily. Network of foot paths bisect all major habitats. Public hides overlook freshwater and brackish lagoons. Wash viewpoint overlooks saltmarsh and mudflats.
Public transport: Bus service from Skegness runs in occasional years but summer service only. Otherwise taxi/car from Skegness. Cycle route in progress.
Habitat: Sand dune grassland and scrub, saltmarshes and mudflats, freshwater marsh and lagoons.
Key birds: Large migration visible during spring and autumn passage - hirundines, chats, pipits, larks, thrushes and occasional rarities. Large numbers of waterfowl including internationally important populations of non-breeding waders. Sept-May impressive wader roosts in high tides. *Summer*: Little Tern and good assemblage of breeding warblers. *Winter*: Shore Lark, raptors, waders and wildfowl.
Contact: Kev Wilson, (Site Manager), Gibraltar Point Field Centre, Gibraltar Road, Skegness, Lincs, PE24 4SU. 01754 762677. e-mail: lincstrust@gibpoint.freeserve.co.uk www.lincstrust.co.uk

SALTFLEETBY-THEDDLETHORPE DUNES

English Nature (East Midlands Team).
Location: TF 46 59 24-TF 49 08 83. Approx two miles N of Mablethorpe. All the following car parks may be accessed from the A1031: Crook Bank, Brickyard Lane, Churchill Lane, Rimac, Sea View.
Access: Open all year at all times. Dogs on leads.

A purpose-built easy access trail suitable for wheelchair users starts adjacent to Rimac car park, just over 0.5 miles long meanders past ponds. Includes pond-viewing platform and saltmarsh-viewing platform.
Facilities: Toilets, including wheelchair suitability at Rimac car park (next to trail) May to end of Sept.
Public transport: Grayscroft coaches (01507 473236) and Lincolnshire Roadcar (01522 532424). Both run services past Rimac entrance (Louth to Mablethorpe service). Lincs Roadcar can connect with trains at Lincoln. Applebys Coaches (01507 357900). Grimsby to Saltfleet bus connects with Grimsby train service.
Habitat: 13th Century dunes, freshwater marsh, new dune ridge with large areas of sea blackthorn, saltmarsh, shingle ridge and foreshore.
Key birds: *Summer*: Small breeding colony of Little Terns. Breeding birds in scrub include Nightingale, Grasshopper Warbler, Whitethroat, Lesser Whitethroat, Redpoll. *Winter*: Large flocks of Brent Goose, Shelduck, Teal and Wigeon. Wintering Short-eared Owl, Hen Harrier.
Contact: Simon Smith,
English Nature, The Maltings, Wharf Road, Grantham, Lincs, NG31 6BH. 01205 311674.
e-mail: simonb.smith@english-nature.org.uk

SNIPE DALES NATURE

Lincolnshire Wildlife Trust.
Location: TF 319 683 (nature reserve) and TF 330 682 (country park). Well signposted off the A158 Skegness-Lincoln Road, W of Hornchurch, and from the B1195 Horncastle-Spilsby road.
Access: Open all year. Dogs on leads. Car park charge. Some disabled access.
Facilities: Toilets, interpretation boards, one small hide, footpaths.
Public transport: Restricted bus service.
Habitat: Nature reserve - steep-sided valleys fretted by streams. Unspoilt wet-valley system. Country park - attractive walks through coniferous woodland, new plantings of broad-leaved trees, plus ponds.
Key birds: *Spring/summer*: Chaffinch, Redpoll, Willow Warbler, Willow Tit, Long-tailed Tit, Siskin, Tawny Owl, Barn Owl, Grasshopper Warbler. *Winter*: Woodcock.
Contact: Peter Graves,
Snipe Dales Country Park, Lusby, Spilsby, PE23 4JB. 01507 588401.
www.lincstrust.co.uk

TETNEY MARSHES

RSPB (North of England Office).
Location: TA 345 025. S of Cleethorpes. Via gate or river bank E of Tetney Lock, which is two miles E of A1031 at Tetney, or through Humberston Fithes.
Access: Access at all times. Visitors are asked to keep to the seawalls, especially during the breeding season (Apr-Aug).
Facilities: None.
Public transport: None.
Habitat: Saltmarsh, sand-dunes and inter-tidal sandflats.
Key birds: *Summer*: Breeding Little Tern, Redshank, Shelduck. *Winter*: Brent Goose, Common Scoter, Wigeon, Bar-tailed Godwit, Knot, Grey and Golden Plovers. All three harriers recorded on passage. Migrant Whimbrel.
Contact: Tetney Warden RSPB,
c/o 4 Benton Terrace, Sandyford Road, Newcastle-upon-Tyne, NE2 1QU,

WHISBY NATURE PARK

Lincolnshire Wildlife Trust.
Location: SK 914 661. W of Lincoln off A46 southern end of Lincoln relief road. Brown tourist signs.
Access: Nature Park open all year but car park closed out of hours. Free entry. Natural World Visitor Centre open (10am-5pm), free entry. Some special exhibitions will have a charge. Disabled access. Dogs on leads.
Facilities: Toilets, visitor centre, café, education centre, waymarked routes, interpretation signs, leaflets.
Public transport: None.
Habitat: Flooded sand and gravel pits.
Key birds: *Summer*: Common Tern on specially-built rafts, Nightingale, Whitethroat, Lesser Whitethroat, Tree Sparrow. *Winter*: Wigeon, Teal, Pochard, Tufted Duck, Goldeneye.
Contact: Phil Porter,
Whisby Nature Park, Moor Lane, Thorpe-on-the-Hill, Lincoln, LN6 9BW. 01522 500676.
e-mail: whisby@cix.co.uk
www.lincstrust.co.uk

London, Greater

BEDFONT LAKES COUNTRY PARK

Hounslow Countryside Parks Service.
Location: TQ 080 728. OS map sheet 176 (west London). 0.5 miles from Ashford, Middx, 0.5 miles S of A30, Clockhouse Roundabout, on B3003 (Clockhouse Lane).
Access: Open 7.30am-9pm or dusk whichever is earlier, all days except Christmas Day. Disabled friendly. Dogs on leads. Main nature reserve area only open Sun (2pm-4pm).
Facilities: Toilets, information centre, several hides, nature trail, free parking, up-to-date information.
Public transport: Train to Feltham and Ashford. Bus – H26 and 116 from Hounslow.
Habitat: Lakes, wildflower meadows, woodland, scrub.
Key birds: *Winter*: Water Rail, Bittern, Smew and other wildfowl, Meadow Pipit. *Summer*: Common Tern, Willow, Garden, Reed and Sedge Warblers, Whitethroat, Lesser Whitethroat, hirundines, Hobby, Blackcap, Chiffchaff, Skylark. *Passage*: Wheatear, Wood Warbler, Spotted Flycatcher, Ring Ouzel, Redstart, Yellow Wagtail.
Contact: Paul Morgan (Ecology Ranger), BLCP, Clockhouse Lane, Bedfont, Middx, TW14 8QA. 01784 423556; Fax: 423451.
e-mail: bedfont-lakes@cip.org.uk

THE CHASE

London Wildlife Trust.
Location: TQ 515 860. Lies in the Dagenham Corridor, an area of green belt between the London Boroughs of Barking & Dagenham and Havering.
Access: Open throughout the year and at all times. Reserve not suitable for wheelchair access. Eastbrookend Country Park which borders The Chase has surfaced footpaths which are easily accessible for wheelchair use.
Facilities: Millennium visitor centre, toilets, ample car parking, Timberland Trail walk.
Public transport: Rail Dagenham East (District Line) 15 minute walk. Bus 174 from Romford five minute walk.
Habitat: Shallow wetlands, reedbeds, horse-grazed pasture, scrub and wetland. These harbour an impressive range of animals and plants including the nationally rare black poplar tree. This site is a haven for birds, with approx 190 different species recorded.
Key birds: *Summer*: Breeding Reed Warbler, Lapwing, Water Rail, Lesser Whitethroat and Little Ringed Plover. *Winter*: Significant numbers of Teal, Shoveler, Redwing, Fieldfare and Snipe dominate the scene. *Spring/autumn migration*: Yellow Wagtail, Wheatear, Ruff, Wood Sandpiper, Sand Martin and Hobby.
Contact: Gareth Winn/Ian Holt, Project Manager/Project Officer, The Millennium Centre, The Chase, Off Dagenham Road, Rush Green, Romford, Essex, RM7 0SS. 020 8593 8096.
e-mail: lwtchase@cix.co.uk
www.wildlifetrust.org.uk/london/

SYDENHAM HILL WOOD

London Wildlife Trust.
Location: TQ 335 722. SE London, SE26, between Forest Hill and Crystal Palace, just off South Circular (A205).
Access: Open at all times, no permits required. Some steep slopes which makes disabled access limited
Facilities: Nature trail, no toilets.
Public transport: Train – Sydenham Hill, Forest Hill. Bus – 63, 202, 356, 185, 312, 176.
Habitat: Oak and hornbeam woodland, small pond, meadow and glades.
Key birds: *Resident*: Kestrel, Sparrowhawk, Tawny Owl, all three woodpeckers, Treecreeper, Nuthatch, Song Thrush. *Summer*: Chiffchaff, Blackcap. *Winter*: Redwing, Fieldfare.
Contact: John White, Horniman Museum, 100 London Road, London, SE23 3PQ. 020 8699 5698. e-mail: lwtsydenham@cix.co.uk
www.wildlifetrust.org.uk/london

THE WETLAND CENTRE

The Wildfowl & Wetlands Trust.
Location: TQ 228 770. In London, S of River Thames at Barnes, Zone 2, one mile from Hammersmith.
Access: Winter (9.30am-5pm: last admission 4pm), summer (9.30am-6pm: last admission

5pm). Some evening opening in summer, please phone for details.
Facilities: Visitor centre, hides, nature trails, art gallery, discovery restaurant (hot and cold food), cinema, shop, observatory centre, seven hides (one with a lift for wheelchair access), three interpretative buildings.
Public transport: Train: Barnes. Tube: Hammersmith then Duckbus 283 (comes into centre). Bus from Hammersmith – 283, 33, 72, 209. Bus from Richmond 33, 72.
Habitat: Main lake, reedbeds, wetland, wader scrape, mudflats, open water lakes, grazing marsh.
Key birds: Nationally important numbers of wintering waterfowl, including Gadwall and Shoveler. Important numbers of wetland breeding birds including grebes, swans, a range of duck species, such as Pochard plus Lapwing, Little Ringed Plover, Redshank, warblers and Reed Bunting.
Contact: John Arbon (Grounds and Facilities Manager), Stephanie Fudge (Manager), The Wetland Centre, Queen Elizabeth Walk, Barnes, London, SW13 9WT. 0208 409 4400. e-mail: info@wetlandcentre.org.uk www.wetlandcentre.co.uk

---

Manchester, Greater

ASTLEY MOSS

Lancashire Wildlife Trust.
Location: Lancs WT SJ692975. S of A580 at Astley, between Leigh and Swinton, W of city centre. Follow Higher Green Lane to Rindle farm.
Access: Permit from Trust required.
Facilities: None.
Public transport: None.
Habitat: Remnant peat bog, scrub, oak/birch woodland.
Key birds: *Spring/summer*: Breeding Tree Pipit. *Winter*: Raptors (inc. Merlin, Hen Harrier), finch flocks, thrush flocks; Long- and Short-eared Owl.
Contact: Dave Woodward, 54 Windermere Road, Leigh, Lancs, WN7 1UZ.

AUDENSHAW RESERVOIRS

North West Water, Bottoms Office.
Location: SJ915965. E of Droylsden between A628 and M60 (junction 24), E of city centre. Access and parking on Audenshaw Road B6390 at N end of site.
Access: No disabled access.
Facilities: Hide (contact R Travis on 0161 330 2607). Permit (free) from D Tomes, NWW Bottoms Office, Woodhead Road, Tintwistle, Glossop SK13 1HS.
Habitat: Reservoir.
Key birds: Major migration point; *Winter*: Notable gull roost inc. regular Mediterranean Gull; large Goosander roost; many rarities.

ETHEROW COUNTRY PARK

Stockport Metropolitan Borough Council.
Location: SJ 965 908. Located NE of Stockport. Take A626(Marple to Glossop road) and B6104 into Compstall near Romiley, Stockport.
Access: Open at all times; permit required for conservation area. Keep to paths.
Facilities: Reserve area has SSSI status. Hide, nature trail, visitor centre, scooters for disabled.
Public transport: None.
Habitat: River Etherow, woodlands, marsh.
Key birds: Sparrowhawk, Buzzard, Dipper, all three woodpeckers, Pied Flycatcher, warblers. *Winter*: Brambling, Siskin, Water Rail. Frequent sightings of Merlin and Raven over hills.
Contact: John Rowland, Etherow Country Park, Compstall, Stockport, Cheshire, SK6 5JD. 0161 427 6937; fax 0161 427 3643.

HOLLINGWORTH LAKE

Hollingworth Lake Country Park-Rochdale MBC.
Location: SD 939 153 (visitor centre). Four miles NE of Rochdale, signed from A58 Halifax Road. Near J21 of M62 – B6225 to Littleborough.
Access: Access open to lake and surroundings at all times.
Facilities: Cafes, hide, trails and education service, car parks. Visitor centre open 10.30am-6pm (Mon-Fri), 10.30am-7pm (Sat & Sun) in summer, 11am-4pm (Mon-Fri), 10.30am-5pm (Sat & Sun) in winter.
Public transport: Bus Nos 452, 450. Train to

Manchester, Greater

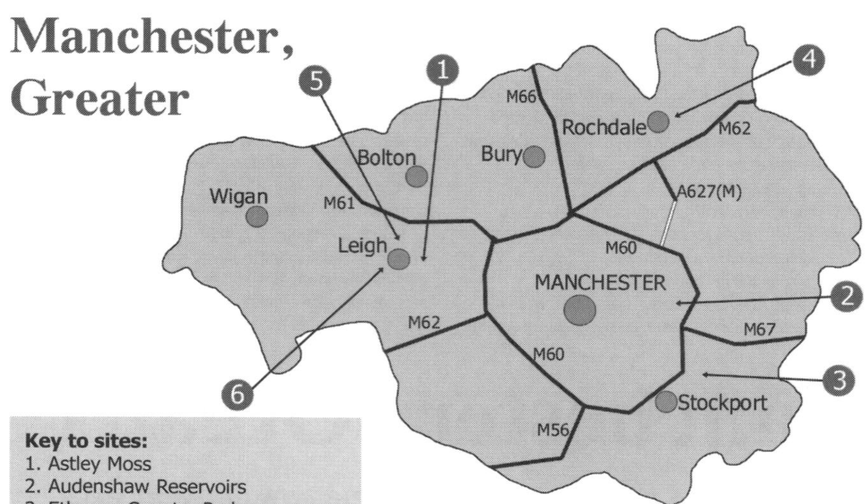

Key to sites:
1. Astley Moss
2. Audenshaw Reservoirs
3. Etherow Country Park
4. Hollingworth Lake Country Park
5. Hope Carr Nature Reserve
6. Pennington Flash Country Park

Littleborough or Smithy Bridge.
Habitat: Lake (116 acres 47 ha includes 20 acre nature reserve), woodland, streams, marsh, willow scrub.
Key birds: *All year*: Great Crested Grebe, Kingfisher, Lapwing, Little Owl, Bullfinch, Cormorant. Occasional Peregrine, Sedge Warbler, Water Rail, Snipe. *Spring/autumn*: passage waders, wildfowl, Kittiwake. *Summer*: Reed Bunting, Dipper, Common Sandpiper, Curlew, Oystercatcher, Black Tern, 'Commic' Tern, Grey Partridge, Blackcap. *Winter*: Golden Plover, Goosander, Goldeneye, Siskin, Redpoll.
Contact: The Ranger, Hollingworth Lake Visitor Centre, Rakewood Road, Littleborough, OL15 0AQ. 01706 373421.
e-mail: holl.lakecp@rochdale.gov.uk

HOPE CARR NATURE RESERVE

North West Water.
Location: SJ 664 986. In Leigh, W of Salford. From A580 E Lancs Road turn N at Greyhound Motel roundabout, L at first lights, first L at mini roundabout.
Access: Open all year.
Facilities: Free parking, disabled access. Hide (access by prior arrangement).
Habitat: Purpose-built scrapes and lake adjoining sludge lagoons of Leigh ETW.
Key birds: Wide variety of breeding and wintering wildfowl; excellent for passage waders; wintering Water Pipit, Green Sandpiper.
Contact: Joe Grima, Leigh Environmental, Education Centre, Hope Carr, Hope Carr Lane, Leigh, WN7 3XB. 01942 269027; fax 01942 269028; mobile 0790 9996272.

PENNINGTON FLASH

Wigan Council
Location: SJ 640 990. One mile from Leigh town centre. Main entrance on A572 (St Helens Road).
Access: Country Park is signposted from A580 (East Lancs Road) and is permanently open. Four largest hides, toilets and information point open 9am-dusk (except Christmas Day). Main paths flat and suitable for disabled.
Facilities: Toilets including disabled toilet and information point. Total of seven bird hides. Site leaflet available and Rangers based on site.
Public transport: None.
Habitat: Lake, ponds and scrapes, fringed with reeds, rough grassland, scrub and woodland.
Key birds: Waterfowl all year, waders mainly passage spring and autumn (14-plus species). Breeding Common Tern and Little Ringed Plover. Feeding station attracts Willow Tit and Bullfinch all year.
Contact: Peter Alker, Pennington Flash Country Park, St Helens Road, Leigh, WN7 3PA. 01942 605253 (also fax number).

Merseyside

DEE ESTUARY

Wirral Country Park Centre (Metropolitan Borough of Wirral).
Location: SJ 255 815. Leave A540 Chester to Hoylake road at Heswall and head downhill (one mile) to the free car park at the shore end of Banks Road. Heswall is 30 minutes from South Liverpool and Chester by car.
Access: Open at all times. Best viewpoint 600 yards along shore N of Banks Road. No disabled access along shore, but good birdwatching from bottom of Banks Road. Arrive 2.5 hours before high tide.
Facilities: Toilets in car park and information board. Wirral Country Park Centre three miles N off A540 has toilets, hide, café, kiosk (all accessible to wheelchairs). Birdwatching events programme available from visitor centre.
Public transport: Bus service to Banks Road car park from Heswall bus station. Contact Mersey Travel (tel 0151 236 7676).
Habitat: Saltmarsh and mudflats.
Key birds: *Autumn/winter*: Large passage and winter wader roosts - Redshank, Curlew, Black-tailed Godwit, Oystercatcher, Golden Plover, Knot, Shelduck, Teal, Red-breasted Merganser, Peregrine, Merlin, Hen Harrier, Short-eared Owl. Smaller numbers of Pintail, Wigeon, Bar-tailed Godwit, Greenshank, Spotted Redshank, Grey and Ringed Plovers, Whimbrel, Curlew Sandpiper, Little Stint, occasional Scaup and Little Egret.
Contact: Martyn Jamieson, Head Ranger, Wirral Country Park Centre, Station Road, Thustaston, Wirral, Merseyside, CH61 0HN. 0151 648 4371/3884.
e-mail: wirralcountrypark@wirral.gov.uk
www.wirral.gov.uk/leisure/ranger

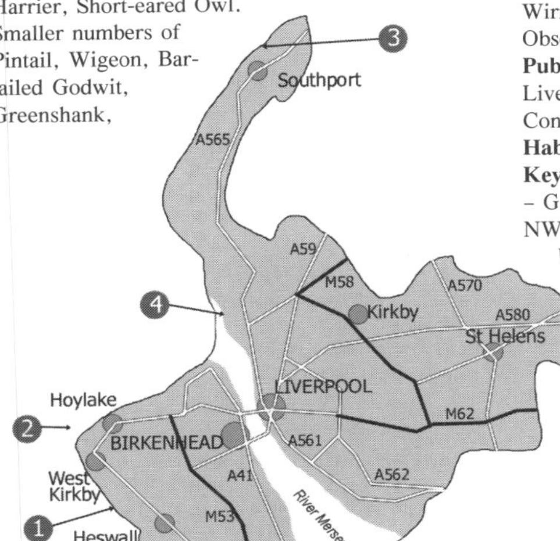

HILBRE ISLAND

Wirral Country Park Centre (Metropolitan Borough of Wirral).
Location: SJ 184 880. Three tidal islands in the mouth of the Dee Estuary. Park in West Kirby which is on the A540 Chester-to-Hoylake road - 30 minutes from Liverpool, 45 minutes from Chester. Follow the brown Marine Lake signs to Dee Lane pay and display car park.
Access: Two mile walk across the sands from Dee Lane slipway. No disabled access. Do not cross either way within 3.5 hours of high water - tide times and suggested safe route on noticeboard at slipway. Prior booking and permit needed for parties of six or more - maximum of 50. Book early.
Facilities: Toilets at Marine Lake and Hilbre (primitive!). Permits, leaflets and tide times from Wirral Country Park Centre. Hilbre Bird Observatory (details as before).
Public transport: Bus and train station (from Liverpool) within 0.5 mile of Dee Lane slipway. Contact Mersey Travel, tel 0151 236 7676.
Habitat: Sandflats, rocky shore and open sea.
Key birds: *Late summer/autumn*: Seabird passage - Gannets, terns, skuas, shearwaters and after NW gales good numbers of Leach's Petrel. *Winter*: Wader roosts at high tide, Purple Sandpiper, Turnstone, sea ducks, divers, grebes. Passage migrants.
Contact: Martyn Jamieson, Head Ranger, Wirral Country Park Centre, Station Road, Thustaston, Wirral,

Key to sites:
1. Dee Estuary
2. Hilbre Island
3. Marshside
4. Seaforth Nature Reserve

Merseyside, CH61 0HN. 0151 648 4371/3884.
e-mail: wirralcountrypark@wirral.gov.uk
www.wirral.gov.uk/leisure/ranger

MARSHSIDE

RSPB (North West England Office).
Location: SD 355 202. On south shore of Ribble Estuary, one mile north of Southport centre on Marine Drive.
Access: Open 8.30am-5pm all year. No toilets. No dogs please. Coach parties please book in advance. No charges but donations welcomed.
Facilities: Two hides and trails accessible to wheelchairs.
Public transport: Bus service to Elswick Road/ Marshside Road half-hourly, bus No 44. Contact Southport Buses (01704 536137).
Habitat: Coastal grazing marsh and lagoons.
Key birds: *Winter*: Pink-footed Goose, wildfowl, waders, raptors. *Spring*: Breeding waders and wildfowl, Garganey, migrants. *Autumn*: Migrants. *All year*: Black-tailed Godwit.
Contact: Tony Baker, RSPB, Beechwood, Cat Tail Lane, Scarisbrick, Southport, FR8 5LW. 01704 233003. e-mail: c/o RSPB@rspb.org.uk

SEAFORTH NATURE RESERVE

Lancashire, Manchester & North Merseyside Wildlife Trust.
Location: SJ 315 970. Five miles from Liverpool city centre. From M57/M58 take A5036 to docks.
Access: Open dawn-dusk daily. £1 donation expected. No dogs. Wheelchairs possible but difficult.
Facilities: Toilets when visitor centre open, three hides.
Public transport: Train to Waterloo or Seaforth stations from Liverpool. Buses to dock gates from Liverpool.
Habitat: Saltwater and freshwater lagoons, scrub grassland.
Key birds: Little Gull on passage (Apr) plus Roseate, Little and Black Terns. Breeding and passage Common Tern (Apr-Sept) plus Roseate, Little and Black Terns on passage. Passage and winter waders and gulls. Passage passerines, especially White Wagtail, pipits and Wheatear.
Contact: Steve White, Seaforth Nature Reserve, Port of Liverpool, L21 1JD. 0151 9203769. e-mail: lwildlife@cix.co.uk

Norfolk

BERNEY MARSHES

RSPB (East Anglia Office).
Location: TG 465 055. W of Great Yarmouth. In the Halvergate Marshes.
Access: Public footpath by Berney Arms Station on the Norwich to Yarmouth railway line NE of Reedham.
Boat service to reserve departs from Burgh Castle Marina first Sun of month at 10am & 2pm, returning 1pm & 4pm (phone 01493 700645 to book).
Facilities: None.
Public transport: Train to Berney Arms.
Habitat: Marsh.
Key birds: *Winter*: Bewick's Swan, Wigeon, birds of prey (inc. Hen Harrier, Merlin, Peregrine, Short-eared Owl). *Spring:* Migrants can include Spoonbill, Little Egret, Ruff.
Contact: Chris Gregory, Warden, Ashtree Farm, Goodchild Marine, Butt Lane, Burgh Castle, Great Yarmouth, Norfolk, NR31 9PE.

BLAKENEY POINT

The National Trust.
Location: TG 000 465. Famous sand and shingle spit N of Morston and Blakeney on A149 coast road.
Access: Free access, open all year, dogs on leads at all times. Restricted access to parts of the reserve, Apr-Aug. Difficult access for wheelchairs.
Facilities: Toilets open Apr-Oct, visitor centre, guided walks by wardens (booked in advance), bird hide.
Public transport: Norbic (tel 0845 3006116).
Habitat: Sand dunes, saltmarsh, shingle ridges.
Key birds: Spring and autumn passage migrants. *Spring/summer*: Breeding seabirds including terns, gulls, Shelduck, Oystercatcher, Ringed Plover.
Contact: Joe Reed, Property Manager, 35 The Cornfield, Langham, Holt, Norfolk, NR25 7DQ. 01263 740241.e-mail: abyjrx@smtp.ntrust.org.uk

BUCKENHAM MARSHES

RSPB (East Anglia Office).
Location: TG 352 056. Located N of River Yare, SE of Norwich. From A47 take minor road S to Strumpshaw and Buckenham. Park at Buckenham Station.
Access: Open at all times, dogs on leads.
Facilities: Public footpaths run from station to riverbank, and along riverbank to hide.
Public transport: Some trains from Norwich to Great Yarmouth will stop on request. Information from National Train enquiries (tel 0845 748 4950).
Habitat: Grazing marshes with shallow flooding in winter.
Key birds: *Winter*: Bean and White-fronted Goose, wildfowl, raptors.
Contact: Mark Smart, Staithe Cottage, Low Road, Strumpshaw, Norwich, Norfolk, NR13 4HS. 01603 715191. www.rspb.org.uk
e-mail strumpshaw@rspb.org.uk

CLEY MARSHES

Norfolk Wildlife Trust.
Location: TG 054 441. NWT Cley Marshes is situated three miles N of Holt on A149 coast road, half a mile E of Cley-next-the-Sea. Visitor centre and car park on inland side of the road.
Access: Open all year round (closed Mon – except Bank Holidays). Visitor centre open Apr-Oct (10am-5pm daily), Nov-mid Dec (10am-4pm Wed-Sun). Cost: adults £3.50, children under 16 free. NWT members free.
Facilities: Visitor centre, birdwatching hides, wildlife gift shop, refreshments, toilets, coach parking, car park, disabled access to centre, boardwalk and hides and toilets, groups welcome.
Public transport: Bus service from Norwich, Fakenham and Holt Mon-Sat. The Coasthopper service stops outside daily. Connections for train and bus services at Sheringham. Special discounts to visitors arriving by bus.
Habitat: Reedbeds, salt and freshwater marshes, scrapes and shingle ridge with international reputation as one of the finest birdwatching sites in Britain.
Key birds: *Feb:* Brent Goose, warblers, Wigeon, Teal, Mallard, Shoveler, Pintail. *Spring*: Chiffchaff, Wheatear, Sandwich Tern, Reed and Sedge Warblers, Ruff, Black-tailed Godwit. *Jun*: Spoonbill, Avocet, Bittern, Bearded Tit. *Autumn*: Green and Wood Sandpiper, Greenshank, Whimbrel, Little Ringed Plover.
Contact: Dick Bagnall, Oakeley Centre, NWT Cley Marshes, Cley, Holt, Norfolk, NR25 7RZ. 01263 740008. www.wildlifetrust.org.uk.Norfolk
e-mail BernardB@nwt.cix.co.uk

EAST WRETHAM HEATH

Norfolk Wildlife Trust.
Location: TL 913 887. Site lies in the centre of Breckland N of Thetford. From A11 take turning for A1075 to Watton and travel for about two miles over the level crossing and pass the lay-by to the left. Car park and entrance to reserve are by the first house on the left.
Access: Open all year (10am-5pm).
Facilities: Car park. Trail.
Public transport: None.
Habitat: Breckland grass heath and meres.
Key birds: Wildfowl, wading birds.
Contact: Bev Nichols, The Wardens House, East Wretham Heath, Thetford Road, Wretham, Thetford, IP24 1RU. 01953 498339.
e-mail BevN@nwt.cix.co.uk
www.wildlifetrust.org.uk/Norfolk

FOXLEY WOOD

Norfolk Wildlife Trust.
Location: TG 049 229. Foxley Wood is situated 12 miles NW of Norwich on A1067, signposted at Foxley village from main road.
Access: Open all year (10am-5pm).
Facilities: Trails, car park, no toilets, groups welcome.
Public transport: Bus – Norwich to Fakenham services stop at Foxley War Memorial approximately 15 minutes' walk. Sanders Coaches Sun service.
Habitat: Norfolk's largest ancient woodland.
Key birds: Woodland birds including Great Spotted and Green Woodpeckers, Woodcock, Blackcap, Garden Warbler. Swallowtail and white admiral butterfles.
Contact: Trust HQ, 01953 498339.

HICKLING BROAD

Norfolk Wildlife Trust.
Location: TG 428 222. Approx four miles SE of Stalham, just off A149 Yarmouth Road. From Hickling village, follow the brown 'duck' tourist

Key to sites:

1. Berney Marshes
2. Blakeney Point
3. Buckenham Marshes
4. Cley Marshes
5. East Wretham Heath
6. Foxley Wood
7. Hickling Broad
8. Holkham
9. Holme Bird Observatory
10. Nunnery Lakes
11. Ranworth Broad
12. Redwell Marsh
13. Scolt Head Island
14. Snettisham
15. Strumpshaw Fen
16. Surlingham Church Marsh
17. Titchwell Marsh
18. Walsey Hills
19. The Wash NNR
20. Weeting Heath
21. Welney

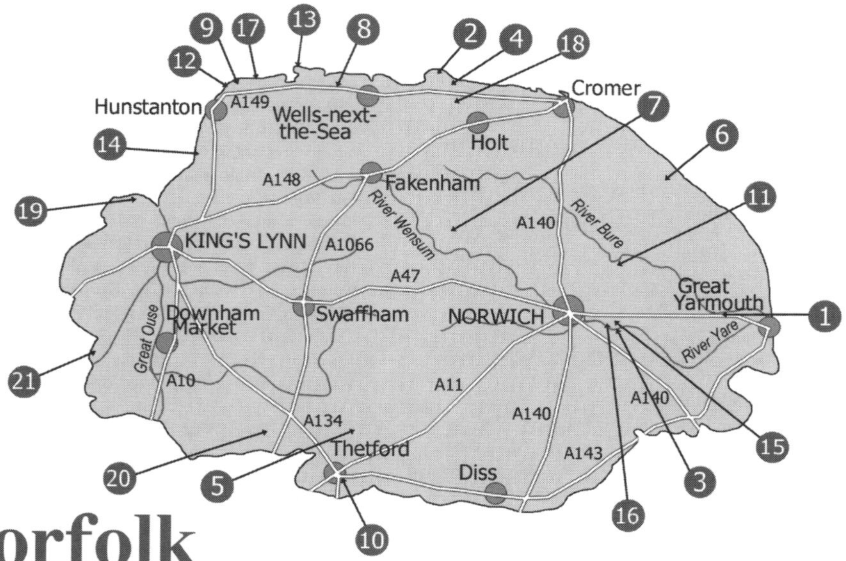

Norfolk

signs into Stubb Road at the Greyhound Inn. Take first turning left to follow Stubb Road for another mile. Turn right at the for the nature reserve. The car park is ahead of you.

Access: Open all year. Visitor centre open Apr-Sept (10am-5pm daily). Cost: adults £2.50, children under 16 free. NWT members free.

Facilities: Visitor centre, boardwalk trail through reedbeds to open water, birdwatching hides, wildlife gift shop, refreshments, picnic site, toilets, coach parking, car parking, disabled access to broad, boardwalk and toilets. Groups welcome. Water trail (additional charge - booking essential).

Public transport: Morning bus service only Mon-Fri from Norwich (Neaves Coaches) Cromer to North Walsham (Sanders). Buses stop in Hickling village, a 20 minute walk away.

Habitat: Hickling is the largest and wildest of the Norfolk Broads with reedbeds, grazing marshes and wide open skies.

Key birds: Marsh Harriers, Bittern. Swallowtail butterfly, Norfolk hawker (rare dragonfly).

Contact: John Blackburn, Hickling Broad Visitor Centre, Stubb Road, Hickling, NR12 0BN, e-mail johnb@nwt.cix.co.uk www.wildlifetrust.org.uk/norfolk

HOLKHAM

English Nature (Norfolk Team).

Location: TF 890 450. From Holkham village turn N off A149 down Lady Ann's Drive, for safe parking.

Access: Access unrestricted, but keep to paths and off grazing marshes and farmland.

Facilities: None.

Public transport: Norfolk Green Bus, 01553 766980.

Habitat: Sandflats, dunes, marshes, pinewoods.
Key birds: *Passage*: Migrants. *Winter*: Wildfowl, inc. Brent, Pink-footed and White-fronted Geese. *Summer*: Breeding Little Tern.
Contact: R Harold, Hill Farm Offices, Main Road, Holkham, Wells-next-the-Sea, NR23 1AB. 01328 711183; fax 01328 711893.

HOLME BIRD OBSERVATORY

Norfolk Ornithologist's Association.
Location: TF 717 450. E of Hunstanton, at Holme-nest-the-Sea, signposted from A149.
Access: Reserve open daily to members dawn to dusk; non-members (9am-5pm) by permit from the Observatory. Parties by prior arrangement.
Facilities: Several hides (seawatch hide reserved for NOA members).
Public transport: Coastal bus service runs from Hunstanton to Sheringham every 30mins but is seasonal. Phone Norfolk Green Bus, 01553 776 980.
Habitat: In ten acres of diverse habitat: sand dunes, Corsican pines, scrub and reed-fringed lagoon.
Key birds: Species list over 320. Ringed species 141. Recent rarities have included Ortolan Bunting, Radde's Warbler, Tawny Pipit and Bee-Eater.
Contact: Jed Andrews, Holme Bird Observatory, Broadwater Road, Holme, Hunstanton, Norfolk, PE36 6LQ. 01485 525406. www.noa.org.uk
e-mail: jedandrews@shrike4.freeserve.co.uk

NUNNERY LAKES

British Trust for Ornithology.
Location: TL 873 815. On the S edge of Thetford, adjacent to the BTO's headquarters at The Nunnery, off Nun's Bridges Road. Main access point is about 60 yards upriver of Nun's Bridges car park (TL 874 825) on the opposite side of the River Little Ouse.
Access: Open during daylight hours. No permits required for access along permissive paths; authorisation required from the BTO to gain access to other parts of the reserve. Dogs must be kept on leads at all times.
Facilities: Waymarked paths with information panels, bird hide. No toilets or visitors centre but enquiries are welcome at Reception at the BTO's headquarters during office hours.
Public transport: Various bus services to Thetford Bus Terminal, off Bridge Street (about a ten minute walk to site alongside river). Thetford Railway Station - Station Road (about 20 minutes' walk across town to the reserve).
Habitat: Flood meadows, flooded gravel pits, woodland, grass heath.
Key birds: *Spring*: Passage waders, Little Ringed Plover, Wheatear. *Summer*: Hobby, breeding Oystercatcher and Lapwing, Skylark, warblers. *Winter*: Water Rail, Snipe, Goosander, Gadwall, Siskin, Lesser Redpoll, Hawfinch. *All year*: Kingfisher, Grey Wagtail, Nuthatch, Willow Tit.
Contact: Chris Gregory, The British Trust for Ornithology, The Nunnery, Thetford, Norfolk, IP24 2PU. 01842 750050. www.bto.org
e-mail: chris.gregory@bto.org

RANWORTH BROAD

Norfolk Wildlife Trust.
Location: TG 357 149. Ranworth is approx four miles SE of Wroxham, signposted on the B1140 Norwich to Acle road at South Walsham. At Ranworth village look out for the signs to the centre and the Norfolk Wildlife Trust car park.
Access: Boardwalk open all year. Broads Wildlife Centre open Apr-Oct (10am-5pm daily).
Facilities: Inter-active displays, wildlife gift shop, refreshments, car park and toilet 400 yards at village, disabled access along trail and into centre, groups welcome. Guided boat trip operates at certain times (additional charge - booking essential on 01603 270479).
Public transport: Nearest bus service is the 704 and 705 service to/from Norwich or Yarmouth to South Walsham. Five to ten minute walk from bus stop.
Habitat: Broadland reedbeds, grazing marsh.
Key birds: Large Cormorant roost, Common Tern, Great Crested Grebe, warblers and winter wildfowl.
Contact: Trust HQ, 01953 498339.

REDWELL MARSH

Norfolk Wildlife Trust.
Location: TF 702 436. In Holme, off A149, E of Hunstanton.
Access: View from public footpath from centre of Holme village to Broadwater Road. Open at all times.
Facilities: Member's hide, offering wheelchair access, (access from Broadwater road).

Public transport: As for Holme Bird Observatory.
Habitat: Wet grazing marsh with ditches, pond and large wader scrape.
Key birds: Wildfowl and waders (inc. Avocet, Black-tailed Godwit, Curlew/Green/Wood Sandpipers, Greenshank, Spotted Redshank). Recent sightings include Little Egret, Arctic Skua, Temminck's Stint, Ring Ouzel and Grasshopper Warbler.
Contact: Jed Andrews,
Holme Bird Observatory, Broadwater Road, Holme, Hunstanton, Norfolk, PE36 6LQ. 01485 525406. www.noa.org.uk
e-mail: jedandrews@shrike4.freeserve.co.uk

SCOLT HEAD ISLAND

English Nature (Norfolk Team).
Location: TF 810 465. Access by ferry from Brancaster Staithe.
Access: Open at all times, apart from ternery at western end between Apr-Aug. No dogs allowed on reserve Apr-Aug. Must be under control at all other times.
Facilities: Short, self-guided nature trail. No other facilities.
Public transport: Coastal road bus stops in Brancaster Staithe.
Habitat: Sand dunes, saltmarsh, intertidal mud and sand.
Key birds: *Summer*: Breeding colony of gulls and terns. *Winter*: Large numbers of wildfowl and waders.
Contact: Michael E S Rooney,
English Nature, Hill Farm Offices, Main Road, Holkham, Norfolk, NR23 1AB. 01328 711866

SNETTISHAM

RSPB (East Anglia Office).
Location: TF 630 310. Car park two miles along Beach road, signposted off A149 King's Lynn to Hunstanton, opposite Snettisham village.
Access: Open at all times. £2 car parking fee for non-members. Dogs to be kept on leads. Two hides are suitable for wheelchairs. Disabled access is across a private road. Please phone office number for permission and directions.
Facilities: Four birdwatching hides, connected by reserve footpath. No toilets on site.
Public transport: Nearest over two miles away.
Habitat: Intertidal mudflats, saltmarsh, shingle beach, brackish lagoons, and unimproved grassland/scrub. Best visited on a high tide.
Key birds: *Autumn/winter/spring*: Waders (particularly Knot, Bar and Black-tailed Godwits, Dunlin, Grey Plover), wildfowl (particularly Pink-footed and Brent Geese, Wigeon, Gadwall, Goldeneye), Peregrine, Hen Harrier, Merlin, owls. Migrants in season. *Summer*: Breeding Ringed Plover, Redshank, Avocet, Common Tern. Marsh Harrier regular.
Contact: Jim Scott,
RSPB, 43 Lynn Road, Snettisham, King's Lynn, Norfolk, PE31 7LR. 01485 542689.

STRUMPSHAW FEN

RSPB (East Anglia Office).
Location: TG 33 06. Seven miles ESE of Norwich. Follow signposts. Entrance across level-crossing from car park, reached by turning sharp right and right again into Low Road from Brundall, off A47 to Great Yarmouth.
Access: Open dawn-dusk. RSPB members free, adults £2.50, children 50p, family £5. Guide dogs only. Viewing platform for wheelchair users.
Facilities: Toilets, reception hide and two other hides, two walks, five miles of trails.
Public transport: Brundall train station about one mile. Bus stop half a mile – contact Norbic (0845 300 6116).
Habitat: Reedbed and reedfen, wet grassland and woodland.
Key birds: *Summer*: Bittern, Bearded Tit, Marsh Harrier, Cetti's Warbler and other reedbed birds. *Winter*: Bean and White-fronted Geese, Hen Harrier. Swallowtails in Jun.
Contact: Tim Strudwick,
Staithe Cottage, Low Road, Strumpshaw, Norwich, Norfolk, NR13 4HS. 01603 715191.
e-mail: strumpshaw@rspb.org.uk
www.rspb.org.uk

SURLINGHAM CHURCH MARSH

RSPB (East Anglia Office).
Location: TG 304 066. Six miles E of Norwich, S of River Yare, N of A146 Norwich to Lowestoft road.
Access: Open at all times (NB: nearby shooting on Wed and Sun).
Facilities: Footpaths from Surlingham church run around reserve. Two hides.

Public transport: None.
Habitat: Broadland marsh with dykes, shallow pools, reedfen and sedge beds, alder and willow carr.
Key birds: *Spring/summer*: Breeding Reed, Sedge and Grasshopper Warblers, Cuckoo, Marsh Harrier. Passage waders (including Green Sandpiper). *Winter*: Hen Harrier, wildfowl (including Gadwall, Teal, Shoveler, Shelduck, geese) and waders (including Snipe and Jack Snipe).
Contact: Tim Strudwick, Staithe Cottage, Low Road, Strumpshaw, Norwich, NR15 4HS. 01603 715191. e-mail: strumpshaw@rspb.org.uk www.rspb.org.uk

TITCHWELL MARSH

RSPB (East Anglia Office).
Location: TF 749 436. Near Hunstanton. Footpath along sea wall from A149 between Thornham and Titchwell.
Access: Fen and meadow trails are new additions allowing further access to the reserve. Reserve and hides open at all times.
Facilities: Visitor centre, shop and servery open every day as follows: summer (BST) Mon-Fri (10am-5pm), Sat-Sun (9.30am-5pm), winter Mon-Fri (10am-4pm), Sat-Sun (9.30am-5pm). Closed Christmas and Boxing Days.
Public transport: Phone Norfolk Green Bus 01553 776980.
Habitat: Reedbed, brackish & freshwater pools, saltmarsh, dunes, shingle.
Key birds: *Spring/summer*: Nesting Avocet, Bearded Tit, Water Rail, Marsh Harrier, Reed and Sedge Warblers. *Autumn*: Knot. *Winter*: Brent Geese, Goldeneye, Scoter, Eider, Hen Harrier roost, Snow Bunting and Shorelark.
Contact: Warden, Titchwell Marsh Reserve, King's Lynn, Norfolk, PE31 8BB. Tel/fax 01485 210779.

WALSEY HILLS

Norfolk Wildlife Trust.
Location: TG 062 441. Up footpath and steps from A149 at Cley.
Access: Open daily throughout year.
Facilities: Wardened visitor centre providing up-to-date birding information. Short walk through scrub and beside Snipe's Marsh (Norfolk WT). Excellent views across adjoining reserves between Cley and Salthouse. Important migration watchpoint.
Public transport: Phone Norfolk Green Bus 01553 776980.
Habitat: Scrub.
Key birds: Recent sightings include Bittern, White Stork, Rough-legged Buzzard, Osprey, Merlin, Crane, Red-necked Phalarope, Wryneck, Marsh Warbler, Bluethroat, Rustic Bunting.
Contact: Tom Fletcher, 01263 740875.

THE WASH NNR

English Nature East Midlands Team.
Location: TR 49 22 57. 7.5 miles West of King's Lynn. From A17, follow road along East bank of River Nene at Sutton Bridge.
Access: Open access, though remain on public footpaths along seabank and keep dogs under control.
Facilities: Car park.
Public transport: None.
Habitat: Saltmarsh and mudflats.
Key birds: *Summer*: Breeding Redshank and Oystercatcher. Massive numbers of passage and wintering waterfowl including Brent Goose, Knot, Oystercatcher, Lapwing, Redshank, Shelduck and raptors.
Contact:
English Nature East Midlands, The Maltings, Wharf Road, Grantham, Lincs, NG31 6BH. 01205 311674. www.english-nature.org.uk
e-mail: simonb.smith@english-nature.org.uk

WEETING HEATH

Norfolk Wildlife Trust.
Location: TL 756 881. Weeting Heath is signposted from the Weeting-Hockwold road, two miles W of Weeting near to Brandon in Suffolk. Nature reserve can be reached via B1112 at Hockwold or B1106 at Weeting.
Access: Open daily from Apr-Aug. Cost: adults £2.00, children free. NWT members free. Disabled access to visitor centre only.
Facilities: Visitor centre, birdwatching hides, wildlife gift shop, refreshments, toilets, coach parking, car park, groups welcome (book first).
Public transport: Train services to Brandon and bus connections from Brandon High Street.
Habitat: Breckland.
Key birds: Stone Curlew, migrant passerines.
Contact: Bev Nichols,
The Wardens House, East Wretham Heath,

Thetford Road, Wretham, Thetford, IP24 1RU. 01842 827615.
e-mail: BevN@nwt.cix.co.uk
www.wildlifetrust.org.uk/Norfolk

WELNEY

The Wildfowl & Wetlands Trust.
Location: TL 546 944. Ten miles N of Ely, signposted from A10 and A1101.
Access: Open daily (10am-5pm) except Christmas Day. Free admission to WWT members, otherwise £3.50 (adult), £2.75 (senior), £2 (child).
Facilities: Visitor centre, cafe open 10am-4pm daily. Large, heated observatory, plus six other birdwatching hides. Provision for disabled visitors.
Public transport: Poor. Train to Littleport (six miles away), but from there, taxi is only option. Excellent cycling country!
Habitat: 1000 acres of washland reserve, damp meadows in spring, winter wildfowl marsh.
Key birds: *Winter*: Bewick's Swan, Whooper Swan, winter wildfowl. *Spring*: Breeding/ migrant waders, warblers.
Contact: Carl Mitchell,
WWT, Hundred Foot Bank, Welney, Nr Wisbech, PE14 9TN. 01353 860711.
e-mail: welney@wwt.org.uk
www.wwt.org.uk

Northants

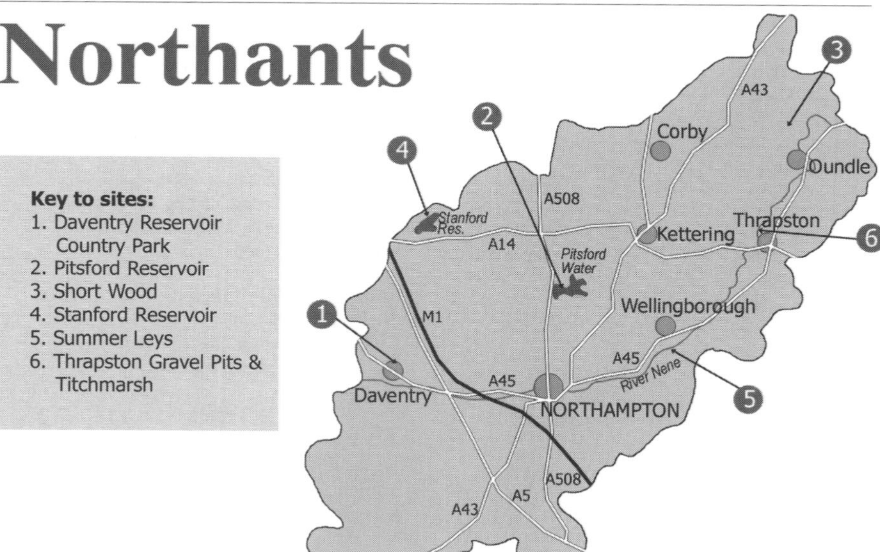

DAVENTRY RESERVOIR

Daventry District Council.
Location: SP 577 642. Country Park signposted from B4036 Daventry to Welton road.
Access: Open at all times
Facilities: Two hides (combinations for locks from Rangers - bring proof of identity), cafe, visitor centre.
Public transport: None.
Habitat: Open water, wetlands, reed, meadows, woodland.
Key birds: *Autumn*: Passage waders inc. Dunlin, Ruff, Greenshank, Green Sandpiper; nesting Common Tern, Arctic and sometimes Black Tern on passage; gull roost; rare species inc. Pacific Swift, Baird's Sandpiper, Wilson's Phalarope, Sabine's Gull. More than 180 species recorded; 60 have bred.
Contact: Dewi Morris, Daventry Country Park, Reservoir Cottage, Northern Way, Daventry, Northants, NN11 5JB. 01327 877193.
e-mail dmorris1@daventrydc.gov.uk

PITSFORD RESERVOIR

Beds, Cambs & Northants Wildlife Trust.
Location: SP 787 702. Five miles N of Northampton. On A43 take turn to Holcot and Brixworth. On A508 take turn to Brixworth and Holcot.
Access: Lodge open mid-Mar to mid-Nov from 8am-dusk. Winter opening times variable, check in advance. Permits for reserve available from Lodge on daily or annual basis. Reserve open to permit holders 365 days a year. No dogs. Not suitable for disabled at present.
Facilities: Toilets available in Lodge, 15 miles of paths, eight bird hides, car parking.
Public transport: None.
Habitat: Open water (up to 120 ha), marginal vegetation and reed grasses, wet woodland, grassland and mixed woodland (40 ha).
Key birds: 174 species in 2000. *Summer*: Breeding warblers, terns, Hobby, Tree Sparrow. *Autumn*: Waders only if water levels suitable. *Winter*: Wildfowl, feeding station with Tree Sparrow and Corn Bunting.
Contact: Dave Francis, Pitsford Water Lodge, Brixworth Road, Holcot, Northampton, NN6 9SJ. 01604 780148.
e-mail: pitsford@cix.compulink.co.uk

SHORT WOOD

Beds, Cambs & Northants Wildlife Trust.
Location: TL 015 913. Via bridle path from minor road between Glapthorn and Southwick, NW of Oundle. Park on roadside verge.
Access: Open all year.
Facilities: None.
Public transport: Not known.
Habitat: Primary and secondary mixed woodland (oak, ash, field maple, hazel), coppiced.
Key birds: Woodcock, Marsh Tit, warblers, Redpoll.
Contact: Trust HQ, 01223 712400.

STANFORD RESERVOIR

Severn Trent Water/Northants Wildlife Trust.
Location: SP 600 805. One mile SW of South Kilworth off Kilworth/Stanford-on-Avon road.
Access: Daytime, permits from Northants Wildlife Trust. No dogs. Limited access for wheelchair users.
Facilities: Toilets (inc disabled). Two hides, perimeter track. Disabled parking.
Public transport: None.
Habitat: Reservoir with willow, reed and hedgerow edges.
Key birds: *Winter*: Wildfowl, especially Ruddy Duck. *Spring*: migratory terns and warblers. *Late summer*: Terns, Hobby, waders.
Contact: Northants Wildlife Trust, Ling House, Billing Lings, Northampton, NN3 8BE. 01604 405285.

SUMMER LEYS

Nene Valley Project.
Location: SP 886 634. Three miles from Wellingborough, accessible from A45 and A509, situated on Great Doddington to Wollaston Road.
Access: Open 24 hours a day, 365 days a year, no permits required. Dogs welcome but must be kept on leads at all times. 40 space car park, small tarmaced circular route suitable for wheelchairs.
Facilities: Three hides, one feeding station. No toilets, nearest are at Irchester Country Park on A509 towards Wellingborough.
Public transport: Nearest main station is Wellingborough. No direct bus service, though buses run regularly to Great Doddington and Wollaston, both about a mile away. Tel: 01604 236712 (24 hrs) for copies of timetables.
Habitat: Scrape, two ponds, lake, scrub, grassland, hedgerow.
Key birds: Hobby, Lapwing, Golden Plover, Ruff, Gadwall, Garganey, Pintail, Shelduck, Shoveler, Little Ringed Plover, Tree Sparrow, Redshank, Green Sandpiper, Oystercatcher, Black-headed Gull colony, terns.
Contact: Cheryl Joyce,
Nene Valley Project, c/o Planning, Transport and Environment, Northamptonshire Council, PO Box 163, County Hall, Northampton, NN1 1AX. 01604 236633 – please ring for a leaflet about the reserve.
e-mail: cmjoyce@northamptonshire.gov.uk

THRAPSTON GRAVEL PITS & TITCHMARSH

Beds, Cambs & Northants Wildlife Trust.
Location: TL 008 804.
Access: Public footpath from layby on A605 N

of Thrapston.
Facilities: Two hides.
Public transport: Bus service to Thrapston.
Habitat: Alder/birch/willow wood; old duck decoy, series of water-filled gravel pits.
Key birds: *Summer*: Breeding Grey Heron (no access to Heronry), Common Tern, Little Ringed Plover; warblers. Migrants, inc. Red-necked and Slavonian Grebes, Bittern and Marsh Harrier recorded. *Winter:* Wildfowl, including Goosander, Redpoll and thrushes.
Contact: Trust HQ, 01223 712400.

Northumberland

ARNOLD RESERVE, CRASTER

Northumberland Wildlife Trust.
Location: NU255197. Lies NE of Alnwick and SW of Craster village.
Access: Public footpath from car park in disused quarry.
Facilities: Intrpretation boards, information centre open in Summer. Toilets (incl disabled) and picnic site in quarry car park.
Public transport: None.
Habitat: Semi-natural woodland and scrub near coast.
Key birds: Good site for migrant passerines to rest and feed. Intersting visitors can inc. Bluethroat, Red-breasted Flycatcher, Barred and Icterine Warblers, Wryneck; moulting site for Lesser Redpoll. Breeding warblers in *Summer*.
Contact: Trust HQ, 0191 284 6884

BRIARWOOD BANKS

Northumberland Wildlife Trust.
Location: NY 791 620. From Haydon Bridge, take minor road from A686 to Plankey Mill, three miles away at junction of Kingswood Burn and River Allen.
Access: Footpaths open to public. One steep route may be impassable after heavy rain.
Facilities: Parking at Plankey Mill. Picnic site and toilets at NT carpark at Allenbanks.
Public transport: None.
Habitat: Ancient woodland along steep valley.
Key birds: Pied Flycatcher, Wood Warbler, Redstart, Dipper, Woodcock, Treecreeper, Nuthatch.
Contact: Trust HQ, 0191 284 6884.

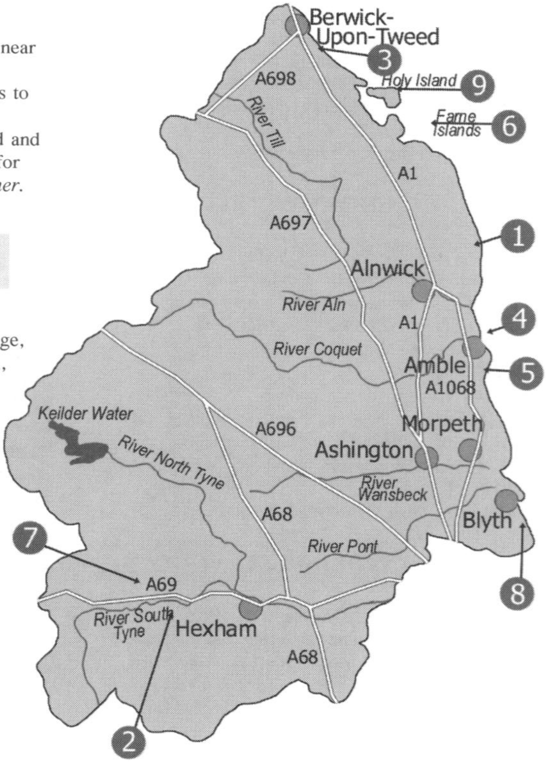

Key to sites:
1. Arnold Reserve, Craster
2. Briarwood Banks
3. Cocklawburn Dunes
4. Coquet Island
5. Druridge Bay Reserves
6. Farne Islands
7. Grindon Lough
8. Holywell Pond
9. Lindisfarne

COCKLAWBURN DUNES

Northumberland Wildlife Trust.
Location: NU 033 481. SE of Scremerston off A1, four miles S of Berwick.
Access: Open access.
Facilities: None.
Public transport: None.
Habitat: Dunes, rocky shore.
Key birds: Eider, waders, (including Turnstone, Purple Sandpiper in winter) good seawatching.
Contact: Trust HQ, 0191 284 6884

COQUET ISLAND

RSPB (North of England Office).
Location: NU 294 046. Small island E ofAmble. Take A1068 SE from Alnwick.
Facilities: Boat trips around island arranged with Dave Gray (tel: 01665 711975). No landings.
Public transport: None.
Habitat: Rocky island
Key birds: Colonies of Eider, Puffin, terns (inc. Roseate).
Contact: RSPB Warden,
c/o RSPB North of England Office.

DRURIDGE BAY RESERVES

Northumberland Wildlife Trust.
Location: 1. NU 285 023. S of Amble. Hauxley (67a) approached by track from road midway between High and Low Hauxley. 2. Druridge Pools NZ 272 965. 3. Cresswell Pond NZ 283 945. Half mile N of Cresswell.
Access: Day permits for all three reserves.
Facilities: 1. Visitor centre, five hides (one suitable for disabled). Disabled toilet. Lake with islands behind dunes. 2. Three hides. 3. Hide.
Public transport: None.
Habitat: 2. Deep lake and wet meadows with pools behind dunes. 3. Shallow brackish lagoon behind dunes fringed by saltmarsh and reedbed, some mudflats.
Key birds: 1. *Spring and autumn*: Good for passage birds (inc. divers, skuas). *Summer*: Coastal birds, esp. terns (inc. Roseate). 2. Especially good in spring. Winter and breeding wildfowl; passage and breeding waders. 3. Good for waders, esp. on passage.
Contact: Jim Martin,
Hauxley Nature Reserve, Low Hauxley, Amble, Morpeth, Northumberland. 01665 711578.

FARNE ISLANDS

The National Trust.
Location: NU 230 370. Access by boat from Seahouses Harbour. Access from A1.
Access: Apr, Aug-Sept: Inner Farne and Staple 10.30am-6pm (majority of boats land at Inner Farne). May-Jul: Staple Island 10.30am-1.30pm, Inner Farne: 1.30pm-5pm. Disabled access possible on Inner Farne, telephone Property Manager for details. Dogs allowed on boats – not on islands.
Facilities: None.
Public transport: Nearest rail stations at Alnmouth and Berwick.
Habitat: Maritime islands, 15-28 depending on state of tide.
Key birds: 18 species of seabirds/waders, four species of tern (including Roseate), 34,000-plus pairs of Puffin, Rock Pipit, Pied Wagtail, Starling, 1,200 Eider etc.
Contact: John Walton, 8 St Aidans, Seahouses, Northumberland, NE68 7SR. 01665 720651

GRINDON LOUGH

Northumberland Wildlife Trust.
Location: NY 806 677. View from unclassified road W of Grindon Hill, three miles NW of Haydon Bridge.
Access: No access to lakeside.
Facilities: None.
Public transport: None.
Habitat: Shallow natural lake.
Key birds: *Winter*: Noted for geese (esp Greylag and Pink-footed) and Whooper Swans. Tufted Duck and Goldeneye regular.
Contact: Trust HQ, 0191 284 6884.

HOLYWELL POND

Northumberland Wildlife Trust.
Location: NZ 319 752. N of Holywell near Seaton Delaval on A192.
Access: Open all year.
Facilities: Public hide (suitable for disabled) accessed from public footpath leading from housing estate.
Public transport: None.
Habitat:
Key birds: Good for winter wildfowl (inc. Goldeneye, Greylag Geese) and passage species.
Contact: Trust HQ, 0191 284 6884.

LINDISFARNE

English Nature (Northumbria Team).
Location: NU 090 430. Island lying two miles E of A1 at Beal, eight miles S of Berwick-on-Tweed.
Access: Open all hours. Some restricted access (refuges).
Facilities: Toilets, visitor centre in village. Hide on island (new hide with disabled access planned for 2002/3). Nature trail on island.
Public transport: Irregular bus service to Holy Island, mainly in summer. Bus route follows mainland boundary of site north-south.
Habitat: Dunes, sand and mudflats.
Key birds: *Passage and winter*: Wildfowl and waders, including pale-bellied Brent Goose, Long-tailed Duck and Whooper Swan. Rare migrants.
Contact: Phil Davey,
Beal Station, Berwick-on-Tweed, TD15 2SP.
01289 381470

Nottinghamshire

ATTENBOROUGH GRAVEL PITS

Nottinghamshire Wildlife Trust.
Location: SK 523 343. On A6005, seven miles SW of Nottingham alongside River Trent. Signed from main road.
Access: Open at all times. Dogs on leads. Paths suitable for disabled access.
Facilities: Nature trail (leaflet from Notts WT), one hide (key £2.50 from Notts WT).
Public transport: Railway station at Attenborough, several buses pass close to reserve (Rainbow 525A from Nottingham every ten minutes).
Habitat: Disused, flooded gravel workings with associated marginal and wetland vegetation.
Key birds: *Spring/summer*: Breeding Common Tern (40-plus pairs), Reed Warbler, Black Tern regular (bred once). *Winter*: Wildfowl (Bittern has wintered for last two years), Grey Heron colony, adjacent Cormorant roost.
Contact: Notts WT Office,
The Old Ragged School, Brook Street, Nottingham, NG1 1EA. 0115 958 8242.
e-mail: nottswt@cix.co.uk
www.wildlifetrust.org.uk/nottinghamshire

BESTHORPE NATURE RESERVE

Nottinghamshire Wildlife Trust.
Location: SK 817 640 and SK813 646 (access points). Take A1133 N of Newark. Turn into Trent Lane S of Besthorpe village, reserve entrances second turn on left and right turn at end of lane (at River Trent).
Access: Open access to two hides (one with disabled access from car park at present). Open access to SSSI meadows. Limited access to areas grazed with sheep. Dogs on leads.
Facilities: No toilets (pubs etc in Besthorpe village), two hides, paths, nature trail (northern part).
Public transport: Buses (numbers 22, 67, 68, 6,

S7L) run by Marshalls, Lincs, Road Car and Travel Wright along A1133 to Besthorpe village (0.75 mile away). Tel: 0115 924 0000 or 01777 710550 for information.
Habitat: Gravel pit with islands, SSSI neutral grasslands, hedges, reedbed, etc.
Key birds: *Spring/summer:* Breeding Grey Heron, Cormorant, Little Ringed Plover, Kingfisher, Grasshopper Warbler. *Winter:* Large numbers of ducks (Pochard, Tufted Duck, Pintail, Wigeon) and Peregrine.
Contact: Contact Notts WT Office, Nottinghamshire Wildlife Trust, The Old Ragged School, Brook Street, Nottingham, NG1 1EA. 0115 958 9242. e-mail: nottswt@cix.co.uk www.wildlifetrust.org.uk/nottinghamshire

COLWICK COUNTRY PARK

Nottingham City Council.
Location: SK 610 395. Off A612 three miles E of Nottingham city centre.
Access: Open at all times, but no vehicle access after dusk or before 7am.
Facilities: Nature trails. Sightings log book in Fishing Lodge.
Public transport: Call park office for advice
Habitat: Lakes, pools, woodlands, grasslands, new plantations, River Trent.
Key birds: *Summer*: Warblers, Hobby, Common Tern (15+ pairs). *Winter*: Wildfowl and gulls. Passage migrants.
Contact: Mark Dennis,
The Fishing Lodge, Colwick, Country Park, River Road, Colwick, Nottingham, NG4 2DW. 0115 987 0785.
www.colwick2000.freeserve.co.uk

LOUND WATERFOWL RESERVE

Lound Bird Club.
Location: SK 690 856. Two miles N of Retford off A638 adjacent to Sutton village.
Access: Open at all times. Use public rights of way only.
Facilities: None.
Public transport: Call club for advice.
Habitat: Working gravel quarries, fish ponds, river valley, infilled and disused fly ash tanks, farmland, scrub, open water.
Key birds: *Summer*: Gulls and terns. Passage waders and raptors. *Winter*: Wildfowl, rarities inc. Ring-billed Gull, Caspian and White-winged Black Terns, Lesser Scaup, Richard's Pipit, Baird's Sandpiper.
Contact: Lound Bird Club,
c/o 23 Milne Road, Bircotes, Doncaster, DN11 8AL. 01302 742779.
www.loundgravelpits.org.uk.

Oxfordshire

ASTON ROWANT

English Nature (Thames & Chilterns).
Location: SW 730 965. Six miles NW of High Wycombe. Leave M40 at either J5 and J6 and take minor road to village.
Access: Open at all times. Dogs on leads.
Facilities: On-site parking, easy access path to viewpoint, seats, interpretation panels.
Public transport: None.
Habitat: Chalk land, chalk scrub, beech woodland.
Key birds: *Summer*: Breeding warblers, passage Wheatear, Hawfinch, occasional Turtle Dove. *Winter*: Brambling. *All year*: Red Kite, Buzzard.
Contact: Aston Rowant Reserve Office, Aston Hill, Lewknor, Watlington, OX9 5SG. 01844 351833. www.english-nature.org.uk

OTMOOR NATURE RESERVE

RSPB (Central England).
Location: SP 570 126. Car park seven miles NE of Oxford city centre. From B4027, take turn to Horton-cum-Studley, then first left to Beckley. After 0.67 miles at the bottom of a short hill turn (before the Abingdon Arms public house). After 200 yards, turn left into Otmoor Lane. Car park is at the end of the lane (approx one mile).
Access: Open dawn-dusk. No permits or fees. No dogs allowed on the reserve visitor trail (except public rights of way). In wet conditions, the public bridleway (which forms part of the visitor trail) can become virtually impassable and wellington boots are essential.
Facilities: Limited. Small car park with cycle racks, visitor trail (just over one mile round trip)

and screened viewpoint. Not accessible by coach and unsuitable for large groups.
Public transport: None.
Habitat: Wet grassland and open water lagoons. The lagoons are in the process of being converted into a reedbed.
Key birds: *Summer*: Breeding birds include Lapwing, Redshank, Curlew, Snipe, Yellow Wagtail, Shoveler, Gadwall, Pochard, Tufted Duck, Little Grebe, Great Crested Grebe. Hobby breeds locally. *Winter*: Wigeon, Teal, Shoveler, Pintail, Gadwall, Pochard, Tufted Duck, Lapwing, Golden Plover, Hen Harrier, Peregrine, Merlin. *Autumn and spring passage*: Marsh Harrier, Short-eared Owl, Greenshank, Green Sandpiper, Common Sandpiper, Spotted Redshank and occasional Black Tern.
Contact: Neil Lambert, Site Manager, RSPB , c/o Lower Farm, Noke, Oxford, OX3 9TX. 01865 848385. www.rspb.org.uk

Shropshire

Key to sites:
1. Clunton Coppice
2. Llynclys Hill
3. Wood Lane

CLUNTON COPPICE

Shropshire Wildlife Trust.
Location: SO 343 806. Take B4385 S from Bishop's Castle. After two miles take road to Brockton, Lower Down and Clunton. Park in Clunton village and walk S into the woodland.
Access: Open at all times. Access along road and public rights of way only.
Facilities: Limited parking in small lquarry entrance on R, or opposite The Crown pub.
Habitat: Oak coppice. Good for ferns, mosses and fungi.
Key birds: Buzzard and Raven regular. *Spring/summer*: Wide range of woodland birds, inc. Redstart, Wood Warbler and Pied Flycatcher.
Contact: Trust HQ, 01743 241691.

LLYNCLYS HILL

Shropshire Wildlife Trust.
Location: SJ 273 237. SSW of Oswestry. Park in layby on A495 at SJ277242 and walk up Turner's Lane.
Access: Open at all times.
Facilities: None.
Public transport: None.
Habitat: Old mixed limestone sward with some woodland and scrub, small pond.
Key birds: Sparrowhawk, Green Woodpecker, Goldcrest, large warbler population. Occasional Peregrine, Buzzard. Eight species of orchid.
Contact: Trust HQ, 01743 241691.

WOOD LANE

Shropshire Wildlife Trust.
Location: SJ 425 327. Turn off A528 at Spurnhill near Ellesmere.
Access: Open at all times.
Facilities: Car parks. Hides (access by permit).
Public transport: None.
Habitat: Gravel pit.
Key birds: *Summer*: Breeding Sand Martins. Popular staging post for waders (inc. Redshank, Greenshank, Ruff, Dunlin, Little Stint, Green and Wood Sandpiper). *Winter*: Lapwing and Curlew.
Contact: Trust HQ, 01743 241691

Somerset

AVONMOUTH SEWAGE WORKS

Avon Wildlife Trust.
Location: Avon WT/Wessex Water ST533797. Lane connecting Kings Weston and Lawrence Weston Lanes near Avonmouth.
Access: Some of reserve visible from road. Permits from Wildlife Trust (members only).
Facilities: Hide.
Public transport: Call Trust for advice.
Habitat: Artificial pools, rough grassland.
Key birds: *Winter*: Wildfowl (inc. Gadwall, Shoveler, Pochard). *Autumn*: Waders (inc. Common and Green Sandpipers); occasional terns; good site in area for Tree Sparrow.
Contact: Trust HQ, 0117 926 8018.

BLAGDON LAKE

Bristol Waterworks.
Location: ST 510 600. Reservoir between Butcombe and Blagdon, 11 miles SW of Bristol. Overlooked from A368, with a mile of public footpath (outside the reservoir enclosure) along SE side from E tip of lake near Ubley westwards to Holt Farm; also public access to wooded N tip, from N end of dam wall carrying Blagdon/ Butcombe byway.
Access: Birds and permits as Chew (below), though birds fewer; permits give access to private paths and two hides.
Facilities: Two hides.
Habitat: Reservoir.
Key birds: Wildfowl, gulls.

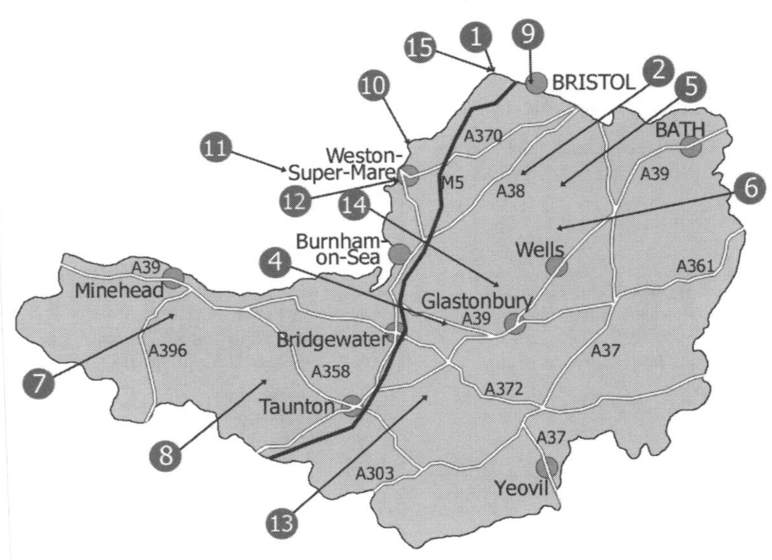

Key to sites:

1. Avonmouth Sewage Works
2. Blagdon Lake
3. Bridgwater Bay
4. Catcott Lows
5. Chew Valley Lake
6. Ebbor Gorge
7. Hurscombe-Wimbleball Lake
8. Langford Heathfield
9. Leigh Woods
10. Sand Point/Middle Hope
11. Steep Holm Island
12. Walborough
13. West Sedgemoor
14. Westhay Moor
15. Willsbridge Mill

BRIDGWATER BAY

English Nature (Somerset Team).
Location: ST 270 470. Nine miles N of Bridgwater. Take J23 or 24 off M5. Turn N off A39 at Cannington.
Access: Hides open every day except Christmas Day. Permits needed for Steart Island (by boat only). Dogs on leads - grazing animals/nesting birds. Disabled access to hides by arrangement, other areas accessible.
Facilities: Car park at Steart. Footpath approx 0.5 miles to tower and hides.
Public transport: None.
Habitat: Estuary, intertidal mudflats, saltmarsh.
Key birds: *Winter:* Wildfowl and waders, birds of prey. *Spring/autumn:* passage migrants.
Contact: Robin Prowse, Dowells Farm, Steart, Bridgwater, Somerset, TA5 2PX. 01278 652426. www.english-nature.org.uk

CATCOTT LOWS

Somerset Wildlife Trust.
Location: ST 400 415. Approx one mile N of Catcott village (off A39 from J23 of M5).
Access: Open at all times.
Facilities: Two hides, one with ramp, one with steps. Car park by ramped hide at ST 400 416. No toilets.
Public transport: None.
Habitat: Wet meadows with winter flooding and summer grazing.
Key birds: *Winter*: Wigeon, Teal, Pintail, Shoveler, Gadwall, Bewick's Swan, Peregrine. *Spring*: Little Egret, passage waders, breeding Lapwing, Snipe, Redshank, Yellow Wagtail.
Contact: D E Read,
SWT, Fyme Court, Broomfield, Bridgwater, Somerset, TA5 2EQ. 01823 451587.

CHEW VALLEY LAKE

Avon Wildlife Trust/Bristol Water Plc.
Location: ST 570 600. Reservoir (partly a Trust reserve) between Chew Stoke and West Harptree, crossed by A368 and B3114, nine miles S of Bristol.
Access: Permit for access to hides (five at Chew, two at Blagdon). Best roadside viewing from causeways at Herriott's Bridge (nature reserve) and Herons Green Bay. Day, half-year and year permits from Bristol Water, Recreation Department, Woodford Lodge, Chew Stoke, Bristol BS18 8SH. Tel/fax 01275 332339.
Facilities: Hides.
Public transport: Call Trust for advice.
Habitat: Reservoir.
Key birds: *Autumn/winter*: Concentrations of wildfowl (inc. Bewick's Swan, Goldeneye, Smew, Ruddy Duck), gull roost (inc. regular Mediterranean, occasional Ring-billed). Migrant waders and terns (inc. Black). Recent rarities inc. Blue-winged Teal, Spoonbill, Alpine Swift, Citrine Wagtail, Little Bunting, Ring-necked Duck, Kumlien's Gull.
Contact: Trust HQ, 0117 926 8018.

EBBOR GORGE

English Nature (Somerset Team).
Location: ST 521 484. Approx two miles from the centre of Wells. Access via Wookey Hole from A39, A371 or via Priddy village from B3135.
Access: Open 9am-dusk all year. No permit required. Limited disabled trail available.
Facilities: Display and nature trails.
Public transport: Not accessible from public transport.
Habitat: Broadleaf woodland and small area of limestone grassland and scrub.
Key birds: Larely spring/summer interest. Buzzard, Sparrowhawk, Greater Spotted and Green Woodpecker, Great and Blue Tit, Whitethroat, Willow Warbler, Chiffchaff, Blackcap. Regular Peregrine Falcon and Raven.
Contact: Bob Corns,
English Nature, Rough Moor, Bishops Hull, Taunton, Somerset, TA1 5AA. 01823 283211.

HURSCOMBE-WIMBLEBALL LAKE

Somerset Wildlife Trust.
Location: SS 974 317. Four miles NE of Dulverton in Exmoor National Park.
Access: Keep to public rights of way.
Facilities: Nature trail. Leaflets from dispenser.
Public transport: None.
Habitat: Reservoir, mud, woodland, scrub, grassland, (formerly farmland).
Key birds: *Winter*: Wildfowl.
Contact: Miss Joan Loraine,
Greencombe, Porlock, Minehead, Somerset, TA24 8NU. 01643 862363.

LANGFORD HEATHFIELD

Somerset Wildlife Trust.
Location: ST 106 227. Lies NW of Wellington (junction 26 of M5).
Access: Open all year. Permit only off footpaths.
Facilities: None.
Public transport: None.
Habitat: Oak/ash woodland, birch/willow scrub, wet heath.
Key birds: Lesser Spotted Woodpecker, Marsh Tit, warblers (inc. Wood, Garden), Pied Flycatcher, Redstart, Tree Pipit.
Contact: Trust HQ, 01823 451587.

LEIGH WOODS

National Trust (Bristol).
Location: ST 560 736. Two miles W from centre of Bristol. Pedestrian access from North Road, Leigh Woods or via Forestry Commission car park at end of Coronation Avenue, Abbots Leigh. Access to both roads is from A369 which goes from Bristol to J19 of M5.
Access: Open all year. A good network of paths around the plateau. The paths down to the towpath are steep and uneven.
Facilities: Two waymarked trails from Forestry Commission car park: purple trail (1.75 miles) on level, red trail (2.5 miles) more undulating.
Public transport: Bristol-Portishead. Bus service (358/658 and 359/659) goes along A369. Leaves Bristol generally at 20 and 50 minutes past the hour. More details from First Badgerline. Tel: 0117 955 3231.
Habitat: Ancient woodland, former wood pasture, two grassland areas, calcareous grassland and scree by towpath.
Key birds: *Summer:* Peregrine, Blackcap, Chiffchaff, Spotted Flycatcher. *Winter:* Great Spotted and Green Woodpeckers, Song Thrush, Long-tailed, Marsh and common tits.
Contact: Bill Morris,
Reserve Office, Valley Road, Leigh Woods, Bristol, 0117 973 1645.
e-mail: wlwbgm@smtp.ntrust.org.uk

SAND POINT/MIDDLE HOPE

National Trust (North Somerset).
Location: ST 330 660. 05283 map. Headland three miles N of Weston-super-Mare. J21 off M5, head for Kewstoke, then N along Beach Road.
Access: Open all year. Dogs on lead. Steep slope – not suitable for wheelchair-users.
Facilities: Toilets (not NT), two mile walks over property.
Public transport: Call Tourist Information Centre for details 01934 888800 (different in winter/summer).
Habitat: Limestone grassland, scrub, saltmarsh.
Key birds: *Summer*: Blackcap, Garden Warbler, Whitethroat, Stonechat. *Winter*: Curlew, Shelduck, Dunlin on mudflat.
Contact:
The National Trust, Barton Rocks, Barton, Winscombe, North Somerset, BS25 1DU. 01934 844518.
e-mail: wmegen@smtp.ntrust.org.uk

STEEP HOLM ISLAND

Kenneth Allsop Memorial Trust.
Location: ST 229 607. Small island in Severn River, five miles NW from Weston-super-Mare harbour.
Access: Scheduled service depending on tides, via ferry. Advance booking advisable to ensure a place. No animals allowed. Not suitable for disabled.
Facilities: Visitor centre, toilets, trails, basic refreshments and sales counter, postal service.
Public transport: None.
Habitat: Limestone grassland, scrub, rare flora, small sycamore wood.
Key birds: Important breeding station for Greater and Lesser Black-backed and Herring Gulls, largest colony of Cormorants in south-west of England. On migration routes.
Contact: Mrs Joan Rendell,
Stonedale, 11 Fairfield Close, Milton, Weston-super-Mare, BS22 8EA. 01934 632307.
www.steepholm.org.uk

WALBOROUGH

Avon Wildlife Trust.
Location: ST 315 579. On S edge of Weston-super-Mare at mouth of River Axe.
Access: Access from Uphill boatyard. Special access trail suitable for less able visitors.
Facilities: None.
Public transport: Call Trust for advice.
Habitat: Limestone grassland, scrub, saltmarsh, estuary.

Key birds: The Axe Estuary holds good numbers of migrant and wintering wildfowl (inc. Teal, Shelduck) and waders (inc. Black-tailed Godwit, Lapwing, Golden Plover, Dunlin, Redshank). Other migrants inc. Little Stint, Curlew Sandpiper, Ruff. Little Egret occurs each year, mostly in late summer.
Contact: Trust HQ, 0117 926 8018

WEST SEDGEMOOR

RSPB (South West England Office).
Location: ST 361 238. Entrance down by-road off A378 Taunton-Langport road, one mile E of Fivehead.
Access: Access at all times to woodland car park and both hides.
Facilities: Heronry hide, nature trail and moorland hide.
Public transport: None.
Habitat: Semi-natural ancient oak woodland and wet grassland. Part of the Somerset Levels and Moors.
Key birds: *Spring/summer*: Breeding Grey Heron, Curlew, Lapwing, Redshank, Snipe, Buzzard, Sedge Warbler, Nightingale. Passage Whimbrel and Hobby. *Winter*: Large flocks of waders and wildfowl (including Lapwing, Golden Plover, Shoveler, Teal and Wigeon).
Contact: The Warden,
Dewlands Farm, Redhill, Curry Rivel, Langport, Somerset, TA10 0PH. 01457 262805, fax 01458 252184. www.rspb.org.uk
e-mail: sally.brown@rspb.org.uk

WESTHAY MOOR

Somerset Wildlife Trust.
Location: ST 458 438. From Glastonbury, take B3151 to site approx one mile NW of Westhay village on minor road to Godney.
Access: Open at all times.
Facilities: Hides and viewing screens, no toilets. Hides have disabled access.
Public transport: None.
Habitat: Open water and reedbeds.
Key birds: *Winter*: Bittern and wildfowl, Red-breasted Merganser, Water Rail, Goosander. *Summer*: Hobby, Reed, Sedge and Cetti's Warblers, Whitethroat.
Contact: David Reid,
SWT, Fyme Court, Broomfield, Bridgwater, Somerset, TA5 2EQ. 01823 451587

WILLSBRIDGE MILL

Avon Wildlife Trust.
Location: ST 665 708. Turn N off A431 at Longwell Green along Long Beach Road, park after quarter mile in car park overlooking valley.
Access: Unrestricted access
Facilities: Visitor centre, nature trail.
Public transport: None.
Habitat: Broadleaved woodland, grassland, scrub, stream, pond.
Key birds: High densities of birds of woodland and scrub. *Winter*: Kingfisher and Dipper regular.
Contact: Ruth Worsley, Willsbridge Mill, Willsbridge Hill, Bristol, BS30 6EX. 0117 932 6885; fax 0117 932 9440.
e-mail wtwmill@cix.co.uk

Staffordshire

BELVIDE RESERVOIR

British Waterways Board and West Midland Bird Club.
Location: SJ865102. Near Brewood, seven miles NW of Wolverhampton.
Access: Access only by permit from the West Midland Bird Club.
Facilities: Hides.
Public transport: Not known.
Habitat: Canal feeder reservoir with marshy margins and gravel islands.
Key birds: Important breeding, moulting and wintering ground for wildfowl, (including Ruddy Duck, Goldeneye and Goosander), passage terns and waders. Night roost for gulls.
Contact: Miss M Surman, 6 Lloyd Square, 12 Niall Close, Edgbaston, Birmingham, B15 3LX,

Staffordshire

Key to sites:
1. Belvide Reservoir
2. Black Brook
3. Blithfield Reservoir
4. Castern Wood
5. Coombes Valley
6. Doxey Marshes
7. Longsdon Woods

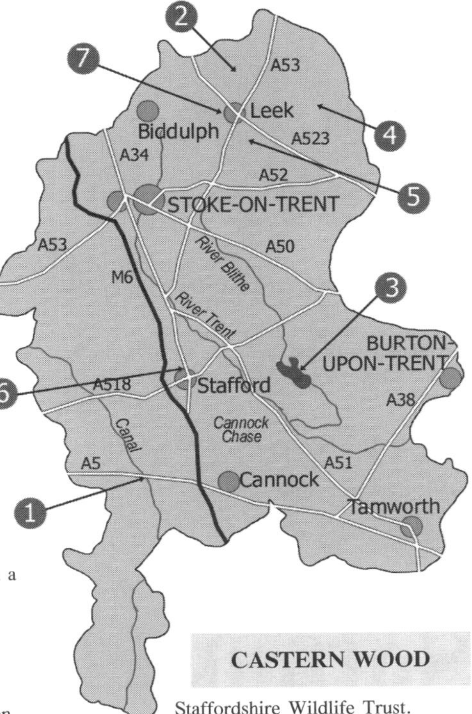

BLACK BROOK

Staffordshire Wildlife Trust.
Location: SK 020 645. N of Leek, W of A53. West of road from Royal Cottage to Gib Tor.
Access: Access is via public footpath from Gib Tor to Newstone Farm; this first passes through a conifer plantation which is outside the reserve.
Facilities: None.
Public transport: None.
Habitat: Heather and bilberry moorland, and upland acidic grassland.
Key birds: Merlin, Kestrel, Red Grouse, Golden Plover, Snipe, Curlew, Dipper, Wheatear, Whinchat, Twite.
Contact: Trust HQ, 01889 508534.

BLITHFIELD RESERVOIR

South Staffs Waterworks Co.
Location: SK 058 237. Large resersvoir lying W of Burton-upon-Trent. View from causeway on B5013 (Rugeley/Uttoxeter).
Access: Access to reservoir and hides by permit from West Midland Bird Club.
Facilities: None.
Public transport: None.
Habitat: Large reservoir.
Key birds: *Winter*: Good populations of wildfowl (inc. Bewick's Swan, Goosander, Goldeneye, Ruddy Duck), large gull roost (can inc. Glaucous, Iceland). Passage terns (Common, Arctic, Black) and waders, esp. in autumn (Little Stint, Curlew Sandpiper, Spotted Redshank regular).
Contact: Miss M Surman,
6 Lloyd Square, 12 Niall Close, Edgbaston, Birmingham, B15 3LX,

CASTERN WOOD

Staffordshire Wildlife Trust.
Location: SK 119 537. E of Leek. Unclassified road SE of Wetton, seven miles NW of Ashbourne, close to Dove Dale.
Access: Use parking area at end of minor road running due SE from Wetton.
Facilities: None.
Public transport: None.
Habitat: Limestone grassland and woodland, spoil heaps from former lead mines.
Key birds: All three woodpeckers, warblers, Pied Flycatcher, Redstart, Sparrowhawk, Tawny Owl.
Contact: Trust HQ, 01889 508534.

COOMBES VALLEY

RSBP (North West England Office).
Location: SK 005 530. Four miles from Leek along A523 between Leek and Ashbourne and 0.5 miles down unclassified road - signposted.
Access: No dogs allowed. Most of the trails are unsuitable for disabled. Open daily - no charge.
Facilities: Visitor centre, toilets, two miles of nature trail, one hide. Events and guided walks.

Public transport: None.
Habitat: Sessile oak woodland, unimproved pasture and meadow.
Key birds: *Spring:* Pied Flycatcher, Redstart, Wood Warbler. *Jan-Mar*: Displaying raptors.
Contact: Nick Chambers, Six Oaks Farm, Bradnop, Leek, Staffs, ST13 7EU. 01438 384017. e-mail: nick.chambers@RSBP.org.uk www.RSBP.org.uk

DOXEY MARSHES

Staffordshire Wildlife Trust.
Location: SJ 903 250. In Stafford. Parking 0.25 miles off M6 J14/A5013 or walk from town centre.
Access: Open at all times. Dogs on leads. Disabled access being improved 2001.
Facilities: Two hides - accessible to wheelchairs.
Public transport: Walk from town centre via Sainsbury's.
Habitat: Marsh, pools, reedbeds, hedgerows, reed sweet-grass swamp.
Key birds: *Spring/summer*: Breeding Snipe, Lapwing, Redshank, warblers, buntings, Skylark, Water Rail. *Winter*: Snipe, wildfowl, thrushes, Short-eared Owl. Passage waders, vagrants.
Contact: Rachel Wheatcroft, Coutts House, Sandon, Staffs, ST18 0DN. 01889 508534. e-mail: staffsut@cix.co.uk www.wildlifetrust.org.uk/staffs

LONGSDON WOODS

Staffordshire Wildlife Trust.
Location: SK 965 555. Reserve lies off A53 Leek - Burton road. Can be approached from Ladderedge near Leek; City Lane, Longsdon; or Rudyard Station.
Access: Public rights of way only.
Facilities: None.
Habitat: Woodland and wet grassland.
Key birds: Heronry, Sparrowhawk, Curlew, Snipe, Jack Snipe, Woodcock, Little and Tawny Owls, all three woodpeckers, Redstart, Blackcap, Garden Warbler.
Contact: Trust HQ, 01889 508534.

Suffolk

BRADFIELD WOODS

Suffolk Wildlife Trust.
Location: TL 935 581. Off minor road from Bradfield St George S of A14, seven miles SE of Bury St Edmunds.
Access: Open during daylight hours.
Facilities: Hide. Visitor centre open Sun (1pm-5pm Easter to end Sep), also Bank Hol Mons.
Public transport: None.
Habitat: Ancient coppiced working woodland.
Key birds: *Summer*: Wide range of breeding woodland species (inc. Nightingale).
Contact: Peter Fordham, Felsham Road, Bradfield St George, Bury St Edmunds, Suffolk, IP30 0HU. 01449 737996.

CARLTON MARSHES

Suffolk Wildlife Trust.
Location: TM 508 920. SW of Lowestoft, at W end of Oulton Broad. Take A146 towards Beceles and turn R after Esso garage.
Access: Open during daylight hours. Keep to marked paths.
Facilities: Information centre.
Public transport: None.
Habitat: 100 acres of grazing marsh, peat pools and fen.
Key birds: Wide range of wetland and Broadland birds, including Marsh Harrier.
Contact: Nick Sanderson, Suffolk Broads Wildlife Centre, Carlton Colville, Lowestoft, Suffolk, NR33 8HU. 01502 564250.

DINGLE MARSHES, DUNWICH

Suffolk Wildlife Trust/RSPB.
Location: TM 48 07 20. Eight miles from Saxmundham. Follow brown signs from A12 to Minsmere and continue to Dunwich. Forest carpark (hide) - TM 46 77 10. Beach carpark - TM 479 707.
Access: Open at all times. Access via public rights of way and permissive path along beach. Dogs on lead please.
Facilities: Toilets at beach car park, Dunwich. Hide in Dunwich Forest overlooking reedbed,

Suffolk

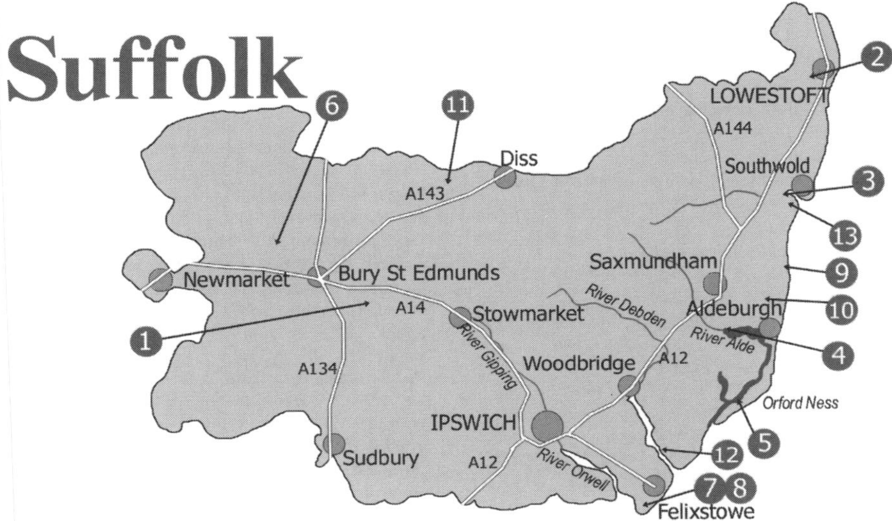

Key to sites:
1. Bradfield Woods
2. Carlton Marshes
3. Dingle Marshes,
4. Hazelwood Marshes
5. Havergate Island
6. Lackford Wildfowl Reserve
7. Landguard
8. Landguard Bird Observatory
9. Minsmere
10. North Warren & Aldringham Walks
11. Redgrave And Lopham Fens
12. Trimley Marshes
13. Walberswick

accessed via Forest car park. Circular trail waymarked from carpark.
Habitat: Grazing marsh, reedbed, shingle beach and saline lagoons
Key birds: Reedbed: Bittern, Marsh Harrier, Bearded Tit (*all year*), Hobby (*Summer*), Hen Harrier (*Winter*). Grazing marsh: Lapwing, Avocet, Snipe, Black-tailed Godwit (Summer) White-fronted Goose, Wigeon, Teal, Snipe (*Winter*). Good for passage waders.
Contact: Alan Miller, Suffolk Wildlife Trust, 9 Valley Terrace, Valley Road, Leiston, Suffolk, IP16 4AP. 01728 833405.
e-mail: alanm@suffolkwildife.cix.co.uk

HAZELWOOD MARSHES

Suffolk Wildlife Trust.
Location: TM 435 575. Four miles W of Aldeburgh. Small car park on A1094. Mile walk down sandy track.
Access: Open dawn to dusk.
Facilities: Hide.
Habitat: Estuary, marshes.
Key birds: Marshland and estuary birds; spring and autumn migrants.
Contact: Rodney West, Flint Cottage, Stone Common, Blaxhall, Woodbridge, Suffolk, IP12 2DP. 01728 689171; fax 01728 688044;
e-mail rodwest@ndirect.co.uk.

HAVERGATE ISLAND

RSPB (East Anglia Office).
Location: TM 425 496. Part of the Orfordness NNR at the mouth of the River Alde.
Access: Open Apr-Aug (1st & 3rd weekends and every Thu), Sep-Mar (1st Sat every month). Book in advance, in writing. Park in Orford.
Facilities: None.
Public transport: Boat trips from Orford (one mile)
Habitat: Shallow brackish water, lagoons with islands, saltmarsh, shingle beaches.
Key birds: *Summer*: Breeding Arctic, Common and Sandwich Terns, migrants. Leading site for Avocet. *Winter*: Wildfowl.
Contact: John Partridge, Manager,
30 Mundays Lane, Orford, Woodbridge, Suffolk, IP12 2LX. 01394 450732.

LACKFORD WILDFOWL RESERVE

Suffolk Wildlife Trust and Atlas Aggregates.
Location: TL 803 708. Via track off N side of A1101 (Bury to Mildenhall road), between Lackford and Flempton. Five miles from Bury.
Access: Open daytime. Access to hides and visitor hut only. No dogs.
Facilities: Eight hides, visitor hut.
Habitat: Restored gravel pit with open water, lagoons, islands, willow scrub.
Key birds: Winter: Large gull roost. Wide range of waders and wildfowl (inc. Goosander, Pochard, Tufted Duck, Shoveler. No1 hide excellent for Kingfisher). *Spring/autumn*: Migrants, inc. raptors. Breeding Shelduck, Little Ringed Plover and reed warblers.
Contact: Colin Jakes, 7 Maltward Avenue, Bury St Edmunds, IP33 3XN. 01284 702215.

LANDGUARD

Suffolk Wildlife Trust.
Location: TM 285 315. Take A154 S from Felixtowe town centre.
Access: Open at all times. Both for reserve and observatory all group visits and guided walks are arranged via the Ranger.
Facilities: None
Habitat: Grassland, shingle bank.
Key birds: The reserve is located on a prime migration route. *Summer:* Nesting Little Tern, Ringed Plover, Wheatear and Black Redstart. Seabirds.
Contact: Paul Holmes,
Landguard Bird Observatory, (see next entry).

LANDGUARD BIRD OBSERVATORY

Location: TM 283 317. Road S of Felixstowe to Landguard Nature Reserve and Fort.
Access: Visiting by appointment.
Facilities: Migration watch point and ringing station.
Public transport: Call for advice.
Habitat: Close grazed turf, raised banks with holm oak, tamarisk, etc.
Key birds: Unusual species and common migrants. Seabirds.
Contact: Paul Holmes, Landguard Bird Observatory, View Point Road, Felixstowe, Suffolk, IP11 8TW. 01394 673782; mobile 0850 427928.

MINSMERE

RSPB (East Anglia Office).
Location: TM 452 680. Six miles NE of Samundham. From A12 head for Westleton, N of Yoxford. Access from Westleton (follow the brown tourist signs).
Access: Open every day, except Tue, Christmas Day and Boxing Day (9am-9pm or dusk if earlier). Visitor centre open 9am-5pm (9am-4pm Nov-Jan). Tea-room 10.30am-4.30pm (10am-4pm Nov-Jan). Free to RSPB members, otherwise £5 adults, £1.50 children, £3 concession.
Facilities: Toilets, visitor centre, hides, trails.
Public transport: Train to Saxmundham then taxi.
Habitat: Woodland, wetland – reedbed and grazing marsh, heathland, dunes and beach, farmland – arable conversion to heath, coastal lagoons, 'the scrape'.
Key birds: *Summer*: Avocet, Bittern, Marsh Harrier, Bearded Tit, Redstart, Nightingale, Nightjar. *Winter*: Wigeon, White-fronted Goose, Bewick's Swan. *Autumn/spring*: Passage migrants, waders etc.
Contact: Geoff Welch, Minsmere RSPB Reserve, Westleton, Saxmundham, Suffolk, IP17 3BY. 01728 648281. www.rspb.org.uk

NORTH WARREN & ADRINGHAM WALKS

RSBP (East Anglia Office).
Location: TM 468 575. Directly N of Aldeburgh on Suffolk coast. Use signposted main car park on beach.
Access: Open at all times. Please keep dogs under close control. Beach area suitable for disabled.
Facilities: Three nature trails, leaflet available from TIC Aldeburgh or Minsmere RSBP. Toilets in Aldeburgh and Thorpeness.
Public transport: Bus service to Aldeburgh. First Eastern Counties (08456 020121).
Habitat: Grazing marsh, lowland heath, reedbed, woodland.
Key birds: *Winter*: White-fronted Goose, Tundra Bean Goose, Wigeon, Shoveler, Teal, Gadwall, Pintail, Snow Bunting. *Spring/summer*: Breeding Bittern, Marsh Harrier, Hobby, Nightjar, Wood Lark, Nightingale, Dartford Warbler.
Contact: Rob Macklin, Racewalk, Priory Road, Snape, Suffolk, IP17 1SD. 01728 688481.
e-mail: rob.macklin@tesco.net

REDGRAVE & LOPHAM FENS

Suffolk Wildlife Trust.
Location: TM 05 07 97. Five miles from Diss, signposted and easily accessed from A1066 and A143 roads.
Access: Open all year, dogs strictly on leads only. Visitor centre open all year at weekends. Summer opening up to six days a week, call for details on 01379 688333.
Facilities: Visitor centre with coffee shop, toilets, including disabled toilets, disabled/ wheelchair accessible boardwalk and viewing platform. Other general circular trails (not wheelchair access).
Public transport: Buses and trains to Diss town – Simonds coaches to local villages of Redgrave and South Lopham from Diss.
Habitat: Calcareous fen, wet acid heath, scrub and woodland
Key birds: *All year*: Water Rail, Snipe, Teal, Woodcock, Sparrowhawk, Kestrel, all three woodpeckers, Tawny and Little Owls, Shelduck. *Summer*: Reed, Sedge and Grasshopper Warblers, other leaf and *Sylvia* warblers, Hobby. *Winter/ occasional on passage*: Bearded Tit, Marsh Harrier, greenshank, Green Sandpiper, Shoveler, Gadwall.
Contact: Andrew Excell, Redgrave and Lopham Fens, Low Common Road, South Lopham, Diss, Norfolk, IP22 2HX. 01379 687618.
e-mail: redgrave@suffolkwildlife.cix.co.uk

TRIMLEY MARSHES

Suffolk Wildlife Trust.
Location: TM 260 352. Main Road A14 – Felixstowe two miles – Ipswich ten miles. Parking at top of Cordy's Lane, Trimley St Mary one mile from reserve.
Access: Reserve open at all times. Visitor centre open at weekends. Dogs on lead. Best time to visit – all year.
Facilities: Visitor centre, toilets (open at weekends), five hides.
Public transport: Train station at Trimley (Station Road/Cordy's Lane).
Habitat: Wetland (84 hectares).
Key birds: *Summer:* Avocet, Marsh Harrier, Redshank, Garganey, etc. *Passage*: Curlew Sandpiper, Wood Sandpiper. *Winter:* Wildfowl.
Contact: Mick Wright, 15 Avondale Road, Ipswich, Suffolk, IP3 9JT. 01473 710032.
e-mail: mickwright@btinternet.com
www.wildlifetrust.org.uk/suffolk

WALBERSWICK

English Nature (Suffolk Team).
Location: TM 475 733. Good views from B1387 and from lane running W from Walberswick towards Westwood Lodge; elsewhere keep to public footpaths or shingle beach.
Access: Parties and coach parking by prior arrangement.
Facilities: Hide on S side of Blyth estuary, E of A12.
Public transport: Call Trust for advice.
Habitat: Tidal estuary, fen, freshwater marsh and reedbeds, heath, mixed woodland, carr.
Key birds: *Spring/summer*: Marsh Harrier, Bearded Tit, Water Rail, Bittern, Nightjar. *Passage/winter*: Wildfowl, waders and raptors.
Contact: Adam Burrows, English Nature, Regent House, 110 Northgate Street, Bury St Edmunds, IP33 1HP. 01502 676171.

Surrey

FRENSHAM COMMON

Waverley Borough Council and National Trust.
Location: SU 855 405. Common and country park lie on either side of A287 between Farnham and Hindhead.
Access: Open at all times. Car park (locked 9pm-9am). Keep to paths.
Facilities: Information rooms, toilets and refreshment kiosk at Great Pond.
Public transport: Call Trust for advice.
Habitat: Dry and humid heath, woodland, two large ponds, reedbeds.
Key birds: *Summer*: Dartford Warbler, Woodlark, Hobby, Nightjar, Stonechat. *Winter*: Wildfowl (inc. occasional Smew), Bittern, Great Grey Shrike.

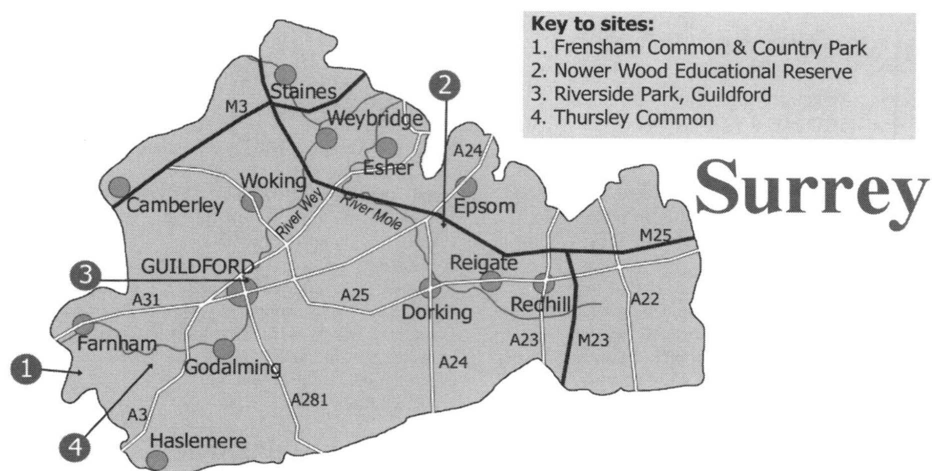

Contact: Mike Coates, Rangers Office, Bacon Lane, Churt, Surrey, GU10 2QB. 01252 792416.

NOWER WOOD EDUCATIONAL RESERVE

Surrey Wildlife Trust.
Location: TQ 193 546. SE of Leatherhead (junction 9 of M25). Then take B2033 Leatherhead to Headley road.
Access: Open days Apr-Oct (call for dates and times).
Facilities: Refreshments. Hide, nature trail, visitor centre.
Public transport: None.
Habitat: Ancient deciduous woodland with ponds.
Key birds: *Summer*: 35 breeding species include, Sparrowhawk, all three woodpeckers, Tawny Owl, Spotted Flycatcher, Woodcock, common warblers, Mandarin Duck.
Contact: Education Department, Surrey Wildlife Trust, Nower Wood, Mill Way, Leatherhead, KT22 8QA. 01372 379509; fax 01372 363964.

RIVERSIDE PARK

Guildford Borough Council.
Location: TQ 005515 (Guildford BC). From car park at Bowers Lane, Burpham (TQ 011 527). Three miles from town centre.
Access: Open at all times. Follow marked paths. Access to far side of lake and marshland area via boardwalk.
Facilities: Boardwalk.
Public transport: Guildford town centre to Burpham (Sainsburys) No 36 Bus (Arriva timetable information. Tel 0870 608 2608).
Habitat: Wetland, lake, meadow, woodland.
Key birds: *Summer*: Sedge, Reed and Garden Warblers, Common Tern, Lesser Whitethroat, Hobby. *Winter*: Jack Snipe, Chiffchaff, Water Rail. *Passage*: Common Sandpiper, Whinchat, Water Pipit (up to 12 most years).
Contact:: Parks Helpdesk, Guildford Borough Council, Millmead House, Millmead, Guildford, Surrey, GO2 5BB. 01483 444715.
e-mail: parks@guildford.gov.uk
www.guildfordborough.co.uk/pages/leisure/parks/parks.htm

THURSLEY COMMON

English Nature (Sussex & Surrey Team).
Location: SU 900 417. From Guildford, take A3 SW to B3001 (Elstead/Churt road). Use the Moat car park.
Access: Open access. Parties must obtain prior permission.
Facilities: Boardwalk in wetter areas.
Public transport: None.
Habitat: Wet and dry heathland, woodland, bog.
Key birds: *Winter*: Hen Harrier and Great Grey Shrike. *Summer*: Hobby, Woodlark, Dartford Warbler, Stonechat, Curlew, Snipe, Nightjar.
Contact: Simon Nobes,
English Nature, Uplands Stud, Brook, Godalming, Surrey, GU8 5LA. 01428 685878.

Sussex, East

FORE WOOD

RSPB (South East England Office).
Location: TQ 758 123. From the A2100 (Battle to Hastings) take lane to Crowhurst at Crowhurst Park Caravan Park. Park at Crowhurst village hall and walk back up Forwood Lane for 0.5 miles. Entrance to reserve on left at top of hill.
Access: Open all year. Closed Christmas Day. No disabled facilities. No dogs.
Facilities: Two nature trails.
Public transport: Station at Crowhurst, about 0.5 mile walk. Charing Cross/Hastings line.
Habitat: Semi-natural ancient woodland.
Key birds: Three species woodpecker, Nuthatch, Treecreeper, Sparrowhawk, Marsh Tit. *Spring/ summer*: Blackcap, Nightingale, Spotted Flycatcher.
Contact: Martin Allison,
12 The Grove, Crowborough, East Sussex, TN6 1NY. 01273 775333 (South East Regional Office). e-mail: allison@rspb.org.uk
www.rspb.org.uk

LULLINGTON HEATH

English Nature (Sussex & Surrey Team).
Location: TQ 525 026. W of Eastbourne, after six miles on A259 turn N on minor road to Lullington Court for parking, then one mile up hill (bridleway).
Access: Permit only off rights of way
Facilities: None.
Public transport: None.
Habitat: Chalk downland and heath, dense woodland scrub and areas of gorse.
Key birds: *Summer*: Breeding Nightingale, Nightjar and Grasshopper Warbler, Turtle Dove. *Winter*: Raptors (inc. Hen Harrier), Woodcock.
Contact: Malcolm Emery, English Nature, Phoenix House, 32-33 North Street, Lewes, E Sussex, BN7 2PH. 01273 476595; fax 01273 483063; e-mail sussex.surrey@english-nature.org.uk; www.english-nature.org.uk.

PETT POOL

Sussex Wildlife Trust.
Location: TQ 903 145. NE of Hastings on A259.
Access: Good views from Rye/Hastings coast road.
Facilities: None.
Public transport: Call Trust for advice.

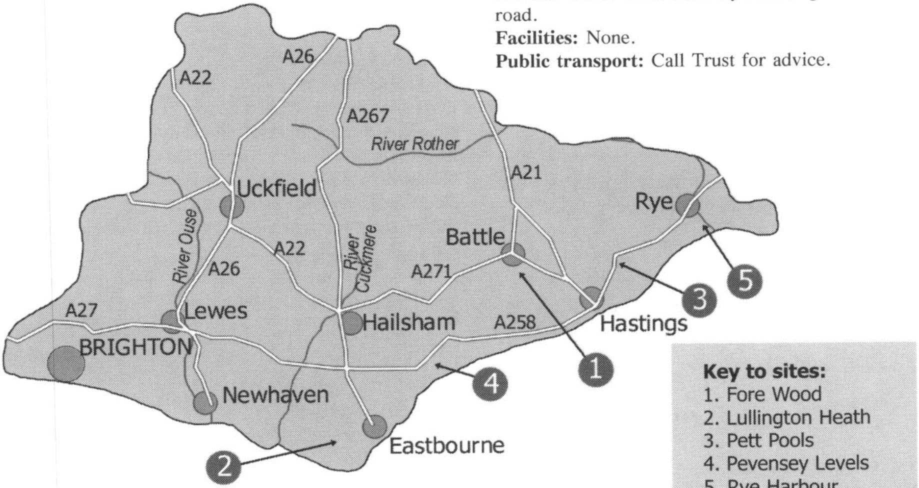

Key to sites:
1. Fore Wood
2. Lullington Heath
3. Pett Pools
4. Pevensey Levels
5. Rye Harbour

Habitat: Man-made shallow pools.
Key birds: *Autumn*: Good wader passage. *Winter*: Bearded Tit.
Contact: Trust HQ, 01273 492630.

PEVENSEY LEVELS

English Nature (Sussex & Surrey Team).
Location: TQ 665 054. NE of Eastbourne. S of A259, one mile along minor road from Pevensey E to Norman's Bay.
Access: Good views from road.
Facilities: None.
Public transport: Call for advice.
Habitat: Freshwater grazing marsh, subject to light flooding after rains.
Key birds: *Summer*: Breeding Reed and Sedge Warblers, Yellow Wagtail, Snipe, Redshank, Lapwing. *Winter*: Large numbers of wildfowl (inc. some Bewick's and Whooper Swans) and waders (inc. Golden Plover). Birds of prey (inc. Merlin, Peregrine, Hobby, Short-eared Owl).
Contact: Malcolm Emery,
English Nature, Phoenix House, 32-33 North Street, Lewes, E Sussex, BN7 2PH. 01273 476595; fax 01273 483063; e-mail sussex.surrey@english-nature.org.uk; www.english-nature.org.uk.

RYE HARBOUR

Rye Harbour Local Nature Reserve Management Committee.
Location: TQ 941 188. One mile from Rye off A259 signed Rye Harbour. From J10 of M20 take A2070 until it joins A259.
Access: Open at all times by footpaths. Organised groups please book.
Facilities: Car park in Rye Harbour village. Information kiosk in car park. Toilets and disabled facilities near car park, four hides (one with wheelchair access), information centre open at weekends.
Public transport: Train (tel: 08457 484950), bus (tel: 0870 608 2608), Rye tourist information (tel: 01797 226696).
Habitat: Sea, sand, shingle, pits and grassland.
Key birds: *Spring*: Passage waders, especially roosting Whimbrel. *Summer*: Breeding terns, waders, Wheatear, Yellow Wagtail, Tree Sparrow. *Winter*: Wildfowl, Water Rail, Bittern.
Contact: Barry Yates, (Manager),
2 Watch Cottages, Winchelsea, East Sussex, TN36 4LU. 01797 223862.
e-mail: yates@clara.net
www.natureserve.ryeharbour.org

Sussex, West

ADUR ESTUARY

RSPB (South East England Office).
Location: TQ211050. On W side of Shoreham-on-Sea.
Access: Good views from riverside paths between footbridge in Shoreham town centre and A259 Norfolk bridge (car park).
Facilities: None.
Public transport: Call RSPB for advice.
Habitat: Mudflats and saltmarsh.
Key birds: Small area but good for easy viewing of waders.
Contact: RSPB office, 01273 775333.

ARUNDEL

The Wildfowl and Wetlands Trust.
Location: TQ 020 081. Clearly signposted from Arundel, just N of A27.
Access: Summer (9.30am-5.30pm) winter (9.30am-4.30pm). Closed Christmas Day. Approx 1.5 miles of level footpaths, suitable for wheelchairs. No dogs except guide dogs.
Facilities: Visitor centre, restaurant, shop, hides, picnic area, seasonal nature trails.
Public transport: Arundel station, 15-20 minute walk. Tel: 01903 882131.
Habitat: Lakes, wader scrapes, reedbed.
Key birds: *Summer*: Nesting Redshank, Lapwing, Oystercatcher, Common Tern, Sedge, Reed and Cetti's Warblers, Peregrine, Hobby. *Winter*: Teal, Wigeon, roosting Bewick's Swan, Water Rail, Cetti's Warbler.
Contact: David Julian,
Mill Road, Arundel, West Sussex, BN18 9PB. 01903 883355.
e-mail: wwt.arundel@virgin.org.uk
www.wwt.org.uk

Sussex, West

KINGLEY VALE

English Nature (Sussex & Surrey Team).
Location: SU 825 088. West Stoke car park. Approx three miles NW of Chichester town centre. Travel W along B2178 from Chichester, approx three miles, to East Ashling. Immediately after village turn right (on sharp left hand bend). After approx 0.5 miles turn left (off sharp right hand bend) and car park is on the right.
Access: Always open, no permits, no disabled access, no toilets. Dogs on a lead please.
Facilities: There is a nature trail (posts 1-24) and an information centre - no toilets, plenty of trees and bushes!
Public transport: Nearest railway station approx four miles walking distance. Nearest main bus route just over one mile on A286 at Mid Lavant.
Habitat: Greatest yew forest in Europe (more than 30,000 trees). Chalk grassland, mixed oak/ ash woodland and scrub. Chalk heath.
Key birds: *Spring/summer*: Nightingale, Golden Pheasant, Whitethroat, Blackcap, Lesser Whitethroat. *Autumn/winter*: Hen Harrier, Buzzard, Hobby on migration, Red Kite.
Contact: Simon Nobes, English Nature, Game Keeper's Lodge, West Stoke House Farm, Downs Road, West Stoke, Chichester, West Sussex, PO18 9BN. 01243 575353.

PAGHAM HARBOUR

West Sussex County Council.
Location: SZ 857 966. National Nature Reserve, five miles S of Chichester on B2145 towards Selsey.
Access: Open at all times, dogs must be on leads, disabled trail with accessible hide.
Facilities: Visitor centre open at weekends (10am-4pm), toilets (including disabled), three hides, one nature trail.
Public transport: Bus stop by visitor centre.
Habitat: Intertidal saltmarsh, shingle beaches, lagoons and farmland.
Key birds: *Spring*: Passage migrants. *Autumn*: Passage waders, other migrants. *Winter*: Brent Goose, Slavonian Grebe, wildfowl. *All year*: Little Egret.
Contact: Sarah Patton, Pagham Harbour NNR, Selsey Road, Sidlesham, Chichester, West Sussex, PO20 7NE. 01243 641508.
e-mail: pagham.nr@westsussex.gov.uk

PULBOROUGH BROOKS

RSPB (South East England Office).
Location: TQ 054 170. Signposted on A283 between Pulborough (via A29) and Storrington

(via A24). Two miles SE of Pulborough.
Access: Open daily. Visitor centre 10am-5pm (Tea-room 4.45pm, 4pm Mon-Fri in winter), closed Christmas Day and Boxing Day. Nature trail and hides (9am-9pm or sunset), closed Christmas Day. Admission fee for nature trail (free to RSPB members). No dogs. Three of the four hides accessible to wheelchair users, although a strong helper is needed.
Facilities: Visitor centre (incl RSPB shop, tea room with terrace, displays, toilets). Nature trail and four hides and one viewpoint. Large car park. Play and picnic areas.
Public transport: Two miles from Pulborough train station. Connecting bus service regularly passes reserve entrance (not Suns). Compass Travel (01903 233767). Cycle stands.
Habitat: Lowland wet grassland (wet meadows and ditches). Hedgerows and woodland.
Key birds: *Winter*: Wintering waterbirds, Bewick's Swan. *Spring*: Breeding wading birds and songbirds (incl Lapwing and Nightingale). *Summer*: Butterflies and dragonflies, warblers. *Autumn*: Passage wading birds, Redstart.
Contact: Tim Callaway,
Site Manager,
Upperton's Barn, Wiggonholt, Pulborough, West Sussex, RH20 2EL. 01798 875851.
e-mail: pulborough.brooks@rspb.org.uk

WALTHAM BROOKS

Sussex Wildlife Trust.
Location: TQ 026 159. SW of Pulborough. On S side of minor road E of Coldwaltham on A29.
Access: Park at Greatham Bridge car park, not on roadside. Permit only.
Facilities: None.
Public transport: None.
Habitat: Wet grassland with muddy pools in spring, flooded meadows in winter.
Key birds: *Winter:* Waders, wildfowl (inc. Bewick's Swan, Shoveler, Teal, Wigeon). *Spring/ summer:* Redshank, Lapwing, Gadwall and Shelduck.
Contact: Trust HQ, 01273 492630.

WARNHAM NATURE RESERVE

Horsham District Council.
Location: TQ 167 324. One mile from Horsham Town Centre. Reserve located off A24 at the 'Robin Hood' roundabout, on B2237.
Access: Open Thu-Sun throughout the year and Bank Holidays (10am-6pm or dusk). Free access over part of reserve, permits required for some areas (small charge day or annual permits). No dogs allowed. Hide nearest visitor centre has good disabled access, otherwise no hardstanding paths.
Facilities: Visitor centre and café open Sat and Sun in summer, Sun only in winter. Toilets (including disabled) available, two hides, nature reserve leaflets available to lead you round.
Public transport: From Horsham Railway Station it is a mile walk along Hurst Road, with a right turn onto Warnham Road. A bus from the 'Carfax' in Horsham Centre can take you to within 150 yards of the reserve. Travel line, 0870 608 2608.
Habitat: Millpond with reedbeds, marsh, meadow and woodland (broadleaf and coniferous).
Key birds: Heronry, Great Crested Grebe, Kingfisher. *Summer*: Swift, Swallow, House Martin, Sedge Warbler, Reed Warbler, Garden Warbler, Willow Warbler, Whitethroat, Blackcap, Chiffchaff, Spotted Flycatcher. *Winter*: Cormorant, Teal, Pochard, Tufted Duck, Black-headed Gull, Meadow Pipit, Siskin.
Contact: Julia Hargreaves, Leisure Services, Park House Lodge, North Street, Horsham, W Sussex, RH12 1RL. 01403 256890

WOODS MILL

Sussex Wildlife Trust.
Location: TQ 218 138. Located NW of Brighton, one mile S of Henfield on A2037.
Access: Nature trail - every day except Christmas week (9am-5pm). Muddy in winter, access by wheelchair in summer. Headquarters of Sussex Wildlife Trust.
Facilities: Toilets, hide, nature trail, car park, centre open summer on Sun (11am-5pm). Events programme.
Public transport: From Henfield hourly. Compass Travel 01903 233767.
Habitat: Woodland, reedbeds, wet meadow, lake.
Key birds: General woodland birds and Kingfisher all year. *Summer*: Warblers (Reed, Blackcap, Garden, Whitethroat, Lesser Whitethroat) and Nightingale.
Contact: Steve Tillman, Woods Mill, Henfield, West Sussex, BN5 9SD. 01273 492630.

Tyne & Wear

Key to sites:
1. Big Waters
2. Boldon Flats
3. Derwent Walk Country Park
4. Maze Park & Portrack Marsh
5. Ryton Willows
6. Shibdon Pond
7. Wallsend Swallow Pond
8. Washington
9. Washingwell Wood/Watergate Park
10. Whitburn Bird Observatory

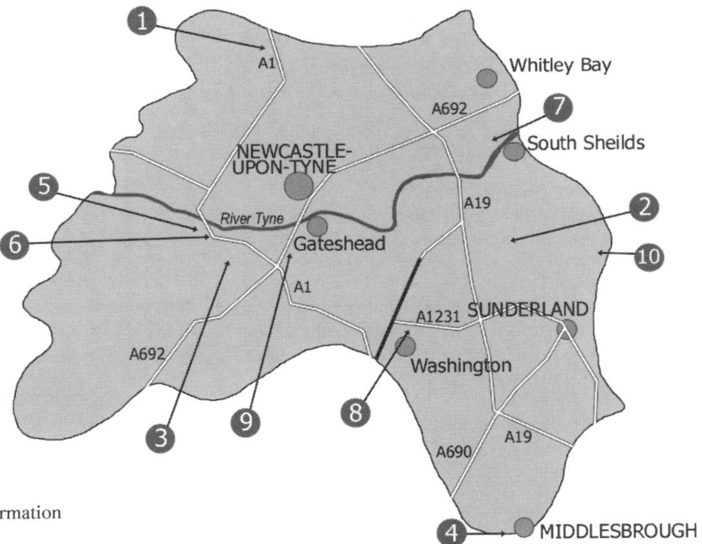

BIG WATERS

Northumberland Wildlife Trust.
Location: NZ 227 734. S along track off Wide Open/Dinnington road.
Access: View from public hide (suitable for disabled) at E end of recreation area; permit for further access from NWT.
Facilities: Public hide.
Public transport: No information available.
Habitat: Pond, fen/wet grassland.
Key birds: Breeding & winter wildfowl; Swallow roost.
Contact: Trust HQ, 0191 284 6884

BOLDON FLATS

South Tyneside Metropolitan Council.
Location: NZ 377 614. Take A184 N from Sunderland to Boldon.
Access: View from Moor Lane on minor road NE of East Boldon station towards Whitburn.
Facilities: None.
Public transport: None.
Habitat: Meadows, part SSSI, managed flood in winter, pond, ditches.
Key birds: *Passage/winter*: Wildfowl and waders. Gull roost may inc. Mediterranean, Glaucous, Iceland; Merlin fairly regular.

DERWENT WALK

Gateshead Council.
Location: NZ 178 604. Along River Derwent, four miles SW of Newcastle and Gateshead. Several car parks along A614.
Access: Site open all times. Thornley visitor centre open weekends and Bank Holidays (12-5pm). Keys for hides available from Thornley Woodlands Centre (£2).
Facilities: Toilets at Thornley visitor centre. Toilets at Swalwell visitor centre. Hides at Far Pasture Ponds and Thornley feeding station.
Public transport: 45, 46, 46A, M20 and 611 buses from Newcastle/Gateshead to Swalwell/ Rowlands Gill. Bus stop Thornley Woodlands Centre. (Regular bus service from Newcastle).

Information from News Travel Line. Tel: 0191 2325325.
Habitat: Mixed woodland, river, ponds, meadows.
Key birds: *Summer*: Wood Warbler, Pied Flycatcher, Green Sandpiper, Kingfisher, Dipper, Great Spotted and Green Woodpeckers, Blackcap, Garden Warbler, Nuthatch. *Winter*: Brambling, Marsh Tit, Willow Tit, Bullfinch, Great Spotted Woodpecker, Nuthatch, Goosander, Kingfisher.
Contact: Stephen Westerberg, Thornley Woodlands Centre, Rowlands Gill, Tyne & Wear, NE39 1AU. 01207 545212.
e-mail: thornleywoodlandscentre@unisonFree.net
www.gateshead.gov.uk

MAZE PARK AND PORTRACK MARSH

Tees Valley Wildlife Trust.
Location: NZ 463 190. Located midway between Middlesbrough and Stockton. Access from A66 at Tees Barrage. Sites are located on opposite banks to the River Tees, E of the barrage.
Access: No permits required. National cycle route passes through Maze Park. Surfaced paths at both sites. Hide suitable for disabled users at Portrack Marsh. Please keep to the permissive paths and public rights of way.
Facilities: Hide at Portrack Marsh. No toilets or visitor centre.
Public transport: Regular buses between Middlesbrough and Stockton stop at the Tees Barrage (Arriva, tel 0870 6082608). Thornaby Station one mile. Frequent trains from Darlington and Middlesbrough.
Habitat: Freshwater marsh, scrub, post-industrial grassland, riverside.
Key birds: *Winter*: Ducks, passage waders, Redshank, Snipe, Lapwing, Grey Heron, Skylark, Grey Partridge, Sand Martin, occasional Kingfisher.
Contact: Bill Ashton-Wickett, Bellamy Pavilion, Kirkleatham Old Hall, Kirkleatham, Redcar, TS10 5NW. 01642 759900.
e-mail: teesvalleywt@cix.co.uk
www.wildlifetrust.org.uk/teesvalley

RYTON WILLOWS

Gateshead Council.
Location: NZ 155 650. Five miles W of Newcastle. Access along several tracks running N from Ryton.
Access: Open at all times.
Facilities: Nature trail and free leaflet.
Public transport: Regular service to Ryton from Newcastle/Gateshead. Information from Nexus Travelline on 0191 232 5325.
Habitat: Deciduous woodland, scrub, riverside, tidal river.
Key birds: *Winter*: Goldeneye, Goosander, Green Woodpecker, Nuthatch, Treecreeper. *Autumn*: Greenshank. *Summer*: Lesser Whitethroat, Sedge Warbler, Yellowhammer, Linnet, Reed Bunting, Common Sandpiper.
Contact: Andrew McLay, Thornley Woodlands Centre, Rowlands Gill, Tyne & Wear, NE39 1AU. 1208 545212.
e-mail: thornleywoodlandscentre@unisonFree.net
www.gateshead.gov.uk

SHIBDON POND

Gateshead Council.
Location: NZ 192 628. E of Blaydon, S of Scotswood Bridge, close to A1. Car park at Blaydon swimming baths. Open access from B6317 (Shibdon Road).
Access: Open at all times. Disabled access to hide. Key for hide available from Thornley Woodlands Centre (£2).
Facilities: Hide in SW corner of pond. Free leaflet available.
Public transport: At least six buses per hour from Newcastle/Gateshead to Blaydon (bus stop Shibdon Road). Information from Nexus Travel Line (0191 232 5325).
Habitat: Pond, marsh, scrub and damp grassland.
Key birds: *Winter*: Wildfowl, Water Rail, white-winged gulls. *Summer*: Reed Warbler, Sedge Warbler, Lesser Whitethroat, Grasshopper Warbler, Water Rail. *Autumn*: Passage waders and wildfowl, Kingfisher.
Contact: Brian Pollinger, Thornley Woodlands Centre, Rowlands Gill, Tyne & Wear, NE39 1AU. 1209 545212.
e-mail: thornleywoodlandscentre@unisonFree.net
www.gateshead.gov.uk

WALLSEND SWALLOW POND

Northumberland Wildlife Trust.
Location: NZ 301 693. Halfway between Whitley Bay and Gosforth in the Rising Sun

Country Park. S off A191 by garden centre.
Access: View from public hide on bridleway.
Facilities: Parking, toilets and picnic area at Rising Sun Centre. Two hides, one adapted for wheelchairs. Pond-dipping platforms.
Public transport: None.
Habitat: Shallow pool created by mining subsidence, mixed woodland.
Key birds: Breeding & winter wildfowl including Teal and Whooper Swan. Pasage waders include Redshank, Greenshank.
Contact: Trust HQ, 0191 284 6884.

WASHINGTON

The Wildfowl & Wetlands Trust.
Location: NZ 331 566. In Washington. On N bank of River Wear, W of Sunderland. Signposted from A195, A19, A1231 and A182.
Access: Open 9.30am-5pm (summer), 9.30am-4pm (winter). Free to WWT members. Admission charge for non-members. No dogs except guide dogs. Good access for people with disabilities.
Facilities: Visitor centre, toilets, parent and baby room, range of hides.
Public transport: Buses to Waterview Park (250 yards walk) from Washington, from Sunderland, Newcastle-upon-Tyne, Durham and South Shields. Tel: 0845 6060260 for details.
Habitat: Wetlands and woodland.
Key birds: *Spring/summer*: Nesting colony of Grey Heron, other breeders include Common Tern, Oystercatcher, Lapwing. *Winter*: Bird-feeding station visited by Great Spotted Woodpecker, Bullfinch, Jay and Sparrowhawk. Goldeneye and other ducks.
Contact: Andrew Donnison, (Grounds Manager), Wildfowl & Wetlands Trust, District IF, Washington, NE38 8LE. 0191 4165454. e-mail: wetlands@euphony.net www.wwt.org.uk

WASHINGWELL WOOD WATERGATE PARK

Gateshead Council.
Location: NZ 229 606. Two miles SW of Newcastle.
Access: Open at all times. Access for all on several paths.
Facilities: Nature trails.
Public transport: Regular bus service to Lobley Hill Farm Newcastle/Gateshead. Information from Nexus Travel Line 0191 232 5325.
Habitat: Lake, conifer wood, grassland (young tree planting areas).
Key birds: *Winter*: Wildfowl, Siskin, finches. *Summer*: Wildfowl, Common Sandpiper, Skylark, Linnet.
Contact: Melanie Bowden, Thornley Woodlands Centre, Rowlands Gill, Tyne & Wear, NE39 1AU. 1210 545212. www.gateshead.gov.uk e-mail: thornleywoodlandscentre@unisonFree.net

WHITBURN BIRD OBSERVATORY

National Trust/Durham Bird Club.
Location: NZ 414 633.
Access: Access details from Recorder.
Facilities: None.
Public transport: None.
Habitat: Cliff top location.
Key birds: Esp. seawatching but also passerine migrants inc. rarities.
Contact: Tony Armstrong, 39 Western Hill, Durham City, DH1 4RJ. 0191 386 1519; e-mail ope@globalnet.co.uk.

Warwickshire

ALVECOTE POOLS

Warwickshire Wildlife Trust.
Location: SK 253 034. Located alongside River Anker E of Tamworth. Access via Robey's Lane (off B5000) just past Alvecote Priory car park. Also along towpath via Pooley Hall visitor centre, also number of points along towpath.
Access: Some parts of extensive path system is accessible to disabled. Parking Alvecote Priory car park.
Facilities: Nature trail.
Public transport: None.
Habitat: Marsh, pools (open and reedbeds) and woodland.
Key birds: *Spring/summer*: Breeding Oystercatcher, Common Tern and Little Ringed Plover. Common species include Great Crested

Grebe, Tufted Duck and Snipe. Important for wintering, passage and breeding wetland birds.
Contact: D G Rogerson,
Brandon Marsh Nature Centre, Brandon Lane, Brandon, Coventry, CV3 3GW. 01276 308993.
e-mail: drogerson@warkswt.cix.co.uk
www.wildlifetrust.org.uk

BRANDON MARSH

Warwickshire Wildlife Trust.
Location: SP 386 762. Three miles SE of Coventry, 200 yards SE of A45/A46 junction (Tollbar End). Turn E off A45 into Brandon Lane. Reserve entrance 1.25 miles on right.
Access: Open weekdays (9am-5pm), weekends (10am-4.30pm). Entrance charge currently £2.50 (free to Wildlife Trust members). Wheelchair access to nature trail and Wright hide. No dogs.
Facilities: Visitor centre, toilets, tea-rooms (open at above times), nature trail, six hides.
Public transport: Bus service from Coventry to Tollbar End then 1.25 mile walk. Tel Travel West Midlands 02476 817032 for bus times.
Habitat: Ten pools, together with marsh, reedbeds, willow carr, scrub and small mixed woodland in 260 acres, designated SSSI in 1972.
Key birds: *Spring/summer*: Garden Warbler, Grasshopper Warbler, Whitethroat, Lesser Whitethroat, Hobby, Little Ringed Plover, Whinchat, Wheatear. *Autumn/winter*: Dunlin, Ruff, Snipe, Greenshank, Green and Common Sandpipers, Wigeon, Shoveler, Pochard, Goldeneye, Siskin, Redpoll. *All year*: Cetti's Warbler, Kingfisher, Water Rail, Gadwall, Little Grebe.
Contact: Ken Bond, Hon. Sec. Brandon Marsh Sanctuary Conservation Team,
54 Wiclif Way, Stockingford, Nuneaton, Warwickshire, CV10 8NF. 02476 328785.

HARTSHILL HAYES

Warwickshire County Council.
Location: SP 317 943. Signposted as 'Country Park' from B4114 W of Nuneaton.
Access: Open all year. Closed Christmas Day. No disabled facilities. No dogs.
Facilities: Three waymarked walks.
Public transport: None.
Habitat: Mixed woodland, grassland hillside.
Key birds: Warblers, woodpeckers, tits, Goldcrest.
Contact: Country Park Manager's Office, Kingsbury Water Park, Bodymoor Heath Lane, Sutton Coldfield, West Midlands, B76 0DY. 01827 872660; e-mail parks@warwickshire.gov.uk.

Warwickshire

Key to sites:

1. Alvecote Pools
2. Brandon Marsh
3. Hartshill Hayes Country Park
4. Kingsbury Water Park
5. Ufton Fields
6. Whitacre Heath

KINGSBURY WATER PARK

Warwickshire County Council.
Location: SP 203 960. Signposted 'Water Park' from J9 M42, A4097 NE of Birmingham.
Access: Closed on Christmas Day.
Facilities: Four hides, interpretative centre, waymarked walks.
Public transport: Call for advice.
Habitat: Open water; numerous small pools, some with gravel islands; gravel pits; silt beds with reedmace, reed, willow and alder; rough areas and grassland.
Key birds: *Summer*: Breeding warblers (nine species), Little Ringed Plover, Great Crested and Little Grebes. Shoveler, Shelduck and a thriving Common Tern colony. Passage waders (esp. spring). *Winter*: Wildfowl, Short-eared Owl.
Contact: Country Park Manager's Office, Kingsbury Water Park, Bodymoor Heath Lane, Sutton Coldfield, West Midlands, B76 0DY. 01827 872660; e-mail parks@warwickshire.gov.uk.

UFTON FIELDS

Warwickshire Wildlife Trust.
Location: SP 378 615. Located SE of Leamington Spa off A425. At South Ufton village, take B4452.
Access: Open at all times. Access via Ufton Fields Lane, South Ufton village.
Facilities: Two hides, nature trail.
Public transport: None.
Habitat: Grassland, woodland, pools with limestone quarry.
Key birds: Usual species for pools/woodland/ grassland including Willow Tit, Goldcrest, Green Woodpecker, Little Grebe and up to nine warbler species.
Contact: D G Rogerson,
Brandon Marsh Nature Centre, Brandon Lane, Brandon, Coventry, CV3 3GW. 01276 308993.
e-mail: drogerson@warkswt.cix.co.uk
www.wildlifetrust.org.uk

WHITACRE HEATH

Warwickshire Wildlife Trust.
Location: SP 209 931. Three miles N of Coleshill, just W of Whitacre Heath village.
Access: Trust members only.
Facilities: Three hides.
Public transport: None.
Habitat: Pools, wet woodland and grassland.
Key birds: *Summer*: Sedge Warbler, Reed Warbler, Lesser Whitethroat, Whitethroat, Garden Warbler, Willow Warbler and Blackcap. Migrant Curlew, Whinchat. Also Snipe, Water Rail and Kingfisher.
Contact: D G Rogerson,
Brandon Marsh Nature Centre, Brandon Lane, Brandon, Coventry, CV3 3GW. 01276 308993.
e-mail: drogerson@warkswt.cix.co.uk
www.wildlifetrust.org.uk

West Midlands

MARSH LANE

Packington Estate Enterprises Limited.
Location: SP 217 804. The Nature Reserve is equidistant between Birmingham and Coventry, both approx 7-8 miles away. Off A452 between A45 and Balsall Common. Turn right into Marsh Lane and immediately right onto Old Kenilworth Road (now a public footpath), to locked gate. Key required for access.
Access: Only guide dogs allowed. Site suitable for disabled. Access is by day or year permit only. Membership rates: annual – adult £20, OAP £15, children (under 16) £10 (special opening offer of two years for the price of one starting Jul 1 2001). Contact address below (9am-5.15pm). Regular newsletter provided to annual permit holders; day adult £3, OAP £2.50, children (under 16) £2 obtained from Golf Professional Shop, Stonebridge Golf Centre, Somers Road, off Hampton Lane, Meriden, nr Coventry CV7 7PL

(tel 01676 522442) only three to four minutes car journey from site. Open Mon-Sun (7am-7pm). Stonebridge Golf Centre open to non-members. Visitors can obtain drinks and meals on site. £10 depost required for key. No toilets or visitor centre. Four hides and hard tracks between hides. Car park behind locked gates.
Public transport: Hampton-in-Arden railway station within walking distance on footpath loop. Bus no 194 stops at N end of Old Kenilworth Road one mile from reserve gate.
Habitat: Two large pools with islands, three small areas of woodland, five acre field set aside for arable growth for finches and buntings as winter feed.
Key birds: 152 species. *Summer:* Breeding birds include Little Ringed Plover, Common Tern, most species of warbler including Grasshopper. Good passage of waders in Apr, May, Aug and Sept. Hobby and Buzzard breed locally.
Contact: Nicholas P Barlow,
Packington Hall, Packington Park, Meriden, Nr Coventry, CV7 7HF. 01676 522020.
www.packingtonestate.net

SANDWELL VALLEY

Metropolitan Borough Council.
Location: 1. SP 012 918 & SP 028 992. 2. SP 036 931. Park located alongside Spagetti Junction (M5 and M6).
Access: 1. Access and car park from Dagger Lane or Forge Lane, West Bromwich. 2. access and car park off Tanhouse Avenue, Great Barr.
Facilities: 1. Mainly public open space. 2. RSPB reserve with nature centre. Nature trails, hides.
Public transport: Call for advice.
Habitat: 1. Nature reserve, lakes, woods and farmland. 2. Lake, freshwater marsh, woodland.
Key birds: *Summer*: Breeding Lapwing, Little Ringed Plover, Sparrowhawk. All three woodpeckers, Tawny Owl, Reed Warbler. Passage waders.
Contact: Senior Ranger,
Sandwell Valley Country Park, Salters Lane, West Bromwich, W Midlands, B71 4BG. 0121 553 0220 or 2147.

SMESTOW VALLEY

Wolverhampton Council.
Location: SJ 895 005. Main entrance of the Local Nature Reserve is at Henwood Road, Tettenhall near junction of A41 and A454, W of Wolverhampton.
Access: Open at all times.
Facilities: None.
Public transport: None.
Habitat: Woodland, meadowland, canal.
Key birds: *Summer*: Breeding Nuthatch, Great Spotted and Green Woodpeckers, Treecreeper, Reed Bunting, Skylark, warblers (seven species). *Winter*: Little Grebe, Siskin, Redwing, Fieldfare, Snipe, Water Rail.
Contact: Chris Jones, (Leisure Services), 01902 555133.

Wiltshire

SWILLBROOK LAKES

Wiltshire Wildlife Trust.
Location: SU 018 934. NW of Swindon, one mile S of Somerford Keynes on Cotswold Water Park spine road; turn off down Minety Lane (parking).
Access: Open at all times.
Facilities: Footpath along N and E sides of lakes.
Public transport: None.
Habitat: Gravel pits with shallow pools, rough grassland and scrub around edges.
Key birds: *Winter*:Wildfowl (inc. Gadwall, Pochard, Smew, Goosander). *Summer*: Breeding Reed and Sedge Warblers; best site for Hobby in Cotswold WP.
Contact: Trust HQ, 01380 725670.

Worcestershire

KNAPP AND PAPERMILL

Worcestershire Wildlife Trust.
Location: SO 749 522. Take A4103 SW from Worcester; R at Bransford roundabout then L towards Suckley and reserve is approx three miles (do not turn off for Alfrick). Park at Bridges Stone layby (SO 751 522), cross road and follow path to the Knapp House.
Access: Open daily exc Christmas Day. Large parties should contact Warden.
Facilities: Hide, nature trail, small visitor centre, wildlife garden.
Public transport: None.
Habitat: Broadleaved woodland, unimproved grassland, fast stream, old orchard in Leigh Brook Valley.
Key birds: *Summer*: Breeding Grey Wagtail, Kingfisher, Pied Flycatcher, all three woodpeckers. Buzzard, Sparrowhawk and Redstart also occur. Also otter.
Contact: Warden, Regional Reserves Manager, The Knapp, Alfrick, Worcester, WR6 5HR. 01886 832065.

TRENCH WOOD

Worcestershire Wildlife Trust.
Location: SO 931 585. NE of Worcester.
Access: Open daily exc Christmas Day.
Facilities: Car park.
Public transport: None.
Habitat: (NB mature trees to SW and SE of wood are not part of reserve). Young broadleaved woodland, mixed scrub.
Key birds: Very good for warblers; Woodcock.
Contact: Trust HQ, 01905 754919.

UPTON WARREN

Worcestershire Wildlife Trust.
Location: SO 936 675. Two miles S of Bromsgrove on A38.
Access: Always open except Christmas Day. Trust membership gives access, or day permit from sailing centre. Disabled access to west hide at moors only. Dogs on leads.
Facilities: Seven hides, maps at entrances, can be very muddy.
Public transport: Birmingham/Worcester bus passes reserve entrance.
Habitat: Fresh and saline pools with muddy islands, some woodland and scrub.
Key birds: *Winter*: Wildfowl. *Spring/autumn*: Passage waders, Common Tern, Cetti's Warbler, Oystercatcher and Little Ringed Plover, many breeding warblers.
Contact: A F Jacobs, 3 The Beeches, Upton Warren, Bromsgrove, Worcs, B61 7EL. 01527 861370.

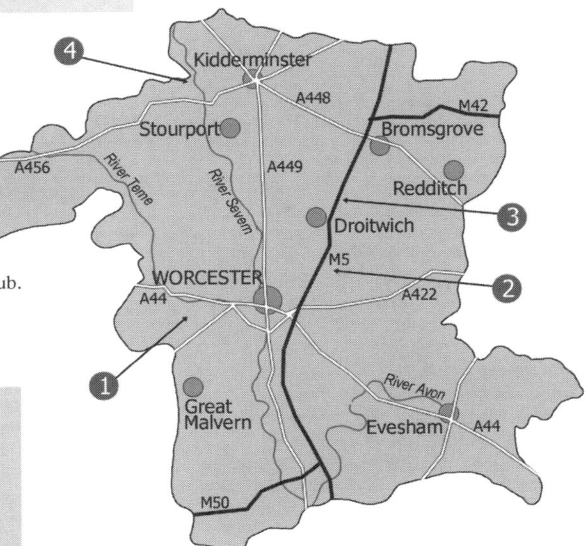

Key to sites:
1. Knapp And Papermill
2. Trench Wood
3. Upton Warren
4. Wyre Forest

WYRE FOREST

English Nature/Worcs Wildlife Trust.
Location: SO 750 760. A456 out of Bewdley.
Access: Observe reserve signs and keep to paths. Forestry Commission visitor centre at Callow Hill. Fred Dale Reserve is reached by footpath W of B4194 (parking at SO776763).
Facilities: Facilities for disabled (entry by car) if Warden telephoned in advance.
Public transport: None.
Habitat: Oak forest, conifer areas, birch heath, stream.
Key birds: Buzzard, Pied Flycatcher, Wood Warbler, Redstart, all three woodpeckers, Woodcock, Crossbill, Siskin, Hawfinch, Kingfisher, Dipper, Grey Wagtail, Tree Pipit.
Contact: Michael Taylor,
Lodge Hill Farm, Bewdley, Worcs, DY12 2LY. 01299 400686.

Yorkshire, East

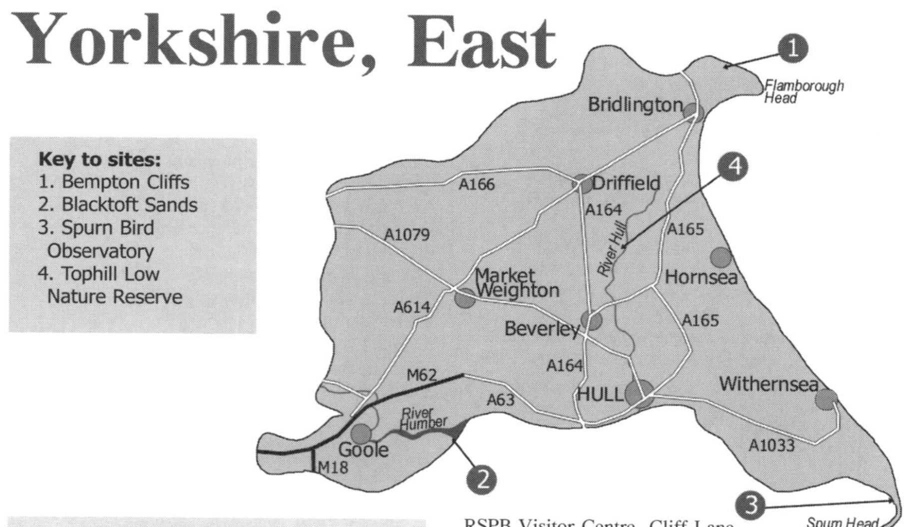

BEMPTON CLIFFS

RSPB (North of England Office).
Location: TA 197 738. Near Bridlington. Take cliff road N from Bempton Village off B1229 to car park and visitor centre.
Access: Visitor centre open Mar-Nov. Public footpath along cliff top with observation points. Four miles of chalk cliffs, highest in the country.
Facilities: Visitor centre, toilets. Viewing platforms.
Public transport: None.
Habitat: Seabird nesting cliffs, farmland, scrub.
Key birds: Best to visit May to mid-July for Puffin, Gannet (only colony on English mainland), Fulmar, Kittiwake; also nesting Tree Sparrow, Corn Bunting. Good migration watchpoint for skuas, shearwaters and terns.
Contact: Site Manager,
RSPB Visitor Centre, Cliff Lane, Bempton, Bridlington, E Yorks, YO15 1JF. 01262 851179.

BLACKTOFT SANDS

RSBP (North of England Office).
Location: SE 843 232. Eight miles E of Goole on minor road between Ousefleet and Adlingfleet.
Access: Open 9am-9pm or dusk if earlier. RSBP members free, £3 permit for non-members, £2 concessionary, £1 children, £6 family.
Facilities: Car park, toilets, visitor centre, six hides, footpaths suitable for wheelchairs.
Public transport: Goole/Scunthorpe bus (Sweynes' Coaches stops at reserve entrance).
Habitat: Reedbed, saline lagoons, lowland wet grassland, willow scrub.
Key birds: *Summer*: Breeding Avocet, Marsh Harrier, Bearded Tit, passage waders (exceptional

list inc many rarities). *Winter*: Hen Harrier, Merlin, Peregrine, wildfowl.
Contact: Pete Short (Warden) & Simon Wellock (Asst Warden), Hillcrest, Whitgift, Nr Goole, E Yorks, DN14 8HL. 01405 704665. www.rspb.org e-mail: simonwellock@RSBP.org

SPURN BIRD OBSERVATORY

Yorkshire Wildlife Trust.
Location: Entrance Gate TA 417 151. 26 miles from Hull. Take A1033 from Hull to Patrington (via Hedon) then B1445 from Patrington to Easington and unclassed roads on to Kilnsea and Spurn Head.
Access: Normally open at all times. Vehicle admission fee (at present £2.50 from Apr 1-Oct 31 and £1.50 from Nov 1-Mar 31). No charge for pedestrians. No dogs allowed under any circumstances, not even in cars. Coaches by permit only (must be in advance).
Facilities: Chemical portaloos next to information centre. Information centre open weekends, Bank Holidays, school holidays, but not Fri (10am-5pm). Two hides.
Public transport: Nearest bus service is at Easington (3.5 miles away).
Habitat: Sand dunes with marram and sea buckthorn scrub. Mudflats around Humber Estuary.
Key birds: *Spring*: Many migrants on passage and often rare birds such as Red-backed Shrike, Bluethroat etc. *Autumn*: Passage migrants and rarities like Wryneck, Pallas's Warbler. *Winter*: Waders and Brent Goose.
Contact: B R Spence, Spurn NNR, Kilnsea, Hull, HU12 0UG.

TOPHILL LOW

Yorkshire Water.
Location: TA 071 482. Nine miles SE of Driffield and ten miles NE of Beverley. Signposted from village of Watton on A164.
Access: Open Wed-Sun and Bank Holiday Mon. Apr-Oct (9am-6pm). Nov-Mar (9am-4pm). Charges: £2.50 per person. £1 concessions. No dogs allowed. Provision for disabled visitors (paths, ramps, hides, toilet etc).
Facilities: Visitor centre with toilets, CCTV camera, displays etc. 13 hides (five with access for wheelchairs). Nature trails.
Public transport: None.
Habitat: Open water (two reservoirs), marshes, wader scrapes, woodland and thorn scrub.
Key birds: *Winter*: Wildfowl, gulls, Water Rail, Kingfisher. *Spring/early summer*: Passage Black-necked Grebe and Black Tern. Breeding Pochard, Kingfisher and Grasshopper Warbler.
Contact: Peter Izzard,
Tophill Low Nature Reserve, Watton Carrs, Driffield, East Yorkshire, YO25 9RH. 01377 270690

Yorkshire, North

BOLTON ON SWALE LAKE

Yorkshire Wildlife Trust.
Location: SE 248 985. From B6721 Northallerton/Catterick road turn left to Ellerton at Ellerton Cross.
Access: Open all year. Closed Christmas Day. No disabled facilities. No dogs.
Facilities: None.
Public transport: None.
Habitat: Former gravel workings.
Key birds: *Summer*: Breeding Shelduck, Oystercatcher, Ringed Plover. *Winter*: Wildfowl inc. 1300 Wigeon, 400 Greylag, Bewick's and Whooper Swans.
Contact: Trust HQ, 01904 659570.

COATHAM MARSH

Tees Valley Wildlife Trust.
Location: NZ 585 250. Located on W edge of Redcar. Access from minor road to Warrenby from A1085/A1042.
Access: Reserve is open throughout daylight hours. Please keep to permissive footpaths only.
Facilities: Two hides. Key required for one of these - available to Tees Valley Wildlife Trust members for £10 deposit. No toilets or visitor centre.
Public transport: Very frequent bus service between Middlesbrough and Redcar. Nearest stops are in Coatham 0.25 mile from reserve (Arriva tel 0870 6082608). Redcar Central

Yorkshire, North

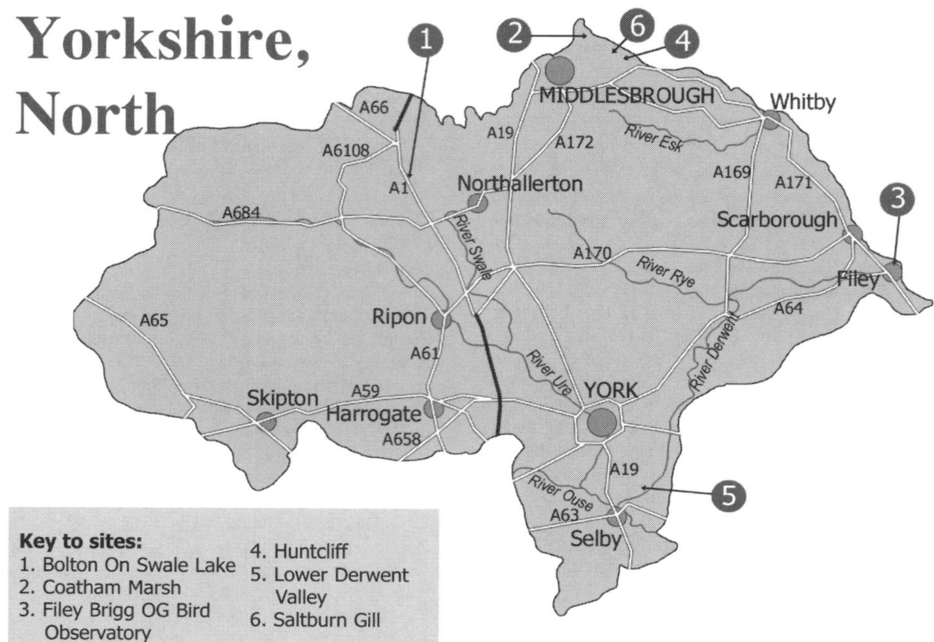

Station one mile from site. Frequent trains from Middlesbrough and Darlington.
Habitat: Freshwater wetlands, lakes, reedbeds.
Key birds: *Spring/autumn*: Wader passage (including Wood Sandpiper and Greenshank). *Summer:* Passerines (including Sedge Warbler, Yellow Wagtail). *Winter:* Ducks (including Smew). Occasional rarities, Water Rail.
Contact: Mark Fishpool,
Tees Valley Wildlife Trust, Bellamy Pavilion, Kirkleatham, Redcar, TS50 5NW. 01642 759900.
e-mail: teesvalleywt@cix.co.uk
www.wildlifetrust.org.uk/teesvalley

FILEY BRIGG BIRD OBSERVATORY

FBOG and Yorkshire Wildlife Trust (The Dams).
Location: TA 10 68 07. Two access roads into Filey from A165 (Scarborough to Bridlington road). Filey is ten miles N of Bridlington and eight miles S of Scarborough.
Access: Opening times – no restrictions. Dogs only in Parish Wood and The Old Tip (on lead).
Facilities: No provisions for disabled at present. Two hides at The Dams, one on The Brigg (open most weekends from late Jul-Oct, key can be hired from Country Park café). Toilets in Country Park (Apr-Nov 1) and town centre.
Nature trails at The Dams, Parish Wood/Old Tip. Cliff top walk for seabirds along Cleveland Way.
Public transport: All areas within a mile of Filey railway station. Trains into Filey tel. 08457 484950; buses into Filey tel. 01723 503020.
Habitat: The Dams – two freshwater lakes, fringed with some tree cover and small reedbeds. Parish Wood – a newly built wood which leads to the Old Tip, the latter has been fenced (for stock and crop strips) though there is a public trail. Carrnaze has a pond, crops and rough areas.
Key birds: The Dams: Breeding and wintering water birds, breeding Sedge Warbler, Reed Warbler and Tree Sparrow. The Tip: important for breeding Sky Lark, Meadow Pipit, common warblers. *Winter:* Area for buntings including Lapland. Seawatch Hide: *Jul-Oct*. All four skuas, shearwaters, terns. *Winter*: Divers and grebes. Totem Pole Field: A new project should encourage breeding species and wintering larks, buntings etc. Many sub-rare/rare migrants possible at all sites.
Contact: Lez Gillard, Recorder, 12 Sycamore Avenue, Filey, N Yorks, YO14 9NU. 01723 516383. e-mail: lez.gillard@talk21.com
www.fbog.co.uk

HUNTCLIFF

Tees Valley Wildlife Trust.
Location: NZ 674 215. Along Cleveland Way footpath from Saltburn or Skinningrove.
Access: Open all year.
Facilities: None.
Public transport: None.
Habitat: Strip of coastal grassland and cliff face.
Key birds: Large colony of Kittiwakes and some Cormorants.
Contact: Trust HQ, 01642 759900.

LOWER DERWENT VALLEY

English Nature (North & East Yorks).
Location: SC 691 444. Six miles SE of York, stretching 12 miles S along the River Derwent from Newton-on-Derwent to Wressle and along the Pocklington Canal. Visitor facilities at Bank Island, Wheldrake (SC 691 444), Thorganby (SE 693 422) and North Duffield Carrs (SE 698 366).
Access: Open all year, 24 hours. No dogs. Disabled access at North Duffield Carrs (two hides and car park). 600 yard path.
Facilities: North Duffield Carrs - two hides, wheelchair access. Wheldrake Ings (YWT) - five hides. Bank Island - two hides. Thorganby - viewing platform.
Public transport: Bus from York/Selby - contact Rider York (01904 435600). Bicycle stands planned for car parks (2001).
Habitat: Hay meadow and pasture, swamp, open water and alder carr woodland.
Key birds: *Spring/summer:* Breeding wildfowl and waders including Garganey and Ruff. Barn Owl and warblers. *Winter:* 20,000-plus waterfowl including Whooper Swan, Bewick's Swan and wild geese. Large gull roost including white-winged gulls. Also passage waders including Whimbrel.
Contact: Site Manager,
English Nature, Genesis 1, Heslington Road, York, YO10 5ZQ. 01904 435500.
e-mail: york@english-nature.org.uk

SALTBURN GILL

Tees Valley Wildlife Trust.
Location: NZ 674 2OS. From Middlesbrough take A174 to Saltburn-by-the-Sea. Access from the Cat Nab Car Park on the seafront.
Access: Public footpaths through the site, therefore open at all times. Paths can be muddy after rain. Some steep gradients.
Facilities: No visitor centre or hides. Parking at Cat Nab Car Park, Saltburn (charges). Toilets in car park.
Public transport: Bus - frequent buses to Saltburn town centre from Middlesbrough. 0.75 mile walk to site. The hourly 62 bus from Middlesbrough to Loftus stops at the seafront (Arriva tel 0870 6082608). Train - frequent services to Saltburn from Middlesbrough and Darlington. Reserve is 0.75 mile walk from station.
Habitat: Semi-natural deciduous woodland. Some grassland and scrub, stream.
Key birds: Typical woodland species, Dipper, Marsh Tit, Woodcock, Grey Wagtail.
Contact: Bill Ashton-Wickett, Bellamy Pavilion, Kirkleatham Old Hall, Kirkleatham, Redcar, TS10 5NW. 01642 759900.
e-mail: teesvalleywt@cix.co.uk
www.wildlifetrust.org.uk/teesvalley

Yorkshire, South & West

ANGLERS COUNTRY PARK

Wakefield Metropolitan Borough Council.
Location: SE380160. SE of Wakefield. Leave A638 at signpost for Crofton. Turn left in village on road to Ryhill, turning just past Anglers pub in Wintersett hamlet.
Access: Open at all times.
Facilities: Two hides.
Habitat: Three lakes.
Key birds: *Winter*: Wildfowl (inc. Wigeon, Goosander), plus large gull roost with regular Iceland, Glaucous, Mediterranean. Passage waders and passerines. *Spring/summer*: Breeding Little Ringed Plover, Redshank, Lapwing, and warblers (inc. Grasshopper Warbler and Lesser Whitethroat).
Contact: 01924 302360.

CARLTON MARSH

Barnsley MBC Countryside Unit.
Location: SE 379 103. Small car park off Weet

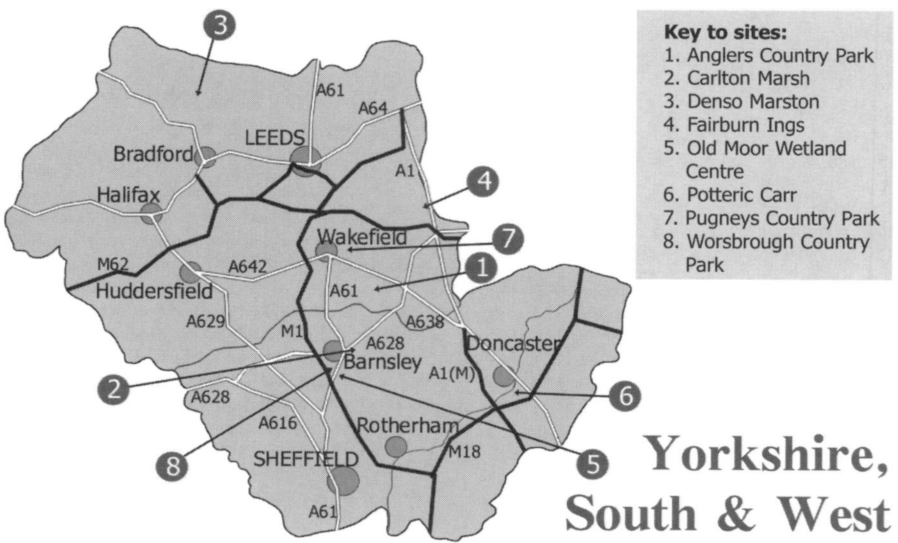

Yorkshire, South & West

Shaw Lane, Cudworth, Barnsley.
Access: Access only along public rights of way and disused railway.
Facilities: Two hides.
Public transport: None.
Habitat: Marsh with reed and sedge, some open water.
Key birds: *Summer*: Breeding Water Rail, Little Ringed Plover, Sedge, Reed and Grasshopper Warblers. *Autumn*: Swallow roost; Barn Owl, Jack Snipe.
Contact: Nigel Labdon, Melanie Perkins, Leisure Services, Berneslai Close, Barnsley, S Yorks, S70 2HS. 01226 774478; fax 01226 773599. e-mail nigellabdon@barnsley.gov.uk

DENSO MARSTON

Denso Marston.
Location: SE 167 389. Two miles N of Shipley on Otley Road (A6038), entrance through kissing gate past end of factory.
Access: Open at all times.
Facilities: None.
Public transport: Bus from Bradford and Leeds 655, 652, 755.
Habitat: Two pools, woodland areas, meadow areas, site next to River Aire.
Key birds: *Summer*: Garden Warbler, Blackcap, Whitethroat. Good selection of insects such as common blue and brimstone butterflies and common hawker, migrant hawker, four-spotted chaser dragonflies. *Winter*: Lesser Redpoll, Siskin, Water Rail.
Contact: Stephen Warrillow, Denso Marston, Otley Road, Baildon, Shipley, West Yorkshire, BD17 7UR. 01274 582266.

FAIRBURN INGS

RSPB (North West England Office).
Location: SE 452 277. 12.5 miles from Leeds, six miles from Pontefract, 3.5 miles from Castleford next to A1 at Fairburn turn-off.
Access: Reserve and hides open every day (9am-dusk). Centre with shop open weekdays (11am-4pm) and weekends (10am-5pm) and Bank Holidays. Hot and cold drinks available. Dogs on leads at all times. Boardwalk leading to Pickup Pool and feeding station and paths to centre wheelchair-friendly.
Facilities: Reserve hides include three open at all times with one locked at dusk. Toilets open when centre open or 9am-5pm. Disabled access to toilets. All nature trails follow public paths and are open at all times.
Public transport: Nearest train stations are Castleford or Pontefract. Buses approx every hour from Pontefract and Tadcaster. Infrequent from Castleford and Selby.

Habitat: Open water due to mining subsidence, wet grassland, marsh and willow scrub, reclaimed colliery spoil heaps.
Key birds: *Winter*: A herd of Whooper Swan usually roost. Normally up to five Smew including male, Wigeon, Gadwall, Goosander, Goldeney. *Spring*: Osprey, Wheatear, Little Gull and five species of tern pass through. *Summer*: Breeding birds include Reed and Sedge Warblers, Shoveler, Gadwall, Cormorant.
Contact: Chris Drake, Information Warden, Fairburn Ings Visitor Centre, Newton Lane, Fairburn, Castleford, WF10 2BH. 01977 603796.

OLD MOOR WETLAND CENTRE

Barnsley MBC Countryside Unit.
Location: SE 422 011. From M1 J36, then A6195. From A1 J37, then A635 and A6195 – follow brown signs.
Access: Open Apr 1-Oct 31 (Wed-Sun 9am-5pm), Nov 1-Mar 31 (Wed/Thu-Sat/Sun 10am-4pm). Entry fee with annual membership available.
Facilities: Toilets (including disabled), large visitor centre and shop, five superb hides. All sites including hides fully accessible for disabled.
Public transport: Buses – information from South Yorkshire Passenger Transport, 01709 589200.
Habitat: Lakes and flood meadows, wader scrape and reedbeds.
Key birds: *Winter*: Large numbers of wildfowl. *Summer*: Breeding waders and wildfowl. Rare vagrants recorded annually.
Contact: Debra Bushby,
Old Moor Wetland Centre, Off Manvers Way, Broomhill, Wombwell, Barnsley, South Yorkshire, S73 0YF. 01226 751593 Fax: 01226 751617.
e-mail: oldmoor@barnsley.gov.uk
www.barnsley.gov.uk

POTTERIC CARR

Yorkshire Wildlife Trust.
Location: SE 589 007. From M18 junction 3 take A6182 (Doncaster) and at first roundabout take third exit; entrance and car park are on R after 50m.
Access: Access by permit only (01302 530778, answerphone). Parties must obtain prior permission.
Facilities: Field Centre (light refreshments, toilet) open (10am-3pm Sun) all year. Eight hides (three for disabled).
Public transport: None.
Habitat: Reed fen, subsidence ponds, artificial pools, grassland, woodland.
Key birds: Nesting waterfowl (inc. Shoveler, Gadwall, Pochard), Water Rail, Little Ringed Plover, Snipe, Kingfisher, all three woodpeckers, Lesser Whitethroat, Reed and Sedge Warblers also breed. *Passage/winter*: Wildfowl, Bittern, Marsh Harrier, Black Tern, waders.
Contact: Trust HQ, 01904 659570.

PUGNEYS COUNTRY PARK

Wakefield Metropolitan District Council.
Location: SE 330 180. Leave M1 at J29 towards Wakefield; reserve signposted from first roundabout.
Access: Open daily 9am to one hour before sunset.
Facilities: Two hides.
Public transport: None.
Habitat: Three lakes, one of which is in reserve area.
Key birds: *Winter*: Large gull roost, Bittern, good range of wildfowl (inc. Smew), Short-eared Owl. *Summer*: Breeding Common Tern, Sedge and Reed Warblers. Passage waders.
Contact: 01924 302360.

WORSBROUGH

Barnsley MBC Countryside Unit.
Location: SE 345 034. South of Barnsley, N of Junction 36 of M1. CP car park is off A61.
Access: Open access at all times.
Facilities: Hide, toilets.
Public transport: None.
Habitat: Open water, willow carr, phragmites and typha reedbed, deciduous wood and meadow land.
Key birds: *Summer*: Breeding Ruddy Duck, Sparrowhawk, Sedge and Reed Warblers, Kingfisher, Common Tern. *Autumn*: Swallow roost. *Winter*: Gulls.
Contact:
Cultural Services, Worsborough Mill, Barnsley, S Yorks, S70 5LJ. 01226 774527.

SCOTLAND

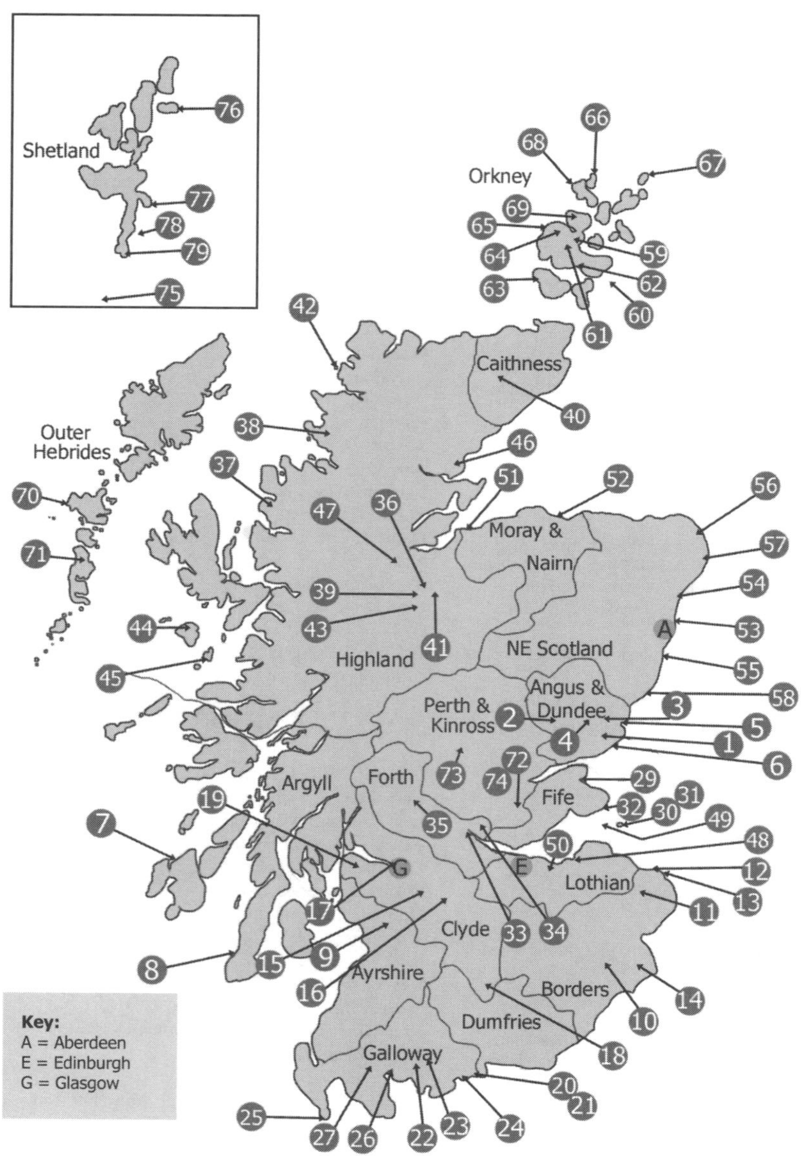

NB: Reserves in Scotland have been listed alphabetically by region (following the arrangement of the Scottish recording areas as set out by the Scottish Ornithologist's Club).

Key to sites:

1. Balgavies Loch
2. Killiecrankie
3. Loch of Kinnordy
4. Loch of Lintrathen
5. Montrose Basin
6. Seaton Cliffs
7. Loch Gruinart, Islay
8. Machrihanish Seabird Observatory
9. Ayr Gorge Woodlands
10. Bemersyde Moss
11. Duns Castle
12. Pease Dean
13. St Abb's Head
14. Yetholm Loch
15. Barons Haugh
16. Falls of Clyde
17. Hogganfield Park
18. Knockshinnock Lagoons
19. Lochwinnoch
20. Caerlaverock
21. Caerlaverock WWT
22. Carstramon Wood
23. Ken/Dee Marshes
24. Mersehead
25. Mull of Galloway
26. Wigtown Bay
27. Wood of Cree
28. Cameron Reservoir
29. Eden Estuary
30. Isle of May NNR
31. Isle of May Bird Observatory
32. Kilminning Coast
33. Cambus Pools
34. Gartmorn Dam
35. Inversnaid
36. Abernethy Forest Reserve – Loch Garten
37. Beinn Eighe
38. Ben More Coigach
39. Cairngorm NNR
40. Forsinard
41. Glenmore Forest Park
42. Handa
43. Insh Marshes
44. Isle of Eigg
45. Isle of Rum
46. Loch Fleet
47. Loch Ruthven
48. Aberlady Bay
49. Bass Rock
50. Bawsinch & Duddingston Loch
51. Culbin Sands
52. Lein, Spey Bay
53. Cullaloe
54. Forvie
55. Fowlsheugh
56. Loch of Strathbeg
57. Longhaven Cliffs
58. St Cyrus
59. Birsay Moors
60. Copinsay
61. Cottescarth & Rendall Moss
62. Hobbister
63. Hoy
64. Loons (The)
65. Marwick Head
66. North Hill, Papa Westray
67. North Ronaldsay Bird Observatory
68. Noup Cliffs, Westray
69. Trumland, Rousay
70. Balranald
71. Loch Druidibeg
72. Loch Leven
73. Loch of The Lowes
74. Vane Farm
75. Fair Isle Bird Observatory
76. Fetlar
77. Isle of Noss
78. Mousa
79. Sumburgh Head

Angus & Dundee

BALGAVIES LOCH

Scottish Wildlife Trust.
Location: Scottish WT NO523 516. From car park on A932, four miles E of Forfar.
Access: All areas apart from hide restricted. Groups apply in advance.
Facilities: Hide open at weekends.
Public transport: None.
Habitat: Loch, fen and woodland.
Key birds: *Winter*: Wildfowl and wetland breeding birds.
Contact: Montrose Basin Wildlife Centre, 01674 676336.

KILLIECRANKIE

RSPB (East Scotland Office).
Location: NN 907 627. W of A9 Pitlochry-Blair Atholl road, B8079 to Killiecrankie, then minor road SW to reserve.
Access: Open dawn to dusk, no dogs. £1 non-member - donations cairn. Not suitable for disabled.
Facilities: None.
Public transport: Train occasionally stops at Blair Atholl and Pitlochry.
Habitat: Upland birch wood, crags, moorland and larch.
Key birds: Buzzard, Crossbill, Wood Warbler, Redstart, Tree Pipit; Black Grouse and Whinchat on moorland fringe; occasional Golden Eagle, Peregrine, Raven.
Contact: Alan Leitch,
1 Atholl Crescent, Perth, PH1 5NG. 01738 630783.
e-mail: alan.leitch@rspb.org.uk
www.rspb.org.uk

LOCH OF KINNORDY

RSPB (East Scotland Office).
Location: NO 351 539. Car park on B951 one mile W of Kirriemuir. Perth 45 minutes drive, Dundee (30 minutes drive), Aberdeen (one hour).
Access: Open dawn-dusk. Disabled access to two hides via short trails.
Facilities: Three birdwatching hides.
Public transport: Nearest centre is Kirriemuir.
Habitat: Freshwater loch, fen, carr, marsh.
Key birds: *Spring/summer*: Osprey, Black-necked Grebe, Black-headed Gull. *Winter*: Wildfowl including Goosander, Goldeneye and Whooper Swan.
Contact: Alan Leitch, RSPB, 1 Atholl Crescent, Perth, PH1 5NG. 01738 639783.
e-mail: alan@leitch@rspb.org www.rspb.org

LOCH OF LINTRATHEN

Scottish Wildlife Trust.
Location: NO 27 54. Seven miles W of Kirriemuir. Take B951 and choose circular route on unclassified roads round loch.
Access: Public hide planned but to date, Scottish Wildlife Trust hide (members permit system). Good viewing points from several places along unclassified roads.
Facilities: None.
Public transport: None.
Habitat: Oligatrophic/mesotrophic loch. Surrounded by mainly coniferous woodland.
Key birds: *Summer*: Osprey. *Winter*: Greylag Goose, Goosander, Whooper Swan, Wigeon, Teal.
Contact: Rick Goater,
SWT, Annat House, South Anag, Ferryden, Montrose, Angus, DD10 9UT. 01674 676555.
e-mail: swtnero@cix.co.uk

MONTROSE BASIN

Scottish Wildlife Trust on behalf of Angus Council.
Location: NO 690 580 Centre of Basin. NO 702 565 Wildlife SWT Centre on A92. 1.5 miles from centre of Montrose.
Access: Apr 1-Oct 31 (10.30am-5pm). Nov 1-Mar 31 (10.30am-4pm). Centre open July.
Facilities: Visitor centre, shop, vending machine, toilets, disabled access to centre, two hides on western half of reserve.
Public transport: Train 1.5 miles in Montrose. Buses same as above.
Habitat: Estuary, saltmarsh, reedbeds, farmland.
Key birds: Pink-footed Goose – up to 35,000 arrive Oct. Wintering wildfowl and waders. Breeding Eider Ducks.
Contact: Karen Spalding, Scottish Wildlife Trust, Montrose Basin Wildlife Centre, Rossie Braes, Montrose, DD10 9TJ. 01674 676336.
e-mail: karen@montrosebasin.cix.co.uk
www.montrosebasin.org.uk

SEATON CLIFFS

Scottish Wildlife Trust.
Location: NO 667 416. 30 acre cliff reserve, less than a mile from Arbroath town centre. Car parking at N end of promenade at Arbroath.
Access: Open all year.
Facilities: Nature trail with interpretation boards.
Public transport: None.
Habitat: Red sandstone cliffs with nature trail.
Key birds: Seabirds inc. Eider, auks, terns; Rock Dove and House Martin breed.
Contact: Trust HQ, 0131 312 7765.

Argyll

LOCH GRUINART, ISLAY

RSPB (South and West Scotland Office).
Location: Sea loch on N coast, seven miles NW from Bridgend.
Access: Hide open all hours, no dogs, visitor centre open (10am-5pm), disabled access to hide, toilets.
Facilities: Toilets, visitor centre, hide, trail.
Public transport: None.
Habitat: Low wet grasslands, moorland.
Key birds: *Sept-Apr*: Barnacle and Greenland White-fronted Goose. *May-Aug*: Corncrake. *Sept-Nov*: Migrating wading birds.
Contact: Yvonne Armitage,
RSPB, Bushmills Cottage, Gruinart, Isle of Islay, PH44 7PR. 01496 850505.
e-mail yvonne.armitage@rspb.org.uk
www.rspb.org.uk

MACHRIHANISH SEABIRD OBSERVATORY

Eddie Maguire and John McGlynn.
Location: NR 628 209. Six miles W of Campbeltown on A83 then B843.
Access: Daily May-Oct. Wheelchair access. Dogs welcome. Parking for three cars.
Facilities: Seawatching hide, toilets in nearby village.
Public transport: Regular buses from Campbeltown (West Coast Motors, tel 01586 552319).
Habitat: Marine, rocky shore and upland habitats.
Key birds: *Summer:* Golden Eagle, Peregrine and Twite. *Autumn:* Passage seabirds and waders. Gales often produce inshore movements of Leach's Petrel and other scarce seabirds including Balearic Shearwater and Grey Phalarope. *Winter:* Great Northern Diver.

Contact: Eddie Maguire, 25B Albyn Avenue, Campbeltown, Argyll, PA28 6LX. 07979 395269. www.mso.1c24.net

Ayrshire

AYR GORGE WOODLANDS

Scottish Wildlife Trust.
Location: NS457249. Wooded ravine in River Ayr valley. At Failford, off A758 Mauchline to Ayr road. Park in lay-by in Failford village.
Access: Access by well-maintained path along west bank of River Ayr.
Facilities: None.
Public transport: None.
Habitat: Woodland.
Key birds: Woodland and riverside birds.
Contact: Trust HQ, 0131 312 7765.

Borders

BEMERSYDE MOSS

Scottish Wildlife Trust.
Location: NT 614 340. Four miles E of Melrose on minor road. Between Melrose and Smailholm.
Access: Permit required.
Facilities: Hide with parking nearby.
Public transport: None.
Habitat: Shallow Loch and marsh.
Key birds: *Summer*: Large Black-headed Gull colony, Black-necked Grebe, Grasshopper Warbler. *Winter:* Wildfowl, waders on migration, raptors.
Contact: Trust HQ, 0131 312 7765

DUNS CASTLE

Scottish Wildlife Trust.
Location: NT 778 550. Located N of the centre of Duns (W of Berwick upon Tweed).
Access: Access from Castle Street or at N end of reserve from B6365.
Facilities: Leaflet available from Trust.
Public transport: None.
Habitat: Loch and woodland.
Key birds: Woodland birds, including Marsh Tit, Chiffchaff and Pied Flycatcher, waterfowl. Also occasional otter an red squirrel.
Contact: Trust HQ, 0131 312 7765.

PEASE DEAN

Scottish Wildlife Trust.
Location: NT 790 705. W of St Abb's Head. Park at Pease Bay Caravan Park off A1107.
Access: Open all year.
Facilities: Leaflet available from the tourist office in Eyemouth.
Public transport: None.
Habitat: Valley woodland.
Key birds: Valuable landfall, feeding and sheltering site for migrants.
Contact: Trust HQ, 0131 312 7765.

ST ABB'S HEAD

National Trust for Scotland.
Location: NT 914 693. Lies five miles N of Eyemouth. Follow A1107 from A1.
Access: Reserve open all year. Keep dogs on lead. Cliff path is not suitable for disabled visitors.
Facilities: Visitor centre and toilets open daily Apr-Oct.
Public transport: Nearest rail station is Berwick-upon-Tweed. Bus service from Berwick, tel 018907 81533.
Habitat: Cliffs, coastal grasslands and freshwater loch.
Key birds: *Apr-Aug*: Seabird colonies with large numbers of Kittiwake, auks, Shag, Fulmar. *Apr-May and Sept-Oct*: Good autumn seawatching.
Contact: Kevin Rideout, Rangers Cottage, Northfield, St Abbs, Borders, TD14 5QF. 018907 71443. e-mail: krideout@nts.org.uk www.nts.org.uk

YETHOLM LOCH

Scottish Wildlife Trust.
Location: NT 803 279. Six miles SE of Kelso. Off B6352, turning to Lochtower (unmetalled road).
Access: No access to marsh during breeding season.
Facilities: Hide. Car park along rough track.

Public transport: None.
Habitat: Marshland and loch.
Key birds: *Summer:* Breeding wildfowl (including Great Crested Grebe, Shoveler and Teal). *Winter:* Whooper Swan, Pink-footed Goose and wide range of ducks.
Contact: Trust HQ, 0131 312 7765.

Clyde

BARONS HAUGH

RSPB (South & West Scotland Office).
Location: RSPB NS755552. On SW edge of Motherwell, overlooking River Clyde. Via Adele Street, then lane off North Lodge Avenue.
Access: Open all year.
Facilities: Four hides.
Public transport: None.
Habitat: Marshland, flooded areas, woodland, parkland, meadows, scrub, river.
Key birds: *Summer*: Breeding Gadwall, warblers (inc. Garden, Grasshopper); Whinchat, Common Sandpiper, Kingfisher. *Autumn*: Excellent for waders (22 species). *Winter*: Whooper Swan.
Contact: RSPB office, Lochwinnoch.

FALLS OF CLYDE

Scottish Wildlife Trust.
Location: NS 88 34 14. Approx one mile S of Lanark. Directions from Glasgow – travel S on M74 until J7 then along A72, following signs for Lanark and New Lanark.
Access: Open daylight hours all year. Partial disabled access.
Facilities: Visitor centre open 11am-5pm all year. Toilets and cafeteria on site. Seasonal viewing facility for Peregrines. Numerous walkways and ranger service offers comprehensive guided walks programme.
Public transport: Scotrail trains run to Lanark (0845 7484950). Local bus service from Lanark to New Lanark.
Habitat: River Clyde gorge, waterfalls, mixed riparian/conifer woodlands, meadow, pond.
Key birds: More than 100 species of bird recorded on the reserve including unrivalled views of breeding Peregrine. Others include Goshawk, Barn Owl, Kingfisher, Dipper, Lapwing, Pied Flycatcher and Skylark.
Contact: Dr Stuart Glen,
The Scottish Wildlife Trust Visitor Centre, The Falls of Clyde Reserve, New Lanark, South Lanark, ML11 9DB. 01555 665262.
e-mail: fallsofclyde@cix.co.uk
www.swt.org.uk

HOGGANFIELD PARK

Glasgow City Council (LNR).
Location: Free car park at entrance on Cumbernauld Road (A80), three miles NE of Glasgow city centre.
Access: Open all year.
Facilities: None.
Public transport: Call for advice.
Habitat: Loch with island, marsh, woodland, grassland.
Key birds: Wildfowl include Tufted Duck, Goldeneye and Goosander. *Autumn*: Ruddy Duck. *Winter*: Whooper Swan and Smew, Jack Snipe on marsh. Occasional Slavonian Grebe. *Summer*: Breeding Reed Bunting and woodland birds.
Contact: Iain Gibson, 0141 287 5665;
e-mail: iain.gibson@land.glasgow.gov.uk.

KNOCKSHINNOCK LAGOONS

Scottish Wildlife Trust.
Location: NS 776 113. Car park off B741 (New Cumnock to Dalmellington road), or from Kirkbrae in New Cumnock.
Access: Open all year. Access from Church Lane, New Cumnock.
Facilities: None.
Public transport: None.
Habitat: Mining spoil, lagoons, meadows, woodland.
Key birds: *Summer*: Breeding Redshank, Lapwing, Snipe, Curlew, Shoveler, Teal, Pochard and Garganey. *Winter*: Whooper Swan and large number of ducks. *Spring/autumn*: Good for migrating waders.
Contact: Trust HQ, 0131 312 7765.

LOCHWINNOCH

RSPB (South & West Scotland Office).
Location: NS 358 582. 18 miles SW of Glasgow, adjacent to A760.
Access: Open every day except Christmas Day &

New Year (10am-5pm).
Facilities: Special facilities for schools and disabled. Refreshments available. Nature centre, hides.
Public transport: None.
Habitat: Shallow lochs, marsh, mixed woodland.
Key birds: *Winter*: Wildfowl (esp. Whooper Swan, Greylag, Goosander, Goldeneye). Occasional passage migrants inc. Whimbrel, Greenshank. *Summer*: Breeding Great Crested Grebe, Water Rail, Sedge and Grasshopper Warblers.
Contact: RSPB Nature Centre, Largs Road, Lochwinnoch, Renfrewshire, PA12 4JF. 01505 842663; fax 01505 843026; e-mail lochwinnoch@interramp.co.uk.

Dumfries & Galloway

CAERLAVEROCK SNH

SNH (Dumfries & Galloway Area Office).
Location: NY 040 645. Overlooks Solway W of Annan. From Dumfries go SE on B725 via Caerlaverock Castle.
Access: Open all year. Visitors may enter most of the reserve, except sanctuary area. The saltmarsh (merse) can be dangerous at high tides; visitors should consult the Reserve Manager for advice. No permit, but organised groups should apply to Reserve Manager well in advance. Research and surveys require approval of SNH Area Manager.
Facilities: None.
Public transport: None.
Habitat: Saltmarsh, grassland.
Key birds: *Winter*: Barnacle, Pink-footed and Greylag Geese, Whooper and Bewick's Swans, ducks, waders and raptors.
Contact: Wally Wright, SNH Reserve Office, Hollands Farm Road, Caerlaverock, Dumfries, DG1 4RS. 01387 770275.

CAERLAVEROCK WWT

The Wildfowl & Wetlands Trust.
Location: NY 051 656. From Dumfries take B725 at Bankend.
Access: Open daily except Christmas Day.
Facilities: 20 hides, heated observatory, three towers, sheltered picnic area. Self-catering accommodation and camping facilities. Nature trails in summer.
Public transport: None.
Habitat: Saltmarsh, grassland.
Key birds: *Winter*: Wildfowl esp. Barnacle Goose (max 13,700), Whooper and Bewick's Swans.
Contact: John Doherty, Centre Manager, The Wildfowl & Wetlands Trust, Eastpark Farm, Caerlaverock, Dumfries, DG1 4RS. 01387 770200.

CARSTRAMON WOOD

Scottish Wildlife Trust.
Location: NT 592 605. Take A75 from Castle Douglas. Reserve is two miles N of Gatehouse of Fleet on minor road off B796.
Access: Open all year.
Facilities: Car parking alongside road. Network of paths. Information boards. Leaflet from tourist office in gatehouse.
Public transport: None.
Habitat: Ancient deciduous oak woodland.
Key birds: Typical woodland birds (inc. Pied Flycatcher, Redstart, Green Woodpecker, Wood Warbler and Tree Pipit).
Contact: Trust HQ, 0131 312 7765.

KEN/DEE MARSHES

RSPB (South and West Scotland Office).
Location: NX 699 684. Six miles from Castle Douglas – good views from A762 and A713 roads to New Galloway.
Access: From car park at entrance to farm Mains of Duchrae. Open during daylight hours. No dogs.
Facilities: Hides, nature trails. Three mile walk to hide and back, nearer parking for elderly and disabled, but phone warden first.
Public transport: None.
Habitat: Marshes, woodlands, open water.
Key birds: *All year:* Mallard, Grey Heron, Buzzard. *Spring/summer*: Pied Flycatcher, Redstart, Tree Pipit, Sedge Warbler. *Winter*: Greenland White-fronted and Greylag Geese, birds of prey (Hen Harrier, Peregrine, Merlin).
Contact: Paul Collin, Gairland, Old Edinburgh Road, Minnigaff, Newton Stewart, DG8 6PL. 01671 402861.

MERSEHEAD

RSPB (South & West Scotland Office).
Location: NX 925 560. From Dalbeattie, take B793 or A710 to Caulkerbush.
Access: Open at all times.
Facilities: Hide, nature trails, information centre and toilets.
Public transport: None.
Habitat: Wet grassland, arable farmland, saltmarsh, inter-tidal mudflats.
Key birds: *Winter*: Up to 9,500 Barnacle Geese, 4,000 Teal, 2,000 Wigeon, 1,000 Pintail, waders (inc. Dunlin, Knot, Oystercatcher). *Summer:* Breeding birds include Lapwing, Redshank, Skylark.
Contact: Eric Nielson, Mersehead, Southwick, Mersehead, Dumfries, DG2 8AH. 01387 780298.

MULL OF GALLOWAY

RSPB (South and West Scotland Office).
Location: NX 156 304. Most southerly tip of Scotland - five miles from village of Drummore, S of Stranraer.
Access: Open at all times. Access suitable for disabled, disabled parking by centre. Centre open summer only (Apr-Sept).
Facilities: Visitor centre, toilets, nature trails.
Public transport: None.
Habitat: Sea cliffs, coastal heath.
Key birds: *Spring/summer*: Guillemot, Razorbill, Kittiwake, Black Guillemot, Puffin, Fulmar, Raven, Wheatear, Rock Pipit, Twite. Migrating Manx Shearwater. *All year*: Peregrine.
Contact: Paul Collin,
Gairland, Old Edinburgh Road, Minnigaff, Newton Stewart, DG8 6PL. 01671 402851

WIGTOWN BAY

Dumfries & Galloway Council.
Location: NX 465 545. Between Wigtown and Creetown. It is the largest LNR in Britain at 2845 ha. The A75 runs along the east side with the A714 S to Wigtown and B7004 providing superb views of the LNR.
Access: Open at all times - permits are not required. The hides are disabled friendly. Main accesses: Roadside lay-bys on A75 near Creetown and parking at Martyr's Stake and Wigtown Harbour.
Facilities: A hide at Wigtown Harbour with views over the River Bladnoch, saltmarsh and fresh water wetland has disabled access from harbour car park. There is also a small hide at the Martyr's Stake car park and walks and interpretation in this area.
Public transport: Travel Information Line 08457 090510 (local rate 9am-5pm Mon-Fri). Bus No 415 for Wigtown and West side. Bus No 431 or 500 X75 for Creetown and E side.
Habitat: Estuary with extensive saltmarsh/merse and mudflats with newly developed fresh water wetland at Wigtown Harbour.
Key birds: *Winter*: Internationally important for Pink-footed Goose, nationally important for Curlew, Whooper Swan and Pintail, with major gull roost and other migratory coastal birds. *Summer*: Breeding waders and duck.
Contact: Elizabeth Tindal,
County Buildings, Wigtown, DG8 9JH. 01988 402 401, mobile 07702 212 728.
e-mail: Elizabeth.Tindal@dumgal.gov.uk

WOOD OF CREE

RSPB (South and West Scotland Office).
Location: NX 382 708. Four miles N of Newton Stewart on minor road from Minnigaff, parallel to A714.
Access: Open during daylight hours. Dogs on lead. Not suitable for disabled.
Facilities: Nature trails.
Public transport: None.
Habitat: Oak woodland, marshes, river.
Key birds: *Spring/summer*: Pied Flycatcher, Wood Warbler, Tree Pipit, Redstart, Buzzard, Great Spotted Woodpecker, red squirrel, otter.
Contact: Paul Collin, Gairland, Old Edinburgh Road, Minnigaff, Newton Stewart, DG8 6PL. 01671 402861.

Fife

CAMERON RESERVOIR

Scottish Wildlife Trust.
Location: NO 478 115. Four miles SSW of St Andrews. Off A915.
Access: Open access to walk round reservoir. Path liable to flooding on south side. Wellington

boots advised. Dogs on leads only. Car park at NE corner of reservoir.
Facilities: SWT hide. Key available from Ian Cumming, 11 Canongate, St Andrews. Tel 01334 473773.
Public transport: None.
Habitat: Decaying pinewoods round shore of reservoir and drowning willows.
Key birds: *Winter*: Pink-footed and Greylag Goose, Wigeon, Tufted Duck, Pochard, Mallard. Also Whooper Swan, Mute Swan, Gadwall, Pintail, Shoveler, Red-breasted Merganser, Great Crested Grebe.
Contact: Ian Cumming (as above).

EDEN ESTUARY

Fife Council.
Location: NO 470 195. The reserve can be accessed from Guardbridge, St Andrews (one mile) on A91, and from Leuchars via Tentsmuir Forest off A919 (four miles).
Access: The Eden Estuary Centre is open (9am-5pm) every day except Christmas Day, New Year's Day and the day of the Leuchars airshow. Reserve is open all year but a permit (from Ranger service) is required to access the N shore.
Facilities: Visitor centre at Guardbridge.
Public transport: Leuchars train station. Regular buses Cupar-Dundee-St Andrews. Tel: 01334 474238.
Habitat: Saltmarsh, river, tidal flats, sand dunes.
Key birds: *Winter*: Main interest is wildfowl and waders, best place in Scotland to see Black-tailed Godwit. Other species include Grey Plover, Shelduck, Bar-tailed Godwit. Offshore Common and Velvet Scoter occur and Surf Scoter is regularly seen. Peregrine, Merlin and Short-eared Owl occur in winter.
Contact: Les Hatton, Fife Ranger Service, Silverburn House, Largo Road, By Leven, Fife, KY8 5PU. 01333 429785/07939 169291 (mobile). e-mail: refrs@craigtoun.freserve.co.uk

ISLE OF MAY

Scottish Natural Heritage.
Location: NT 655 995. This small island lying six miles off Fife Ness in the Firth of Forth is a National Nature Reserve.
Access: Contact boatman for day trips: J Reaper tel 01333 310103. Keep to paths. Fishing boat from Anstruther, arranged by the Observatory. Rock landings mean that delays are possible, both arriving and leaving, because of weather.
Facilities: No dogs; no camping; no fires. Prior permission required if scientific work is to be carried out.
Habitat: Sea cliffs, rocky shoreline.
Key birds: *Summer*: Breeding auks and terns, Kittiwake, Shag, Eider, Fulmar. *Autumn/spring:* Weather-related migrations include rarities each year.
Contact: David Thorne, Craigurd House, Blyth Bridge, West Linton, Peeblesshire, EH46 7AH,

ISLE OF MAY BIRD OBSERVATORY

Facilities: Hostel accommodation in disused lighthouse (the Low Light) for up to six, Apr-Oct; usual stay is one week. No supplies on island; visitors must take own food and sleeping bag. Five Heligoland traps used for ringing migrants when qualified personnel present. SNH Warden usually resident Apr-Sep.
Bookings: Mike Martin, 2 Manse Park, Uphall, W Lothian EH52 6NX, tel 01506 855285.

KILMINNING COAST

Scottish Wildlife Trust.
Location: NO 633 090. Take A917 from St Andews SE towards Crail. Off minor road 1.5 NE of Crail turn R past disused airfield. Park next to coast at NO 43 20 88.
Access: Open all year.
Facilities: Coastal footpath, information board.
Public transport: None.
Habitat: Scrub, grassland, rocky shoreline.
Key birds: Eider, waders, terns, Gannet. *Spring and autumn*: Excellent for passage migrants.
Contact: Trust HQ, 0131 312 7765.

Forth

CAMBUS POOL

Scottish Wildlife Trust.
Location: NS 846 937. ENE of Alloa on A907. Park by river in Cambus village.
Access: Cross River Devon by bridge at

NS853940 and walk down stream on R bank past bonded warehouses. Open all year.
Facilities: None.
Public transport: None.
Habitat: Wet grassland and pools.
Key birds: Used extensively by migrants, inc. wildfowl and waders.
Contact: Trust HQ, Regional Reserves Manager 0131 312 7765.

GARTMORN DAM

Clackmannanshire Council.
Location: NS 912 940. Approx one mile NE of Alloa, signposted from A908 in Sauchie.
Access: Open at all times. No charge.
Facilities: Visitor centre with toilets. Open 8.30am-8.30pm daily (Apr-Sept) inclusive and 1pm-4pm (weekends only Oct-Mar). One hide, key from visitor centre. Provision for disabled.
Public transport: Bus service to Sauchie. First Bus, 01324 613777. Stirling Bus Station, 01786 446 474.
Habitat: Open water (with island), woodland - deciduous and coniferous, farmland.
Key birds: *Summer*: Great Crested Grebe, breeding Sedge and Reed Warblers. *Autumn*: Migrant waders. *Winter*: Wildfowl (regionally important site), Kingfisher, Water Rail.
Contact: Clackmannanshire Ranger Service, Lime Tree House, Alloa, Clackmannanshire, FK10 1EX. 01259 450000.
www.clacksweb.org.uk
e-mail: rangers@clacks.gov.uk

INVERSNAID

RSPB (South & West Scotland Office).
Location: NN 337 088. On E side of Loch Lomond. Via B829 W from Aberfoyle, then along minor road to car park by Inversnaid Hotel.
Access: Open all year.
Facilities: None.
Public transport: None.
Habitat: Deciduous woodland rises to craggy ridge and moorland.
Key birds: *Summer*: Breeding Buzzard, Blackcock, Grey Wagtail, Dipper, Wood Warbler, Redstart, Pied Flycatcher, Tree Pipit. The loch is on a migration route, especially for wildfowl and waders.
Contact: RSPB, 0141 576 4100.

Highland & Caithness

ABERNETHY FOREST RESERVE - LOCH GARTEN

RSPB (North Scotland Office).
Location: NH 981 184. 2.5 miles from Boat of Garten, eight miles from Aviemore. Off B970, follow 'RSPB Ospreys' roadsigns.
Access: Osprey Centre open daily 10am-6pm (Apr to end Aug). Disabled access. No dogs (guide dogs only). No charge to RSPB members. Non-members: adults £2.50, senior citizens £1.50, children 50p.
Facilities: Osprey Centre overlooking nesting Ospreys, toilets, optics and CCTV live pictures.
Public transport: Bus service to Boat of Garten from Aviemore, 2.5 mile footpath to Osprey Centre. Steam railway to Boat of Garten from Aviemore.
Habitat: Caledonian pine wood.
Key birds: Ospreys nesting from Apr to Aug, Crested Tit, Crossbill, red squirrel. In 2001 hide provided views of lekking Capercaillies.
Contact: R W Thaxton,
RSPB, Grinian, Tulloch, Nethybridge, Inverness-shire, PH25 3EF. 01479 831694.

BEINN EIGHE

Scottish Natural Heritage.
Location: NG 990 620. By Kinlochewe, Wester Ross, 50 miles from Inverness and 20 miles from Gairloch on A832.
Access: Reserve open at all times, no charge. No dogs. Visitor centre open Easter-Sept (10am-5pm).
Facilities: Visitor centre, toilets, woodland trail and mountain trail - self-guided with leaflets.
Public transport: Very limited.
Habitat: Caledonian pine forest, dwarf shrub heath, mountain tops, freshwater loch shore.
Key birds: Golden Eagle, Scottish Crossbill, Ptarmigan, Red Grouse, Siskin. *Summer*: Black-throated Diver, Redwing, Snow Bunting.
Contact: David Miller, Reserve Manager, Scottish Natural Heritage, Anancaun, Kinlochewe, Ross-shire, IV22 2PD. 01445 760254. e-mail: david.miller@snh.gov.uk

BEN MORE COIGACH

Scottish Wildlife Trust.
Location: NC 075 065. 10 miles N of Ullapool, W of A835.
Access: Access at several points from minor road off A835 to Achiltibuie. Open all year, do not enter croftland without permission.
Facilities: None.
Public transport: None.
Habitat: Loch, bog mountain and moorland.
Key birds: Upland birds (inc. Ptarmigan, Raven, Ring Ouzel, Golden Plover, Twite). *Winter:* Grazing Barnacle Goose.
Contact: John Smith,
North Keanchullish, Ullapool, Wester Ross, IV26 2TW. 01854 612531.

CAIRNGORM NNR

SNH (East Highland Area).
Location: NJ 010 010. Largest NNR in Britain, surrounding Aviemore.
Access: Unrestricted but certain areas out of bounds during deer cull season.
Facilities: Visitor Centre open May-Sept. Full information from Aviemore tourist office.
Public transport: Call tourist office for advice.
Habitat: Mountain, moorland, pine woodland and lochs.
Key birds: Goosander, Crested Tit, Siskin, Redstart, Crossbill, Capercaillie, Black Grouse, Ptarmigan, Dotterel, Golden Eagle.
Contact: SNH,
Achantoul, Aviemore, Inverness-shire, PH22 1QD. 01479 810477; (Fax) 01479 811363.

FORSINARD

RSPB (North Scotland Office).
Location: NC 89 04 25. 30 miles SW of Thurso on A897. Turn off A9 at Helmsdale from the South (24 miles) or A836 at Melvich from the N coast road (14 miles).
Access: Open at all times. Contact visitor centre during breeding season (mid-Apr to end Jun) and during deerstalking season (Jul 1-Feb 15) for advice. Self-guided trail open all year, no dogs, not suitable for wheelchairs.
Facilities: Visitor centre open Apr 1-Oct (9am-6pm), seven days per week. Static and AV displays, live CCTV and webcam link to Hen Harrier nest in breeding season. Wheelchair access to centre and toilet. Guided walks Tue and Thu. Tea-room nearby.
Public transport: Train from Inverness and Thurso (0845 484950) visitor centre in Forsinard Station building.
Habitat: Blanket bog, upland hill farm.
Key birds: Golden Plover, Greenshank, Dunlin, Hen Harrier, Merlin, Short-eared Owl.
Contact: Norrie Russell,
RSPB Forsinard, Forsinard, Sutherland, KW13 6YT. 01641 571225. www.rspb.org.uk
e-mail: forsinard@rspb.org.uk

GLENMORE

Scottish Wildlife Trust/Forest Enterprise.
Location: NH 998 104. Park at Glenmore seven miles E of Aviemore, opposite campsite.
Access: Access over a comprehensive network of paths.
Facilities: Visitor centre at Glenmore, with maps and guidebook.
Public transport: None.
Habitat: Native Caledonian pinewood, heather moorland.
Key birds: Crossbill, Crested Tit, Redstart, Siskin, Dipper, occasional Osprey fishing in Loch Morlich.
Contact: Scottish Trust HQ, 0131 312 7765.

HANDA

Scottish Wildlife Trust.
Location: NC 138 480. Accessible by boat from Tarbet, near Scourie - follow A894 N from Ullapool 40 miles. Continue another three miles, turn left down single track road another three miles to Tarbet.
Access: Open April-Sept. Boats leave 9.30am-2pm (last boat back 5pm). Dogs not allowed. Visitors are asked for a contribution of £1.50 towards costs. Not suitable for disabled due to uneven terrain.
Facilities: Three mile circular path, shelter (no toilets on island - use those in Tarbet car park). Visitors are given introductory talk and a leaflet with map on arrival.
Public transport: Post bus to Scourie (tel 01549 402357 Lairg Post Office). Train to Lairg (tel 0845 484950 National Train enquiries). No connecting public transport between Scourie and Tarbet.

Habitat: Sea cliffs, blanket bog.
Key birds: *Spring/summer*: Biggest Guillemot and Razorbill colony in Britain and Ireland. Also nationally important for Kittiwakes, Arctic and Great Skuas. Puffin, Shag, Fulmar and Common and Arctic Terns also present.
Contact: Liz Lee, (Office Administrator), Unit 4A, 3 Carsegate Road North, Inverness, IV3 8PU, 01463 714746.
Charles Thomson (Boatman) 01971 502347.
e-mail: swtnorth@cix.co.uk
www.swt.org.uk

INSH MARSHES

RSPB (North Scotland Office).
Location: NN 775 999. In Spey Valley, two miles NE of Kingussie on B970 minor road.
Access: Open at all times. No disabled access.
Facilities: Information viewpoint, two hides, three nature trails. Not suitable for disabled. No toilets.
Public transport: Nearest rail station Kingussie (two miles). Bus from Kingussie on Tue only!
Habitat: Marshes, woodland, river, open water.
Key birds: *Spring/summer*: Waders (Lapwing, Curlew, Redshank, Snipe), wildfowl (including Goldeneye and Wigeon), Spotted Crake, Wood Warbler, Redstart, Tree Pipit. *Winter*: Hen Harrier, Whooper Swan, other wildfowl.
Contact: Tom Prescott/Pete Moore, Ivy Cottage, Insh, Kingussie, Inverness-shire, PH21 1NT. 01540 661518.
e-mail: tomprescott@rspb.org.uk or petemoore@rspb.org.uk
www.kincraig.com/rspb.htn

ISLE OF EIGG

Scottish Wildlife Trust.
Location: NM 38 48. Small island S of Skye, reached by ferry from Maillaig or Arisaig (approx 12 miles).
Access: Ferries seven days per week (weather permitting) during summer. Four days per week (weather permitting) Sept-Apr.
Facilities: Pier centre – shops/Post Office, tea-room, craftshop, toilets.
Public transport: Caledonian MacBrayne Ferries NE from Mallaig (tel: 01687 462403), *MV Shearwater* from Arisaig (tel: 01678 450 224).
Habitat: Moorland (leading to sgurr pitchstone ridge), wood and scrub, hay fields, shoreline.
Key birds: Red-throated Diver, Golden Eagle, Buzzard, Raven. *Summer*: Manx Shearwater, Arctic Tern, various warblers, Twite, etc.
Contact: John Chester, Millers Cottage, Isle of Eigg, Small Isles, PH42 4RL. 01687 482477.
www.isleofeigg.org

ISLE OF RUM

SNH (North West Region).
Location: NM 370 970. Island lying S of Skye. To reach Passenger ferry at Mallaig, take A830 from Fort William.
Access: Contact Reserve Office for details of special access arrangements relating to breeding birds, deer stalking and deer research.
Facilities: Prior booking needed to stay overnight. General store and Post Office (01687 462744). Self-guided trails.
Public transport: Passenger ferry to island.
Habitat: Coast, moorland, woodland restoration, montane.
Key birds: *Summer:* Large Manx Shearwater colonies on hill tops; breeding auks (inc. Black Guillemot), Kittiwake, Fulmar, Eider, Golden Plover, Merlin, Red-throated Diver, Golden Eagle.
Contact: SNH Reserve Office, Isle of Rum PH43 4RR, 01687 462026; fax 01687 462805.

LOCH FLEET

Scottish Wildlife Trust.
Location: NH 794 965. Site lies two miles S of Golspie on the A9 and five miles N of Dornoch. View across tidal basin from A9 or unclassified road to Skelbo.
Access: Park at Little Ferry or in lay-bys around the basin.
Facilities: Guided walks in Summer. Interpretive centre.
Public transport: None.
Habitat: Tidal basin, sand dunes, shingle, woodland, marshes.
Key birds: *Winter*: Important feeding place for ducks and waders. The sea off the mouth of Loch Fleet is a major wintering area for Long-tailed Duck, Common and Velvet Scoters, Eider Duck. Pinewood off minor road S from Golspie to Little Ferry, has Crossbill, occasional Crested Tit.
Contact: Trust HQ, 0131 312 7765.

LOCH RUTHVEN

RSPB (North Scotland Office).
Location: H 638 281. From Inverness, take A9 SE to junction with B851. Head SW until the minor road NE at Croachy; car park one mile.
Access: Open at all times.
Facilities: None.
Public transport: None.
Habitat: Freshwater loch and woodland.
Key birds: Best breeding site in Britain for Slavonian Grebe. Teal, Wigeon and other wildfowl. Peregrine, Hen Harrier and Osprey often seen.
Contact: RSPB North Scotland Office.

Lothian

ABERLADY BAY

East Lothian Council (LNR).
Location: NT 472 806. From Edinburgh take A198 E to Aberlady. Reserve is 1.5 miles E of Aberlady village.
Access: Open at all times. Please stay on footpaths to avoid disturbance. Disabled access from reserve car park. No dogs.
Facilities: Small car park and toilets. Notice board with recent sightings at end of footbridge.
Public transport: Edinburgh to N Berwick bus service stops at reserve (request), service no124. Railway four miles away at Longniddry.
Habitat: Tidal mudflats, saltmarsh, freshwater marsh, dune grassland, scrub, open sea.
Key birds: *Summer*: Breeding birds include Shelduck, Eider, Reed Bunting and up to eight species of warbler. Passage waders inc. Green, Wood and Curlew Sandpipers, Little Stint, Greenshank, Whimbrel, Black-tailed Godwit. *Winter*: Divers (esp. Red-throated), Red-necked and Slavonian grebes and geese (large numbers of Pink-footed roost); sea-ducks, waders.
Contact: Ian Thomson,
4 Craigielaw, Longniddry, East Lothian, EH32 0PY. 01875 870588.

BASS ROCK

Location: NT602873. Island in Firth of Forth, lying E of North Berwick.
Access: Private property. Regular daily sailings from N Berwick around Rock; local boatman has owner's permission to land individuals or parties by prior arrangement. For details contact Fred Marr, N Berwick on 01620 892838.
Facilities: None.
Habitat: Sea cliffs.
Key birds: The spectacular cliffs hold a large Gannet colony, (up to 9000 pairs), plus auks, Kittiwake, Shag and Fulmer.

BAWSINCH & DUDDINGSTON LOCH

Scottish Wildlife Trust.
Location: NT 003 631. Centre of Edinburgh below Arthur's Seat. Car park on Duddingston Road West for Bawsinch or by Holyrood Park Gate for views across loch.
Access: Open access to N shore of loch; to remainder of site and hide by prior arrangement with Colin McLean, 27 Manse Road, Roslin, Midlothian, (SWT members only).
Facilities: Hide with bird and plant list.
Public transport: Call Trust for advice.
Habitat: Marsh, loch, ponds, trees and scrub, developed from former waste area.
Key birds: *Nearly 70 species recorded. Summer*: Loch has breeding wildfowl. *Winter*: Wildfowl, Bittern.
Contact: Trust HQ, 0131 312 7765.

Moray & Nairn

CULBIN SANDS

RSPB (North Scotland Office).
Location: NH 900 580. Approx 0.5 miles from Nairn. Access to parking at East Beach car park, signed off A96.

Access: Open at all times. Not suitable for wheelchairs.
Facilities: Toilets at car park. Track along dunes and saltmarsh.
Public transport: Buses stop in Nairn. Train station in Nairn .75 miles W of reserve.
Habitat: Saltmarsh, sandflats, dunes.
Key birds: *Winter*: Flocks of Common Scoter, Long-tailed Duck, Knot, Bar-tailed Godwit, Red-breasted Merganser. Rapters like Peregrine, Merlin and Hen Harrier attracted by wader flocks. Roosting geese. *Summer:* Breeding Ringed Plover, Oystercatcher and Common Tern.
Contact: RSPB North Scotland Office., Etive House, Beechwood Park, Inverness, IV2 3BW. 01463 715000.
e-mail: nsro@rspb.org.uk
www.rspb.org.uk

LEIN, SPEY BAY

Scottish Wildlife Trust.
Location: NJ 325 657. Eight miles NE of Elgin. From Elgin take A96 and B9015 to Kingston. Reserve is immediately E of village. Car parks at Kingston and Tugnet.
Access: Open all year.
Facilities: Wildlife centre.
Public transport: None.
Habitat: Shingle, rivermouth and coastal habitats.
Key birds: *Summer*: Osprey, waders, wildfowl. *Winter*: Seaduck and divers offshore (esp. Long-tailed Duck, Common and Velvet Scoters, Red-throated Diver).
Contact: Trust HQ 0131 312 7765.

NE Scotland

CULLALOE

Scottish Wildlife Trust.
Location: NT 188 877. On loop of B9157 just N of Aberdeen. Car parking at the disused filter beds below the old dam.
Access: Open all year. Disabled access.
Facilities: Car parking on reserve.
Public transport: None.
Habitat: Loch, scrub willow, woodland, meadow.
Key birds: Good for wildfowl (inc. Teal) and passage waders.
Contact: Trust HQ, 0131 312 7765.

FORVIE

Scottish Natural Heritage.
Location: NK 034 289.
Access: Dogs on leads only. Reserve open at all times but ternery closed Apr 1- end of Aug annually. Stevenson Forvie Centre open every day (Apr-Sept) and when staff are available outside those months.
Facilities: Interpretive display and toilets in Stevenson Forvie Centre. Bird hide, waymarked trail.
Public transport: Bluebird No 263 to Cruden Bay. Ask for the Newburgh or Collieston Crossroads stop. Tel: 01224 591381.
Habitat: Estuary, dunes, coastal heath.
Key birds: *Spring/summer*: Eider and terns nesting. *Winter*: Waders and wildfowl on estuary.
Contact: Alison Matheson (Area Officer), Scottish Natural Heritage, Stevenson Forvie Centre, Little Collieston Croft, Collieston, Aberdeenshire, AB41 8RU. 01358 751330.
www.snh.org.uk

FOWLSHEUGH

RSPB (East Scotland Office).
Location: NO 879 80. Cliff top path N from Crawton, signposted from A92, three miles S of Stonehaven.
Access: Unrestricted. Boat trips Tue and Fri evenings (May-Jul) from Stonehaven Harbour. Booking essential. Contact East Scotland regional office. Tel: 01224 624824.
Facilities: New car park (council) with limited number of spaces 200 yards from reserve (replaced following the storm damage of 1999).
Public transport: None.
Habitat: Sea cliffs.
Key birds: Large seabird colony, Kittiwake, auks.
Contact: Warden, Starnafin, Crimond, Fraserburgh, AB43 8QN. 01346 532017.
e-mail: esro@rspb.org.uk
www.rspb.org.uk

LOCH OF STRATHBEG

RSPB (East Scotland Office).
Location: NK 057 581. Near Crimond on the A90, nine miles S of Fraserburgh.
Access: Open at all times dawn-dusk. No dogs except guide dogs please. One hide with wheelchair access. Visitor centre not fully accessible to wheelchairs and disabled visitors.
Facilities: Visitor centre at Starnatin Farm, four hides, toilets (with disabled access), car parking.
Public transport: Access to whole of reserve is difficult without a vehicle. Bus service runs between Fraserburgh and Peterhead, stopping at Crimond just over one mile from visitor centre.
Habitat: Dune loch with surrounding marshes, reedbeds, grasslands, dunes and agricultural land.
Key birds: *Winter*: Whooper Swan, Pink-footed and Barnacle Geese, large numbers of winter duck including Smew. *Spring/summer*: Lowland waders, Sandwich Tern, Water Rail, Corn Bunting, Skylark all breeding. Passage birds, *Spring/autumn*: Curlew Sandpiper, Marsh Harrier, Spotted Redshank.
Contact: RSPB Warden,
Starnafin, Crimond, Fraserburgh, Aberdeenshire, 01346 532017. e-mail: esro@rspb.org.uk
www.rspb.org.uk

LONGHAVEN CLIFFS

Scottish Wildlife Trust.
Location: NK 116 394. Two miles S of Peterhead. Take A952 S from Peterhead and then A975 to Bullers of Buchan (gorge).
Access: Access from car park at Blackhills quarry or Bullers of Buchan.
Facilities: Leaflet available from Mark Young, Mechlepark, Oldmeldrum, Inverurie, Aberdeenshire, AB5 0DC.
Public transport: None.
Habitat: Rugged red granite cliffs and cliff-top vegetation.
Key birds: *May-July:* Nine species of breeding seabird inc. Kittiwake, Shag, Guillemot, Razorbill, Puffin.
Contact: Trust HQ, Regional Reserves Officer.

ST CYRUS

Scottish Natural Heritage.
Location: NO 764 650. Three miles N of Montrose, follow the sign saying 'Beach' from the main coast road.
Access: The whole reserve is accessible from Sept-Mar. From Apr-Aug the south of the reserve is closed for breeding birds. Disabled access limited to visitor centre and boardwalk. Dogs on leads during the breeding season, but can be let off on the beach.
Facilities: Visitor centre and toilets.
Public transport: None to reserve. Buses to the village of St Cyrus. Walk down the cliff path from there.
Habitat: Narrow dune system, calcareous grassland and cliffs.
Key birds: *Summer*: Grasshopper Warbler, Whitethroat, Willow Warbler. Terns feeding and roosting by river mouth. Nesting Peregrine.
Contact: 1. Summer - Catriona Reid.
Old Lifeboat Station, Nether Warberton, St Cyrus, DD10 0DG. 01674 430736.
2. Winter - Alison Matheson, Little Colliston Croft, By Ellon, Aberdeenshire.

Orkney

BIRSAY MOORS

RSPB (East Scotland Office).
Location: Now part of separate reserve. Separate access to hide at Burgar Hill, signposted from A966 at Evie (HY 346 247). Birsay Moors viewed from B9057 NW of Dounby.
Access: Open access all year round.
Facilities: One hide at Burgar Hill.
Public transport: Orkney Coaches. Service within 0.5 mile of reserve. Tel: 01856 877500.
Habitat: Heather moorland.
Key birds: *Spring/summer*: Nesting Hen Harrier, Merlin, Great and Arctic Skuas, Short-eared Owl, Golden Plover, Curlew, Red-throated Diver. *Winter*: Hen Harrier roost.
Contact: Andy Knight, Warden,
12/14 North End Road, Stromness, Orkney, KW16 3HG. 01856 850176.
e-mail: andy.knight@rspb.org.uk
www.rspb.co.uk

COPINSAY

RSPB (East Scotland Office).
Location: HY 610 010. Access by private boat or hire boat from mainland Orkney.
Access: Open all year round.
Facilities: House on island open to visitors. No toilets or hides.
Public transport: None.
Habitat: Sea cliffs, farmland.
Key birds: *Summer*: Breeding Kittiwake, Guillemot, Black Guillemot, Puffin, Razorbill, Shag, Fulmar, Rock Dove, Eider, Twite, Raven and Greater Black-backed Gull. Passage migrants esp. during periods of E winds.
Contact: Andy Knight, Warden, 12/14 North End Road, Stromness, Orkney, KW16 3AG. 01856 850176.
e-mail: andy.knight@rspb.org.uk
www.rspb.co.uk

COTTESCARTH AND RENDALL MOSS

RSBP (East Scotland Office).
Location: HY 360 200. Orkney reserve off A966, three miles N of Finstown.
Access: Open all year. Hide open all year. Not suitable for dogs.
Facilities: Hide and car park.
Public transport: Orkney Coaches. Tel: 01856 877500.
Habitat: Heather moorland, areas of rushes and wet grassland.
Key birds: *Summer*: Breeding Hen Harrier, Merlin, Redshank, Oystercatcher, Curlew, Reed Bunting.
Contact: Andy Knight, 12/14 North End Road, Stromness, Orkney, KW16 3AG. 01856 850176.
e-mail: andy.knight@RSBP.org.uk
www.RSBP.co.uk

HOBBISTER

RSPB (East Scotland Office).
Location: HY 396 070 or HY 381 068. Near Kirkwall.
Access: Open access between A964 and the sea.
Facilities: None.
Public transport: Orkney Coaches. Tel: 01856 877500.
Habitat: Orkney moorland, bog, fen, saltmarsh, coastal cliffs.
Key birds: *Summer*: Breeding Hen Harrier, Merlin, Short-eared Owl, Red Grouse, Red-throated Diver, Eider, Merganser, Black Guillemot. Wildfowl and waders at Waulkmill Bay.
Contact: Andy Knight, Mainland Warden, 12/14 North End Road, Stromness, Orkney, KW16 3AG. 01856 850176.
e-mail: andy.knight@rspb.org.uk
www.rspb.co.uk

HOY

RSPB (East Scotland Office).
Location: HY 210 025. Located in NW of Hoy, a large island S of mainland Orkney. Car ferry from Houten to Lyness.
Access: Open all year round. Keep dogs on lead. Unsuitable for disabled people - rough terrain.
Facilities: Toilet facilities at Moaness Pier and at Rackwick. Nature trail - circular route from Moaness Pier to Old Man of Hoy via Old Rackwick Post Road.
Public transport: None.
Habitat: Coastal maritime heath, moorland, fellfield, woodland and cliffs.
Key birds: *Spring/summer:* Red-throated Diver, Merlin, Peregrine, Golden Plover, Dunlin, Great Skua, Arctic Skua, Short-eared Owl, Guillemot, Razorbill, Puffin, Fulmar, Kittiwake, Stonechat, Wheatear. *Autumn/winter:* Long-eared Owl, Whooper Swan, Snow Bunting. Migration species: Redwing, Whimbrel, Brambling.
Contact: RSPB Mainland Orkney Office, 12-14 North End Road, Stromness, Orkney, KW16 3AG. 01856 850176.
e-mail: keith.fairclough@rspb.org.uk
www.rspb.org.uk

LOONS (THE)

RSPB (East Scotland Office).
Location: HY 246 242. Access to hide (only) via minor road from A986, three miles N of Dounby.
Access: Hide open all year.
Facilities: One hide. No nature trail nor toilets.
Public transport: Orkney Coaches (01856 877500).
Habitat: Marsh.
Key birds: *Summer*: Breeding Pintail, Red-

breasted Merganser and waders (inc. Snipe, Redshank, Black-tailed Godwit), Common and Black-headed Gulls, Arctic Tern. *Winter*: Regular flock of Greenland White-fronted Goose.
Contact: Andy Knight,
12/14 North End Road, Stromness, Orkney, KW16 3AG. 01856 850176.
e-mail: andy.knight@rspb.org.uk
www.rspb.co.uk

MARWICK HEAD

RSPB (East Scotland Office).
Location: HY 229 242. On W coast of mainland Orkney, near Dounby. Path N from Marwick Bay, or from car park at Cumlaquoy at HY 232 252.
Access: Open all year. Not suitable for disabled.
Facilities: Cliff top path.
Public transport: Orkney Coaches (01856 877500).
Habitat: Rocky bay, sandstone cliffs.
Key birds: May-Jul best. Large numbers of Kittiwakes and auks, inc. Puffins, also nesting Fulmar, Rock Dove, Raven, Rock Pipit.
Contact: Andy Knight, Mainland Warden, 12/14 North End Road, Stromness, Orkney, KW16 3AG. 01856 850176.www.rspb.co.uk
e-mail: andy.knight@rspb.org.uk

NORTH HILL, PAPA WESTRAY

RSPB (East Scotland Office).
Location: HY 496 538. Small island lying NE of Westray, reserve at N end of island's main road.
Access: Access at all times. During breeding season report to summer warden at Rose Cottage, 650 yards S of reserve entrance. Tel 01857 644240.
Facilities: Nature trails.
Public transport: Orkney Ferries (01856 872044).
Habitat: Sea cliffs, maritime heath.
Key birds: *Summer*: Close views of colony of Puffin, Guillemot, Razorbill and Kittiwake. Black Guillemot nest under flagstones around reserve's coastline. One of UK's largest colonies of Arctic Tern, also Arctic Skua.
Contact: Keith Fairclough, Reserves Manager, Orkney, 12/14 North End Road, Stromness, Orkney, KW16 3AG. 01856 850176.
e-mail: keith.fairclough@rspb.org.uk
www.rspb.co.uk

NORTH RONALDSAY BIRD OBSERVATORY

Location: HY 64 52. 35 miles from Kirkwall, Orkney mainland
Access: Open all year except Christmas.
Facilities: Accommodation, display room, meals, snacks etc for non-residents, toilets, croft walk.
Public transport: Twice daily (Mon-Sat) subsidised flights from Kirkwall (Loganair 01856 872494). Once weekly ferry from Kirkwall (Fri or Sat), some Sun sailings in summer (Orkney Ferries Ltd 01856 872044).
Habitat: Crofting island with a number of eutrophic and oligotrophic wetlands. Coastline has both sandy bays and rocky shore. Walled gardens concentrate passerines.
Key birds: Prime migration site in *Spring/ Autumn* including regular BBRC species. Wide variety of breeding seabirds, wildfowl and waders. *Winter:* Waders and wildfowl include Whooper Swan and hard weather movements occur.
Contact: Alison Duncan,
North Ronaldsay Bird Observatory, Twingness, North Ronaldsay, Orkney, KW17 2BE. 01857 633200.
e-mail: alison@nrbo.prestel.co.uk
www.nrbo.f2s.com

NOUP CLIFFS WESTRAY

RSPB (East Scotland Office).
Location: HY 392 500. Westray lies NE of Mainland and Rousay. Take minor road to Pierowall and Noup Farm then track NW to lighthouse.
Access: No restrictions.
Facilities: None.
Public transport: Flights from Kirkwall daily (Loganair 01856 872494). Daily ferry (Orkney Ferries 01856 872044).
Habitat: 1.5 miles of sandstone cliffs.
Key birds: *Summer*: May-Jul best. Huge seabird colony, breeding Rock Dove, Raven, Shag, auks, Rock Pipit.
Contact: Keith Fairclough, (Reserves Manager), 12/14 North End Road, Stromness, Orkney, KW16 3EQ. 01856 850176.
e-mail: keith.fairclough@rspb.org.uk
www.rspb.co.uk

TRUMLAND, ROUSAY

RSPB (East Scotland Office).
Location: HY 427 276. Ferry from Tingwall in NE Mainland to Rousay.
Access: Reserve and nature trail (access at all times) from entrance to Taversoe Tuick Cairn.
Facilities: Nature trail.
Public transport: Orkney Ferries to Rousay from Tingwall Pier Tel: 01856 751360.
Habitat: None.
Key birds: *Summer*: Breeding Hen Harrier, Merlin, Short-eared Owl, Red-throated Diver, Golden Plover, Great and Arctic Skuas, Common Gull.
Contact: Andy Mitchell, Egilsay Warden, 01856 821395. e-mail: andy.mitchell@rspb.org.uk www.rspb.co.uk

---

Outer Hebrides

BALRANALD

RSPB (North Scotland Office).
Location: NF 705 707. From Skye take ferry to Lochmaddy, North Uist. Drive W on A867 for 20 miles to reserve. Turn off main road three miles NW of Bayhead at signpost to Houghharry.
Access: Open at all times, no charge. Dogs on leads. Disabled access.
Facilities: Visitor Centre and toilets - disabled access. Marked nature trail.
Public transport: Bus service (tel 01876 560244).
Habitat: Freshwater loch, machair, coast and craglands.
Key birds: *Summer*: Corncrake, Corn Bunting, Lapwing, Oystercatcher, Dunlin, Ringed Plover, Redshank, Snipe. *Winter*: Twite, Greylag Goose, Wigeon, Teal Shoveler. *Passage*: Barnacle Goose, Pomarine Skua, Long-tailed Skua.
Contact: Jamie Boyle,
9 Grenitote, Isle of North Uist, H56 5BP. 01876 560287. e-mail: james.boyle3@btinternet.com

LOCH DRUIDIBEG

SNH (North West Region).
Location: NF 782 378. South Uist.
Access: Restricted access during breeding season.
Facilities: None.
Public transport: None.
Habitat: Loch, machair, coast.
Key birds: Summer: Breeding Greylag, waders.
Contact: SNH Area Officer,
Stilligarry, South Uist, HS8 5RS. 01870 620238; (Fax) 01870 620350.

Perth & Kinross

LOCH LEVEN

SNH, Loch Leven Laboratory.
Location: NO 150 010. Head S from Perth and leave M90 at exit 5, S of Kinross.
Access: Public access restricted to three short stretches of shoreline. Most birdwatchers visiting the reserve go to the RSPB nature centre at Vane Farm (qv) overlooking the loch.
Facilities: Extensive ornithological research programme.
Public transport: None.
Habitat: Lowland loch with islands.
Key birds: *Winter*: Flocks of geese (over 20,000 Pinkfeet), ducks, Whooper Swan. *Summer*: Greatest concentration of breeding ducks in Britain (10 species) and grebes. *Passage*: Waders (Golden Plover flocks up to 500).
Contact: Paul Brooks,
SNH, Loch Leven Laboratory, The Pier, Kinross, KY13 8UF. 01577 864439.

LOCH OF LOWES

Scottish Wildlife Trust.
Location: NO 042 435. Sixteen miles N of Perth, two miles NE of Dunkeld - just off A923 (signposted).
Access: Visitor centre open Apr-Sept inclusive (10am-5pm), mid-Jul to mid-Aug (10am-6pm).

Observation hide open all year – daylight hours. No dogs allowed. Partial access for wheelchairs.
Facilities: Visitor centre with toilets, observation hide.
Public transport: Railway station – Birnam/ Dunkeld – three miles from reserve. Bus from Dunkeld – two miles from reserve.
Habitat: Freshwater loch with fringing woodland.
Key birds: Breeding Ospreys (Apr-end Aug). Nest in view, 250 yards from hide. Wildfowl and woodland birds. Greylag roost (Oct-Mar).
Contact: Dr Alan Barclay, (Manager), Scottish Wildlife Trust, Loch of the Lowes, Visitor Centre, Dunkeld, Perthshire, PH8 0HH. 01350 727337.

VANE FARM

RSPB (East Scotland Office).
Location: NT 160 993. By Loch Leven. Take exit 5 from M90 onto B9097.
Access: Open daily (10am-5pm) except Jan 1 and Christmas Day. Cost £3 adults, £2 concessions, 50p children, £6 family. Free to members. No dogs except guide dogs. Disabled access to shop, coffee shop, observation room and toilets.
Facilities: Shop, coffee shop and observation room overlooking Loch Leven and the reserve. There is a 1.25 mile hill trail through woodland and moorland. Wetland trail with three observation hides. Toilets, including disabled.
Public transport: Nearest train station Cowdenbeath (nine miles away). Nearest bus station Kinross at Green Hotel (five miles away).
Habitat: Wet grassland and flooded areas by Loch Leven. Arable farmland. Native woodland and heath moorland.
Key birds: *Spring/summer*: Breeding and passage waders (including Lapwing, Redshank, Snipe, Curlew). Farmland birds (including Skylark and Yellowhammer). *Winter*: Whooper Swan, Bewick's Swan, Pink-footed Goose.
Contact: Ken Shaw, Site Manager, Vane Farm Nature Centre, Kinross, Tayside, KY13 9LX. 01577 862355.
e-mail: vanefarm@rspb.co.uk

Shetland

FAIR ISLE BIRD OBSERVATORY

Fair Isle Bird Observatory.
Location: HZ 2172.
Access: Open from end Apr-end Oct. Free to roam everywhere except one croft (Lower Leogh).
Facilities: Public toilets at Airstrip and Stackhoull Stores (shop). Accommodation at Fair Isle Bird Observatory (phone/e-mail: for brochure/details). Guests can be involved in observatory work and get to see birds in the hand. Slide shows, guided walks through Ranger Service.
Public transport: Tue, Thurs, Sat – ferry (12 passengers) from Grutness, Shetland. Tel: Jimmy or Florrie Stout 01595 760222. Mon, Wed, Fri, Sat – air (7 seater) from Tingwall, Shetland. Tel: Loganair 01595 840246.
Habitat: Heather moor and lowland pasture/ crofting land.
Key birds: Large breeding seabird colonies (auks, Gannet, Arctic Tern, Arctic Skua and Great Skua). Many common and rare migrants Apr/May/early Jun, late Aug-Nov.
Contact: Deryk Shaw (Warden), Hollie Shaw (Administrator), Fair Isle Bird Observatory, Fair Isle, Shetland, ZE2 9JG. 01595 760258.
e-mail: fairisle.birdobs@zetnet.co.uk
www.fairislebirdobs.co.uk

FETLAR

RSPB (East Scotland Office).
Location: HU 603 917. Lies W of Yell. Take car ferry from Gutcher, N Yell. Booking advised. Tel: 01957 722259.
Access: Part of RSPB reserve (Vord Hill) closed mid-May-end Jul. Entry during this period is only by arrangement with warden.
Facilities: Hide at Mires of Funzie. Displays etc at interpretive centre, Houbie. Toilets at ferry terminal, shop and interpretive centre.
Public transport: None.
Habitat: Serpentine heath, rough hill lane,

upland mire.
Key birds: *Summer*: Breeding Red-throated Diver, Eider, Shag, Whimbrel, Golden Plover, Dunlin, skuas, Manx Shearwater, Storm Petrel. Red-necked Phalarope on Loch of Funzie (HU 655 899) viewed from road or RSPB hide overlooking Mires of Funzie.
Contact: RSPB North Isles Officer, Bealance, Fetlar, Shetland, ZE2 9DJ. Tel/Fax: 01957 733246.
e-mail: malcolm.smith@rspb.org.uk

ISLE OF NOSS

Scottish Natural Heritage (Shetland Office).
Location: HU 531 410. Four miles by car ferry and road to the E of Lerwick. Take ferry to Bressay and follow signs for Noss. Park at end of road and walk to shore (600 yards) where ferry to island will collect you (if red flag is flying, island is closed due to sea conditions).
Access: Access (Mon, Wed, Thu, Sat, Sun) 10am-5pm, late May-late Aug. (Note – foot and mouth restrictions in place mid-2001 – phone for latest position.) Access by zodiac inflatable so unsuitable for disabled. No dogs allowed.
Facilities: Visitor centre, toilets.
Public transport: None.
Habitat: Dune grassland, moorland, blanket bog, sea cliffs.
Key birds: *Spring/summer:* Fulmar, Shag, Gannet, Arctic Tern, Kittiwake, Great Black-backed Gull, Great Skua, Arctic Skua, Guillemot, Razorbill, Puffin, Black Guillemot, Eider.
Contact: Jonathan Swale, Scottish Natural Heritage, Stewart Building, Alexandra Wharf, Lerwick, Shetland, ZE1 0LL. 01595 693345.
e-mail: jonathan.swale@snh.gov.uk

MOUSA

RSBP (Shetland Office).
Location: HU 460240. Small uninhabited island east of Sandwick in South Mainland of Shetland.
Access: By ferry from Leebitton Pier, Sandwick, Shetland – mid-Apr–mid-Sept.
Facilities: The Mousa Broch is the best preserved Iron Age tower in the world (World Heritage Site).
Public transport: Buses run to Sandwick from Lerwick. Details of ferry available from Tom Jamieson (01950 431367) or his web site (www.mousaboattrips.co.uk).
Habitat: A small uninhabited island with maritime grassland and a small area of shell sand.
Key birds: *Summer*: Storm Petrels can be seen on the special night trips run by Tom Jamieson. Arctic Tern, Arctic and Great Skuas, Black Guillemot and Puffin.
Contact: Tom Jamieson, RSBP Shetland Office, East House, Sumburgh Head Lighthouse, Virkie, Shetland, ZE3 9JN. 01950 460800.

SUMBURGH HEAD

RSPB (Shetland Office).
Location: HU 407 079. S tip of mainland Shetland.
Access: Open all year, but seabirds best May-mid Aug.
Facilities: View points.
Public transport: None.
Habitat: Sea cliffs.
Key birds: Breeding Puffin, Guillemot, Razorbill, Kittiwake, Shag, also minke and killer whales. Humpback whale seen occasionally.
Contact: RSPB Shetland Office, East House, Sumburgh Head Lighthouse, Virkie, Shetland, ZE3 9JN. 01950 460 800.

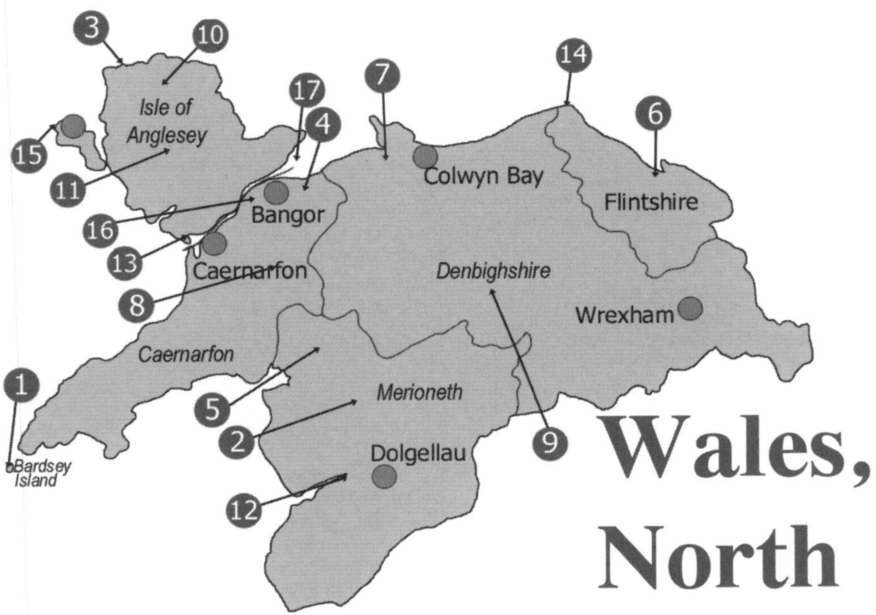

Wales, North

Key to sites:
1. Bardsey Bird Observatory
2. Cadair Idris
3. Cemlyn
4. Coedydd Aber
5. Coedydd Maentwrog
6. Connahs Quay
7. Conwy
8. Cwm Idwal
9. Gors Maen Llwyd
10. Llyn Alaw
11. Llyn Cefni
12. Mawddach Valley
13. Newborough Warren
14. Point Of Air
15. South Stack Cliffs
16. Spinnies
17. Traeth Lafan

BARDSEY BIRD OBSERVATORY

Bardsey Bird Observatory.
Location: SH 11 21. Private 444 acre island. One hour boat journey from Pwllheli (18 miles SW of Bangor).
Access: Mar-Nov. No dogs. Visitor accommodation in 150-year-old farmhouse (two single, two double, two four berth dorms). To stay at the Observatory contact Alicia Normand (tel 01626 773908, e-mail bob&lis@solfach.freeserve.co.uk) Day visitors by Bardsey Island Trust (tel Simon Glyn 01758 730326).
Facilities: Public toilets available for day visitors. Three hides, one on small bay, two seawatching.
Public transport: Trains from Birmingham to Pwllheli. Tel: 0345 484950. Arriva bus from Bangor to Pwllheli. Tel: 0870 6082608.
Habitat: Sea-birds cliffs viewable from boat only. Farm and scrubland, Spruce plantation, willow copses and gorse-covered hillside.
Key birds: *All Year*: Chough, Peregrine. *Spring/ summer*: Manx Shearwaters 7,500 pairs, other seabirds. Migrant warblers, chats, Redstart, thrushes. *Autumn*: Many rarities including Eye-browed Thrush, Lanceolated Warbler, Iberian Chiffchaff, Collared Flycatcher, etc.
Contact: Steven Stansfield, Cristen, Ynys Enlli (Bardsey), off Aberaron, via Pwllheli, Gwynedd, LL53 8DE. 07855 264151. www.bbfo.org.uk e-mail: steve@bbfo.freeserve.co.uk

CADAIR IDRIS

CCW (North West Area).
Location: SH 728 116. Three miles SW of Dolgellau. Take A487 SE to junction with B4405.
Access: Permit for enclosed woodland. Footpath to lake of Llyn Cau, a superb upland cwm.
Facilities: Leaflet.
Public transport: None.
Habitat: Cliffs, heath.
Key birds: *Summer*: Breeding Raven, Wheatear, Ring Ouzel, Pied Flycatcher.
Contact: CCW North West Area. Tel/fax 01766 780868; mobile 07771 925885.

CEMLYN

North Wales Wildlife Trust.
Location: SH 337 932. Ten miles from Holyhead, Anglesey, minor roads from A5025 at Tregele.
Access: Open all the time. Dogs on leads. Disabled viewing from adjacent road. During summer months walk on seaward side of ridge and follow signs.
Facilities: None.
Public transport: None.
Habitat: Brackish lagoon, shingle, ridge.
Key birds: *Summer*: Breeding terns. *Winter*: Waders/ducks (including Little Grebe, Goldeneye and Shoveler).
Contact: Chris Wynne, North Wales Wildlife Trust, 376 High Street, Bangor, Gwynedd, LL57 1YE. 01248 351541. e-mail: nwwt@cix.co.uk www.wildlifetrust.org.uk/northwales

COEDYDD ABER

CCW (North West Area).
Location: SH 660 710. E of Bangor.
Access: From car park at Bont Newydd, SE of Aber Falls. Permit required for places away from designated routes.
Facilities: Small visitor centre. Leaflets.
Public transport: None.
Habitat: Upland valley, deciduous woodland, river and spectacular waterfall.
Key birds: *All year:* Dipper, Grey Wagtail, Buzzard, Raven, woodland birds. *Summer:* Warblers and Ring Ouzel.
Contact: Duncan Brown, Tel/fax 01286 650547; mobile 0421 869263.

COEDYDD MAENTWROG

CCW (North West Area).
Location: SH 667 416. Smallest of three woodland blocks high above Vale of Festiniog.
Access: From car park on B4410 Maentwrog/ Rhyd road.
Facilities: Coed Llyn Mair Nature Trail.
Public transport: None.
Habitat: Oak woodland; views over lake.
Key birds: *Summer*: Redstart, Wood Warbler, Pied Flycatcher. *Winter*: Goldeneye, Pochard.
Contact: Doug Oliver, Tel/fax 01766 530461; mobile 07771 925888.

CONNAHS QUAY POWERGEN RESERVE

Deeside Naturalists' Society.
Location: SJ 275 715. NW of Chester. Take B5129 from Queensferry towards Flint, two miles.
Access: Advance permit required.
Facilities: Field studies centre, four hides.
Public transport: None.
Habitat: Saltmarsh, mudflats, grassland scrub, open water, wetland meadow.
Key birds: High water roosts of waders, inc. Black-tailed Godwit, Oystercatcher, Redshank, Spotted Redshank. Passage waders. *Winter*: Wildfowl (inc. Teal, Pintail, Goldeneye), Merlin, Peregrine.
Contact: R A Roberts, 38 Kelsterton Road, Connahs Quay, Flints, CH5 4BJ.

CONWY

RSBP (North Wales Office).
Location: SH 799 771. On E bank of Conwy Estuary. Access from A55 at exit signed to Conwy and Deganwy.
Access: Open daily (10am-5pm) or dusk if earlier. Closed for Christmas Day.
Facilities: Visitor centre, toilets including disabled. Two hides, all accessible to wheelchairs. Trails firm and level, though a little rough in places. Two further hides accessible to pedestrians.
Public transport: Train service to Llandudno Junction. Bus service to Tesco supermarket, Llandudno Junction. Tel: 08706 082 608.
Habitat: Open water, islands, reedbeds, grassland, estuary.

Key birds: *Spring/summer*: Breeding Reed and Sedge Warblers, Lapwing, Redshank, Skylark, Reed Bunting and rarities. *Autumn*: Passage waders and rarities. *Winter*: Kingfisher, Goldeneye, Red-breasted Merganser, wildfowl.
Contact: Ian Higginson, Conwy RSBP Nature Reserve, Llandudno Junction, Conwy, North Wales, LL33 9XZ. 01492 584091.

CWM IDWAL

CCW (North West Area).
Location: SH 648 603. Head for the Snowdonia National Park car park on A5 between Bethesda and Capel Curig.
Access: Do not enter experimental enclosures. Keep to marked paths.
Facilities: None.
Habitat: Mountain crags, river, shallow lake.
Key birds: *Summer:* Grey Heron, gulls, Dipper, Ring Ouzel, Wheatear, Raven, Common Sandpiper. *Winter:* Goldeneye, Pochard.
Contact: Hywel Roberts, Tel/fax 01248 362312; mobile 0468 918573.

GORS MAEN LLWYD

North Wales Wildlife Trust.
Location: SH 975 580. Follow A5 to Cerrigydrudion (seven miles S of site), then take B4501 and go past the Llyn Brennig Visitor Centre. Approx two miles beyond centre, turn right (still on B4501). First car park on right approx 300 yards after the cattle grid.
Access: Open all the time. Dogs on leads. Keep to the paths. Rare breeding birds on the heather so keep to paths.
Facilities: In second car park by lake shore there are toilets and short walk to bird hide. Paths are waymarked, but can be very wet and muddy in poor weather.
Public transport: None.
Habitat: Heathland. Heather and grass overlooking large lake.
Key birds: *Summer*: Red and Black Grouse, Hen Harrier, Merlin, Skylark, Curlew. *Winter*: Wildfowl on lake.
Contact: Neil Griffiths, Reserves Officer, NWWT, 376 High Street, Bangor, Gwynedd, LL57 1YE. 01248 351541.
e-mail: nwwt@cix.co.uk
www.wildlifetrust.org.uk/northwales

LLYN ALAW

Welsh Water/Hamdden Ltd.
Location: SH 390 865. Large lake five miles from Amlwch in northern part of Anglesey. Signposted from A55/A5/B5112/B5111/B5109.
Access: Open all year. No dogs to hides or sanctuary area but dogs allowed (maximum two per adult) other areas.
Facilities: Toilets (including disabled), two hides, two nature trails, information centre, car parks, network of mapped walks, picnic sites, information boards.
Public transport: Not to within a mile.
Habitat: Large area of standing water, shallow reedy bays, hedges, scrub, woodland, marsh, grassland.
Key birds: *Summer*: Lesser Whitethroat, Sedge and Grasshopper Warblers, Little and Great Crested Grebes, Tawny Owl, Barn Owl, Buzzard. *Winter*: Whooper Swan, Goldeneye, Hen Harrier, Short-eared Owl, Redwing, Fieldfare, Peregrine, Raven. *All year*: Bullfinch, Siskin, Redpoll, Goldfinch, Stonechat. *Passage waders*: Ruff, Spotted Redshank, Curlew Sandpiper, Green Sandpiper.
Contact: Jim Clark, Llyn Alaw, Llantrisant, Holyhead, LL65 4TW. 01407 730762.
e-mail: llynalaw@amserve.net

LLYN CEFNI

Welsh Water/Hamdden Ltd.
Location: SH 440 775. A reservoir located two miles NW of Llangefni, in central Anglesey. Follow B5111 or B5109 from the village.
Access: Open at all times. Dogs allowed except in sanctuary area.
Facilities: Toilets (near waterworks), picnic site, hide, information boards.
Public transport: Bus 32, 4 (45 Sat only, 52 Tue and Thu only). Tel 0870 6082608 for information.
Habitat: Large area of open water, reedy bays, coniferous woodland, carr, scrub.
Key birds: *Summer*: Sedge, Whitethroat and Grasshopper Warblers, Buzzard, Tawny Owl, Little Grebe, Gadwall, Shoveler. *Winter*: Waterfowl (Whooper Swan, Goldeneye), Crossbill, Redpoll, Siskin, Redwing. *All year*: Stonechat, Treecreeper, Song Thrush.
Contact: Jim Clark, (see Llyn Alaw above).

MAWDDACH VALLEY

RSPB (North Wales Office).
Location: SH 696 185 (information centre). Two miles W of Dolgellau on A493. Next to toll bridge at Penmaenpool.
Access: Reserve open at all times. Information centre open daily during Easter week and from Whitsun to first weekend of Sept (11am-5pm). Between Easter week and Whitsun, weekends only (noon-4pm).
Facilities: Toilets and car park at information centre.
Public transport: Buses run along A493. Morfa Mawddach railway halt four miles from information centre.
Habitat: Oak woodlands of Coed Garth Gell and willow/alder scrub at Arthog Bog SSSI.
Key birds: *Spring/summer*: Pied Flycatcher, Redstart and Tree Pipit. *Winter*: Raven, roving flocks of Siskin, Redpoll with Goosander and Goldeneye on the estuary.
Contact: The Warden, Mawddach Valley Nature Reserves, Abergwynant Lodge, Penmaenpool, Dolgellau, Gwynedd, LL40 1YF. 01341 422071. e-mail: mawddach@rspb.org.uk
www.rspb.org.uk

NEWBOROUGH WARREN

CCW (North West Area).
Location: SH 406 670/430 630. In SE corner of Anglesey. From Menai Bridge head SW on A4080 to Niwbwrch or Malltraeth.
Access: Permit required for places away from designated routes.
Facilities: None.
Public transport: None.
Habitat: Sandhills, estuaries, saltmarshes, dune grasslands, rocky headlands.
Key birds: Wildfowl and waders at Malltraeth Pool (visible from road), Braint and Cefni estuaries (licensed winter shoot on marked areas of Cefni estuary administered by CCW); waterfowl at Llyn Rhosddu (public hide).
Contact: W Sandison, CCW North West Area,Tel/fax 01248 716422; mobile 0468 918572.

POINT OF AIR

RSPB (North Wales Office).
Location: SJ 140 840. At mouth of the Dee Estuary. Three miles E of Prestatyn. Access from A548 coast road to Talacre village. Park at end of Station Road.
Access: Open at all times.
Facilities: Car park, public hide overlooking saltmarsh and mudflats, accessible to wheelchairs. No visitor centre. Toilets in Talacre village. Group bookings, guided walks and events.
Public transport: Bus – not known. Rail – Prestatyn.
Habitat: Intertidal mud/sand, saltmarsh, shingle.
Key birds: *Spring/summer*: Breeding Skylark, Meadow Pipit, Reed Bunting. *Late summer*: Pre-migratory roost of Sandwich and Common Terns. *Autumn*: Passage waders. *Winter*: Roosting waterfowl (eg Shelduck, Pintail), Oystercatcher, Curlew, Redshank, Merlin, Peregrine, Short-eared Owl. Rarities have occurred.
Contact: Gareth Stamp, Burton Point Farm, Station Road, Burton, Nr Neston, Cheshire, CH64 5SB. 0151 3367681.
e-mail: colin.wells@rspb.org.uk

SOUTH STACK CLIFFS

RSPB (North Wales Office).
Location: SH 205 823. W of Holyhead, Anglesey. Take A5 to Tyn-y-nant.
Access: No restrictions.
Facilities: Car parks. Information centre (Ellin's Tower) with windows overlooking main auk colony open daily (11am-5pm Easter-Sep), with live TV of the seabirds. Public footpaths.
Habitat: Sea cliffs, maritime heath.
Key birds: Peregrine, Chough, Fulmar, Puffin, Guillemot, Razorbill, Kittiwake, Shag, migrant warblers. Seabirds on passage.
Contact: Alastair Moralee, Plas Nico, South Stack, Holyhead, Anglesey, LL65 1YH. 01407 764973.

SPINNIES

North Wales Wildlife Trust.
Location: SH 613 721. Three miles from Bangor, Gwynedd. Use minor roads from A5122 or A55.
Access: Open all the time. Dogs on leads. Main path suitable for wheelchair users.
Facilities: Two hides, one suitable for wheelchair users.
Public transport: None.
Habitat: Woodland, tidal pool.
Key birds: Waders and passage species, woodland birds, Kingfisher, Little Egret.

Contact: Chris Wynne, North Wales Wildlife Trust, 376 High Street, Bangor, Gwynedd, LL57 1YE. 01248 351541. e-mail: nwwt@cix.co.uk www.wildlifetrust.org.uk/northwales

TRAETH LAFAN

Gwynedd Council.
Location: NE of Bangor, stretching to Penmaenmawr. 1) Minor road from old A55 near Tal-y-Bont (SH 610 710) to Aber Ogwen car park by coast (SH 614 723). 2) Also access from minor road from Aber village to Morfa Aber LNR (SH 646 731) 3) track to Morfa Madryn LNR (SH 667 743), and 4) Llanfairfechan promenade (SH 679 754).
Access: Open access from 1,2, 3 and 4.
Facilities: Public paths. 2) Car park and hide. 3) Hides. 4) Toilets and cafés.
Public transport: Call council for advice.
Habitat: Intertidal sands and mudflats, wetlands, streams. SPA and SSSI.
Key birds: Third most important area in Wales for wintering waders; of national importance for moulting Great Crested Grebe and Red-breasted Merganser; internationally important for Oystercatcher and Curlew; passage waders; winter concentrations of Goldeneye and Greenshank, and of regional significance for wintering populations of Black-throated, Red-throated & Great Northern Divers and Black-necked & Slavonian Grebes.
Contact: Planning and Economic, Development Dept, Gwynedd Council, Council Offices, Caernarfon, LL55 1SH. 01286 679381; fax 01286 673324;
e-mail ruralservices@gwynedd.gov.uk.

Wales, South

ABERTHAW SALTMARSH

Glamorgan Wildlife Trust.
Location: ST045657. E of Aberthaw Power Station, W of Barry.
Access: Open access. Park in lay-by on main road.
Facilities: None.
Public transport: Call Trust for advice.
Habitat: Lias limestone cliffs, saltmarsh (very mobile), pebble beach.
Key birds: *Spring*: Whimbrel. *Autumn*: Migrant waders and passerines. *Winter*: Peregrine in winter. Good seawatching.
Contact: Trust HQ, 01656 724100.

CWM CLYDACH

RSBP (South Wales Office).
Location: SN 584 026. Three miles N of J45 on M4, through the village of Clydach on B4291.
Access: Open at all times along public footpaths and waymarked trails.
Facilities: Nature trails, car park, information boards.
Public transport: Buses from Swansea stop at reserve entrance. Nearest railway station is eight miles away in Swansea.
Habitat: Oak woodland on steep slopes lining the banks of the fast-flowing Lower Clydach River.
Key birds: *Spring/summer*: Nesting Buzzard, Sparrowhawk and Raven. Nestboxes are used by Pied Flycatcher, Redstart and tits while Wood Warbler, all three species of woodpecker, Nuthatch, Treecreeper and Tawny Owl also nest. Dipper and Grey Wagtail frequent the river.
Contact: Martin Humphreys,
2 Tyn y Berllan, Craig Cefn Par, Clydach, Swansea, SA6 5TL. 01792 842927.

CWM COL-HUW

Glamorgan Wildlife Trust.
Location: SS 957 674. On site of 2700-year-old Iron Age fort, overlooking Bristol Channel. From Bridgend take B4265 S to Llanwit Major. Follow beach road from village.
Access: Park in seafront car park. Climb steps. Open all year.
Facilities: All year toilets and café. Information boards.
Public transport: None.
Habitat: Unimproved grassland, woodland, scrub and Jurassic blue lias cliff.
Key birds: Cliff-nesting House Martin colony, breeding Fulmar, Grasshopper Warbler. Large autumn passerine passage. Peregrine.
Seawatching vantage point.
Contact: Trust HQ, 01656 724100.

NATURE RESERVES - WALES

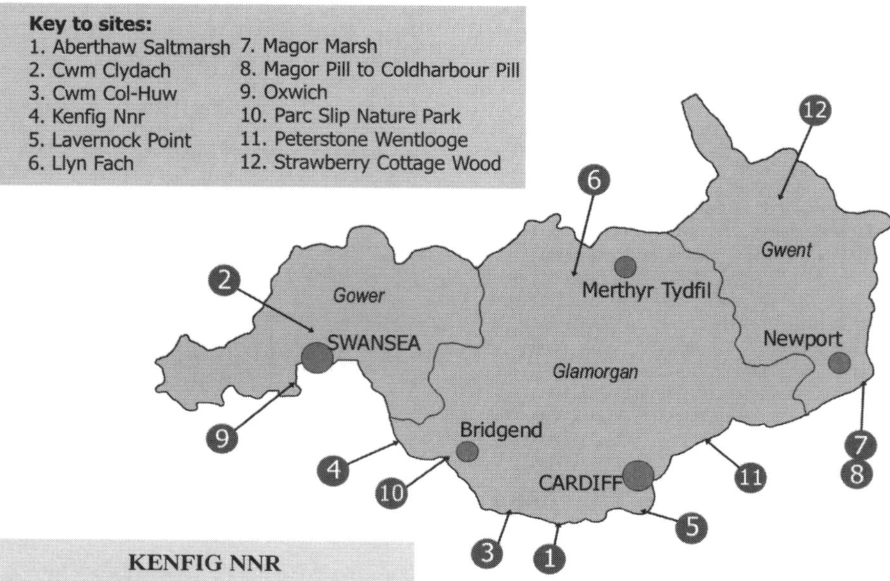

KENFIG NNR

Bridgend County Borough Council.
Location: SS 802 811. Seven miles W of Bridgend. From J37 on M4, drive towards Porthcawl, then North Cornelly, then follow signs.
Access: Open at all times.
Facilities: Toilets, hides, free car parking and nature trail for visually impaired. Visitor centre open weekends and holidays (10am-4.30pm), weekdays (2pm-4.30pm).
Public transport: None.
Habitat: Sand dunes, dune slacks, Kenfig Pool, Sker Beach.
Key birds: *Summer*: Warblers including Cetti's, Grasshopper, Sedge, Reed, Willow and Whitethroat. One of the UK's best sites for orchids. *Winter*: Wildfowl, Water Rail, Bittern, grebes.
Contact: David Carrington, Ton Kenfig, Bridgend, CF33 4PT. 01656 743386.
e-mail: carridg@bridgend.gov.uk

LAVERNOCK POINT

Glamorgan Wildlife Trust.
Location: ST 182 680. Public footpaths S of B4267 between Barry & Penarth.
Access: No restrictions.
Facilities: None.
Habitat: Cliff top, unimproved grassland, dense hawthorn, scrub.
Key birds: Seawatching in late summer; Glamorgan's best migration hotspot in autumn.
Contact: Trust HQ, 01656 724100.

LLYN FACH

Glamorgan Wildlife Trust.
Location: SN 905 038. From Merthyr Tydfil take A465 W to Hirwaun, then head S on A4061 to car park 1.8 miles away.
Access: Open dawn to dusk.
Facilities: None.
Public transport: None.
Habitat: Lake, bog, cliff and scree, surrounded by plantations.
Key birds: Nesting Raven, Ring Ouzel. Also Buzzard, Sparrowhawk.
Contact: Trust HQ, 01656 724100.

MAGOR MARSH

Gwent Wildlife Trust.
Location: ST 425 867. Leave M4 at exit 23, turning R onto B4245. S of Magor village, look for gate on Whitewall Common on E side of

reserve.
Access: Keep to path. Parties give advance notice.
Facilities: Hide. Information centre.
Public transport: None.
Habitat: Last remnant of fenland on Gwent levels, including marsh, reeds, pond, willow and alders, scrub.
Key birds: Waterfowl (inc. breeding Garganey); reedbed warblers; Water Rail, Kingfisher. *Winter:* Teal and raptors.
Contact: Derek Upton, 14 Westfield, Caldicot, Newport, Gwent, NP6 4HE. 01291 420137.

MAGOR PILL TO COLDHARBOUR PILL

Gwent Wildlife Trust.
Location: ST 437 847. Overlooks River Severn, E of Newport.
Access: Access from Magor Pill Farm track down to sea wall.
Facilities: None.
Public transport: None.
Habitat: Foreshore, intertidal mudflats.
Key birds: Passage and winter waders.
Contact: Derek Upton, 14 Westfield, Caldicot, Newport, Gwent, NP6 4HE. 01291 420137.

OXWICH

CCW (Swansea Office).
Location: SS 872 773. 12 miles from Swansea, off A4118.
Access: NNR open at all times. No permit required for access to foreshore. Dunes, woodlands and facilities.
Facilities: Private car park, summer only. Toilets summer only. Bird hide, marsh boardwalk and marsh lookout. No visitor centre, no facilities for disabled visitors.
Public transport: Bus service Swansea/Oxwich. First Cymru, tel 01792 580580.
Habitat: Freshwater marsh, saltmarsh, foreshore, dunes, woodlands.
Key birds: *Summer*: Breeding Reed, Sedge and Cetti's Warblers, Treecreeper, Nuthatch, woodpeckers. *Winter*: Wildfowl.
Contact: Countryside Council for Wales, RVB House, Llys Felin Newydd, Phoenix Way, Swansea, SA7 9FG. 01792 763500.

PETERSTONE WENTLOOGE

Gwent Wildlife Trust.
Location: ST 269 800. Reserve over looks River Severn, between Newport and Cardiff.
Access: Public footpaths to sea wall, use B4239.
Facilities: None.
Public transport: None.
Habitat: Foreshore, inter-tidal mudflats, grazing.
Key birds: Passage waders and winter wildfowl.
Contact: Trust HQ, 01600 715501.

PARC SLIP NATURE PARK

Glamorgan Wildlife Trust.
Location: SS 880 840. Tondu, half mile W of Aberkenfig. From Bridgend take A4063 N, turning L onto B4281 after passing M4. Reserve is signposted from this road.
Access: Open dawn to dusk.
Facilities: Three hides, nature trail, interpretation centre.
Public transport: None.
Habitat: Restored opencast mining site, wader scrape, lagoons.
Key birds: *Summer*: Breeding Tufted Duck, Lapwing, Skylark. Migrant waders (inc. Little Ringed Plover, Green Sandpiper), Little Gull. Kingfisher, Green Woodpecker. Badgers on site.
Contact: Trust HQ, 01656 724100.

STRAWBERRY COTTAGE WOOD

Gwent Wildlife Trust.
Location: SO 315 214. N of Abergavenny. Leave A465 at Llanvihangel Crucorney on minor road to Llanthony, about 1.25 miles.
Access: Open at all times. Keep to waymarked trail.
Facilities: None.
Public transport: None.
Habitat: Mixed woodland on valley side.
Key birds: Buzzard, Redstart, Pied Flycatcher, Wood Warbler.
Contact: Jerry Lewis,
Y Bwthyn Gwyn, Coldbrook, Abergavenny, Monmouthshire, NP7 9TD. 01873 855091.

Wales, East

Key to sites:
1. Brechfa Pool
2. Bwlchcoediog Nature Reserve
3. Dolydd Hafren
4. Elan Valley
5. Gilfach
6. Glaslyn, Plynlimon
7. Llyn Coed Y Dinas
8. Llyn Mawr
9. Pwll-Y-Wrach
10. Pwll Penarth
11. Roundton Hill
12. Talybont Reservoir
13. Vyrnwy (Lake)

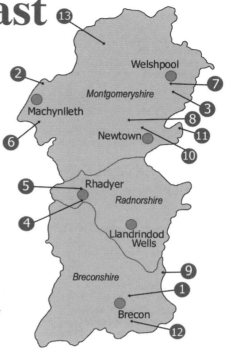

BRECHFA POOL

Brecknock Wildlife Trust.
Location: SO 118 377. Travelling NE from Brecon look for lane off A470, 1.5 miles SW of Llyswen; on Brechfa Common, pool is on right after cattle grid.
Access: Open dawn to dusk.
Facilities: None.
Public transport: None.
Habitat: Marshy grassland, large shallow pool.
Key birds: Teal, Wigeon, Bewick's Swan, Redshank, Lapwing, Dunlin
Contact: Trust HQ, 1874625708.

BWLCHCOEDIOG

W K and Mrs J Evans.
Location: SH 878 149. From Machynlleth take A489 NE for 14 miles. Half mile east of Mallwyd, turn left into Cwm Cewydd, then 1.25 miles up the valley. Park at Bwlchcoediog House.
Access: Open all year round. No dogs, in fenced areas, please keep to paths.
Facilities: None.
Public transport: None.
Habitat: Farmland, woodland, streams, two ponds, lake.
Key birds: *Summer:* Breeding Tree Pipit, Redstart, Garden and Wood Warblers, Pied and Spotted Flycatchers. *Winter:* Woodcock, Brambling, Raven, Buzzard, Sparrowhawk. *All Year*: Siskin, occasional Peregrine, Red Kite, Dipper.
Contact: W K and Mrs J Evans, Bwlchcoediog Isaf, Cwm Cewydd, Mallwyd, Machynlleth, Powys, SY20 9EE. 01650 531243.

DOLYDD HAFREN

Montgomeryshire Wildlife Trust.
Location: SJ 208 005. W of B4388. Go through Forden village S of Welshpool and on about 1.5 miles. Turn right at sharp left bend at Gaer Farm and down farm track to car park at the other end.
Access: Open at all times – dogs to be kept on lead at all times.
Facilities: Two bird hides.
Public transport: None.
Habitat: Riverside flood meadow – bare shingle, permanent grassland, ox-bow lakes and new pools.
Key birds: Goosander, Redshank, Lapwing, Snipe, Oystercatcher, Little Ringed Plover.

Winter: Curlew.
Contact: Al Parrot, c/o Montgomeryshire Wildlife Trust,
Collot House, 20 Severn Street, Welshpool, Powys, SY21 7AD. 01938 555654.
e-mail: montwt@cixcompulink.co.uk
www.wildlifetrust.org.uk/montwt

ELAN VALLEY

Dwr Cymm/Welsh Water & Elan Valley Trust.
Location: SN 928 646 (visitor centre). Three miles SW of Rhayader, off B4518.
Access: Mostly open access.
Facilities: Visitor centre and toilets (open mid Mar-end Oct), nature trails all year and hide at SN 905 617.
Public transport: Post bus from Rhayader and Llandrindod Wells.
Habitat: Seventy square miles of moorland, woodland, river and reservoir.
Key birds: *Spring/summer*: Birds of prey, upland birds including Golden Plover and Dunlin. Woodland birds include Redstart and Pied Flycatcher.
Contact: Pete Jennings,
Rangers Office, Elan Valley Visitor Centre, Rhayader, Powys, LD6 5HP. 01597 810880.
e-mail: pete@elanvalley.org.uk
www.elanvalley.org.uk

GILFACH

Radnorshire Wildlife Trust.
Location: SN 952 714. Two miles NW from Rhayader/Rhaeadr-Gwy. Take minor road to St Harmon from A470 at Marteg Bridge.
Access: Centre Easter-Sept 31 (10am-5pm). Apr (every day). May/Jun (Fri-Mon). Jul/Aug (every day). Sept (Fri-Mon). Reserve open every day all year. Dogs on leads only. Disabled access and trail.
Facilities: Visitor centre – open as above. Way-marked trails.
Habitat: Upland hill farm, river, oak woods, meadows, hill-land.
Key birds: *Spring/summer*: Pied Flycatcher, Redstart. *All year*: Dipper, Red Kite.
Contact: Tim Thompson, Gilfach, St Harmon, Rhaeadr-Gwy, Powys, CD6 5LF. 01597 870 301.
e-mail: tim@ratgilfoelfisnet.co.uk http//westwales.co.uk/gilfach.htm

GLASLYN, PLYNLIMON

Montgomeryshire Wildlife Trust.
Location: SN 826 941. Nine miles SE of Machynlleth. Off minor road between the B4518 near Staylittle and the A489 at Machynlleth. Go down the track for about a mile.
Access: Open at all times – dogs on a lead at all times.
Facilities: Footpath.
Public transport: None.
Habitat: Heather moorland and upland lake.
Key birds: Red Grouse, Short-eared Owl, Meadow Pipit, Skylark, Wheatear and Ring Ouzel, Red Kite, Merlin, Peregrine. Goldeneye – occasional. *Winter*: Greenland White-fronted Goose.
Contact: Montgomeryshire Wildlife Trust,
Collot House, 20 Severn Street, Welshpool, Powys, SY21 7AD. 01938 555654.
e-mail: montwt@cix.compulink.co.uk
www.wildlifetrust.org.uk/montwt

LLYN COED Y DINAS

Montgomeryshire Wildlife Trust.
Location: SJ 223 052. On A490, one mile S of Welshpool, just before roundabout at Welshpool by-pass (A483).
Access: Open at all times (subject to Little Ringed Plovers nesting in car park). Suitable for disabled access.
Facilities: Wide and footpaths.
Public transport: No 75 bus running from Shrewsbury/Welshpool/Llanidloes. Bus stop at reserve. Arriva Bus Company, tel 01970 617951. Approx two mile walk through town from Welshpool train station.
Habitat: Eight ha/20 acre site. Lake and haymeadow.
Key birds: *Summer*: Canada Goose, Sand Martin, Little Ringed Plover, Mute Swan, Mallard, Tufted Duck, Wigeon. *Winter*: Whooper Swan.
Contact: Glyn Roberts, Montgomeryshire Wildlife Trust,
Collot House, 20 Severn Street, Welshpool, Powys, SY21 7AD. 01938 555654.
e-mail: montwt@cix.compulink.co.uk
www.wildlifetrust.org.uk/montwt

LLYN MAWR

Montgomeryshire Wildlife Trust.
Location: SO 009 971. From Newtown, head

NW on A470 and then take minor 'no through' road N of Clatter. Stay close to shore.
Access: Permit required.
Facilities: None.
Public transport: None.
Habitat: Upland lake, wetland, scrub.
Key birds: *Summer*: Breeding Great Crested Grebe, Black-headed Gull, Snipe, Curlew, Whinchat. *Winter*: occasional Goldeneye, Goosander, Whooper Swan.
Contact: Trust HQ, 01938 555654.

PWLL-Y-WRACH

Brecknock Wildlife Trust.
Location: SO 165 327. Between Hay-on-Wye and Brecon at foot of Black Mountains. Half mile SE of Talgarth, access is from the minor road.
Access: Limited car parking. In Talgarth use Pentent Road, go over river and follow lane 250 yards, past hospital.
Facilities: Keep to public footpaths (inc. one for disabled).
Public transport: None.
Habitat: Steep valley woodland, stream and waterfall.
Key birds: Dipper, Grey Wagtail, woodland species (inc. Pied Flycatcher, Wood Warbler). Dormouse colony.
Contact: Trust HQ, 01874 625708.

PWLL PENARTH

Montgomeryshire Wildlife Trust.
Location: SO 137 926. Take B4568 from Newtown to Llanllwchaiarn, turn down by the church and follow lane for a mile to sewage works gates.
Access: Open at all times. Disabled access via Severn Trent sewage works between 9am-4pm, Mon-Fri only. Dogs to be kept on lead at all times.
Facilities: Two hides.
Public transport: None.
Habitat: Lake, Sand Martin bank, arable crops.
Key birds: *Late spring/summer*: Sand Martin, Lapwing, Skylark, Grey Wagtail. *Winter*: buntings, finches. *All year*: Kingfisher, Mallard, Coot, Canada Goose, Ruddy Duck.
Contact: Mike Green, Montgomeryshire Wildlife Trust, Collot House, 20 Severn Street, Welshpool, Powys, SY21 7AD. 01938 555654. e-mail: montwt@cix.compulink.co.uk
www.wildlifetrust.org.uk/montwt

ROUNDTON HILL

Montgomeryshire Wildlife Trust.
Location: SO 293 947. SE of Montgomery. From Churchstoke on A489, take minor road to Old Churchstoke, R at phone box, then first R.
Access: Open access. Tracks rough in places.
Facilities: Car park. Waymarked trails.
Habitat: Ancient hill grassland, woodland, streamside wet flushes, scree, rock outcrops.
Key birds: Buzzard, Raven, Wheatear, all three woodpeckers, Tawny Owl, Redstart, Linnet, Goldfinch.
Contact: Trust HQ, 01938 555654.

TALYBONT RESERVOIR

Brecknock Wildlife Trust.
Location: SO 100 190. Take minor road off B4558 S of Talybont, SE of Brecon.
Access: No access to reservoir area, view from road.
Facilities: Displays at the Glyn Collwm information centre at Aber, between the reservoir and Talybont.
Public transport: None.
Habitat: Reservoir, woodland.
Key birds: *Winter*: Wildfowl (inc. Goldeneye, Goosander, Whooper Swan), Redpoll, Siskin. Migrant waders.
Contact: Trust HQ, 01874 625708.

VYRNWY (LAKE)

RSPB (North Wales Office).
Location: SJ 020 193. Located WSW of Oswestry. Nearest village is Llanfyllin on A490. Take B4393 to lake.
Access: Reserve open all year. Visitor centre open Apr-Dec (10.30am-4.30pm), Dec-Apr weekends only (10.30am-4.30pm).
Facilities: Toilets, visitor centre, hides, nature trails, coffee shop, RSPB shop, craft workshops.
Public transport: Train and bus Welshpool (25 miles away).
Habitat: Heather moorland, woodland, meadows, rocky streams and large reservoir.
Key birds: Dipper, Kingfisher, Pied Flycatcher, Wood Warbler, Redstart, Peregrine and Buzzard.
Contact: Jo Morris, Centre Manager, RSPB Lake Vyrnwy Reserve, Bryn Awel, Llanwddyn, Oswestry, Salop, SY10 0LZ. 01691 870278. e-mail: lake.vyrnwy@rspb.org.uk

Wales, West

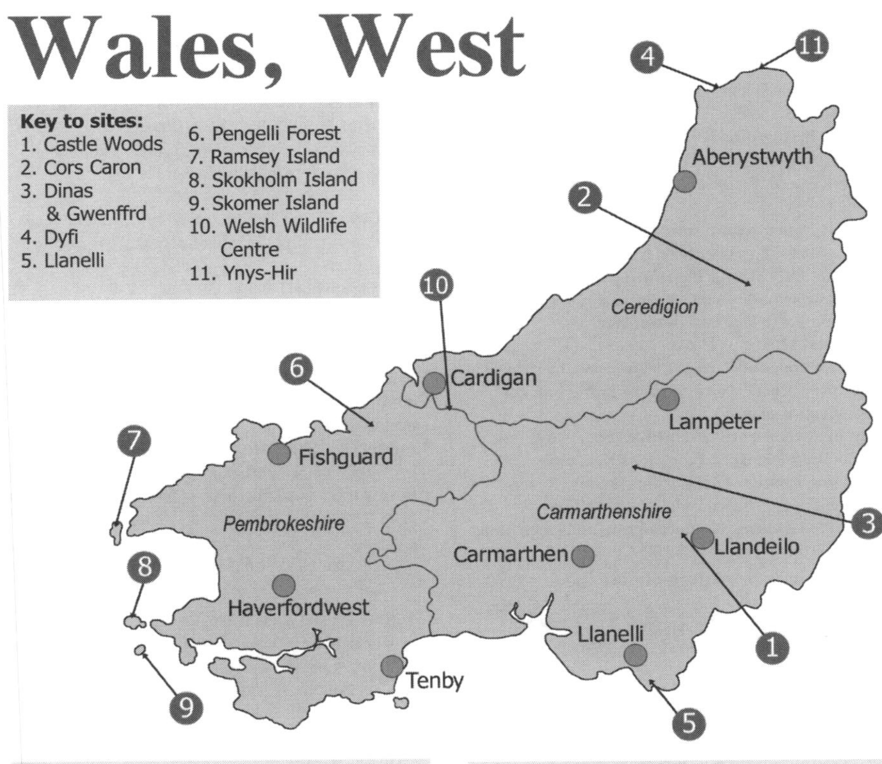

CASTLE WOODS

Wildlife Trust: West Wales.
Location: SN 615 217. About 60 acres of woodland overlooking River Tywi, W of Llandeilo town centre.
Access: Open all year by footpath from Tywi Bridge, Llandeilo (SN 627 221).
Facilities: Call for advice.
Public transport: None.
Habitat: Old mixed deciduous woodlands.
Key birds: All three woodpeckers, Buzzard, Raven, Sparrowhawk. *Summer:* Pied and Spotted Flycatchers, Redstart, Wood Warbler. *Winter:* On water meadows below, look for Teal, Wigeon, Goosander, Shoveler, Tufted Duck and Pochard.
Contact: Steve Lucas, Area Officer,
35 Maesquarre Road, Betws, Ammanford, Carmarthenshire, SA18 2LF. 01269 594293.

CORS CARON

CCW (West Wales Area).
Location: SN 697 632 (car park). Reached from B4343 N of Tregaron.
Access: Old railway walk open all year. Access to rest of the reserve by permit. Dogs on lead.
Facilities: Observation tower on railway walk.
Public transport: None.
Habitat: Raised bog, river, fen, wet grassland, willow woodland, reedbed.
Key birds: *Summer*: Lapwing, Redshank, Curlew, Red Kite, Grasshopper Warbler, Whinchat. *Winter:* Teal, Wigeon, Whooper Swan, Hen Harrier, Red Kite.
Contact: Paul Culyer,
CCW, Neuaddlas, Tregaron, Ceredigion, 01974 298480.
e-mail: p.culyer@ccw.gov.uk
www.ccw.gov.uk

DINAS & GWENFFRWD

RSPB (South Wales Office).
Location: SN 788 472. Dinas car park off B road to Llyn Brianne Reservoir. Gwenffrwd (SN 749 460) off minor road to Rhandirmwyn from Llandovery or Pumpsaint, approx ten miles N of Llandovery.
Access: Public nature trail at Dinas open at all times. Access to Gwenfrwd trails for RSPB members only (Good Fri to Aug). Obtain details at Dinas car park. Some steep and rugged paths requiring particular care when wet.
Facilities: Office at Dinas.
Public transport: Nearest station at Llandovery.
Habitat: Hillside oakwoods, streams, bracken slopes and moorland.
Key birds: Buzzard, Pied Flycatcher, Redstart, Wood Warbler, Tree Pipit, Red Kite and Peregrine in area. Dipper, Goosander, Raven.
Contact: c/o RSPB (South Wales Office), Sutherland House, Castlebridge, Cowbridge Road East, Cardiff, CF11 9AB. 02920 353000.B. 02920 353000. www.rspb.org.uk

DYFI

CCW (West Wales Area).
Location: SN 610 942. Large estuary area W of Machynlleth. Public footpaths off A493 E of Aberdyfi, and off B4353 (S of river); minor road from B4353 at Ynyslas to dunes and parking area.
Access: Ynyslas dunes and the estuary have unrestricted access. No access to Cors Fochno (raised bog) for casual birdwatching; permit required for study and research purposes. Good views over the bog and Aberleri marshes from W bank of Afon Leri.
Facilities: Public hide overlooking marshes beside footpath at SN 611 911.
Public transport: None.
Habitat: Sandflats, mudflats, saltmarsh, creeks, dunes, raised bog, grazing marsh.
Key birds: *Winter:* Greenland White-fronted Goose, wildfowl, waders and raptors. *Summer*: Breeding wildfowl and waders (inc. Teal, Shoveler, Merganser, Lapwing, Curlew, Redshank).
Contact: Mike Bailey,
CCW Warden, Plas Gogerddan, Aberystwyth, Ceredigion, SY23 3EE. 01970 821100.

LLANELLI

The Wildfowl & Wetlands Trust.
Location: SS 533 984. Leave M4 at junction 47. Signposted from A484, E of Llanelli.
Access: Open daily (9.30am-5.30am summer, earlier in winter) except Christmas Eve and Christmas Day.
Facilities: Visitor centre, restaurant, hides, education facilities, disabled access. Overlooks Burry Inlet.
Public transport: None.
Habitat: Inter-tidal mudflats, reedbeds, pools, marsh, waterfowl collection.
Key birds: Large flocks of Curlew, Oystercatcher, Redshank on saltmarsh. *Winter*: Pintail, Wigeon, Teal. Also Little Egret, Short-eared Owl, Peregrine.
Contact: Dr Geoff Proffitt, Centre Manager, The Wildfowl & Wetlands Trust, Penclacwydd, Llwynhendy, Llanelli, SA14 9SH. 01554 741087.

PENGELLI FOREST

Wildlife Trust (West Wales).
Location: SN 123 396. Between Fishguard and Cardigan. Take minor road off A487 from Felindre Farchog/Eglwyswrw.
Access: Open all year. No permit, but keep to trails.
Facilities: Trails.
Public transport: None.
Habitat: 40 acre sessile oak wood, 120 acre mixed oak/ash wood (inc. scrub, rides).
Key birds: *Summer:* Pied Flycatcher, Redstart, Wood Warbler. *All year:* Buzzard, Raven, woodpeckers.
Contact: Lin Gander,
Welsh Wildlife Centre, Cilgerran, Cardigan, SA43 2TB. 01269 621600.

RAMSEY ISLAND

RSBP (South Wales Office).
Location: SM 706237. One mile offshore St Justinians, slipway, two miles W of St Davids.
Access: Open every day, except Fri, Apr 1-Oct 31.
Facilities: Toilets, small RSBP shop, tuck shop, hot drinks and snacks, self-guiding trail.
Public transport: Trains to Haverfordwest

Station. Hourly buses to St Davids, taxi to St Justinians.
Habitat: Acid grassland, maritime heath, seacliffs.
Key birds: *Spring/summer*: Cliff-nesting auks (Guillemot, Razorbill). Kittiwake, Lesser, Great Black-backed, Herring Gulls, Shag, Peregrine, Raven, Chough, Lapwing, Wheatear, Stonechat.
Contact: Ian Bullock, Tegfan, Caerbwdi, St Davids, Pembs, SA62 6QP. 07836 535733. www.rspb.org.uk

SKOKHOLM ISLAND

Wildlife Trust (West Wales).
Location: SM 738 037. Island lying S of Skomer.
Access: Day visits, Mon only Jun-Aug from Martins Haven. Weekly accomm. Apr-Sep, tel 01437 765462 for details and booking.
Facilities: Call for details.
Public transport: None.
Habitat: Cliffs, bays and inlets.
Key birds: *Summer*: Large colonies of Razorbill, Puffin, Guillemot, Manx Shearwater, Storm Petrel, Lesser Black-backed Gull. Migrants inc. rare species.
Contact: Trust HQ, 01437 765462.

SKOMER ISLAND

Wildlife Trust (West Wales).
Location: SM 725 095. Fifteen miles from Haverfordwest. Take B4327 turn-off for Marloes, embarkation point at Martin's Haven, two miles past village.
Access: Apr 1-Oct 31. Boats sail at 10am, 11am and noon every day except Mon (Bank Holidays excluded). Closed four days beginning of Jun for seabird counts. Not suitable for infirm (steep landing steps and rough ground).
Facilities: Information centre, toilets, two hides, wardens, booklets, guides, nature trails.
Public transport: None.
Habitat: Maritime cliff, bracken, bluebells and red campion, heathland, freshwater ponds.
Key birds: Largest colony of Manx Shearwater in the world (overnight). Puffin, Guillemot, Razorbill (Apr-end Jul). Kittiwake (until end Aug), Fulmar (absent Oct), Short-eared Owl (during day Jun and Jul), Chough, Peregrine, Buzzard (all year), migrants.
Contact: Juan Brown, Skomer Island, Marloes, Pembs, SA63 2BJ. 07971 114302. e-mail: skomer@wtww.co.uk

WELSH WILDLIFE CENTRE

Wildlife Trust West Wales.
Location: SN 188 451. Two miles SE of Cardigan. River Teifi is N boundary. Sign posted from Cardigan to Fishguard Road.
Access: Open 10am-5pm all year. Free parking for WTWW members, £5 non-members. Dogs welcome – on a lead. Disabled access to visitor centre, paths, four hides.
Facilities: Visitor centre, restaurant, network of paths and seven hides.
Public transport: Train station, Haverfordwest (23 miles). Bus station in Cardigan. Access on foot from Cardigan centre, ten mins.
Habitat: Wetlands, marsh, swamp, reedbed, open water, creek (tidal), river, saltmarsh, woodland.
Key birds: Cetti's Warbler, Kingfisher, Water Rail, Greater Spotted Woodpecker, Dipper, gulls, Marsh Harrier, Sand Martin, Hobby, Redstart, occasional Bittern.
Contact: Chris Lawrence, Welsh Wildlife Centre, Cillgerran, Pembrokeshire, SA43 2TB. 01239 621212. e-mail: chris@wtww.co.uk www.wildlife@wtww.co.uk

YNYS-HIR

RSPB (CYMRU).
Location: SN 68 29 63. Off A487 Aberystwyth - Machynlleth road in Eglwys-fach village. Six miles SW of Machynlleth.
Access: Open every day (9am-9pm or dusk if earlier). Visitor centre open daily Apr-Oct (10am-5pm), weekends only Nov-Mar (10am-4pm).
Facilities: Visitor centre and toilets, both with disabled access. Numerous trails and seven hides.
Public transport: Bus service to Eglwys-fach from either Machynlleth or Aberystwyth, tel. 01970 617951. Rail service to Machynlleth.
Habitat: Estuary, freshwater pools, woodland and wet grassland.
Key birds: *Winter*: Greenland White-fronted Goose, Wigeon, Hen Harrier, Barnacle Goose. *Spring/summer*: Wood Warbler, Redstart, Pied Flycatcher. *All year*: Peregrine, Red Kite, Buzzard, Goshawk.
Contact: Dick Squires, Ynys-Hir RSPB Nature Reserve, Eglwys-fach, Machynlleth, Powys, SY20 8TA. 01654 781265.
e-mail: dick.squires@rspb.org.uk

Isle of Man

CALF OF MAN BIRD OBSERVATORY

Administration Department, Manx National Heritage.
Location: SC 15 65. Small island off the SW tip of the Isle of Man. Local boat from Port Erin or Port St Mary.
Access: Apr-Oct. No dogs, fires or camping.
Facilities: Accommodation for eight people in three bedrooms at Observatory Apr-Oct. Bookings: Administration Department (address below).
Public transport: Local boat from Port Erin or Port St Mary.
Habitat: Heather/bracken moor and cliffs.
Key birds: *All year*: Hen Harrier, Peregrine and Chough. *Summer*: Breeding seabirds (nine species including Storm Petrel, Manx Shearwater). Excellent spring and autumn migration, seabird migration best in autumn.
Contact: Tim Bagworth, (Warden), Manx National Heritage, Manx Museum, Douglas, Isle of Man, IM1 3LY.

CLOSE SARTFIELD

Manx Wildlife Trust.
Location: SC 361 956. From Ramsey drive W on A3. Turn on to B9, take third right and follow this road for nearly a mile. Reserve entrance is on right.
Access: Open all year round. No dogs. Path and boardwalk suitable for wheelchairs from car park through wildflower meadow and willow scrub to hide.
Facilities: Car park, hide, reserve leaflet (50p, available from office) outlines circular walk.
Public transport: None.
Habitat: Wildflower-rich hay meadow, marshy grassland, willow scrub/developing birch woodland, bog.
Key birds: *Winter*: Large roost of Hen Harrier. *Summer*: Corncrake (breeding 1999 and 2000 after 11 years' absence), Curlew, warblers.
Contact: Tricia Sayle, Reserves Officer, Manx Wildlife Trust, Tynwald Mills, St John's, Isle of Man, IM4 3AE. 01624 801985.
e-mail: tricia@manxwt.cix.co.uk

COOILDARRY

Manx Wildlife Trust.
Location: SC 319 896. Entrance approximately one mile S of Kirk Michael village, left of A3.
Access: Open all year round. Not suitable for disabled. Dogs to be kept on a lead.
Facilities: Well-maintained paths throughout. Leaflet (50p) available from office. Nearest toilets in Kirk Michael village.
Public transport: Buses run regularly past the lower entrance off A4.
Habitat: Woodland.
Key birds: Raven, Sparrowhawk.
Contact: Tricia Sayle, Reserves Officer, Manx Wildlife Trust HQ.
e-mail: tricia@manxwt.cix.co.uk

CRONK Y BING

Manx Wildlife Trust.
Location: NX 381 017. Take A10 coast road N from Jurby. Approx two miles along there is a sharp right hand turn over a bridge. Before the bridge there is a track to the left. A parking area is available at the end of the track.
Access: Open all year round. Dogs to be kept on a lead. Not suitable for the disabled.
Facilities: None.
Public transport: None.
Habitat: Open dune and dune grassland.
Key birds: *Summer*: Terns. *Winter*: Divers, grebes, skuas, gulls.
Contact: Tricia Sayle, Reserves Officer, Manx Wildlife Trust, (see above)

DALBY MOUNTAIN

Manx Wildlife Trust.
Location: SC 233769. Approx two miles S of Dalby village, lying adjacent to the A27.
Access: Open all year round. Dogs to be kept on a lead. Not suitable for wheelchairs.
Facilities: None.
Public transport: None.
Habitat: Heathland.
Key birds: Hen Harrier, Red Grouse.
Contact: Tricia Sayle, Reserves Officer, Manx Wildlife Trust, (see above).

Channel Islands

COLIN McCATHIE RESERVE (VALE POND)

La Société Guernesiaise.
Location: On Guernsey. Perry's Island Guide (page 6 B5).
Access: Open at all times.
Facilities: Hide on road to Vale Church must be used.
Public transport: Hourly bus service 7/7A (island circular)., tel: 01481 720210.
Habitat: Brackish tidal pond, reed fringes.
Key birds: Passage waders. *Summer*: Breeding Reed Warbler, Moorhen, Coot. *Winter*: Wildfowl, Water Rail, Little Egret, Snipe, Kingfisher.
Contact: Vic Froome (Section Secretary), La Cloture, Courtil de Bas Lane, St Sampson's, Guernsey, GY2 4XJ. 01481 254841.

LA CLAIRE MARE

La Société Guernesiaise.
Location: On Guernsey. Perry's Island Guide (page 12 C5).
Access: Open at all times.
Facilities: Hide down concrete track off the Rue de la Rocque Road then boardwalk to second hide.
Public transport: Hourly bus service 7/7A (island circular), tel: 01481 720210.
Habitat: Reedbeds, pasture, willow thickets, scrape.
Key birds: Passage waders and passerines. *Summer*: Breeding Reed Warbler, Moorhen, Coot, Kestrel. *Winter*: Wildfowl, Water Rail, Snipe, Kingfisher.
Contact: Vic Froome, (see above).

PLEINMONT

La Société Guernesiaise.
Location: On Guernsey. Perry's Island Guide Page 32 B3.
Access: Open at all times.
Facilities: Public footpath around reserve.
Public transport: Hourly bus service 7/7A (island circular) 0.5 miles from Imperial Hotel, tel 01481 720210.
Habitat: Cliff-top headland of scrub, remnant heathland and small fields.
Key birds: Passage passerines. *Summer*: Breeding Dartford Warbler, Whitethroat, Stonechat and Linnet.
Contact: Vic Froome, (see above).

Northern Ireland

Co. Antrim

BOG MEADOWS

Ulster Wildlife Trust.
Location: J 315 726. Two miles from Belfast city centre. Signposted from the Falls Road.
Facilities: Car park, bird hide, disabled access, high quality paths.
Public transport: City bus from city centre or taxi.
Habitat: Wet grassland, scrub, ponds, reedbed.
Key birds: *Summer:* Breeding Sedge Warbler, Grasshopper Warbler, Grey Wagtail, Blackcap, Reed Bunting. *Winter*: Snipe, Teal, occasional Long-eared Owl.
Contact: Trust HQ (see Glenarm)

BREEN OAKWOOD

Department of the Environment NI.
Location: D 125 338. Off the Armoy-Glenshesk-Ballycastle road.
Access: No restrictions.
Facilities: None.
Public transport: None.
Habitat: Oak and birch woodland, a rare habitat in N Ireland.
Key birds: Wood Warbler.
Contact: Darrell Stanley,
Portrush Countryside Centre, 8 Bath Road, Portrush, Co Antrim, BT56 8AP. 028 7082 3600.

GLENARM

Ulster Wildlife Trust.
Location: J 335 703. Within Lagan Valley Regional Park, two miles from Belfast city centre, off Malone Road - signposted at Bladon Drive.
Access: Open at all times.
Facilities: Main paths suitable for disabled access - from Lagan towpath.
Public transport: No 71 bus from Belfast city centre.
Habitat: Ponds, wet unimproved grassland, marsh, tussock sedge, scrub.
Key birds: *Summer*: Sedge Warbler, Blackcap. *Winter*: Redpoll, Teal.
Contact: Andrew Upton, Ulster Wildlife Trust, 3 New Line, Crossgar, Co Down, BT30 9EP. 028 4483 0282.
e-mail: ulsterwt@cix.co.uk

KEBBLE

Department of the Environment NI.
Location: D 095 515. W end of Rathlin Island, off coast from Ballycastle.
Access: Scheduled ferry service from Ballycastle.
Facilities: None.
Public transport: None.
Habitat: Sea cliffs, grass, heath, lake, marsh.
Key birds: Major cliff nesting colonies of auks (inc. Puffin), Fulmar and Kittiwake; also Buzzard and Peregrine. Manx Shearwater and other seabirds on passage.
Contact: Darrell Stanley,
Portrush Countryside Centre, 8 Bath Road, Portrush, Co Antrim, BT56 8AP. 028 7082 3600.

LAGAN MEADOWS

Ulster Wildlife Trust.
Location: D 301 152. Gate by B97 0.5 mile SW Glenarm, 15 miles from Ballymena. OS 1:50 000 sheet 9.
Access: Permit required.
Facilities: None.
Public transport: Ulsterbus - from Ballymena.
Habitat: Species rich grassland, oak woodland.
Key birds: *Summer*: Breeding Sedge Warbler, Blackcap, Garden Warbler. *Winter*: Teal, Snipe, Redpoll, Woodcock, Buzzard, Dippers, Bullfinches, Kingfisher etc.
Contact: Andrew Upton, Ulster Wildlife Trust, 3 New Line, Crossgar, Co Down, BT30 9EP. 028 4483 0282. e-mail: ulsterwt@cix.co.uk

LOUGH NEAGH ISLANDS

c/o Department of the Environment NI.
Location: The largest body of water in Ireland, due W of Belfast.

Access: Landing is only by arrangement with Warden.
Facilities: None.
Key birds: On most of the 80 islands within the reserve there are breeding wildfowl (inc. Gadwall, Shelduck), gulls, terns.
Contact: EHS Central Region Office, Peatlands Country Park, 33 Derryhubbert Road, Dungannon, Co Tyrone, BT71 6NW. 028 3885 1102.

PORTMORE LOUGH

RSPB (Northern Ireland Office).
Location: J 107 685. Eight miles from Lurgan. Signposted from Aghalee village.
Access: Open every day, unmanned. No access to meadows during winter. Limited disabled facilities.
Facilities: Car park, toilets, information shelter and one hide.
Public transport: None.
Habitat: Lowland wet grassland, scrub and reedbed.
Key birds: *Spring/summer*: Breeding Curlew, Snipe, Lapwing. *Winter*: Greylag Goose, Whooper Swan and a variety of wildfowl.
Contact: Eddie Franklin, 7 Derryola Bridge Road, Aghalee, Co Armagh, BT67 0DJ. 012892 652406. e-mail: eddie.franklin@rspb.org.uk

RANDALSTOWN FOREST

c/o Department of the Environment NI.
Location: 088 872. Two miles S of Randalstown, lying alongside N edge of Lough Neagh.
Access: Permit only.
Facilities: Public hide.
Habitat: Mixed woodland and scrub.
Key birds: *Summer:* Breeding Great Crested Grebe, Sedge Warbler, Blackcap. *Winter:* Teal, Gadwall, Goldeneye. Also Kingfisher.
Contact: EHS Central Region Office, Peatlands Country Park, 33 Derryhubbert Road, Dungannon, Co Tyrone, BT71 6NW. 028 3885 1102.

RATHLIN ISLAND CLIFFS

RSBP (Northern Ireland Office).
Location: Five mile ferry journey from Ballycastle.
Access: Apr-Aug by appointment with warden only. Four miles from harbour, approx 100 steps. No toilets. Small shelter.
Facilities: Viewing with binoculars and telescopes.
Public transport: Caledonian MacBrayne ferry service from Ballycastle to Rathlin, tel 028 207 69299. Minibus availability on island, tel 028 207 63909.
Habitat: Sea cliffs and offshore stacks.
Key birds: *Spring/summer*: Puffin, Guillemot, Razorbill, Fulmar, Kittiwake.
Contact: Liam Mcfaul/Alison Hurst, South Cleggan, Rathlin Island, Ballycastle, Co Antrim, 028 207 63948.

REA'S WOOD

c/o Department of the Environment NI.
Location: J 142 855. One mile S of Antrim.
Access: Open all year. No permit, but keep to trails.
Facilities: None.
Habitat: Lough Neagh shore, wet alder woodland and scrub.
Key birds: Wildfowl and woodland species (inc. Blackcap, Siskin).
Contact: EHS Central Region Office, Peatlands Country Park, 33 Derryhubbert Road, Dungannon, Co Tyrone, BT71 6NW. 028 3885 1102.

Co. Armagh

OXFORD ISLAND

Craigavon Borough Council.
Location: J 061 608. On shores of Lough Neagh, 2.5 miles from Lurgan, Co Armagh. Signposted from J10 of M1.
Access: Site open at all times. Car parks are locked at varying times depending on seasons (see signs). Lough Neagh Discovery Centre open every day Apr-Sept (10am-7pm) inclusive and Wed-Sun, Oct-Mar (10am-5pm). Dogs on leads please. Most of site and all of Centre accessible for wheelchairs.
Facilities: Public toilets, Lough Neagh Discovery Centre with exhibitions, loop system for hard-of-hearing, shop and café. Four miles of footpaths, five birdwatching hides, children's play area,

picnic tables, public jetties.
Public transport: Waterbus Park'n Ride at Lough Road, Lurgan is 0.5 miles from reserve entrance. Tel 028 9033 3000.
Habitat: Freshwater lake, ponds, wet grassland, reedbed, woodland.
Key birds: *Winter*: More than 7000 wildfowl in Dec/Jan, especially Pochard, Tufted Duck, Goldeneye and Scaup. Whooper and Bewick's Swans (Oct-Apr). *Summer*: Sedge Warbler and Great Crested Grebe (mainly Apr-Aug).
Contact: Rosemary Mulholland, Conservation Officer, Lough Neagh Discovery Centre, Oxford Island NNR, Lurgan, Co Armagh, N Ireland, BT66 6NJ. 028 383 322205.
e-mail: oxford.island@craigavon.gov.uk
www.craigavon.gov.uk

Co. Down

BELFAST LOUGH RESERVE

RSPB (Northern Ireland Office).
Location: Take A2 N from Belfast and follow signs to Belfast Harbour Estate. Both entrances to reserve have checkpoints. From Dee Street two miles to reserve, from Tillysburn entrance one mile.
Access: Dawn to dusk.
Facilities: Lagoon overlooked by observation room (check for opening hours), two view points.
Public transport: None.
Habitat: Mudflats, wet grassland, freshwater lagoon.
Key birds: Noted for Black-tailed Godwit numbers and excellent variety of waterfowl in spring, autumn and winter. Rarities have included Buff-breasted, Pectoral, White-rumped and Semi-palmated Sandpipers, Spotted Crake, American Wigeon, Laughing Gull.
Contact: Anthony McGeehan, 028 9147 9009.

CASTLE ESPIE

The Wildfowl & Wetlands Trust.
Location: J 474 672. On Strangford Lough ten miles E of Belfast, signposted from A22 in the Comber area.
Access: Open daily except Christmas Day (10.30am Mon-Sat, 11.30am Sun).
Facilities: Visitor centre, educational facilities, views over lough, three hides, woodland walk.
Public transport: Call for advice.
Habitat: Reedbed filtration system with viewing facilities.
Key birds: *Winter*: Wildfowl esp. pale-bellied Brent Goose, Scaup. *Summer:* Warblers. Wader scrape has attracted Little Egret, Ruff, Long-billed Dowitcher, Killdeer.
Contact: James Orr, Centre Manager, The Wildfowl & Wetlands Trust, Castle Espie, Ballydrain Road, Comber, Co Down, BT23 6EA. 028 9187 4146.

COPELAND BIRD OBSERVATORY

Location: Situated on a 40-acre island on outer edge of Belfast Lough, four miles N of Donaghadee.
Access: Access is by chartered boat from Donaghadee.
Facilities: Observatory open Apr-Oct most weekends and some whole weeks. Hostel-type accommodation for up to 20. Daily ringing, bird census, sea passage recording. General bookings: Neville McKee, 67 Temple Rise, Templepatrick, Co. Antrim BT39 0AG (tel 028 9443 3068).
Public transport: None.
Habitat: Grassy areas, rock foreshore.
Key birds: Large colony of Manx Shearwaters; Black Guillemot, Eider, Water Rail also nest. *Summer*: Visiting Storm Petrels. Moderate passage of passerine migrants.
Contact: Dr Peter Munro, Talisker Lodge, 54B Templepatrick Road, Ballyclare, Co Antrim, BT39 9TX. 028 9332 3421.

CRAWFORDSBURN COUNTRY PARK

Department of the Environment NI.
Location: J 467 826. Signposted off A2 Belfast-Bangor road.
Access: Open at all times.
Facilities: Car parks.
Habitat: Sea, shore (rocky and sandy), woodland, glen, open fields.
Key birds: Woodland and grassland species; Dipper; Eider, gulls, divers, terns, shearwaters can all be seen offshore, esp. in autumn.
Contact: Ciaran McLarnon, Crawfordsburn Country Park, Bridge Road South, Helen's Bay, Co Down, BT19 1LD. 028 9185 3621.

DORN

c/o Department of the Environment NI.
Location: J 593 568. On the Ards Peninsula, E of Strangford Loch, near Ardkeen on Kircubbin to Portaferry coastal route.
Access: Access only by arrangement with Warden.
Facilities: None.
Habitat: Marine foreshore, mudflats and seabed.
Key birds: Waders; wildfowl (inc. pale-bellied Brent Goose). Common seal.
Contact: Quoile Countryside Centre, 5 Quay Road, Downpatrick, Co Down, BT30 7JB. 028 4461 5520.

KILLARD

c/o Department of the Environment NI.
Location: J 610 433. Access from Millquarter Bay on coastal road four miles S of Strangford village.
Access: Open all year. No permit, but keep to trails.
Facilities: None.
Public transport: None.
Habitat: Varied rocky and sandy shoreline.
Key birds: Waders (inc. Purple Sandpiper in winter). Good seawatching (esp. shearwaters, skuas). *Summer*: Breeding Fulmar, Shelduck, Stonechat and Sand Martin. Rare orchids.
Contact: Warden, Quoile Countryside Centre, 5 Quay Road, Downpatrick, Co Down, BT30 7JB. 028 4461 5520.

MURLOUGH

National Trust.
Location: J 394 338. Ireland's first nature reserve, between Dundrum and Newcastle, close to Mourne Mountains.
Access: Permit needed except on marked paths.
Facilities: Visitor centre.
Public transport: None.
Habitat: Sand dunes, heathland.
Key birds: Waders and wildfowl occur in Inner Dundrum Bay adjacent to the reserve; divers and large numbers of Scoter (inc. regular Surf Scoter) and Merganser in Dundrum Bay.
Contact: Head Warden, Murlough NNR, The Stable Yard, Keel Point, Dundrum, Newcastle, Co Down, BT33 0NQ. Tel/fax 028 437 51467; e-mail umnnrw@smtp.ntrust.org.uk.

NORTH STRANGFORD LOUGH

National Trust.
Location: J 510 700. View from adjacent roads and car parks; also from hide at Castle Espie (J 492 675).
Access: Call for advice.
Facilities: Hide.
Habitat: Extensive tidal mudflats, limited saltmarsh.
Key birds: Major feeding area for pale-bellied Brent Goose, also Pintail, Wigeon, Whooper Swan. Waders (inc. Dunlin, Knot, Oystercatcher, Bar-tailed Godwit).
Contact: Head Warden, National Trust, Strangford Lough Wildlife Scheme, Strangford Lough Wildlife Centre, Castle Ward, Strangford, Co Down, BT30 7LS. Tel/fax 028 4488 1411; e-mail uslwcw@smtp.ntrust.org.uk.

QUOILE PONDAGE

c/o Department of the Environment NI.
Location: J 500 478. One mile N of Downpatrick on road to Strangford, at S end of Strangord Lough.
Access: Open all year. No permit, but keep to trails.
Facilities: Large modern hide, visitor centre. Nature trail.
Public transport: None.
Habitat: Freshwater pondage to control flooding, with many vegetation types on shores.
Key birds: Many wildfowl species, woodland birds; migrant and wintering waders including Spotted Redshank, Ruff and Black-tailed Godwit.
Contact: Warden, Quoile Countryside Centre, 5 Quay Road, Downpatrick, Co Down, BT30 7JB. 028 4461 5520.

Co. Fermanagh

LOWER LOUGH ERNE ISLANDS

RSPB (Northern Ireland Office).
Location: H O15 605 (Castlecaldwell) H 104 615 (Lusty More). A total of 39 islands with access from adjacent roads especially A47. Castlecaldwell located five miles E of Belfast. Lusty More Island (accessible only by private boat) located S of Lusty Beg off Boa Island near

N shore of Lower Lough Erne.
Access: Castlecaldwell footpaths are open from dawn-dusk. Dogs allowed, paths rather rough, not suitable without assistance. Lusty More Island access by own boat to rough path and picnic area. No dogs.
Facilities: Castlecaldwell - information board, footpaths, picnic area. Lusty More - footpaths, information board, picnic area. No dogs.
Public transport: None.
Habitat: Castlecaldwell - conifer plantation and mixed woodland and shore edge to large open freshwater lough. Lusty More - damp alder woodland and small area of limestone grassland.
Key birds: *Winter:* Common woodland birds including Siskin, Redpoll, and occasional Crossbill at Castlecaldwell with some wintering wildfowl including occasional Scaup. *All year:* Woodland species common plus including breeding migrants, eg Spotted Flycatcher. Lusty More - common woodland species with Sandwich and Common Terns offshore.
Contact: Brad Robson, Randalshough, Monlea, Co Fermanagh. 02868 658835.
e-mail: bradr@hsads.kitaonline.co.uk

Co. Londonderry

LOUGH FOYLE

RSPB (Northern Ireland Office).
Location: C 545 237. Large sea lough NE of Londonderry. Take minor roads off Limavady-Londonderry road to view-points (choose high tide) at Longfield Point, Ballykelly, Faughanvale.
Access: Open all year. No permit, but keep to trails.
Facilities: None.
Public transport: None.
Habitat: Beds of eel-grass, mudflats, surrounding agricultural land.
Key birds: Staging-post for migrating wildfowl (eg. 15,000 Wigeon, 4,000 pale-bellied Brent Geese in Oct/Nov). *Winter*: Slavonian Grebe, divers, Bewick's and Whooper Swans, Bar-tailed Godwit, Golden Plover, Snow Bunting. *Autumn*: Waders (inc. Ruff, Little Stint, Curlew Sandpiper, Spotted Redshank).
Contact: RSPB N Ireland HQ (01232 491547),

ROE ESTUARY

c/o Department of the Environment NI.
Location: C 640 295. Access off A2 coast road between Castlerock and Limavady. E of Londonderry.
Access: Open all year. No permit, keep to trails.
Facilities: None.
Public transport: None.
Habitat: Mudflats and saltings (beware soft mud), sand dunes.
Key birds: Pale-bellied Brent Goose, many wildfowl and wader species.
Contact: Warden, NW Nature Reserves Office, The Cornstore, Dogleap Road, Limavady, Co Londonderry, BT49 9NN. 028 7776 3982.

ROE VALLEY COUNTRY PARK

c/o Department of the Environment NI.
Location: C 678 203. Signposted off Belfast-Londonderry and Limavady-Dungiven roads.
Access: Open at all times.
Facilities: Car parks, visitor centre, nature trail, pathways.
Public transport: None.
Habitat: Mixed woodland and gorge.
Key birds: Typical woodland and river species, inc. Wood Warbler, Dipper, Grey Wagtail.
Contact: Warden, Roe Valley Country Park, 41 Dogleap Road, Limavady, Co Londonderry, BT49 9NN. 028 7112 2074.

UMBRA

Ulster Wildlife Trust.
Location: C 725 355. Ten miles from Coleraine on A2 - entrance beside automatic railway crossing about 1.5 miles W of Downhill. OS 1:50 000 sheet 4. Access from beach or off sea coast road where railway line crosses.
Access: Open.
Facilities: None.
Public transport: Ulsterbus service to Downhill from Coleraine.
Habitat: Sand dunes.
Key birds: *Summer*: Breeding Skylark. *Winter*: Peregrine, plus Great Northern Diver offshore.
Contact: Ulster Wildlife Trust, 3 New Line, Crossgar, Co Down, BT30 9EP. 028 4483 0282.
e-mail: ulsterwt@cix.co.uk

ADDENDUM

Late-arriving information and the sheer weight of entries to be inputted in a short period of time has inevitably led to some errors and omissions in the County Directory. As we are committed to giving our readers information that is as accurate and up to date as possible, we would like you to note the following amendments.

We apologise for any inconvenience this may cause.

Page 255 – Reading Ornithological Club – W:0207 728 2496, (no fax/eve number) website www.roc.care4free.net.

Page 255 – Theale Area Bird Conservation Group – W:0207 728 2496, (no fax/eve number) - website http://www.bramblingphotos.com/tabcgweb/

Page 258 – Wilmslow Guild Ornithological Society – change of contact as follows: Tom Gibbons, Chestnut Cottage, 37 Strawberry Lane, Wilmslow, Cheshire SK9 6AQ. 01625 520317.

Page 260 – South Peak Raptor Group – telephone 01246 277749.

Page 275 – Sefton Coast RSPB Group – telephone 0151 524 1905.

Page 275 – Wirral RSPB Group – email: s.woolfall@btinternet.com website: http://website.lineone.net/~dave.jowitt/

Page 277 – BTO RDO for Northamptonshire – telephone 01832 274797.

Page 290 – York Ornithological Club – email: info@yorkbirding.org.uk website: www.yorkbirding.org.uk

Page 290 – East Yorks RG – email: pjd@fbog.co.uk

Page 291 – Craven & Pendle RSPB Group –
email: ian@cravenandpendlerspb.org
website: www.cravenandpendlerspb.org

Page 307 – BTO Ireland Officer – fax: 028 7032 8053.

Page 308 – BTO Ireland Officer – telephone numbers – from Eire: (048) 7034 2985; fax: (048) 7032 8053 - from UK (028) 7034 2985; fax: (028) 7032 8053.

COUNTY DIRECTORY

No trip to Shetland is complete without a sighting of the island's race of Wren. Drawing by Craig Chapman of West Yorkshire.

ENGLAND

The information in the directory has been obtained either from the persons listed or from the appropriate national or other bodies. In some cases, where it has not proved possible to verify the details directly, alternative responsible sources have been relied upon. When no satisfactory record was available previously included entries have sometimes had to be deleted. Readers are requested to advise the editor of any errors or omissions.

BEDFORDSHIRE

Bird atlas/Avifauna
An Atlas of the Breeding Birds of Bedfordshire 1988-92 by R A Dazley and P Trodd (Bedfordshire Natural History Society, 1994).

Bird Recorders
Dave Odell, The Hobby, 74 The Links, Kempston, Bedford, MK42 7LT. 01234 857149.
Bedfordshire Bird Club Records & Research Committee, Phil Cannings, 30 Graham Gardens, Luton, LU3 1NQ. H:01582 400394; W:01234 842220; e-mail: philcannings@ntlworld.com

Bird Report
BEDFORDSHIRE BIRD REPORT (1946-), From Gill Dickens, 9 Ullswater Road, Dunstable, Beds, LU6 3PX. 01582 609864.

BTO Regional Representative & Regional Development Officer
RR, Phil Cannings, 30 Graham Gardens, Luton, Beds, LU3 1NQ. H:01582 400394; W:01234 842220; e-mail: philcannings@ntlworld.com
RDO, Judith Knight, 381 Bideford Green, Linslade, Leighton Buzzard, Beds, LU7 7TY. Home 01525 378161; Work 01923 229079; e-mail: judy.knight@tinyonline.co.uk

Club
BEDFORDSHIRE BIRD CLUB, (1992; 220). Miss Sheila Alliez, Flat 67 Adamson Court, Hillgrounds Road, Kempston, Bedford, MK42 8QT. www.bedsbirdclub.org.uk

Ringing Groups
IVEL RG, Errol Newman, 29 Norse Road, Goldington, Bedford, MK41 0NR. 01234 343119; e-mail: lew.n@virgin.net

RSPB, Dr A D Evans, 6 Jennings Close, Potton, Sandy, Beds, SG19 2SE.

RSPB Members' Groups
BEDFORD, (1970; 80). Barrie Mason, 6 Landseer Walk, Bedford, MK41 7LZ. 01234 262280.
EAST BEDFORDSHIRE, (1973; 75). Terence C Park, 8 Back Street, Biggleswade, Beds, SG18 8JA. 01767 221363.
SOUTH BEDFORDSHIRE, (1973; 150). Brian Payne, 13A Sowerby Avenue, Luton, LU2 8AF. 01582 723330.

Wetland Bird Survey Organiser
Kevin Sharpe, 22 Russet Close, Stewartby, Beds, MK43 9LG. 07949 173588; e-mail: kevinmark.sharpe@virgin.net

Wildlife Trust
See Cambridgeshire.

BERKSHIRE

Bird atlas/Avifauna
The Birds of Berkshire by P E Standley et al (Berkshire Atlas Group/Reading Ornithological Club, 1996).

Bird Recorder
Peter Standley, Siskins, 7 Llanvair Drive, South Ascot, Berks, SL5 9HS. 01344 623502.

Bird Reports
BERKSHIRE BIRD BULLETIN (Monthly, 1986-), From Brian Clews, 118 Broomhill, Cookham, Berks, SL6 9LQ. 01628 525314.
BIRDS OF BERKSHIRE (1974-), From Recorder.
BIRDS OF THE THEALE AREA (1988-), From Secretary, Theale Area Bird Conservation Group.
NEWBURY BIRD REPORT (1959-), From Secretary, Newbury District Ornithological Club.

BTO Regional Representative & Regional Development Officer
RR, Chris Robinson, 2 Beckfords, Upper Basildon, Reading, RG8 8PB. 01491 671420; e-mail: robinsochr@compaq.com

MAIDENHEAD RDO, Jeremy Langham, 23 Gorse Road, Cookham, Maidenhead, Berks, SL6 9LL. 01628 526552.

Clubs

BERKSHIRE BIRD BULLETIN GROUP, (1986; 100). Berkshire Bird Bulletin Group, PO Box 680, Maidenhead, Berks, SL6 9ST. 01628 525314.

NEWBURY DISTRICT ORNITHOLOGICAL CLUB, (1959; 120). Jim Burnett, 44 Bourne Vale, Hungerford, Berks, RG1 0LL. 01488 681344.

READING ORNITHOLOGICAL CLUB, (1945; 200). Mike Smith, 5 Nabbs Hill Close, Tilehurst, Reading, RG31 4SG. H:0118 941 3365; W:0118 950 0336; fax (evg) 0118 960 7703; email: msmith8741@aol.com

THEALE AREA BIRD CONSERVATION GROUP, (1988; 75). Mike Smith, 5 Nabbs Hill Close, Tilehurst, Reading, RG31 4SG. H:0118 941 3365; W:0118 950 0336; fax (evg) 0118 960 7703; email: msmith8741@aol.com

Ringing Groups

NEWBURY RG, J Legg, 1 Malvern Court, Old Newtown Road, Newbury, Berks, RG14 7DR. e-mail: janlegg@talk21.com

RUNNYMEDE RG, D G Harris, 22 Blossom Waye, Hounslow, TW5 9HD. e-mail: daveharris@tinyonline.co.uk

RSPB Members' Groups

EAST BERKSHIRE, (1974; 200). Brian Clews, 118 Broomhill, Cookham, Maidenhead, Berks, SL6 9LQ. 01628 525314.

READING, (1986; 80). Carl Feltham, 39 Moriston Close, Reading, RG30 2PW. 0118 941 1713.

WOKINGHAM & BRACKNELL, (1979; 200). Patrick Crowley, 56 Ellis Road, Crowthorne, Berks, RG45 6PT. 01344 776473. e-mail: patrick.crowley@btinternet.com www.wbrspb.btinternet.co.uk

Wetland Bird Survey Organiser

Neil Bucknell, 10 Cleeve Court, Streatley, Reading, RG8 9PS. e-mail; neil-bucknell@laytons.com

Wildlife Hospitals

KESTREL LODGE, D J Chandler, 101 Sheridan Avenue, Caversham, Reading, RG4 7QB. 01189 477107.
Birds of prey, ground feeding birds, waterbirds, seabirds. Temporary homes for all except large birds of prey. Veterinary support. Small charge.

SWAN LIFELINE, Chairman, Tim Heron, Swan Treatment Centre, Cuckoo Weir Island, South Meadow Lane, Eton, Windsor, Berks, SL4 6SS. 01753 859397; fax 01753 622709; www.swanlifeline.org.uk
Registered charity. Thames Valley 24-hour swan rescue and treatment service. Veterinary support and hospital unit. Operates membership scheme.

Wildlife Trust

Director, See Oxfordshire.

BUCKINGHAMSHIRE

Bird atlas/Avifauna

The Birds of Buckinghamshire ed by P Lack and D Ferguson (Buckinghamshire Bird Club, 1993).

Bird Recorder

Andy Harding, 15 Jubilee Terrace, Stony Stratford, Milton Keynes, MK11 1DU. H:01908 565896; W:01908 653328.

Bird Reports

AMERSHAM BIRDWATCHING CLUB ANNUAL REPORT (1975-), From Secretary.

BUCKINGHAMSHIRE BIRD REPORT (1980-), From Rosie Hamilton, 56 Church Hill, Cheddington, Leighton Buzzard, Beds, LU7 0SY.

NORTH BUCKS BIRD REPORT (10 pa), From Recorder.

BTO Regional Representative & Regional Development Officer

RR, Mick A'Court, 29A Amersham Hill, High Wycombe, Bucks, HP13 6NU. H:01494 536734; W:01494 462246; e-mail: mick@focusrite.com

RDO, Peter Hearn, 160 High Street, Aylesbury, Bucks, HP20 1RE. Home & fax 01296 581520; Work 01296 424145.

Clubs

AMERSHAM BIRDWATCHING CLUB, (1973; 70). Mary Mackay, 26A Highfield Close, Amersham, Bucks, HP6 3HG. 07980 503879.

BUCKINGHAMSHIRE BIRD CLUB, (1981; 300). Roger S Warren, Bakery Lodge, Skirmett, Henley on Thames, Oxon, RG9 6TD. 01491 638544.
NORTH BUCKS BIRDERS, (1977; 50). Andy Harding, 15 Jubilee Terrace, Stony Stratford, Milton Keynes, MK11 1DU. H:01908 565896; W:01908 653328.

Ringing Groups

HUGHENDEN RG, Mr S. Avery, 5 Park Close, Lane End, High Wycombe, Bucks, HP14 3LF.

RSPB Members' Groups

See also Herts: Chorleywood,
AYLESBURY, (1981; 220). Barry Oxley, 3 Swan Close, Station Road, Blackthorn, Bicester, Oxon, OX25 1TU. 01869 247780.
NORTH BUCKINGHAMSHIRE, (1976; 400). Jim Parsons, 8 The Mount, Aspley Guise, Milton Keynes, MK17 8EA. 01908 582450.

Wetland Bird Survey Organiser

Graeme Taylor, 54 Halton Lane, Wendover, Aylesbury, Bucks, HP22 6AU. 01296 625796.

Wildlife Hospitals

MILTON KEYNES WILDLIFE HOSPITAL, Mr & Mrs V Seaton, 150 Bradwell Common Blvd, Milton Keynes, MK13 8BE. 01908 604198;
www-tec.open,ac.uk/staff/robert/robert.html
Registered charity. All species of British birds and mammals. Veterinary support.
WILDLIFE HOSPITAL TRUST,
St Tiggywinkles, Aston Road, Haddenham, Aylesbury, Bucks, HP17 8AF. 01844 292292;
fax: 01844 292640;
e-mail: tiggys@globalnet.co.uk
www.sttiggywinkles.org.uk
Registered charity. All species. Veterinary referrals and helpline for vets and others on wild bird treatments. Full veterinary unit and staff. Pub: *Bright Eyes* (free to members - sae).

Wildlife Trust

Director, See Oxfordshire.

CAMBRIDGESHIRE

Bird atlas/Avifauna

An Atlas of the Breeding Birds of Cambridgeshire (VC 29) P M M Bircham et al (Cambridge Bird Club, 1994).
The Birds of Cambridgeshire: checklist 2000 (Cambridge Bird Club).

Bird Recorders

CAMBRIDGESHIRE, Richard Allison, Kingsfold, 38 Cootes Lane, Fen Drayton, Cambridge, CB4 5SL. Tel/fax 01954 231217;
e-mail: rallison@fendrayton.fsnet.co.uk
HUNTINGDON & PETERBOROUGH, John Clark, 7 Westbrook, Hilton, Huntingdon, Cambs, PE28 9NW. 01480 830472.

Bird Reports

CAMBRIDGESHIRE BIRD REPORT (1925-), From Secretary, Cambridge Bird Club.
PAXTON PITS BIRD REPORT (1994-), From Trevor Gunton, 15 St James Road, Little Paxton, Cambs, PE19 4QW. 01480 473562.

PETERBOROUGH BIRD CLUB REPORT (1999-), From Secretary, Peterborough Bird Club.

BTO Regional Representatives

CAMBRIDGESHIRE, John Le Gassick, 17 Acacia Avenue, St Ives, Cambs, PE27 6TN. 01480 391991;
e-mail: john.legassick@ntlworld.com
HUNTINGDON & PETERBOROUGH, Position vacant.

Clubs

CAMBRIDGE BIRD CLUB, (1925; 270). Bruce Martin, 178 Nuns Way, Cambridge, CB4 2NS. 01223 700656;
e-mail: bruce.s.martin@ntlworld.com
www.cambridgebirdclub.org.uk
GREATER PETERBOROUGH ORNITHOLOGICAL GROUP, (1983; 20). Martin Coates, 63 Primrose Way, Stamford, PE9 4BU. 01780 755016;
e-mail: martin.shelagh@virgin.net
PETERBOROUGH BIRD CLUB, (1999; 90). Jane Williams, The Old Rectory, Church St, Market Deeping, Lincs, 01778 345711;
e-mail: jane@oldrectory.screaming.net
www.peterboroughbirdclub.org.uk

ST NEOTS BIRD & WILDLIFE CLUB, (1993; 150). Tim Watling, 39 Shakespeare Road, Eaton Socon, St Neots, Cambs, PE19 8HG. 01480 212763; e-mail: tim@watling2000.fsnet.co.uk www.paxton-pits.org.uk

Ringing Group
WICKEN FEN RG, Dr C J R Thorne, Norden House, 17 The Footpath, Coton, Cambs, CB3 7PX. e-mail: cjrt@cam.ac.uk

RSPB Members' Groups
CAMBRIDGE, (1977; 290). Colin Kirtland, 22 Montgomery Road, Cambridge, CB4 2EQ. 01223 363092.
HUNTINGDON, (1982; 200). Pam Peacock, Old Post Office, Warboys Road, Pidley, Huntingdon, Cambs, PE28 3DA. 01487 840615;
e-mail: pam.peacock@care4free.net
www.huntsrspb.co.uk

Wetland Bird Survey Organisers
CAMBRIDGESHIRE (Old), Bruce Martin, 178 Nuns Way, Cambridge, CB4 2NS. 01223 700656; e-mail: bruce.s.martin@ntlworld.com
HUNTINGDONSHIRE, Graham Elliott, 3 Greenway, Buckden, Huntingdon, Cambs, PE18 9TU.
NENE WASHES, Charlie Kitchin, 21a East Delph, Whittlesey, Peterborough, PE7 1RH. 01733 205140.
OUSE WASHES, Cliff Carson, Ouse Washes Reserve, Welches Dam, Manea, March, Cambs, PE15 0NF. 01354 680212.
PETERBOROUGH, John Redshaw, 7 Fennell Road, Pinchbeck, Spalding, Lincs, PE11 3RP. 01775 768227;
e-mail: jredshaw@fennell97.fsnet.co.uk

Wildlife Trust
BEDS, CAMBS, NORTHANTS & PETERBOROUGH WILDLIFE TRUST, (1990; 12,000). 3B Langford Arch, London Road, Sawston, Cambridge, CB2 4EE. 01223 712400; fax 01223 712412; e-mail: cambswt@cix.co.uk

CHESHIRE

Bird atlas/Avifauna
The Breeding Bird Atlas of Cheshire and Wirral by J Guest et al (Cheshire & Wirral Ornithological Society, 1992) out of print.
The Birds of Sandbach Flashes 1935-1999 by Andrew Goodwin and Colin Lythgoe (The Printing House, Crewe, 2000).

Bird Recorder (inc Wirral)
Tony Broome, 4 Larchwood Drive, Wilmslow, Cheshire, SK9 2NU. 01625 540434.

Bird Report
CHESHIRE & WIRRAL BIRD REPORT (1969-), From Dr P Brewster, 23 Verdin Close, Moulton, Northwich, Cheshire, CW9 8RL. 01606 590491.

BTO Regional Representatives & Regional Development Officer
MID RR, Roy Leigh, 10 Mere Road, Higher Marston, Northwich, Cheshire, CW9 6DR. 01606 892032; e-mail: roysleigh@aol.com
NORTH & EAST RR, David B Jones, 8 Wey Gates Drive, Hale Barns, Cheshire, WA15 0BW. 0161 980 5273; e-mail: d.b.jones@lineone.net
SOUTH RR & RDO, Charles Hull, Edleston Cottage, Edleston Hall Lane, Nantwich, Cheshire, CW5 8PL. 01270 628194;
e-mail; edleston@yahoo.co.uk

Clubs
CHESHIRE & WIRRAL ORNITHOLOGICAL SOCIETY, (1988; 340). David Cogger, 113 Nantwich Road, Middlewich, Cheshire, CW10 9HD. 01606 832517; e-mail: memsec@cawos.org www.cawos.org
CHESTER & DISTRICT ORNITHOLOGICAL SOCIETY, (1967; 50). David King, 13 Bennett Close, Willaston, South Wirral, CH64 2XF. 0151 327 7212
KNUTSFORD ORNITHOLOGICAL SOCIETY, (1974; 45). Roy Bircumshaw, 267 Longridge, Knutsford, Cheshire, WA16 8PH. 01565 634193; www.10x50.com
LANCASHIRE & CHESHIRE FAUNA SOCIETY, (1914; 130). Dave Bickerton, 64 Petre Crescent, Rishton, Lancs, BB1 4RB. 01254 886257; e-mail: bickertond@cs.com
LYMM ORNITHOLOGY GROUP, (1975; 65). Mrs Ann Ledden, 4 Hill View, Widnes, WA8 9AL. 0151 424 0441.
MID-CHESHIRE ORNITHOLOGICAL SOCIETY, (1963; 80). Les Goulding, 7 Summerville Gardens, Grappenhall, Warrington, WA4 2EG. 01925 265578; www.hems.u-net.com
e-mail: les@goulding7.fsnet.co.uk

SOUTH EAST CHESHIRE ORNITHOLOGICAL SOCIETY, (1964; 105). Colin Lythgoe, 11 Waterloo Road, Haslington, Crewe, CW1 5TF. 01270 582642.
WILMSLOW GUILD ORNITHOLOGICAL SOCIETY, (1965; 60). Mrs Brenda Webb, 26 Lowfield Road, Shaw Heath, Stockport, Cheshire, SK2 6RN. 0161 480 5855.

Ringing Groups

MERSEYSIDE RG, P Slater, 45 Greenway Road, Speke, Liverpool, L24 7RY.
SOUTH MANCHESTER RG, C M Richards, Fairhaven, 13 The Green, Handforth, Wilmslow, Cheshire, SK9 3AG. 01625 524527;
e-mail: cliveandray.richards@care4free.net

RSPB Members' Groups

CHESTER, (1987; 350). Bernard Wright, Carden Smithy, Clutton, Chester, CH3 9EP. 01829 782243; e-mail: knoydart@globalnet.co.uk
MACCLESFIELD, (1979; 347). Peter Kirk, Field Rise, Dumbah Lane, West Bollington, Macclesfield, Cheshire, SK10 5AB. 01625 829119; email: peter@kirk199.freeserve.co.uk
NORTH CHESHIRE, (1976; 132). Steve Kemp, 7 Denehurst Close, Penketh, Warrington, WA5 2ES. 01925 723835;
e-mail: steve@wfskemp.fsnet.com.uk

Wetland Bird Survey Organisers

DEE ESTUARY, Colin Wells, Burton Point Farm, Station Road, Burton, Nr Neston, South Wirral, CH64 5SB. 0151 336 7681.
MERSEY ESTUARY, Graham Thomason, 110 Coroners Lane, Widnes, Cheshire, WA8 9HZ. 0151 424 7257.
INLAND, Tony O'Neill, 742 Hyde Road, Gorton, Manchester, M18 7EF.

Wildlife Hospitals

RSPCA STAPELEY GRANGE WILDLIFE HOSPITAL, London Road, Stapeley, Nantwich, Cheshire, CW5 7JW. 0870 442 7102.
All wild birds. Oiled bird wash facilities and pools. Veterinary support.
SWAN SANCTUARY, Mrs C Clements, 24 St David's Drive, Callands, Warrington, WA5 5SB. 01925 636245.
Veterinary support.

Wildlife Trust

CHESHIRE WILDLIFE TRUST, (1962; 3600). Grebe House, Reaseheath, Nantwich, Cheshire, CW5 6DG. 01270 610180; fax 01270 610430;
e-mail: cheshirewt@cix.co.uk
www.wildlifetrust.org.uk/cheshire

CORNWALL

Bird Recorders

CORNWALL, K Wilson, No.1 Tol-pedn House, School Hill Road, St Levan, Penzance, Cornwall, TR19 6LP. 01736 871800;
e-mail: kesteraw@yahoo.co.uk
ISLES OF SCILLY, Paul Stancliffe, 1 Heydor Flats, Garrison Lane, St Mary's, Isles of Scilly, TR21 0JD; e-mail: paulnabby@supanet.com

Bird Reports

BIRDS IN CORNWALL (1931-), From Keith Harris, Lowena, Chyvarloe, Gunwalloe, Helston, Cornwall, TR12 7PY.
ISLES OF SCILLY BIRD REPORT and NATURAL HISTORY REVIEW 2000 (1969-), From A.J.Martin, Nornour Parade, St Mary's, Isles of Scilly, TR21 0LP.

BTO Regional Representatives & Regional Development Officers

CORNWALL RR & RDO, Position vacant.
ISLES OF SCILLY RR & RDO, Will Wagstaff, 42 Sally Port, St Mary's, Isles of Scilly, TR21 0JE. 01720 422212;
e-mail: william.wagstaff@virgin.net

Clubs

CORNWALL BIRDWATCHING & PRESERVATION SOCIETY, (1931; 990). Steve Rogers, Roseland, Cyril Road, Truro, TR1 3TA. 01872 273004.
ISLES OF SCILLY BIRD GROUP, (2000; 20). A J Martin, Nornour, Hugh Town, St Mary's, Isles of Scilly; 01720 422871;
e-mail: martinamanda@talk21.com

Ringing Group

SCILLONIA SEABIRD GROUP, Peter Robinson, 19 Pine Park Road, Honiton, Devon, EX14 2HR. 01404 549873;
e-mail: pjrobinson2@compuserve.com

RSPB Members' Group
CORNWALL, (1972; 550). Michael Lord, Gue Gassel, Church Cove, The Lizard, Cornwall, TR12 7PH. 01326 290981.

Wetland Bird Survey Organisers
TAMAR COMPLEX, Gladys Grant, 32 Dunstone Close, Plymstock, Plymouth, PL9 8SG. 01752 406287.
CORNWALL (excl Tamar complex), Dave Conway, Tregenna, Cooksland, Bodmin, Cornwall, PL31 2AR. 01208 77686.

Wildlife Hospital
MOUSEHOLE WILD BIRD HOSPITAL & SANCTUARY ASSOCIATION LTD, Raginnis Hill, Mousehole, Penzance, Cornwall, TR19 6SR. 01736 731386.
All species. No ringing.

Wildlife Trust
CORNWALL WILDLIFE TRUST, (1962; 6000). Five Acres, Allet, Truro, Cornwall, TR4 9DJ. 01872 273939; fax 01872 225476;
e-mail: cornwt@cix.co.uk

CUMBRIA

Bird Recorders
COUNTY, Colin Raven, 18 Seathwaite Road, Barrow-in-Furness, Cumbria, LA14 4LX.
NORTH EAST (Carlisle & Eden), Michael F Carrier, Lismore Cottage, 1 Front St, Armathwaite, Carlisle, CA4 9PB, 01697 472218.
NORTH WEST (Allerdale & Copeland), J K Manson, Fell Beck, East Road, Egremont, Cumbria, CA22 2ED. 01946 822947; e-mail: jake@jakemanson.freeserve.co.uk
SOUTH (South Lakeland & Furness), Ronnie Irving, 24 Birchwood Close, Kendal, Cumbria, LA9 5BJ. 01539 727523;
e-mail: ronald.irving@virginnet.co.uk

Bird Reports
BIRDS AND WILDLIFE IN CUMBRIA (1970-), From D Clarke, Tullie House Museum, Castle Street, Carlisle, Cumbria, CA3 8TP. DavidC@carlisle-city.gov.uk
WALNEY BIRD OBSERVATORY REPORT, From Warden, see Reserves,

BTO Regional Representatives
NORTH RR, John Callion, The Cherries, 2 Scawfield, Scaw Road, High Harrington, Workington, Cumbria, CA14 4LZ.
H:01946 830651; W:01946 830694.
SOUTH RR, Stephen Dunstan, 29 Greenfinch Court, Herons Reach, Blackpool, FY3 8FG. 01253 301009;
e-mail: stephen@greenfinch.fslife.co.uk

Clubs
ARNSIDE & DISTRICT NATURAL HISTORY SOCIETY, (1967; 170). Mrs GM Smith, West Wind, Orchard Road, Arnside, via Carnforth, Cumbria, LA5 0DP. 01524 762522.

CUMBRIA BIRD CLUB, (1989; 215). Peter Ullrich, 25 Arlecdon Parks Road, Arlecdon, Frizington, Cumbria, CA26 3XG. 01946 861376.

CUMBRIA RAPTOR STUDY GROUP, (1992). P N Davies, Snowhill Cottage, Caldbeck, Wigton, Cumbria, CA7 8HL. 016973 71245;
e-mail: pete.caldbeck@virgin.net

Ringing Groups
EDEN RG, G Longrigg, Mere Bank, Bleatarn, Warcop, Appleby, Cumbria, CA16 6PX.
MORECAMBE BAY WADER RG, J Sheldon, 415 West Shore Park, Barrow-in-Furness, Cumbria, LA14 3XZ. 01229 473102.
WALNEY BIRD OBSERVATORY, K Parkes, 176 Harrogate Street, Barrow-in-Furness, Cumbria, LA14 5NA. 01229 824219.

RSPB Members' Groups
CARLISLE, (1974; 400). Alistair Leslie, 15 High Garth Meadows, Ivegill, Carlisle, CA4 0PA. 01697 473138.
SOUTH LAKELAND, (1973; 350). Ms Kathleen Atkinson, 2 Langdale Crescent, Windermere, Cumbria, LA23 2HE. 01539 444254.
WEST CUMBRIA, (1986; 200). Neil Hutchin, Orchard House, Main Street, Greysouthen, Cockermouth, Cumbria, CA13 0UG. 01900 825231; e-mail: neil@hutchin50.fsnet.co.uk

Wetland Bird Survey Organisers

DUDDON ESTUARY, Bob Treen, 5 Rydal Close, Dalton-in-Furness, Cumbria, LA15 8QU. 01229 464789

IRT, MITE & ESK ESTUARIES, Graeme Prest, 5 Fallowfield, Ulverston, Cumbria, CA19 1YQ.

MORECAMBE BAY (North), Nick Littlewood, Coastguard Cottages, South Walney, Barrow-in-Furness, Cumbria, LA14 3YQ.

SOLWAY ESTUARY (Inner South), Norman Holton, North Plain Farm, Bowness-on-Solway, Wigton, CA7 5AG.
e-mail: norman.holton@rspb.org.uk

SOLWAY ESTUARY (Outer South), John C Callion, The Cherries, 2 Scawfield, Scaw Road, High Harrington, Workington, Cumbria, CA14 4LZ.

INLAND, Ms Kathleen Atkinson, 2 Langdale Crescent, Windermere, Cumbria, LA23 2HE.

Wildlife Trust

CUMBRIA WILDLIFE TRUST, (1962; 5000). Brockhole, Windermere, Cumbria, LA23 1LJ. 01539 448280; fax 01539 448281;
e-mail: cumbriawt@cix.co.uk

DERBYSHIRE

Bird Recorders

1. Rare breeding records, Roy A Frost, 66 St Lawrence Road, North Wingfield, Chesterfield, Derbyshire, S42 5LL. 01246 850037.
2. Records Committee & rarity records, Rodney W Key, 3 Farningham Close, Spondon, Derby, DE21 7DZ. 01332 678571;
e-mail: rod.key@talk21.co.uk
3. Annual Report editor, Richard M R James, 10 Eastbrae Road, Littleover, Derby, DE23 7WA. 01332 771787.

Bird Reports

BENNERLEY MARSH WILDLIFE GROUP ANNUAL REPORT, From Secretary.

CARSINGTON BIRD CLUB ANNUAL REPORT, From Secretary.

DERBYSHIRE BIRD REPORT (1954-), From Andrew Hattersley, 104 Longedge Lane, Wingerworth, Chesterfield, S42 6PQ.

OGSTON BIRD CLUB REPORT (1970-), From Secretary.

BTO Regional Representatives

NORTH RR, Dave Budworth, 121 Wood Lane, Newhall, Swadlincote, Derbys, DE11 0LX. 01283 215188; e-mail: dbud01@aol.com

SOUTH RR, Dave Budworth, 121 Wood Lane, Newhall, Swadlincote, Derbys, DE11 0LX. 01283 215188; e-mail: dbud01@aol.com

Clubs

BENNERLEY MARSH WILDLIFE GROUP, (1995; 135). Mark Keighley, 64 Highgate Drive, Ilkeston, Derbys, DE7 9HU. 0115 944 4726.

BAKEWELL & DISTRICT BIRD STUDY GROUP, (1987; 70). Anne Wrench, Longstone Byre, Little Longstone, Nr Bakewell, Derbyshire, DE45 1NN; e-mail: ann.wrench@btinternet.com

BUXTON FIELD CLUB, (1946; 78). B Aries, 1 Horsefair Avenue, Chapel-en-le-Frith, High Peak, Derbys, SK23 9SQ. 01298 815291.

CARSINGTON BIRD CLUB, (1992; 257). Mrs Dorothy Evans, 41 Belvedere Avenue, Walton, Chesterfield, Derbys, S40 3HY. 01246 238421.

DERBYSHIRE ORNITHOLOGICAL SOCIETY, (1954; 515). Steve Shaw, 84 Moorland View Road, Walton, Chesterfield, Derbys, S40 3DF. 01246 236090;
e-mail: steveshaw@ornsoc.freeserve.co.uk

OGSTON BIRD CLUB, (1969; 480). Mrs Ann Hunt, 2 Sycamore Avenue, Glapwell, Chesterfield, S44 5LH. 01623 812159.

SOUTH PEAK RAPTOR STUDY GROUP, (1998; 12). M E Taylor, 76 Hawksley Avenue, Newbold, Chesterfield, Derbys, S40 4TL. 01246 277748.

Ringing Groups

DARK PEAK RG, W M Underwood, 56 Bank Street, Hadfield, Glossop, Derbys, SK13 1BB.
e-mail: w.m.underwood@talk21.com

SORBY-BRECK RG, Geoff P Mawson, Moonpenny Farm, Farwater Lane, Dronfield, Sheffield, S18 1RA. 01246 415097;
e-mail: gpmawson@hotmail.com

SOUDER RG, Dave Budworth, 121 Wood Lane, Newhall, Swadlincote, Derbys, DE11 0LX. 0121 6953384.

RSPB Members' Groups

CHESTERFIELD, (1987; 274). Brian Quinney, 6 Hallfield Close, Wingerworth, Chesterfield, S42 6RP. 01246 221033; mobile 0773 021 2240; e-mail: brian.quinney@tinyworld.co.uk

DERBY, (1973; 3800). Brian Myring, 74 The Bancroft, Etwall, Derby, DE65 6NF. 01283 734851.

HIGH PEAK, (1974; 250). Peter Griffiths, 17 Clifton Drive, Marple, Stockport. 0161 427 5325.

Wetland Bird Survey Organiser

Chris Burnett, 23 The Potlocks, Willington, Derbys, DE65 6YA. 01283 703634; e-mail: tweetyburnett@aol.com

Wildlife Trust

DERBYSHIRE WILDLIFE TRUST, (1962; 5000). Elvaston Castle, Derby, DE72 3EP. 01332 756610; fax 01332 758872; e-mail: derbywt@cix.co.uk

DEVON

Bird atlas/Avifauna

Tetrad Atlas of Breeding Birds of Devon by H P Sitters (Devon Birdwatching & Preservation Society, 1988).

Bird Recorder

Mike Langman, 38 Brantwood Drive, Paignton, Devon, TQ4 5HZ. 01803 528008; e-mail: mikelangman38@aol.com

Bird Reports

DEVON BIRD REPORT (1928-), From H Kendall, 33 Victoria Road, Bude, Cornwall, EX23 8RJ. 01288 353818.

LUNDY FIELD SOCIETY ANNUAL REPORT (1946-), From Secretary. Index to Report is on Society's website.

BTO Regional Representative & Regional Development Officer

John Woodland, Glebe Cottage, Dunsford, Exeter, EX6 7AA. Tel/fax 01647 252494; e-mail: jwoodland@btodv.fsnet.co.uk

Clubs

DEVON BIRDWATCHING & PRESERVATION SOCIETY, (1928; 1400). Mrs Joy Vaughan, 28 Fern Meadow, Okehampton, Devon, EX20 1PB. 01837 53360.

KINGSBRIDGE & DISTRICT NATURAL HISTORY SOCIETY, (1989; 120). Martin Catt, Migrants Rest, East Prawle, Kingsbridge, Devon, TQ7 2DB. 01548 511443; e-mail: martincatt@btinternet.com

LUNDY FIELD SOCIETY, (1946; 450). Chris Webster, 38 Greenway Avenue, Taunton, Somerset, TA2 6HY. 01823 282889; e-mail: chris@webster5.demon.co.uk www.lundy.org.uk

TOPSHAM BIRDWATCHING & NATURALISTS' SOCIETY, (1969; 100). Mrs Janice Vining, 2 The Maltings, Fore Street, Topsham, Exeter, EX3 0HF. 01392 873514; e-mail: tbns@talk21.com

Ringing Groups

DEVON & CORNWALL WADER RG, R C Swinfen, 72 Dunraven Drive, Derriford, Plymouth, PL6 6AT. 01752 633253.

LUNDY FIELD SOCIETY, A M Taylor, 26 High Street, Spetisbury, Blandford, Dorset, DT11 9DJ. 01258 857336.

SLAPTON BIRD OBSERVATORY, Peter Ellicott, 10 Chapel Road, Alphington, Exeter, EX2 8TB. 01392 277387.

RSPB Members' Groups

EXETER & DISTRICT, (1974; 535). Allan Hancock, Pineta, Sand Down Lane, Newton St Cyres, Exeter, EX5 5DE. 01392 851744; e-mail: allan.h@care4free.net

NORTH DEVON, (1970; 96). David Gayton, 29 Merrythorne Road, Fremington, Barnstaple, Devon, EX31 3AL. 01271 371092.

PLYMOUTH, (1974; 850). Mrs Eileen Willey, 11 Beverstone Way, Roborough, Plymouth, PL6 7DY. 01752 208996.

Wetland Bird Survey Organisers

TAMAR COMPLEX, Gladys Grant, 32 Dunstone Close, Plymstock, Plymouth, PL9 8SG. 01752 406287; e-mail: gladysgrant@onetel.net.uk

TAW & TORRIDGE ESTUARY, Terry Chaplin, Little Orchard, Braunton Road, Barnstaple, Devon, EX31 1JY.

OTHER SITES, Philip Stidwill, 80 Stuart Road, Pennycomequick, Plymouth, PL1 5LP. 01752 559332.

Wildlife Hospitals

BIRD OF PREY CASUALTY CENTRE, Mrs J E L Vinson, Crooked Meadow, Stidston Lane, South Brent, Devon, TQ10 9JS. 01364 72174. Birds of prey, with emergency advice on other species. Aviaries, releasing pen. Veterinary support.
BONDLEIGH BIRD HOSPITAL, Manager, Samantha Hart, North Tawton, Devon, EX20 2AJ. 01837 82328.
All species. 14 aviaries, 2 aquapens. Veterinary support available, if requested, with payment of full charges.
CATT, Martin, Migrants Rest, East Prawle, Kingsbridge, Devon, TQ7 2DB. 01548 511443; e-mail: martincatt@btinternet.com
Collects oiled birds and gives initial treatment before forwarding to cleaning station.
HURRELL, Dr L H, 201 Outland Road, Peverell, Plymouth, PL2 3PF. 01752 771838
Birds of prey only. Veterinary support.
TORBAY WILDLIFE RESCUE CENTRE, Malcolm Higgs, 6A Gerston Place, Paignton, S Devon, TQ3 3DX. 01803 557624.
www.twrs.fsnet.co.uk
All wild birds, inc. oiled. Pools, aviaries, intensive care, washing facilities. Open at all times. 24-hr veterinary support. Holding areas off limits to public as all wildlife must be returned to the wild.

Wildlife Trust

DEVON WILDLIFE TRUST, (1962; 10,600). Shirehampton House, 35-37 St David's Hill, Exeter, EX4 4DA. 01392 279244; fax 01392 433221; e-mail: devonwt@cix.co.uk

DORSET

Bird atlas/Avifauna

Dorset Breeding Bird Atlas (working title). In preparation.

Bird Recorder

Neil Gartshore, 54 Corfe Road, Stoborough, Wareham, Dorset, BH20 5AF. 01929 552560; e-mail: neil&yuki@onaga54.freeserve.co.uk

Bird Reports

DORSET BIRDS (1987-), From Miss J W Adams, 16 Sherford Drive, Wareham, Dorset, BH20 4EN. 01929 552299.
THE BIRDS OF CHRISTCHURCH HARBOUR (1959-), From General Secretary, Christchurch Harbour, Ornithological Group.
PORTLAND BIRD OBSERVATORY REPORT, From Warden, see Reserves.

BTO Regional Representatives

Catherine and Graham Whitby, 2 Helston Close, Portesham, Weymouth, Dorset, DT3 4EY. 01305 871301.

Clubs

CHRISTCHURCH HARBOUR ORNITHOLOGICAL GROUP, (1956; 150). John Hall, 15 Kingsbere Gardens, Haslemere Avenue, Highcliffe, Dorset, BH23 5BQ. 01425 275610
DORSET BIRD CLUB, (1987; 550). Mrs Eileen Bowman, 53 Lonnen Road, Colehill, Wimborne, Dorset, BH21 7AT. 01202 884788.
DORSET NATURAL HISTORY & ARCHAEOLOGICAL SOCIETY, (1845; 2188). Kate Hebditch, Dorset County Museum, High West Street, Dorchester, Dorset, DT1 1XA. 01305 262735; e-mail: dorsetcountymuseum@dor-mus.demon.co.uk
www.dorsetcountymuseum.co.uk

Ringing Groups

CHRISTCHURCH HARBOUR RS, E C Brett, 3 Whitfield Park, St Ives, Ringwood, Hants, BH24 2DX.
PORTLAND BIRD OBSERVATORY, Martin Cade, Old Lower Light, Portland Bill, Dorset, DT5 2JT. 01305 820553;
e-mail: obs@btinternet.com
www.portlandbirdobs.btinternet.co.uk
STOUR RG, R Gifford, 62 Beacon Park Road, Upton, Poole, Dorset, BH16 5PE.

RSPB Members' Groups

BLACKMOOR VALE, (1981; 120). Mrs Margaret Marris, 15 Burges Close, Marnhull, Sturminster Newton, Dorset, DT10 1QQ. 01258 820091.
EAST DORSET, (1974; 310). Brian Morgan, 50 Lowther Road, Bournemouth, BH8 8NR. 01202 293372.
POOLE, (1982; 305). John Derricott, 51

Dacombe Drive, Upton, Poole, Dorset, BH16 5JJ. 01202 776312.
SOUTH DORSET, (1976; 400). Marion Perriss, Old Barn Cottage, Affpuddle, Dorchester, Dorset, DT2 7HH. 01305 848268.

Wetland Bird Survey Organisers
EXCLUDING ESTUARIES, John Jones, Blackbird Cottage, 14 Church Lane, Sutton Waldron, Dorset, DT11 8PA. 01747 811490
THE FLEET & PORTLAND HARBOUR, Steve Groves, Abbotsbury Swannery, New Barn Road, Abbotsbury, Dorset, DT3 4JG. 01305 871 684
POOLE HARBOUR, Steve Smith, 7 South Road, Corfe Mullen, Wimborne, Dorset, BH21 3HY.
RADIPOLE & LODMOOR, Keith Ballard, 52 Goldcroft Avenue, Weymouth, DT4 0ES.

Wildlife Hospital
SWAN RESCUE SANCTUARY, Ken and Judy Merriman, The Wigeon, Crooked Withies, Holt, Wimborne, Dorset, BH21 7LB. 01202 828166; mobile 0385 917457;
e-mail: ken@swan-rescue.fsnet.co.uk
www.swan-rescue.co.uk
Swans. Hospital unit with indoor ponds and recovery pens. Outdoors: 35 ponds and lakes, and recovery pens. 24-hr veterinary support. Viewing by appointment only.

Wildlife Trust
DORSET WILDLIFE TRUST, (1961; 8000). Brooklands Farm, Forston, Dorchester, Dorset, DT2 7AA. 01305 264620; fax 01305 251120;
e-mail: dorsetwt@cix.co.uk
www.wildlifetrust.org.uk/dorset

DURHAM

Bird atlas/Avifauna
A Summer Atlas of Breeding Birds of County Durham by Stephen Westerberg/Keith Bowey. (Durham Bird Club, 2000).

Bird Recorders
Tony Armstrong, 39 Western Hill, Durham City, DH1 4RJ. 0191 386 1519;
e-mail: ope@globalnet.co.uk
CLEVELAND, Graeme Joynt, 3 Brigandine Close, Warrior Park, Seaton Carew, Hartlepool, TS25 1ES. 01429 289968.

Bird Reports
BIRDS IN DURHAM (1971-),
From D Sowerbutts, 9 Prebends Fields, Gilesgate, Durham, DH1 1HH.
CLEVELAND BIRD REPORT (1974-), From Mr J Sharp, 10 Glendale, Pinehills, Guisborough, TS14 8JF. 01287 633976.

BTO Regional Representatives
David L Sowerbutts, 9 Prebends Field, Gilesgate Moor, Durham, DH1 1HH. H:0191 386 7201; W:0191 374 3011;
e-mail: d.l.sowerbutts@durham.ac.uk
CLEVELAND RR, Russell McAndrew, 5 Thornhill Gardens, Hartlepool, TS26 0HX. 01429 277291.

Clubs

DURHAM BIRD CLUB, (1975; 263). Kevin Spindloe, 30 Swinburne Road, Hartlepool, TS25 4JQ. 01429 292622.
www.durhambirdclub.org.uk
SUMMERHILL (HARTLEPOOL) BIRD CLUB, (2000; 57). Kevin Spindloe, 30 Swinburne Road, Hartlepool, 01429 292622.
TEESMOUTH BIRD CLUB, (1960; 220). Chris Sharp, 20 Auckland Way, Hartlepool, TS26 0AN. 01429 865163.

Ringing Groups
DURHAM RG, S Westerberg, 32 Manor Road, Medomsley, Consett, Co Durham, DH8 6QW. 01207 563862.
DURHAM DALES RG, J R Hawes, Fairways, 5 Raby Terrace, Willington, Crook, Durham, DL15 0HR.

RSPB Members' Group
DURHAM, (1974; 150). Joe Bray, 34 Langley Road, Newton Hall, Durham, DH1 5LR. 0191 386 5838.

Wetland Bird Survey Organisers
TEES ESTUARY, Mike Leakey, English Nature, Visitor Centre, British Energy, Tees Road, Hartlepool, TS25 2BZ. Tel/fax 01429 853325;
e-mail; mike.leakey@english-nature.org.uk

CLEVELAND (excl Tees Estuary), Graeme Joynt, 3 Brigandine Close, Warrior Park, Seaton Carew, Hartlepool, TS25 1ES. 01429 289968.
DURHAM COAST, Robin Ward, Dept of Biological Sciences, University of Durham, South Road, Durham, DH1 3LE. H:0191 383 1259; W:0191 374 3350;
e-mail: r.m.ward@durham.ac.uk
TYNE & WEAR SOUTH (Inland), Andrew Donnison, WWT Washington, District 15, Washington, Tyne & Wear, NE38 8LE. 0191 416 5454 ext 222; fax 0191 416 5801;
e-mail: wetlands@euphony.net

Wildlife Trust

DURHAM WILDLIFE TRUST, (1971; 3500). Rainton Meadows, Chilton Moor, Houghton-le-Spring, Tyne & Wear, DH4 6PU. 0191 5843112; fax 0191 584 3934; e-mail: durhamwt@cix.co.uk

ESSEX

Bird Atlas/Avifauna

Birds of Essex (provisional title) by Simon Woods (Essex Birdwatching Society, date to be announced).
The Breeding Birds of Essex by M K Dennis (Essex Birdwatching Society, 1996). New county avifauna, edited by Simon Wood, to be published during 2001.

Bird Recorder

Mike Dennis, 173 Collier Row Lane, Romford, RM5 3ED. 01708 761865.

Bird Report

ESSEX BIRD REPORT (inc Bradwell Bird Obs records) (1950-), from Dr G Gibbs, 72 Orchard Place, Blackmore, Essex, CM4 0RZ.

BTO Regional Representatives & Regional Development Officer

NORTH-EAST RR & RDO, Peter Dwyer, 48 Churchill Avenue, Halstead, Essex, CO9 2BE. Tel/fax 01787 476524; e-mail: petedwyer@aol.com or pete@northessex.co.uk
NORTH-WEST RR, Geoff Gibbs, 72 Orchard Piece, Blackmore, Ingatestone, Essex, CM4 0RZ. 01277 823007; e-mail: geoffg@essexwt.org.uk
SOUTH RR, Jean Stone, Topcroft, 8 Hillview Road, Rayleigh, Essex, SS6 7HX. 01268 775328.

Club

ESSEX BIRDWATCHING SOCIETY, (1949; 750). Roy Ledgerton, 25 Bunyan Road, Braintree, Essex, CM7 2PL. 01376 326103; e-mail: r.ledgerton@virgin.net

Ringing Groups

ABBERTON RG, C P Harris, Wylandotte, Seamer Road, Southminster, Essex, CM0 7BX.
BASILDON RG, B J Manton, 72 Leighcliff Road, Leigh-on-Sea, Essex, SS9 1DN. 01702 475183; e-mail: bjmanton@lineone.net
BRADWELL BIRD OBSERVATORY, C P Harris, Wyandotte, Seamer Road, Southminster, Essex, CM0 7BX.

RSPB Members' Groups

CHELMSFORD, (1976; 5500). Mike Logan Wood, Highwood, Ishams Chase, Wickham Bishops, Essex, CM8 3LG. 01621 892045.
COLCHESTER, (1981; 250). Graham Browne, Oakdene, Inworth Lane, Wakes Colne, Colchester, CO6 2BE. 01787 227629.
SOUTHEND, (1983; 400). Keith Crees, 178 Rawreth Lane, Rayleigh, Essex, SS6 9RN. 01268 781843; www.southendrspb.co.uk

Wetland Bird Survey Organisers

STOUR ESTUARY, Russell Leavett, 24 Orchard Close, Great Oakley, Harwich, Essex, CO12 5AX. Tel/fax 01255 886043;
e-mail; russell.leavett@rspb.org.uk
THAMES ESTUARY (FOULNESS), Dr Chris Lewis, 166 Kings Road, Westcliff-on-Sea, Essex, SS0 8PP. 01702 712863.
LEE VALLEY, Ian Kendall, Lee Valley Reg Park Authority, Abbey Mills, Highbridge Street, Waltham Abbey, Essex, EN9 1BZ. Tel/fax 01992 714610;
e-mail: rangerscentral@leevalleypark.org.uk
OTHER SITES, Jeremy Alderton, 367 Baddow Road, Chelmsford, CM2 7QF. 01245 471400.

Wildlife Trust

ESSEX WILDLIFE TRUST, (1959; 15,500). Fingringhoe Wick Nature Reserve, South Green Road, Fingringhoe, Colchester, CO5 7DN. 01206 729678; fax 01206 729298;
e-mail: admin@essexwt.org.uk
www.essexwt.org.uk

GLOUCESTERSHIRE

Bird Atlas/Avifauna

Atlas of Breeding Birds of the North Cotswolds. (North Cotswold Ornithological Society, 1990).

Bird Recorder

Gordon Avery, 12 Hemmingsdale Road, Hempsted, Gloucester, GL2 5HN. 01452 305002; e-mail: gravery@hembirds.freeserve.co.uk

Bird Reports

CHELTENHAM BIRD CLUB BIRD REPORT (1998-), From M Sutcliffe, 18 Carlton Street, Cheltenham, GL52 6AQ.
e-mail: michael.sutcliffe2@virgin.net
GLOUCESTERSHIRE BIRD REPORT (1953-), From Peter Jones, 2 Beech Close, Highnam, Gloucester, GL2 8EG. 01452 413561;
e-mail: peter@joneshighnam.freeserve.co.uk
NORTH COTSWOLD ORNITHOLOGICAL SOCIETY ANNUAL REPORT (1983-), from Secretary.

BTO Regional Representative

Mike Smart, 143 Cheltenham Road, Gloucester, GL2 0JH. Home/work 01452 421131;
e-mail: smartmike@email.msn.com

Clubs

CHELTENHAM BIRD CLUB, (1976; 78). Mrs Frances Meredith, 14 Greatfield Drive, Charlton Kings, Cheltenham, GL53 9BU. 01242 516393.

DURSLEY BIRDWATCHING & PRESERVATION SOCIETY, (1952; 403). Maurice Bullen, 20 South Street, Uley, Dursley, Glos, GL11 5SP. 01453 860004.

GLOUCESTERSHIRE NATURALISTS' SOCIETY, (1948; 600). John McLellan, 15 Charlton Road, Tetbury, Glos, GL8 8DX. 01666 504757; e-mail: johnmclellan.birds@virgin.net (for membership info) losnats@blueyonder.co.uk

NORTH COTSWOLD ORNITHOLOGICAL SOCIETY, (1982; 55). T Hutton, 15 Green Close, Childswickham, Broadway, Worcs, WR12 7JJ. 01386 858511.

Ringing Groups

SEVERN ESTUARY GULL GROUP, M E Durham, 6 Glebe Close, Frampton-on-Severn, Glos, GL2 7EL. 01452 741312.
SEVERN VALE RG, R Hearn, Wildfowl & Wetlands Trust, Slimbridge, Glos, GL2 7BT. 01453 891900 ext 185;
e-mail: richard.hearn@wwt.org.uk
WILDFOWL & WETLANDS TRUST, R Hearn, Wildfowl & Wetlands Trust, Slimbridge, Glos, GL2 7BT. 01453 891900 ext 185;
e-mail: richard.hearn@wwt.org.uk

RSPB Members' Group

GLOUCESTERSHIRE, (1972; 700). David Cramp, 2 Ellenor, Alderton, Tewkesbury, GL20 8NZ. 01242 620281.

Wetland Bird Survey Organisers

SEVERN ESTUARY, Mark Pollitt, Wildfowl & Wetlands Trust, Slimbridge, Glos, GL2 7BT. 01453 890333.
INLAND, Dr Leslie Jones, Chestnut House, Water Lane, Somerford Keynes, Cirencester, Glos, GL7 6DS. 01285 861545.
INLAND NORTH AVON, David Pryce, 5 The Knapp, Dursley, Glos, GL11 4BT. 01453 543440.

Wildlife Hospitals

GLOUCESTER WILDLIFE RESCUE CENTRE, Alan and Louise Brockbank, 2 Home Farm, Hartpury, Glos, GL19 3DE. 01452 700038; http://beehive.thisisgloucestershire.co.uk/gloswildliferescue
Intensive care, treatment and rehabilitation facilities. Vetinary support. No restrictions or conditions.
VALE WILDLIFE RESCUE - WILDLIFE HOSPITAL & REHABILITATION CENTRE, Ms Caroline Gould, Station Road, Beckford, Tewkesbury, Glos, GL20 7AN. 01386 882288; (Fax)01386 882299; e-mail: info@vwr.org.uk www.vwr.org.uk
All wild birds. Intensive care. Registered charity. Veterinary support.

Wildlife Trust
GLOUCESTERSHIRE WILDLIFE TRUST, (1961; 6200). Dulverton Building, Robinswood Hill Country Park, Reservoir Road, Gloucester, GL4 6SX. 01452 383333; fax 01452 383334; e-mail: info@gloucswt.cix.co.uk www.gloucesterwildlife.co.uk

HAMPSHIRE

Bird Atlas/Avifauna
Birds of Hampshire by J M Clark and J A Eyre (Hampshire Ornithological Society, 1993).

Bird Recorder
John Clark, 4 Cygnet Court, Old Cove Road, Fleet, Hants, GU15 2RL. Tel/fax 01252 623397; e-mail: johnclark@cygnetcourt.demon.co.uk

Bird Reports
HAMPSHIRE BIRD REPORT (1955-), From Mrs Margaret Boswell, 5 Clarence Road, Lyndhurst, Hants, SO43 7AL. 023 8028 2105; e-mail: mag.bos@btinternet.com
HANTS/SURREY BORDER BIRD REPORT (1971-), From Recorder.

BTO Regional Representative & Regional Development Officer
Glynne C Evans, Waverley, Station Road, Chilbolton, Stockbridge, Hants, SO20 6AL. H:01264 860697; W:01962 847435; e-mail: hantsbto@hotmail.com

Clubs
HAMPSHIRE ORNITHOLOGICAL SOCIETY, (1979; 955). Alan Snook, 16 Emmett Road, Rownhams, Southampton, SO16 8JB. Tel/fax Home 023 8073 0009; Work 01425 657988; e-mail: alan.snook@dial.pipex.com
SOUTHAMPTON & DISTRICT BIRD GROUP, (1994; 100). Les Stride, 196 Calmore Road, Calmore, Southampton, SO40 2RA. 023 8086 8058.

Ringing Groups
FARLINGTON RG, D A Bell, 38 Holly Grove, Fareham, Hants, PO16 7UP.
ITCHEN RG, W F Simcox, 10 Holdaway Close, Kingsworthy, Winchester, SO23 7QH.
LOWER TEST RG, J Pain, Owlery Holt, Nations Hill, Kingsworthy, Winchester, SO23 7QY. 023 8066 7919; e-mail: jessp@hwt.org.uk

RSPB Members' Groups
BASINGSTOKE, (1979; 90). Peter Hutchins, 35 Woodlands, Overton, Whitchurch, RG25 3HN. 01256 770831.
NORTH EAST HAMPSHIRE, (1976; 350). Graham Dumbleton, 28 Castle Street, Fleet, Hants, GU13 9ST. 01252 622699.
PORTSMOUTH, (1974; 205). Gordon Humby, 19 Charlesworth Gardens, Waterlooville, Hants, PO7 6AU. 02392 353949.
WINCHESTER & DISTRICT, (1974; 152). Maurice Walker, Jesmond, 1 Compton Way, Olivers Battery, Winchester, SO22 4EY. 01962 854033.

Wetland Bird Survey Organisers
ESTUARIES & COASTAL SITES, Dave Unsworth, Flat 3, 142 Malmesbury Road, Shirley, Southampton, SO15 5FQ.
INLAND, Keith Wills, 51 Peabody Road, Farnborough, Hants, GU14 6EB. 01252 548408; e-mail: KeithB.Wills@ukgateway.net

Wildlife Hospital
NEW FOREST OWL SANCTUARY, Bruce Berry, New Forest Owl Sanctuary, Crow Lane, Crow, Ringwood, Hants, BH24 1EA. 01425 476487; e-mail: nfosowls@aol.com www.owlsanctuary.co.uk
A selection of owls, hawks and falcons from around the world with flying demonstrations at set times throughout the day. An opportunity to observe birds of prey at close range, an enjoyable day for the whole family. Open daily Feb to Nov.

Wildlife Trust
HAMPSHIRE WILDLIFE TRUST, (1960; 11,295). 8 Romsey Road, Eastleigh, Hants, SO50 9AL. 023 8061 3636; fax 023 8061 2233; e-mail: hampswt@cix.co.uk

HEREFORDSHIRE

Bird Recorder
Steve Coney, Lion's Den, Bredwardine, Hereford, HR3 6DE. 01981 500236; e-mail: coney@bluecarrots.com

Bird Report
HEREFORDSHIRE ORNITHOLOGICAL CLUB ANNUAL REPORT (1951-), from Mr I Evans, 12 Brockington Drive, Tupsley, Hereford, HR1 1TA.

BTO Regional Representative
Steve Coney, Lion's Den, Bredwardine, Hereford, HR3 6DE. 01981 500236; e-mail: coney@bluecarrots.com

Club
HEREFORDSHIRE ORNITHOLOGICAL CLUB, (1950; 391). C E Lankester, 6 Biddulph Way, Ledbury, Herefs, HR8 2HN. 01531 633530.

Ringing Group
LLANCILLO RG, Dr G R Geen, 6 The Copse, Bannister Green, Felsted, Dunmow, Essex, CM6 3NP. 01371 820189; e-mail: thegeens@aol.com

Wetland Bird Survey Organiser
Steve Coney, Lion's Den, Bredwardine, Hereford, HR3 6DE. 01981 500236; e-mail: coney@bluecarrots.com

Wildlife Hospital
ATHENE BIRD SANCTUARY, B N Bayliss, 61 Chartwell Road, Hereford, HR1 2TU. 01432 273259. Birds of prey, ducks and waders, seabirds, pigeons and doves. Heated cages, small pond. Veterinary support.

Wildlife Trust
HEREFORDSHIRE NATURE TRUST, (1962; 1450). Lower House Farm, Ledbury Road, Tupsley, Hereford, HR1 1UT. 01432 356872; fax 01432 275489;
e-mail: herefordwt@cix.co.uk
www.wildlifetrust.org.uk/hereford

HERTFORDSHIRE

Bird Atlas/Avifauna
Birds at Tring Reservoirs by R Young et al (Hertfordshire Natural History Society, 1996).
The Breeding Birds of Hertfordshire by K W Smith et al (Herts NHS, 1993).

Bird Recorder
Mike Ilett, 14 Cowper Crescent, Bengeo, Hertford, Herts, SG14 3DY.
e-mail: michael.ilett@uk.tesco.com

Bird Report
HERTFORDSHIRE BIRD REPORT (1908-1998), From Hon Secretary, Herts Bird Club, 46 Manor Way, Boreham Wood, Herts, WD6 1QY.

BTO Regional Representative & Regional Development Officer
Chris Dee, 26 Broadleaf Avenue, Thorley Park, Bishop's Stortford, Herts, CM23 4JY. H:01279 755637; e-mail: chris_w_dee@hotmail.com

Clubs

FRIENDS OF TRING RESERVOIRS, (1993; 350). Judith Knight, 381 Bideford Green, Linslade, Leighton Buzzard, Beds, LU7 7TY. 01525 378161.
www.tringreservoirs.btinternet.co.uk

HERTFORDSHIRE BIRD CLUB, (1971; 290). Jim Terry, 46 Manor Way, Borehamwood, Herts, WD6 1QY. 020 8905 1461;
e-mail: jim@jayjoy.fsnet.co.uk

Ringing Groups
AYLESBURY VALE RG (main activity at Marsworth), S M Downhill, 12 Millfield, Berkhamsted, Herts, HP4 2PB. 01442 865821;
e-mail: smdjbd@waitrose.com
MAPLE CROSS RG, P Delaloye, 34 Watford Road, Croxley Green, Herts, WD3 3BJ. 01923 442182; e-mail: delaloye34@lineone.net
RYE MEADS RG, D G Baggott, 86 Fordwich Rise, Hertford, SG14 2DE.
www.rmrg.care4free.net
TRING RG, Mick A'Court, 29A Amersham Hill, High Wycombe, Bucks, HP13 6NU. H:01494 536734; W:01494 462246;
e-mail: mick@focusrite.com

RSPB Members' Groups
CHORLEYWOOD & DISTRICT, (1977; 128). Dennis A Spooner, Old Tannery House, 333 Uxbridge Road, Rickmansworth, Herts, WD3 2DT. 01923 776854.

HARPENDEN, (1974; 900). Peter Thomley, 10 Lea Road, Harpenden, Herts, AL5 4PG. 01582 620755.
HEMEL HEMPSTEAD, (1973; 130). Paul Green, 310 North Ridgeway, Hemel Hempstead, HP1 2AB. 01442 266637.
HITCHIN & LETCHWORTH, (1973; 106). Tim Goose, 2 Masefield Road, Hitchin, Herts, SG4 0QB. 01462 435605;
e-mail: tim@twgoose.freeserve.co.uk
www.twgoose.freeserve.co.uk
POTTERS BAR & BARNET, (1977; 1800). Stan Bailey, 23 Bowmans Close, Potters Bar, Herts, EN6 5NN. 01707 646073.
ST ALBANS, (1979; 1500). John Maxfield, 46 Gladeside, Jersey Farm, St Albans, Herts, AL4 9JA. 01727 832688;
e-mail: peterantram@antram.demon.co.uk
www.antram.demon.co.uk/
SOUTH EAST HERTS, (1971; 2000). Phil Blatcher, 3 Churchfields, Broxbourne, Herts, EN10 7JU. 01992 441024;
e-mail: SE_Herts_RSPB@hotmail.com
STEVENAGE, (1982; 1000). Mrs Sue Pople, 633 Lonsdale Road, Stevenage, Herts, SG1 5ED. 01438 232508.
WATFORD, (1974; 480). John Britten, Harlestone, 98 Sheepcot Lane, Garston, Watford, WD25 0EB. 01923 673205;
e-mail: john.britten@btinternet.com; http://members.tripod.co.uk/watford_rspb/

Wetland Bird Survey Organisers

ALL EXCEPT LEE VALLEY, Jim Terry, 46 Manor Way, Borehamwood, Herts, WD6 1QY. 020 8905 1461; e-mail: jim@jayjoy.fsnet.co.uk
LEE VALLEY, Ian Kendall, Lee Valley Reg Park Authority, Abbey Mills, Highbridge Street, Waltham Abbey, Essex, EN9 1BZ.
Tel/fax 01992 714610;
e-mail: rangerscentral@leevalleypark.org.uk

Wildlife Hospital

SWAN CARE, Secretary, Swan Care, 14 Moorland Road, Boxmoor, Hemel Hempstead, Herts, HP1 1NH. 01442 251961.
Swans. Sanctuary and treatment centre. Veterinary support.

Wildlife Trust

HERTS & MIDDLESEX WILDLIFE TRUST, (1964; 8500). Grebe House, St Michael's Street, St Albans, Herts, AL3 4SN. 01727 858901; fax 01727 854542; e-mail: hertswt@cix.co.uk

ISLE OF WIGHT

Bird Recorder

Position vacant,

Bird Reports

ISLE OF WIGHT BIRD REPORT (1996-) (various titles 1920-95), From Mr DJ Hunnybun, 40 Churchill Road, Cowes, Isle of Wight, PO31 8HH.

BTO Regional Representative

James C Gloyn, 3 School Close, Newchurch, Isle of Wight, PO36 0NL. 01983 865567;
e-mail: gloynjc@yahoo.com

Clubs

ISLE OF WIGHT NATURAL HISTORY & ARCHAEOLOGICAL SOCIETY, (1919; 450). Dr Margaret Jackson, The Fruitery, Brook Hill, Brook, Newport, Isle of Wight, PO30 6EP. 01983 740015.
ISLE OF WIGHT ORNITHOLOGICAL GROUP, (1986; 135). G Sparshott, Leopards Farm, Main Road, Havenstreet, Isle of Wight, PO33 4DR. 01983 882549.

RSPB Members' Group

ISLE OF WIGHT, (1979; 188). John Cole, 12 Monterey Road, Ryde, Isle of Wight, PO33 3JR. 01983 611797.

Wetland Bird Survey Organisers

ESTUARIES & COASTAL SITES, James C Gloyn, 3 School Close, Newchurch, Isle of Wight, PO36 0NL. 01983 865567;
e-mail: gloynjc@yahoo.com
INLAND, John Stafford, Westering, Moor Lane, Brighstone, Newport, Isle of Wight, PO30 4DL. 01983 740280.

Wildlife Trust

Director, See Hampshire,

KENT

Bird Atlas/Avifauna

The Birds of Kent by D W Taylor et al (Kent Ornithological Society, 1981).
Kent Ornithological Society Winter Bird Survey by N Tardivel (KOS, 1984).

Bird Recorder

Don Taylor, 1 Rose Cottages, Old Loose Hill, Loose, Maidstone, Kent, ME15 0BN. 01622 745641; e-mail: Don.Taylor@care4free.net

Bird Reports

DUNGENESS BIRD OBSERVATORY REPORT (1989-), From Warden, see Reserves.
KENT BIRD REPORT (1952-), From Dave Sutton, 61 Alpha Road, Birchington, Kent, CT7 9ED. 01843 842541;
e-mail: dave@sutton8.freeserve.co.uk
SANDWICH BAY BIRD OBSERVATORY REPORT, From Warden, see Reserves.

BTO Regional Representative & Regional Development Officer

RR, Martin Coath, 77 Oakhill Road, Sevenoaks, Kent, TN13 1NU. 01732 460710;
e-mail: mcoath@waitrose.com

Club

KENT ORNITHOLOGICAL SOCIETY, (1952; 771). Dr Grant Hazlehurst, PO Box 1211, London, NW1 1AE. 020 8650 7063.

Ringing Groups

DARTFORD RG, P E Jones, Sheppards Barn, Hurst Green, Oxted, Surrey, RH8 9BS.
DUNGENESS BIRD OBSERVATORY, David Walker, Dungeness Bird Observatory, Dungeness, Romney Marsh, Kent, TN29 9NA. 01797 321309;
e-mail: dungeness.obs@tinyonline.co.uk
RECULVER RG, Chris Hindle, 42 Glenbervie Drive, Herne Bay, Kent, CT6 6QL. 01227 373070; e-mail: christopherhindle@hotmail.com
SANDWICH BAY BIRD OBSERVATORY, K J Webb, Sandwich Bay Bird Observatory, Guilford Road, Sandwich, Kent, CT13 9PF. 01304 617341; e-mail: kevinjwebb@hotmail.com
SWALE WADER RG, Rod Smith, 67 York Avenue, Chatham, Kent, ME5 9ES. 01634 865863; e-mail: rod.Smith@care4free.net

RSPB Members' Groups

CANTERBURY, (1973; 230). Jean Bomber, St Heliers, 30a Castle Road, Tankerton, Whitstable, Kent, CT5 2DY. 01227 277725.
GRAVESEND & DISTRICT, (1977; 250). Peter Heathcote, 9 Greenfinches, New Barn, Kent, DA3 7ND. 01474 702498.
www.gravesend-rspb.freeserve.co.uk
MAIDSTONE, (1973; 250). Dick Marchese, 11 Bathurst Road, Staplehurst, Tonbridge, Kent, TN12 0LG. 01580 892458.
MEDWAY, (1974; 230). Sue Carter, 31 Ufton Lane, Sittingbourne, ME10 1JB. 01795 427854.
www.medway-rspb.pwp.blueyonder.co.uk
SEVENOAKS, (1974; 350). Bernard Morris, New House Farm, Kilkhampton, Bude, Cornwall, EX23 9RZ. 01288 321727; or 07967 564699; (Fax)01288 321838;
e-mail: bernard@amorris32.freeserve.co.uk
SOUTH EAST KENT, (1981; 260). Keith Shepherd, 23 Barton Road, Dover, Kent, CT16 9NF. 01304 225757.
THANET, (1976; 200). Paul Hale, 2 Shutler Road, Broadstairs, Kent, CT10 1HD. 01843 601482; e-mail: paul.hale@care4free.net
TONBRIDGE, (1975; 1430). Ms Gabrielle Sutcliffe, 1 Postern Heath Cottages, Postern Lane, Tonbridge, Kent, TN11 0QU. 01732 365583.

Wetland Bird Survey Organisers

INNER THAMES ESTUARY, Jeremy Alderton, 367 Baddow Road, Chelmsford, CM2 7QF. 01245 471400.
EAST, Ken Lodge, 14 Gallwey Avenue, Birchington, Kent, CT7 9PA. 01843 843105;
e-mail: kenlodge@minnisbay15.freeserve.co.uk
MEDWAY ESTUARY & NORTH KENT MARSHES, Alan Johnson, RSPB Bromhey Farm, Eastborough, Cooling, Rochester, Kent, ME3 8DS.
PEGWELL BAY, Pete Findley, Sandwich Bay Bird Observatory, Guilford Road, Sandwich, Kent, CT13 9PF. 01304 617341;
e-mail: sbbot@talk21.com
SWALE ESTUARY, Bob Gomes, Kingshill Farm, Elmley, Sheerness, Kent, ME12 3RW. 01795 665969.

DUNGENESS AREA, David Walker, Dungeness Bird Observatory, Dungeness, Romney Marsh, Kent, TN29 9NA. 01797 321309; e-mail: dungeness@tinyonline.co.uk
WEST, Vacant,

Wildlife Hospital
RAPTOR CENTRE, Eddie Hare, Ivy Cottage, Groombridge Place, Groombridge, Tunbridge Wells, Kent, TN3 9QG. 01892 861175; fax 01892 863761. www.raptorcentre.co.uk
Birds of prey. Veterinary support.

Wildlife Trust
KENT WILDLIFE TRUST, (1958; 10500). Tyland Barn, Sandling, Maidstone, Kent, ME14 3BD. 01622 662012; fax 01622 671390; kentwildlife@cix.co.uk
www.wildlifetrust.org.uk/kent

LANCASHIRE

Bird Atlas/Avifauna
An Atlas of Breeding Birds of Lancaster and District by Ken Harrison (Lancaster & District Birdwatching Society, 1995).
Breeding Birds of Lancashire and North Merseyside (2001), sponsored by North West Water. Contact: Bob Pyefinch, 12 Bannistre Court, Tarleton, Preston PR4 6HA.

Bird Recorder
(See also Manchester),
Inc North Merseyside, Steve White, 102 Minster Court, Crown Street, Liverpool, L7 3QD. 0151 707 2744; e-mail: lwildlife@cix.co.uk

Bird Reports
BIRDS OF LANCASTER & DISTRICT (1959-from Secretary, Lancaster & District BWS,
EAST LANCASHIRE ORNITHOLOGISTS' CLUB BIRD REPORT (1998-), from Secretary.
BLACKBURN & DISTRICT BIRD CLUB ANNUAL REPORT (1992-), from Doreen Bonner, 6 Winston Road, Blackburn, BB1 8BJ. Tel/fax; 01254 261480.
FYLDE BIRD REPORT (1983-), from Secretary, Fylde Bird Club.
LANCASHIRE BIRD REPORT (1914-), from Secretary, Lancs & Cheshire Fauna Soc.

BTO Regional Representatives & Regional Development Officer
EAST RR, Tony Cooper, 28 Peel Park Avenue, Clitheroe, Lancs, BB7 1ET. 01200 424577; e-mail: tonycooper@beeb.net
NORTH & WEST RR & RDO, Dave Sharpe, 17 Greenwood Avenue, Bolton-le-Sands, Carnforth, Lancs, LA5 8AN. H:01524 822492; e-mail: dave.s@airtime.co.uk
SOUTH RR, Philip Shearwood, Netherside, Green Lane, Whitestake, Preston, PR4 4AH. 01772 745488; e-mail: phil.shearwood@virgin.net

Clubs
BLACKBURN & DISTRICT BIRD CLUB, (1991; 134). Jim Bonner, 6 Winston Road, Blackburn, BB1 8BJ. Tel/fax;01254 261480.
CHORLEY & DISTRICT NATURAL HISTORY SOCIETY, (1979; 170). Phil Kirk, Millend, Dawbers Lane, Euxton, Chorley, Lancs, PR7 6EB. 01257 266783; e-mail: philkirk@clara.net
www.philkirk.clara.net/cdnhs/

EAST LANCASHIRE ORNITHOLOGISTS' CLUB, (1955; 45). Doug Windle, 39 Stone Edge Road, Barrowford, Nelson, Lancs, BB9 6BB. 01282 617401; e-mail: doug.windle@care4free.net
FYLDE BIRD CLUB, (1982; 60). Paul Ellis, 18 Staining Rise, Blackpool, FY3 0BU. 01253 891281; e-mail: paulellis@fyldebirdclub.freeuk.com
www.fyldebirdclub.freeuk.com
FYLDE NATURALISTS' SOCIETY, (1946; 120). Gerry Stephen, 10 Birch Way, Poulton-le-Fylde, Blackpool, FY6 7SF. 01253 895195.
LANCASHIRE & CHESHIRE FAUNA SOCIETY, (1914; 130). Dave Bickerton, 64 Petre Crescent, Rishton, Lancs, BB1 4RB. 01254 886257; e-mail: bickertond@cs.com
LANCASHIRE BIRD CLUB, (1996). Dave Bickerton, 64 Petre Crescent, Rishton, Lancs, BB1 4RB. 01254 886257; e-mail: bickertond@cs.com
LANCASTER & DISTRICT BIRD WATCHING SOCIETY, (1959; 205). Andrew Cadman, 57

Greenways, Over Kellet, Carnforth, Lancs, LA6 1DE. 01524 734462.
ROSSENDALE ORNITHOLOGISTS' CLUB, (1976; 35). Ian Brady, 25 Chur ch St, Newchurch, Rossendale, Lancs, BB4 9RX. 01706 222120.

Ringing Groups

FYLDE RG, G Barnes, 17 Lomond Avenue, Marton, Blackpool, FY3 9QL.
MORECAMBE BAY WADER RG, J Sheldon, 415 West Shore Park, Barrow-in-Furness, Cumbria, LA14 3XZ. 01229 473102
NORTH LANCS RG, John Wilson BEM, 40 Church Hill Avenue, Warton, Carnforth, Lancs, LA5 9NU.
SOUTH WEST LANCASHIRE RG, J D Fletcher, 4 Hawksworth Drive, Freshfield, Formby, Merseyside, L37 7EZ. 01704 877837.

RSPB Members' Groups

BLACKPOOL, (1983; 170). Alan Stamford, Flat 3, Fairhurst Court, Rossall Road, Cleveleys, FY5 1HA. 01253 859662.
LANCASTER, (1972; 210). John Wilson BEM, 40 Church Hill Avenue, Warton, Carnforth, Lancs, LA5 9NU.

Wetland Bird Survey Organisers

MORECAMBE BAY (South), Mr Jon Carter, 61 Sibsey Street, Lancaster, 01524 842738.
RIBBLE ESTUARY, Mike Gee, English Nature, Old Hollow, Marsh Road, Banks, Southport, PR9 8DU. 01704 229624.
INLAND, NORTH, Dave Sharpe, 17 Greenwood Avenue, Bolton-le-Sands, Carnforth, Lancs, LA5 8AN. H:01524 822492; W:01524 64160
EAST, Stephen Dunstan, 29 Greenfinch Court, Herons Reach, Blackpool, FY3 8FG. 01253 301009.
INLAND, WEST, Chris Tomlinson, WWT Martin Mere, Burscough, Ormskirk, Lancs, L40 0TA. H:01704 895181.

Wildlife Trust

LANCASHIRE WILDLIFE TRUST, (1962; 3500). Cuerden Park Wildlife Centre, Shady Lane, Bamber Bridge, Preston, PR5 6AU. 01772 324129; fax: 01772 628849;
e-mail: lancswt@cix.co.uk
www.wildlifetrust.org.uk/lancashire

LEICESTERSHIRE & RUTLAND

Bird Recorder

Rob Fray, 5 New Park Road, Aylestone, Leicester, LE2 8AW. 0116 223 8491;
e-mail: robfray@fray-r.freeserve.co.uk

Bird Reports

LEICESTERSHIRE & RUTLAND BIRD REPORT (1941-), From Mrs S Graham, 5 Brading Road, Leicester, LE3 9BG. 0116 262 5505;
e-mail: jsgraham83@aol.com
RUTLAND NAT HIST SOC ANNUAL REPORT (1965-), from Secretary.

BTO Regional Representative

LEICESTER & RUTLAND, Jim Graham, 5 Brading Road, Leicester, LE3 9BG. 0116 262 5505; e-mail: jsgraham83@aol.com

Clubs

BIRSTALL BIRDWATCHING CLUB, (1976; 50). Ken J Goodrich, 6 Riversdale Close, Birstall, Leicester, LE4 4EH. 0116 267 4813.

LEICESTERSHIRE & RUTLAND ORNITHOLOGICAL SOCIETY, (1941; 462). Mrs Marion Vincent, 48 Templar Way, Rothley, Leicester, LE7 7RB. 0116 230 3405.
www.lros.org.uk

MARKET HARBOROUGH & DISTRICT NATURAL HISTORY SOCIETY, (1971; 40). Mrs Sue Allibone, 20 Smyth Close, Market Harborough, Leics, LE16 7NS. 01858 410385.
RUTLAND NATURAL HISTORY SOCIETY, (1964; 256). Mrs L Worrall, 6 Redland Close, Barrowden, Oakham, Rutland, LE15 8ES. 01572 747302.

Ringing Groups

RUTLAND WATER RG, D Roizer, 38 Kestrel Road, Oakham, Rutland, LE15 6BU.
STANFORD RG, M J Townsend, 87 Dunton Road, Broughton Astley, Leics, LE9 6NA.

RSPB Members' Groups

LEICESTER, (1969; 1200). Peter Kightley, 16 Barwell Road, Kirby Muxloe, Leics, LE9 2AA. 0116 239 4271; e-mail: joan.kightley@virgin.net
LOUGHBOROUGH, (1970; 300). Keith Freeman, 2 Leckhampton Road, Loughborough, Leics, LE11 4TH. 01509 230908.

Wetland Bird Survey Organisers

ALL EXCEPT RUTLAND WATER, Andrew Harrop, 30 Dean Street, Oakham, Leics, LE15 6AF. 01572 757134;
e-mail: andrew.harrop@virgin.net
RUTLAND WATER, Tim Appleton, Fishponds Cottage, Stamford Road, Oakham, Rutland, Leics, LE15 8AB. 01572 770651;
e-mail: tim@rutlandwater.org.uk

Wildlife Trust

LEICESTERSHIRE & RUTLAND WILDLIFE TRUST, (1956; 3000). Longfellow Road, Knighton Fields, Leicester, LE2 6BT.
0116 270 2999; fax 0116 270 9555;
e-mail: leicswt@cix.co.uk

LINCOLNSHIRE

Bird Recorders

NORTH, Position vacant.
SOUTH, Position vacant.

Bird Reports

LINCOLNSHIRE BIRD REPORT inc Gibraltar Point Bird Obs(1979-), from R K Watson, 8 High Street, Skegness, Lincs, PE25 3NW. 01754 763481.
SCUNTHORPE & NORTH WEST LINCOLNSHIRE BIRD REPORT (1973-), from Secretary, Scunthorpe Museum Society, Ornithological Section.

BTO Regional Representatives & Regional Development Officer

EAST RR, Position vacant,
NORTH RR, Position vacant,
SOUTH RR, Richard & Kay Heath, 56 Pennytoft Lane, Pinchbeck, Spalding, Lincs, PE11 3PQ. 01775 767055; e-mail: heathsrk@bigfoot.com
WEST RR, Peter Overton, Hilltop Farm, Welbourn, Lincoln, LN5 0QH. Work 01400 273323; e-mail: nyika@biosearch.org.uk
RDO, Nicholas Watts, Vine House Farm, Deeping St Nicholas, Spalding, Lincs, PE11 3DG. 01775 630208.

Club

LINCOLNSHIRE BIRD CLUB, (1979; 220). M Harrison, Sherbrooke, Holme Road, Kirton Holme, Boston, Lincs, PE20 1SY.
01205 290575.
SCUNTHORPE MUSEUM SOCIETY (Ornithological Section), (1973; 50). Craig Nimick, 115 Grange Lane South, Scunthorpe, N Lincs, DN16 3BW. 01724 339659.

Ringing Groups

GIBRALTAR POINT BIRD OBSERVATORY, Adrian Blackburn, Suleska, 1 Richmond Road, Retford, Notts, DN22 6SJ. 01777 706516; (M)07718 766873.
MID LINCOLNSHIRE RG, J Mawer, 18 Standish Lane, Immingham, Lincs, DN40 2HA. 01469 518549.
WASH WADER RG, P L Ireland, 27 Hainfield Drive, Solihull, W Midlands, B91 2PL. 0121 704 1168; e-mail: phil_ireland@bigfoot.com

RSPB Members' Groups

GRIMSBY, (1986; 1580). Brian Sykes, 93 Humberstone Road, Grimsby, Lincs, 01472 320418. www.birds.ic24.act
LINCOLN, (1974; 250). Peter Skelson, 26 Parksgate Avenue, Lincoln, LN6 7HP. 01522 695747; e-mail: peter.skelson@care4free.net www.lincoln.rspb.care4free.net
SOUTH LINCOLNSHIRE, (1987; 200). Barry Hancock, The Limes, Mere Booth Road, Antons Gowt, Boston, Lincs, PE22 7BG. 01205 280057.

Wetland Bird Survey Organisers

HUMBER, INNER SOUTH, Keith Parker, 7 Ryedale Avenue, Winterton, Scunthorpe, Lincs, DN15 9BJ. 01724 734261.
HUMBER, MID SOUTH SHORE, Ian Shepherd, 38 Lindsey Road, Cleethorpes, DN35 8TN. 01472 697142.
HUMBER, OUTER SOUTH ESTUARY, John Walker, 3 Coastguard Cottages, Churchill Lane, Theddlethorpe, Mablethorpe, Lincs, LN12 1PQ. H:01507 338038.
NORTH LINCS (Inland), John Hollis, c/o Hartsholme Country Park, Skellingthorpe Road, Lincoln, LN6 0EY. W:01522 873577; mobile 0771 2437426; e-mail: jp hollis@talk21.com

SOUTH, John Redshaw, 7 Fennell Road, Pinchbeck, Spalding, Lincs, PE11 3RP. 01775 768227; e-mail: jredshaw@fennell97.fsnet.co.uk
WASH, Lewis James, 157 Freiston Road, Boston, Lincs, PE21 0JR.
e-mail: lewis.james@rspb.org.uk

Wildlife Hospital
FEATHERED FRIENDS WILD BIRD RESCUE, Colin Riches, 5 Blacksmith Lane, Thorpe-on-the-Hill, Lincoln, LN6 9BQ. 01522 684874.
All species. Purpose-built hospital unit. Heated cages, etc. Membership and adoption scheme available. Quarterly newsletter. Veterinary support.

Wildlife Trust
LINCOLNSHIRE WILDLIFE TRUST, (1948; 10,800). Banovallum House, Manor House Street, Horncastle, Lincs, LN9 5HF. 01507 526667; fax 01507 525732; www.lincstrust.co.uk
e-mail: info@lincstrust.co.uk

LONDON, GREATER

Bird Atlas/Avifauna
New Atlas of Breeding Birds of the London Area by Keith Betton (London Natural History Society, in preparation).

Bird Recorder see also Surrey
Andrew Self, 16 Harp Island Close, Neasden, London, NW10 0DF.
e-mail: andrewself@lineone.net
www.users.globalnet.co.uk/~lnhsweb

Bird Report
CROYDON BIRD SURVEY (1995), from Secretary, Croydon RSPB Group.
LONDON BIRD REPORT (20-mile radius of St Paul's Cath) (1936-), from Catherine Schmitt, 4 Falkland Avenue, London, N3 1QR.

BTO Regional Representative & Regional Development Officer
LONDON & MIDDLESEX RR, Derek Coleman, Flat 9, 52 Nightingale Road, Carshalton, Surrey, SM5 2EL. 020 8669 7421.
SOUTH WEST RDO, Position vacant.

Clubs
LONDON NATURAL HISTORY SOCIETY (Ornithology Section), (1858; 1100). Ms N Duckworth, 9 Abbey Court, Cerne Abbas, Dorchester, Dorset, DT2 7JH. 01300 341 195.

MARYLEBONE BIRDWATCHING SOCIETY, (1981; 92). Judy Powell, 7 Rochester Terrace, London, NW1 9JN. 020 7485 0863; e-mail: birdsmbs@yahoo.co.uk www.geocities.com/birdsmbs

Ringing Groups
LONDON GULL STUDY GROUP, Mark Fletcher, 24 The Gowans, Sutton-on-the-Forest, York, YO61 1DJ.
RUNNYMEDE RG, D G Harris, 22 Blossom Waye, Hounslow, TW5 9HD.
e-mail: daveharris@tinyonline.co.uk

RSPB Members' Groups
BEXLEY, (1979; 3500). David James, 78 Colney Road, Dartford, DA1 1UH. 01322 274791.
BROMLEY, (1972; 273). Bob Francis, 2 Perry Rise, Forest Hill, London, SE23 2QL.
020 8669 9325.
www.bromleyrspb.org.uk
CENTRAL LONDON, (1970; 250). Miss Annette Warrick, 12 Tredegar Sq, London, E3 5AD. 020 8981 9624;
e-mail: annette@warricka.freeserve.co.uk
www.janja@dircon.co.uk/rspb
CROYDON, (1973; 4000). Sheila Mason, 5 Freshfields, Shirley, Croydon, CR0 7QS.
020 8777 9370.
www.croydon-rspb.org.uk
ENFIELD, (1971; 2700). Norman G Hudson, 125 Morley Hill, Enfield, Middx, EN2 0BQ. 020 8363 1431.
HAVERING, (1972; 270). Eric Hammond, 33 Canterbury Avenue, Upminster, Essex, RM14 3LD. 01708 222230.
NORTH LONDON, (1974; 3000). John Parsons, 65 Rutland Gardens, Harringay, London, N4 1JW. 020 8802 9537.
NORTH WEST LONDON, (1983; 800). Bob Husband, The Firs, 49 Carson Road, Cockfosters, Barnet, Herts, EN4 9EN. 020 8441 8742.

PINNER & DISTRICT, (1972; 300). Dennis Bristow, 118 Crofts Road, Harrow, Middx, HA1 2PJ. 020 8863 5026.
RICHMOND & TWICKENHAM, (1979; 2300). Steve Harrington, 93 Shaftesbury Way, Twickenham, TW2 5RW. 020 8898 4539.
WEST LONDON, (1973; 400). Alan Bender, 6 Allenby Road, Southall, Middx, UB1 2HQ. 020 8571 0285.

Wetland Bird Survey Organiser

Helen Baker, 60 Townfield, Rickmansworth, Herts, WD3 7DD. 01923 772441.

Wildlife Hospitals

WILDLIFE RESCUE & AMBULANCE SERVICE, Barry and June Smitherman, 19 Chesterfield Road, Enfield, Middx, EN3 6BE. 020 8292 5377.
All categories of wild birds. Emergency ambulance with full rescue equipment, boats, ladders etc. Own treatment centre and aviaries. Veterinary support. Essential to telephone first.

Wildlife Trust

LONDON WILDLIFE TRUST, (1981; 7500). Harling House, 47-51 Great Suffolk Street, London, SE1 0BS. 0207 261 0447; fax: 0207 261 0538; e-mail: londonwt@cix.co.uk
www.wildlifetrust.org.uk/london

MANCHESTER, GREATER

Bird Atlas/Avifauna

Breeding Birds in Greater Manchester by Philip Holland et al (1984).

Bird Recorder

Mrs A Judith Smith, 12 Edge Green Street, Ashton-in-Makerfield, Wigan, WN4 8SL. 01942 712615; e-mail: judith@gmbirds.freeserve.co.uk
www.gmbirds.freeserve.co.uk

Bird Reports

BIRDS IN GREATER MANCHESTER (1976-), from Recorder,
LEIGH ORNITHOLOGICAL SOCIETY BIRD REPORT (1971-), From J Critchley, 2 Albany Grove, Tyldesley, Manchester, M29 7NE. 01942 884644.

BTO Regional Representative & Regional Development Officer

RR, Mrs A Judith Smith, 12 Edge Green Street, Ashton-in-Makerfield, Wigan, WN4 8SL. 01942 712615; e-mail: judith@gmbirds.freeserve.co.uk
www.gmbirds.freeserve.co.uk
RDO, Jim Jeffery, 20 Church Lane, Romiley, Stockport, Cheshire, SK6 4AA.
H:0161 494 5367; W:01625 522107 ext 112; e-mail: j.jeffery@kudos-idd.com

Clubs

GREATER MANCHESTER BIRD CLUB, (1954; 60). Dr R Sandling, 17 Range Road, Stalybridge, Cheshire SK15 Z44.
HALE ORNITHOLOGISTS, (1968; 58). Ms Diana Grellier, 8 Apsley Grove, Bowdon, Altrincham, Cheshire, WA14 3AH. 0161 928 9165.
LEIGH ORNITHOLOGICAL SOCIETY, (1971; 150). Mr D Shallcross, 10 Holden Brook Close, Leigh, Lancs, WN7 2HL. 01942 607206.
www.leighos.org.uk
ROCHDALE FIELD NATURALISTS' SOCIETY, (1970; 90). Mrs J P Wood, 196 Castleton Road, Thornham, Royton, Oldham, OL2 6UP. 0161 345 2012.
STOCKPORT BIRDWATCHING SOCIETY, (1972; 60). Dave Evans, 36 Tatton Road South, Stockport, Cheshire, SK4 4LU. 0161 432 9513.

Ringing Groups

LEIGH RG, A J Gramauskas, 21 Elliot Avenue, Golborne, Warrington, WA3 3DU. 0151 929215.
SOUTH MANCHESTER RG, C M Richards, Fairhaven, 13 The Green, Handforth, Wilmslow, Cheshire, SK9 3AG. 01625 524527; e-mail: cliveandray.richards@care4free.net

RSPB Members' Groups

BOLTON, (1978; 550). Peter Young, 83 Church Street, Blackrod, Bolton, BL6 5EE. 01204 692213; email: peterfy@lineone.net
MANCHESTER, (2000). Peter Wolstenholme, 31 South Park Road, Gatley, Cheshire, SK8 4AL. 0161 428 2175.
STOCKPORT, (1979; 250). Brian Hallworth, 69 Talbot Street, Hazel Grove, Stockport, SK7 4BJ. 0161 456 5328.
WIGAN, (1973; 80). Allan Rimmer, 206 Hodges Street, Wigan, Lancs, WN6 7JG. 01942 241402.

Wetland Bird Survey Organiser
Robin Crompton, 56 Palmerston Road, Denton, Manchester, M34 2NY. 0161 320 3048.

Wildlife Hospital
THREE OWLS BIRD SANCTUARY AND RESERVE, Trustee, Nigel Fowler, Wolstenholme Fold, Norden, Rochdale, OL11 5UD. 01706 642162; 24-hr helpline 07973 819389;

e-mail: mail@threeowls.co.uk
www.threeowls.co.uk
Registered charity. All species of wild bird. Rehabilitation and release on Sanctuary Reserve. Open every Sunday 1200-1700, otherwise visitors welcome by appointment. Bi-monthly newsletter. Veterinary support.

Wildlife Trust
Director, See Lancashire,

MERSEYSIDE & WIRRAL

Bird Atlas see Cheshire.

Bird Recorders see Cheshire; Lancashire.

Bird Reports see also Cheshire.
HILBRE BIRD OBSERVATORY REPORT, from Warden, see Reserves.
NORTHWESTERN BIRD REPORT (1938-irregular), from Secretaries, Merseyside Naturalists' Assoc.

BTO Regional Representatives
MERSEYSIDE RR, Bob Harris, 2 Dulas Road, Wavertree Green, Liverpool, L15 6UA. Work 0151 706 4311; e-mail: harris@liv.ac.uk
WIRRAL RR, Kelvin Britton, 9B Kingsmead Road South, Prenton, Birkenhead, Merseyside, CH43 6TA. 0151 653 9751.

Clubs
LIVERPOOL ORNITHOLOGISTS' CLUB (membership by invitation), (1953; 40). Mrs V McFarland, The Cedars, Quakers Lane, Heswall, Wirral, CH60 6RD.
MERSEYSIDE NATURALISTS' ASSOCIATION. (1938; 250). Joint Hon Secretaries, Eric Hardy, 47 Woodsorrel Road, Liverpool, L15 6UB. 0151 722 2819.
Also Steven Cross, 58 Kinstwood Avenue, Liverpool L22 4RL; 0151 920 5718.
WIRRAL BIRD CLUB, (1977; 150). Mrs Hilda Truesdale, Cader, 8 Park Road, Meols, Wirral, CH47 7BG. 0151 632 2705.

Ringing Groups
HILBRE BIRD OBSERVATORY, John C Gittins, 17 Deva Road, West Kirby, Wirral, CH48 4DB. 0151 625 5428.
MERSEYSIDE RG, P Slater, 45 Greenway Road, Speke, Liverpool, L24 7RY.
SOUTH WEST LANCASHIRE RG, J D Fletcher, 4 Hawksworth Drive, Freshfield, Formby, Merseyside, L37 7EZ. 01704 877837.

RSPB Members' Groups
LIVERPOOL, (1966; 162). Chris Tynan, 10 Barker Close, Huyton, Liverpool, L36 0XU. 0151 480 7938.
SEFTON COAST, (1980; 199). Peter Taylor, 26 Tilshon Road, Walton, L9 6AJ. 0151 474 9129.
SOUTHPORT, (1974; 250). Group Leader, 01704 872421.
WIRRAL, (1982; 120). Steve Woolfall, 85 Ridgemere Road, Pensby, Wirral, Merseyside, CH61 8RR. 0151 648 6007;
e-mail: swoolfall@chestercc.gov.uk
www.users.globalnet.co.uk/~jowitt/rspb.htm

Wetland Bird Survey Organisers
ALT ESTUARY, Jack Taylor, 4 Whitham Avenue, Crosby, Merseyside, L23 0RD.
DEE ESTUARY, Colin Wells, Burton Point Farm, Station Road, Burton, Nr Neston, South Wirral, CH64 5SB. 0151 336 7681.
MERSEY ESTUARY, Graham Thomason, 110 Coroners Lane, Widnes, Cheshire, WA8 9HZ. 0151 424 7257.
INLAND, Steven Cross, 58 Kingswood Ave, Waterloo, Liverpool, L22 4RL. 0151 920 5718.

Wildlife Trust
Director, see Lancashire.

NORFOLK

Bird Atlas/Avifauna

The Birds of Norfolk by Moss Taylor, Michael Seago, Peter Allard & Don Dorling (Pica Press, 1999).

Bird Recorder

Giles Dunmore, 49 NelsonRoad, Sheringham, Norfolk, NR26 8DA. 01263 822550.

Bird Reports

CLEY BIRD CLUB 10-KM SQUARE BIRD REPORT (1987-), fFrom Secretary.
NAR VALLEY ORNITHOLOGICAL SOCIETY ANNUAL REPORT (1976-), from Secretary.
NORFOLK BIRD & MAMMAL REPORT (1953-), from Secretary, Norfolk and Norwich Naturalists Society, Castle Museum, Norwich, NR1 3JU.
NORFOLK ORNITHOLOGISTS' ASSOCN ANNUAL REPORT (1961-), from Secretary.

BTO Regional Representatives

NORTH-EAST RR, Chris Hudson, Cornerstones, Ringland Road, Taverham, Norwich, NR8 6TG. 01603 868805.
NORTH-WEST RR, Nick Gallichan, Walnut Cottage, High Road, Tilney cum Islington, King's Lynn, PE34 3BN. 01553 617310; e-mail: nick@strange-brew.freeserve.co.uk
SOUTH-EAST RR, Graham Coxall, 4 Shirley Close, Frettenham, Norwich, NR12 7LW. 01603 737486.
SOUTH-WEST RR, Vince Matthews, Rose's Cottage, The Green, Merton, Thetford, Norfolk, IP25 6QU. 01953 884125.

Clubs

CLEY BIRD CLUB, (1986; 300). Peter Gooden, 45 Charles Road, Holt, Norfolk, NR25 6DA. 01263 712368.
GREAT YARMOUTH BIRD CLUB, (1989; 79). Keith R Dye, 104 Wolseley Road, Great Yarmouth, Norfolk, NR31 0EJ. 01493 600705.
NAR VALLEY ORNITHOLOGICAL SOCIETY, (1976; 100). Ian Black, Three Chimneys, Tumbler Hill, Swaffham, Norfolk, PE37 7JG. 01760 724092; e-mail: ian_a_black@hotmail.com
NORFOLK & NORWICH NATURALISTS' SOCIETY, (1869; 490). Dr Tony Leech, 3 Eccles Road, Holt, Norfolk, NR25 6HJ. 01263 712282; e-mail: leecha@dialstart.net
NORFOLK BIRD CLUB, (1992; 350). Vernon Eve, Pebble House, The Street, Syderstone, King's Lynn, Norfolk, PE31 8SD. 01485 578121.
NORFOLK ORNITHOLOGISTS' ASSOCIATION, (1962; 1100). Jed Andrews, Broadwater Road, Holme-next-Sea, Hunstanton, Norfolk, PE36 6LQ. 01485 525406.

Ringing Groups

BTO NUNNERY RG, Dawn Balmer, 39 Station Road, Thetford, Norfolk, IP24 1AW. e-mail: dawn.balmer@bto.org www.nunnery-ringing.org.uk
HOLME BIRD OBSERVATORY, J M Reed, 21 Hardings, Panshanger, Welwyn Garden City, Herts, AL7 2EQ. 01707 336351.
NORTH WEST NORFOLK RG, J M Reed, 21 Hardings, Panshanger, Welwyn Garden City, Herts, AL7 2EQ. 01707 336351.
SHERINGHAM RG, D Sadler, Denver House, 25 Holt Road, Sheringham, Norfolk, NR26 8NB. 01263 821904. e-mail: dhsadler@hotmail.com
UEA RG, D Thomas, 15 Grant Street, Norwich, NR2 4HA.
WASH WADER RG, P L Ireland, 27 Hainfield Drive, Solihull, W Midlands, B91 2PL. 0121 704 1168; e-mail: phil_ireland@bigfoot.com
WISSEY RG, S J Browne, End Cottage, 24 Westgate Street, Hilborough, Norfolk, IP26 5BN. e-mail: sjbathome@aol.com

RSPB Members' Groups

NORWICH, (1971; 259). Charles Seagrave, 2 Riverside Cottages, Barford, Norwich, NR9 4BE. 01603 759752; e-mail: seagrave@connectfree.co.uk
WEST NORFOLK, (1977; 247). David Lake, 194B Wootton Road, King's Lynn, Norfolk, PE30 3BQ. 01553 673873.

Wetland Bird Survey Organisers

BREYDON WATER, Peter R Allard, 39 Mallard Way, Bradwell, Great Yarmouth, Norfolk, NR31 8JY. 01493 657798; e-mail; peter.allard@rjt.co.uk

NORTH NORFOLK COAST, Michael Rooney, English Nature, Hill Farm Offices, Main Road, Wells-next-the-Sea, Norfolk, NR23 1AB. 01328 711866;
e-mail: micheal.rooney@english-nature.org.uk
WASH, James Cadbury, RSPB, The Lodge, Sandy, Beds, SG19 2DL. 01767 680551.
INLAND, Tim Strudwick, RSPB Strumpshaw Fen, Staithe Cottage, Low Road, Strumpshaw, Norfolk, NR13 4HS. 01603 715191;
e-mail: tim.strudwick@rspb.org.uk

Wildlife Hospitals
RSPCA NORFOLK WILDLIFE HOSPITAL, Administrator, Mrs A Smith, Station Road, East Winch, King's Lynn, Norfolk, PE32 1NR. 01553 842336.
All species. Specialist treatment of oiled birds. Purpose-built surgery, x-ray, isolation, bird washing rooms, rehabilitation pools, aviaries. Group visits by appointment, with open days for the general public. Full-time veterinary surgeon and qualified staff.
SHAW, Mrs Brenda, Fourways, Litcham, King's Lynn, Norfolk, PE32 2NZ. 01328 701383.
All species of wild bird. Veterinary support.

Wildlife Trust
NORFOLK WILDLIFE TRUST, (1926; 17,500). 72 Cathedral Close, Norwich, NR1 4DF. 01603 625540; fax 01603 630593;
e-mail: admin@nwt.cix.co.uk

NORTHAMPTONSHIRE

Bird Recorder
Paul Gosling, 23 Newtown Road, Little Irchester, Northants, NN8 2DX. 01933 227709;
e-mail: paul_gosling@lineone.net

Bird Report
NORTHAMPTONSHIRE BIRD REPORT (1969-), from Recorder.

BTO Regional Representative & Regional Development Officer
RR, Phil W Richardson, 10 Bedford Cottages, Great Brington, Northampton, NN7 4JE. 01604 770632.
RDO, Bill Metcalfe, Blendon, Rockingham Hills, Oundle, Peterborough, PE8 4QA. 01832 274647.

Clubs
DAVENTRY NATURAL HISTORY SOCIETY, (1970; 18). Leslie G Tooby, The Elms, Leamington Road, Long Itchington, Southam, Warks, CV47 9PL. 0192 681 2269.

NORTHAMPTONSHIRE BIRD CLUB, (1973; 100). Mrs Eleanor McMahon, Oriole House, 5 The Croft, Hanging Houghton, Northants, NN6 9HW. 01604 880009.

Ringing Group
NORTHANTS RG, D M Francis, 2 Brittons Drive, Billing Lane, Northampton, NN3 5DP.

RSPB Members' Groups
MID NENE, (1975; 250). Michael Ridout, Melrose, 140 Northampton Road, Rushden, Northants, NN10 6AN. 01933 355544.
NORTHAMPTON, (1978; 3000). Liz Wicks, 6 Waypost Court, Lings, Northampton, NN3 8LN. 01604 513991.

Wetland Bird Survey Organiser
Robert Ratcliffe, 173 Montague Road, Bilton, Rugby, Warks, CV22 6LG. 01788 336983.

Wildlife Trust
Director, see Cambridgeshire.

NORTHUMBERLAND

Bird Atlas/Avifauna
The Atlas of Breeding Birds in Northumbria edited by J C Day et al (Northumberland and Tyneside Bird Club, 1995).

Bird Recorder
Ian Fisher, 74 Benton Park Road, Newcastle upon Tyne, NE7 7NB. 0191 266 7900;
e-mail: ian@hauxley.freeserve.co.uk
www.ntbc.org.uk

Bird Reports
BIRDS IN NORTHUMBRIA (1970-), from Muriel Cadwallender, 22 South View, Lesbury, NE66

3PZ. 01665 830884;
e-mail: tmcadwallender@lineone.net
BIRDS ON THE FARNE ISLANDS (1971-), from Secretary, Natural History Society of Northumbria.

BTO Regional Representative & Regional Development Officer

RR, Tom Cadwallender, 22 South View, Lesbury, Alnwick, Northumberland, NE66 3PZ. H:01665 830884; W:01670 533039;
e-mail: tmcadwallender@lineone.net
RDO, Muriel Cadwallender, 22 South View, Lesbury, Alnwick, Northumberland, NE66 3PZ. 01665 830884.
e-mail: tmcadwallender@lineone.net

Clubs

NATURAL HISTORY SOCIETY OF NORTHUMBRIA, (1829; 900). David C Noble-Rollin, Hancock Museum, Barras Bridge, Newcastle upon Tyne, NE2 4PT. 0191 232 6386;
e-mail: david.noble-rollin@ncl.ac.uk
NORTH NORTHUMBERLAND BIRD CLUB, (1984; 210). David Welch, 26 Armstrong Cottages, Bamburgh, Northumberland, NE69 7BA. 01668 214403.
NORTHUMBERLAND & TYNESIDE BIRD CLUB, (1958; 270). Sarah Barratt, 3 Haydon Close, Red House Farm, Gosforth, Newcastle upon Tyne, NE3 2BY. 0191 213 6665.

Ringing Groups

BAMBURGH RS, Mike S Hodgson, 31 Uplands, Monkseaton, Whitley Bay, Tyne & Wear, NE25 9AG. 0191 252 0511.
NATURAL HISTORY SOCIETY OF NORTHUMBRIA, Dr C P F Redfern, Westfield House, Acomb, Hexham, Northumberland, NE46 4RJ.
NORTHUMBRIA RG. Secretary, B Galloway, 34 West Meadows, Stamfordham Road, Westerhope, Newcastle upon Tyne, NE5 1LS. 0191 286 4850.

Wetland Bird Survey Organisers

LINDISFARNE, Phil Davey, English Nature, Beal Station, Berwick-upon-Tweed, TD15 2SP. 01289 381470.
NORTHUMBERLAND COAST (excl Lindisfarne), Dr Roger Norman, 1 Prestwick Gardens, Kenton, Newcastle upon Tyne, NE3 3DN. Tel/fax 0191 285 8314;
e-mail: r.norman@clara.net
INLAND, Steve Holliday, 2 Larriston Place, Cramlington, Northumberland, NE23 8ER.

Wildlife Hospitals

BERWICK SWAN & WILDLIFE TRUST, M L Allport, Keld, 4 Ryecroft Park, Wooler, Northumberland, NE71 6AS. 01668 281249;
e-mail: mail@swan-trust.org.uk
Registered charity. All categories of birds. Indoor pool for swans. Veterinary support.
WILDLIFE IN NEED SANCTUARY, Mrs Lisa Bolton, Shepherds Cottage, Chatton, Alnwick, Northumberland, NE66 5PX. 01668 215281.
All categories of birds. Number of gulls restricted. Oiled birds sent to Swan & Wildlife Trust, Berwick. Heated bird room. Aviaries. Veterinary support. Visiting strictly by appointment.

Wildlife Trust

NORTHUMBERLAND WILDLIFE TRUST, (1962; 5000). The Garden House, St Nicholas Park, Jubilee Road, Newcastle upon Tyne, NE3 3XT. 0191 284 6884; fax 0191 284 6794;
e-mail: mail@northwt.org.uk

NOTTINGHAMSHIRE

Bird Recorders

Steve Keller, 17 Suffolk Avenue, Beeston Rylands, Notts, NG9 1NN. 0115 917 1452;
e-mail: s.keller@ntlworld.com

Bird Reports

LOUND BIRD REPORT (1990-), From Secretary, Lound Bird Club, 01302 745594;
e-mail: tichodroma@btinternet.com
BIRDS OF NOTTINGHAMSHIRE (1943-), From Howard Broughton, 5 Park Road, Plumtree Park, Nottingham, NG12 5LX. 0115 937 4474.

BTO Regional Representative & Regional Development Officer

RR, Mrs Lynda Milner, 6 Kirton Park, Kirton, Newark, Notts, NG22 9LR. 01623 862025;
e-mail: lyndamilner@hotmail.com

Clubs

COLWICK PARK WILDLIFE GROUP, (1994; 150). Michael Walker, 14 Ramblers Close, Colwick, Nottingham, NG4 2DN. 0115 961 5494. www.colwick2000.freeserve.co.uk

LOUND BIRD CLUB, (1991; 50). P Hobson, 6 St Mary's Crescent, Tickhill, Doncaster, DN11 9JW. 01302 745594; e-mail: tichodroma@btinternet.com

NETHERFIELD WILDLIFE GROUP, (1999; 95). Philip Burnham, 38 Gedling Road, Arnold, Nottingham, NG5 6NW. 0115 953 5817.

NOTTINGHAMSHIRE BIRDWATCHERS, (1935; 420). Mark Keighley, 64 Highgate Drive, Ilkeston, Derbys, DE7 9HU. 0115 944 4726.

WOLLATON NATURAL HISTORY SOCIETY, (1976; 105). Mrs P Price, 33 Coatsby Road, Hollycroft, Kimberley, Nottingham, NG16 2TH. 0115 938 4965.

Ringing Groups

BIRKLANDS RG, A D Lowe, 12 Midhurst Way, Clifton Estate, Nottingham, NG11 8DY. e-mail: birklandsringinggroup@lineone.net

NORTH NOTTS RG, Adrian Blackburn, Suleska, 1 Richmond Road, Retford, Notts, DN22 6SJ. 01777 706516; (M)07718 766873.

SOUTH WEST NOTTINGHAMSHIRE RG, K J Hemsley, 8 Grange Farm Close, Toton, Beeston, Notts, NG9 6EB. e-mail: k.hemsley@ntlworld.com

TRESWELL WOOD INTEGRATED POPULATION MONITORING GROUP, Chris du Feu, 66 High Street, Beckingham, Notts, DN10 4PF. e-mail: chris@beckingham0.demon.co.uk

RSPB Members' Groups

MANSFIELD AND DISTRICT, (1986; 205). Chris Watkinson, 9 Ash Ford Rise, Sutton-in-Ashfield, Notts, NG17 2BB. 01623 403669.

NOTTINGHAM, (1974; 399). Andrew Griffin, Hawthorn Cottage, Thornton, Notts, NG13 9DS. 01949 851426; e-mail: andrew@thoroton.f.sworld.co.uk www.notts-rspb.org.uk

Wetland Bird Survey Organiser

Steve Branch, 145 Kilton Road, Worksop, Notts, S80 2ED. 01909 488079.

Wildlife Trust

NOTTINGHAMSHIRE WILDLIFE TRUST, (1963; 4300). The Old Ragged School, Brook Street, Nottingham, NG1 1EA. 0115 958 8242; fax: 0115 924 3175; e-mail: nottswt@cix.co.uk www.wildlifetrust.org.uk/nottinghamshire

OXFORDSHIRE

Bird Atlas/Avifauna

Birds of Oxfordshire by J W Brucker et al (Oxford, Pisces, 1992).

The New Birds of the Banbury Area by T G Easterbrook (Banbury Ornithological Society, 1995).

Bird Recorder

Ian Lewington, 119 Brasenose Road, Didcot, Oxon, OX11 7BP. 01235 819792; e-mail: ian@recorder.fsnet.co.uk

Bird Reports

BIRDS OF OXFORDSHIRE (1920-), from Roy Overall, 30 Hunsdon Road, Iffley, Oxford, OX4 4JE. 01865 775632.

BANBURY ORNITHOLOGICAL SOCIETY ANNUAL REPORT (1952-), from A Turner, 33 Newcombe Close, Milcombe, Nr Banbury, Oxon, OX15 4RN. 01295 720938.

BTO Regional Representatives & Regional Development Officer

NORTH, Frances Marks, 15 Insall Road, Chipping Norton, Oxon, OX7 5LF. 01608 644425.

SOUTH RR & RDO, Peter Abbott, The Mallards, 109 Brook Street, Benson, Oxon, OX10 6LJ. 01491 837529.

Clubs

BANBURY ORNITHOLOGICAL SOCIETY, (1952; 100). Tony Clark, 11 Rye Close, Banbury, Oxon, OX16 7XG. 01295 268900.

OXFORD ORNITHOLOGICAL SOCIETY, (1921; 300). David Hawkins, The Long House, Park Lane, Long Hanborough, Oxon, OX29 8RD. 01993 880027; e-mail: dhawkins@dircon.co.uk www.oos.org.uk

Ringing Group
EDWARD GREY INSTITUTE, Dr A G Gosler, c/o Edward Grey Institute, Department of Zoology, South Parks Road, Oxford, OX1 3PS. 01865 271158.

RSPB Members' Groups
OXFORD, (1977; 100). Ian Kilshaw, 6 Queens Court, Bicester, Oxon, OX26 6JX. Tel 01869 601901; (fax) 01869 600565;
e-mail: ian.kilshaw@ntlworld.com
www.rspb-oxford.org.uk
VALE OF WHITE HORSE, (1977; 250). Margaret Meardon, 7 Tavistock Avenue, Didcot, Oxon, OX11 8NA. 01235 210525.

Wetland Bird Survey Organisers
NORTH, Mrs Sandra Bletchly, 11 Orchard Grove, Bloxham, Banbury, Oxon, OX15 4NZ. 01295 721048;
e-mail: sandra@banornsoc.fsnet.co.uk
SOUTH, Mrs Catherine Ross, Duck End Cottage, 40 Sutton, Witney, Oxon, OX29 5RU.

Wildlife Trust
BBOWT, (1959; 11,000). The Lodge, 1 Armstrong Road, Littlemore, Oxford, OX4 4XT. 01865 775476; fax 01865 711301;
e-mail: bbowt@cix.co.uk

SHROPSHIRE

Bird Atlas/Avifauna
Atlas of the Breeding Birds of Shropshire (Shropshire Ornithological Society, 1995).

Bird Recorder
Geoff Holmes, 22 Tenbury Drive, Telford Estate, Shrewsbury, SY2 5YF. 01743 364621.

Bird Report
SHROPSHIRE BIRD REPORT (1956-) Annual, from Secretary, Shropshire, Ornithological Society,

BTO Regional Representative
Allan Dawes, Rosedale, Chapel Lane, Trefonen, Oswestry, Shrops, SY10 9DX. 01691 654245;
e-mail: dawes.rosedale@talk21.com

Club
SHROPSHIRE ORNITHOLOGICAL SOCIETY, (1955; 750). John Turner, 1 Brookside Gardens, Yockleton, Shrewsbury, SY5 9PR. 01743 821678;
e-mail: peregrineleada@aol.com

RSPB Members' Group
SHROPSHIRE, (1992; 240). Roger Evans, 31 The Wheatlands, Bridgenorth, WV16 5BD. 01746 766042.

Wetland Bird Survey Organiser
Bill Edwards, Hopton Villa, Maesbury Marsh, Oswestry, Shrops, SY10 8JA. 01691 656679.

Wildlife Trust
SHROPSHIRE WILDLIFE TRUST, (1962; 2000). 167 Frankwell, Shrewsbury, SY3 8LG. 01743 241691; fax 01743 366671;
e-mail: shropshirewt@cix.co.uk
www.shropshirewildlifetrust.org.uk

SOMERSET & BRISTOL

Bird Atlas/Avifauna
Atlas of Breeding Birds in Avon 1988-91 by R L Bland and John Tully (John Tully, 6 Falcondale Walk, Westbury-on-Trym, Bristol BS9 3JG, 1992).

Bird Recorders
Brian D Gibbs, 23 Lyngford Road, Taunton, Somerset, TA2 7EE. 01823 274887;
e-mail: brian.gibbs@virgin.net
www.somornithosoc.freeserve.co.uk
BATH, NE SOMERSET, BRISTOL, S GLOS, Harvey Rose, 12 Birbeck Road, Bristol, BS9 1BD. H:0117 968 1638; W:0117 928 7992;
e-mail: h.e.rose@bris.ac.uk

Bird Reports
AVON BIRD REPORT (1979-), from Harvey Rose, as above.
EXMOOR NATURALIST (1974-), from Secretary, Exmoor Natural History Society.
SOMERSET BIRDS (1913-), from David Ballance, Flat 2, Dunboyne, Bratton Lane, Minehead, Somerset, TA24 8SQ. 01643 706820.

BTO Regional Representatives, Development Officer & Secretary

AVON RR, Richard L Bland, 11 Percival Road, Bristol, BS8 3LN. Home/W:01179 734828; e-mail: rbland1@compuserve.com

AVON REGIONAL SECRETARY, John Tully, 6 Falcondale Walk, Westbury-on-Trym, Bristol, BS9 3JG. 0117 950 0992; e-mail: johntully4@aol.com

SOMERSET RR, Eve Tigwell, Hawthorne Cottage, 3 Friggle Street, Frome, Somerset, BA11 5LP. 01373 451630; e-mail: evetigwell@aol.com

SOMERSET RDO, Position vacant,

Clubs

BRISTOL NATURALISTS' SOCIETY (Ornithological Section), (1936; 550). Dr Mary Hill, 15 Montrose Avenue, Redland, Bristol, BS6 6EH. 0117 942 2193; e-mail: terry@jhill15.fsnet.co.uk

BRISTOL ORNITHOLOGICAL CLUB, (1966; 650). Mrs Judy Copeland, 19 St George's Hill, Easton-in-Gordano, North Somerset, BS20 0PS. Tel/fax 01275 373554; e-mail: judy.copeland@ukgateway.net

EXMOOR NATURAL HISTORY SOCIETY, (1974; 450). Miss Caroline Giddens, 12 King George Road, Minehead, Somerset, TA24 5JD. 01643 707624.

MID-SOMERSET NATURALISTS' SOCIETY, (1949; 20). Roy Brearly, 2 Quayside, Bridgwater, Somerset, TA6 3TA. 01278 427100.

SOMERSET ORNITHOLOGICAL SOCIETY, (1923; 350). Miss Sarah Beavis, The Old Surgery, 4 The Barton, Hatch Beauchamp, Somerset, TA3 6SG. 01823 480948.

Ringing Groups

CHEW VALLEY RS, W R White, Church View Cottage, Mead Lane, Blagdon, N Somerset, BS40 7UA. 01761 463157 (evgs); e-mail: warwickw@architen.com

GORDANO VALLEY RG, Lyndon Roberts, 20 Glebe Road, Long Ashton, Bristol, BS41 9LH. 01275 392722; e-mail: lyndonroberts@bigfoot.com

RSPCA, S Powell, 1 Rosemill Cottage, Rosemill Lane, Ilminster, Somerset, TA19 5PR.

STEEP HOLM RS, A J Parsons, Barnfield, Tower Hill Road, Crewkerne, Somerset, TA18 8BJ. 01460 73640.

RSPB Members' Groups

BATH (NE SOMERSET), (1989; 240). Gordon Rich, 9 Cranwells Park, Bath, BA1 2YD. 01225 422541.

CREWKERNE & DISTRICT, (1979; 325). Denise Chamings, Daniels Farm, Lower Stratton, South Petherton, Somerset, TA13 5LP. 01460 240740.

TAUNTON, (1975; 148). Eric Luxton, 33 Hoveland Lane, Taunton, Somerset, TA1 5DD. 01823 283033.

WESTON-SUPER-MARE (N SOMERSET), (1976; 215). Don Hurrell, Freeways, Star, Winscombe, BS25 1PS. 01934 842717.

Wetland Bird Survey Organisers

BRIDGWATER BAY, Harvey Rose, 12 Birbeck Road, Bristol, BS9 1BD. H:0117 968 1638; W:0117 928 7992; e-mail: h.e.rose@bris.ac.uk

SEVERN ESTUARY, Harvey Rose, 12 Birbeck Road, Bristol, BS9 1BD. H:0117 968 1638; W:0117 928 7992; e-mail: h.e.rose@bris.ac.uk

SOMERSET LEVELS & MOORS, Warden, RSPB, West Sedgemoor, Dewlands Farm, Redhill, Curry Rivel, Langport, Somerset, TA10 0PH. (Work) 01458 252805.

OTHER SITES, Keith Fox, Vernwood, 32 Ash Hayes Road, Nailsea, North Somerset, BS48 2LW. 01275 854678.

Wildlife Trusts

AVON WILDLIFE TRUST, (1980; 4500). Wildlife Centre, 32 Jacobs Wells Road, Bristol, BS8 1DR. 0117 926 8018; fax 0117 929 7273; e-mail: avonwt@cix.co.uk

SOMERSET WILDLIFE TRUST, (1964; 8000). Fyne Court, Broomfield, Bridgwater, Somerset, TA5 2EQ. 01823 451587; fax 01823 451671; e-mail: somwt@cix.co.uk www.wildlifetrust.org.uk/somerset

STAFFORDSHIRE

Bird Recorder

Mrs Gilly Jones, 4 The Poplars, Lichfield Road, Abbots Bromley, Rugeley, Staffs, WS15 3AA. 01283 840555.

Bird Report See West Midlands

BTO Regional Representatives
NORTH, position vacant.
SOUTH & CENTRAL, Liz Palmer, 58 Fontenaye Road, Coton Green, Tamworth, Staffs, B79 8JU. Tel/fax 01827 52715.

Clubs
WEST MIDLAND BIRD CLUB (STAFFORD BRANCH), Andy Lawrence, 14 Jack Haye Lane, Light Oaks, Stoke-on-Trent, ST2 7NG. 01782 253502. www.westmidlandbirdclub.com
WEST MIDLAND BIRD CLUB (TAMWORTH BRANCH), (1992). Barbara Stubbs, 19 Alfred Street, Tamworth, Staffs, B79 7RL. 01827 57865.

RSPB Members' Groups
BURTON-ON-TRENT, (1976; 50). Dave Lummis, 121 Wilmot Road, Swadlincote, Derbys, DE11 9EN. 01283 219902.
LICHFIELD & DISTRICT, (1977; 1150). Ray Jennett, 12 St Margarets Road, Lichfield, Staffs, WS13 7RA. 01543 255195.
NORTH STAFFORDSHIRE, (1982; 211). John Booth, 32 St Margaret Drive, Sneyd Green, Stoke-on-Trent, ST1 6EW. 01782 262082.
SOUTH WEST STAFFORDSHIRE, (1972; 171). Mrs Theresa Dorrance, 39 Wilkes Road, Codsall, Wolverhampton, WV8 1RZ. 01902 847041.

Wetland Bird Survey Organiser
Maurice Arnold, 58 Overwoods Road, Hockley, Tamworth, Staffs, B77 5LZ.

Wildlife Hospitals
BRITISH WILDLIFE RESCUE CENTRE, Alfred Hardy, Amerton Working Farm, Stowe-by-Chartley, Stafford, ST18 0LA. 01889 271308. On A518 Stafford/Uttoxeter road. All species, including imprints and permanently injured. Hospital, large aviaries and caging. Open to the public every day. Veterinary support.
GENTLESHAW BIRD OF PREY HOSPITAL, Robert A Smith, 5 Chestall Road, Cannock Wood, Rugeley, Staffs, WS15 4RB. 01543 676372. www.gentleshawwildlife.co.uk
Registered charity. All birds of prey (inc. owls). Hospital cages and aviaries; release sites. Veterinary support. Also GENTLESHAW BIRD OF PREY AND WILDLIFE CENTRE, Fletchers Country Garden Centre, Stone Road, Eccleshall, Stafford. 01785 850379 (10am - 5pm).
RAPTOR RESCUE, J M Cunningham, 8 Harvey Road, Handsacre, Rugeley, Staffs, WS15 4HF. 01543 491712; (Nat. advice line) 0870 241 0609; e-mail: mickcunningham@btinternet.com
www.raptorrescue.org.uk
Birds of prey only. Heated hospital units. Indoor flights, secluded aviaries, hacking sites, rehabilitation aviaries/flights. Falconry rehabilitation techniques, foster birds for rearing young to avoid imprinting. Veterinary support. Reg charity no. 283733.

Wildlife Trust
STAFFORDSHIRE WILDLIFE TRUST, (1969; 4000). Coutts House, Sandon, Stafford, ST18 0DN. 01889 508534; fax 01889 508422; e-mail: staffswt@cix.co.uk

SUFFOLK

Bird Atlas/Avifauna
Birds of Suffolk by S H Piotrowski (Pica, expected 2001).

Bird Recorders
NORTH EAST, Richard Walden, 21 Kilbrack, Beccles, Suffolk, NR34 9SH. 01502 713521; e-mail: walden1@supanet.com
SOUTH EAST (inc. coastal region from Slaughden Quay southwards), Position vacant
WEST (whole of Suffolk W of Stowmarket, inc. Breckland), Colin Jakes, 7 Maltward Avenue, Bury St Edmunds, Suffolk, IP33 3XN. 01284 702215; e-mail: cjjakes@supanet.com

Bird Report
SUFFOLK BIRDS (inc Landguard Bird Observatory Report) (1950-), from Secretary, Suffolk Ornithologists' Group.

BTO Regional Representative
Mick T Wright, 15 Avondale Road, Ipswich, IP3 9JT. 01473 710032;
e-mail: micktwright@btinternet.com

Clubs

LAVENHAM BIRD CLUB, (1972; 54). Richard Michette, 7 Clopton Drive, Long Melford, Sudbury, Suffolk, CO10 9LJ. 01787 377741 (day).

SUFFOLK ORNITHOLOGISTS' GROUP, (1973; 650). Andrew M Gregory, 1 Holly Road, Ipswich, IP1 3QN. 01473 253816.

Ringing Groups

DINGLE BIRD CLUB, Dr D Pearson, 4 Lupin Close, Reydon, Southwold, Suffolk, IP18 6NW.
LACKFORD RG, Dr Peter Lack, 11 Holden Road, Lackford, Bury St Edmunds, Suffolk, IP28 6HZ.
e-mail: peter.diane@tinyworld.co.uk
LANDGUARD RG, M C Marsh, 5 Ennerdale Close, Felixstowe, Suffolk, IP11 9SS. 01394 674888.
MARKET WESTON RG, Dr R H W Langston, Walnut Tree Farm, Thorpe Street, Hinderclay, Diss, Norfolk, IP22 1HT.
e-mail: rlangston@wntfarm.demon.co.uk

RSPB Members' Groups

BURY ST EDMUNDS, (1982; 150). Trevor Hart, 7 Westgart Gardens, Bury St Edmunds, Suffolk, IP33 3LB. 01284 705165.
IPSWICH, (1975; 200). PL Wright, 116 Bucklesham Rd, Ipswich, Suffolk, IP3 8TU. 01473 273737;
e-mail: plwright@compuserve.com
LOWESTOFT & DISTRICT, (1976; 170). Brian Sivyer, 39 Fern Avenue, Lowestoft, Suffolk, NR32 3JF. 01502 560414;
e-mail: brian.sivyer@lineone.net
WOODBRIDGE, (1986; 350). Colin Coates, 42A Bredfield Road, Woodbridge, Suffolk, IP12 1JE. 01394 385209.

Wetland Bird Survey Organisers

ALDE COMPLEX, Rodney West, Flint Cottage, Stone Common, Blaxhall, Woodbridge, Suffolk, IP12 2DP. 01728 689171; fax 01728 688044;
e-mail: rodwest@ndirect.co.uk
ALTON WATER, John Glazebrook, 61 Woodlands, Chelmondiston, Suffolk, IP9 1DU.
BLYTH ESTUARY, Cliff Waller, Angel Cottage, Blythburgh, Halesworth, Suffolk, IP19 9LQ. 01502 478239.
DEBEN ESTUARY, Nick Mason, Evening Hall, Hollesley, Woodbridge, Suffolk, IP12 3QU.
ORWELL ESTUARY, Mick T Wright, 15 Avondale Road, Ipswich, IP3 9JT. 01473 710032; e-mail: mick.wright@talk21.com
STOUR ESTUARY, Russell Leavett, 24 Orchard Close, Great Oakley, Harwich, Essex, CO12 5AX. Tel/fax 01255 886043;
e-mail; russell.leavett@rspb.org.uk
OTHER SITES, Post vacant.

Wildlife Trust

SUFFOLK WILDLIFE TRUST, (1961; 15,000). Brooke House, The Green, Ashbocking, Ipswich, IP6 9JY. 01473 890089; fax 01473 890165;
e-mail: suffolkwildlife@cix.co.uk
www.wildlifetrust.org.uk/suffolk

SURREY

Bird Atlas/Avifauna

Birds of Surrey (avifauna). Due 2001.

Bird Recorder (inc London S of Thames & E to Surrey Docks)

Jeffery Wheatley, 9 Copse Edge, Elstead, Godalming, Surrey, GU8 6DJ. 01252 702450; 01252 703650.

Bird Report

SURREY BIRD REPORT (1952-), from J Gates, 90 The Street, Wrecclesham, Farnham, Surrey, GU10 4QR.

BTO Regional Representative

Hugh Evans, 31 Crescent Road, Shepperton, Middx, TW17 8BL. 01932 227781;
e-mail: hugh_w_evans@lineone.net

Clubs

SURBITON & DISTRICT BIRDWATCHING SOCIETY, (1954; 200). Norman Ford, 25 Canada Road, Cobham, Surrey, KT11 1BB. 01932 863475; e-mail: birds@sdbws.ndo.co.uk
www.sdbws.ndo.co.uk

SURREY BIRD CLUB, (1957; 420). Mrs Jill Cook, Moorings, Vale Wood Drive, Lower Bourne, Farnham, Surrey, GU10 3HW. 01252 792876; e-mail: jilck@lineone.net http://website.lineone.net/~jilck/index.sbc.html

Ringing Groups

HERSHAM RG, A J Beasley, 29 Selbourne Avenue, New Haw, Weybridge, Surrey, KT15 3RB. e-mail: abeasley00@hotmail.com

RUNNYMEDE RG, D G Harris, 22 Blossom Waye, Hounslow, TW5 9HD. e-mail: daveharris@tinyonline.co.uk

RSPB Members' Groups

DORKING & DISTRICT, (1982; 320). Peter H Crook, 33 The Park, Bookham, Surrey, KT23 3LN. 01372 458175.

EAST SURREY, (1984; 3000). Brian Hobley, 26 Alexandra Road, Warlingham, Surrey, CR6 9DU. 01883 625404.

EPSOM & EWELL, (1974; 168). Janet Gilbert, 78 Fairfax Avenue, Ewell, Epsom, Surrey, KT17 2QQ. 0208 394 0405.

GUILDFORD, (1971; 500). Alan Bowen, Newlands, 13 Mountside, Guildford, Surrey, GU2 4JD. 01483 567041.

NORTH WEST SURREY, (1973; 125). Ms Mary Harris, 20 Meadway Drive, New Haw, Surrey, KT15 2DT. 01932 858692; e-mail: mary.harris2@virgin.net

Wetland Bird Survey Organiser

Mr J Wheatley, 9 Copse Edge, Elstead, Godalming, Surrey, GU8 6DJ.

Wildlife Hospitals

THE SWAN SANCTUARY, See National Directory.

WILDLIFE AID, Simon Cowell, Randalls Farm House, Randalls Road, Leatherhead, Surrey, KT22 0AL. 01372 377332; 24-hr emergency line 09061 800 132 (50p/min); fax 01372 375183; e-mail: wildlife@pncl.co.uk www.wildlife-aid.org.uk/wildlife

Registered charity. Wildlife hospital and rehabilitation centre helping all native British species. Special housing for birds of prey. Membership scheme and fund raising activities. Veterinary support.

Wildlife Trust

SURREY WILDLIFE TRUST, (1959; 7500). School Lane, Pirbright, Woking, Surrey, GU24 0JN. 01483 488055; fax 01483 486505; e-mail: surreywt@cix.co.uk www.surreywildlifetrust.co.uk

SUSSEX

Bird Atlas/Avifauna

The Birds of Selsey Bill and the Selsey Peninsular (a checklist to year 2000) from: Mr O Mitchell, 21 Trundle View Close, Barnham, Bognor Regis, PO22 0JZ.

Birds of Sussex ed by Paul James (Sussex Ornithological Society, 1996).

Bird Recorder

John A Hobson, 23 Hillside Road, Storrington, W Sussex, RH20 3 LZ. 01903 740155; e-mail: janthobson@aol.com

Bird Reports

FRIENDS OF RYE HARBOUR NR ANNUAL REPORT (1977-), from Dr Barry Yates, see Clubs.

PAGHAM HARBOUR LOCAL NATURE RESERVE ANNUAL REPORT, from Warden, see Reserves.

SHOREHAM DISTRICT ORNITHOLOGICAL SOCIETY ANNUAL REPORT (1952-), from Secretary.

SUSSEX BIRD REPORT (1963-), from J E Trowell, Lorrimer, Main Road, Icklesham, Winchelsea, E Sussex, TN36 4BS. e-mail: membership@susos.org.uk www.susos.org.uk

BTO Regional Representative

Dr A Barrie Watson, 83 Buckingham Road, Shoreham-by-Sea, W Sussex, BN43 5UD. 01273 452472; e-mail: abwatson@mistral.co.uk

Clubs

FRIENDS OF RYE HARBOUR NATURE RESERVE, (1973; 1500). Dr Barry Yates, 2 Watch Cottages, Nook Beach, Winchelsea, E Sussex, TN36 4LU. 01797 223862; e-mail: yates@clara.net www.yates.clara.net

HENFIELD BIRDWATCH, (1999; 60). Mike Russell, 31 Downsview, Small Dole, Henfield, West Sussex, BN5 9YB. 01273 494311.

SHOREHAM DISTRICT ORNITHOLOGICAL SOCIETY, (1953; 120). Mrs B Reeve, The Old Rectory, Coombes, Lancing, W Sussex, BN15 0RS. 01273 452497.
SUSSEX ORNITHOLOGICAL SOCIETY, (1962; 1500). Mrs V P Bentley, Chetsford, London Road, Henfield, W Sussex, BN5 9JJ. 01273 494723 www.susos.org.uk

Ringing Groups
BEACHY HEAD RS, R D M Edgar, 6 Turnpike Close, Ringmer, Lewes, E Sussex, BN8 5PD.
CUCKMERE RG, Tim Parmenter, 22 The Kiln, Burgess Hill, W Sussex, RH15 0LU. 01444 236526.
RYE BAY RG, S J R Rumsey, Elms Farm, Pett Lane, Icklesham, Winchelsea, E Sussex, TN36 4AH. 01797 226137;
e-mail: srumsey@europeancredit.com
STEYNING RG, B R Clay, 30 The Drive, Worthing, W Sussex, BN11 5LL.
e-mail: brclay@compuserve.com

RSPB Members' Groups
BATTLE, (1973; 100). Miss Lynn Jenkins, 61 Austen Way, Guestling, Hastings, E Sussex, TN35 4JH. 01424 432076;
e-mail: battlerspb@freewire.co.uk
www.battlerspb.freewire.co.uk
BRIGHTON & DISTRICT, (1974; 800). Colin Upton, 2 Montford Close, Shoreham-by-Sea, W Sussex, BN43 6YP. 01273 593938;
e-mail: colin.upton@care4free.net
CHICHESTER & SW SUSSEX, (1979; 245). Dominic Carlton, Pipits, Park Road, Barnham, Bognor Regis, W Sussex, PO22 0AQ. 01243 552716.
CRAWLEY & HORSHAM, (1978; 148). Andrea Saxton, 104 Heath Way, Horsham, W Sussex, RH12 5XS.
EAST GRINSTEAD, (1998; 218). Nick Walker, 14 York Avenue, East Grinstead, W Sussex, RH19 4TL. 01342 315825.
EASTBOURNE & DISTRICT, (1993; 520). AM Squires, 5 Hyperion Ave, Polegate, E Sussex, BH26 5HG.
HASTINGS & ST LEONARDS, (1983; 145). Richard Prebble, 1 Wayside, 490 Sedlescombe Road North, St Leonards-on-Sea, E Sussex, TN37 7PH. 01424 751790.
HEATHFIELD, (1979; 75). Mrs Dorothy Cull, 33 Horam Park Close, Horam, E Sussex, TN21 0HW. 01435 812093.

Wetland Bird Survey Organisers
CHICHESTER HARBOUR, Anne de Potier, Chichester Harbour Conservancy, The Harbour Office, Itchenor, Chichester, W Sussex, PO20 7AW. 01243 512301; fax 01243 513026;
e-mail: anne@conservancy.co.uk
OTHER SITES, Chris Lowmass, 33 Barn Close, Seaford, E Sussex, BN25 3EW. 01323 897758.

Wildlife Hospital
BRENT LODGE BIRD & WILDLIFE TRUST, Penny Cooper, Brent Lodge, Cow Lane, Sidlesham, Chichester, West Sussex, PO20 7LN. 01243 641672. All species of wild birds. Full surgical and medical facilities (inc. X-ray). Purpose-built oiled bird washing unit. Veterinary support.

Wildlife Trust
SUSSEX WILDLIFE TRUST, (1961; 11000). Woods Mill, Shoreham Road, Henfield, W Sussex, BN5 9SD. 01273 492630; fax 01273 494500; e-mail: sussexwt@cix.co.uk

TYNE & WEAR

Bird Recorders
See Durham; Northumberland.

Bird Report See Durham; Northumberland.

Clubs
NATURAL HISTORY SOCIETY OF NORTHUMBRIA, (1829; 900). David C Noble-Rollin, Hancock Museum, Barras Bridge, Newcastle upon Tyne, NE2 4PT. 0191 232 6386;
e-mail: david.noble-rollin@ncl.ac.uk
NORTHUMBERLAND & TYNESIDE BIRD CLUB, (1958; 270). Sarah Barratt, 3 Haydon Close, Red House Farm, Gosforth, Newcastle upon Tyne, NE3 2BY. 0191 213 6665.

RSPB Members' Groups
NEWCASTLE UPON TYNE, (1969; 300). John Evans, 21 Beacon Drive, Brunswick Green,

Wideopen, Newcastle upon Tyne, NE13 7HB. 0191 236 2369.
SUNDERLAND & SOUTH TYNESIDE, (1982; 25). Paul Metters, Almonte, 1 Bloomfield Drive, Elemore View, East Rainton, Houghton-le-Spring, Tyne & Wear, DH5 9SF.

Wetland Bird Survey Organisers
NORTHUMBERLAND COAST (excl Lindisfarne), Dr Roger Norman, 1 Prestwick Gardens, Kenton, Newcastle upon Tyne, NE3 3DN. Tel/fax 0191 285 8314;
e-mail: r.norman@clara.net
SOUTH COAST, Robin Ward, Dept of Biological Sciences, University of Durham, South Road, Durham, DH1 3LE. H:0191 383 1259; W:0191 374 3350;
e-mail: r.m.ward@durham.ac.uk
INLAND, NORTH, Mrs Margaret MacFarlane, 7 Wildshaw Close, Southfield Lea, Cramlington, Northumberland, NE23 6LH.
INLAND, SOUTH, Andrew Donnison, WWT Washington, District 15, Washington, Tyne & Wear, NE38 8LE. 0191 416 5454 ext 222; fax 0191 416 5801; e-mail: wetlands@euphony.net

WARWICKSHIRE

Bird Recorder
Jonathan Bowley, 17 Meadow Way, Fenny Compton, Southam, Warks, CV47 2WD. 01295 770069; e-mail: bowley@tesco.net

Bird Report See West Midlands.

BTO Regional Representatives
WARWICKSHIRE, Joe A Hardman, Red Hill House, Red Hill, Alcester, Warks, B49 6NQ. 01789 763159;
e-mail: annandjoe.hardman@lineone.net
RUGBY, Barrington Jackson, 5 Harris Drive, Rugby, Warks, CV22 6DX. 01788 814466;
e-mail: jacksonbj2@aol.com

Clubs
NUNEATON & DISTRICT BIRDWATCHERS' CLUB, (1950; 76). Alvin K Burton, 23 Redruth Close, Horeston Grange, Nuneaton, Warwicks, CV11 6FG. 024 7664 1591.
WEST MIDLAND BIRD CLUB SOLIHULL BRANCH, George Morley, 64 Cambridge Avenue, Solihull, West Midlands, B91 1QF.

Ringing Groups
ARDEN RG, Joe A Hardman, Red Hill House, Red Hill, Alcester, Warks, B49 6NQ. 01789 763159; e-mail: annandjoe.hardman@lineone.net
BRANDON RG, David Stone, Overbury, Wolverton, Stratford-on-Avon, Warks, CV37 0HG. 01789 731488.

RSPB Members' Group
See West Midlands.

Wetland Bird Survey Organiser
Maurice Arnold, 58 Overwoods Road, Hockley, Tamworth, Staffs, B77 5LZ.

Wildlife Trust
WARWICKSHIRE WILDLIFE TRUST, (1970; 7000). Brandon Marsh Nature Centre, Brandon Lane, Coventry, CV3 3GW. 024 7630 2912; fax 024 7663 9556;
e-mail: admin@warkswt.cix.co.uk
www.wildlifetrust.org.uk

WEST MIDLANDS

Bird Atlas/Avifauna
The Birds of the West Midlands edited by Graham Harrison et al (West Midland Bird Club, 1982). Rev ed due 2000/2001.

Bird Recorder
Tim Hextell, 39 Windermere Road, Handsworth, Birmingham, B21 9RQ. 0121 551 9997;
www.westmidlandbirdclub.com

Bird Reports
THE BIRDS OF SMESTOW VALLEY AND DUNSTALL PARK (1988-), From Secretary, Smestow Valley Bird Group.
WEST MIDLAND BIRD REPORT (inc Staffs, Warks, Worcs) (1934-), From Mrs D Dunstan, 4 Blossomfield Road, Solihull, West Midlands, B91 1LD. 0121 705 1601.

BTO Regional Representative
BIRMINGHAM & WEST MIDLANDS, Position vacant.

Clubs

SMESTOW VALLEY BIRD GROUP, (1988; 56). Frank Dickson, 11 Bow Street, Bilston, Wolverhampton, WV14 7NB. 01902 493733

WEST MIDLAND BIRD CLUB, (1929; 2000). Mrs Hilary Brittain, 13 Lawford Avenue, Lichfield, Staffs, WS14 9XJ. 01543 254443.

WEST MIDLAND BIRD CLUB BIRMINGHAM BRANCH, (1995; 800). John N Sears, 14 Ingram Street, Malmesbury, Wilts, SN16 9BX. 01666 824417. www.westmidlandbirdclub.com

Ringing Groups

MERCIAN RG (Sutton Coldfield), R L Castle, 91 Maney Hill Road, Sutton Coldfield, West Midlands, B72 1JT. 0121 686 7568.

RSPB Members' Groups

BIRMINGHAM, (1975; 100). John Bailey, 52 Gresham Road, Hall Green, Birmingham, B28 0HY. 0121 777 4389. www.rspb-birmingham.org.uk

COVENTRY & WARWICKSHIRE, (1969; 130). Alan King, 69 Westmorland Road, Coventry, CV2 5BO. 024 7672 7348.

SOLIHULL, (1983; 2350). John Roberts, 115 Dovehouse Lane, Solihull, West Midlands, B91 2EQ. 0121 707 3101; e-mail: d.john.roberts@care4free.net

STOURBRIDGE, (1978; 150). Paul Banks, 4 Sandpiper Close, Wollescote, Stourbridge, DY9 8TD. 01384 898948.

SUTTON COLDFIELD, (1986; 250). Paul Hobbs, 12 Hurlingham Road, Kingstanding, Birmingham, B44 0LT. 0121 382 7154.

WALSALL, (1970; 80). Peter Hunt, 26 Dumblederry Lane, Aldridge, Staffs, WS9 0DH. 01922 456908.

WOLVERHAMPTON, (1974; 90). Ian Wiltshire, 25 Oakridge Drive, Willenhall, WV12 4EN. 01902 630418.

Wetland Bird Survey Organiser

Maurice Arnold, 58 Overwoods Road, Hockley, Tamworth, Staffs, B77 5LZ.

Wildlife Hospitals

KIDD, D J, 20 Parry Road, Ashmore Park, Wednesfield, Wolverhampton, WV11 2PS. 01902 863971. All birds of prey, esp. owls. Aviaries, isolation pens. Veterinary support.

REPTILE & WILDLIFE RESCUE, Warren Davis, 103 Beauchamp Road, Billesley, Birmingham, B13 0NN. 0121 444 3944; mobile 07979 370525. All species of wild birds. Full hand-rearing care. Veterinary support.

WEDNESFIELD ANIMAL SANCTUARY, Jimmy Wick, 92 Vicarage Road, Nordley, Wednesfield, Wolverhampton, WV11 1SF. 01902 823064. Birds of prey, softbills, seed-eaters. Brooders, incubators, outdoor aviaries, heated accommodation. Telephone first. Veterinary support.

Wildlife Trust

BIRMINGHAM AND BLACK COUNTRY WILDLIFE TRUST, (1980; 900). 28 Harborne Road, Edgbaston, Birmingham, B15 3AA. 0121 454 1199; fax 0121 454 6556; e-mail: urbanwt@cix.co.uk

WILTSHIRE

Bird Recorder

Rob Turner, 14 Ethendun, Bratton, Westbury, Wilts, BA13 4RX. 01380 830862.

Bird Report

Published in Hobby (journal of the Wiltshire OS) *(1975-)*, from Nigel Pleass, The Curlews, 22 Ferrers Drive, Swindon, SN5 6HJ. 01793 873251; e-mail: nigelpleass@aol.com

BTO Regional Representatives

NORTH, Mark Lang, 1 Sherington Mead, Pewsham, Wilts, SN15 3TU. e-mail: mark@marknsams.fsnet.co.uk

SOUTH, Andrew Carter, Standlynch Farm, Downton, Salisbury, SP5 3QR. 01722 710382; e-mail: A_G_Carter@compuserve.com

Clubs

SALISBURY & DISTRICT NATURAL HISTORY SOCIETY, (1952; 167). J Pitman, 10 The Hardings, Devizes Road, Salisbury, SP2 9LZ. 01722 327395.

WILTSHIRE ORNITHOLOGICAL SOCIETY, (1974; 490). Mrs EM Nuttall, 11 Kingsfirld Close, Bradford-on-Avon, Wilts, BA15 1AW. 01225 863816.

Ringing Group

WEST WILTSHIRE RG, Mr M.J. Hamzij, 13 Halfway Close, Trowbridge, Wilts, BA14 7HQ.

RSPB Members' Groups

NORTH WILTSHIRE, (1973; 130). Derek Lyford, 9 Devon Road, Swindon, SN2 1PQ. 01793 520997;
e-mail: derek.lyford@care4free.net
SOUTH WILTSHIRE, (1986; 870). Tony Goddard, Clovelly, Lower Road, Charlton All Saints, Salisbury, SP5 4HQ. 01725 510309.

Wetland Bird Survey Organiser

Julian Rolls, 110 Beanacre, Melksham, Wilts, SN12 7PZ. 01225 790495.

Wildlife Hospital

CALNE WILD BIRD AND ANIMAL RESCUE CENTRE, Tom and Caroline Baker, 2 North Cote, Calne, Wilts, SN11 9DL. 01249 817893. All species of birds. Large natural aviaries (all with ponds), release areas, incubators, heated cages. Day and night collection. Veterinary support.

Wildlife Trust

WILTSHIRE WILDLIFE TRUST, (1962; 10,000). Elm Tree Court, Long Street, Devizes, Wilts, SN10 1NJ. 01380 725670; fax 01380 729017; e-mail: admin@wiltshirewildlife.org www.wiltshire-web.co.uk/wildlife

WORCESTERSHIRE

Bird Recorder

Richard Harbird, Flat 4, Buckley Court, 16 Woodfield Rd, Moseley, Birmingham B13 9UJ. 0121 441 2459. Resigns at the end of 2001.

Bird Report See West Midlands,

BTO Regional Representative

G Harry Green, Windy Ridge, Pershore Road, Little Comberton, Pershore, Worcs, WR10 3EW. 01386 710377; e-mail: harrygreen@zetnet.co.uk

Ringing Group

WYCHAVON RG, J R Hodson, 15 High Green, Severn Stoke, Worcester, WR8 9JS. 01905 754919.

RSPB Members' Group

WORCESTER & MALVERN, (1980; 400). Garth Lowe, Sunnymead, Old Storridge, Alfrick, Worcester, WR6 5HT. 01886 833362.

Wetland Bird Survey Organiser

Maurice Arnold, 58 Overwoods Road, Hockley, Tamworth, Staffs, B77 5LZ.

Wildlife Trust

WORCESTERSHIRE WILDLIFE TRUST, (1968; 8000). Lower Smite Farm, Smite Hill, Hindlip, Worcester, WR3 8SZ. 01905 754919; fax 01905 755868; e-mail: worcswt@cix.co.uk www.worcswildlifetrust.co.uk

YORKSHIRE

Bird Atlas/Avifauna

Atlas of Breeding Birds in the Leeds Area 1987-1991 by Richard Fuller et al (Leeds Birdwatchers' Club, 1994).
The Birds of Yorkshire by John Mather (Croom Helm, 1986).
An Atlas of the Breeding Birds of the Huddersfield Area, 1987-1992. by Brian Armitage et al (2000).
Birds of Barnsley by Nick Addey (Pub by author, 114 Everill Gate Lane, Broomhill, Barnsley S73 0YJ, 1998).

Bird Recorders

VC61 (East Yorkshire), Geoff Dobbs, 12 Park Avenue, Hull, HU5 3ER. 01482 341524;
e-mail: geoffdobbs@aol.com
VC62 (North Yorkshire East), Russell Slack, 64 Sundew Gardens, High Green, Sheffield, S35 4DU. 01142 845300.
VC63 (South & West Yorkshire), Lance Degnan, 14 Fiddlers Drive, Armthorpe, Doncaster, DN3 4TT. 01302 835094;
e-mail: lance.degnan@lineone.net
VC64 (West Yorkshire)/HARROGATE & CRAVEN, John Pewtress, 31 Piercy End,

Kirbymoorside, York, YO62 6DQ. 01751 431001; e-mail: jim@pewtress.co.uk
VC65 (North Yorkshire West), Nick Morgan, Linden, Church View, Ainderby Steeple, Northallerton, N Yorks, DL7 9PU. 01609 770168; e-mail: nick.morgan1@virgin.net

Bird Reports

BARNSLEY & DISTRICT BIRD STUDY GROUP REPORT (1971-), from Secretary.
BRADFORD NATURALISTS' SOCIETY ANNUAL REPORT, from Mr I Hogg, 23 St Matthews Road, Bankfoot, Bradford, BD5 9AB.
BRADFORD ORNITHOLOGICAL GROUP REPORT (1987-), from Shaun Radcliffe, Bradford Ornithological Group.
DONCASTER BIRD REPORT (1955-), From Mr M Roberts, 30 St Cecillia's Road, Belle Vue, Doncaster, DN4 5EG.
FILEY BRIGG BIRD REPORT (1976-), from John Harwood, 13 West Garth Gardens, Cayton, Scarborough, N Yorks, YO11 3SF. 01723 584373 www.fbog.co.uk
FIVE TOWNS BIRD REPORT (1995-), from Secretary, Five Towns Bird Group.
HALIFAX BIRDWATCHERS' CLUB ANNUAL REPORT (1991-), from Nick Garter, 72 Townsgate, Midgley, Halifax, HX2 6HJ.
HARROGATE & DISTRICT NATURALISTS' ORNITHOLOGY REPORT (1996-), from Secretary.
BIRDS IN HUDDERSFIELD (1966-), from Secretary, Huddersfield Bird Club.
LEEDS BIRDWATCHERS' CLUB ANNUAL REPORT (1949-), from Secretary.
BIRDS OF ROTHERHAM (1975-), from Secretary, Rotherham Orn Soc.
BIRDS IN THE SHEFFIELD AREA (1973-), from Tony Morris, 4A Raven Road, Sheffield, S7 1SB. e-mail: tonyjmorris@thesbsg.f9.co.uk www.thesbsg.f9.co.uk
THE BIRDS OF SK58 (1993-), from Secretary, SK58 Birders.
SPURN BIRD OBSERVATORY ANNUAL REPORT, from Warden, see Reserves,
TOPHILL LOW BIRD REPORT (1996-), from Recorder for VC61.
YORK ORNITHOLOGICAL CLUB ANNUAL REPORT (1970-), from T Lawson, Burton Garth, Main Street, Knapton, York, YO26 6QG. 01904 795489: e-mail: info@yorkbirding.org.uk www.yorkbirding.org.uk
YORKSHIRE NATURALISTS' UNION: BIRD REPORT (1940-), from John A Newbould, Stonecroft, 3 Brookmead Close, Sutton Poyntz, Wemouth, Dorset, DT3 6RS.

BTO Regional Representatives & Regional Development Officers

NORTH-EAST RR, Peter Ottaway, 7 Marshall Drive, Pickering, N Yorks, YO18 7JT. 01751 476714; e-mail: peter.ottaway@lineone.net
NORTH-WEST RR & RDO, Malcolm M Priestley, Havera Bank, Howgill Lane, Sedbergh, Cumbria, LA10 5HB. H:01539 620104; W:01539 620535.
SOUTH RR, Chris Falshaw, 6 Den Bank Crescent, Sheffield, S10 5PD. 0114 230 3857; e-mail: chris.falsh@virgin.net
EAST RR, Position vacant.
BRADFORD RR & RDO, Mike L Denton, 77 Hawthorne Terrace, Crosland Moor, Huddersfield, HD4 5RP. 01484 646990.
HARROGATE RR, Mike Brown, 48 Pannal Ash Drive, Harrogate, N Yorks, HG2 0HU. H:01423 567382; W:01423 507237; e-mail: mike.brown17@btinternet.com
HARROGATE RDO, Hamish Roberton, H:01423 879480; W:01423 561614.
LEEDS & WAKEFIELD RR & RDO, Peter Smale, 2A Hillcrest Rise, Leeds, LS16 7DL. 0113 226 9526; e-mail: petersmale@cwcom.net
RICHMOND RR, John Edwards, 7 Church Garth, Great Smeaton, Northallerton, N Yorks, DL6 2HW. H:01609 881476; W:01609 780780 extn 2452; e-mail: john@garthwards.fsnet.co.uk
YORK RR, Rob Chapman, 12 Moorland Road, York, YO10 4HF. 01904 633558; e-mail: robert.chapman@tinyworld.co.uk

Clubs

BARNSLEY & DISTRICT BIRD STUDY GROUP, (1970; 35). Dave Pearce, 15 Bleakley Terrace, Notton, Wakefield, WF4 2NS. 01226 723646.
BRADFORD NATURALISTS' SOCIETY, (1875; 50). D R Grant, 19 The Wheatings, Ossett, W Yorks, WF5 0QQ. 01924 273628.
BRADFORD ORNITHOLOGICAL GROUP, (1987; 170). Shaun Radcliffe, 8 Longwood Avenue, Bingley, W Yorks, BD16 2RX. 01274 770960.
CASTLEFORD & DISTRICT NATURALISTS' SOCIETY, (1956; 30). Michael J Warrington, 31 Mount Avenue, Hemsworth, Pontefract, W Yorks, WF9 4QE. 01977 614954.

DONCASTER & DISTRICT ORNITHOLOGICAL SOCIETY, (1955; 40). Mrs C McKee, 14 Poplar Close, Branton, Doncaster, DN3 3QA. 01302 532454.

FILEY BRIGG ORNITHOLOGICAL GROUP, (1977; 50). Jack Whitehead, 15 The Beach, Filey, N Yorkshire, YO14 9LA. 01723 514565

FIVE TOWNS BIRD GROUP, (1994; 20). Robert Knight, 2 Milnes Grove, Airedale, Castleford, W Yorkshire, WF10 3EZ. 01977 510761; e-mail: f.t.b.g@lineone.net

HALIFAX BIRDWATCHERS' CLUB, (1992; 33). Nick C Dawtrey, 14 Moorend Gardens, Pellon, Halifax, W Yorks, HX2 0SD. 01422 364228.

HARROGATE & DISTRICT NATURALISTS' SOCIETY, (1947; 430). Mrs J McClean, 6 Rossett Park Road, Harrogate, N Yorks, HG2 9NP. 01423 879095;
e-mail: joan mcclean@hotmail.com

HORNSEA BIRD CLUB, (1967; 40). John Eldret, 44 Rolston Road, Hornsea, HU18 1UH. 01964 532854.

HUDDERSFIELD BIRDWATCHERS' CLUB, (1966; 80). David Butterfield, 15 Dene Road, Skelmanthorpe, Huddersfield, HD8 9BU. 01484 862006; e-mail: dbutt52@hotmail.com

HULL VALLEY WILDLIFE GROUP, (1997; 175). F X Moffatt, 102 Norwood, Beverley, E Yorks, HU17 9HL. 01482 882791.

LEEDS BIRDWATCHERS' CLUB, (1949; 60). Mrs Shirley Carson, 2 Woodhall Park Gardens, Stanningley, Pudsey, W Yorks, LS28 7XQ. 0113 255 2145; e-mail: shirley.carson@care4free.net

NEW SWILLINGTON INGS BIRD GROUP, (1989; 20). Nick Smith, 40 Holmsley Lane, Woodlesford, Leeds, LS26 8RN. 0113 282 6154.

PUDSEY ORNITHOLOGY GROUP, (1989; 22). Mrs Joan Thornes, 8 Newlands, Farsley, Leeds, LS28 5BB. 0113 229 8356.

ROTHERHAM & DISTRICT ORNITHOLOGICAL SOCIETY, (1974; 80). Malcolm Taylor, 18 Maple Place, Chapeltown, Sheffield, S35 1QW. 0114 246 1848

SCALBY NABS ORNITHOLOGICAL GROUP, (1993; 15). Ian Glaves, Halleykeld House, Chapel Lane, Sawdon, Scarborough, N Yorkshire, YO13 9DZ. 01723 859766.

SHEFFIELD BIRD STUDY GROUP, (1972; 170). Ron Walker, 22 Parkers Lane, Sheffield, S17 3DP. 0114 236 6150;
e-mail: ronw@erod.demon.co.uk

SK58 BIRDERS, (1993; 60). Andy Hirst, 15 Hunters Drive, Dinnington, Sheffield, S25 2TG. 01909 560310;
e-mail: sk58birders@sk58.freeserve.co.uk
www.sk58.freeserve.co.uk

SORBY NHS (ORNITHOLOGICAL SECTION), (1918; 40). Chris Falshaw, 6 Den Bank Crescent, Sheffield, S10 5PD. 0114 230 3857;
e-mail: chris.falsh@virgin.net

SPEN BIRD CLUB, (2001; 14). Stephen Warrillow, 17 Shirley Mount, Gomersal, W.Yorks, BD19 4Nl. 01274 875220;
e-mail: chozthebaldingbirder@btinternet.com

WAKEFIELD NATURALISTS' SOCIETY, (1851; 40). Philip Harrison, 392 Dewsbury Road, Wakefield, W Yorks, WF2 9DS. 01924 373604.

YORK ORNITHOLOGICAL CLUB, (1967; 80). Ian Traynor, The Owl House, 137 Osbaldwick Lane, York, YO10 3AY.
e-mail: yoc@tka.co.uk
www.tka.co.uk/yoc/

YORKSHIRE NATURALISTS' UNION (Ornithological Section), (1940; 500). W F Curtis, Farm Cottage, Atwick, Driffield, YO25 8DH. 01964 532477.

Ringing Groups

BARNSLEY RG, M C Wells, 715 Manchester Road, Stocksbridge, Sheffield, S36 1DQ. 0114 288 4211.

DONCASTER RG, D Hazard, 41 Jossey Lane, Scawthorpe, Doncaster, S Yorks, DN5 9DB. 01302 788044;
e-mail: davehazard@netscapeonline.co.uk

EAST DALES RG, S P Worwood, 18 Coltsgate Hill, Ripon, N Yorks, HG4 2AB.

EAST YORKS RG, Peter J Dunn, 43 West Garth Gardens, Cayton, Scarborough, N Yorks, YO11 3SF. 01723 583149;
e-mail: jd@fbog.co.uk
www.eyrg.freeserve.co.uk

SORBY-BRECK RG, Geoff P Mawson, Moonpenny Farm, Farwater Lane, Dronfield, Sheffield, S18 1RA. 01246 415097;
e-mail: gpmawson@hotmail.com

SOUTH CLEVELAND RG, W Norman, 2 Station Cottages, Grosmont, Whitby, N Yorks, YO22 5PB. 01947 895226;
e-mail: wilfgros@lineone.net

SPURN BIRD OBSERVATORY, I D Walker, 31 Walton Park, Pannal, Harrogate, N Yorks, HG3 1EJ. 01423 879408.

TEES RG, E Wood, Southfields, 16 Marton Moor Road, Nunthorpe, Middlesbrough, Cleveland, TS7 0BH. 01642 323563; e-mail; redshank@ntlworld.co.uk
WINTERSETT RG, P Smith, 16 Templar Street, Wakefield, W Yorks, WF1 5HB. 01924 375082.

RSPB Members' Groups

AIREDALE AND BRADFORD, (1972; 3500). Peter Sutcliffe, 10 Southfield Mount, Riddlesden, Keighley, W Yorks, BD20 5HS. 01535 600937.
CLEVELAND, (1974; 200). Mark Stokeld, 38 Ash Grove, Kirklevington, Cleveland, TS15 9NQ. 01642 783819;
e-mail: mark@stokeld.demon.co.uk
www.stokeld.demon.uk
CRAVEN & PENDLE, (1986; 250). Ian Cresswell, Dove House, Skyreholme, Skipton, N Yorks, BD23 6DE. 01756 720355; fax 01756 720407; e-mail: iancresswell@lentoid.com
www.airenct.co.uk/rspb
DONCASTER, (1984; 100). Sue Clifton, West Lodge, Wadworth Hall Lane, Wadworth, Doncaster, DN11 9BH. Tel/fax 01302 854956;
e-mail: sue@westlodge53.freeserve.co.uk
EAST YORKSHIRE, (1986; 90). Keith & Sal Barrow, 17 St Aidan Road, Bridlington, E Yorks, YO16 7SP. 01262 679685;
e-mail: keith.barrow@btinternet.com
sal.barrow@btinternet.com
www.eymg.freeserve.co.uk
HUDDERSFIELD & HALIFAX, (1981; 200). David Hemingway, 267 Long Lane, Dalton, Huddersfield, HD5 9SH. 01484 301920.
HULL & DISTRICT, (1983; 334). Derek Spencer, The Old Brewhouse, Main Road, Burton Pidsea, Hull, HU12 9AX. 01964 670024.
LEEDS, (1975; 450). Linda Jenkinson, 112 Eden Crescent, Burley, Leeds, LS4 2TR.
0113 230 4595.
SHEFFIELD, (1983; 500). John Badger, 24 Athersley Gardens, Owlthorpe, Sheffield, S20 6RW. 0114 247 6622.
WAKEFIELD, (1987; 170). Paul Disken, 6 Northfield Road, Dewsbury, W Yorks, WF13 2JX. 01924 456352.
WHITBY, (1977; 120). Fred Payne, 16 Hermitage Way, Sleights, Whitby, N Yorks, YO22 5HG. 01947 810022.
YORK, (1973; 600). Chris Lloyd, 7 School Lane, Upper Poppleton, York, YO26 6JS. 01904 794865.

Wetland Bird Survey Organisers

N YORKS, SCARBOROUGH, Mrs Shirley Pashby, 10 Ambrey Close, Hunmanby, Filey, N Yorks, YO14 0LZ. 01723 891377.
HARROGATE & YORKSHIRE DALES, Bill Haines, 14 Railway Terrace, Knaresborough, N Yorks, HG5 0JB. 01423 869789.
DONCASTER AREA, Hugh Parkin, 25 Hyman Close, Warmsworth, Doncaster, S Yorks, DN4 9PB. 01302 857684.
SHEFFIELD AREA, Carl Corbridge, 74 Well Green Road, Stannington, Sheffield, S6 6DF. 0114 234 8795
E YORKS (excl Humber estuary), Mrs Shirley Pashby, 10 Ambrey Close, Hunmanby, Filey, N Yorks, YO14 0LZ. 01723 891377.
HUMBER, NORTH ESTUARY, Nick Cutts, 1 Castle Mews, West End, South Cave, E Yorks, HU15 2EX.
BRADFORD/HUDDERSFIELD/HALIFAX AREA, position vacant.
WAKEFIELD/BARNSLEY AREA, John Cudworth, 17A Prospect Road, Ossett, W Yorks, WF5 8AE.

Wildlife Hospital

ANIMAL HOUSE WILDLIFE WELFARE, Mrs C Buckroyd, 14 Victoria Street, Scarborough, YO12 7SS. 01723 371256; shop 01723 375162. All species of wild birds. Oiled birds given treatment before forwarding to cleaning stations. Incubators, hospital cages, heat pads, release sites. Birds ringed before release. Prior telephone call requested. Collection if required. Veterinary support. Charity shop at 127 Victoria Road.

Wildlife Trusts

TEES VALLEY WILDLIFE TRUST, (1979; 4000). Bellamy Pavilion, Kirkleatham Old Hall, Kirkleatham, Redcar, Cleveland, TS10 5NW. 01642 759900; fax 01642 480401;
e-mail: teesvalleywt@cix.co.uk
SHEFFIELD WILDLIFE TRUST, (1985; 250). Norfolk House, Stafford Lane, Sheffield, S2 5HR. 0114 272 2377; fax 0114 279 6458;
e-mail: sheffieldwt@cix.co.uk
YORKSHIRE WILDLIFE TRUST, (1946; 8000). 10 Toft Green, York, YO1 6JT. 01904 659570; fax 01904 613467;
e-mail: yorkshirewt@cix.co.uk

SCOTLAND

For this section we are following the arrangement of the Scottish recording areas as set out by the Scottish Ornithologists' Club.

Bird Report
See Scottish Ornithologists' Club in National Directory.

Club
See Scottish Ornithologists' Club in National Directory.

ANGUS & DUNDEE

Bird Recorder
ANGUS & DUNDEE, Dan A Carmichael, 2a Reres Road, Broughty Ferry, Dundee, DD5 2QA. 01382 779981;
e-mail: dan_a_carmichael@email.msn.com

Bird Report
ANGUS & DUNDEE BIRD REPORT (1974-), from Secretary, SOC Tayside Branch.

BTO Regional Representatives & Regional Development Officer
ANGUS RR & RDO, Ken Slater, Braedownie Farmhouse, Glen Cova, Kirriemuir, Angus, DD8 4RD. 01575 550233.

Clubs
ANGUS & DUNDEE BIRD CLUB, (1997; 116). Bob McCurley, 22 Kinnordy Terrace, Dundee, DD4 7NW. 01382 462944.
SOC TAYSIDE BRANCH, (145). James Whitelaw, 36 Burn Street, Dundee, DD3 0LB. 01382 819391.

Ringing Group
TAY RG, Ms S Millar, Edenvale Cottage, 1 Lydox Cottages, Dairsie, Fife, KY15 4RN.

RSPB Members' Groups
DUNDEE, (1972;110). Ron Downing, 3 Lynnewood Place, Dundee, DD4 7HB. 01382 451987.

Wetland Bird Survey Organisers
MONTROSE BASIN, Ian Hutchison, 13 Eddie Avenue, Brechin, Angus, DD9 6YD. 01356 624851.
TAY ESTUARY, Norman Elkins, 18 Scotstarvit View, Cupar, Fife, KY15 5DX. 01334 654348;
e-mail: jandnelkins@rapidial.co.uk
INLAND ANGUS (excl Montrose Basin), position vacant..

ARGYLL

Bird Recorder
ARGYLL, Paul Daw, Tigh-na-Tulloch, Tullochgorm, Minard, Argyll, PA32 8YQ. 01546 886260;
e-mail: monedula@globalnet.co.uk

Bird Reports
ARGYLL BIRD REPORT (1984-), from W J Staley, 16 Glengilp, Ardrishaid, Lochgilphead, Argyll, PA30 8HT.
e-mail: pabstaley@freeuk.com
MACHRIHANISH SEABIRD OBSERVATORY REPORT (1992-), from Observatory, see Reserves & Observatories.

BTO Regional Representatives
ARGYLL (NORTH & MULL), Richard Evans, East Croft, Lochdon, Isle of Mull, PA64 6AP. 01680 812430; e-mail: rjevans6@aol.com
ARGYLL (SOUTH & GIGHA), David Wood, Drover's House, Bellanoch, Lochgilphead, Argyll, PA31 8SN. Home 01546 830272;
e-mail: puffinus@stormie.idps.co.uk
ISLAY, JURA, COLONSAY RR, Dr Malcolm Ogilvie, Glencairn, Bruichladdich, Isle of Islay, PA49 7UN. 01496 850218;
e-mail: maogilvie@indaal.demon.co.uk

Club
ARGYLL BIRD CLUB, (1983;170). Pam Staley, 16 Glengilp, Ardrishaig, Argyll, PA30 8HT.
e-mail: pabstaley@freeuk.com

Ringing Group

TRESHNISH AUK RG, S W Walker, Snipe Cottage, Hamsterley, Bishop Auckland, Co Durham, DL13 3NX.
e-mail: snipe@snipe.screaming.net

Wetland Bird Survey Organisers

ARGYLL & ISLANDS, Dr Malcolm Ogilvie, Glencairn, Bruichladdich, Isle of Islay, PA49 7UN. 01496 850218;
e-mail: maogilvie@indaal.demon.co.uk

AYRSHIRE

Bird Recorder

AYRSHIRE, Angus Hogg, 11 Kirkmichael Road, Crosshill, Maybole, Ayrshire, KA19 7RJ. 01655 740317; e-mail: dcgos@globalnet.co.uk

Bird Reports

AYRSHIRE BIRD REPORT (1976-), from Ayrshire Recorder.

BTO Regional Representatives

AYRSHIRE RR, Paul Darnbrough, 65 Loreny Drive, Kilmarnock, Ayrshire, KA1 4RH. 0775 953 7856; e-mail: pauldarnbrough@hotmail.com

Club

SOC AYRSHIRE BRANCH, (1962; 100). Henry Martin, 9 Shawfield Avenue, Ayr, KA7 4RE. 01292 442086.

RSPB Members' Groups

CENTRAL AYRSHIRE, (1978; 70). James Thomson, Sundrum Smithy, Ayr, KA6 6LR. 01292 570351.
NORTH AYRSHIRE, (1976; 180). Duncan Watt, 28 Greenbank, Dalry, Ayrshire, KA24 5AY.

Wetland Bird Survey Organisers

AYRSHIRE, Dave Grant, 16 Thorn Ave, Coylton, Ayrshire, KA6 6NL.
e-mail: d.grant@au.sac.ac.uk

Wildlife Hospital

HESSILHEAD WILDLIFE RESCUE CENTRE, Gay & Andy Christie, Gateside, Beith, Ayrshire, KA15 1HT. 01505 502415. All species. Releasing aviaries. Veterinary support.

BORDERS

Bird Atlas/Avifauna

The Breeding Birds of South-east Scotland, a tetrad atlas 1988-1994 by R D Murray et al. (Scottish Ornithologists' Club, 1998).

Bird Recorder

Ray Murray, 4 Bellfield Crescent, Eddleston, Peebles, EH45 8RQ. 01721 730677;
e-mail: ray.d.murray@ukgateway.net

Bird Report

BORDERS BIRD REPORT (1979-), From Malcolm Ross, The Tubs, Dingleton Road, Melrose, Borders.

BTO Regional Representative & Regional Development Officer

RR, Alex Copland, Keeraun Hill, Banagher, Co Offaly, Ireland; Home 00 353 509 51076; Work 00 353 509 51676; e-mail crex@eircom.net
RDO, Position vacant.

Club

SOC BORDERS BRANCH, (90). Vicky McLellan, 18 Glen Crescent, Peebles, EH45 9BS. 01721 724580.

Ringing Group

BORDERS RG, Dr T W Dougall, 62 (1F2) Leamington Terrace, Edinburgh, EH10 4JL. Fax 0131 469 5599.

RSPB Members' Group

BORDERS, (1995; 94). Nancy Marshall, The Birches, Leydon Grove, Clovenfords, Galashiels, TD1 3NF. 01896 850564.

Wetland Bird Survey Organiser

Andrew Bramhall, 2 Abbotsferry Road, Tweedbank, Galashiels, Selkirkshire, TD1 3RX.

CAITHNESS

Bird Recorders

CAITHNESS, Peter Miller, 10 Harrold Cottages, Reiss Wick, Caithness, KW1 4RU.

Bird Reports

CAITHNESS BIRD REPORT (1983-), From Julian Smith, St John's, Brough, Dunnet, Caithness; 01847 851280; e-mail: designsmith@madasafish.com

BTO Regional Representatives & Regional Development Officers

CAITHNESS, Hugh Clark, Bellfield, 3 Lindsay Place, Wick, Caithness, KW1 4PF. 01955 605372; e-mail: hugh@lindsayplace.fsnet.co.uk

Clubs

SOC CAITHNESS BRANCH, (51). Stan Laybourne, Old Schoolhouse, Harpsdale, Halkirk, Caithness, KW12 6UN. 01847 841244.

Wetland Bird Survey Organisers

CAITHNESS, Stan Laybourne, Old Schoolhouse, Harpsdale, Halkirk, Caithness, KW12 6UN. 01847 841244.

CLYDE

Bird Atlas/Avifauna

Clyde Breeding Bird Atlas (working title). In preparation.

Bird Reports

CLYDE BIRDS (1973-), from Jim & Valerie Wilson, 76 Laigh Road, Newton Mearns, Glasgow, G77 5EQ. 0141 639 2516; e-mail: jim.val@btinternet.com

Bird Recorder

CLYDE ISLANDS, Bernard Zonfrillo, 28 Brodie Road, Glasgow, G21 3SB. 0141 557 0791.
CLYDE, Iain P Gibson, 8 Kenmure View, Howwood, Johnstone, Renfrewshire, PA9 1DR. 01505 705874.

BTO Regional Representatives

ARRAN, BUTE, CUMBRAES, Position vacant.
LANARK, RENFREW, DUMBARTON, Position vacant.

Club

SOC CLYDE BRANCH, (300). Liz Parsons, 22 Braehead, Lochwinnoch, PA12 4AS. 01505 843849.

Ringing Groups

CLYDE RG, I Livingstone, 57 Strathview Road, Bellshill, Lanarkshire, ML4 2UY. 01698 749844.
GLASGOW UNIVERSITY RG, Prof P Monaghan, Dept of Zoology, University of Glasgow, Glasgow, G12 8QQ.

RSPB Members' Groups

GLASGOW, (1972;146). Jim Coyle, 6 Westerlands, Anniesland, Glasgow, G12 0FB. 0141 579 7565.
HAMILTON AREA, (1976;90). Mrs Isabel Crinean, 15A Central Avenue, Cambuslang, Glasgow, G72 8AY. 0141 641 1292.
HELENSBURGH, (1975; 75). Alistair McIntyre, Craggan, Rosneath Road, Helensburgh, Dunbartonshire, G84 0EJ.
e-mail: almc@jameswatt.co.uk
RENFREWSHIRE, (1986; 200). Ms Alison Purssell, 2 Glencairn Place, High Street, Kilmacolm, PA13 4BT. 01505 872576.

Wetland Bird Survey Organisers

ARRAN, Mrs Audrey Walters, Sula, Margnaheglish Road, Lamlash, Isle of Arran, KA27 8LE.
CLYDE ESTUARY, Jim & Valerie Wilson, 76 Laigh Road, Newton Mearns, Glasgow, G77 5EQ. 0141 639 2516;
e-mail: jim.val@btinternet.com
BUTE, Ian Hopkins, 2 Eden Place, High Street, Rothesay, Isle of Bute, PA20 9BS. 01700 50 4042; e-mail: ian@hopkins0079.freeserve.co.uk
GLASGOW, RENFREWSHIRE, DUNBARTONSHIRE & LANARKSHIRE, Jim & Valerie Wilson, 76 Laigh Road, Newton Mearns, Glasgow, G77 5EQ. 0141 639 2516;
e-mail: jim.val@btinternet.com
ISLE OF CUMBRAE, Dr Rupert Ormond, Bellevue, 15 Kames Bay, Millport, Isle of Cumbrae, KA28 0EA.
e-mail: rupert.ormond@millport.gla.ac.uk

DUMFRIES & GALLOWAY

Bird Recorders

NITHSDALE, ANNANDALE & ESKDALE, 1, Steve Cooper, WWT Caerlaverock, Eastpark Farm, Caerlaverock, Dumfries, DG1 4RS. 01387 770200; fax 01387 770539;
e-mail: steve.cooper@wwt.org.uk;
www.wwtck.free-online.co.uk

2, Paul N Collin, Gairland, Old Edinburgh Road, Minnigaff, Newton Stewart, Wigtownshire, DG8 6PL. 01671 402861.

Bird Report

DUMFRIES & GALLOWAY REGION BIRD REPORT (1985-), from Peter Norman, Low Boreland, Tongland Road, Kirkcudbright, DG6 4UU.

BTO Regional Representatives & Regional Development Officer

DUMFRIES RR, Richard Mearns, Connansknowe, Kirkton, Dumfries, DG1 1SX. 01387 710031.
DUMFRIES RDO, Ken Bruce, Mallaig, Wellington Street, Glencaple, Dumfries, DG1 4RA. 01387 770336.
KIRKCUDBRIGHT RR, Andrew Bielinski, 41 Main Street, St Johns Town of Dalry, Castle Douglas, Kirkcudbright, DG7 3UP. 01644 430418.
WIGTOWN RR, Geoff Sheppard, The Roddens, Leswalt, Stranraer, Wigtownshire, DG9 0QR. 01776 870685;
e-mail: geoff_sheppard@lineone.net

Clubs

SOC DUMFRIES BRANCH, (1961; 105). Brian Smith, Rockiemount, Colvend, Dalbeattie, Dumfries, DG5 4QW. 01556 620617.
SOC STEWARTRY BRANCH, (1976; 76). Miss Joan Howie, 60 Main Street, St Johns Town of Dalry, Castle Douglas, Kirkcudbrightshire, DG7 3UW. 01644 430226.
SOC WEST GALLOWAY BRANCH, (1975; 50). Geoff Sheppard, The Roddens, Leswalt, Stranraer, Wigtownshire, DG9 0QR. 01776 870685; e-mail: geoff_sheppard@lineone.net

Ringing Group

NORTH SOLWAY RG, Geoff Sheppard, The Roddens, Leswalt, Stranraer, Wigtownshire, DG9 0QR. 01776 870685;
e-mail: geoff_sheppard@lineone.net

RSPB Members' Group

GALLOWAY, (1985;150). Robert M Greenshields, Nether Linkins, Gelston, Castle Douglas, DG7 1SU. 01556 680217.

Wetland Bird Survey Organisers

FLEET BAY, David Hawker, Windywalls, Upper Drumwall, Gatehouse of Fleet, Castle Douglas, Kirkcudbrightshire, DG7 2DE. Tel/fax 01557 814249; e-mail: david_hawker@quista.net
KIRKCUDBRIGHT BAY, position vacant.
LOCH RYAN, Geoff Sheppard, The Roddens, Leswalt, Stranraer, Wigtownshire, DG9 0QR. 01776 870685;
e-mail: geoff_sheppard@lineone.net
ROUGH FIRTH, Judy Baxter, Saltflats Cottage, Rockcliffe, Dalbeattie, DG5 4QQ. 01556 630262.
SOLWAY ESTUARY NORTH, Steve Cooper, WWT Caerlaverock, Eastpark Farm, Caerlaverock, Dumfries, DG1 4RS. 01387 770200; fax 01387 770539;
e-mail: steve.cooper@wwt.org.uk;
www.wwtck.free-online.co.uk
WIGTOWN BAY, Paul N Collin, Gairland, Old Edinburgh Road, Minnigaff, Newton Stewart, Wigtownshire, DG8 6PL. 01671 402861.
OTHER SITES, Steve Cooper, WWT Caerlaverock, Eastpark Farm, Caerlaverock, Dumfries, DG1 4RS. 01387 770200; fax 01387 770539; e-mail: steve.cooper@wwt.org.uk;
www.wwtck.free-online.co.uk

FIFE

Bird Recorders

FIFE REGION INC OFFSHORE ISLANDS (NORTH FORTH), Douglas Dickson, 2 Burrelton Court, Bankhead, Glenrothes, Fife, KY7 4UN. 01592 774066;
e-mail: douglasdickson@excite.co.uk
ISLE OF MAY BIRD OBSERVATORY, Iain English, 21 Grant Court, Avon Grove, Hamilton, S Lanarks, ML3 7UT.
e-mail: i.english@talk21.com

Bird Reports

FIFE BIRD REPORT (1988-) (FIFE & KINROSS BR 1980-87), From Fife recorder.
ISLE OF MAY BIRD OBSERVATORY REPORT (1985-), From David Thorne, Craigurd House, Blyth Bridge, West Linton, Peeblesshire, EH46 7AH.

BTO Regional Representative

FIFE & KINROSS RR, Norman Elkins, 18 Scotstarvit View, Cupar, Fife, KY15 5DX. 01334 654348; e-mail: jandnelkins@rapidial.co.uk

Clubs

LOTHIANS AND FIFE MUTE SWAN STUDY GROUP, Allan & Lyndesay Brown, 61 Watts Gardens, Cupar, Fife, KY15 4UG. 01334 656804; e-mail: swans@allanwbrown.co.uk

SOC FIFE BRANCH, (1956;190). Donald R Stewart, 18 Newmill Gardens, St Andrews, Fife, KY16 8RY. 01334 475763.

Ringing Groups

ISLE OF MAY BIRD OBSERVATORY, D Robertson, Woodlands, Bandrum, Nr Carnock, Dunfermline, KY12 9HR. 01383 852997; e-mail: derek@woodlandstudios.fsnet.co.uk

TAY RG, Ms S Millar, Edenvale Cottage, 1 Lydox Cottages, Dairsie, Fife, KY15 4RN.

Wetland Bird Survey Organisers

EDEN ESTUARY, Les Hatton, Fife Ranger Service, Silverburn House, Largo Road, By Leven, Fife, KY8 5PU. 01333 429785; e-mail; nefrs@craigtoun.freeserve.co.uk

FORTH, NORTH ESTUARY, Simon Burton, 51 Double Row, Charlestown, Fife, KY11 3EJ.

TAY ESTUARY (South), Norman Elkins, 18 Scotstarvit View, Cupar, Fife, KY15 5DX. 01334 654348; e-mail: jandnelkins@rapidial.co.uk

INLAND (also Goose Count Co-ordinator, Fife & Lothians), Allan Brown, 61 Watts Gardens, Cupar, Fife, KY15 4UG. 01334 656804; e-mail: swans@allanwbrown.co.uk

Wildlife Hospital

SCOTTISH SPCA WILD LIFE REHABILITATION CENTRE, Middlebank Farm, Masterton Road, Dunfermline, Fife, KY11 8QN. All species. Open to visitors, groups and school parties. Illustrated talk on oiled bird cleaning and other aspects of wildlife rehabilitation available. Veterinary support.

FORTH

Bird Recorder

FORTH AREA, Dr C J Henty, Edgehill East, 7b Coneyhill Road, Bridge of Allan, Stirling, FK9 4EL. 01786 832166.

Bird Report

CENTRAL REGION BIRD REPORT (1976-), From Lindsay Corbett, 30 Dunmar Drive, Alloa, Clacks.

BTO Regional Representative

Neil Bielby, 56 Ochiltree, Dunblane, Perthshire, FK15 0DF. 01786 823830; e-mail: neil.bielby@ntlworld.com

Club

SOC STIRLING BRANCH, (1968; 90). Duncan J Cameron, Allt Beithe, Keip Road, Strathyre, FK18 8NQ. 01877 384246.

RSPB Members' Group

FORTH VALLEY, (1996; 150). Alex Downie, 2 St Lawrence Avenue, Dunblane, Perthshire, FK15 9DE. 01786 825228.

Wetland Bird Survey Organisers

FORTH INNER ESTUARY (Blackness to Fallin), Professor David Bryant, Institute of Biological Sciences, University of Stirling, Stirling, FK9 4LA. 01786 467755; e-mail: dmb1@stirling.ac.uk

INLAND, Neil Bielby, 56 Ochiltree, Dunblane, Perthshire, FK15 0DF. 1787 823830; e-mail: neil.bielby@ntlworld.com

HIGHLAND

Bird Atlas/Avifauna

The Birds of Sutherland by Alan Vittery (Colin Baxter Photography Ltd, 1997).

Birds of Skye by Andrew Currie. In preparation.

Bird Recorders

ROSS-SHIRE, INVERNESS-SHIRE, SUTHERLAND, Colin Crooke, RSPB, Etive House, Beechwood Park, Inverness, IV2 3BW. 01463 715000.

Bird Reports

HIGHLAND BIRD REPORT (1991-), from Recorder.

BTO Regional Representatives & Regional Development Officers

INVERNESS & SPEYSIDE RR & RDO, Hugh Insley, 1 Drummond Place, Inverness, IV2 4JT. H:01463 230652; W:01463 232811; e-mail: hugh.insley@tinyworld.co.uk

RUM, EIGG, CANNA & MUCK RR & RDO, Bob Swann, 14 St Vincent Road, Tain,

Ross-shire, IV19 1JR. 01862 894329; e-mail: bob.swann@hcs.uhi.ac.uk
ROSS-SHIRE RR (Acting), David Butterfield, 1 Calrichie Cottages, Kindeace, Invergordon, Ross-shire, IV18 0LN. 01349 854434 evgs.
SKYE RR & RDO, Position vacant.
SUTHERLAND, Position vacant.

Clubs

EAST SUTHERLAND BIRD GROUP, (1976; 80). Alan Vittery, Elmag Croft, 164 West Clyne, Brora, Sutherland, KW9 6NH. 01408 621827.
SOC HIGHLAND BRANCH, (1955; 171). Janet Crummy, Coalhaugh, Tomatin, Inverness, IV13 7YS. 01808 511261.

Ringing Groups

EAST ROSS RG, Ivan Brockway, Courthill, Tain, Ross-shire, IV19 1NE. 01349 852521.
HIGHLAND RG, Bob Swann, 14 St Vincent Road, Tain, Ross-shire, IV19 1JR. 01862 894329; e-mail: bob.swann@hcs.uhi.ac.uk

RSPB Members' Group

HIGHLAND, (1987; 225). Richard Prentice, Lingay, Lewiston, Drumnadrochit, Inverness, IV63 6UW. 01456 450526.

Wetland Bird Survey Organisers

LOCHABER, John Dye, Toad Hall, Dalnabreac, Acharacle, Argyll, PH36 4JX. 01967 431222.
MORAY BASIN COAST, Bob Swann, 14 St Vincent Road, Tain, Ross-shire, IV19 1JR. 01862 894329; e-mail: bob.swann@hcs.uhi.ac.uk
WEST INVERNESS, LOCHALSH & WESTER ROSS, Vacant.
SKYE, Vacant.
EAST INVERNESS, EASTER ROSS (Inland), Colin Crooke, RSPB, Etive House, Beechwood Park, Inverness, IV2 3BW. 01463 715000.
INLAND, SPEYSIDE, Keith Duncan, SNH, Achantoul, Aviemore, Inverness-shire, PH22 1QD. 01479 810477; e-mail: keith.duncan@snh.gov.uk
BADENOCH & STRATHSPEY, Keith Duncan, details as above.

Bird Atlas/Avifauna

The Breeding Birds of South-east Scotland, a tetrad atlas 1988-1994 by R D Murray et al. (Scottish Ornithologists' Club, 1998).

LOTHIAN

Bird Recorder

David J Kelly, 149 High Street, Prestonpans, East Lothian, EH32 9AX. 01875 810827; e-mail: dj_kelly@btinternet.com

Bird Reports

LOTHIAN BIRD REPORT (1979-), from Recorder.
WEST LOTHIAN BIRD CLUB REPORT (1991-), from Secretary, West Lothian Bird Club,

BTO Regional Representative

Alan Heavisides, 9 Addiston Crescent, Balerno, Edinburgh, EH14 7DB. 0131 449 3816; e-mail: a.heavisides@napier.ac.uk

Clubs

EDINBURGH NATURAL HISTORY SOCIETY, (1869; 200). Mr Michael Osborne, 2 Old Woodside, Bush Estate, Penicuik, Midlothian, EH26 0PQ. 0131 445 3824.
FOULSHIELS BIRD GROUP, (1991; 7). Frazer Henderson, 2 Elizabeth Gardens, Stoneyburn, W Lothian, EH47 8BP. 01501 762972.
LOTHIANS AND FIFE MUTE SWAN STUDY GROUP, Allan & Lyndesay Brown, 61 Watts Gardens, Cupar, Fife, KY15 4UG. 01334 656804; e-mail: swans@allanwbrown.co.uk
SOC LOTHIAN BRANCH, (1936; 440). Ian Thomson, 4 Craigielaw, Longniddry, E Lothian, EH32 0PY. 01875 870588; e-mail: imt.aberlady@ic24.net
WEST LOTHIAN BIRD CLUB, (1990; 67). Martin Collinson, 22 Tippet, Knowes Park, Winchburgh, W Lothian, EH52 6UJ. 01506 890089; e-mail: martin.collinson@ed.ac.uk

Ringing Group

LOTHIAN RG, A F Leitch, 2 Burgess Terrace, Edinburgh, EH9 2BD.

RSPB Members' Group

EDINBURGH, (1974;450). Michael Betts, 10 St Bernard's Row, Edinburgh, EH4 1HW. 0131 332 1708; e-mail: hmc@cee.hw.ac.uk; http://www.cee.hw.ac.uk/~hmc/rspb.html

Wetland Bird Survey Organisers
FORTH, OUTER SOUTH ESTUARY, Mr Duncan Priddle, Countryside Ranger Service, Hermitage House, 69a Braid Road Edinburgh, EH10 6JF.
TYNINGHAME ESTUARY, Bobby Anderson, John Muir Country Park, Town House, Dunbar, East Lothian, EH42 1ER. 01620 827318; (Fax)01620 827459;
e-mail: randerson@eastlothian.gov.uk
INLAND, Miss Joan Wilcox, 18 Howdenhall Gardens, Edinburgh, EH16 6UN. 0131 664 8893.

MORAY & NAIRN

Bird Recorder
MORAY & NAIRN , Martin J H Cook, Rowanbrae, Clochan, Buckie, Banffshire, AB56 5EQ. 01542 850296.

Bird Reports
MORAY & NAIRN BIRD REPORT (1985-), from Moray Recorder.

BTO Regional Representatives & Regional Development Officer
NAIRN RR, Bob Proctor, 94 Reid Street, Bishopmill, Elgin, Moray, IV30 4HH. H:01343 548395 (w/e); W:01479 821409; F:01479 821069; e-mail: bobproctor@rspb.org.uk
MORAY RR, Bob Proctor, 94 Reid Street, Bishopmill, Elgin, Moray, IV30 4HH. H:01343 548395 (w/e); W:01479 821409; F:01479 821069; e-mail: bobproctor@rspb.org.uk

Wetland Bird Survey Organisers
LOSSIE ESTUARY, Bob Proctor, 94 Reid Street, Bishopmill, Elgin, Moray, IV30 4HH. H:01343 548395 (w/e); W:01479 821409;
e-mail: bobproctor@rspb.org.uk
MORAY BASIN COAST, Bob Swann, 14 St Vincent Road, Tain, Ross-shire, IV19 1JR. 01862 894329; e-mail: bob.swann@hcs.uhi.ac.uk
INLAND, MORAY, Martin J H Cook, Rowanbrae, Clochan, Buckie, Banffshire, AB56 5EQ. 01542 850296.
INLAND, NAIRN, Martin J H Cook, Rowanbrae, Clochan, Buckie, Banffshire, AB56 5EQ. 01542 850296.

NORTH EAST SCOTLAND

Bird Atlas/Avifauna
The Birds of North East Scotland by S T Buckland, M V Bell & N Picozzi (North East Scotland Bird Club, 1990).

Bird Recorder
NORTH-EAST SCOTLAND, Andrew Thorpe, 30 Monearn Gardens, Milltimber, Aberdeen, AB13 0EA. 01224 733296;
e-mail: andrewthorpe@tinyworld.co.uk

Bird Reports
NORTH-EAST SCOTLAND BIRD REPORT (1974-), from Dave Gill, Drakemyre Croft, Cairnorrie, Methlick, Aberdeenshire, AB41 0JN. 01651 806252.
NORTH SEA BIRD CLUB ANNUAL REPORT (1979-), from NSBC Recorder, see below.

BTO Regional Representatives & Regional Development Officer
ABERDEEN RDO, Kath Hamper, 9 Mid Street, Inverallochy, Fraserburgh, Aberdeenshire, AB43 8YA. 01346 583015.
ABERDEEN NORTH RR, Peter Walker, Westgate House, Udny, Ellon, Aberdeenshire, AB41 6SD. 01651 842163;
e-mail: pkwalkers@aol.com
KINCARDINE & DEESIDE, Graham Cooper, Westbank, Beltie Road, Torphins, Banchory, Aberdeen, AB31 4JT. H:01339 882706.

Clubs
NORTH SEA BIRD CLUB, (1979; 200). Andrew Thorpe, (Recorder), Aberdeen University, Culterty Field Station, Newburgh, Ellon, Aberdeenshire, AB41 0AA. 01358 789631; fax: 01358 789214; e-mail: nsbc@abdn.ac.uk
SOC GRAMPIAN BRANCH, (1956; 110). John Wills, Bilbo, Monymusk, Inverurie, Aberdeenshire, AB51 7HA. 01467 651296;
e-mail: bilbo@monymusk.freeserve.co.uk

Ringing Groups
ABERDEEN UNIVERSITY RG, Andrew Thorpe, Culterty Field Station, Newburgh, Ellon, Aberdeenshire, AB41 0AA.
e-mail: andrewthorpe@tinyworld.co.uk

GRAMPIAN RG, R Duncan, 86 Broadfold Drive, Bridge of Don, Aberdeen, AB23 8PP.

RSPB Members' Group

ABERDEEN, (1977; 180). Bob Littlejohn, 28 Seafield Drive East, Aberdeen, AB15 7UR. 01224 313576.

Wetland Bird Survey Organisers

ABERDEENSHIRE, Alistair Duncan, 12 Cairncry Avenue, Aberdeen, AB16 5DS. 01224 483717; e-mail: alistair@cairncry.freeserve.co.uk

Wildlife Hospital

GRAMPIAN WILDLIFE REHABILITATION TRUST, 40 High Street, New Deer, Turriff, Aberdeenshire, AB53 6SX. Veterinary surgeon. Access to full practice facilities. Will care for all species of birds.

OUTER HEBRIDES

Bird Recorder

Andrew Stevenson, Mill House, Snishival, Isle of South Uist, HS8 5SG. 01870 620317;
e-mail: andrew.stevenson@snh.gov.uk

Bird Report

OUTER HEBRIDES BIRD REPORT (1989-), from Recorder.

BTO Regional Representatives & Regional Development Officer

BENBECULA & THE UISTS RR & RDO, Paul R Boyer, 96 Carnan, South Uist, Eochar, Lochboisdale, Western Isles, HS8 5QX. H:01870 610253; W:01896 754333 & ask to bleep.
LEWIS & HARRIS RR. 1, Tony Pendle, 3 Linsiadar, Isle of Lewis, HS2 9DR. 01851 621311; e-mail: ellerpendle@madasafish.com
2, Chris Reynolds, 11 Reef, Isle of Lewis, HS2 9HU. 01851 672376;
e-mail: juliareynolds@btinternet.com

Ringing Group

SHIANTS AUK RG, David Steventon, Welland House, 207 Hurdsfield Road, Macclesfield, Cheshire, SK10 2PX. 01625 421936.

Wetland Bird Survey Organisers

HARRIS & LEWIS, Peter Cunningham, Aros, 10 Barony Square, Stornoway, Isle of Lewis, HS1 2TQ. 01851 702423;
e-mail: wajcunningham@lineone.net
BENBECULA & THE UISTS, Paul R Boyer, 96 Carnan, Eochar, Lochboisdale, South Uist, Western Isles, HS8 5QX. 01870 610253.

ORKNEY

Bird Atlas/Avifauna

The Birds of Orkney by CJ Booth et al (The Orkney Press, 1984).

Bird Recorder

Tim Dean, Echna View, Burray, Orkney, KW17 2SX. 01856 731445.

Bird Report

ORKNEY BIRD REPORT (inc North Ronaldsay Bird Report) (1974-), from Mr EJ Williams, Fairholm, Finstown, Orkney, KW17 2EQ.
e-mail: jim@geniefea.freeserve.co.uk

BTO Regional Representative & Regional Development Officer

Colin Corse, Garrisdale, Lynn Park, Kirkwall, Orkney, KW15 1SL. H:01856 874484;
e-mail: ccorse@aol.com

Club

SOC ORKNEY BRANCH, (1993; 15). Stuart Williams, Crafty, Firth, Orkney, KW17 2ES. 01856 761742;
e-mail: stuart@gavia.freeserve.co.uk

Ringing Groups

NORTH RONALDSAY BIRD OBSERVATORY, Ms A E Duncan, Twingness, North Ronaldsay, Orkney, KW17 2BE. 01857 633267; e-mail: alison@nrbo.prestel.co.uk www.nrbo.f2s.com
ORKNEY RG, Colin J Corse, Garrisdale, Lynn Park, Kirkwall, Orkney, KW15 1SL. H:01856 874484; W:01856 884156.
SULE SKERRY RG, Dave Budworth, 121 Wood Lane, Newhall, Swadlincote, Derbys, DE11 0LX. 0121 6953384.

RSPB Members' Group
ORKNEY, (1985;250). Kate Barrett, 30 Queen Sonja Kloss, Kirkwall, Orkney, KW15 1FJ. 01856 875562.

Wetland Bird Survey Organisers
OPEN COASTAL SITES, Colin J Corse, Garrisdale, Lynn Park, Kirkwall, Orkney, KW15 1SL. H:01856 874484; W:01856 884156.
OTHER SITES, Eric Meek, RSPB, 12/14 North End Road, Stromness, Orkney, KW16 3AG. 01856 850176.

PERTH & KINROSS

Bird Recorder
PERTH & KINROSS, Ron Youngman, Blairchroisk Cottage, Ballinluig, Pitlochry, Perthshire, PH9 0NE. 01796 482324;
e-mail: blairchroisk@aol.com

Bird Report
PERTH & KINROSS BIRD REPORT (1974-), from Recorder.

BTO Regional Representatives & Regional Development Officer
PERTHSHIRE RR, Position vacant.

Clubs
PERTHSHIRE SOCIETY OF NATURAL SCIENCE (Ornithological Section), (1964; 60). Miss Esther Taylor, 23 Verena Terrace, Perth, PH2 0BZ. 01738 621986.

RSPB Members' Groups
TAYSIDE, (1988; 160). Alan Davis, 6 Grey Street, Perth, PH2 0JJ. 01738 622480.

Wetland Bird Survey Organisers
PERTHSHIRE, position vacant.

SHETLAND

Bird Recorders
FAIR ISLE, Deryk Shaw, Bird Observatory, Fair Isle, Shetland, ZE2 9JU. 01595 760258;
e-mail: fairisle.birdobs@zetnet.co.uk
SHETLAND, Kevin Osborn, Inkleholme, Swinister, Sandwick, Shetland ZE2 9HH. 01950 431286. e-mail: k.o@virgin.net

Bird Reports
FAIR ISLE BIRD OBSERVATORY REPORT (1949-), from Scottish Ornithologists' Club, 21 Regent Terrace, Edinburgh, EH7 5BT. 0131 556 6042.
SHETLAND BIRD REPORT (1969-), from Martin Heubeck, East House, Sumburgh Lighthouse, Virkie, Shetland, ZE3 9JN.
e-mail: martinheubeck@btinterenet.com

BTO Regional Representative
Dave Okill, Heilinabretta, Cauldhame, Trondra, Shetland, ZE1 0XL. H:01595 880450; W:01595 696926.

Club
SHETLAND BIRD CLUB, (1973; 200). Wendy Dickson, Flat 4, Muckle Flugga Shore Station, Burrafirth, Unst, Shetland, ZE2 9EQ. 01957 711275.
www.zetnet.co.uk/sigs/birds/links.html

Ringing Groups
FAIR ISLE BIRD OBSERVATORY, Deryk Shaw, Bird Observatory, Fair Isle, Shetland, ZE2 9JU. Tel/fax 01595 760258;
e-mail: fairisle.birdobs@zetnet.co.uk
SHETLAND RG, Dave Okill, Heilinabretta, Cauldhame, Trondra, Shetland, ZE1 0XL. H:01595 880450; W:01595 696926.

Wetland Bird Survey Organiser
Dr Roger Riddington, Shetland Biological, Records Centre, 22-24 North Road, Lerwick, Shetland, ZE1 0NQ. 01595 694688;
e-mail: sbrc@zetnet.co.uk

WALES

Bird Report & Club See Welsh Ornithological Society in National Directory.

BTO Honorary Wales Officer

Dr Derek Thomas, Laburnum Cottage, 12 Mansfield Rd, Murton, Swansea SA3 3AR. Home: 01792 232623; work; 01792 205698 ext 4630. e-mail: d.k.thomas@swansea.ac.uk

NORTH WALES

Bird Atlas/Avifauna

The Birds of Caernarfonshire (1998, from Lionel Pilling, 51 Brighton Close, Rhyl LL18 3HL).

Bird Recorders

ANGLESEY, Stephen Culley, Millhouse, Penmynydd Road, Menai Bridge, Anglesey, LL59 5RT. e-mail: SteCul10@aol.com
CAERNARFON, John Barnes, Fach Goch, Waunfawr, Caernarfon, LL55 4YS. 01286 650362.
DENBIGHSHIRE & FLINTSHIRE, Norman Hallas, 63 Park Avenue, Wrexham,LL12 7AW. Tel/fax 01978 290522.
MEIRIONNYDD, RI Thorpe, 2 Tan-y-Garth, Friog, Fairbourne, Gwynedd, Ll38 5RJ.

Bird Reports

BARDSEY BIRD OBSERVATORY ANNUAL REPORT, from Warden, see Reserves.
CAMBRIAN BIRD REPORT (sometime Gwynedd Bird Report) (1953-), from Mr Rhion Pritchard, Pant Afonig, Hafod Lane, Bangor, Gwynedd, LL57 4BU. 01248 671301.
e-mail: rhion@pritchardr.freeserve.co.uk
CLWYD BIRD REPORT, from Dr Anne Brenchley, Tyr Fannog, 43 Black Brook, Sychdyn, Mold, Flints, CH7 6LT. 01352 750118
MEIRIONNYDD BIRD REPORT Published in *Cambrian Bird Report* (above).
WREXHAM BIRDWATCHERS' SOCIETY ANNUAL REPORT (1982-), from Secretary, Wrexham Birdwatchers Society.

BTO Regional Representatives & Regional Development Officer

ANGLESEY RR & RDO, Jim Clark, Glan Dwr, Llyn Traffwll, Caergeiliog, Holyhead, LL65 3LR. H:01407 741536; W:01407 730762.
CAERNARFON RR, John Barnes, Fach Goch, Waunfawr, Caernarfon, LL55 4YS. 01286 650362.
CLWYD EAST RR, Dr Anne Brenchley, Ty'r Fawnog, 43 Black Brook, Sychdyn, Mold, CH7 6LT. 01352 750118.
e-mail: ian.anne@imsab.idps.co.uk
CLWYD WEST RR, Mel ab Owain, 31 Coed Bedw, Abergele, Conwy, LL22 7EH.
e-mail: malabowain@cix.compulink.co.uk
MEIRIONNYDD RR, Peter Haveland, Ty Manceinion, Penmachno, Betws-y-Coed, Gwynedd, LL24 0UD.
e-mail: peter.haveland@tesco.net

Clubs

BANGOR BIRD GROUP, (1947; 100). Secretary, Bangor Bird Group, Treborth Botanic Gardens, University of Wales, Bangor, LL57 2RQ. e-mail: n.brown@bangor.ac.uk
CAMBRIAN ORNITHOLOGICAL SOCIETY, (1952; 162). Mr Rhion Pritchard, Pant Afonig, Hafod Lane, Bangor, Gwynedd, LL57 4BU. 01248 671301.
CLWYD ORNITHOLOGICAL SOCIETY, (1956; 45). Miss Lynn Davies, Preswylfa, Berthen Rd, Lixwm, Holywell, Flints, CH8 8LT. 01352 781106.
DEE ESTUARY CONSERVATION GROUP, (1973; 22 grps). N J Friswell, 8 Oaklands Crescent, Tattenhall, Chester, CH3 9QT. 01829 770463.
DEESIDE NATURALISTS' SOCIETY, (1973; 300). Brian Grey, 10 Heswall Avenue, Higher Bebington, Wirral, CH63 5QD. 0151 608 4167.
WREXHAM BIRDWATCHERS' SOCIETY, (1974; 90). Miss Marian Williams, 10 Lake View, Gresford, Wrexham, Clwyd, LL12 8PU. 01978 854633.

Ringing Groups

BARDSEY BIRD OBSERVATORY, Steven Stansfield, Bardsey Island, off Aberdaron, Pwllheli, Gwynedd, LL53 8DE. 08312 55569.
MERSEYSIDE RG, P Slater, 45 Greenway Road, Speke, Liverpool, L24 7RY.
SCAN RG, D J Stanyard, Court Farm, Groeslon, Caernarfon, Gwynedd, LL54 7UE.01286 881 669

RSPB Members' Group

NORTH WALES, (1986; 130). Maureen Douglas, 57 Penrhyn Beach East, Penrhyn Bay, Llandudno, Gwynedd, LL30 3RW. 01492 547768.

Wetland Bird Survey Organisers

ARTRO, MAWDDACH & TRAETH BACH ESTUARIES, Vacant.
CEFNI & BRAINT ESTUARIES, Will Sandison, CCW Hafod Elfyn, Penrhos, Bangor, Gwynedd.
CONWY ESTUARY, Ian Higginson, Conwy RSPB Nature Reserve, Llandudno Junction, Conwy, North Wales, LL31 9XZ. 01492 584091.
DEE ESTUARY, Colin Wells, Burton Point Farm, Station Road, Burton, Nr Neston, South Wirral, CH64 5SB. 0151 336 7681.
DULAS BAY, David Wright, Graig Eithin, Mynydd Bodafon, Llanerchymedd, Anglesey, LL71 8BG.
DYFI ESTUARY, Dick Squires, Cae'r Berllan, Eglwysfach, Machynlleth, Powys, SY20 8TA. 01654 781265. e-mail: dick.squires@rspb.org.uk
FORYD BAY, Simon Hugheston-Roberts, Oakhurst, St David's Road, Caernarfon, LL55 1EL. 01286 672155.
e-mail: hrsimon.oakhurst@virgin.net
INLAND SEA, Ivor McLean, 32 Lon-y-Bryn, Bangor, LL57 2LD. 01248 362112.
RED WHARF BAY, Dr Richard Arnold, 8 Helen Terrace, Y Felinheli, Gwynedd, LL57 2UW.
ANGLESEY & CAERNARFON (other sites), Jim Clark, Glan Dwr, Llyn Traffwll, Caergeiliog, Holyhead, LL65 3LR. 01407 741536.
CLWYD (INLAND), Elvet Jones, Sandiway, Llanasa, Holywell, Flints, CH8 9NE.01745 852984.
MERIONETH, OTHER SITES, Trefor Owen, Crochendy Twrog, Maentwrog,LL41 3YU. 01766 590302.
CLWYD (coastal) & RIVER CLWYD, Peter Wellington, 4 Cheltenham Avenue, Rhyl, Denbighs, LL18 4DN. 01745 354232.

Wildlife Trust

NORTH WALES WILDLIFE TRUST, (1963; 2400). 376 High Street, Bangor, Gwynedd, LL57 1YE. 01248 351541; fax 01248 353192.
e-mail: nwwt@cix.co.uk

SOUTH WALES

Bird Atlas/Avifauna

An Atlas of Breeding Birds in West Glamorgan by David M Hanford et al (Gower Ornithological Society, 1992).
Birds of Glamorgan by Clive Hurford and Peter Lansdown (Published by the authors, c/o National Museum of Wales, Cardiff, 1995)

Bird Recorders

GLAMORGAN (EAST), Steve Moon, 36 Rest Bay Close, Porthcawl, Bridgend, CF36 3UN. 01656 786571; work 01656 643170.
e-mail: moonsj@bridgend.gov.uk
GOWER (WEST GLAMORGAN), Robert Taylor, 285 Llangyfelach Road, Brynhyfryd, Swansea, SA5 9LB. 01792 464780; mobile 07970 567007.

Bird Reports

EAST GLAMORGAN BIRD REPORT (title varies 1963-95) 1996-, from Richard G Smith, 35 Manor Chase, Gwaun Miskin, Pontypridd, Rhondda Cynon Taff, S Wales.
GOWER BIRDS (1965-), from Secretary, Gower Ornithological, Society.

BTO Regional Representatives & Regional Development Officer

EAST GLAMORGAN RR, Rob Nottage, 32 Village Farm, Bonvilston, Cardiff, CF5 6TY. 01446 781423.
e-mail: rob@nottages.freeserve.co.uk
WEST RR, Bob Howells, Ynys Enlli, 14 Dolgoy Close, West Cross, Swansea, SA3 5LT. 01792 405363. e-mail: bobhowells31@hotmail.com
GLAMORGAN RDO, Dr Derek Thomas, 12 Manselfield Road, Murton, Swansea, SA3 3AR. Home 01792 232623; work 01792 205678 ext 4630. e-mail: d.k.thomas@swansea.ac.uk

Clubs

CARDIFF NATURALISTS' SOCIETY, (1867; 250). Stephen R Howe, Department of Geology, National Museum of Wales, Cardiff, CF10 3NP. 029 2057 3363 e-mail: steve.howe@nmgn.ac.uk
GLAMORGAN BIRD CLUB, (1990; 170). Steve Moon, Kenfig National Nature Reserve, Ton Kenfig, Pyle, Bridgend, CF33 4PT. 01656 743386. e-mail: moonsj@bridgend.gov.uk
GOWER ORNITHOLOGICAL SOCIETY, (1956; 120). Audrey Jones, 24 Hazel Road, Uplands, Swansea, SA2 0LX. 01792 298859.

Ringing Groups

FLAT HOLM RG, Brian Bailey, Tamarisk House, Wards Court, Frampton-on-Severn, Glos, GL2 7DY.
e-mail: brianhbailey98@freeserve.co.uk
KENFIG RG, Mr D.G. Carrington, 25 Bryneglwys Gardens , Porthcawl, Bridgend, Mid Glamorgan, CF36 5PR.

RSPB Members' Groups

CARDIFF & DISTRICT, (1973; 4500). Mrs Margaret Read, 121 Lavernock road, Penarth, South Wales, CF64 3QG. 029 2070 9537. e-mail: mereadcmt@aol.com
WEST GLAMORGAN, (1985; 421). Mark Johnson, 16 Pant y Telin Road, Portardulais, Swansea, SA4 1PZ. 01792 882140.

Wetland Bird Survey Organisers

EAST GLAMORGAN (former Mid & South Glam), Rob Nottage, 32 Village Farm, Bonvilston, Cardiff, CF5 6TY. 01446 781423. e-mail: rob@nottages.freeserve.co.uk
SEVERN ESTUARY, Niall Burton, c/o BTO, The Nunnery, Thetford, Norfolk, IP24 2PU. 01842 750050. e-mail: niall.burton@bto.org
WEST, Bob Howells, Ynys Enlli, 14 Dolgoy Close, West Cross, Swansea, SA3 5LT. 01792 405363.

Wildlife Hospitals

GOWER BIRD HOSPITAL, Karen Kingsnorth and Simon Allen, Valetta, Sandy Lane, Parkmill, Swansea, SA3 2EW. 01792 371630 fax 01792 371412. e-mail: gbh@valetta.u-net.com
All species of wild birds also hedgehogs and small mammals. **Prior phone call essential**. The purpose the hospital is to care for sick, injured and orphaned wild birds and animals with the sole intention of returning them to the wild. Newsletter available.
LLEWELLYN, Paul, 104 Manselfield Road, Murton, Swansea, SA3 3AG. 01792 233712. e-mail: p.j.llewellyn@swansea.ac.uk
All species of birds but specialist knowledge of raptors. Veterinary support.

Wildlife Trust

GLAMORGAN WILDLIFE TRUST, (1961; 1300). Fountain Road, Tondu, Bridgend, CF32 0EH. 01656 724100; fax 01656 729880. e-mail: glamorganwt@cix.co.uk

EAST WALES

Bird Atlas/Avifauna

Birds of Radnorshire. In preparation.
The Gwent Atlas of Breeding Birds by Tyler, Lewis, Venables & Walton (Gwent Ornithological Society, 1987).

Bird Recorders

BRECONSHIRE, Martin F Peers, Cyffylog, 2 Aberyscir Road, Cradoc, Brecon, Powys, LD3 9PB. 01874 623774.
GWENT, Chris Jones, 22 Walnut Drive, Caerleon, Newport, Gwent, NP6 1SB. 01633 423439.
MONTGOMERYSHIRE, Brayton Holt, Scops Cottage, Pentrebeirdd, Welshpool, Powys, SY21 9DL. 01938 500266.
RADNORSHIRE, Pete Jennings, Penbont House, Elan Valley, Rhayader, Powys, LD6 5HS. H:01597 811522; W:01597 810880.

Bird Reports

BRECONSHIRE BIRDS (1962-), from Brecknock Wildlife Trust.
GWENT BIRD REPORT (1964-), from Jerry Lewis, Y Bwthyn Gwyn, Coldbrook, Abergavenny, Monmouthshire, NP7 9TD. (H)01873 855091; (W)01633 644856.
MONTGOMERYSHIRE BIRD REPORT (1981-82-), From Montgomeryshire Wildlife Trust.
RADNOR BIRDS (1987/92-), from Recorder.

BTO Regional Representatives & Regional Development Officer

BRECKNOCK RR, John Lloyd, Cynghordy, Llandovery, Carms, SA20 0LN. 01550 750202. e-mail; thelloyds@dial.pipex.com
GWENT RR, Jerry Lewis, Y Bwthyn Gwyn, Coldbrook, Abergavenny, Monmouthshire, NP7 9TD. H:01873 855091; W:01633 644856.
MONTGOMERY RR, Brayton Holt, Scops Cottage, Pentrebeirdd, Welshpool, Powys, SY21 9DL. 01938 500266.
RADNORSHIRE RR & RDO, Pete Jennings, Penbont House, Elan Valley, Rhayader, Powys, LD6 5HS. H:01597 811522; W:01597 810880.

Clubs

BRECKNOCK WILDLIFE TRUST BIRD CLUB, (1993; 80). Jim Vale, c/o Brecknock Wildlife Trust, Lion House, Bethel Square, Brecon, Powys, LD3 7AY. 01874 625708.
GWENT ORNITHOLOGICAL SOCIETY, (1964; 350). T J Russell, The Pines, Highfield Road, Monmouth, Gwent, NP25 3HR. 01600 716266.
MONTGOMERYSHIRE FIELD SOCIETY, (1946; 170). Maureen Preen, Ivy House, Deep Cutting, Pool Quay, Welshpool, Powys, SY21 9LJ. Tel: Mary Oliver, 01686 413518.
MONTGOMERYSHIRE WILDLIFE TRUST BIRD GROUP, (1997; 104). A M Puzey, Four Seasons, Arddleen, Llanymynech, Powys, SY22 6RU. 01938 590578.

RADNOR BIRD GROUP, (1986; 600). Pete Jennings, Penbont House, Elan Valley, Rhayader, Powys, LD6 5HS. H:01597 811522; W:01597 810880.

Ringing Groups

GOLDCLIFF RG, Vaughan Thomas, Gilgal Cottage, Gilfach, Llanvaches, S Wales, NP26 3AZ. 01633 817161.
LLANGORSE RG, Jerry Lewis, Y Bwthyn Gwyn, Coldbrook, Abergavenny, Monmouthshire, NP7 9TD. H:01873 855091; W:01633 644856.

Wetland Bird Survey Organisers

SEVERN ESTUARY, Niall Burton, c/o BTO, The Nunnery, Thetford, Norfolk, IP24 2PU. 01842 750050. e-mail: niall.burton@bto.org
GWENT (excl Severn Estuary), Chris Jones, 22 Walnut Drive, Caerleon, Newport, Gwent, NP6 1SB. 01633 423439.
POWYS, Martin F Peers, Cyffylog, 2 Aberyscir Road, Cradoc, Brecon, Powys, LD3 9PB. 01874 623774.

Wildlife Trusts

BRECKNOCK WILDLIFE TRUST, (1963; 893). Lion House, Bethel Square, Brecon, Powys, LD3 7AY. 01874 625708.
e-mail: brecknockwt@cix.co.uk
GWENT WILDLIFE TRUST, (1963;1200). 16 White Swan Court, Church Street, Monmouth, Gwent, NP25 3NY. 01600 715501; fax 1600715832. e-mail: gwentwildlife@cix.co.uk
MONTGOMERYSHIRE WILDLIFE TRUST, (1982; 1000). Collot House, 20 Severn Street, Welshpool, Powys, SY21 7AD. 01938 555654; fax 07938 556161. e-mail: montwt@cix.co.uk
RADNORSHIRE WILDLIFE TRUST, (1987; 789). Warwick House, High Street, Llandrindod Wells, Powys, LD1 6AG. 01597 823298; fax 01597 823274. e-mail: radnorshirewt@cix.co.uk

WEST WALES

Bird Atlas/Avifauna

Birds of Pembrokeshire by Jack Donovan and Graham Rees (Dyfed Wildlife Trust, 1994).

Bird Recorders

CEREDIGION, Hywel Roderick, 32 Prospect Street, Aberystwyth, Ceredigion, SY23 1JJ. 01970 617681.
e-mail: hywel@ador.freeserve.co.uk
CARMARTHENSHIRE, Rob Hunt, 9 Waun Road, Llanelli, Carmarthenshire, SA15 3RS. 01554 778729.
From January 2002: Tony Foster, Ffosddu, Salem, Llandeilo, Carmathenshire, SA19 7NS; 01558 824237; e-mail: tony-foster@supanet.com
PEMBROKESHIRE. 1, Jack Donovan MBE, The Burren, 5 Dingle Lane, Crundale, Haverfordwest, Pembrokeshire, SA62 4DJ. 01437 762673.
2, Graham Rees, 22 Priory Avenue, Haverfordwest, Pembrokeshire, SA61 1SQ. 01437 762877.

Bird Reports

CARMARTHENSHIRE BIRDS (1982-), from Carmarthenshire Recorder,
CEREDIGION BIRD REPORT (biennial 1982-87; annual 1988-), from Wildlife Trust West Wales,
PEMBROKESHIRE BIRD REPORT (1981-), from TJ Price, 2 Wordsworth Ave, Haverfordwest, Pembrokeshire, SA61 1SN.

BTO Regional Representatives & Regional Development Officer

CARDIGAN RR, Moira Convery, 41 Danycoed, Aberystwyth,SY23 2HD.
e-mail: moira@mconvery.freeserve.co.uk
CARMARTHEN RR, David Poulter, Ty Isaf, Pentrepoeth, Idole, Carmarthen, SA32 8DH. 01267 233816; work 01267 224322.
e-mail: david.poulter@ic24.net
PEMBROKE RR, Roderick Hadfield, 104 Nun Street, St David's, Haverfordwest, SA62 6NX. 01437 720572.
PEMBROKE RDO, Position vacant.

Clubs

LLANELLI NATURALISTS, (1971; 100). Richard Pryce, Trevethin, School Road, Pwll, Llanelli, Carmarthenshire, SA15 4AL. 01554 775847. e-mail: pryceeco@aol.com
PEMBROKESHIRE BIRD GROUP, (1993; 60). T J Price, 2 Wordsworth Ave, Haverfordwest, Pembs, SA61 1SN. 01437 779667.

Ringing Group

PEMBROKESHIRE RG, J Hayes, 3 Wades Close, Holyland Road, Pembroke, SA71 4BN. 01646 687036.

Wetland Bird Survey Organisers

BURRY, NORTH, Graham Rutt, c/o 13 St James Gardens, Uplands, Swansea, SA1 6DY. 01792 458245.
DYFI & DYSINNI ESTUARIES, Dick Squires,

Cae'r Berllan, Eglwysfach, Machynlleth, Powys, SY20 8TA. e-mail: dick.squires@rspb.org.uk
GWENDRAETH, TYWI & TAFF ESTUARIES, Gavin Hall, Visitor Centre, Pembrey Country Park, Pembrey, Carmarthenshire, SA16 0EJ. 01269 871580.
NYFER ESTUARY, position vacant.
CARDIGAN (excl Dyfi Estuary), Peter Davis, Felindre, Aberarth, Aberaeron, SA46 0LP. 01545 570870. e-mail; pedavis@supanet.com
CARMARTHEN, INLAND, position vacant,
PEMBROKESHIRE, Ms Annie Poole, 1 Rushmoor, Martletwy, Narberth, Pembs, SA67 8BB. 01834 891667. e-mail: annie@clara.net

Wildlife Hospitals
NEW QUAY BIRD HOSPITAL, Jean Bryant, Penfoel, Cross Inn, Llandysul, Ceredigion, SA44 6NR. 01545 560462. All species of birds. Fully equipped for cleansing oiled seabirds. Veterinary support.
WEST WILLIAMSTON OILED BIRD CENTRE, Mrs J Hains, Lower House Farm, West Williamston, Kilgetty, Pembs, SA68 0TL. 01646 651236. Facilities for holding up to 200 Guillemots, etc. for short periods. Initial treatment is given prior to despatch to other washing centres during very large oil spills; otherwise birds are washed at the Centre with intensive care and rehabilitation facilities. Also other species. Veterinary support.

Wildlife Trust
WILDLIFE TRUST WEST WALES, (1938; 3100). Welsh Wildlife Centre, Cilgerran, Cardigan, SA43 2TB. 01239 621212.
e-mail: june@wildlife-wales.org.uk
www.wildlife-wales.org.uk

ISLE OF MAN

Bird Atlas/Avifauna
Manx Bird Atlas. 2002 is fifth year of five-year research programme. Contact: Chris Sharpe (see below, BTO).

Bird Recorder
Dr Pat Cullen, Troutbeck, Cronkbourne, Braddan, Isle of Man, IM4 4QA. 01624 623308; work 01624 676744.
e-mail: bridgeen@mcb.net

Bird Reports
MANX BIRD REPORT (1947-), published in *Peregrine*. From G D Craine, 8 Kissack Road, Castletown, Isle of Man, IM9 1NP.
e-mail: g.craine@adusys.co.uk
CALF OF MAN BIRD OBSERVATORY ANNUAL REPORT, From Secretary, Manx National Heritage, Manx Museum, Douglas, Isle of Man, IM1 3LY.

BTO Regional Representative & Regional Development Officer
RR, Dr Pat Cullen, as above,
RDO, Chris Sharpe, 33 Mines Road, Laxey, Isle of Man, IM4 7NH. 01624 861130.
e-mail: chris@manxbirdatlas.org

Club
MANX ORNITHOLOGICAL SOCIETY, (1967; 150). Mrs A C Kaye, Cronk Ny Ollee, Glen Chass, Port St Mary, Isle of Man, IM9 5PL. 01624 834015.

Ringing Group
CALF OF MAN BIRD OBSERVATORY, Tim Bagworth, Calf of Man, c/o Kionsleau, Plantation Road, Port St Mary, Isle of Man, IM9 5AY. Mobile 07624 462858.

Wetland Bird Survey Organiser
Dr Pat Cullen, as above.

Wildlife Trust
MANX WILDLIFE TRUST, (1973;900). Tynwald Mills, St Johns, Isle of Man, IM4 3AE. 01624 801985; fax 01624 801022.
e-mail: manxwt@cix.co.uk
www.mcb.net./mwt/

CHANNEL ISLANDS

BTO Regional Representative
Jamie Hooper, Old Rocquaine Hotel, Torteval, Guernsey, GY8 0QE. Tel/fax 01481 266924.

Ringing Group
The Channel Islands ringing scheme is run by the Société Jersiaise,

Wetland Bird Survey Organiser
INLAND, Glyn Young, Société Jersiase, The Museum, 9 Pier Road, St Helier, Jersey, JE2 4XW. 01481 822414.
e-mail: gyoung@durrell.org

ALDERNEY

Bird Recorder
Mrs Jill Watson, Huitrier Pies, 9 Rue de Beaumont, Alderney, GY9 3XU. 01481 822414.
e-mail: jillwatson@beeb.net

Bird Report
ALDERNEY SOCIETY ORNITHOLOGY REPORT (1992-), from Recorder,

GUERNSEY

Bird Atlas/Avifauna
Birds of the Bailiwick of Guernsey (working title). In preparation.

Bird Recorder
Wayne Turner, Pumpkin Cottage, La Route des Adams, St Peters, Guernsey, GY7 9LH. 01481 263403.

Bird Report
REPORT & TRANSACTIONS OF LA SOCIÉTÉ GUERNESIAISE (1882-), From Wayne Turner, Bird Recorder,

Clubs
LA SOCIÉTÉ GUERNESIAISE (Ornithological Section), (1882; 30). Vic Froome, La Cloture, Coutil de Bas Lane, St Sampsons, Guernsey, GY2 4XJ. 01481 254841.
www.societe.org.gg

RSPB Members' Group
GUERNSEY, (1975;800+). Michael Bairds, Le Quatre Vents, La Passee, St Sampsons, Guernsey, GY2 4TS. 01481 255524;
e;mail: mikebairds@gtonline.net

Wetland Bird Survey Organiser
COASTAL SITES, Wayne Turner, Pumpkin Cottage, La Route des Adams, St Peters, Guernsey, GY7 9LH. 01481 263403

Wildlife Hospital
GUERNSEY. GSPCA ANIMAL SHELTER, Mrs Jayne Le Cras, Rue des Truchots, Les Fiers Moutons, St Andrews, Guernsey, Channel Islands, GY6 8UD. 01481 57261
All species. Modern cleansing unit for oiled seabirds. 24-hour emergency service. Veterinary support.

JERSEY

Bird Recorder
Tony Paintin, 16 Quennevais Gardens, St Brelade, Jersey, Channel Islands, JE3 8LH.
e-mail: cavokjersey@hotmail.com

Bird Report
JERSEY BIRD REPORT, From Secretary (Publications), Société Jersiase.

Club
SOCIETE JERSIAISE (Ornithological Section), (1948; 40). Roger Noel, 7 Pier Road, St Helier, Jersey, JE2 4XW. 01534 758314.

RSPB Members' Group
JERSEY, Robert Burrow, 1 Southlands, Green Road, St Clements, Jersey, JE2 6QA. 01534 32167.

Wetland Bird Survey Organiser
COASTAL SITES, Roger Noel, Ilanda, 4 Le Petite Piéce, St Peters, Jersey, JE3 7AE. 01534 481409.

Wildlife Hospital
JERSEY. JSPCA ANIMALS' SHELTER, Pru Bannier, 89 St Saviour's Road, St Helier, Jersey, JE2 4GJ. e-mail: jspca@super.net
All species. Expert outside support for owls and raptors. Oiled seabird unit. Veterinary surgeon on site. Educational Centre.

NORTHERN IRELAND

Bird Recorder

George Gordon, 2 Brooklyn Avenue, Bangor, Co Down, BT20 5RB. 028 9145 5763.
e-mail: gordon@ballyholme2.freeserve.co.uk

Bird Reports

NORTHERN IRELAND BIRD REPORT, From Secretary, Northern Ireland, Birdwatchers' Association (see, National Directory).
IRISH BIRD REPORT, Included in Irish Birds, BirdWatch Ireland in National, Directory.
COPELAND BIRD OBSERVATORY REPORT, From, (see Reserves).

BTO Regional Representatives

BTO IRELAND OFFICER, Ken Perry, 43 Portstewart Road, Coleraine, Co Londonderry, BT52 1RW. 028 7034 2985; fax 0287033 8053.
e-mail: kennethwilliamperry@hotmail.com
ANTRIM & BELFAST, Position vacant,
ARMAGH, David W A Knight, 20 Mandeville Drive, Tandragee, Craigavon, Co Armagh, BT62 2DQ. 028 3884 0658.
DOWN, Position vacant.
LONDONDERRY, Charles Stewart, Bravallen, 18 Duncrun Road, Bellarena, Limavady, Co Londonderry, BT49 0JD. 028 7775 0468.
TYRONE SOUTH & FERMANAGH, Philip S Grosse, 30 Tullybroom Road, Clogher, Co Tyrone, BT76 0UW. 028 8554 8606.
e-mail: phigro@aol.com
TYRONE NORTH, Mary Mooney, 20 Leckpatrick Road, Ballymagorry, Strabane, Co Tyrone, BT82 0AL. 028 7188 2442.
e-mail: memooney@foxlodge.healthnet.co.uk

Clubs

NORTHERN IRELAND BIRDWATCHERS' ASSOCIATION See National Directory.
NORTHERN IRELAND ORNITHOLOGISTS' CLUB See National Directory.
CASTLE ESPIE BIRDWATCHING CLUB, (1995; 60). Dot Blakely, 31 Clandeboye Way, Bangor, Co Down, BT19 1AD. 028 9145 0784.

Ringing Groups

ANTRIM & ARDS RG, M McNeely, 35 Balleyvalley Heights, Banbridge, Co Down, BT32 4AQ. 028 4062 9823.
COPELAND BIRD OBSERVATORY, C W Acheson, 28 Church Avenue, Dunmurry, Belfast, BT17 9RS.
NORTH DOWN RG, Hugh Thurgate, 24 Church Court, Clough, Downpatrick, Co Down, BT30 8QX.

RSPB Members' Groups

ANTRIM, (1977; 23). Agnes Byron, 59 Tirgracey Road, Mucamore, Co Antrim, BT41 4PS. 028 9446 2207.
BANGOR, (1973; 45). Michael Richardson, 10 Belgravia Road, Bangor, Co Down, BT19 6XJ. 028 9146 2705.
BELFAST, (1970;130). Ron Houston, 7 Kingsdale Park, Belfast,BT5 7BY.
028 9079 6188
COLERAINE, (1978; 45). John Clarke, 48 Shelbridge Park, Coleraine, Co Londonderry, BT52 2HP. 028 7032 1239.
FERMANAGH, (1977; 28). Doreen Morrison, 91 Derrin Road, Cornagrade, Enniskillen, Co Fermanagh, BT74 6BA. 028 6632 6654.
LARNE, (1974; 55). Jimmy Christie, 314 Coast Road, Ballygally, Co Antrim, BT40 2QZ.
028 2858 3223.
LISBURN, (1978; 30). John Scott, 22 Whitla Road, Lisburn, Co Antrim, BT28 3PP.
028 9260 1864.

Wetland Bird Survey Organisers

ANTRIM, BELFAST LOUGH, John O'Boyle, 3 Killeen Park, Belfast, BT11 8HH.
ANTRIM, LARNE LOUGH, position vacant.
ANTRIM, LOUGHS NEAGH & BEG, Stephen Foster, Peatlands Park, 33 Derryhubbert Road, Verner's Bridge, Dungannon, BT71 6NW.
ANTRIM, OTHER SITES, Jim Wells, 16 Bridge Road, Lurgan, Co Armagh, BT67 9LA.
028 3832 1837.
ARMAGH, LOUGHS NEAGH & BEG, Warden, Lough Neagh Nature Reserves, as above.
DOWN, BELFAST LOUGH, John O'Boyle, as above.
DOWN, CARLINGFORD LOUGH, Frank Carroll, 292 Barcroft Park, Newry, Co Down, BT35 8ET. 028 3026 8015.
DOWN, DUNDRUM BAY, Cormac Loughron, Murlough NNR, The Stableyard, Keel Point, Dundrum, Newcastle, Co Down, BT33 0NQ.
028 437 51467.
DOWN, LOUGHS NEAGH & BEG, Warden,

Lough Neagh Nature Reserves, as above.
DOWN, OUTER ARDS, Ian Enlander, Environment & Heritage Service, Commonwealth House, 35 Castle Street, Belfast, BT1 1GU. 028 9054 6610
DOWN, STRANGFORD LOUGH, Paddy Mackie, Mahee Island, Comber, Newtownards, Co Down, BT23 6EP. Tel/fax 028 9754 1420
FERMANAGH, Ian Enlander, as above.
LONDONDERRY, BANN ESTUARY, Hill Dick, 33 Hopefield Avenue, Portrush, Co Antrim, BT56 8HB.
LONDONDERRY, LOUGH FOYLE, Dave Allen, RSPB, Belvoir Park Forest, Belfast, BT8 4QT. 028 9049 1547.
LONDONDERRY, LOUGHS NEAGH & BEG, Warden, Lough Neagh Nature Reserves, as above.
TYRONE, LOUGHS NEAGH & BEG, Warden, Lough Neagh Nature Reserves, as above.

Wildlife Hospital

TACT WILDLIFE CENTRE, Mrs Patricia Nevines, 2 Crumlin Road, Crumlin, Co Antrim, BT29 4AD. 028 9442 2900.
e-mail: t.a.c.t@care4free.net
All categories of birds treated and rehabilitated; released where practicable, otherwise given a home. Visitors (inc. school groups and organisations) welcome by prior arrangement. Veterinary support.

Wildlife Trust

ULSTER WILDLIFE TRUST, (1978; 2100). 3 New Line, Crossgar, Co Down, BT30 9EP. 028 4483 0282. e-mail: ulsterwt@cix.co.uk

REPUBLIC OF IRELAND

Bird Recorders

1, Oran O'Sullivan, BirdWatch Ireland, Ruttledge House, 8 Longford Place, Monkstown, Co Dublin; +353 (0) 1280 4322; fax +353 (0) 1284 4407. e-mail: bird@indigo.ie
2. Rarities, Paul Milne, 100 Dublin Road, Sutton, Dublin 13; +353 (0) 1832 5653.
e-mail: paul.milne@oceanfree.net

Bird Reports

IRISH BIRD REPORT, Included in *Irish Birds*, (see BirdWatch Ireland in National Directory).
CAPE CLEAR BIRD OBSERVATORY ANNUAL REPORT.
CORK BIRD REPORT (1963-71; 1976-), (contact BirdWatch Ireland).
EAST COAST BIRD REPORT (1980-), (contact BirdWatch Ireland).

BTO Regional Representative

BTO IRELAND OFFICER, Ken Perry, 43 Portstewart Road, Coleraine, Co Londonderry, BT52 1RW. From Ireland: 08 028 7034 2985; fax 08 028 7033 8053. From UK: 028 7034 2985; fax 028 7033 8053.
e-mail: kennethwilliamperry@hotmail.com

BirdWatch Ireland Branches

Branches may be contacted in writing via BirdWatch Ireland HQ.

Ringing Groups

CAPE CLEAR BIRD OBSERVATORY, S Wing, 30 Irsher Street, Appledore, Devon, EX39 1RZ.
GREAT SALTEE RS, O J Merne, 20 Cuala Road, Bray, Co Wicklow.
MUNSTER RG, K P Collins, Ballygambon, Lisronagh, Clonmel, Co Tipperary;
e-mail: kevcoll@indigo.ie
SHANNON WADER RG, P A Brennan, The Crag, Stonehall, Newmarket-on-Fergus, Co Clare.

ARTICLES IN BIRD REPORTS

Argyll Bird Report Vol 16 (For 1999) 2000
Argyll Bird Checklist – 2000 Update by Tristan ap Rheinallt and Paul Daw.
Breeding of Red-throated Divers *Gavia Stellata* on Islay 1992-1998 by Aubrey and Edith Colling.

Ayrshire Bird Report 2000
Ailsa Craig – Before and after the Eradication of Rats in 1991 by Bernard Zonfrillo.
Kestrels in Ayrshire in 2000 by Gordon Riddle.

Beds Bird Report 2000
The Honey Buzzard influx by Dave Odell.
Ringing Report by Erroll Newman.
Plus many other articles.

Cambridgeshire Bird Report 1999
Identification of Siberian Chiffchaff in Somersham by A Hitchings.
Are Summer Migants Arriving Earlier in Cambridgeshire? by BG Martin.

Ceredigion Bird Report 1999
Colour Ringed Lapwings by Ray Bomford.
Changing Pattern of Little Gull *Larus Minutus* and Mediteranean Gull *L.Melanocepalus* Records in Ceredigion by Hywel Podouk.
Aberystwyth Starlings by Peter Walters Davies and Tony Cross.
Ceredigion Bird Ringing Report 1999 by Tony Cross.

Cleveland Bird Report 2000
Desert Wheatear – New To Cleveland by H Mitchell.
Desert Lesser Whitethroat – New To Cleveland by DA Money.
The Status of Green-winged Teal and Common Redpoll in Cleveland by RC Taylor.

Clwyd Bird Report 1999
Birds And Biodiversity by Dr Anne Brenchley.
Bird of the Year: Black Grouse *Tetrao Tetrix* by Ron Plummer.
Gronant Little Tern Colony by Gareth Stamp.

Birds in Cornwall 1999
Analysis of Cornwall's Farmland Birds 1968-1999.
Seabird 2000 Results.
Ongoing Cornwall Bird Atlas Results (Highlights).

Derbyshire Bird Report 1999
General Secretary's Report for 1999 by Steve Shaw.
Wetland Bird Surveys, Winter 1999-2000 by Chris Burnett.
Spotted Sandpiper at Willington GP - a New Species for Derbyshire by Rodney Key.
Cetti's Warbler at Drakeland WR – a New Species for Derbyshire by Rodney Key.
Pallas's Warbler at Bondhay – a New Species For Derbyshire by David Fell.
Green Sandpiper Apparently 'Holding Territory' in Derbyshire, Summer 1999 by Stephen Jackson.
The Status of the Raven in Derbyshire by Mick Lacey.

Devon Bird Report 2000
Sora Rail – a New Bird For Devon by Brian Heasman.
The Kenwith *Acrocephalus* Warbler by D Churchill, A Jewels, T Whiley.

Dorset Bird Report 1999
Report on Bird Ringing in Dorset in 1999 by Roger Peart.
The 1999 Nightingale Survey by Graham And Catherine Whitby.
The Portland Olivaceous Warbler by Martin Cade.
Breeding Farmland Birds in Dorset 1999 by John Day, Julie Walker and Leigh Lock.
Iberian Chiffchaff at Verne Common by Charles Richards.
The Swanage Serins by WG Teagle.
Breeding Bird Survey by Graham and Catherine Whitby.
The Status of the Avocet in Poole Harbour by Colin Williams.

Fair Isle Bird Observatory 2000
Report on Causes of Death in Birds on Fair Isle in 2000 by Jason Waine.
Trip Durations of Gannets on Fair Isle by Sue Lewis.
Fair Isle ....Shetland, Scotland 1950 by Michael Wolton.
The Luckiest Young Ornithologist by Oliver Slessor.
Moth Report by Nick Riddiford.
Other Wildlife by Alan Bull.

Forth Naturalist And Historian Journal Vol 23. 2000
Forth Area Bird Report 1999 by CJ Henty and WR Brackenridge.
Wintering and Breeding Birds of long-term set-aside in the Forth Valley by CJ Henty.

Gower Birds 2000
Arrival Dates of Spring Migrants to Gower 1967-1998 by DK Thomas.

Hampshire Bird Report 1999
Low Tide Counts of the Solent 1997 and 1999 by DJ Unsworth and AJ Musgrove.
Report on the Hampshire Sand Martin Survey 1999 by Tony Blander.
Nightingales Breeding in Hampshire in 1999 by Norman Pratt.

Isle of May Report 2000
Systematic List and Migration Summary Notes on Balearic Shearwater.
Autumn Seabird Passage.
Shag Ringing on the Isle of May by M Harris and S Lawless.
Extracts from chatty log.
Ringing Report.

Kent Bird Report 1999
Rare Waders in Kent 1960-1999 by Chris Bradshaw.
KOS Hobby Survey 1999 by Rob Clements and Adam Rowlands.
Blyth's Reed Warbler – New To Kent by Dave Walker.
Nightingale Survey by Andrew Henderson.
Alpine Swifts by Phil Chantler.
Tree Pipit – Unusual Behaviour by Murray Orchard.

Lancashire Bird Report 1999
Butterflies of Lancashire and North Merseyside by S Hayhow.
The Plight of Lancashire's Twite by T Melling And SJ White.
Seawatching in Lancashire by B McCarthy.
Lancashire Bird Report 2000.
Mammals of Lancashire And North Merseyside by S Cross.
Honey Buzzards in Lancashire in 2000 by S Dunstan and P Crooks.
Increasing And Declining Bird Species in Lancashire by SJ White.

This list is based on information supplied by recorders and bird report editors.

ARTICLES IN BIRD REPORTS

London Bird Report 1998
Ringing Report For 1998 by G Elton.
Breeding Bird Survey in London 1998 by DA Coleman.
Year-listing in the London Area by S Connor.
Crossbills in the London Area by PJ Oliver.

Montgomershire Bird Report 1998/99
Montgomery Canal Mute Swan Survey by Roger Matthews.
Fluctuations in Bird Populations by Brayton Holt.
Windows of a Saltmarsh by Jim Marshall.

Birds in Moray And Nairn 2000
Birds New To Moray And Nairn: Corys Shearwater by Bob Proctor; Balearic Shearwater by Martin Cook; Red-breasted Goose, by Dick Hewitt; Green-winged Teal by Bob Proctor; Steller's Eider by Dave Pullan; Wryneck by Bob Proctor; Icterine Warbler by Martin Cook.
The Breeding Population of Water Rails in Moray and Nairn in 1995-2000 by Alistair Young and Martin Cook.

Norfolk Bird Report 2000
Breydon Water and Its Birdlife by Peter Allard.
The House Sparrow in Norwich – Autumn/Winter 2000 by Stuart Paston.
Norfolk Bird Atlas by Moss Taylor.
Norfolk 75 Years Ago by Don Dorling: 50 Years Ago by John Williamson; 25 Years Ago by Giles Dunmore.
Slender-billed Gulls at Cley by Bernard Dawson.
Isabelline Wheatear at Blakeney Point by Andy Stoddart.
Bee Eaters at Burgh Castle by Paul Noakes.
Eleonora's Falcon at Blickley 1987 by Peter Morris.
Plus systematic review of the year.

North East Scotland Bird Report 1999
Collared Flycatcher at Cover – the First Record For NE Scotland by PAA Baxter.
Short-Billed Dowitcher at Rosehearty Sept 1999 – First Record For Britain by P Crockett.
Water Pipit at Burnmervie – the First Record For NE Scotland by A Stalker.
Breeding Ecology of Ring Ouzels in Glen Clunie Report For 1998/1999 by I Sim, R Duncan et al.
Corn Buntings in and around Aberdeen by R Rae and E Duthie.
Colour-ringed Spoonbill at Loch of Strathbeg 1999 by PAA Baxter.

Northamptonshire Bird Report 2000
Red Kites in East Midlands by Ian Carter.
Honey Buzzard influx in Northants in Autumn 2000 by Mike Alibone.

Northern Ireland Bird Report 1999
Synopsis of recent research (1995-99) examining the ecology and conservation of a Great Crested Grebe population on Lough Neagh by Kenneth W Perry.
Goshawk – Breeding in Northern Ireland by Don Scott.
Influx of Short-eared Owls and Hen Harriers into Northern Ireland During 1999 by Don Scott.
A Norwegian Rock Pipit near Groomsport (Down) during the late Autumn of 1996 by George Henderson.

Birds in Northumbria 2000
Birding Sites VII – Caistron by Mike Richardson.
Birding Sites VIII – Hauxley by Ian Fisher.
Isabelline Shrike – An Addition To the County List by Nick Dales.
Pied Flycatchers – A Long Term Review by Mike Carr.
Naturalised Goose Survey 2000 by Roger Norman.
Seasonal Variation in Numbers of Immature Great Black-backed Gulls in the Mouths of the Rivers Tyne and Blyth during 1999 and 2000 by Dan Turner.
Lindisfarne Refuge by Matthew Denny.
Survey Summary 2000 by Tom And Muriel Cadwallender.
A Review of the Status of Roseate Tern in Northumberland by Tom Cadwallender.

Orkney Bird Report 1999
North Ronaldsay Bird Observatory Report by Alison Duncan.
Stronsay Bird Reserve Report by John and Sue Holloway.
The Decline of the Kestrel as a Breeding Species in Orkney by Chris Booth.

Outer Hebrides (Western Isles) Bird Report 2000
Species New to the Outer Hebrides – Pacific Golden Plover at Peninerine, South Uist by Digger Jackson; Long-tailed Shrike at Howbeg and Howmore, South Uist by Andrew Stevenson; Hooded Merganser at Oban Trumisgarry, North Uist by Brian Rabbitts.
Uist Wader Surveys 2000 – Provisional Estimates and Recent Trends by Digger Jackson.
Long-tailed Tit Nesting and Being Evicted by Blue Tit by Bob Wemyss.
The Abundance and Distribution of Birds on the Peatlands of Lewis and Harris by Phil Whitfield and Paul Haworth.
Sporadic Late Autumn Occurrences of Pomarine Skua off Wester Scotland by Eddie Maguire.

Shetland Bird Report 2000
Seasonal summary by Mike Pennington.
Early and Late Dates for Summer Migrants.
A Census of the Seabirds of Foula by P Harvey, S Gear, J Swale, A Upton.
Breeding birds on the Unst Islands by M Pennington.
A Review of the Birds of Noss NNR by A Upton and P Harvey.
A Census of Breeding Blackbirds on Unst by M Pennington.
Bird ringing in Shetland by D Okill.

The Shopshire Bird Report 1999
Long Mynd Breeding Bird Project, the Ring Ouzel by L Smith.
Shropshire Raven Study Group Report 1999 by L Smith.
Venus Pool 1999 by Helen Griffiths.
The BTO Breeding Bird Survey 1994-1999 by AP Dawes.
Birds of the Severn Gorge, Leighton To Coalport 1999 by Glen Bishton.
Long-tailed Skua At Westwood Farm, Bourton by J Sankey.

The Sussex Bird Report No 52, 1999
A Review of the Status of Tundra Bean Geese in Sussex by Richard Fairbank.
A Review of the Current Status and Distribution of the Hobby in Sussex by Martin Kalaher.
The Population and Distribution of the Nightingale in Sussex in 1999 by John Newnham and Matthew Sennitt.

West Midland Bird Club Annual Report No 66. 1999
Observations at a Eurasian Hobby's Nest in West Midlands County 1999 by Brian L Kinton.
Wintering Blackcaps in Worcestershire 1998/1999 by Dave Ratcliffe.
Movements of Greenfinch to and from the West Midland Bird Club Area Between 1910 and 1985 by JT Coleman and AE Coleman.

NATIONAL DIRECTORY

The increase in wintering Cormorants in Britain is the subject of a joint WWT and JNCC study. Drawing by Simon Patient of Essex.

ARMY ORNITHOLOGICAL SOCIETY (1960; 250).
Activities include field meetings, expeditions, checklists of birds on Ministry of Defence property, conservation advice and an annual bird count. Publishes an annual journal called *The Osprey*, published with the *RNBWS* and *RAFOS* from Easter 2001 and bulletins/newsletters twice a year. Open to MOD employees and civilians who have an interest in their local MOD estate.
Contact: Hon Secretary, Lt Col P S Bennett, SO1 DEF LOG(OPS/EX), HQ DLO, Room 7261, MOD Main Building, Whitehall, London, SW1A 2HB, 020 7218 6750.

ASSOCIATION FOR THE PROTECTION OF RURAL SCOTLAND (1926).
Works to protect Scotland's countryside from unnecessary or inappropriate development, recognising the needs of those who live and work there and the necessity of reconciling these with the sometimes competing requirements of recreational use.
Contact: Director, Mrs Joan Geddes, Gladstone's Land, 3rd Floor, 483 Lawnmarket, Edinburgh, EH1 2NT, 0131 225 7012; (Fax)0131 225 6592;
e-mail: aprs@aprs.org.uk

ASSOCIATION OF COUNTY RECORDERS AND EDITORS (1993; 120).
The basic aim of ACRE is to promote best practice in the business of producing county bird reports, in the work of recorders and in problems arising in managing record systems and archives. Organises periodic conferences and publishes *newsACRE.*
Contact: Secretary, M J Rogers, 2 Churchtown Cottages, Towednack, St Ives, Cornwall, TR26 3AZ, 01736 796223.
e-mail: judith@gmbirds.freeserve.co.uk

BARN OWL TRUST
Registered charity. Aims to conserve the Barn Owl and its environment through conservation, education, research and information. Free leaflets on all aspects of Barn Owl conservation. Educational material inc. video and resource pack. Book '*Barn Owls on Site*', is a guide for planners and developers. Works with and advises landowners, farmers, planners, countryside bodies and others to promote a brighter future for Britain's Barn Owls. Currently pursuing pro-active conservation schemes in SW England to secure breeding sites and form a stable basis for population expansion. Phone on Tues and Thu only; send SAE for information.
Contact: Secretary, Barn Owl Trust, Waterleat, Ashburton, Devon, TQ13 7HU, 01364 653026;
e-mail: info@barnowltrust.org.uk
www.barnowltrust.org.uk

BIRD OBSERVATORIES COUNCIL
The BOC replaced the Bird Observatories Committee in 1970. Its objectives are to provide a forum for establishing closer links and co-operation between individual autonomous observatories and to help co-ordinate the work carried out by them. All accredited bird observatories affiliated to the Council undertake a ringing programme and provide ringing experience to those interested. Most also provide accommodation for visiting birdwatchers.
Contact: Secretary, Peter Howlett, c/o Dept of Biodiversity, National Museums & Galleries, Cardiff, CF10 3NP, 0292 057 3233; (Fax)0292 023 9009;
e-mail: peter.howlett@nmgw.ac.uk

BIRD STAMP SOCIETY (1986; 250).
Quarterly journal *Flight* contains philatelic and ornithological articles. Lists all new issues and identifies species. Runs a quarterly Postal Auction; number of lots range from 400 to 800 per auction.
Contact: Secretary, Graham Horsman, 9 Cowley Drive, Worthy Down, Winchester, Hants, SO21 2QW, 01962 889381; (Fax)01962 887423.

BIRDWATCH IRELAND
The trading name of the Irish Wildbird Conservancy, a voluntary body founded in 1968 by the amalgamation of the Irish Society for the Protection of Birds, the Irish Wildfowl Conservancy and the Irish Ornithologists' Club. Now the BirdLife International partner in Ireland. Supported by more than 5,000 members and 21 voluntary branches. Conservation policy is based on formal research and surveys of birds and their habitats. Owns or manages an increasing number of reserves to protect threatened species and habitats. Publishes *Wings* quarterly and *Irish Birds* annually, in addition to annual project reports and survey results.
Contact: Oran O'Sullivan, Ruttledge House, 8 Longford Place, Monkstown, Co Dublin, Ireland, +353 (0)1 2804322; (Fax)+353 (0)1 2844407;
e-mail: bird@indigo.ie
www.birdwatchireland.ie

BRITISH BIRDS RARITIES COMMITTEE
Set up in 1959, the Committee's function is to adjudicate records of species of rare occurrence in Britain (marked 'R' in the Log Charts). Its annual report, which includes records accepted by the Northern Ireland Birdwatchers' Association, is published in *British Birds.* As from 1981, the BBRC also assesses records from the Channel Islands and includes them in its report. In the case of rarities trapped for ringing, records should be sent to the Ringing Office of the British Trust for Ornithology, who will in turn forward them to the BBRC.
Contact: Hon Secretary, M J Rogers, 2 Churchtown Cottages, Towednack, St Ives, Cornwall, TR26 3AZ, 01736 796223.
www.bbrc.org.uk

Figures appearing in brackets following the names of organisations indicate the date of formation and, if relevant, the current membership.

BRITISH FALCONERS' CLUB (1927; 200).
A national body with regional branches. Largest falconry club in Europe. Its aim is to encourage falconers in the responsible practice of their sport and in their efforts to conserve birds of prey by breeding, holding educational meetings and providing facilities, guidance and advice to those wishing to take up the sport. Publishes *The Falconer* annually.
Contact: Director, John R Fairclough, Home Farm, Hints, Tamworth, Staffs, B78 2DW, Tel/(Fax)01543 481737;
e-mail: falconers@zetnet.co.uk
www.users.zetnet.co.uk/bfc

BRITISH MUSEUM (NAT HIST) see Walter Rothschild Zoological Museum.

BRITISH ORNITHOLOGISTS' CLUB (1892; 600).
Membership open only to members of the British Ornithologists' Union. A registered charity, the Club's objects are 'the promotion of scientific discussion between members of the BOU, and others interested in ornithology, and to facilitate the publication of scientific information in connection with ornithology'. The Club maintains a special interest in avian systematics, taxonomy and distribution. About eight evening dinner meetings are held each year. Publishes the *Bulletin of the British Ornithologists' Club* quarterly, also (since 1992) a continuing series of occasional publications.
Contact: Hon Secretary, Cdr M B Casement OBE RN, Dene Cottage, West Harting, Petersfield, Hants, GU31 5PA, 01730 825280;
e-mail: mbcasement@aol.com.uk

BRITISH ORNITHOLOGISTS' UNION
The BOU, founded in 1858 by Professor Alfred Newton FRS, is one of the world's oldest and most respected ornithological societies. With a membership of 2,000 worldwide, it aims to promote ornithology within the scientific and birdwatching communities, both in Britain and around the world. This is largely achieved by the publication of its quarterly, *Ibis* (1859-), one of the world's leading ornithological journals featuring work at the cutting edge of our understanding of the world's birdlife. The BOU also has an active programme of meetings, seminars and conferences at which birdwatchers and ornithologists can learn more about the work being undertaken around the world. This often includes research projects that have received financial assistance from the BOU's ongoing programme of Ornithological Research Grants, which includes student sponsorship. The BOU also runs the Bird Action Grant scheme to assist projects aimed at conserving or researching species on the UK's Biodiversity Action
Contact: Administrator, Steve Dudley, c/o Natural History Museum, Akeman Street, Tring, Herts, HP23 6AP, 01442 890080; (Fax)0207 942 6150; e-mail: bou@bou.org.uk
www.bou.org.uk

BRITISH ORNITHOLOGISTS' UNION RECORDS COMMITTEE
The BOURC is a standing committee of the British Ornithologists' Union. Its function is to maintain the British List, the official list of birds recorded in Great Britain. Up-to-date versions are published annually as *The British List* which is distributed free to British birdwatchers via the popular birdwatching magazines. Where vagrants are involved it is concerned only with those which relate to potential additions to the British List (ie first records). In this it differs from the British Birds Rarities Committee (qv). In maintaining the British List, it also differs from the BBRC in that it examines, where necessary, important pre-1950 records, monitors introduced species for possible admission to or deletion from the List, and reviews taxonomy and nomenclature generally. BOURC reports are published in the BOU's journal, *Ibis.* Decisions contained in these reports which affect the List are also announced via the popular birdwatching press and incorporated in *The British List.*
Contact: Secretary, Dr Tim Melling, c/o The Natural History Museum, Akeman Street, Tring, Herts, HP23 6AP, 01442 890080; (Fax)0207 942 6150; e-mail: bourc.sec@bou.org.uk

BRITISH TRUST FOR ORNITHOLOGY
A registered charity formed in 1933, the BTO is financed by membership subscriptions, by a partnership contract from the Joint Nature Conservation Committee on behalf of English Nature, Scottish Natural Heritage, the Countryside Council for Wales and the Environment and Heritage Service in Northern Ireland; and by contracts from other Government organisations, industry and voluntary conservation bodies. Governed by an elected Council, it has a rapidly growing membership of over 12,500 birdwatchers and enjoys the support of a large number of county and local birdwatching clubs and societies through the BTO/Bird Clubs Partnership. Its aims are: 'To promote and encourage the wider understanding, appreciation and conservation of birds through scientific studies using the combined skills and enthusiasm of its members, other birdwatchers and staff.' Through the fieldwork of its members and other birdwatchers, the BTO is responsible for the majority of the monitoring of British birds, British bird population and their habitats. BTO surveys include the National Ringing Scheme, the Nest Record Scheme, the Breeding Bird Survey (in collaboration with JNCC and RSPB), and the Waterways Bird Survey - all contributing to an integrated programme of population monitoring. The BTO also runs projects on the birds of farmland and woodland, also (in collaboration with WWT, RSPB and JNCC) the Wetland Bird Survey, in particular Low Tide Counts. Garden Birdwatch, which started in 1995, now has over 14,000 participants. The Trust has 140 voluntary regional representatives (see County Directory) who organise fieldworkers for the BTO's programme of national surveys in which members participate. The results of these co-operative efforts are communicated to government departments,

local authorities, industry and conservation bodies for effective action. For details of current activities see National Projects. Members receive *BTO News* six times a year and have the option of subscribing to the thrice-yearly journal, *Bird Study* and twice-yearly *Ringing & Migration*. Local meetings are held in conjunction with bird clubs and societies; there are regional and national birdwatchers' conferences, and specialist courses in modern censusing techniques. Grants are made for research, and members have the use of a lending and reference library at Thetford and the Alexander Library at the Edward Grey Institute of Field Ornithology (qv).
Contact: Director,Dr Jeremy J D Greenwood, British Trust for Ornithology, The Nunnery, Thetford, Norfolk, IP24 2PU, 01842 750050; (Fax)01842 750030;
e-mail: btostaff@bto.org
www.bto.org

BRITISH WATERFOWL ASSOCIATION
The BWA is an association of enthusiasts interested in keeping, breeding and conserving all types of waterfowl, including wildfowl and domestic ducks and geese. It is a registered charity, without trade affiliations, dedicated to educating the public about waterfowl and the need for conservation as well as to raising the standards of keeping and breeding ducks, geese and swans in captivity.
Contact: Mrs Rachel Boer, Oaklands, Blind Lane, Tamworth in Arden, Solihull, B94 5HS, Tel/(Fax)01564 741821.
www.waterfowl.org.uk

BRITISH WILDLIFE REHABILITATION COUNCIL
Established in 1987. Supported by many national bodies including the Zoological Society of London, the British Veterinary Zoological Society, the RSPCA, the SSPCA, and the Vincent Wildlife Trust. Its aim is to promote the care and rehabilitation of wildlife casualties through the exchange of information between people such as rehabilitators, zoologists and veterinary surgeons who are active in this field. Organises an annual symposium or workshop. Publishes a regular newsletter.
Contact: Secretary, Tim Thomas, Wildlife Department, RSPCA, Causeway, Horsham, W Sussex, RH12 1HG, 0870 010 1181.
www.nimini.demon.co.uk/bwrc

BTCV (formerly British Trust for Conservation Volunteers)
Set up in 1959 to involve people of all ages in practical conservation work, much of which directly affects bird habitats. There are over 2500 local conservation groups affiliated to BTCV, which also provides a service to many other bodies including the JNCC, RSPB, WWT and county wildlife trusts, national parks, water authorities, local authorities and private landowners. Over 750 training courses are run annually on the theory of management and practical techniques, for example woodland and wetland management, hedging, etc. Runs working holidays in UK and overseas. Publishes a quarterly newsletter, *The Conserver*, a series of practical handbooks and a wide range of other publications. Further information and a list of local offices is available from the above address.
Contact: Chief Executive, Tom Flood, 80 York Way, London, N1 9NG, 020 7713 5327; (Fax)020 7278 8967;
e-mail: tflood@btcv.org.uk
www.btcv.org.uk

BTCV SCOTLAND
Runs 7-14 day 'Action Breaks' in Scotland during which participants undertake conservation projects; weekend training courses in environmental skills; midweek projects in Edinburgh, Glasgow, Aberdeen and Stirling.
Contact: Balallan House, 24 Allan Park, Stirling, FK8 2QG, 01786 479697; (Fax)01786 465359;
e-mail: stirling@btcv.org.uk
www.btcv.org.uk

CAMPAIGN FOR THE PROTECTION OF RURAL WALES
Contact: Director, Merfyn Williams, Ty Gwyn, 31 High Street, Welshpool, Powys, SY21 7YD, 01938 552525/ 556212; (Fax)552741;
e-mail: director@cprw.org.uk
www.cprw.org.uk

CANADA GOOSE STUDY GROUP
No longer active in ringing, the group still functions to monitor records.
Contact: Dr C B Thomas, Dept of Chemistry, University of York, Heslington, York, YO10 5DD, 01904 432532; (Fax)01904 432516;
e-mail: cbt1@york.ac.uk

CENTRE FOR ECOLOGY & HYDROLOGY
The work of the CEH, a component body of the Natural Environment Research Council, includes a range of ornithological research, covering population studies, habitat management and work on the effects of pollution. The CEH has a long-term programme to monitor pesticide and pollutant residues in the corpses of predatory birds sent in by birdwatchers, and carries out detailed studies on affected species. The Biological Records Centre (BRC), which is part of the CEH, is responsible for the national biological data bank on plant and animal distributions (except birds).
Contact: Director, Prof Pat Nuttall, Monks Wood, Abbots Ripton, Huntingdon, PE28 2LS, 01487 773381.
www.ceh.ac.uk

COUNTRY LANDOWNERS' ASSOCIATION
The CLA is at the heart of rural life and is the voice of the countryside for England and Wales, campaigning on issues which directly affect those who live and work

in rural communities. It represents the interests of 50,000 members who together manage 60% of the countryside. CLA members range from some of the largest landowners, with interests in forest, moorland, water and agriculture, to some of the smallest with little more than a paddock or garden.
Contact: Secretary, 16 Belgrave Square, London, SW1X 8PQ, 020 7235 0511.

COUNTRYSIDE AGENCY
The Countryside Agency advises the Government on countryside issues and is the leading organisation concerned with landscape conservation and public access to the countryside, as well as promoting social equity and economic opportunity for the people who live there. The Agency works by leading with research and advice, influencing others, expecially central and local government and demonstrating ways forward through practical projects. Its responsibilities include designating national parks, areas of outstanding natural beauty and national trails.
Contact: Chief Executive, Richard Wakeford, John Dower House, Crescent Place, Cheltenham, Glos, GL50 3RA, 01242 521381; (Fax)01242 584270; e-mail: info@countryside.gov.uk
www.countryside.gov.uk
Offices
North East Region. Cross House, Westgate Road, Newcastle upon Tyne NE1 4XX, 0191 269 1600; (Fax)0191 269 1601
North West Region. 7th Floor, Bridgewater House, Whitworth Street, Manchester M1 6LT. 0161 237 1061; fax 0161 237 1062
South West Region. Bridge House, Sion Place, Clifton Down, Bristol BS8 4AS. 0117 973 9966; fax 0117 923 8086
Yorkshire & The Humber Region. 4th Floor Victoria Wharf, No 4 The Embankment, Sovereign Street, Leeds LS1 4BA. 0113 246 9222; fax 0113 246 0353
East Midlands Region. Regional Office 18, Market Place, Bingham, Nottingham NG13 9AP. 01949 876200; fax 01949 876222
West Midlands Region. 1st Floor, Vincent House, Tindal Bridge, 92-93 Edward Street, Birmingham B1 2RA. 0121 233 9399: fax 0121 233 9286
Eastern Region. Ortona House, 110 Hills Road, Cambridge CB2 1LQ. 01223 354462, fax 01223 313850
South East Region. Dacre House, Dacre Street, London SW1H 0DH, 020 7340 2900; fax 020 7340 2911

COUNTRYSIDE COUNCIL FOR WALES
CCW is the Government's statutory adviser on wildlife, countryside and maritime conservation matters in Wales. It is the executive authority for the conservation of habitats and wildlife. Through partners, CCW promotes protection of landscape, opportunities for enjoyment, and support of those who live, work in, and manage the countryside. It enables these partners, including local authorities, voluntary organisations and interested individuals, to pursue countryside management projects through grant aid. CCW is accountable to the National Assembly for Wales which appoints its Council members and provides its annual grant-in-aid.
Contact: Plas Penrhos, Ffordd Penrhos, Bangor, Gwynedd, LL57 2LQ, 01248 385500; (Fax)01248 355782; www.ccw.gov.uk
Area Offices
West Area. Plas Gogerddan, Aberystwyth, Ceredigian, SY23 3EE. 01970 821100
North West Area. Llys y bont, Ffordd y Parc, Parc Menai, Bangor, Gwynedd, LL57 4BH. 01248 672500
South Area. Unit 4, Castleton Court, Fortran Road, St Mellons, Cardiff CF3 0LT. 02920 772400
East Area. Eden House, Ithon Road, Llandrindod, Powys, LD1 6AS, 01597 827400
North East Area. Victoria House, Grosvenor Street, Mold CH7 1EJ. 01352 706600

THE COUNTRYSIDE RESTORATION TRUST
A charity dedicated to the protection and restoration of a countryside where quality food is produced usng frming methods that encourag wildlife and enable more people to earn their living from the land. We protect traditional farms and acquire, for restoration, farmland that has been managed over-intensively. We work closely with other conservation organisations, local communities and tenant farmers who are sypathetic to our aims.
Address: Barton, Cambridgeshire, CB3 7AG. Tel/fax: 01223 870932.
e-mail: crtbarton@care4free.net
www.crtbarton.com

CPRE (formerly Council for the Protection of Rural England)
Patron HM The Queen. Formed in 1926, CPRE now has 43 county branches, 200 local groups and 45,000 members. It seeks to provide well researched and practical solutions to problems affecting the English countryside. Membership open to all.
Contact: Director, Ms K Parminter, Warwick House, 25 Buckingham Palace Road, London, SW1W 0PP, 020 7976 6433; (Fax)020 7976 6373; e-mail: info@cpre.org.uk
www.cpre.org.uk

DEPARTMENT OF THE ENVIRONMENT FOR NORTHERN IRELAND
EHS is responsible for the declaration and management of National Nature Reserves, the declaration of Areas of Special Scientific Interest, the administration of Wildlife Refuges, the classification of Special Protection Areas under the EC Birds Directive, and the designation of Ramsar sites and of Special Areas of Conservation under the EC Habitats Directive. It administers the Nature Conservation and Amenity Lands (Northern Ireland) Order 1985, the Wildlife (Northern Ireland) Order 1985, the Game Acts and the Conservation (Natural Habitats, etc) Regulations (NI) 1995.
Contact: Gordon Hatkick, Environment and Heritage Service, Commonwealth House, 35 Castle Street, Belfast, BT1 1GU, 028 9054 6450.

EDWARD GREY INSTITUTE OF FIELD ORNITHOLOGY

The EGI takes its name from Edward Grey, first Viscount Grey of Fallodon, a life-long lover of birds and former Chancellor of the University of Oxford, who gave his support to an appeal for its foundation capital. Formally set up in 1938, the Institute now has a permanent research staff; it usually houses some twelve to fifteen research students, two or three senior visitors and post-doctoral research workers. The EGI also houses Prof Sir John Krebs's Ecology & Behaviour Group, which has specialised in the study of the ecology, demography and conservation of declining farmland birds. Field research is carried out mainly in Wytham Woods near Oxford and on the island of Skomer in West Wales. In addition there are laboratory facilities and aviary space for experimental work and members of the Institute have access to departmental and university computers. The Institute houses the Alexander Library, one of the largest collections of twentieth-century material on birds in the world. The library is supported by the British Ornithologists Union which provides much of the material. Included in its manuscript collections are diaries, notebooks and papers of ornithologists. It also houses the British Falconers Club library. The Library is open to members of the BOU and the Oxford Ornithological Society. Other bona fide ornithologists may use the library by arrangement.

Director, Prof C M Perrins LVO, FRS, Department of Zoology, South Parks Road, Oxford, OX1 3PS, 01865 271274, Alexander Library 01865 271143.

EGI web-site: http://egiwcruzool.zoo.ox.ac.uk/EGI/egihome.htm

Library web-site: http://users.ox.ac.uk/~zoolib/

ENGLISH NATURE

Established by Parliament in April 1991, English Nature advises Government on nature conservation in England. It promotes, directly and through others, the conservation of England's wildlife and geology within the wider setting of the UK and its international responsibilities. It selects, establishes and manages National Nature Reserves (many of which are described in Reserves and Observatories), and identifies and notifies Sites of Special Scientific Interest. It provides advice and information about nature conservation and supports and conducts research relevant to these functions. Through the Joint Nature Conservation Committee (qv), English Nature works with sister organisations in Scotland and Wales on UK and international nature conservation issues.

Northminster House, Peterborough, PE1 1UA, 01733 455100; (Fax)01733 455103;
e-mail: enquiries@english-nature.org.uk
www.english-nature.org.uk

Local teams:

Bedfordshire, Cambridgeshire & Northants. Ham Lane House, Ham Lane, Nene Park, Orton Waterville, Peterborough PE2 5UR, 01733 405850; (Fax)01733 394093; e-mail: beds.cambs.nhants@english-nature.org.uk

Cornwall & Isles of Scilly. Trevint House, Strangways Villas, Truro TR1 2PA. 01872 265710; (Fax)01872 262551;
e-mail: cornwall@english-nature.org.uk

Cumbria. Juniper House, Murley Moss, Oxenholme Road, Kendal LA9 7RL. 01539 792800; (Fax)01539 792830;
e-mail; cumbria@english-nature.org.uk

Devon. Level 2, Rensdale House, Bonhay Rd, Exeter, EX4 3AW, 01392 889770; fax 01392 437999; e-mail: devon@english-nature.org.uk

Dorset. Slepe Farm, Arne, Wareham, Dorset BH20 5BN. 01929 557450; (Fax)01929 554752;
e-mail: dorset@english-nature.org.uk

East Midlands. The Maltings, Wharf Road, Grantham, Lincs NG31 6BH. 01476 584800; (Fax)01476 570927;
e-mail: eastmidlands@english-nature.org.uk

Essex, London and Hertfordshire. Harbour House, Hythe Quay, Colchester CO2 8JF. 01206 796666; (Fax)01206 794466;
e-mail: essex.herts@english-nature.org.uk

Hampshire and Isle of Wight. 1 Southampton Road, Lyndhurst, Hants SO43 7BU. 02380 283944; (Fax)02380 283834;
e-mail: hants.iwight@english-nature.org.uk

Humber to Pennines. Bull Ring House, Northgate, Wakefield, W Yorks WF1 1HD. 01924 334500; (Fax)01924 201507;
e-mail: humber.pennines@english-nature.org.uk

Kent. The Countryside Management Centre, Coldharbour Farm, Wye, Ashford, Kent TN25 5DB. 01233 812525; (Fax)01233 812520;
e-mail: kent@english-nature.org.uk

Norfolk. 60 Bracondale, Norwich NR1 2BE. 01603 598400; (Fax)01603 762552;
e-mail: norfolk@english-nature.org.uk

North and East Yorkshire. Genesis 1, University Road, Heslington, York YO10 5ZQ. 01904 435500; (Fax)01904 435520;
e-mail: york@english-nature.org.uk

North West. Pier House, 1st Floor, Wallgate, Wigan WN3 4AL. 01942 820342; (Fax)01942 820364; e-mail: northwest@english-nature.org.uk

Northumbria. Stocksfield Hall, Stocksfield, Northumberland NE4 7TN. 01661 845500; (Fax)01661 845501;
e-mail: northumbria@english-nature.org.uk

Peak District and Derbyshire. Manor Barn, Over Haddon, Bakewell, Derbyshire DE45 1JE. 01629 816640; (Fax)01629 815091;
e-mail: peak.derbys@english-nature.org.uk

Somerset. Roughmoor, Bishop's Hull, Taunton, Somerset TA1 5AA. 01823 283211; C01823 272978; e-mail: somerset@english-nature.org.uk

Suffolk. Regent House, 110 Northgate Street, Bury St Edmunds, Suffolk IP33 1HP. 01284 762218;

(Fax)01284 764318;
e-mail: suffolk@english-nature.org.uk
Sussex and Surrey. Phoenix House, 32-33 North Street, Lewes, E Sussex BN7 2PH. 01273 476595; (Fax)01273 483063;
e-mail: sussex.surrey@english-nature.org.uk
Thames and Chilterns. Foxhold House, Thornford Road, Crookham Common, Thatcham, Berks RG19 8EL. 01635 268881; fax 01635 268940;
e-mail thames.chilterns@english-nature.org.uk.
Three Counties (Gloucestershire, Hereford and Worcester). Bronsil House, Eastnor, Nr Ledbury HR8 1EP. 01531 638500; (Fax)01531 638501;
e-mail: three.counties@english-nature.org.uk
West Midlands (Ches, Shrops, Staffs, Warks, W Mid). Attingham Park, Shrewsbury SY4 4TW. 01743 709611; (Fax)01743 709303;
e-mail: westmidlands@english-nature.org.uk
Wiltshire. Prince Maurice Court, Hambleton Avenue, Devizes, Wilts SN10 2RT. 01380 726344; (Fax)01380 721411;
e-mail: wiltshire@english-nature.org.uk

ENVIRONMENT AGENCY (THE)

A non-departmental body, created in 1996, sponsored by the Department of the Environment, Transport and the Regions, MAFF and the Welsh Office. Primary aim: to protect and improve the environment and to contribute towards the delivery of sustainable development through the integrated management of air, land and water. Functions include pollution prevention and control, waste minimisation, management of water resources, flood defence, improvement of salmon and freshwater fisheries, conservation of aquatic species, navigation and use of inland and coastal waters for recreation.
Contact: Rio House, Waterside Drive, Aztec West, Almondsbury, Bristol, BS32 4UD, 01454 624400; (Fax)01454 624409;
www.environment-agency.gov.uk
Regional offices:
Anglian. Kingfisher House, Goldhay Way, Orton Goldhay, Peterborough PE2 5ZR. 01733 371811; (Fax)01733 231840.
North East. Rivers House, 21 Park Square South, Leeds LS1 2QG. 0113 244 0191; (Fax)0113 246 1889.
North West. Richard Fairclough House, Knutsford Road, Warrington WA4 1HG. 01925 653999; (Fax)01925 415961.
Midlands. Sapphire East, 550 Streetsbrook Road, Solihull B91 1QT. 0121 711 2324; (Fax)0121 711 5824.
Southern. Guildbourne House, Chatsworth Road, Worthing, W Sussex BN11 1LD. 01903 832000; (Fax)01903 821832.
South West. Manley House, Kestrel Way, Exeter EX2 7LQ. 01392 444000; fax 01392 444238.
Thames. Kings Meadow House, Kings Meadow Road, Reading RG1 8DQ. 0118 953 5000; (Fax)0118 950 0388.
Wales. Rivers House, St Mellons Business Park, St Mellons, Cardiff CF3 0EY. 029 2077 0088; (Fax)029 2079 8555.

FARMING AND WILDLIFE ADVISORY GROUP (FWAG)

Technical Director, Richard Knight. Founded in 1969, FWAG is an independent UK registered charity led by farmers and supported by government and leading countryside organisations. Its aim is to unite farming and forestry with wildlife and landscape conservation. Has FWAG's in most UK counties. There are 85 Farm Conservation Advisers who give practical advice to farmers and landowners to help them integrate environmental objectives with commercial farming practices.
Contact: Chief Executive, Robert Bettley-Smith, National Agricultural Centre, Stoneleigh, Kenilworth, Warwickshire, CV8 2RX, 024 7669 6699; (Fax)024 7669 6760;
e-mail: info@fwag.org.uk
www.fwag.org.uk

FIELD STUDIES COUNCIL

The Council was created in 1943 to establish Centres where students from schools, universities and colleges of education, as well as individuals of all ages, could stay and study various aspects of the environment under expert guidance. The courses include many for birdwatchers, from beginners to those with experience, providing opportunities to study birdlife on coasts, estuaries, mountains and islands. There are some courses demonstrating bird ringing and others for members of the Wildlife Explorers. The length of the courses varies: many are for a weekend, but there are some of 4, 5, 6 or 7 days' duration. Research workers and naturalists wishing to use the records and resources are welcome. FSC Overseas includes birdwatching in its programme of overseas courses.
Contact: Kathleen Howe, Preston Montford, Montford Bridge, Shrewsbury, SY4 1HW, 01743 852100; (Fax)01743 852101;
e-mail: fsc.headoffice@ukonline.co.uk
www.field-studies-council.org
Centres:
Blencathra Field Centre, Threlkeld, Keswick, Cumbria CA12 4SG, 017687 79601;
e-mail: fsc.blencathra@ukonline.co.uk
Castle Head Field Centre, Grange-over-Sands, Cumbria LA11 6QT, 015395 34300,
e-mail: fsc,castlehead@ukonline.co.uk
Dale Fort Field Centre, Haverfordwest, Pembs SA62 3RD, 01646 636205,
e-mail: fsc.dalefort@ukonline.co.uk
Derrygonnelly, Tir Navar, Creamery St, Derrygonnelly, Co Fermanagh, BT93 6HN
Epping Forest Field Centre, High Beach, Loughton, Essex, IG10 4AF, 020 8508 7714,

e-mail: fsc.epping@ukonline,co.uk
Flatford Mill Field Centre, East Bergholt, Suffolk, CO7 6UL, 01206 298283,
e-mail: fsc.flatford@ukonline.co.uk
Juniper Hall Field Centre, Dorking, Surrey, RH5 6DA, 0845 458 3507,
e-mail: fsc.juniper@ukonline.co.uk
Malham Tarn Field Centre, Settle, N Yorks, BD24 9PU, 01729 830331,
e-mail: fsc.malham@ukonline.co.uk
Nettlecombe Court, The Leonard Wills Field Centre, Williton, Taunton, Somerset, TA4 4HT, 01984 640320,
e-mail: fsc.nettlecombe@ukonline.co.uk
Orielton Field Centre, Pembroke, Pembs,SA71 5EZ, 01646 661225,
e-mail: fsc.orielton@ukonline.co.uk
Preston Montford Field Centre, Montford Bridge, Shrewsbury, SY4 1DX, 01743 850380,
e-mail: fsc.montford@ukonline.co.uk
Rhyd-y-creuau, the Drapers' Field Centre Betws-y-coed, Conwy, LL24 0HB, 01690 710494,
e-mail: fsc.ryc@ukonline.co.uk
Slapton Ley Field Centre, Slapton, Kingsbridge, Devon, TQ7 2QP, 01548 580466,
e-mail: fsc.slapton@ukonline.co.uk

FLIGHTLINE
Northern Ireland's daily bird news service. Run under the auspices of the Northern Ireland Birdwatchers' Association (qv).
Contact: George Gordon, 2 Brooklyn Avenue, Bangor, Co Down, BT20 5RB, 028 9146 7408.

FORESTRY COMMISSION
Forest Enterprise is the executive agency which manages the Commission's forest estate.
Contact: Head of Communication Branch, 231 Corstorphine Road, Edinburgh, EH12 7AT, 0131 334 0303; (Fax)0131 334 4473;
www.forestry.gov.uk
Forestry Commission National Offices
England. Great Eastern House, Tenison Road, Cambridge CB1 2DU. 01223 314546; (Fax)01223 460699.
Scotland. As HQ above
Wales. Victoria Terrace, Aberystwyth, Ceredigion SY23 2DQ. 01970 625866; (Fax)01970 626177.
Forest Enterprise Territorial Offices:
England. 340 Bristol Business Park, Coldharbour Lane, Bristol BS16 1AJ. 0117 906 6000; (Fax)0117 931 2859.
*Scotland. North.*1 Highlander Way, Inverness Retail and Business Park, Inverness, IV2 7GB, 01463 232811; (Fax)01463 243846.
Scotland South. 55/57 Moffat Road, Dumfries DG1 1NP. 01387 272440; (Fax)01387 251491.
Wales. Victoria Terrace, Aberystwyth, Ceredigion SY23 2DQ. 01970 612367; (Fax)01970 625282.

FRIENDS OF THE EARTH
(1971; 150,000).
One of UK's leading pressure groups, campaigning on a wide range of local, national and international environmental issues. Local groups in England, Wales and Northern Ireland.
Contact: 26/28 Underwood Street, London, N1 7JQ, 020 7490 1555; e-mail: info@foe.co.uk
www.foe.co.uk

GAME CONSERVANCY TRUST
(1933; 27,000).
A registered charity which researches the conservation of game and other wildlife in the British countryside. Over 60 scientists are engaged in detailed work on insects, pesticides, birds (30 species inc. raptors) mammals (inc. foxes), and habitats. The results are used to advise government, landowners, farmers and conservationists on practical management techniques which will benefit game species, their habitats, and wildlife. Each June an *Annual Review* of 100 pages lists about 60 papers published in the peer-reviewed scientific press.
Contact: Director General, Dr G R Potts, Fordingbridge, Hampshire, SP6 1EF, 01425 652381; (Fax)01425 651026;
e-mail: info@gct.org.uk
www.gct.org.uk

GOLDEN ORIOLE GROUP (1987)
Organises censuses of breeding Golden Orioles in parts of Cambridgeshire, Norfolk and Suffolk. Maintains contact with a network of individuals in other parts of the country where Golden Orioles may or do breed. Studies breeding biology, habitat and food requirements of the species.
Contact: Secretary, Jake Allsop, 5 Bury Lane, Haddenham, Ely, Cambs, CB6 3PR, 01353 740540; e-mail: jakeallsop@aol.com

HAWK AND OWL TRUST (1969)
Registered charity dedicated to the conservation and appreciation of all birds of prey including owls. Publishes a newsletter *Peregrine* and educational materials for all ages. The Trust achieves its major aim of creating and enhancing wild habitats for birds of prey through projects which involve practical research, creative conservation and education. Projects are often conducted in close partnership with landowners, farmers and others. Members are invited to take part in population studies, field surveys, etc. Studies of Barn and Little Owls, Hen Harrier, and Goshawk are in progress. In 1988 a major project, the Barn Owl Conservation Network was launched in an effort to implement a country-wide programme of habitat creation and enhancement, and provision of artificial nest sites which is achieving considerable success. The Trust's National Conservation and Education Centre at Newland Park, Gorelands Lane, Chalfont St Giles, Bucks, is now open to the public and offers schools and other groups cross-curricular environmental activities.

Contact: Membership administration: 11 St Mary's Close, Abbotskerswell, Newton Abbot, Devon, TQ12 5QF. Director, Colin Shawyer, c/o Zoological Society of London, Regents Park, London, NW1 4RY, Tel/(Fax)01582 832182;
e-mail: hawkandowltrust@aol.com
www.hawkandowl.org

IRISH RARE BIRDS COMMITTEE (1985)
Assesses records of species of rare occurrence in the Republic of Ireland. Details of records accepted and rejected are incorporated in the Irish Bird Report, published annually in *Irish Birds*. In the case of rarities trapped for ringing, ringers in the Republic of Ireland are required to send their schedules initially to the National Parks and Wildlife Service, 51 St Stephen's Green, Dublin 2. A copy is taken before the schedules are sent to the British Trust for Ornithology.
Contact: Hon Secretary, Paul Milne, 100 Dublin Road, Sutton, Dublin 13, +353 (0)1 8325653;
e-mail: paul.milne@oceanfree.net

JOINT NATURE CONSERVATION COMMITTEE
Established under the Environmental Protection Act 1990, the JNCC is a committee of the three country agencies (English Nature, Scottish Natural Heritage, and the Countryside Council for Wales), together with independent members and representatives from Northern Ireland and the Countryside Agency. It is supported by specialist staff. Its statutory responsibilities include the establishment of common standards for monitoring, the analysis of information and research; advising Ministers on the development and implementation of policies for or affecting nature conservation; the provision of advice and the dissemination of knowledge to any persons about nature conservation; and the undertaking and commissioning of research relevant to these functions. JNCC additionally has the UK responsibility for relevant European and wider international matters. The Species Team, located at the HQ address below, is responsible for terrestrial bird conservation.
Contact: Monkstone House, City Road, Peterborough, PE1 1JY, 01733 562626; (Fax)01733 555948;
e-mail: feedback@jncc.gov.uk
www.jncc.gov.uk

LINNEAN SOCIETY OF LONDON (1788)
Named after Carl Linnaeus, the eighteenth-century Swedish biologist, who created the modern system of scientific biological nomenclature, the Society promotes all aspects of pure and applied biology. It houses Linnaeus's collection of plants, insects and fishes, library and correspondence. The Society has a major reference library of some 100,000 volumes. Publishes the *Biological, Botanical and Zoological Journals*, and the *Synopses of the British Fauna*.
Contact: Executive Secretary, Dr J C Marsden, Burlington House, Piccadilly, London, W1J 0BF, 020 7434 4479; (Fax)020 7287 9364;
e-mail: john@linnean.org
www.linnean.org

MANX ORNITHOLOGICAL SOCIETY see County Directory.

MANX WILDLIFE TRUST see County Directory.

NATIONAL BIRDS OF PREY CENTRE (1967).
Concerned with the conservation and captive breeding of all raptors. Approx 85 species on site. Birds flown daily. Open Feb-Nov.
Contact: Mrs J Parry-Jones MBE, Newent, Glos, GL18 1JJ, 0870 9901992;
e-mail: jpj@nbpc.demon.co.uk
www.nbpc.co.uk

NATIONAL SOUND ARCHIVE WILDLIFE SECTION (1969).
(Formerly BLOWS - British Library of Wildlife Sounds). The most comprehensive collection of bird sound recordings in existence: more than 120,000 recordings of over 7000 species of birds worldwide, available for free listening. Copies or sonograms of most recordings can be supplied for private study or research and, subject to copyright clearance, for commercial uses. Contribution of new material and enquiries on all aspects of wildlife sounds and recording techniques are welcome. Publishes *Bioacoustics* journal, CD and cassette guides to bird songs.
Contact: Curator, Richard Ranft, British Library, National Sound Archive, 96 Euston Road, London, NW1 2DB, 020 7412 7402/3;
e-mail: nsa-wildsound@bl.uk
www.bl.uk/nsa

NATIONAL TRUST
Charity depending on voluntary support of its members and the public. Largest private landowner with over 603,862 acres of land and nearly 600 miles of coast. Conservation society with over 2.6 million members in Britain. Founded in 1895. Works for the preservation of places of historic interest or natural beauty, in England, Wales and N Ireland. Under Acts of Parliament it is empowered to declare its land inalienable and has a right to appeal to Parliament against compulsory orders affecting such land. The Trust's coast and countryside properties are open to the public at all times, subject only to the needs of farming, forestry and the protection of wildlife. Over a quarter of the Trust's land holding is designated SSSI or ASSI (N Ireland) and about 10% of SSSIs in England and Wales are wholly or partially owned by the Trust, as are 31 NNRs (eg Blakeney Point, Farne Islands, Wicken Fen and large parts of Strangford Lough, N Ireland). Fifteen per cent of Ramsar Sites include Trust land, as do 27% of SPAs. 71 of the 117 bird species listed in the UK Red Data Book are found on Trust land.
Contact: Emily Brooks, Communications, 36 Queen Anne's Gate, London, SW1H 9AS, 020 7222 9251.
www.nationaltrust.org.uk
Head of Nature Conservation: Dr H J Harvey, Estates Dept, 33 Sheep Street, Cirencester, Glos GL7 1RQ. 01285 651818.

Welsh office: Trinity Square, Llandudno, LL30 2DE, 01492 860123; (Fax)01492 860233.
Northern Ireland Office: Rowallane House, Saintfield, Ballynahinch, Co. DownBT24 7LH. 028 975 10721.

NATIONAL TRUST FOR SCOTLAND
An independent charity formed in 1931. 230,000 members. Its 90 properties open to the public are described in its annual guide.
Contact: Head of Public Affairs, Ian Gardner, Wemyss House, 28 Charlotte Square, Edinburgh, EH2 4ET, 0131 243 9300; www.nts.org.uk

NATURE PHOTOGRAPHERS' PORTFOLIO (1944)
A small society for photographers of wildlife, especially birds. Circulates postal portfolios of prints and transparencies.
Contact: Hon Secretary, A Winspear-Cundall, 8 Gig Bridge Lane, Pershore, Worcs, WR10 1NH, 01386 552103.

NORTHERN IRELAND BIRDWATCHERS' ASSOCIATION (1991; 90).
The NIBA Records Committee, established in 1997, has full responsibility for the assessment of records in N Ireland. NIBA also publishes the *Northern Ireland Bird Report*.
Contact: Hon Secretary, William McDowell, 4 Gairloch Park, Holywood, Co Down, BT18 0LZ, 028 9059 4390; e-mail: williamm.mcdowell@ntlworld.com

NORTHERN IRELAND ORNITHOLOGISTS' CLUB (1965;150)
Operates two small reserves in Co Down. Operates a Barn Owl nestbox scheme and a winter feeding programme for Yellowhammers. Has a regular programme of lectures and field trips for members. Publishes *The Harrier* quarterly.
Contact: Gary Wilkinson, The Roost, 139 Windmill Road, Hillsborough, Co Down, BT26 6NP, 028 9263 9254. www.nioc.fsnet.co.uk

PEOPLE'S DISPENSARY FOR SICK ANIMALS (1917)
Registered charity. Provides free veterinary treatment for sick and injured animals whose owners qualify for this charitable service.
Contact: Director General, Mrs Marilyn Rydstrom, Whitechapel Way, Priorslee, Telford, Shrops, TF2 9PQ, 01952 290999.
e-mail: pr@pdsa.org.uk
www.pdsa.org.uk

RARE BREEDING BIRDS PANEL
Originally formed as a sub-committee of the RSPB in 1968, the RBBP has since 1973 been an independent body funded and supported jointly by the JNCC, the RSPB, *British Birds*, and the BTO. It collects in a central file all information on rare breeding birds in the United Kingdom, so that changes in status can be monitored as an aid to present-day conservation and stored for posterity. Special forms are used (obtainable free from the secretary) and records should if possible be submitted via the county and regional recorders. Since 1996 the Panel also monitors breeding by scarcer non-native species and seeks records of these in the same way. Annual report published in *British Birds*. For details of species covered by the Panel, see Log Charts.
Contact: Secretary, Dr Malcolm Ogilvie, Glencairn, Bruichladdich, Isle of Islay, PA49 7UN, 01496 850218; e-mail: rbbp@indaal.demon.co.uk

ROYAL AIR FORCE ORNITHOLOGICAL SOCIETY (1965; 295).
RAFOS organises regular field meetings for members, carries out ornithological census work on MOD properties and mounts major expeditions annually to various UK and overseas locations. Publishes a Newsletter twice a year and contributes to the Joint Service journal *The Osprey*, annually, and reports on its expeditions and surveys.
Contact: General Secretary, RAFOS, MOD DE(C) Conservation, Blandford House, Farnborough Road, Aldershot, Hants, GU11 2HA,

ROYAL NAVAL BIRDWATCHING SOCIETY (1946; 193 full and 98 associate members and library)
Cover all the main ocean routes, and the Society has developed a system for reporting the positions and identity of seabirds and landbirds at sea by means of standard sea report forms, much of the system being computerised. Members are encouraged to photograph birds while at sea and a library of photographs and slides is maintained. Publishes a Bulletin and an annual report entitled *The Sea Swallow*.
Contact: Hon Secretary, Col P J S Smith RM (Ret'd), 19 Downlands Way, South Wonston, Winchester, Hants, SO21 3HS, 01962 885258.

ROYAL PIGEON RACING ASSOCIATION (46,000)
Exists to promote the sport of pigeon racing and controls pigeon racing within the Association. Organises liberation sites, issues rings, calculates distances between liberation sites and home lofts, and assists in the return of strays. May be able to assist in identifying owners of ringed birds caught or found.
Contact: General Manager, RPRA, The Reddings, Cheltenham, GL51 6RN, 01452 713529;
e-mail: gm@rpra.org or strays@rpra.org
www.rpra.org

ROYAL SOCIETY FOR THE PREVENTION OF CRUELTY TO ANIMALS (1824).
In addition to its animal homes the Society also runs a woodland study centre and nature reserve at Mallydams Wood in East Sussex and specialist wildlife rehabilitation centres at:
West Hatch, Taunton, Somerset TA3 5RT (01823 480156).
Station Road, East Winch, King's Lynn, Norfolk PE32 1NR (01553 842336).
London Road, Stapeley, Nantwich, Cheshire CW5 7JW (01270 610347).

Inspectors are contacted through their Regional Communications Centres, which can be reached via the Society's national telephone number: 08705 555 999.
Contact: Causeway, Horsham, West Sussex, RH12 1HG, 01403 264181. www.rspca.co.uk

ROYAL SOCIETY FOR THE PROTECTION OF BIRDS
UK partner of BirdLife International. The RSPB, founded in 1889, is Europe's largest voluntary wildlife conservation body. A registered charity, governed by an elected body,with a subscribing membership of 1,011,416 (see also RSPB Phoenix and RSPB Wildlife Explorers). Its work in the conservation of wild birds and habitats covers the acquisition and management of nature reserves; research and surveys; monitoring and response to development proposals, land use practices and pollution which threaten wild birds; protection of rare and endangered species, and the provision of an advisory service on wildlife law enforcement. Work in the education and information field includes formal education in schools and colleges, and informal activities for children through the Wildlife Explorers; publications (including *Birds*, a quarterly magazine for members, *Bird Life*, a bi-monthly magazine for RSPB Wildlife Explorers, *Wild Times* for under-8s, and *Conservation Review* published annually); displays and exhibitions; the distribution of moving images about birds; and the development of membership involvement through Members' Groups. The activities of sales and funding involve direct mail and sale of goods designed to promote an interest in birds, and fund raising by appeals and other means. The RSPB currently manages 161 reserves throughout Britain and Northern Ireland, covering over 275,000 acres. Sites are carefully selected, most being officially recognised as of national or international importance to nature conservation. The policy is to achieve a countrywide network of reserves with examples of all the main bird communities. Visitors are generally welcome to most reserves, subject to any restrictions necessary to protect the wildlife and habitat. Current national projects include campaigns to safeguard the marine environment, safeguard estuaries, and halt illegal persecution of birds of prey. There is increasing involvement with agriculture, energy and transport, and with biodiversity conservation generally. The International Dept is much involved with projects overseas, especially in Europe and Africa, notably with BirdLife partners.
Chief Executive, Graham Wynne, The Lodge, Sandy, Beds, SG19 2DL, 01767 680551; (Fax)01767 692365; e-mail: (firstname.name)@rspb.org.uk
www.rspb.org.uk

Regional Offices:
RSPB North England, 4 Benton Terrace, Sandyford, Newcastle upon Tyne NE2 1QU. 0191 281 3366.
RSPB North West, Westleigh Mews, Wakefield Road, Denby Dale, Huddersfield HD8 8QD. 01484 861148.
RSPB Central England, 46 The Green, South Bar, Banbury, Oxon OX16 9AB. 01295 253330.
RSPB East Anglia, Stalham House, 65 Thorpe Road, Norwich NR1 1UD. 01603 661662.
RSPB South East, 2nd Floor, Frederick House, 42-46 Frederick Place, Brighton BN1 1AT. 01273 775333.
RSPB South West, 1st Floor, Keble House, Southernhay Gardens, Exeter EX1 1NT. 01392 432691.
RSPB Scotland HQ, Dunedin House, 25 Ravelston Terrace, Edinburgh EH4 3TP. 0131 311 6500.
RSPB North Scotland, Etive House, Beechwood Park, Inverness IV2 3BW. 01463 715000.
RSPB East Scotland, 10 Albyn Terrace, Aberdeen AB1 1YP. 01224 624824.
RSPB South & West Scotland, Unit 3.1, West of Scotland Science Park, Kelvin Campus, Glasgow G20 0SP. 0141 576 4100.
RSPB North Wales, Maes y Ffynnon, Penrhosgarnedd, Bangor, Gwynedd LL57 2DW. 01248 363800.
RSPB South Wales, Sutherland House, Castlebridge, Cowbridge Road East, Cardiff CF11 9AB. 029 2035 3000.
RSPB Northern Ireland, Belvoir Park Forest, Belfast BT8 4QT. 028 9049 1547.

RSPB WILDLIFE EXPLORERS and RSPB PHOENIX (formerly YOC)
(1965; 140,000)
Junior section of the RSPB. There are over 500 groups run by almost 1500 volunteers. Activities include projects, holidays, roadshows, competitions, and local events for children, families and teenagers. Publishes two bi-monthly magazines, *Bird Life* (aimed at 8-12 year olds) and *Wild Times* (aimed under 8s) and one quarterly magazine *Wingbeat* (aimed at teenagers).
Contact: Principal Youth Officer, David Chandler, RSPB Youth Unit, The Lodge, Sandy, Beds, SG19 2DL, 01767 680551;
e-mail: explorers@rspb.org.uk and phoenix@rspb.org.uk
www.rspb.org.uk/youth

SCOTTISH BIRDS RECORDS COMMITTEE
Set up by the Scottish Ornithologists' Club in 1984 to ensure that records of species not deemed rare enough to be considered by the British Birds Rarities Committee, but which are rare in Scotland, are fully assessed; also maintains the official list of Scottish birds.
Contact: Secretary, R W Forrester, The Gables, Eastlands Road, Rothesay, Isle of Bute, PA20 9JZ.
www.the-soc.org.uk

SCOTTISH FIELD STUDIES ASSOCIATION (1950)
Offers residential courses on a variety of environmental subjects, including birdwatching in spring, summer and autumn; weekend and week-long courses.

Contact: Director, SFSA, Kindrogan Field Centre, Enochdhu, Blairgowrie, Perthshire, PH10 7PG, 01250 881286; (Fax)01250 881433;
e-mail: kindrogan@btinternet.com
www.kindrogan.com

SCOTTISH NATURAL HERITAGE
SNH is a statutory body established by the Natural Heritage (Scotland) Act 1991, formed in April 1992 and responsible to Scottish Ministers. Its aim is to promote Scotland's natural Heritage, its care and improvement, its responsible enjoyment, its greater understanding and appreciation and its sustainable use now and for future generations.
Contact: Chief Executive, SNH, Roger Crofts, 12 Hope Terrace, Edinburgh, EH9 2AS, 0131 447 4784;
www.snh.org.uk

SCOTTISH ORNITHOLOGISTS' CLUB (1936; 2500)
The Club has fourteen branches (see County Directory). Each has a programme of meetings during the winter and field trips throughout the year. The Club organises the SOC annual weekend conference in the autumn and the joint SOC/BTO one-day birdwatchers' conference in the spring. Members receive the quarterly newsletter *Scottish Bird News*, the bi-annual *Scottish Birds*, the annual *Scottish Bird Report* and the *Raptor Round Up*. The Waterston Library, housed by the SOC, is the the most comprehensive ornithological reference library in Scotland. Membership of the Club is open to anyone interested in ornithology in Scotland.
Contact: 21 Regent Terrace, Edinburgh, EH7 5BT, 0131 556 6042; (Fax)0131 558 9947;
e-mail: mail@the-soc.org.uk
www.the-soc.org.uk

SCOTTISH SOCIETY FOR THE PREVENTION OF CRUELTY TO ANIMALS
Founded in 1839. Represents animal welfare interests to Government, local authorities and others. Educates young people to realise their responsibilities. Maintains an inspectorate to patrol and investigate and to advise owners of their responsibility for the welfare of animals and birds in their care. Maintains 16 welfare centres, two of which include oiled bird cleaning centres. Bird species, including birds of prey, are rehabilitated and where possible released back into the wild.
Contact: Chief Executive, James Morris, Braehead Mains, 603 Queensferry Road, Edinburgh, EH4 6EA, 0131 339 0222; (Fax)0131 339 4777; e-mail: enquiries@scottishspca.org
www.scottishspca.org

SCOTTISH WILDLIFE TRUST
(1964; 16,500)
Has branches and members' groups throughout Scotland. Aims to conserve all forms of wildlife and has over 123 reserves, many of great birdwatching interest, covering some 55,555 acres. Member of The Wildlife Trusts partnership and organises Scottish Wildlife Watch. Publishes *Scottish Wildlife* three times a year.
Contact: Chief Executive, Steve Sankey, Cramond House, Off Cramond Glebe Road, Edinburgh, EH4 6NS, 0131 312 7765; (Fax)0131 312 8705;
e-mail: enquiries@swt.org.uk
www.swt.org.uk

SEABIRD GROUP (1966;350)
Concerned with conservation issues affecting seabirds. Co-ordinates census and monitoring work on breeding seabirds; has established and maintains the Seabird Colony Register in collaboration with the JNCC; organises triennial conferences on seabird biology and conservation topics. Small grants available to assist with research and survey work on seabirds. Publishes the *Seabird Group Newsletter* every four months and the journal, *Atlantic Seabirds,* quarterly in association with the Dutch Seabird Group.
Contact: Bob Swann, 14 St Vincent Road, Tain, Ross-shire, IV19 1JR, 01862 894329;
e-mail: bob.swann@freeuk.com

SOCIETY OF WILDLIFE ARTISTS (1964)
Registered charity. Annual exhibitions held in Sept/Oct at the Mall Galleries, London. Offers bursaries to young, talented artists.
Contact: President, Bruce Pearson, Federation of British Artists, 17 Carlton House Terrace, London, SW1Y 5BD, 020 7930 6844.
www.swla.co.uk

SWAN SANCTUARY (THE)
Founded by Dorothy Beeson BEM. A registered charity which operates nationally, with 6 rescue centres in the UK and one in Ireland. Has a fully equipped swan hospital with an operating theatre, two treatment rooms, x-ray facilities and a veterinary surgeon. Present site has three lakes and 10 rehabilitation ponds where some 3,000 swans a year are treated. 24-hour service operated, with volunteer rescuers on hand to recover victims of oil spills, vandalism etc. A planned new site will allow visitors. Provides education and training.
Contact: Secretary, Field View, Pooley Green, Egham, Surrey, TW20 8AT, 01784 431667; (Fax)01784 430122;
e-mail: swanuk@dialstart.net
www.swanuk.org.uk

SWAN STUDY GROUP
An association of some 80 swan enthusiasts, both amateur and professional, from around the UK. Most are concerned with Mute Swans, but Bewick's and Whooper Swan biologists are also active members. The aim of the Group is to provide a forum for communication and discussion, and to help co-ordinate co-operative studies. Annual meetings are held at various locations in the UK at which speakers give presentations on their own fieldwork.
Contact: Dr Helen Chisholm, 14 Buckstone Howe, Edinburgh, EH10 6XF, 0131 445 2351;
e-mail: h.chisolm@ed.ac.uk

UK400 CLUB (1981)
Serves to monitor the nation's top twitchers and their life lists, and to keep under review contentious species occurrences. Publishes a bi-monthly magazine *Rare Birds*. Membership open to all.
Contact: L G R Evans, 8 Sandycroft Road, Little Chalfont, Amersham, Bucks, HP6 6QL, 01494 763010;
e-mail: lgre@uk400clubonline.co.uk
www.uk400clubonline.co.uk

ULSTER WILDLIFE TRUST **see County Directory.**

WADER STUDY GROUP (1970; 600)
The WSG is an association of wader enthusiasts, both amateur and professional, from all parts of the world. The Group aims to maintain contact between them, to help in the organisation of co-operative studies, and to provide a vehicle for the exchange of information. Publishes the *Wader Study Group Bulletin* three times a year and holds annual meetings throughout Europe.
Contact: Membership Secretary, Wader Study Group, Rod West, c/o BTO, The Nunnery, Thetford, Norfolk, IP24 2PU,
e-mail: rodwest@ndirect.co.uk

WALTER ROTHSCHILD ZOOLOGICAL MUSEUM
Founded by Lionel Walter (later Lord) Rothschild, the Museum displays British and exotic birds (1500 species) including many rarities and extinct species. Galleries open all year except Dec 24-26. Adjacent to the Bird Group of the Natural History Museum - with over a million specimens and an extensive ornithological library, an internationally important centre for bird research.
Contact: Akeman Street, Tring, Herts, HP23 6AP, 020 7942 6171.
www.nhm.nc.uk/museum/tring

WELSH KITE TRUST
Formed in 1996 by the existing fieldworker network, the Trust is a registered charity that undertakes the conservation and annual monitoring of Red Kites in Wales. It attempts to locate all the breeding birds, to compile data on population growth, productivity, range expansion etc. The Trust liaises with landowners, acts as consultant on planning issues and with regard to filming and photography, and represents Welsh interests on the UK Kite Steering Group. Provides a limited rescue service for injured Kites and eggs or chicks at risk of desertion or starvation. Publishes a newsletter *Boda Wennol* twice a year, sent free to members of Friends of the Welsh Kite and to all landowners with nesting Kites.
Contact: Tony Cross, Samaria, Nantmel, Llandrindod Wells, Powys, LD1 6EN, 01597 860524;
e-mail: tony.cross@welshkitetrust.org
www.welshkitetrust.org

WELSH ORNITHOLOGICAL SOCIETY (1988; 250).
Promotes the study, conservation and enjoyment of birds throughout Wales. Runs the Welsh Records Panel which adjudicates records of scarce species in Wales. Publishes the journal *Welsh Birds* twice a year, along with newsletters, and organises an annual conference.
Contact: Paul Kenyon, 196 Chester Road, Hartford, Northwich, CW8 1LG, 01606 77960;
e-mail: pkenyon196@aol.com
www.members.aol.com/welshos/cac

WETLAND TRUST
Set up to encourage conservation of wetlands and develop study of migratory birds, and to foster international relations in these fields. Destinations for recent expeditions inc. Senegal, The Gambia, Guinea-Bissau, Nigeria, Kuwait, Thailand. Large numbers of birds are ringed each year in Sussex and applications are invited from individuals to train in bird ringing or extend their experience.
Contact: S J R Rumsey, Elms Farm, Pett Lane, Icklesham, Winchelsea, E Sussex, TN36 4AH, 01797 226137;
e-mail: srumsey@europeancredit.com

A drake Tufted Duck at Oare Marsh - drawn by Mark James of Hernhill, Kent.

WILDFOWL & WETLANDS TRUST (THE)
Founded in 1946 by the late Sir Peter Scott. Over 80,000 members and 57,000 bird adopters. A registered charity. Has nine centres with reserves (see Arundel, Caerlaverock, Castle Espie, Llanelli, Martin Mere, Slimbridge, Washington, Welney, and The Wetland Centre in Reserves and Observatories section). The centres are nationally or internationally important for wintering wildfowl; they also aim to raise awareness of, and appreciation for, wetland species, the problems they face and the conservation action needed to help them. Programmes of walks and talks are available for visitors with varied interests - resources and programmes are provided for school groups. Centres, except Caerlaverock and Welney, have wildfowl from around the world, inc. endangered species. Research Department works on population dynamics, species management plans and wetland ecology. The Wetland Advisory Service (WAS) undertakes contracts, and Wetland Link International promotes the role of wetland centres for education and public awarenes
Contact: Managing Director, Tony Richardson, Slimbridge, Glos, GL2 7BT, 01453 890333; (Fax)01453 890827;
e-mail: enquiries@wwt.org.uk
www.wwt.org.uk

WILDLIFE SOUND RECORDING SOCIETY (1968; 327)
Works closely with the Wildlife Section of the National Sound Archive. Members carry out recording work for scientific purposes as well as for pleasure. A field weekend is held each spring, and members organise meetings locally. Four CD sound magazines of members' recordings are produced for members each year, and a journal, *Wildlife Sound*, is published twice a year.
Contact: Hon Membership Secretary, WSRS, Mike Iannantuoni, 36 Wenton Close, Cottesmore, Oakham, Rutland, LE15 7DR, 01572 812447.

WILDLIFE TRUSTS (THE)
A nationwide network of 46 local Wildlife Trusts and 100 urban Wildlife Groups which work to protect wildlife in town and country. The Wildlife Trusts manage more than 2300 nature reserves, undertake a wide range of other conservation and education activities, and are dedicated to the achievement of a UK richer in wildlife. Publishes *Natural World*. See also Wildlife Watch.

Contact: Director-General, Dr Simon Lyster, The Kiln, Waterside, Mather Road, Newark, NG24 1WT, 01636 677711; (Fax)01636 670001;
e-mail: info@wildlife-trusts.cix.co.uk
www.wildlifetrusts.org

WILDLIFE WATCH
The junior branch of The Wildlife Trusts (see previous entry). Founded in 1971 it now has over 20,000 members. It supports 1500 registered volunteer leaders running Watch groups across the UK. Publishes *Watchword* and *Wildlife Extra*.
Contact: Helen Freeston, The Kiln, Waterside, Mather Road, Newark, NG24 1WT, 01636 677711; (Fax)01636 670001;
e-mail: watch@wildlife-trusts.cix.co.uk
www.wildlifewatch.org.uk

WWF-UK (1961)
WWF is the world's largest independent conservation organisation, comprising 27 national organisations. It works to conserve endangered species, protect endangered spaces, and address global threats to nature by seeking long-term solutions with people in government and industry, education and civil society. Publishes *WWF News* (quarterly magazine).
Contact: Chief Executive, Robert Napier, Panda House, Weyside Park, Catteshall Lane, Godalming, Surrey, GU7 1XR, 01483 426444; (Fax)01483 426409; www.wwf-uk.org

ZOOLOGICAL PHOTOGRAPHIC CLUB (1899)
Circulates black and white and colour prints of zoological interest via a series of postal portfolios. Hon Secretary, Martin B Withers, 93 Cross Lane, Mountsorrel, Loughborough, Leics, LE12 7BX, 0116 229 6080.

ZOOLOGICAL SOCIETY OF LONDON (1826)
Carries out research, organises symposia and holds scientific meetings. Manages the Zoological Gardens in Regent's Park (first opened in 1828) and Whipsnade Wild Animal Park near Dunstable, Beds, each with extensive collections of birds. The Society's library has a large collection of ornithological books and journals. Publications include the *Journal of Zoology*, *Animal Conservation*, *The Symposia* and *The International Zoo Yearbook*.
Contact: Director General, Dr Michael Dixon, Regent's Park, London, NW1 4RY, 020 7722 3333. www.zsl.org

NATIONAL PROJECTS

NOTICE TO BIRDWATCHERS

National ornithological projects depend for their success on the active participation of amateur birdwatchers. In return they provide birdwatchers with an excellent opportunity to contribute in a positive and worthwhile way to the scientific study of birds and their habitats, which is the vital basis of all conservation programmes. The following entries provide a description of each particular project and a note of whom to contact for further information (full address details are in the previous section).

BEWICK'S SWAN RESEARCH

A WWF project

Recognition of individual Bewick's Swans by their black and yellow bill markings has been used for an extensive study of the flock wintering at Slimbridge, Gloucestershire since 1964. The swans show a high level of both site and mate fidelity; 10 to 50% of the birds identified each season have been recorded at Slimbridge in previous years. Factors affecting the life cycle of individual birds can therefore be analysed in detail.

A regular ringing programme was introduced in 1967 to identify staging sites used during migration to and from the Russian breeding grounds, and to continue monitoring individuals that transferred to other wintering sites. Bewick's Swans have also been caught and ringed at Caerlaverock (Dumfries & Galloway) and Welney (Norfolk) since 1979, and at Martin Mere (Lancashire) since 1990.

Since 1991 staff have made one or two expeditions to the Russian arctic each summer, to study the swans' breeding biology in collaboration with scientists from Russia, the Netherlands and Denmark. Sightings of marked birds are invaluable for maintaining the life-history records of individual swans.

Contact: Eileen Rees, WWT.

BREEDING BIRD SURVEY

Supported by the BTO, JNCC and the RSPB.

Begun in 1994, the BBS is designed to keep track of the changes in populations of our common breeding birds. It is dependent on volunteer birdwatchers throughout the country who can spare about five hours a year to cover a 1x1km survey square.There are just two morning visits to survey the breeding birds each year.

Survey squares are picked at random by computer to ensure that all habitats and regions are covered, making BBS the most important new survey in many years. Since its inception it has been a tremendous success, with more than 2,300 squares covered and more than 2,200 species recorded. Contact: Mike Raven, BTO, or your local BTO Regional Representative (see County Directory).

BREEDING WADERS OF WET MEADOWS 2002

A BTO project funded by the RSPB English Nature and DEFRA.

A repeat of the 1982 survey. Around 1600 selected sites are to be surveyed across England & Wales. Each site will be visited three times between mid April and late June, to record and map breeding waders. Ducks (except Mallard) and Yellow Wagtails will also be counted.

Contacts: Andy Wilson, BTO.

BTO/JNCC WINTER FARMLAND BIRDS SURVEYS

A BTO project funded by a partnership of the BTO and the JNCC.

Three winters of full surveys 1999/2000, 2000/01, 2001/02. They concentrate on a suite of species found on farmland in winter, including Tree Sparrow, Linnet, Bullfinch, Yellowhammer, Redwing and Fieldfare, Lapwing and Golden Plover. The surveys involve several components, including coverage of random squares, counts along standard routes and casual records. Contact: Andy Wilson, e-mail: wfbs@bto.org.

COMMON BIRDS CENSUS

A BTO project, previously supported by JNCC The Common Birds Census ran from 1962 to 2000. A small group of core plots have been selected and they will continue to be surveyed. Volunteer fieldworkers make ten breeding-season visits each year to a plot of farmland or woodland. Maps are prepared showing the locations of birds' territories on each plot. These are of value both locally and nationally. The BTO uses the data to study bird population changes, the structure of bird communities and the relationships of breeding birds with their habitats. Long-term population trends derived from CBC are used to assess bird conservation priorities.

Contact: Richard Thewlis, BTO.

CONCERN FOR SWIFTS

A Concern for Swifts Group project.

Endorsed by the BTO and the RSPB, the Group monitors Swift breeding colonies, especially where building restoration and maintenance are likely to cause disturbance. Practical information can be provided to owners, architects, builders and others, as well as advice on nest boxes and the use of specially adapted roof tiles. The help of interested birdwatchers is always welcome. Contact: Jake Allsop, 01353 740540; fax 01353 741585.

CONSTANT EFFORT SITES SCHEME
A BTO project for bird ringers, funded by a partnership of the BTO, the JNCC, Duchas the Heritage Service - National Parks & Wildlife Service (Ireland) and the Ringers themselves.
Participants in the Scheme monitor common songbird populations by mist-netting and ringing birds throughout the summer at more than 130 sites across Britain and Ireland. Changes in numbers of adults captured provide an index of population changes between years, while the ratio of juveniles to adults gives a measure of productivity. Between-year recaptures of birds are used to study variations in adult survival rates. Information from CES complements that from other long-term BTO surveys. Contact: Dawn Balmer, BTO.

CORMORANT ROOST SITE INVENTORY AND BREEDING COLONY REGISTER
R Sellers in association with WWT and JNCC.
Daytime counts carried out under the Wetland Bird Survey provide an index of the number of Cormorants wintering in Great Britain, but many birds are known to go uncounted on riverine and coastal habitats.

Dr Robin Sellers, in association with WWT, therefore established the Christmas Week Cormorant Survey which, through a network of volunteer counters, sought to monitor the numbers of Cormorants at about 70 of the most important night roosts in GB. In 1997, this project was extended, in collaboration with JNCC, to produce a comprehensive Cormorant Roost Site Inventory for GB to aid the statutory nature conservation agencies in their advice to government. Over 100 county bird recorders and local bird experts played an integral role in compiling the inventory, which currently lists 291 night roosts, mostly in England.

In 1990, Robin Sellers also established the Cormorant Breeding Colony Survey to monitor numbers and breeding success of Cormorants in the UK at both coastal and inland colonies. Some 1500 pairs of Cormorants, representing perhaps 15% of the local UK population, now breed inland. New colonies are forming every year as the population inland increases annually by 19%.

By 1998, breeding had been attempted at over 50 inland sites and colonies established at 11, mainly in SE England. Recent research has shown that a high proportion of these inland breeders are of the continental race *Phalacrocorax carbo sinensis*. Anyone wishng to take part in either roost or breeding surveys should contact Richard Hearn at WWT. Records of night time roost sites would also be greatly appreciated and individually acknowledged.

GARDEN BIRD FEEDING SURVEY
A BTO project.
The 2000/01 season completed 31 years of the GBFS. Each year 250 observers record the numbers and variety of garden birds fed by man in the 26 weeks between October and March. It is the longest running survey of its type in the world. Gardens are selected by region and type, from city flats, suburban semis and rural houses to outlying farms. Contact: David Glue, BTO.

GARDEN BIRDWATCH
A BTO project, supported by C J WildBird Foods.
Started in January 1995, this project is a year-round survey that monitors the use that birds make of gardens. Approximately 14,000 participants from all over the UK and Ireland keep a weekly log of species using their gardens. The data collected are used to monitor regional, seasonal and year-to-year changes in the garden populations of our commoner birds. To cover costs there is an annual registration fee of £12. There is a quarterly volunteers magazine and all new joiners receive a full-colour, 80 page garden bird handbook.
Contact: Jacky Prior/Carol Povey, BTO.

GOLDEN ORIOLE CENSUS
A Golden Oriole Group project.
With support from the RSPB, the Golden Oriole Group has undertaken a systematic annual census of breeding Golden Orioles in the Fenland Basin since 1987. In recent years national censuses have been made, funded by English Nature and the RSPB, in which some 60 volunteer recorders have participated. The Group is always interested to hear of sightings of Orioles and to receive offers of help with its census work. Studies of breeding biology, habitat and food requirements are also carried out. Contact: Jake Allsop, Golden Oriole Group.

GOOSE CENSUSES
A RW project.
Britain and Ireland support internationally important goose populations. During the day, many of these feed away from wetlands and are therefore not adequately censused by the Wetland Bird Survey. Additional surveys are therefore undertaken to provide estimates of population size. These primarily involve roost counts, supplemented by further counts of feeding birds.

Most populations are censused up to three times a year, typically during the autumn, midwinter, and spring. In addition, counts of the proportion of juveniles in goose flocks are undertaken to provide estimates of annual productivity. Further volunteers are always needed. In particular, counters in Scotland, Lancashire and Norfolk are sought. For more information contact: Richard Hearn, WWT, e-mail richard.hearn@wwt.org.uk.

HERONRIES CENSUS
A BTO project.
This survey started in 1928 and has been carried out under the auspices of the BTO since 1934. It represents the longest continuous series of population data for any European breeding bird.

Counts are made at a sample of heronries each year, chiefly in England and Wales, to provide an index of the current population level; data from Scotland and Northern Ireland are scant and more contributions from these countries would be especially welcomed. Herons may be hit hard during periods of severe weather but benefit by increased survival over mild winters. Their position at the top of a food chain makes them particularly vulnerable to pesticides and pollution. Contact: John Machant, BTO.

IRISH WETLAND BIRD SURVEY (I-WeBS)
A joint project of BirdWatch Ireland, the National Parks & Wildlife Service of the Dept of Arts, Culture & the Gaeltacht, and WWT, and supported by the Heritage Council and WWF-UK.
Established in 1994, I-WeBS aims to monitor the numbers and distribution of waterfowl populations wintering in Ireland in the long term, enabling the population size and spatial and temporal trends in numbers to be identified and described for each species.

Methods are compatible with existing schemes in the UK and Europe, and I-WeBS collaborates closely with the Wetland Bird Survey (WeBS) in the UK. Synchronised monthly counts are undertaken at wetland sites of all habitats during the winter. Counts are straightforward and counters receive a newsletter and full report annually. Additional help is always welcome, especially during these initial years as the scheme continues to grow. Contact: Kendrew Colhoun, BirdWatch Ireland.

LOW TIDE COUNTS SCHEME
see Wetland Bird Survey

MANX CHOUGH PROJECT
A Manx registered charitable trust.
Established in 1990 to help the conservation of the Chough in the Isle of Man, leading to its protection and population increase. The main considerations are the maintenance of present nest sites, provision of suitable conditions for the reoccupation of abandoned sites and the expansion of the range of the species into new areas of the Island. Surveys and censuses are carried out. Raising public awareness of and interest in the Chough are further objects. Contact: Allen S Moore, Lyndale, Derby Road, Peel, Isle of Man IM5 1HH. 01624 843798.

MUTE SWAN CENSUS 2001
A WWT/JNCC project, in collaboration with BTO, Swan Study Group, SOC and others.
This national census of Mute Swans is scheduled to take place in spring 2001, repeating the previous one conducted in 1990. Mute Swans are widespread during the breeding season on all manner of wetlands, including small lakes and particularly on rivers, habitats little visited by waterbird surveys. Complete coverage will be attempted for the most densely populated regions, with options to assist organisers and counters elsewhere. The census will require large numbers of observers. Contact: Peter Cranswick at WWT.

NEST RECORD SCHEME
A BTO project, funded by a partnership of the BTO, the JNCC.
All birdwatchers can contribute to this scheme by completing easy-to-use Nest Record Cards for any nesting attempt they find. The aim is to provide a picture of how Britain's birds are faring in town and countryside, in a way that no single observer could ever do. Even one card is a useful addition. Prospective new participants can obtain a free introductory pack.
Contact: Andy Simpkin, BTO.

PREDATORY BIRDS MONITORING SCHEME
A Centre for Ecology and Hydrology project
This long-running scheme was set up to monitor the effects of pesticides on wildlife and is now largely concerned with checking on the effectiveness of restrictions that have been imposed on some uses of agricultural chemicals.

The species at present studied are Peregrine, Sparrowhawk, Kestrel, Merlin, Long-eared Owl, Barn Owl, Heron, Kingfisher and Great Crested Grebe, and the CEH would be grateful to receive specimens of these. They should be packed in a polythene bag (sealed in some way), then in a padded envelope or box. Mark the outside of the package 'Perishable Goods' and post first class to: Miss L Dale, Centre for Ecology & Hydrology, Monks Wood, Abbots Ripton, Huntingdon, Cambridgeshire PE28 2LS (01487 773381).

The following information is required: name and address of finder, locality in which the bird was found, date collected and the circumstances (eg found dead on road). The whole specimen should be sent. If there is any delay before posting, the dead bird should be put in a plastic bag and stored in a freezer to delay decomposition. Birds which have been kept in captivity are not required. Postage costs are reimbursed in the form of stamps and a copy of the results will be sent to the sender.

RAPTOR AND OWL RESEARCH REGISTER
A BTO project
The Register has helped considerably over the past 26 years in encouraging and guiding research, and in the co-ordination of projects. There are currently almost 500 projects in the card index file through which the Register operates.

The owl species currently receiving most attention are Barn and Tawny, as to raptors, the most popular subjects are Kestrel, Buzzard, Sparrowhawk, Hobby and Peregrine, with researchers showing increasing interest in Red Kite, and fewer large in-depth studies of Goshawk, Osprey and harriers. Contributing is a simple process and involves all raptor enthusiasts, whether it is to describe an amateur activity or professional study. The nature of research on record varies widely - from local pellet analyses to captive breeding and rehabilitation programmes to national surveys of Peregrine, Buzzard and Golden Eagle. Birdwatchers in both Britain and abroad are encouraged to write for photocopies of cards relevant to the species or nature of their work. The effectiveness of the Register depends upon those running projects (however big or small) ensuring that their work is included. Contact: David Glue, BTO.

RED KITE RE-INTRODUCTION PROJECT

An English Nature/SNH/RSPB project supported by Forest Enterprise, Yorkshire Water and authorities in Germany and Spain

The project involves the translocation of birds from Spain, Germany and the expanding Chilterns population for release at sites in England and Scotland. Records of any wing-tagged Red Kites in England should be reported to Ian Carter at English Nature, Northminster House, Peterborough, PEI IUA (tel 01733 455281). Scottish records should be sent to Brian Etheridge at RSPB's North Scotland Regional Office, Etive House, Beechwood Park, Inverness, IV2 3BW (tel 01463 715000).

Sightings are of particular value if the letter/number code (or colour) of wing tags can be seen or if the bird is seen flying low over (or into) woodland. Records should include an exact location, preferably with a six figure grid reference, and as much detail as possible about the bird's behaviour.

RETRAPPING ADULTS FOR SURVIVAL PROJECT

A BTO project for bird ringers, funded by a partnership of the BTO, the JNCC, Duchas the Heritage Service - National Parks & Wildlife Service (Ireland) and the ringers themselves.

This project started in 1998 and is an initiative of the BTO Ringing Scheme. It aims to gather retrap information for a wide range of species, especially those of conservation concern, in a variety of breeding habitats, allowing the monitoring of survival rates.

Detailed information about survival rates from the RAS Project will help in the understanding of changing population trends. Ringers choose a target species, decide on a study area and develop suitable catching techniques. The aim then is to catch all the breeding adults of the chosen species within the study area. This is repeated each breeding season for a minimum of five years. The results will be relayed to conservation organisations who can use the information to design effective conservation action plans. Contact: Dawn Balmer, BTO.

RINGING SCHEME

A BTO project for bird ringers, funded by a partnership of the BTO, the JNCC, Duchas the Heritage Service - National Parks & Wildlife Service (Ireland) and the ringers themselves.

The purpose of the Ringing Scheme is to study mortality, survival and migration by marking birds with individually numbered metal rings which carry a return address. About 2,000 trained and licensed ringers operate in Britain and Ireland, and together they mark around 800,000 birds each year.

All birdwatchers can contribute to the scheme by reporting any ringed birds they find. On finding a ringed bird the information to note is the ring number, species (if known), when and where the bird was found, and what happened to it. If the bird is dead the ring should be removed, flattened and attached to the letter. Finders who send their name and address will be given details of where and when the bird was ringed. About 12,000 ringed birds are reported each year and an annual report is published. Contact: Jacquie Clark, BTO.

SEABIRD COLONY REGISTER, SEABIRD MONITORING PROGRAMME, AND SEABIRD 2000

JNCC projects in collaboration with the Seabird Group, RSPB and Shetland Oil Terminal Environmental Advisory Group.

The SCR is a computer database of numbers of seabirds breeding at colonies throughout the British Isles. It includes records from the comprehensive surveys undertaken in 1969/70 and 1985/87 in addition to more recent records derived from the SMP and other sources.

The SMP monitors seabird numbers and breeding success at a range of colonies each year. Outputs include an annual report, Seabird Numbers and Breeding Success in Britain and Ireland. The aim of the Seabird 2000 project is to carry out a complete census of breeding seabirds in Britain and Ireland between 1999 and 2002. This will provide updated baseline population estimates against which future trends can be assessed.

Anyone wishing to access or submit data to the SCR or with an interest in volunteering to assist with the SMP or Seabird 2000 should contact: Kate Thompson, JNCC, Dunnet House, 7 Thistle Place, Aberdeen AB10 lUZ. 01224 655703; fax 01224 621488; e-mail: thomp@k@jncc. gov.uk; wwwjncc.gov.uk.

SIGHTINGS OF COLOUR-MARKED BIRDS

Various bodies.

Studies of movements of colour-marked birds depend heavily on the help of birdwatchers. On sighting a colour-marked bird full details should be recorded and sent to the appropriate contact below. The information will be passed on to the person who marked the bird, who will send details of marking to the observer. Unfortunately some birds cannot be traced, owing for example to loss of rings or the inadequacy of the central record.

Waders: Wader Study Group, c/o Bob Robinson, BTO.
Wildfowl: Richard Hearn, WWT, Slimbridge, Gloucester GL2 7BT.
Cormorant: Graham Ekins, 35 Church Road, Boreham, Essex CM3 3DN.
Chough: Eric Bignal, Kindrochaid, Bruichladdich, Islay PA44 7PP.
Large gulls: Peter Rock, 59 Concorde Drive, Westbury-on-Trym, Bristol BS10 6PX.
Small gulls: K T Pedersen, Daglykkevej 7, DK-2650 Hridovre, Denmark.
All other species: Linda Milne, Ringing Unit, BTO.

SWIFTS see Concern for Swifts

2002 UK PEREGRINE SURVEY

A joint BTO Raptor Study Groups project, supported by JNCC/EHS/EN/CCW/SNH/SOC/RSPB.

This is the fifth in a series of ten-yearly surveys of the breeding Peregrine population in the UK. The survey in 1961/62 highlighted the plight of Peregrines, badly affected by organochlorine pesticides such as DDT. Subsequent surveys have shown how the population has recovered as the pesticides were withdrawn from use. In 1991 Peregrines were at last beginning to recolonise the southeast coast of England, but there were worrying declines in the north and west of Scotland.

The survey in 2002 aims to provide solid information about the numbers of Peregrines breeding throughout the UK information that is especially important in the light of perceived conflicts between raptors and game rearing and pigeon racing interests.

The Peregrine is listed on Schedule 1 of the Wildlife and Countryside Act 1981 and a licence is required to disturb a bird at its nest. The survey is being organised on the ground through the network of Raptor Study Groups, where they exist, or through designated regional organisers. Volunteer birdwatchers, with experience of raptor survey, who wish to take part and others, who can provide information on the location of territorial Peregrines, particularly those birds located in cities, should contact the national organiser, who will put them in touch with their local raptor study group organiser. National Organiser: Alan Lauder, BTO Scotland.

WATERWAYS BIRD SURVEY

A BTO project

From March to July each year participants survey linear waterways (rivers and canals) to record the position and activity of riparian birds. Results show both numbers and distribution of breeding territories for each waterside species at each site. An annual report on population change is published in *BTO News*. WBS maps show the habitat requirements of the birds and can be used to assess the effects of waterway management. Coverage of new plots is always required, especially in poorly covered areas such as Ireland, Scotland, Wales, SW England and the North East.

Contact: Richard Thewlis, BTO.

WATERWAYS BREEDING BIRD SURVEY

A BTO project, supported by the Environment Agency

WBBS uses transect methods like those of the Breeding Bird Survey to record bird populations along randomly chosen stretches of river and canal throughout the UK Just two survey visits are needed during April-June. WBBS began in 1998 and is currently in a development phase, in which its performance is being assessed against the long established Waterways Bird Survey. Contact BTO Regional Representative (see County Directory) to enquire if any local stretches require coverage, otherwise John Marchant at BTO HO.

WeBS PILOT DISPERSED WATERFOWL SURVEY

A WeBS project funded by the BTO,WWT, RW, RSPB and JNCC

Little is known about the numbers of dabbling ducks, Moorhen, Coot, Little Grebe, Heron, etc that winter on small water bodies, streams, flooded fields, ditches and dykes, away from Wetland Bird Survey (WeBS) sites. Furthermore, there are no reliable population estimates of wintering Ruff or either species of snipe. This survey aims to assess whether it is possible to estimate the size of these populations.

The full survey, planned for 2002/03 winter, would estimate how many of these birds occur in UK habitats not completely covered at present by WeBS. The Pilot will test the value of a tetrad-based approach incorporating intensive coverage of one of the 1Km^2

Seabirds such as Fulmar are monitored in various projects. Here Michael Webb records an incident on the Isle of Wight when a roosting Little Owl appeared on one of the ledges.

units within each tetrad (4Km^2) It is impractical to get whole tetrads intensively covered, but a large count unit is essential for the larger less common species. Therefore, three quarters of each tetrad will be covered for such species as the plovers and herons, which can often be counted from roads and farm tracks. In the intensively covered 1Km^2 all species will be counted according to habitat. The tetrads will be selected by random sampling. BTO Regional Representatives may be asked to help with this survey if it proves too difficlt to obtain sufficient counters from WeBS Local Organsisers. Contacts: Mark Rehfisch, Stephen Holloway, Mike Armitage, BTO.

WeBS RIVERINE SURVEY
A Wetland Bird Survey project (qv)
Whilst the Wetland Bird Survey (WeBS) achieves excellent coverage of estuaries and inland still waters, rivers are poorly monitored by comparison. Consequently, WeBS undoubtedly misses a significant proportion of the UK populations of several species which use rivers, eg. Little Grebe, Mallard, Tufted Duck, Goldeneye and Goosander. The WeBS Riverine Survey in 2001/02 will be the first national survey of waterbirds on rivers during winter. It aims to estimate total numbers of birds on rivers throughout the UK and to identify particularly important river stretches for birds. Exact methods are being finalised following a pilot last winter, but in essence will involve simply counting the numbers of waterbirds (esp. ducks) on particular stretches of river and canal (sections for counts will probably be 2.5 km long). Many counters in addition to those involved in the pilot will be required. Contact: James Robinson at WNT.

WETLAND BIRD SURVEY
A joint scheme of BTO, RW, RSPB & JNCC
The Wetland Bird Survey (WeBS) is the monitoring scheme for non-breeding waterbirds in the UK. The principal aims are:
1. to determine the population sizes of waterbirds:
2. to determine trends in numbers and distribution:
3. to identify important sites for waterbirds:
4. to conduct research which underpins waterbird conservation.

WeBS data are used to designate important waterbird sites and protect them against adverse development, for research into the causes of declines, for establishing conservation priorities and strategies and to formulate management plans for wetland sites and waterbirds.

Once monthly, synchronised Core Counts are made at as many wetland sites as possible. Low Tide Counts are made on about 20 estuaries each winter to identify important feeding areas. Counts take just a few hours and are relatively straightforward. The 3,000 participants receive regular newsletters and a comprehensive annual report. New counters are always welcome. Contacts: WeBS Secretariat, WWT (for Core Counts an dgeneral enquiries) and Andy Musgrove, BTO (Low Tide Count).

WHOOPER SWAN RESEARCH
A WWT/Icelandic Museum of Nature History project
WNW's long-term study of Whooper Swans commenced in 1979 with the completion of swan pipes at Caerlaverock (Dumfries & Galloway) and Welney (Norfolk) and the subsequent development of a ringing programme for this species. Whooper Swans have been ringed at Martin Mere (Lancashire) from 1990 onwards. Since 1988, staff have made regular expeditions to Iceland where they collaborate with Icelandic ornithologists in monitoring clutch and brood sizes, and in catching the families and non-breeding flocks. The study aims to determine factors affecting the reproductive success of the Icelandic-breeding Whooper Swan population which winters mainly in Britain and Ireland. Relocating the families in winter is important for assessing the number of cygnets that survive autumn migration. Efforts made by birdwatchers to read Whooper Swan rings and to report the number of juveniles associated with ringed birds, are therefore particularly useful. The first and last dates on which ringed birds are seen at a site are also valuable for monitoring the movements of the swans in winter. Contact: Eileen Rees, WWT.

WILDFOWL COLOUR RINGING
A WWT project
The Wildfowl & Wetlands Trust co-ordinates all colour ringing of swans, geese and ducks on behalf of the BTO. The use of unique coloured leg-rings enables the movements and behaviour of known individuals to be observed without recapture. The rings are usually in bright colours with engraved letters and/or digits showing as black or white, and can be read with a telescope at up to 200m. Colour-marked neckcollars, and plumage dyes, have also been used on geese and swans. Any records of observations should include species, location, date, ring colour and mark, and which leg the ring was on (most rings read from the foot upwards). Tle main study species are Mute Swan, Bewick's Swan, Whooper Swan, Pink-footed Goose, Greylag Goose, Greenland and European White-fronted Geese, Barnacle Goose, Brent Goose, Shelduck and Wigeon. Records will be forwarded to the relevant study, and when birds are traced ringing details will be sent back to the observer. All sightings should be sent to: Research Dept (Colour-ringed Wildfowl), WWT.

WINTER FARMLAND BIRDS SURVEYS see BTO/ JNCC Winter Farmland Bird Surveys.

INTERNATIONAL DIRECTORY

Thick-billed Larks *(Ramphacoris clothy)* **at Merzouga, Morocco by Ernest Leahy.**

The BirdLife Partnership

BirdLife is a Partnership of non-governmental organisations (NGOs) with a special focus on conservation and birds. Each NGO Partner represents a unique geographic territory/country.

The BirdLife Network explained

Partners: Membership-based NGOs who represent BirdLife in their own territory. Vote holders and key implementing bodies for BirdLife's Strategy and Regional Programmes in their own territories.

Partners Designate: Membership-based NGOs who represent BirdLife in their own territory, in a transition stage to becoming full Partners. Non-vote holders.

Affiliates: Usually NGOs, but also individuals, foundations or governmental institutions when appropriate. Act as a BirdLife contact with the aim of developing into, or recruiting, a BirdLife Partner in their territory.

Secretariat: The co-ordinating and servicing body of BirdLife International.

Secretariat Addresses

BirdLife Cambridge Office
BirdLife International
Wellbrook Court
Girton Road
Cambridge CB3 0NA
United Kingdom
Tel. +44 1 223 277 318
Fax +44 1 223 277200
Email birdlife@birdlife.org.uk
http://www.birdlife.net

BirdLife Americas Regional Office
Birdlife International
Vicente Cárdenas 120 y Japon, 3rd Floor
Quito
Ecuador
Postal address
BirdLife International
Casilla 17-17-717
Quito
Ecuador
Tel. +593 2 453 645
Fax +593 2 459 627
Email birdlife@birdlife.org.ec
http://www.geocities.com/RainForest/Wetlands/6203

BirdLife Asia Regional Office
Jl. Jend. Ahmad Yani No. 11
Bogor 16161
Indonesia
Postal address
PO Box 310/Boo
Bogor 16003
Indonesia
Tel. +62 251 333 234/+62 251 371 394
Fax +62 251 357 961
Email birdlife@indo.net.id
http://www.kt.rim.or.jp/~birdinfo/indonesia

BirdLife European Regional Office
Droevendaalsesteeg 3a PO Box 127
NL- 6700 AC
Wageningen
The Netherlands
Tel. +31 317 478831
Fax +31 317 478844
Email birdlife@birdlife.agro.nl

European Community Office (ECO)
BirdLife International
22 rue de Toulouse
B-1040 Brussels
Belgium
Tel. +32 2280 08 30
Fax +32 2230 38 02
Email bleco@ibm.net

BirdLife Middle East Regional Office
BirdLife International
c/o Royal Society for the Conservation of Nature (RSCN)
PO Box 6354
Amman 11183
Jordan
Tel: +962 6 535-5446
Fax: +962 6 534-7411
Email birdlife@nol.com.jo

FOREIGN NATIONAL ORGANISATIONS

BirdLife Country Programmes

Cameroon
e-mail: birdlife@camnet.cm

Sierra Leone
e-mail: ddsiaffa@hotmail.com

Madagascar
e-mail: zicoma@simicro.mg

Brazil
e-mail: birdlifebrasil@uol.com.br

Indonesia
e-mail: birdlife@indo.net.id

Vietnam
e-mail: birdlife@birdlife.netnam.vn

BirdLife Partner Organisations

AFRICA

Partners

Ethiopia
Ethiopian Wildlife and Natural History Society
e-mail: ewnhs@telecom.net.et
Ghana
Ghana Wildlife Society
e-mail: wildsoc@ighmail.com
Kenya
NatureKenya
e-mail: eanhs@africaonline.co.ke
Sierra Leone
Conservation Society of Sierra Leone
e-mail: cssl@sierratel.sl
South Africa
BirdLife South Africa
e-mail: info@birdlife.org.za
Tanzania
Wildlife Conservation Society of Tanzania
e-mail: wcst@africaonline.co.tz
Uganda
NatureUganda
e-mail: eanhs@infocam.co.ug

Partners Designate

Burkina Faso
Fondation des Amis de la Nature (NATURAMA)
e-mail: naturama@fasonet.bf
Nigeria
Nigerian Conservation Foundation
e-mail: ncf@hyperia.com
Tunisia
Association 'Les Amis des Oiseaux'
e-mail: aao.bird@excite.com
Zimbabwe
BirdLife Zimbabwe
e-mail: birds@zol.co.zw

Affiliates

Botswana
Botswana Bird Club
e-mail: Stephyler@info.bw
Burundi
Dr Laurant Ntahuga
e-mail: arcos.rc@imul.com
Cameroon
Dr Roger Fotso
e-mail: wcscam@aol.com
Egypt
Sherif Baha El Din
e-mail: baha@internetegypt.com
Rwanda
Sam Kanyamibwa
e-mail:
sam.kanyamibwa@wcmc.org.uk
Seychelles
Nirmal Jivan Shah
e-mail: birdlife@seychelles.net
Zambia
Zambian Ornithological Society
e-mail: zos@zamnet.zm

AMERICAS

Partners

Argentina
Aves Argentinas/AOP
e-mail: bosso@aorpla.org.ar
Belize
Belize Audubon Society
e-mail: base@btl.net

Nutcracker *(Nucifraga caryocatactes)* **by Swiss artist Paola Ricceri.**

Bolivia
Asociación Armonía
e-mail: armonia@scbbs-bo.com
Canada
Bird Studies Canada and Canadian Nature Federation
e-mail: mbradstreet@bsc-eoc.org (BSC)
e-mail: cnf@cnf.ca (CNF)
Ecuador
Fundación Ornithológica del Ecuador
e-mail: cecia@uio.satnet.net
Jamaica
BirdLife Jamaica
e-mail: mclevy@cwjamaica.com
Panama
Panama Audubon Society
e-mail: ecoconsult@pty.com
Venezuela
Sociedad Conservacionista Audubon de Venezuela
e-mail: research@telcel.net.ve

Partners Designate

Chile
Unión de Ornitólogos de Chile
e-mail: yerko.vilina@geotecnica.cl
Mexico
CIPAMEX
e-mail: ehma@servidor.unam.mx
Paraguay
Guyra Paraguay (GP) and Fundación Moisés Bertoni (FMB)
e-mail: guyra@highway.com.py (GP)
e-mail: ayanosky@pla.net.py (FMB)
USA
National Audubon Society
e-mail: jwells@audubon.org

Affiliates

Bahamas
Bahamas National Trust
e-mail: bnt@bahamas.net.bs
Cuba
Dr Martín Acosta
e-mail: poey@comuh.uh.cu
El Salvador
Asociación Audubón de El Salvador
e-mail: perezleon@es.com.sv
Falkland Islands
Falklands Conservation
e-mail: info@falklands-nature.demon.co.uk
Honduras
Sherry Thorne
Tel. +504 341 869

Suriname
e-mail: nzcs@cq-link.sr
Uruguay
Grupo Uruguayo para el Estudio y la Conservación de las Aves
e-mail: gupeca@adinet.com.uy

ASIA

Partners

Japan
Wild Bird Society of Japan
vshim@wing-wbsj.or.jp
Malaysia
Malaysian Nature Society
e-mail: natsoc@po.jaring.my
Philippines
Haribon Foundation
vbirdlife@haribon.org.ph
Singapore
The Nature Society Singapore
vkklimsg@singnet.com.sg
Taiwan
Wild Bird Federation Taiwan
cwbf@ms4.url.com.tw
Thailand
Bird Conservation Society of Thailand
bcst@box1.a-net.net.th

Partner Designate

India
Bombay Natural History Society
e-mail: director.bnhs@vsnl.com

Affiliates

Hong Kong
Hong Kong Birdwatching Society
e-mail: chiuylam@asiaonline.net
Nepal
Bird Conservation Nepal
e-mail: birdlife@mos.com.np
Pakistan
Ornithological Society of Pakistan
e-mail: aleemk@usa.net
Sri Lanka
Field Ornithology Group of Sri Lanka
e-mail: fogsl@slt.lk

EUROPE

Partners

Austria
BirdLife Austria
e-mail: birdlife@blackbox.at
Belgium
BNVR-RNOB Belgische Natuur- en Vogelreservaten vzw, Reserves Naturelles et Ornithologique de Belgique asbl.
e-mail: wim.VandenBossche@sec.natuurreservaten.be
Bulgaria
Bulgarian Society for the Protection of Birds
e-mail: bspb_hq@mb.bia-bg.com
Czech Republic
Czech Society for Ornithology
e-mail: cso@bbs.infima.cz
Denmark
Dansk Ornitologisk Forening
e-mail: anita.pederson@dof.dk
Estonia
Estonian Ornithological Society
e-mail: jaanus@linnu.tartu.ee
Finland
BirdLife SUOMI-FINLAND
e-mail: mika.asikainen@birdlife.fi
France
Ligue Pour La Protection des Oiseaux
e-mail: alison.duncan@lpo-birdlife.asso.fr
Germany
Naturschutzbund Deutschland
e-mail: Claus.Mayr@NABU.de
Gibraltar
Gibraltar Ornithological and Natural History Society
e-mail: gonhs@gibnet.gi
Greece
Hellenic Ornithological Society
e-mail: birdlife-gr@ath.forthnet.gr
Hungary
Hungarian Ornithological and Nature Conservation Society
e-mail: mme@mme.hu
Ireland
BirdWatch Ireland
e-mail: bird@indigo.ie
Italy
Lega Italiana Protezione Uccelli
e-mail: lipusede@box1.tin.it
Luxembourg
Lëtzebuerger Natur- a Vulleschutzliga
e-mail: secretary@luxnatur.lu
Malta
BirdLife Malta
e-mail: blm@orbit.net.mt
Netherlands
Vogelbescherming Nederland
e-mail: birdlife@antenna.nl

FOREIGN NATIONAL ORGANISATIONS

Common Cranes *(Grus grus)* **overflying Maremma in Tuscany, by Graziano Offoviani.**

Norway
Norwegian Ornithological Society
e-mail: norornis@online.no
Romania
Romanian Ornithological Society
e-mail: sorcj@codec.ro
Slovakia
Society for the Protection of Birds in Slovakia
e-mail: sovs@changenet.sk
Slovenia
Bird Watching and Bird Study Association of Slovenia
e-mail: dopps@dopps-drustvo.si
Spain
Sociedad Espanola de Ornitologia
e-mail: asanchez@seo.org
Sweden
Swedish Ornithological Society
e-mail: birdlife@sofnet.org
Switzerland
Swiss Association for the Protection of Birds
e-mail: svs@birdlife.ch
Turkey
Dogal Hayati Koruma Dernegi
e-mail: guven.eken@dhkd.org
United Kingdom
Royal Society for the Protection of Birds
e-mail:
alistair.gammell@RSPB.org.uk

Partners Designate

Albania
Albanian Society for the Protection of Birds
e-mail: mns@albmail.com
Belarus
Bird Conservation Belarus
e-mail: APB-Minsk@mail.ru
Israel
Society for the Protection of Nature in Israel
e-mail: ioc@netvision.net.il
Latvia
Latvijas Ornitologijas Biedriba
e-mail: putni@parks.lv
Lithuania
Lithuanian Ornithological Society
e-mail: birdlife@post.5ci.lt
Poland
Polish Society for the Protection of Birds
e-mail: office@otop.most.org.pl
Portugal
Sociedade Portuguesa Para o Estudio das Aves
e-mail: spea@ip.pt
Russia
Russian Bird Conservation Union
e-mail: rbcu@glas.apc.org
Ukraine
Ukrainian Union for Bird Conservation
e-mail: utop@iptelecom.net.ua

Affiliates

Andorra
Associació per a la Defensa de la Natura
e-mail: adn@andorra.ad
Croatia
Croatian Society for Bird and Nature Protection
e-mail: jasmina@mahazu.hazu.hr
Faeroe Islands
Faeroese Ornithological Society
e-mail: doreteb@ngs.fo
Iceland
Icelandic Society for the Protection of Birds
e-mail: fuglavernd@simnet.is
Liechtenstein
Botanish-Zoologische Gesellschaft
vrenat@pingnet.li
Former Yugloslavian Republic of Macedonia
Bird Study and Protection Society of Macedonia
e-mail:
bspsm@iunona.pmf.ukim.edu.mk

MIDDLE EAST

Partner

Jordan
Royal Society for the Conservation of Nature
e-mail: irani@rscn.org.jo
Partner Designate
Lebanon
Society for the Protection of Nature and Natural Resources in Lebanon
r-jaradi@cyberia.net.lb

Affiliates

Bahrain
Dr Saeed A. Mohamed
vsam53@batelco.com.bh
Iran
Dr Jamshid Mansoori
vbirdlife@morva.net
Palestine
Wildlife Palestine Association
vwildlife@palnet.com
Saudi Arabia
National Commission for Wildlife Conservation and Development
vncwcd@zajil.net

PACIFIC

Partner

Australia
Birds Australia
e-mail:
h.phillipps@birdsaustralia.com.au

Affiliates

Fiji
Dr Dick Watling
e-mail: watling@is.com.fj

French Polynesia
Société d'Ornithologie de Polynésie "Manu"
e-mail: sop.manu@mail.pf

New Zealand
The Royal Forest and Bird Protection Society
e-mail: l.bates@wn.forest-bird.org.nz

Western Samoa
O le Si'osi'omaga Society Incorporated
e-mail:
ngo_siosiomaga@samoa.net

INTERNATIONAL ORGANISATIONS

AFRICAN BIRD CLUB.
c/o Birdlife International as below.
e-mail (general): keithbetton@hotmail.com
(membership and sales):
Moira.Y.Hargreaves@btinternet.com
www.africanbirdclub.org
Pub: *Bulletin of the African Bird Club.*

BIRDLIFE INTERNATIONAL.
Wellbrook Court, Girton Road, Cambridge, CB3 ONA, +44 (0)1223 277318; fax +44 (0)1223 277200, Pub: *World Birdwatch.* www.birdlife.net

EAST AFRICA NATURAL HISTORY SOCIETY see Kenya in preceding list.

EURING (European Union for Bird Ringing).
Euring Data Bank, NIOO Centre for Terrestrial Ecology, PO Box 40, NL-6666 ZG Heteren, Netherlands. www.nioo.knaw.nl/euring.htm.

EUROPEAN WILDLIFE REHABILITATION ASSOCIATION (EWRA).
Les Stocker MBE, c/o Wildlife Hospital Trust, Aston Road, Haddenham, Aylesbury, Bucks, HP17 8AF, +44 (0)1844 292292; fax +44 (0)1844 292640, www.sttiggywinkles.org.uk

FAUNA AND FLORA INTERNATIONAL.
Great Eastern House, Tenison Road, Cambridge, CB1 2TT, +44 (0)1223 571000; fax +44 (0)1223 461481, Pub: *Fauna & Flora News; Oryx.* www.ffi.org.uk

LIPU-UK
(the Italian league for the Protection of Birds).
David Lingard, Fernwood, Doddington Road, Whisby, Lincs, LN6 9BX, +44 (0)1522 689030,
e-mail: david@lipu-uk.org
www.lipu-uk.org
Pub: *The Hoopoe,* annually, *Ali Notizie,* quarterley.

NEOTROPICAL BIRD CLUB.
As OSME below. Pub: *Cotinga.*
www.neotropicalbirdclub.org

ORIENTAL BIRD CLUB.
As OSME below. Pub: *The Forktail; Bull OBC.*
www.orientalbirdclub.org

ORNITHOLOGICAL SOCIETY OF THE MIDDLE EAST (OSME).
c/o The Lodge, Sandy, Beds, SG19 2DL.
Pub: *Sandgrouse.*
www.osme.org

TRAFFIC International (formerly Wildlife Trade Monitoring Unit).
219 Huntingdon Road, Cambridge, CB3 ODL, +44 (0)1223 277427; fax +44 (0)1223 277237.
Pub: *TRAFFIC Bulletin.*
e-mail: traffic@trafficint.org

WEST AFRICAN ORNITHOLOGICAL SOCIETY.
R E Sharland, 1 Fisher's Heron, East Mills, Hants, SP6 2JR. Pub: *Malimbus.*

WETLANDS INTERNATIONAL.
PO Box 471, 6700 AL Wageningen, Netherlands, +31 317 478854; fax +31 317 478850, Pub: *Wetlands.*
www.wetlands.org

WORLD OWL TRUST.
The World Owl Centre, Muncaster Castle, Ravenglass, Cumbria, CA18 1RQ, +44 (0)1229 717393; fax +44 (0)1229 717107,
www.owls.org

WORLD PHEASANT ASSOCIATION.
PO Box 5, Lower Basildon, Reading, RG8 9PF, +44 (0)118 984 5140; fax +44 (0)118 984 3369, Pub: *WPA News.* www.pheasant.org.uk

WORLD WIDE FUND FOR NATURE.
Avenue du Mont Blanc, CH-1196 Gland, Switzerland, +41 22 364 9111; fax +41 22 364 5358,
www.panda.org

QUICK REFERENCE SECTION

Goldeneye enjoy special protection during the close season, when they nest in Scottish tree holes and nest boxes. Drawing by Alessandro Troisi.

TIDE TABLES: USEFUL INFORMATION

BRITISH SUMMER TIME

In 2002 BST applies from 0100 on 31 March to 0100 on 27 October.

Note that all the times in the following tables are GMT. **During British Summer Time one hour should be added.**

Predictions are given for the times of high water at Dover throughout the year.

The times of tides at the locations shown here may be obtained by adding or subtracting their 'tidal difference' as shown opposite (subtractions are indicated by a minus sign).

Shetland 42, 43
Orkney 44, 45

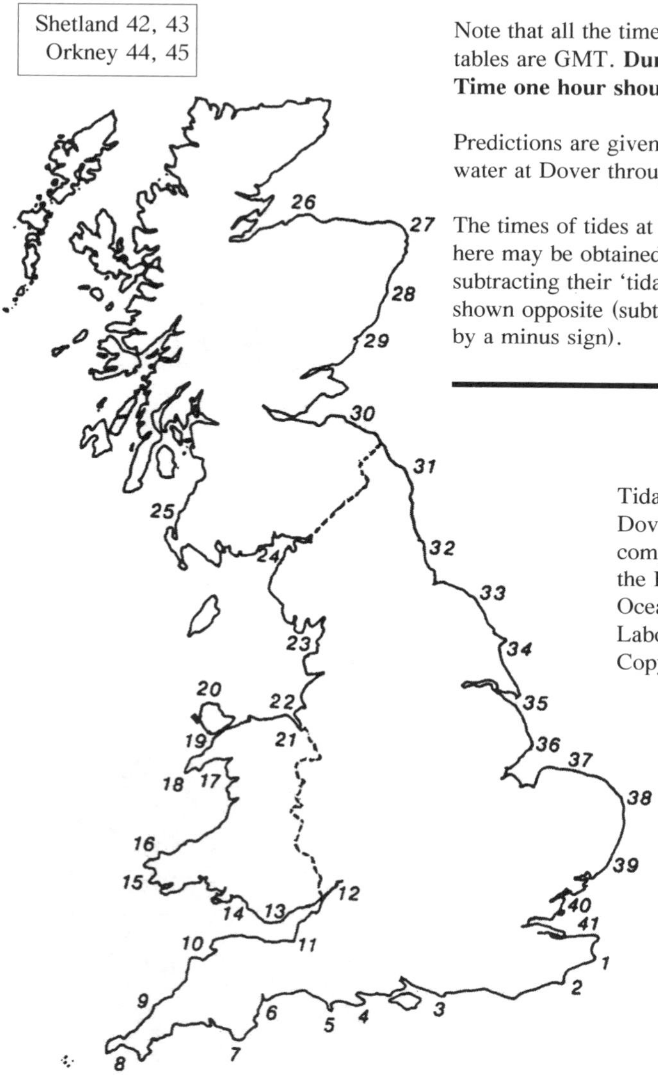

Map showing locations for which tidal differences are given on facing page.

TIDE TABLES 2002

Example 1
To calculate the time of first high water at Girvan on February 24

1. Look up the time at Dover (08 14)* = 8.14 am
2. Add the tidal difference for Girvan = 0.54
3. Therefore the time of high water at Girvan = 9.08 am

Example 2
To calculate the time of second high water at Blakeney on June 16

1. Look up the time at Dover (14 58) = 2.58 pm
2. Add 1 hour for British Summer Time (15 58) = 3.58 pm
3. Subtract the tidal difference for Blakeney = - 4.07
4. Therefore the time of high water at Blakeney = 11.11 am

*All Dover times are shown on the 24-hour clock.
Thus, 08 14 = 08.14 am; 14 58 = 2.58
Following the time of each high water the height of the tide is given, in metres.

(Tables for 2003 are not available at the time of going to press.)

TIDAL DIFFERENCES

1	Dover	See pp 340-341
2	Dungeness	-0 12
3	Selsey Bill	0 09
4	Swanage (lst H.W.Springs)	-2 36
5	Portland	-4 23
6	Exmouth (Approaches)	-4 48
7	Salcombe	-5 23
8	Newlyn (Penzance)	5 59
9	Padstow	-5 47
10	Bideford	-5 17
11	Bridgwater	-4 23
12	Sharpness Dock	-3 19
13	Cardiff (Penarth)	-4 16
14	Swansea	-4 52
15	Skomer Island	-5 00
16	Fishguard	-3 48
17	Barmouth	-2 45
18	Bardsey Island	-3 07
19	Caernarvon	-1 07
20	Amlwch	-0 22
21	Connahs Quay	0 20
22	Hilbre Island (Hoylake/West Kirby)	-0 05
23	Morecambe	0 20
24	Silloth	0 51
25	Girvan	0 54
26	Lossiemouth	0 48
27	Fraserburgh	1 20
28	Aberdeen	2 30
29	Montrose	3 30
30	Dunbar	3 42
31	Holy Island	3 58
32	Sunderland	4 38
33	Whitby	5 12
34	Bridlington	5 53
35	Grimsby	-5 20
36	Skegness	-5 00
37	Blakeney	-4 07
38	Gorleston	-2 08
39	Aldeburgh	-0 13
40	Bradwell Waterside	1 11
41	Herne Bay	1 28
42	Sullom Voe	-1 34
43	Lerwick	0 01
44	Kirkwall	-0 26
45	Widewall Bay	-1 30

NB. Care should be taken when making calculations at the beginning and end of British Summer Time. See worked examples above.

Time Zone **GMT**

Tidal Predictions : **HIGH WATERS 2002**

Units **METRES**

Datum of Predictions = **Chart Datum : 3.67 metres below Ordnance Datum (Newlyn)**

British Summer Time : **31st March to 27th October**

DOVER

January

DATE	DAY	Morning hr min	m	Afternoon hr min	m
1	Tu	** **	* *	12 05	6·7
2	W	00 37	6·7	12 54	6·6
3	Th	01 25	6·7	13 46	6·5
4	F	02 16	6·6	14 41	6·3
5	Sa	03 06	6·4	15 37	6·1
6	Su ☾	04 01	6·2	16 38	5·9
7	M	05 02	6·0	17 42	5·7
8	Tu	06 09	5·9	18 53	5·6
9	W	07 18	5·9	19 59	5·7
10	Th	08 21	5·9	20 59	5·9
11	F	09 19	6·1	21 50	6·1
12	Sa	10 08	6·2	22 35	6·2
13	Su ●	10 53	6·3	23 14	6·4
14	M	11 34	6·3	23 54	6·4
15	Tu	** **	* *	12 12	6·3
16	W	00 30	6·5	12 49	6·2
17	Th	01 05	6·4	13 24	6·1
18	F	01 41	6·3	13 57	6·0
19	Sa	02 14	6·2	14 31	5·8
20	Su	02 48	6·0	15 08	5·6
21	M ☽	03 27	5·8	15 54	5·4
22	Tu	04 15	5·6	16 52	5·2
23	W	05 17	5·4	17 59	5·2
24	Th	06 26	5·4	19 11	5·3
25	F	07 35	5·5	20 17	5·6
26	Sa	08 35	5·8	21 13	5·9
27	Su	09 30	6·1	22 04	6·2
28	M ○	10 19	6·4	22 52	6·5
29	Tu	11 07	6·6	23 38	6·7
30	W	11 55	6·7	** **	* *
31	Th	00 26	6·9	12 44	6·8

DOVER

February

DATE	DAY	Morning hr min	m	Afternoon hr min	m
1	F	01 12	6·9	13 35	6·7
2	Sa	01 59	6·8	14 23	6·5
3	Su	02 44	6·7	15 09	6·3
4	M ☾	03 32	6·4	16 01	6·0
5	Tu	04 25	6·1	17 00	5·7
6	W	05 30	5·8	18 12	5·4
7	Th	06 46	5·6	19 32	5·4
8	F	08 03	5·6	20 42	5·6
9	Sa	09 09	5·7	21 37	5·8
10	Su	10 01	5·9	22 21	6·1
11	M	10 43	6·1	22 59	6·3
12	Tu ●	11 21	6·2	23 35	6·4
13	W	11 55	6·3	** **	* *
14	Th	00 11	6·5	12 29	6·3
15	F	00 44	6·5	13 00	6·2
16	Sa	01 15	6·4	13 28	6·1
17	Su	01 42	6·3	13 55	6·0
18	M	02 09	6·2	14 23	5·9
19	Tu	02 38	6·1	14 59	5·7
20	W ☽	03 19	5·8	15 49	5·5
21	Th	04 15	5·6	16 57	5·3
22	F	05 30	5·3	18 22	5·2
23	Sa	06 57	5·3	19 49	5·4
24	Su	08 14	5·6	20 56	5·8
25	M	09 16	6·0	21 50	6·2
26	Tu	10 07	6·4	22 36	6·6
27	W ○	10 55	6·7	23 23	6·9
28	Th	11 41	6·8	** **	* *

DOVER

March

DATE	DAY	Morning hr min	m	Afternoon hr min	m
1	F	00 08	7·0	12 29	6·9
2	Sa	00 53	7·1	13 14	6·8
3	Su	01 35	7·0	13 57	6·6
4	M	02 17	6·8	14 40	6·4
5	Tu	03 01	6·5	15 27	6·0
6	W ☾	03 53	6·1	16 24	5·6
7	Th	04 56	5·6	17 37	5·3
8	F	06 20	5·3	19 08	5·2
9	Sa	07 50	5·3	20 24	5·4
10	Su	08 59	5·5	21 20	5·7
11	M	09 50	5·8	22 03	6·0
12	Tu	10 29	6·0	22 39	6·2
13	W	11 03	6·2	23 14	6·4
14	Th ●	11 34	6·3	23 47	6·5
15	F	** **	* *	12 04	6·3
16	Sa	00 18	6·5	12 32	6·3
17	Su	00 46	6·5	12 57	6·3
18	M	01 08	6·4	13 21	6·2
19	Tu	01 32	6·3	13 49	6·1
20	W	02 02	6·2	14 23	5·9
21	Th	02 40	6·0	15 09	5·7
22	F ☽	03 34	5·6	16 17	5·4
23	Sa	04 55	5·3	17 51	5·2
24	Su	06 36	5·3	19 28	5·4
25	M	08 02	5·6	20 38	5·8
26	Tu	09 02	6·0	21 32	6·3
27	W	09 53	6·4	22 18	6·7
28	Th ○	10 38	6·7	23 02	6·9
29	F	11 23	6·9	23 45	7·1
30	Sa	** **	* *	12 06	6·9
31	Su	00 29	7·1	12 50	6·8

DOVER

April

DATE	DAY	Morning hr min	m	Afternoon hr min	m
1	M	01 10	7·0	13 31	6·6
2	Tu	01 50	6·7	14 13	6·4
3	W	02 34	6·4	14 59	6·0
4	Th ☾	03 25	5·9	15 54	5·6
5	F	04 29	5·5	17 06	5·3
6	Sa	05 58	5·1	18 37	5·1
7	Su	07 31	5·2	19 56	5·3
8	M	08 38	5·4	20 52	5·7
9	Tu	09 27	5·7	21 37	6·0
10	W	10 04	6·0	22 14	6·2
11	Th	10 36	6·1	22 46	6·3
12	F ●	11 06	6·2	23 19	6·4
13	Sa	11 34	6·3	23 47	6·5
14	Su	** **	* *	12 01	6·3
15	M	00 13	6·5	12 27	6·3
16	Tu	00 37	6·4	12 54	6·3
17	W	01 04	6·3	13 25	6·2
18	Th	01 36	6·2	14 02	6·0
19	F	02 19	6·0	14 51	5·8
20	Sa ☽	03 18	5·6	16 03	5·5
21	Su	04 45	5·3	17 37	5·3
22	M	06 26	5·4	19 08	5·5
23	Tu	07 45	5·7	20 16	5·9
24	W	08 44	6·1	21 08	6·4
25	Th	09 32	6·4	21 54	6·7
26	F	10 17	6·7	22 38	6·9
27	Sa ○	11 00	6·8	23 21	7·0
28	Su	11 44	6·8	** **	* *
29	M	00 04	7·0	12 27	6·7
30	Tu	00 47	6·8	13 10	6·6

Time Zone **GMT** Tidal Predictions : **HIGH WATERS 2002** Units **METRES**

Datum of Predictions = **Chart Datum : 3.67 metres below Ordnance Datum (Newlyn)**

British Summer Time : **31st March to 27th October**

DOVER

May

Date	Day	Morning hr min	m	Afternoon hr min	m
1	W	01 29	6·6	13 52	6·3
2	Th	02 13	6·2	14 37	6·0
3	F	03 04	5·8	15 29	5·7
4	Sa ☾	04 05	5·4	16 32	5·4
5	Su	05 26	5·1	17 55	5·2
6	M	06 53	5·1	19 14	5·3
7	Tu	07 59	5·3	20 14	5·6
8	W	08 49	5·6	21 01	5·9
9	Th	09 29	5·8	21 39	6·1
10	F	10 03	6·0	22 14	6·2
11	Sa	10 32	6·2	22 45	6·3
12	Su ●	11 02	6·3	23 14	6·4
13	M	11 33	6·3	23 42	6·4
14	Tu	** **	* *	12 04	6·3
15	W	00 13	6·4	12 37	6·3
16	Th	00 47	6·3	13 15	6·2
17	F	01 28	6·1	13 59	6·1
18	Sa	02 17	5·9	14 54	5·9
19	Su ☽	03 22	5·7	16 04	5·7
20	M	04 45	5·5	17 23	5·6
21	Tu	06 09	5·6	18 40	5·8
22	W	07 19	5·8	19 45	6·0
23	Th	08 17	6·1	20 40	6·3
24	F	09 08	6·3	21 27	6·6
25	Sa	09 54	6·5	22 14	6·7
26	Su ○	10 41	6·6	22 59	6·8
27	M	11 26	6·6	23 45	6·7
28	Tu	** **	* *	12 11	6·6
29	W	00 29	6·6	12 53	6·5
30	Th	01 12	6·4	13 34	6·3
31	F	01 56	6·1	14 17	6·1

DOVER

June

Date	Day	Morning hr min	m	Afternoon hr min	m
1	Sa	02 44	5·8	15 04	5·8
2	Su	03 37	5·5	15 57	5·6
3	M ☾	04 42	5·2	17 03	5·4
4	Tu	05 56	5·1	18 16	5·4
5	W	07 04	5·2	19 21	5·5
6	Th	07 59	5·4	20 14	5·7
7	F	08 44	5·6	20 58	5·9
8	Sa	09 23	5·8	21 34	6·0
9	Su	09 58	6·0	22 10	6·2
10	M ●	10 34	6·2	22 43	6·3
11	Tu	11 09	6·3	23 20	6·3
12	W	11 48	6·4	23 59	6·4
13	Th	** **	* *	12 30	6·4
14	F	00 43	6·3	13 15	6·4
15	Sa	01 31	6·2	14 04	6·3
16	Su	02 26	6·1	14 58	6·1
17	M	03 27	5·9	15 56	6·0
18	Tu ☽	04 34	5·8	17 00	5·9
19	W	05 41	5·8	18 06	5·9
20	Th	06 47	5·8	19 11	6·0
21	F	07 48	5·9	20 10	6·2
22	Sa	08 44	6·1	21 05	6·3
23	Su	09 37	6·2	21 56	6·4
24	M ○	10 26	6·4	22 45	6·5
25	Tu	11 11	6·5	23 31	6·5
26	W	11 55	6·5	** **	* *
27	Th	00 16	6·4	12 37	6·4
28	F	00 58	6·3	13 17	6·3
29	Sa	01 39	6·1	13 55	6·2
30	Su	02 20	5·9	14 35	6·1

DOVER

July

Date	Day	Morning hr min	m	Afternoon hr min	m
1	M	03 04	5·7	15 20	5·9
2	Tu ☾	03 53	5·4	16 10	5·7
3	W	04 49	5·3	17 07	5·5
4	Th	05 52	5·2	18 11	5·4
5	F	06 56	5·2	19 14	5·4
6	Sa	07 53	5·4	20 09	5·6
7	Su	08 42	5·6	20 56	5·8
8	M	09 27	5·9	21 39	6·0
9	Tu	10 10	6·1	22 21	6·2
10	W ●	10 52	6·3	23 04	6·3
11	Th	11 35	6·5	23 49	6·5
12	F	** **	* *	12 20	6·6
13	Sa	00 37	6·5	13 08	6·6
14	Su	01 28	6·5	13 56	6·6
15	M	02 20	6·4	14 45	6·5
16	Tu	03 13	6·2	15 36	6·4
17	W ☽	04 07	6·0	16 29	6·2
18	Th	05 06	5·8	17 30	6·0
19	F	06 11	5·7	18 37	5·9
20	Sa	07 21	5·7	19 46	5·9
21	Su	08 27	5·8	20 51	6·0
22	M	09 26	6·0	21 47	6·1
23	Tu	10 15	6·2	22 36	6·2
24	W ○	11 00	6·3	23 21	6·3
25	Th	11 40	6·4	** **	* *
26	F	00 02	6·3	12 18	6·5
27	Sa	00 40	6·3	12 56	6·5
28	Su	01 15	6·2	13 31	6·4
29	M	01 50	6·0	14 06	6·3
30	Tu	02 26	5·9	14 40	6·1
31	W	03 01	5·7	15 16	5·9

DOVER

August

Date	Day	Morning hr min	m	Afternoon hr min	m
1	Th ☾	03 41	5·5	16 00	5·7
2	F	04 34	5·3	16 56	5·4
3	Sa	05 40	5·2	18 04	5·3
4	Su	06 54	5·2	19 18	5·4
5	M	08 04	5·4	20 23	5·6
6	Tu	09 04	5·8	21 18	5·9
7	W	09 51	6·1	22 05	6·2
8	Th ●	10 36	6·4	22 50	6·5
9	F	11 20	6·7	23 35	6·7
10	Sa	** **	* *	12 05	6·8
11	Su	00 23	6·7	12 51	6·9
12	M	01 11	6·7	13 36	6·9
13	Tu	02 00	6·6	14 21	6·8
14	W	02 47	6·4	15 06	6·6
15	Th ☽	03 34	6·1	15 57	6·3
16	F	04 31	5·8	16 57	5·9
17	Sa	05 37	5·6	18 11	5·7
18	Su	06 58	5·5	19 34	5·6
19	M	08 17	5·6	20 48	5·7
20	Tu	09 18	5·9	21 44	6·0
21	W	10 05	6·1	22 29	6·1
22	Th ○	10 45	6·3	23 07	6·3
23	F	11 21	6·5	23 42	6·3
24	Sa	11 56	6·6	** **	* *
25	Su	00 16	6·3	12 30	6·6
26	M	00 49	6·3	13 03	6·5
27	Tu	01 18	6·2	13 31	6·4
28	W	01 45	6·1	13 57	6·3
29	Th	02 11	5·9	14 24	6·1
30	F	02 44	5·7	14 59	5·8
31	Sa ☾	03 27	5·5	15 49	5·5

Time Zone **GMT**

Tidal Predictions : **HIGH WATERS 2002**

Units **METRES**

Datum of Predictions = **Chart Datum : 3.67 metres below Ordnance Datum (Newlyn)**

British Summer Time : **31st March to 27th October**

DOVER

September

DATE	DAY	Morning hr min	m	Afternoon hr min	m
1	Su	04 32	5·3	17 03	5·2
2	M	06 01	5·1	18 37	5·2
3	Tu	07 34	5·3	20 02	5·5
4	W	08 42	5·7	21 02	5·9
5	Th	09 33	6·2	21 50	6·3
6	F	10 18	6·6	22 34	6·6
7	Sa ●	11 00	6·9	23 17	6·8
8	Su	11 42	7·0	** **	* *
9	M	00 02	6·9	12 26	7·1
10	Tu	00 47	6·9	13 10	7·1
11	W	01 31	6·7	13 52	6·9
12	Th	02 14	6·5	14 35	6·6
13	F ☽	03 02	6·2	15 26	6·2
14	Sa	03 57	5·8	16 28	5·8
15	Su	05 07	5·5	17 51	5·4
16	M	06 40	5·3	19 29	5·4
17	Tu	08 04	5·5	20 45	5·6
18	W	09 04	5·8	21 37	5·9
19	Th	09 47	6·1	22 17	6·1
20	F	10 24	6·4	22 48	6·3
21	Sa ○	10 57	6·5	23 19	6·4
22	Su	11 30	6·6	23 48	6·4
23	M	** **	* *	12 02	6·6
24	Tu	00 18	6·4	12 30	6·6
25	W	00 43	6·4	12 54	6·5
26	Th	01 07	6·2	13 17	6·4
27	F	01 32	6·1	13 42	6·2
28	Sa	02 03	6·0	14 16	6·0
29	Su ☾	02 44	5·7	15 04	5·6
30	M	03 44	5·4	16 19	5·2

DOVER

October

DATE	DAY	Morning hr min	m	Afternoon hr min	m
1	Tu	05 21	5·2	18 12	5·1
2	W	07 07	5·3	19 43	5·5
3	Th	08 19	5·8	20 44	6·0
4	F	09 11	6·3	21 30	6·4
5	Sa	09 54	6·7	22 14	6·8
6	Su ●	10 36	7·0	22 55	6·9
7	M	11 17	7·2	23 38	7·0
8	Tu	11 59	7·2	** **	* *
9	W	00 20	6·9	12 41	7·1
10	Th	01 04	6·8	13 24	6·9
11	F	01 48	6·5	14 09	6·5
12	Sa	02 34	6·2	14 59	6·1
13	Su ☽	03 29	5·8	16 04	5·6
14	M	04 38	5·4	17 31	5·2
15	Tu	06 12	5·2	19 14	5·3
16	W	07 38	5·4	20 26	5·5
17	Th	08 37	5·8	21 15	5·9
18	F	09 20	6·1	21 51	6·1
19	Sa	09 57	6·3	22 21	6·3
20	Su	10 31	6·5	22 50	6·4
21	M ○	11 02	6·6	23 19	6·4
22	Tu	11 31	6·6	23 47	6·5
23	W	11 58	6·6	** **	* *
24	Th	00 12	6·4	12 22	6·5
25	F	00 39	6·3	12 46	6·4
26	Sa	01 05	6·2	13 15	6·2
27	Su	01 39	6·1	13 52	6·0
28	M	02 23	5·8	14 42	5·6
29	Tu ☾	03 25	5·5	16 03	5·3
30	W	04 59	5·3	17 52	5·3
31	Th	06 36	5·5	19 17	5·6

DOVER

November

DATE	DAY	Morning hr min	m	Afternoon hr min	m
1	F	07 48	5·9	20 17	6·0
2	Sa	08 41	6·3	21 06	6·4
3	Su	09 27	6·7	21 49	6·7
4	M ●	10 10	7·0	22 32	6·9
5	Tu	10 52	7·1	23 14	6·9
6	W	11 35	7·1	23 59	6·9
7	Th	** **	* *	12 19	7·0
8	F	00 43	6·7	13 03	6·7
9	Sa	01 26	6·5	13 48	6·4
10	Su	02 13	6·2	14 38	6·0
11	M ☽	03 04	5·9	15 40	5·5
12	Tu	04 05	5·5	16 59	5·2
13	W	05 26	5·3	18 32	5·2
14	Th	06 51	5·4	19 42	5·4
15	F	07 55	5·6	20 34	5·6
16	Sa	08 44	5·9	21 15	5·9
17	Su	09 25	6·2	21 50	6·1
18	M	10 00	6·3	22 21	6·2
19	Tu	10 32	6·4	22 50	6·3
20	W ○	11 02	6·4	23 20	6·4
21	Th	11 30	6·4	23 49	6·4
22	F	11 58	6·4	** **	* *
23	Sa	00 20	6·3	12 29	6·3
24	Su	00 56	6·3	13 04	6·2
25	M	01 34	6·1	13 48	6·0
26	Tu	02 21	5·9	14 42	5·7
27	W ☾	03 23	5·7	15 57	5·5
28	Th	04 38	5·6	17 24	5·5
29	F	05 58	5·7	18 41	5·7
30	Sa	07 08	5·9	19 43	5·9

DOVER

December

DATE	DAY	Morning hr min	m	Afternoon hr min	m
1	Su	08 07	6·2	20 37	6·2
2	M	08 58	6·5	21 25	6·5
3	Tu	09 44	6·7	22 12	6·6
4	W ●	10 31	6·9	22 59	6·7
5	Th	11 17	6·9	23 45	6·7
6	F	** **	* *	12 04	6·8
7	Sa	00 29	6·6	12 49	6·6
8	Su	01 12	6·5	13 34	6·3
9	M	01 55	6·3	14 20	6·0
10	Tu	02 41	6·0	15 12	5·6
11	W ☽	03 32	5·8	16 12	5·3
12	Th	04 34	5·5	17 26	5·2
13	F	05 45	5·4	18 39	5·2
14	Sa	06 57	5·5	19 41	5·3
15	Su	07 56	5·6	20 31	5·6
16	M	08 44	5·8	21 13	5·8
17	Tu	09 26	6·0	21 51	6·0
18	W	10 01	6·1	22 26	6·1
19	Th ○	10 35	6·2	23 00	6·3
20	F	11 07	6·3	23 35	6·3
21	Sa	11 44	6·3	** **	* *
22	Su	00 12	6·4	12 22	6·3
23	M	00 53	6·4	13 04	6·3
24	Tu	01 36	6·3	13 50	6·1
25	W	02 23	6·2	14 42	6·0
26	Th	03 15	6·1	15 43	5·8
27	F ☾	04 12	6·0	16 49	5·7
28	Sa	05 19	5·9	17 58	5·7
29	Su	06 26	5·9	19 04	5·8
30	M	07 31	6·0	20 07	5·9
31	Tu	08 31	6·2	21 06	6·1

SCHEDULE 1 SPECIES

Under the provisions of the Wildlife and Countryside Act 1981 the following bird species (listed in Schedule 1 - Part I of the Act) are protected by special penalties at all times.

Avocet,
Bee-eater
Bittem
Bittern, Little
Bluethroat
Brambling
Bunting, Cirl
Bunting, Lapland
Bunting, Snow
Buzzard, Honey
Chough
Corncrake
Crake, Spotted
Crossbills (all species)
Curlew, Stone
Divers (all species)
Dotterel
Duck, Long-tailed
Eagle, Golden
Eagle, White-tailed
Falcon, Gyr
Fieldfare
Firecrest
Garganey
Godwit, Black-tailed
Goshawk
Grebe, Black-necked
Grebe, Slavonian
Greenshank
Gull, Little
Gull, Mediterranean
Harriers (all species)
Heron, Purple
Hobby
Hoopoe
Kingfisher
Kite, Red
Merlin
Oriole, Golden
Osprey
Owl, Barn
Owl, Snowy
Peregrine
Petrel, Leach's
Phalarope, Red-necked
Plover, Kentish
Plover, Little Ringed
Quail, Common
Redstart, Black
Redwing
Rosefinch, Scarlet
Ruff
Sandpiper, Green
Sandpiper, Purple
Sandpiper, Wood
Scaup
Scoter, Common
Scoter, Velvet
Serin
Shorelark
Shrike, Red-backed
Spoonbill
Stilt, Black-winged
Stint, Temminck's
Swan, Bewick's
Stone-curlew
Swan, Whooper
Tern, Black
Tern, Little
Tern, Roseate
Tit, Bearded
Tit, Crested
Treecreeper, Short-toed
Warbler, Cetti's
Warbler, Dartford
Warbler, Marsh
Warbler, Savi's
Whimbrel
Woodlark
Wryneck

The following birds and their eggs (listed in Schedule 1 - Part II of the Act) are protected by special penalties during the close season, which is Feb 1 to Aug 31 (Feb 21 to Aug 31 below high water mark), but may be killed outside this period.

NATIONAL AND REGIONAL BIRDLINES

Birdline name	To obtain information	To report sightings (hotlines)
National		
Bird Information Service	09068 700222	01263 741140
www.birdingworld.co.uk		
Regional		
Northern Ireland	028 9146 7408	
Scotland*	09068 700 234	01292 611 994
Wales *	09068 700 248	01492 544 588
East Anglia	09068 700 245	01603 763 388
www.birdnews.co.uk		or 08000 830 803
Midlands *	09068 700 247	01905 754 154
North East*	09068 700 246	01426 983 963
North West *	09068 700 249	0151 336 6188
South East	09068 700 240	07626 933 933
www.southeastbirdnews.co.uk	or 08000 377 240	
South West	09068 700 241	01426 923 923

* www.uk-birding.co.uk

Charges

At the time of compilation, calls to 09068 numbers cost 60p per minute.

SUNRISE AND SUNSET TIMES

Predictions are given for the times of sunrise and sunset on every Sunday throughout the year. For places on the same latitude as the following, add 4 minutes for each degree of longitude west (subtract if east).

These times are in GMT, except between 01 00 on Mar 31 and 01 00 on Oct 27, when the times are in BST (1 hour in advance of GMT).

		London		Manchester		Edinburgh	
		Rise	**Set**	**Rise**	**Set**	**Rise**	**Set**
Jan	6	08 05	16 08	08 24	16 06	08 42	15 56
	13	08 01	16 18	08 19	16 17	08 36	16 07
	20	07 55	16 29	08 12	16 29	08 28	16 21
	27	07 47	16 41	08 02	16 42	08 17	16 35
Feb	3	07 36	16 53	07 51	16 55	08 04	16 50
	10	07 24	17 06	07 38	17 09	07 50	17 05
	17	07 11	17 19	07 24	17 23	07 34	17 21
	24	06 57	17 32	07 09	17 37	07 17	17 36
Mar	3	06 42	17 44	06 53	17 50	07 00	17 51
	10	06 27	17 56	06 36	18 03	06 42	18 06
	17	06 11	18 08	06 19	18 16	06 24	18 20
	24	05 55	18 20	06 02	18 29	06 05	18 34
	31	06 39	19 32	06 45	19 42	06 47	19 49
Apr	7	06 23	19 44	06 29	19 55	06 29	20 03
	14	06 08	19 55	06 12	20 08	06 11	20 17
	21	05 53	20 07	05 56	20 20	05 53	20 31
	28	05 39	20 19	05 41	20 33	05 37	20 45
May	5	05 26	20 30	05 27	20 46	05 21	21 00
	12	05 14	20 41	05 14	20 58	05 06	21 13
	19	05 04	20 52	05 03	21 09	04 54	21 26
	26	04 55	21 01	04 53	21 20	04 43	21 38

SUNRISE AND SUNSET TIMES

		London Rise	London Set	Manchester Rise	Manchester Set	Edinburgh Rise	Edinburgh Set
Jun	2	04 49	21 09	04 46	21 29	04 34	21 48
	9	04 44	21 16	04 41	21 36	04 29	21 56
	16	04 43	21 20	04 39	21 40	04 26	22 01
	23	04 44	21 22	04 40	21 42	04 27	22 03
	30	04 47	21 21	04 43	21 41	04 31	22 02
Jul	7	04 52	21 18	04 49	21 38	04 37	21 58
	14	05 00	21 13	04 57	21 32	04 46	21 50
	21	05 08	21 05	05 07	21 23	04 57	21 40
	28	05 18	20 55	05 18	21 12	05 09	21 28
Aug	4	05 28	20 44	05 29	21 00	05 22	21 14
	11	05 39	20 31	05 41	20 46	05 36	20 59
	18	05 50	20 18	05 53	20 31	05 49	20 43
	25	06 02	20 03	06 05	20 16	06 03	20 26
Sep	1	06 13	19 48	06 18	19 59	06 17	20 08
	8	06 24	19 32	06 30	19 42	06 30	19 50
	15	06 35	19 16	06 42	19 25	06 44	19 31
	22	06 46	19 00	06 54	19 08	06 58	19 13
	29	06 58	18 43	07 07	18 51	07 11	18 54
Oct	6	07 09	18 28	07 19	18 34	07 25	18 36
	13	07 21	18 12	07 32	18 18	07 39	18 18
	20	07 33	17 57	07 45	18 02	07 54	18 01
	27	06 45	16 43	06 58	16 47	07 09	16 44
Nov	3	06 57	16 30	07 11	16 33	07 23	16 29
	10	07 10	16 19	07 25	16 20	07 38	16 15
	17	07 22	16 09	07 38	16 09	07 53	16 02
	24	07 33	16 01	07 50	16 00	08 07	15 52
Dec	1	07 44	15 55	08 02	15 54	08 19	15 44
	8	07 53	15 52	08 11	15 50	08 30	15 40
	15	08 00	15 52	08 19	15 49	08 38	15 38
	22	08 04	15 54	08 23	15 52	08 43	15 40
	29	08 06	15 59	08 25	15 57	08 44	15 46

COUNTY BIRDWATCH TALLIES

The County Birdrace has become an institution in British birdwatching - providing both a personal challenge to those seeking to break records for species seen in one day, but also raising money via sponsorship for local and national conservation projects. Due to restrictions imposed by the foot and mouth crisis, the 2001 event was moved from its traditional May date to October (after *The Yearbook* went to press). For information on how to participate in 2002, contact *Birdwatch* magazine, Solo Publishing, 3D/F Leroy House, 436 Essex Road, Islington, London N1 3QP.

Rules

1. Teams shall comprise four members, all resident in the geographical area of the birdwatch, one of whom may be a driver and/or record-keeper.
2. Geographical areas shall generally be those used by the network of Bird Recorders.
3. A tally must be achieved on one calendar day.
4. No species shall be included in the tally unless seen or heard by at least three members of the team.
5. Team members and birds must be within the defined area at the time of recording.
6. Admitted species shall be those on the relevant official country list (eg. the British List for England, Scotland and Wales), plus Feral Pigeon; rarities must be accepted by the appropriate (county or national) Rarities Committee. Schedule D species shall be excluded.
7. Escapes, sick, injured or oiled birds shall not be admitted.
8. Attracting birds with a tape recording shall not be allowed.
9. The Birdwatchers' Code of Conduct shall be strictly observed.

Tallies opposite are accepted and published in good faith. A listing does not imply that the above rules have been adhered to, nor that any authentication or adjudication has been made. A county or region's best record is used in determining its position in the table. If the same total has been reached in more than one year, only the first is given.

( ) Numbers within curved brackets indicate the latest known total number of species on the county or region's list. In order to ensure consistency as to which species should be included on the list, Rule 6 should be applied.

If the same total has been reached by more than one county or region the names are listed alphabetically and a joint position indicated by an 'equals' sign (=).

Arctic terns mobbing a birdwatcher on the Farne Islands. Drawing by Gerald Russell.

COUNTY BIRDWATCH TALLIES

	County	Race total	County total	Year
1	Norfolk	162	(411)	2000
2	Dorset	158	(400)	1989
3	Yorkshire	155	(428)	1998
4	Kent	153	(400)	1999
5	Grampian	152	(352)	1999
6	Hampshire	151	(357)	1994
7	Cheshire	149	(338)	1993
8	Suffolk	148	(371)	1992
9	Highland	146	(246)	1988
10=	Cleveland	142	(349)	1994
10=	Durham	142	(354)	1999
12	Lancs & N Merseyside	141	(348)	1996
13	Cumbria	140	(344)	1996
14	Northumb	139	(388)	1993
15=	Highland, NE Scotland	136	(?)	1993
15=	Sussex	136	(380)	1996
17=	Gwynedd (old county)	135	(349)	1989
17=	Tayside, Angus/Dundee	135	(306)	1994
19	Highland, N Scotland	134	(?)	1988
20=	Devon	133	(410)	1991
20=	N Ireland	133	(309)	1993
22=	Fife (excl Isle of May)	130	(300)	1996
22=	Cambs	130	(327)	2000
24=	Anglesey	123	(304)	1999
24=	Derbyshire	129	(308)	1998
26=	Cornwall	128	(451)	1992
26=	Lincolnshire	128	(369)	1988
26=	Lothian	128	(345)	1994
29	Ayrshire	127	(288)	1991
30=	Caernarf.	126	(347)	1993
30=	Notts	126	(308)	1991
32=	Clwyd	125	(296)	1995
32=	Staffordshire	125	(293)	1993
34=	Borders	124	(294)	2000
34=	Somerset	124	(336)	2000
34=	Yorkshire, E	124	(353)	1993
37	Essex	123	(365)	1996
38=	Carmarthen	122	(293)	1991
38=	Gloucs	122	(307)	1998
40=	Berkshire	121	(309)	1990
40=	Caithness	121	(292)	1994
40=	Moray & Nairn	121	(291)	1993
43=	Eire	119	(425)	1996
43=	Wexford	119	(?)	1992
45=	Manchester	118	(300)	1992
45=	Wiltshire	118	(305)	1989
47	Merioneth	117	(263)	1989
48=	Cambs, Hunts/P'boro	115	(294)	1989
48=	Dumfries & Galloway	115	(279)	1986
48=	Glams (Old)	115	(300)	1986
48=	Leics/ Rutland	115	(302)	1997
48=	Pembroke	115	(355)	1995
48=	Surrey	115	(321)	1995
54=	Northants	114	(314)	1998
54=	Oxon	114	(297)	2000
54=	Shetland	114	(419)	1992
54=	Worcs	114	(287)	1995
58=	Bucks	113	(276)	1990
58=	Isle of Wight	113	(321)	1989
58=	London	113	(351)	1994
61=	Montgomery	112	(221)	1991
61=	Rutland	112	(275)	1994
63=	Bedfordshire	111	(286)	1996
63=	Glams, East	111	(298)	1993
63=	Gwent	111	(288)	1991
63=	Warwicks	111	(295)	1993
67	Glams, West	110	(288)	1991
68	Leics	109	(290)	1998
69=	Central	108	(248)	1996
69=	Herts	108	(282)	1989
71	Ceredigion	107	(282)	1986
72=	Merseyside	105	(?)	1993
72=	Western Isles	105	(341)	1985
74	Avon	104	(320)	1993
75	Shropshire	103	(263)	1989
76	Radnorshire	97	(235)	1988
77	Guernsey	96	(304)	1992
78	Breconshire	95	(251)	1991
79	West Mid	92	(264)	1995
80	Hereford	90	(250)	1994
81	Cornwall, Scilly	85	(407)	1992

The following do not have a one-day tally but are listed for their County total. Alderney(267), Argyll (316), Clyde (287), Fife, Isle of May (273), Highland, Sutherland (268), Isle of Man (287), Jersey (303), Orkney (364), Shetland, Fair Isle (354).

GRID REFERENCES

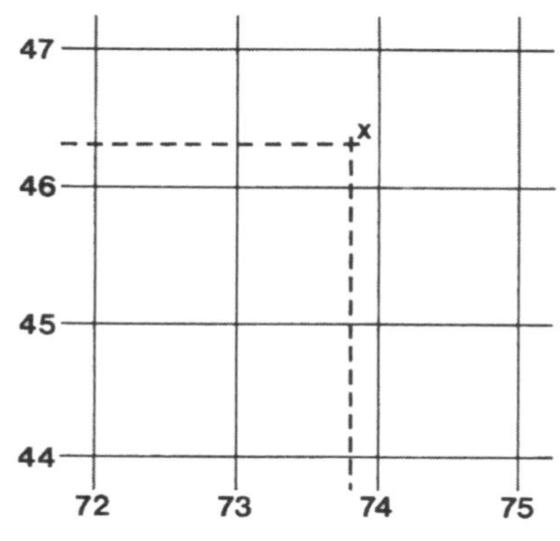

A grid reference is made up of letters and numbers. Two-letter codes are used for 100km squares on the National Grid (opposite) and single-letter codes on the Irish Grid (below).

The squares may be further subdivided into squares of 10km, 1km or 100m, allowing for increasingly specific references. On a given map the lines forming the squares are numbered in the margins, those along the top and bottom being known as 'eastings' and those along the sides as 'northings'. A reference number is made up of the relevant letter code plus two sets of figures, those representing the easting followed by the northing. According to the scale of the map they can either be read off directly or calculated by visually dividing the intervals into tenths. For most purposes three-figure eastings plus three-figure northings are adequate.

The example above, from an Ordnance Survey 'Landranger' map, illustrates how to specify a location on a map divided into lkm squares: the reference for point X is 738463. If that location lies in square SP (see map opposite), the full reference is SP738463.

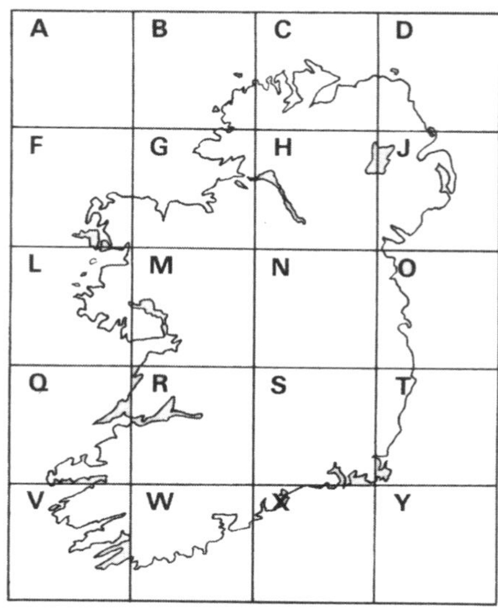

LETTER CODES FOR IRISH GRID 10km SQUARES

LETTER CODES FOR NATIONAL GRID 100km SQUARES

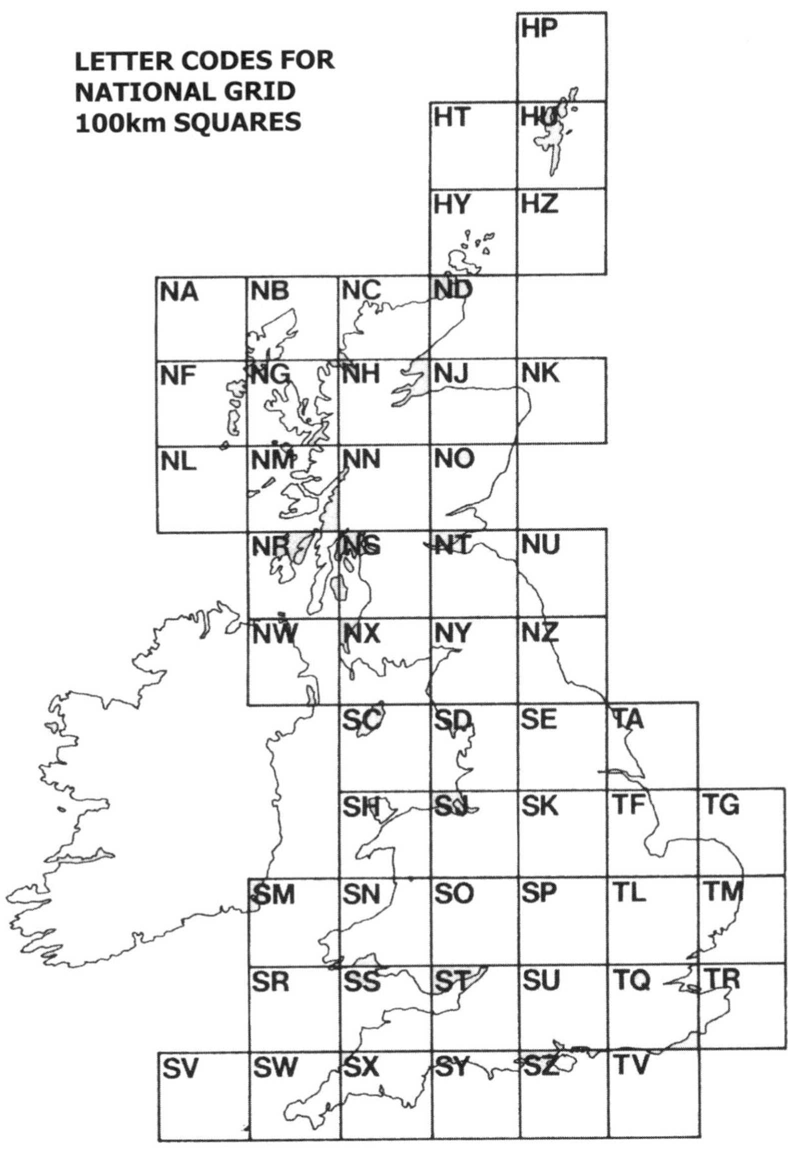

Index to Bird Reserves and Observatories

INDEX TO RESERVES

INDEX TO RESERVES